FRIENDLY FASCISM

OTHER BOOKS
BY BERTRAM GROSS

The Legislative Struggle:
A Study in Social Combat
The Hard Money Crusade
The Managing of Organizations
Organizations and Their Managing
The State of the Nation:
Social Systems Accounting

EDITED BY BERTRAM GROSS

Action Under Planning
The National Planning Series
A Great Society?
Social Intelligence for America's Future
New Styles of Planning in Post-Industrial America

FRIENDLY FASCISM

The New Face of Power in America

by

Bertram Gross

SOUTH END PRESS

Boston

To My Grandchildren

Library of Congress Cataloging in Publication Data

Gross, Bertram Myron, 1912-
Friendly fascism.

Includes index.
1. United States—Politics and government—1945-
2. United States—Economic policy—1971- 3. Elite (Social sciences)—United States. I. Title.
JK271.G745 320.973 80-13035
ISBN 0-87131-317-0

First published in hardcover by
M. Evans and Company, Inc.
216 East 49th Street
New York, New York 10017

Paperback edition published by
South End Press
302 Columbus Avenue
Boston MA 02116

Design by Robert Bull

Cover by Sheila Walsh

Manufactured in the United States of America

Acknowledgments

THE WRITING OF THIS BOOK has been a long voyage of exploration, in the course of which I have learned many new things, changed many old ideas and written far more than there is room to publish in any one volume. Throughout this effort I have been fortunate to receive valuable criticisms, suggestions and other reactions from family members, students, colleagues, editors, and other friends.

I have been particularly helped by the encouragement or ideas given me by the American members of my immediate family—Theodore Gross, Samuel Gross, Larry Gross, David Gross, Shulamith Gross, Nora Gross, Edith Lateiner and Isidore Lateiner—and by the Indian branch as well—Kusum Singh, Nisha Singh, Gayatri Singh, Neera Sen and A. N. Sen. Ungrudging support has been provided by an "extended family" of former doctoral students—David Curzon, Itzhak Galnoor, Michael Marien, Herman Mertins, Stanley Moses, David Porter, Michael Springer and David Warner—and of present doctoral students—Frances Cooper and Stephen Frantz.

With apologies to other students too numerous to list, I also wish to thank: Ann Berson, William Byrnes, Randy Crawford, Marjorie Gellerman, Gregory Gerard, John Goetz, Titiana Hardy, Robert Kraushaar, Marilyn Phelan, Sidney Plotkin, Lenore Rasmussen, Maynard T. Robison, Virginia Sherry, Donna Soucy, Mary Stern, Norma Turner and Marcie Waterman.

Let me also express my appreciation for the help received from other colleagues: Carol and Sandor Agocz, Stephen K. Bailey, Blanche Blank, Karen Bogen, Jean Boudin, Leonard Boudin, Philip Brenner, Carlos Ciaño, Robert Chassell, Richard Cloward, Joe Conason, Loretta Curzon, Paul David, John Dixon, G. William Domhoff, Yehezkel Dror, Joel C. Edelstein, Robert Engler, Julian Friedman, Alan Gartner, Corinne Gilb, Max Gordon, Colin Greer, Larry Hirshhorn, John P. Lewis, Robert McGregor, Harry Magdoff, Mary Lou Marien, Max Mark, Donald Michael, S. M. Miller, Mario Monzon, Paul Orentlich, Saul Padover, Alphonso Pinkney, Frances Piven, Frank Riessman, Philip Roos, Peter Salins, Ned Schneier, G. N. Seetharam, Falguni Sen, Chaim Shatan, Derek

Shearer, Hans Spiegel, Julius Stulman, Miguel Teubal, Terri Thal, Edith Tiger, Geoffrey Vickers, Elizabeth Wickenden and Sol Yurick.

Over the years I have been privileged to enjoy encouragement and advice from Peter Mayer, one of the few creative giants in American and British publishing. I have been particularly privileged to have had the editorial help of Maria Carvainis, Peter Steinfels and Fred Graver. Giving more time to this book than Maria or Peter had a chance to do, Fred has proven to me that a brilliant editor can carve out entire chapters, sections and paragraphs without causing too much pain; the secret, of course, is that by going to the roots of what I had been trying to say, he repeatedly pushed me toward reformulating and improving my entire conception. Indeed, it was only through discussions with Fred that I realized something that had been true from the very beginning—namely, that this is a book about democracy.

BERTRAM GROSS

Contents

Acknowledgments v
Preface to paperback edition xi
Introduction: A Patriotic Warning 1

ONE: The Roots of Friendly Fascism 9

1. The Rise and Fall of Classic Fascism 11
Italy, Germany, Japan · Breeding Grounds of Fascism · The Axis · Anti-Fascist Failures · Fascist Exploits · Fascist Ideologies · Destruction of the Axis · Indestructible Myths

2. The Takeoff Toward a New Corporate Society 32
The Sun Never Sets on America's "Free World" · The Golden International · Big Welfare for Big Business · More Rational Corporate Planning · Technology: Starting, Stopping, Suppressing

3. The Mysterious Establishment 54
The Castles of Power · The Ultra-Rich · The Corporate Overseers · The Chief Executive Network · Executive Managers · Junior and Contingent Members · Conflicts Among the Few · Purges and Conversions · Purifying Ideologies

4. The Side Effects of Success 98
An Abundance of Frustrations · Falling Apart: Work, Community, Family · Loneliness and Alienation · Crime: The Dirty Secrets · The Erosion of Authority

5. The Challenge of a Shrinking Capitalist World 119
New Losses to Communism · Creeping Socialism · Third World Demands · Détente: A Cooler Cold War · Instability at the Top

6. Old Crises in New Forms 139
Untamed Recession · The Hidden Unemployed · The New Inflation: Hyena's Delight · The Dynamite of Class Conflict · Limited War · Unlimited Overkill

TWO: The Specter of Friendly Fascism 159

7. The Unfolding Logic 161
Making the Most of Crises · Consolidating Power · The Cat Feet of Tyranny · Many Paths

8. Trilateral Empire or Fortress America? 173
American Retrenchment · A "True Empire" · Alternative Outcomes

9. The Friendly Fascist Establishment 184
From Floundering Establishment to Super-America, Inc. · A Righteous Presidency · Remolding Militarism · The Restructuring of the Radical Right · New Ideologies of Central Power · Triplespeak

10. Friendly Fascist Economics 209
More Stagflation · More Money Moving Upward · An Abundance of Shortages · More Waste and Pollution · More Nuclear Poison · More Junk and Disservices

11. Subverting Democratic Machinery 229
Integrating Separate Branches · Friendly Fascist Federalism · Community Carnivals · Contrapuntal Party Harmony · Union-Busting and the Slow Meltdown · The Lessons of the Watergate Conspiracy · Unhinging an Anti-Establishment White House · Coups D'Etat American-Style

12. Managing Information and Minds 255
Information as the March · The Symbolic Environment · Image as the Reality · Narrowing the Scope of Controversy · Manufacturing Opinion by Polling · The Electronic Throne · Monitoring as the Message · Womb-to-Tomb Dossiers · Economic and Social Vindicators · Educational Authoritarianism · Custodial Functions

13. Incentives for System Acceptance 280
Extended Professionalism · Job, Prometheus, Faust · For Consumers: Kidnapper Candy · Servitude's Services · Conditional Benefactions · Rationed Payoffs · The Effulgent Aura

14. The Ladder of Terror 294
The Rungs of Violence · Precision Purging · Forceful Confrontation · Personal Injury · Covert Action · Conflict Among the "Slobs" · A Violence-Vigilante Culture

15. Sex, Drugs, Madness, Cults 311
Sex: Through Liberation to Repression · Drugs: Religion of Some People · Madness: Escape from Madness · Cults: Belonging through Submission

16. The Adaptive Hydra 321
Frying Pan-Fire Conflicts · Multilevel Co-optation · Creative Counterresistance · Innovative Apathetics

17. The Myths of Determinism 331
Impossibility: It Couldn't Happen · Inevitability: It Will Happen
Irreversibility: Eternal Servitude or Holocaust

THREE: True Democracy 339

18. It Hasn't Happened Yet 341
The USA Today vs. Friendly Fascism, USA · Why It Has Not Yet Happened

19. The Long-Term Logic of Democracy 349
The Democratic Mystique · Democratic Struggles

20. The Democratic Logic in Action 355
A Good Neighbor in a New World Order · Democratizing the Establishment · Balancing the Economy · Democratizing the Social Base · Information for Human Liberation · Releasing Humanistic Values · Truth and Rationality

21. What Can You Do? 376
Yes, You . . . · Anyone Anywhere, Really? · High Aspirations, Realistic Expectations · My Country, Right and Wrong

Notes 389
About the Author 403
Index 404

PREFACE
TO THE PAPERBACK EDITION

THE NEW BILL OF FRIGHTS

It is right it should be so
Man was made for Joy and Woe
And when this we rightly know
Thro' the World we safely go.
Joy and Woe are woven fine
A clothing for the Soul Divine;
Under every grief and pine
Runs a joy with silken twine

WILLIAM BLAKE
Auguries of Innocence

Hope and fear arc inseparable.

LA ROCHEFOUCALD
Maxims

FRIENDLY FASCISM portrays two conflicting trends in the United States and other countrics of the so-called "free world."

The first is a slow and powerful drift toward greater concentration of power and wealth in a repressive Big Business-Big Government partnership. This drift leads down the road toward a new and subtly manipulative form of corporatist serfdom. The phrase "friendly fascism" helps distinguish this possible future from the patently vicious corporatism of classic fascism in the past of Germany, Italy and Japan. It also contrasts with the unfriendly present of the dependent fascisms propped up by the U.S. government in El Salvador, Haiti, Argentina, Chile, South Korea, the Philippines and elsewhere.

The other is a slower and less powerful tendency for individuals and groups to seek greater participation in decisions affecting themselves and others. This trend goes beyond mere reaction to authoritarianism. It transcends the activities of progressive groups or movements and their use of formal democratic machinery. It is nourished by establishment promises—too often rendered false—of more human rights, civil rights and civil liberties. It is embodied in larger values of community, sharing, cooperation, service to others and basic morality as contrasted with crass materialism and dog-eat-dog competition. It affects power relations in the household, workplace, community, school, church, synagogue, and even the labyrinths of private and public bureaucracies. It could lead toward a truer democracy—and for this reason is bitterly fought...

These contradictory trends are woven fine into the fabric of highly industrialized capitalism. The unfolding logic of friendly fascist corporatism is rooted in "capitalist society's transnational growth and the groping responses to mounting crises in a dwindling capitalist world" (p. 6). Mind management and sophisticated repression become more attractive to would-be oligarchs when too many people try to convert democratic promises into reality. On the other hand, the alternative logic of true democracy is rooted in "humankind's long history of resistance to unjustified privilege" (p. 349) and in spontaneous or organized "reaction (other than fright or apathy) to concentrated power...and inequality, injustice or coercion" (p. 351).

A few years ago too many people closed their eyes to the indicators of the first tendency.

But events soon began to change perceptions.

The Ku Klux Klan and American Nazis crept out of the woodwork. An immoral minority of demagogues took to the airwaves. "Let me tell you something about the character of God," orated Jim Robison at a televised meeting personally endorsed by candidate Ronald Reagan. "If necessary, God would raise up a tyrant, a man who may not have the best ethics, to protect the freedom interests of the ethical and the godly." To protect Western oil companies, candidate Jimmy Carter proclaimed presidential willingness to send American troops into the Persian Gulf. Rosalyn Carter went further by telling an Iowa campaign audience: "Jimmy is not afraid to declare war." Carter then proved himself unafraid to expand unemployment, presumably as an inflation cure, thereby reneging on his party's past full employment declarations.

Reaching the White House with this assist from Carter (as well as from the Klan and the immoral minority of televangelicals), Reagan promptly served the immediate interests of the most powerful and the wealthiest. The Reaganites depressed real wages through the worst unemployment since the 1929-39 depression, promoted "give backs" by labor unions, cut social programs for lower and middle income people, expanded tax giveaways for the truly rich, boosted the military budget and warmed up the cold war. They launched savage assaults on organized labor, civil rights and civil liberties.

Horrified by this new bill of frights, many people who had earlier thought *Friendly Fascism* exaggerated the danger of authoritarianism switched to the other extreme by the end of 1981. Some people donned sweatshirts depicting Reagan as "the fascist gun in the West." Many attacked my use of the world "friendly." Going further than I had ever done, the distinguished economist Robert Lekachman named a name:

> Ronald Reagan must be the nicest president who ever destroyed a union, tried to cut school lunch milk rations from six to four ounces, and compelled families in need of public help to first dispose of household goods in excess of $1,000...If there is an authoritarian regime in the American future, Ronald Reagan is tailored to the image of a friendly fascist...[1]

Today, as the world moves toward 1984 and beyond, too many people fail to see the workings of the alternative logic. Their gloom seems unabated by awareness of the growing sources of hope and joy woven into the current scene of fear and grief. Others seem confused by either-or simplifications. "Which are you?" they ask me, "a pessimist or an optimist?" "Both" is the most sensible answer. To be only the former would be self-defeating—and to be only the latter would be self-deception.

But the questioning continues. "Since *Friendly Fascism* was published, which of the two tendencies has become stronger?"

Let me answer this one by first looking at the bad news, then at the good news—and then at the question of just who is looking how at what...

EVILS AMONG US

> Evil is no faceless stranger
> living in a distant neighborhood.
> Evil has a wholesome, hometown face,
> with merry eyes and an open smile.
> Evil walks among us, wearing a mask
> which looks like all our faces.
>
> THE BOOK OF COUNTED SORROWS

> A naught, a liar, a devil or dunce—
> Could he be possibly all at once?
>
> B.G.

The bad news is that evil now wears a friendlier face than ever before in American history.

"Like a good TV commercial, Reagan's image goes down easy," Mark Crispin Miller has written, "calming his audience with sweet inversions of the truth...He has learned to liven up his every televised appearance with frequent shifts in expression, constant movements of the head, lots of warm chuckles and ironic shrugs and sudden frowns of manly purpose. Reagan is unfailingly attractive—'a nice guy,' pure and simple." But what is really there, he asks, behind the mask?[2]

The President's critics have many answers. Some call him "an amiable dunce." Some see him, reports Miller, as a devil "who takes from the poor to give to the rich, has supported infanticide abroad, ravages his own countryside and props up brutal dictatorships." Others regard him as a congenital falsifier who surrounds any half-truth with a "bodyguard of lies." Miller himself has still another answer: there is nothing behind the mask. "The best way to keep his real self hidden" he suggests, "is not to have one...Reagan's mask and face are as one." To this, one might add that the Reagan image is an artfully designed blend of charisma and machismo, a combination that Kusum Singh calls *charismacho*.[3]

"Princes," wrote Machiavelli many centuries ago, "should delegate the ugly jobs to other people, and reserve the attractive functions for themselves." In keeping with this maxim, Reagan's less visible entourage has surrounded the President with highly visible targets of disaffection: Volcker, Stockman, Haig, Weinberger, Kirkpatrick, and Watt. In comparison, Reagan looks truly wholesome. This makes it all the more difficult to focus attention on the currents and forces behind the people behind the President—or for that matter, other less visible leaders of the American Establishment.

That focus, of course, is at the heart of this book. It is developed throughout the chapters on "The Roots of Friendly Fascism" (Part One) and "The Specter of Friendly Fascism" (Part Two). The more unpleasant of these currents are briefly listed in the right hand column of the table (pp. 344-345) comparing trends toward "Friendly Fascism, U.S.A." (as set forth in Chapters 8—16) with "U.S.A., Early 1980s."

Lamentably, my observations in these nine chapters still hold. They provide a way of looking at Reagan and some Republicans without placing a retrospective halo on the head of Carter or any Democrats. They offer a perspective that places the "new right" and "neo-conservatism"—and also "neo-liberalism"—in the context of the U.S. social system in a period of global stress. Instead of conforming with the current liberal fashion of abstract moaning about threats to democracy, they pinpoint the many paths that tyranny walks as it comes slowly "on little cat feet."

But when I sent the book to the printer in January 1980, I underestimated two factors: the speed with which some of the evils might emerge and the power of the nice guy friendliness that would help disguise their emergence. These factors require an extension of my earlier warning.

When I think of the new dangers from reactionary forces, I remember the famous words used toward the end of the Franco-led rebellion against the Spanish republic: "I have four columns marching on Madrid and a fifth column inside the city itself." Today, I see five columns marching against the people of the United States and our democratic institutions.

In the geography of politics, all five columns come from what is loosely known as "the Right." None of them was first assembled after Reagan's inauguration. All have a long history behind them. Each was helped—openly or secretly—by his campaign organizers. Each contributed to his election. None is separate from the others. Each column mingles with the others and squabbles with them over strategy, tactics and division of the spoils. While each operates both under cover of darkness and in open daylight, the first four can more readily be seen and combatted.

The first is a motley array of fanatical freebooters. The so-called Moral Majority whips up militarism in an effort to stem anti-militarist tides among other evangelicals. The Ku Klux Klan and the American Nazis stir up racism and anti-semitism. Well-financed frenetics lead frenzied campaigns on the so-called "social issues," stirring up both sexism and heterosexism. The so-called "right to life" opponents of abortion often condone the destruction of life through military adventurism and the restoration of the death penalty. Political hucksters capitalize on the fear of "crime in the streets" by promoting the quick fixes of more electrocution and imprisonment, despite clear evidence that these are no more capable of deterring crime than the phlebotomy—blood-letting—used in the Middle Ages was capable of curing disease.[4] Together, these groups focus attention on the many scapegoats—Blacks, Hispanics, Jews, feminists, lesbians, gays, anti-war people and low-income criminals—needed by the larger forces leading what Piven and Cloward call "a new class war against the unemployed, the unemployable, and the working poor."[5] In addition to fostering a "violence-vigilante culture," they distract attention from the many shared interests of the unrich majority and promote divisive tensions among the heterogeneous elements of the low- and middle-income population.

The second is a far-flung suicide squadron. With passionate intensity and compulsive conviction, its leaders flash their instruments of suicidal destruction. Overstating the dangers of a Soviet attack on Western Europe or the Persian Gulf, they flaunt their machismo by reserving the right to make a first strike against the Soviets. Understating the destructive power of U.S. and NATO forces, they seek the charisma (and for the corporations involved, the cost-free capital) derived from resolute dedication to that power's tumescence. For the men and women in military training camps, this glorification of violence is enshrined in the training song: "Kill, Kill/ Hate, Hate/ Murder, Murder/ Mutilate."[6] Behind this bravado is the tacit knowledge that the Reagan administrations's enlargement of overkill capacity breeds insecurity in the first instance and, if ever used, would destroy its users. The unspoken theme song, even more ominous that the "Kill, Kill" chant, is "Spread our missiles far and wide/ Defend ourselves by suicide."

The third is a big money battalion. Under the cover of the maxim "There is no free lunch," the Reagan administration has been giving the truly rich the largest corporate welfare program in U.S. history—through not only military contracts but also an immense variety of tax give-aways, loans, loan guarantees and regulatory or deregulatory favors. The huge handouts promote capital flight, robotization, commodity speculation, merger-mania, condo-mania, speculation in urban and rural real estate and the construction (triply subsidized by federal, state and local government) of luxury hotels and skyscraping office buildings. As a reward for initiative in extracting these benefits from the federal, state and local treasury, top executives get more than free lunch. They get free breakfasts, dinners, cocktail hours, theater tickets, country clubs, vacation resorts and executive planes, boats and limousines. They enjoy free, round-the-clock services by devoted retinues of in-house and out-house academics, lawyers, accountants, public relations people, call-girls, call-boys and other experts. The bill for all this corporate and sensory gratification is paid, of course—but not by them. The money comes, rather, from the pockets of the great majority of Americans. The so-called "trickle down" theory is merely a justification for the actual policy of moving money upward. This is done by cutting income maintenance programs for lower and middle income people, encouraging or tolerating higher unemployment and imposing higher taxes on payrolls and consumption. In "Moving Money Upwards" and the other parts of "Friendly Fascist Economics" (Chapter 10), I outlined the general strategy of doing these things. But in 1980 I didn't anticipate how rapidly and ruthlessly the next administration would start to do them.

The members of the fourth column are sappers of the Constitution. With the active help of the Reaganite White House, they are burrowing deeply under almost every provision of the Bill of Rights. The Department of Justice itself has become a staging ground for those undermining the civil rights of minorities and the First, Fourth, Fifth, Sixth and Eighth Amendment rights of all people. Sixth and Seventh Amendment rights to jury trials are being sidetracked by plea bargaining in criminal cases and "rent-a-judge" schemes in civil cases. Reaganite invasions into the area of personal sexual behavior—through regulations on birth control or abortion—threaten to undermine the Ninth and Tenth Amendments on rights retained by or reserved to the people.

The fifth column is inside our minds. It is composed of the ruling myths that camouflage, encourage and legitimate the other four columns. As shown in "The Friendly Fascist Establishment" (Chapter 9) and "Managing Information and Minds" (Chapter 12), these myths go far beyond "nice guy" imagery. They establish America's symbolic environment. The Reagan administration has triggered a great leap forward in the mobilization and deployment of corporatist myths. Many billions of tax-exempt funds from conservative foundations have gone into the funding of such think tanks as the Heritage Foundation and the American Enterprise Institute. According to the *Wall Street Journal*, nearly three hundred economists on the staffs of conservative think tanks are part of an informal information network organized by the American Heritage Foundation alone.[7] (This contrasts with only about two dozen economists working for trade unions, most of whom are pinned down in researching contract negotiations.) To transmit the myths concocted by the scores of such think tanks, new systems have been put in place. "The fanciest television studio in Washington, D.C. does not belong to ABC, NBC or CBS but to the U.S. Chamber of Commerce," writes Robert K. Massie, Jr. "Through Biznet..." the chamber's president boasts, "we are going to influence the affairs of Congress; we are going to impact on the White House itself for the good of the nation."[8] In 1981, at the White House itself, presidential assistant Wayne Valis organized the Budget Control Working Group, a business coalition that backed up Reagan's personal lobbying by sparking at least half a million telegrams and phone calls to members of Congress from local business executives, particularly campaign contributors. "This business coalition," stated Valis, "is our most reliable, strongest, best organized, most sophisticated support...It's resources are almost scary, they're so big.[9]

Distributing general propaganda, however, is perhaps the scariest operation of the fifth column. Expanded government intervention into the lives of ordinary people is glorified under the slogan "getting the government off our backs." Decriminalization of corporate bribery, fraud and the dumping of health-killing wastes is justified under the banner of "promoting free enterprise" and countering "environmental extremists." Private greed, gluttony and speculation are disguised in "free market" imagery. Business corruption is hidden behind smokescreens of exaggerated attacks on the public sector. Like Trojan horses, these ideas penetrate the defenses of those opposed to any new corporatism. They establish strongholds of false consciousness and treacherous terminology in the minds not only of old-fashioned conservatives but also of the most dedicated liberals and left-wingers.

Hence on many issues the left seems bereft, the middle muddled and the right not always wrong. Other elements are thereby added to the new bill of frights.

One is a frightening retreat by liberals and leftwingers on the key gut issues of domestic policy: full employment, inflation and crime. "Deep cynicism has been engendered in progressive circles by past experiences with 'full employment' legislation (as) the tail on the kite of an ever-expanding military economy."[10] A movement for full employment without militarism or inflation is seen as dangerous by old-time labor leaders, utopian by liberals and by some marxists as impossible under capitalism. Inflation is seen as a conservative issue—or else one that requires the kind of price controls that necessitate more far-reaching social controls over capital. Middle-of-the-roaders try to deal with crime by fussing too much with the details of the police-courthouse-jail-parole complex and too little with the sources of low-income crime, racketeering, political corruption and crime in the executive suites.[11] Thus the demagogues among the Reaganites and their frenetic fringes have been able to seize and keep initiatives on these issues. Those of us who have tried to formulate progressive alternatives too often find ourselves whistling in the dark...

Still more frightening has been the even greater retreat on the subject of *detente*—best defined as the relaxation of tensions in place of confrontation between military powers. In "The Democratic Logic in Action" (Chapter 20), I opened by suggesting a "Detente II" to include all NATO and Warsaw Pact countries, and eventually Third World countries, to replace the shaky, bilateral, and now crumbling Detente I negotiated by Nixon and Brezhnev in 1972. In other First World Countries, action along these lines is taken for granted by anti-war movements and promoted by governments through expanded trade, cultural and scientific exchanges and improved communication at all levels. In the United States, on the contrary, most liberals and left-wingers have dropped the idea entirely. Some dodge the issue because they identify it with Nixon and Kissinger, now outspoken opponents of the detente into which the anti-war movement forced them years ago. Others oppose detente because of the ridiculous idea that U.S.-Soviet tension reduction, which is the precise meaning of the word in Spanish (distension), German (entspannung), and Russian (razrjadka), would result in some "co-dominium," that is, rule of the world by the two superpowers. Others fail to see that relaxation of tensions is a necessary precondition of all anti-war demands: a nuclear freeze, reduction of nuclear and non-nuclear weaponry, cessation of testing and the renunciation by the U.S. of the first strike option. Indeed, members of both the suicide squadron and the big money battalion have exploited Soviet intervention in Afghanistan and influence on Poland in order to raise the high tension level on which increased military spending depends.

Finally, many people allow such "dirty words" as *fascism* (or even *capitalism* and *exploitation*) to cloud their perception of the evils among us. Because *fascism* is often a violent epithet hurled at any user of brute force, they are taken in by the simplistic linkage (dissected on p. 30-31 and again on p. 294) of fascism with brutality alone. Because some think of fascism only in the classic forms they observed (or suffered from) between

World Wars I and II, they reject the term's use in referring to the significantly different corporatist tendencies in countries of highly industrialized (or "post-industrial") capitalism. Other symbols may be O.K.—Nicos Poulantzas' "positive state," Morton Mintz's "America, Inc.," Senator Sam J. Ervin's "post-constitutionalism," Kenneth Dolbeare's "repressive managerialism," the *Wall Street Journal*'s "benign totalitarianism," or even the *New York Times*' "over-all corporate-government complex." But not the nasty seven-letter word—not Stephen Spender's "fascism without tears," nor R.E. Paul's and J.T. Winkler's "fascism with a human face," and, of course, not "friendly fascism." S.J. Woolf, a British analyst, is so upset by the different meanings given the word (a phenomenon characterizing every important word in the dictionary) that he adds to the confusion by suggesting that "perhaps the word *fascism* should be banned." This principle, of course, would also ban ban *dictatorship, authoritarianism* and *totalitarianism,* and such "squeaky clean" terms as *democracy, freedom* and *equality.* The tyranny of emotion-laden terms is to be fought not by avoidance but by clarifying the meanings one gives to them. The fault, dear reader, is not in the stars or the symbols, but in ourselves and how we fail to clarify our usage.

To help clarify my meaning, I have tried to sweep away the myths surrounding classic fascism (p. 28-33) and sharply pinpoint both the similarities and the differences among the varieties of authoritarian capitalism (as briefly summarized on p. 168-172). For those who take "friendly" too seriously, I have focussed sharply in "The Ladder of Terror" (Chapter 14) and elsewhere on the many "iron fists" beneath the velvet gloves of mind management, manipulation, rationed payoffs and co-optation. Occasionally, in deference to some people's overly tender sensibilities, I have identified the sharpening conflict between capitalism and democracy without once using the ugly word beginning with "f."

In a recent interview with *Fortune* I used the word *syzygy* to refer to the repressive conjunction of Big Business and Big Government without either losing tis identity. Attacking "solemnly silly syzygy," the reporter saw "syzygy avoidance...being fiercely debated on *Agronsky and Company,* harmoniously elaborated by all those characters who keep nodding at each other on *Washington Week in Review,* joked about in a Johnny Carson monologue or lengthily testified on before Congress."[12] Despite this *Fortune* fantasy, unfortunately, no euphemistic word play by itself could possibly break through the media's silken controls and focus national attention on the evils among us or the many kinds of action needed to avoid a new authoritarianism. Even a conservative like Kevin Phillips is ignored when in Post-Conservative America (New York: Random House, 1982) he warns against "apple pie authoritarianism" or an American Caesarism that "could make a more triumphal entry through television than was ever possible by chariot."

GOOD TIDINGS

How beautiful upon the mountains are the footsteps of the herald who bringeth good tidings, who publisheth peace...

ISAIAH, III, 7

Helter skelter have I rode to thee
And tidings do I bring and lucky joys
And golden times.

WILLIAM SHAKESPEARE

One cannot find these good ideas wrapped up someplace in a neat package. Helter skelter must one ride to find them, and even then many will not be seen. Moreover, some of the best of these ideas are usually wrecked—like many of the first airplanes—when first tried out.

In explaining why a new corporatism has not yet emerged in a more repressive form, I point out that "despite substantial erosion in constitutional democracy, there are still many people and groups who insist on using the freedoms and opportunities that are available." I also note that the dominant logic of friendly fascism tends to spark an alternative—but still subordinate—logic of true democracy. ("It Hasn't Happened Yet," Chapter 18, and "The Long-Term Logic of Democracy," Chapter 19.) This logic is expressed in the many warm currents that swirl through the cold water and among the ice floes.

Since completing my manuscript at the end of 1979, I have found that while more ice has congealed, more warm currents may also be found. In urban ghettoes and rural slums, unhonored heroes and heroines—poor white, Black, Hispanic and Native American—struggle daily against the fearful odds of desolation and hopelessness. Among workers and technicians, ceaseless creativity, like a wild flower, pushes up through the crevices of corporate and government hierarchies. One can hardly think of an innovative idea for human betterment—whether through group action, self-help, or both together—that is not being tried someplace in this country, perhaps just around your corner.

"The big cliche of this political season," writes Bob Kuttner, "is that the Left has run out of ideas." He then brings good tidings by listing ten good ideas now in the percolation stage; capital allocation, adjustment policies, controlling corporate flight, democratizing pension fund capital, worker ownership, cooperatives, "trickle-up" savings and tax incentives, energy and jobs, public works and full employment.[13] Martin Charnoy, Derek Shearer and Mark Green have developed a large array of similar themes in much greater detail.[14] Robert Lekachman offers a few strategic themes: democratic planning for full employment with a balance between a few strategic themes: democratic planning for full employment with a central direction and local control, worker control in the workplace, a much narrower gap between the rich and the poor, and a tilt in the direction of a more human scale rather than giantism.[15] In various parts of the country "a loose network of community, labor, minority, academic and peace activists has responded (to recession and continuing unemployment) with an innovative economic proposal called 'locally-based national planning' (through) the novel combination of political mobilization and participatory legislation drafting."[16] The ongoing work on this proposal is aimed at breaking the historic connection between full employment and cold war liberalism, healing the breach between national planning that hovers in the air without touching the ground and local planning parochially disconnected from national and global issues. Above all, it is aimed at helping build a locally based national movement with the power to make fundamental changes in the social structure, culture and economy of the United States.

The hope for such a movement lies less in any immediate prospect of a broad-based people's party and more in the growth of smaller movements that may later provide the sinews of majoritarian politics. I see at least ten of these sources of optimism:

1. an anti-war movement which, with a much stronger religious component than during the Vietnam War, has thus far prevented direct U.S. military intervention in El Salvador and has pushed the Reagan administration into arms control negotiations. The huge anti-war demonstration in New York City on June 12, 1982, testifies to the potential power behind efforts to halt the arms race and divert part of the swollen military budget to meeting human needs.
2. an anti-nuclear power and environmental movement that has already been a decisive factor in stopping the growth of the nuclear energy industry in the U.S.
3. a neighborhood movement that has brought millions of ordinary people, conservatives included, into responsible activism against corporate and bureaucratic exploitation and, in the words of Harry Boyte, has provided "a vast schooling in democracy."[17]
4. labor unions, that, according to Francis Fox Piven and Richard A. Cloward, are "likely to be radicalized by the pressure of a rank-and-file indignant over rising unemployment, provocative anti-union federal policies, and intense corporate efforts to roll back earlier wage and workplace victories."[18]
5. government employees who collectively have been joining labor unions in larger numbers and who individually, as with the

Justice Department lawyers in response to the Reaganite efforts to provide tax exemption for racist schools, are often willing to "blow the whistle" in public.

6. civil liberties and civil rights organizations that have followed the lead of the National Emergency Committee on Civil Liberties and the American Civil Liberties Union in fighting back militantly against almost every one of the Reaganite assaults on the Bill of Rights.
7. organizations of older people that have already proved their mettle by beating back one after another of the Reaganite attacks on social security entitlements, by making forward advances toward removing mandatory retirement from the statute books and, as in the case of the Gray Panthers, playing a key role in nursing the embryonic full employment movement.
8. the small beginnings of a more serious socialist presence with the merger of the Democratic Socialist Organizing Committee and the New American Movement into the new Democratic Socialists of America (D.S.A.).
9. continuing progress, despite the regressive forces of sexism and homophobia, in extending the liberating values of the women's movements and the civil and human rights of lesbians and gay men.
10. in the words of Kusum Singh, a warm current of "bottom-sideways communication" among people who are fed up with the elitism, snobbery, and hierarchy of most private and public bureaucracies and are inventing democratic leadership styles that escape "charismacho."

The enlargement of this last current, already discernable in each of the movements referred to above, would be the best guarantee against their being diverted by establishment forces or perverted by the "iron law of oligarchy" in operation among progressives themselves. An important part of this current is the growing body of theory, grounded on the examination of practice, on "community relations" as an integral part of socialism,[19] heterarchy (or polyarchy) instead of hierarchy,[20] and the empowerment of "inferiors" and "non-significant people" through alternatives to bureaucratic decision-making.[21]

And far from scattered activism and anti-establishment theory, untold numbers of people develop new life-styles that challenge establishment hegemony more frontally than some of the external symbols of the old youth culture: e.g., sexual freedom, dress, hair style or drug use. These intimations of a new and non-exploitative culture may now be found at each stage of the life cycle. Many children now come into the world not only through natural child-birth but in a "natural" room where the father is a part of the child-birth process. Many are now growing up without having their minds stuffed into pre-ordained sex roles or twisted by racial bias. For some, education becomes and remains a joyous process of exploration as well as discipline. With maturity, some people attain a new openness, freeing themselves from the repressions and traumas of childhood and adolescence, working with others on behalf of small common interests or avoiding most of the pressures toward rat race competition. With old age, there are trends toward new self-assertion, a political and cultural activism that defies the old waiting-for-death outlook, and tendencies toward bringing grandparents back into the home and rejecting the warehousing of older people in "golden age" projects and nursing homes. At all ages of life, moreover, there are small experiments and initiatives in doing customary things much differently and more creatively than ever before. If one looks hard enough, these may be found in well-baby clinics, classrooms, factories, fields, mines, artists' studios and innovative, experimental or non-commercial theaters near Main Street and off Broadway. Someplace in America—perhaps far away, but maybe around the corner from you—you may find real people really doing some of the things on a small scale that you might have thought could occur only in some never-never dream world. If these activities may be sometimes an alternative to open activism or a refuge for the frustrated, they nonetheless renew and deepen the counter-establishment currents in the heartland of First World capitalism. They are a way in which some people change the world a little as part of changing themselves much more.

VIGILANCE

> Power is always gradually stealing away from the many to the few, because the few are more vigilant and consistent.
>
> SAMUEL JOHNSON

> Tell the truth and run.
>
> YUGOSLAV PROVERB

Many years ago, as touched on in "Economic and Social Vindicators" (pp. 273-277), I helped develop a "social indicator movement" to help monitor the changing nature of U.S. society. Most of the people involved in this effort concentrated on seeking improved measures to supplement the increasingly one-sided supply of economic indicators. My own approach was more ambitious. In *The State of the Nation: Social Systems Accounting*, I constructed a model for continuous reporting on the changing structure and performance of the United States' system in its physical and world environment.[22] I called this framework *social systems accounting* to stress the value of an interrelated set of structured indicators (non-statistical as well as statistical) and the need for such information to hold individuals and institutions accountable for, rather than to vindicate, their behavior. But "the maturation of social accounting concepts," I warned, "will take many decades."

The most constructive criticism of my proposed system came from Gerhard Colm of the National Planning Association, who objected to an abstract strategy of information collection rather than an effort to put it into practice. "Why don't you apply the model to the United States," he asked, "and in the application improve it?"

In writing *Friendly Fascism* I tried to do exactly that. And in the final manuscript, I summed up my efforts in a preface that included the following comment:

> In this volume I have tried to produce my own report on the changing "State of the Nation." In so doing, I have used qualitative information and subjective judgments as well as formal statistics (much of which I look upon with growing suspicion). Like other transdisciplinarians, I have used any kind of information—economic, social, cultural, political, ecological—that may illuminate the nature and future of the American system in the world environment...
>
> Since this is an anti-establishment report, I have often had to revise radically many established concepts, using new conceptual frameworks that challenge the fundamental values, if not the integrity, of official data and data-dispensers. This approach has required somewhat less attention to the details of system performance as usually measured, much more attention to the power, values and thought structures of high technology capitalism. It has demanded frank recognition of capitalism's substantial achievements without translating these into proof of unmodified benevolence or promise of inevitable progress...I see the indicators in this report on the changing state of the nation both as indictors of the system's shortcomings and as vindicators of the struggles and dreams of all those who have envisioned, and fought for, a more human and egalitarian social order in the United States. It is also my hope that the information in this volume may incite people to organized action against the maturation of modern capitalism's most dangerous potentials.[23]

But these words never appeared in the hard-cover edition of *Friendly Fascism*. Nor does that (or this) volume contain the theoretical and historical materials that pulled together in a more integrated fashion the many threads of my analysis.[24]

These portions of my manuscript were not excluded by my original publisher, who consistently supported my effort to monitor the U.S. establishment—despite the fact that his company was a subsidiary of Gulf and Western, the great transnational conglomerate. In June 1978 when he formally accepted the completed manuscript, I asked him, "Are you at all bothered by my rather disrespectful references to Gulf and Western?" He brushed the query aside with a careless wave of his hand.

A few days later, through an act of careful vigilance by Gulf and Western, the publisher and his staff were fired. Descending from the conglomerate's bureaucratic heights, a Gulf and Western accountant broke the news suddenly. The justification: inadequate cash flow. Although the publisher tried to plumb the subject a little further, he was denied access to the less visible higher-ups. The accountant's words were final. But behind "inadequate cash flow," I am sure there were many other reasons—so many that this courageous acceptance of *Friendly Fascism* for publication was probably just the proverbial "straw that broke the camel's back."

While seeking another publisher, I recalled a crucial sentence in "It Hasn't Happened Yet" (Chapter 18): "If friendly fascism had already arrived, a book like this could not be published—unless previously edited to make repression seem more acceptable and its reversal impossible" (p. 342). When I had circulated the draft of this chapter among my graduate students, one of them responded by writing in the margin beside the words "could not be published" the cryptic comment: "It hasn't been..."

For a while, I thought it might never be. And as I have already pointed out, parts of it have not been. The price of publication was the excision of all the theoretical analysis, most of the history and the entire discussion of social monitoring.

On this last theme, unfortunately, there seems to be a strange division of labor between reactionaries and progressives in the United States. With the help of well-paid co-optees, agents provocateurs and sophisticated surveillance technologies, the former monitor the latter. In turn, the progressives try to monitor the former.

This is far from a balanced operation. Progressives have relatively few resources at their disposal. Also, critics of the establishment—even advocates of gradual restructuring rather than longer-range transformation—have many fewer resources at their disposal. Some of the establishment's most persistent demystifiers themselves suffer from the myopia bred by necessity of making a living in a specialized disciplinary niche. Some organizers are street wise and system stupid. Many modern marxists flinch from the task of reconceptualizing such basic concepts as exploitation, accumulation, capital, class, workers, surplus value, profits, and—above all—socialism. Some know full well what Bernard Shaw had in mind when he wrote that "All great truths begin as blasphemies." Rather than stand up to the hazards of heresy (and *then* running, as in the Yugoslav proverb), they run from unpleasant truths by not telling them.

On the other hand, most establishment leaders seem systematically incapable of seeing themselves—and the sources of their own power—clearly. Trapped by the myths needed for legitimation, fouled up by the jargon designed by experts, deceived by their own images of charismacho, they discourage the straight talk required for self-awareness and vigilance with respect to the system as a whole.

The comparative advantage, hopefully, lies with the forces of democracy. Over the long run, we are better able to look at ourselves as well as at U.S. capitalism in a confusing world environment. Our vigilance has a broader scope. It is also more persistent—because it is motivated more by genuine moral commitment than by the personalistic greed for money and power that the ideologues of the "free market" try to dress up in moralistic garb. This preface—as an extension of *Friendly Fascism*'s identification of two conflicting logics—is itself a small exercise in persistence.

A more consistent approach to vigilance by the many has been suggested by Dr. Archie W. Singham, professor of political science at Brooklyn College of City University of New York. "We need a network of monitors, a Democracy Watch," Professor Singham urges, "to keep track of every tendency described in *Friendly Fascism*. An updated report should be published regularly—every year if possible but at least every two years..."

It is too early to tell whether the Singham plan, which marries persistence with consistency, is feasible. But if or when it is attempted, much more would also be needed. No single model or single set of concepts can cope fully with the mysterious dynamics of an extremely complex system undergoing recurrent crisis. Too much consistency in applying a single set of indicators could inhibit the creativity of those who want to develop their own indicators or prefer their own terminology to express similar ideas. It could distract attention from the vital need to counter what I have called "hardening of the categories," the principle disease that can affect any data-processing operation. This disease can be avoided, as I stated in 1966, "only by continuing debate, review and recurrent reconstruction"[25]—and, as I have learned more recently, by direct involvement in efforts to attain a truer democracy...

I hope that this paperback edition of *Friendly Fascism*, along with the updating in this preface, will contribute to such debate, review and reconstruction.

Moraga, California
1982

Notes to Preface.

1. Robert Lekachman, *Greed Is Not Enough* (New York: Pantheon, 1982, pp. 3, 179-180).
2. "Mark Crispin Miller on Television," *The New Republic,* April 7, 1982.
3. Kusum Singh, "People Against Charisma," *Communicator,* Quarterly Journal of the Indian Institute of Mass Communication, October 1981.
4. Bertram Gross, "Reagan's Criminal 'Anti-Crime' Fix," in Frank Riessman, ed., *What Reagan Is Doing To Us* (New York: Harper and Row, 1982).
5. Francis Fox Piven and Richard A. Cloward, *The New Class War* (New York: Pantheon, 1982).
6. Used for warming up women cadets at the Air Force Academy, according to Grace Lichtenstein, *Machisma: Women and Daring* (Garden City: Doubleday, 1981).
7. Bob Kuttner, "The Other Side," *Working Papers,* May-June 1982.
8. Robert K. Massie, Jr., "Giving America the Business," *The Nation,* May 8, 1982.
9. Sidney Blumenthal, "Whose Side Is Business On Anyway?" *New York Times Magazine,* Oct. 25, 1981.
10. Bertram Gross and Stanley Moses, "Full Employment: Planning from the Bottom Up," *The Nation,* April 10, 1982.
11. Bertram Gross, "Is the Left Guilty of Criminal Neglect?" *In These Times,* Nov. 25-Dec. 1, 1981; "Sóme Anti-Crime Proposals for Progressives," *The Nation,* Feb. 6, 1982; and "Reagan's Criminal 'Anti-Crime' Fix," in Frank Riessman, ed. *What Reagan Is Doing To Us* (New York: Harper and Row, 1982).
12. For the use of the word *syzygy* in this connection I am indebted to the work of Arthur S. Miller, the noted constitutional lawyer, in *The Modern Corporate State* (Westport: Greenwood Press, 1976) and also his more recent *Democratic Dictatorship: the Emergent Constitution of Control* (Westport: Greenwood Press, 1981).
    Similar symbolic flexibility has been shown by R.E. Paul and J.T. Winkler who switch back and forth between "fascism with a human face" and "new corporatism" ("The Coming Corporatism," *Challenge,* March April 1975). Russell Baker has gone still further in symbolic analysis in "A Nice Muddle of Meddle" (*New York Times*, June 3, 1981), which ridicules Jean Kirkpatrick's distinction between *authoritarian* and *totalitarian.*
13. Bob Kuttner, "Economic Jeopardy," *Mother Jones,* May 1982. These ten ideas have been sired by, or are the offspring of, many more ideas than could have been covered in one article. In another vital review article, "Democratic Investment" (*democracy*, April 1982), Maurice Zeitlin pulls together new ideas on the possibilitiy of a Public Investment Reserve System that would "balance the private right to earn profits with the public right to decide democratically how to reinvest a portion of them in the public interest."
14. Martin Charnoy and Derek Shearer, *Economic Democracy: The Challenge of the 1980's* (White Plains: M.E. Sharpe, 1980); Mark Greene, *Winning Back America* (New York: Bantam, 1982).
15. Robert Lekachman, *Greed Is Not Enough* (New York: Pantheon, 1982).
16. Bertram Gross and Stanley Moses, "Full Employment: Planning From the Bottom Up," *The Nation,* April 10, 1982. A fuller report on this approach is presented in Bertram Gross and Stanley Moses, "How to Plan for Full Employment," a study prepared for the Institute for Policy Studies.
17. Harry C. Boyte, *The Backyard Revolution: Understanding the New Citizen Movement* (Philadelphia: Temple University Press, 1980).

18. Francis Fox Piven and Richard A. Cloward, *The New Class War: Reagan's Attack on the Welfare State and Its Consequences* (New York: Pantheon, 1982).
19. Michael Albert and Robin Hahnel, *Socialism Today and Tomorrow* and *Marxism and Socialist Theory* (Boston: South End Press, 1981).
20. Hazel Henderson, *The Politics of the Solar Age: Alternatives to Economics* (Garden City: Anchor Press, 1981).
21. William G. Scott and David K. Hart, *Organizational America: Can Individual Freedom Survive Within the Security It Promises?* (Boston: Houghton Mifflin, 1979); and Frederick C. Thayer, *An End to Hierarchy and Competition: Administration in the Post-Affluent World,* 2nd edition (New York: Franklin Watts, 1981). These and similar theoretical currents are being brought together by Kusum Singh and Bertram Gross in an ongoing study. *The Age of Charismacho.*
22. Bertram Gross, *The State of the Nation: Social Systems Accounting* (London: Tavistock, 1966, and New York: Barnes and Noble, 1966). This monograph also appeared as Chapter 3 in Raymond A. Bauer, ed., *Social Indicators* (Cambridge, Mass.: MIT Press, 1966). An historical review and critique of work in this area may be found in Bertram Gross and Jeffrey Straussman, "The Social Indicator Movement,"*Social Policy.* September/October 1974.
23. For the distinction between indicators, indictors and vindicators, I am indebted to Albert D. Biderman's section on "vindicators and indictors" in his "Social Indicators and Goals," Chapter 2 in Raymond A. Bauer, *Social Indicators* (Cambridge, Mass.: MIT Press, 1966).
24. The material expunged from the original manuscript included (1) a preface that summarized my long wanderings through the writings of Marx and Engels and the thick forests of Marxian literature; (2) a first chapter setting forth "the logic of a more perfect capitalism" (the book's original subtitle), in the new era of transnational accumulation; (3) "Imperfect Capitalism and Its Crises," a chapter dissecting the growth of industrial capitalism from its earliest days until World War II; (4) "Imperfect Socialism: The Specter Materializes," a chapter on the nature and impact of the Russian, Chinese and Cuban revolutions; and (5) "The Alternative Logic," a concluding chapter in which I defined three interrelated responses to the threat of friendly fascism: minimal defense of the best in the *status quo*, an in-between effort to attain "capitalism with a difference" (now briefly discussed on pp. 373-375) and a maximum approach to "socialism-with-a-difference." I defined the third approach as the invention of a democratic socialism attuned to the transformation of highly industrialized capitalist countries rather than—as in the Russian, Chinese and Cuban revolutions—the semi-feudal systems of the Tsar, Chiang Kai Shek and Batista. In this presentation I stressed something often ignored by modern socialists: namely, that a growing socialist movement might have the unintended consequence of either (i) provoking stronger counter-tendencies toward a repressive corporate state or (ii) undermining itself by facilitating the kind of reforms that might take the hard edge off exploitation and produce capitalism-with-some-difference. Also, I reluctantly had to omit many of the most trenchant details from "The Rise and Fall of Classic Fascism" (now Chapter 1) and my entire discussion of "A Larger and Abler Working Class" in "The Take-Off Toward a New Corporate Society" (now Chapter 2). Most of this material is being used in a new study, undertaken jointly with Kusum Singh, under the title of *The Dialectics of Heaven and Hell: The Logic of a More Perfect Capitalism.* In doing this, we shall improve the model for social system accounting and give more balanced attention to the indicators of good tidings as well as of the evils among us.
25. Bertram Gross, *The State of the Nation, op. cit.* (Tavistock edition, p. 142, MIT Press edition, p. 260).

Introduction: A Patriotic Warning

THIS IS A BOOK ABOUT DEMOCRACY.

It is a book of realism, fear, and hope.

It is about great achievements and tragic failures in America; about maneuverings that could turn the democracy we now know into a new form of despotism. Above all, it is about a more "true" democracy.

As I look toward the future, I see the possibility in America for a more genuine democracy than has ever existed. Economically, socially, culturally, and politically the people of that America would be able to take part—more directly than ever before—in decisions affecting themselves and others and our nation's role in the world. The country would operate in the best sense of a national "honeycomb" of interrelating groups and individuals. On all sides, I see the potentials for that America. "The spirits of great events," in Johannon von Schiller's words, "stride on before the event/ And in today already walks tomorrow." That kind of future, more than material possessions, has always been the vital center of the American dream.

Looking at the present, I see a more probable future: a new despotism creeping slowly across America. Faceless oligarchs sit at command posts of a corporate-government complex that has been slowly evolving over many decades. In efforts to enlarge their own powers and privileges, they are willing to have others suffer the intended or unintended consequences of their institutional or personal greed. For Americans, these consequences include chronic inflation, recurring recession, open and hidden unemployment, the poisoning of air, water, soil and bodies, and, more important, the subversion of our constitution. More broadly, consequences include widespread intervention in international politics through economic manipulation, covert action, or military invasion. On a world scale, all of this is already producing a heating up of the cold war and enlarged stockpiles of nuclear and non-nuclear death machines.

I see at present members of the Establishment or people on its fringes who, in the name of Americanism, betray the interests of most Americans by fomenting militarism, applauding rat-race individualism, protecting undeserved privilege, or stirring up nationalistic and ethnic hatreds. I see pretended patriots who desecrate the American flag by waving it while waiving the law.

In this present, many highly intelligent people look with but one eye and see only one part of the emerging Leviathan. From the right, we are warned against the danger of state capitalism or state socialism, in which Big Business is dominated by Big Government. From the left, we hear that the future danger (or present reality) is monopoly capitalism, with finance capitalists dominating the state. I am prepared to offer a cheer and a half for each view; together, they make enough sense for a full three cheers. Big Business and Big Government have been learning how to live in bed together, and despite arguments between them, enjoy the cohabitation. Who may be on top at any particular moment is a minor matter—and in any case can be determined only by those with privileged access to a well-positioned keyhole.

I am uneasy with those who still adhere strictly to President Eisenhower's warning in his farewell address against the potential for the disastrous rise of power in the hands of the military-industrial complex. Nearly two decades later, it should be clear to the opponents of militarism that the military-industrial complex does not walk alone. It has many partners: the nuclear-power complex, the technology-science complex, the energy-auto-highway complex, the banking-investment-housing complex, the city-planning-development-land-speculation complex, the agribusiness complex, the communications complex, and the enormous tangle of public bureaucracies and universities whose overt and secret services provide the foregoing with financial sustenance and a nurturing environment. Equally important, the emerging Big Business-Big Government partnership has a global reach. It is rooted in colossal transnational corporations and complexes that help knit together a "Free World" on which the sun never sets. These are elements of the new despotism.

A few years ago a fine political scientist, Kenneth Dolbeare, conducted a series of in-depth interviews totalling twenty to twenty-five hours per person. He found that most respondents were deeply afraid of some future despotism. "The most striking thing about inquiring into expectations for the future," he reported, "is the rapidity with which the concept of fascism (with or without the label) enters the conversation." [1] But not all knowledge serves the cause of freedom. In this case the tendency is to suppress fears of the future, just as most people have learned to repress fears of a nuclear holocaust. It is easier to repress well-justified fears than to control the dangers giving rise to them. Thus Dolbeare found an "air-raid shelter mentality, in which people go underground rather than deal directly with threatening prospects."

Fear by itself, as Alan Wolfe has warned, could help immobilize people and nurture the apathy which is already too large in American society.[2] But repression of fear can do the same thing—and repression of fear is a reality in America.

As I look at America today, I am not afraid to say that I am afraid.

I am afraid of those who proclaim that it can't happen here. In 1935 Sinclair Lewis wrote a popular novel in which a racist, anti-Semitic, flag-waving, army-backed demagogue wins the 1936 presidential election and proceeds to establish an Americanized version of Nazi Germany. The title, *It Can't Happen Here,* was a tongue-in-cheek warning that it might. But the "it" Lewis referred to is unlikely to happen again any place. Even in today's Germany, Italy or Japan, a modern-style corporate state or society would be far different from the old regimes of Hitler, Mussolini, and the Japanese oligarchs. Anyone looking for black shirts, mass parties, or men on horseback will miss the telltale clues of creeping fascism. In any First World country of advanced capitalism, the new fascism will be colored by national and cultural heritage, ethnic and religious composition, formal political structure, and geopolitical environment. The Japanese or German versions would be quite different from the Italian variety—and still more different from the British, French, Belgian, Dutch, Australian, Canadian, or Israeli versions. In America, it would be supermodern and multi-ethnic—as American as Madison Avenue, executive luncheons, credit cards, and apple pie. It would be fascism with a smile. As a warning against its cosmetic facade, subtle manipulation, and velvet gloves, I call it friendly fascism. What scares me most is its subtle appeal.

I am worried by those who fail to remember—or have never learned—that Big Business–Big Government partnerships, backed up by other elements, were the central facts behind the power structures of old fascism in the days of Mussolini, Hitler, and the Japanese empire builders.

I am worried by those who quibble about labels. Some of my friends seem transfixed by the idea that if it is fascism, it must appear in the classic, unfriendly form of their youth. "Why, oh why," they retrospectively moan, "didn't people see what was happening during the 1920s and the 1930s?" But in their own blindness they are willing to use the terms invented by the fascist ideologists, "corporate state" or "corporatism," but not fascism.

I am upset with those who prefer to remain spectators until it may be too late. I am shocked by those who seem to believe—in Anne Morrow Lindbergh's words of 1940—that "there is no fighting the wave of the future" and all you can do is "leap with it." [3] I am appalled by those who stiffly maintain that nothing can be done until things get worse or the system has been changed.

I am afraid of inaction. I am afraid of those who will heed no warnings and who wait for some revelation, research, or technology to offer a perfect solution. I am afraid of those who do not see that some of the best in America has been the product of promises and that the promises of the past are not enough for the future. I am dismayed by those who will not hope, who will not commit themselves to something larger than themselves, of those who are afraid of true democracy or even its pursuit.

I suspect that many people underestimate both the dangers that lie ahead and the potential strength of those who seem weak and powerless. Either underestimation stems, I think, from fear of bucking the Establishment. This is a deep and well-hidden fear that guides the thoughts and actions of many of my warmest friends, closest colleagues, and best students. It is a fear I know only too well, for it has pervaded many years of my life.

I fear any personal arrogance in urging this or that form of action—the arrogance of ideologues who claim a monopoly on truth, of positivists who treat half-truths as whole truths, of theoreticians who stay aloof from the dirty confusions of political and economic combat, and of the self-styled "practical" people who fear the endless clash of theories. I am afraid of the arrogance of technocrats as well as the ultra-rich and their high executives. Some of this arrogance I often find in my own behavior. I am afraid of blind anti-fascism.[4]

One form of blindness was suddenly revealed to me in a graduate seminar in which I was trying out the ideas in this book. One of my brightest students asked me a startling question: "Aren't you a friendly fascist yourself, Professor Gross?"

"How can you possibly ask such a question?" I countered.

She replied with a bill of particulars, which she amplified during a few weeks of disconcerting argument.

First, did not the Employment Act of 1946, which I had helped draft and administer, turn out to strengthen the role not only of the President but also of the corporate-government complex?[5]

She then went on to my writings on management. Didn't they all point in the direction of a centrally managed society? She made a special point of my work on social indicators. Would not an Annual Social Report of the President, as I had proposed to Presidents Johnson and Nixon, concentrate more power in the presidential part of an increasingly imperial Establishment?

A strange answer to her rhetorical question came to me in the form of a dream. I saw myself searching for "friendly fascists" through a huge, rambling house. I climbed upstairs, ran through long corridors and opened the doors of many rooms, but found nobody. At last I came to a half-lit room with many doors. I sensed there was someone there, but saw nobody. Striding across the room, I flung open one of the doors—and there sitting at a typewriter and smiling right back at me, I saw MYSELF . . .

I think I now understand the meaning of this dream: For many years I sought solutions for America's ills—particularly unemployment, ill health, and slums—through more power in the hands of central government. In this I was not alone. Almost all my fellow planners, reformers, social scientists, and urbanists presumed the benevolence of more concentrated government power. The major exceptions were those who went to the other extreme of presuming the benevolence of concentrated corporate power, often hiding its existence behind sophistical litanies of praise for the "rationality," "efficiency," or "democracy" of market systems and "free competitive" private enterprise. Thus the propensity toward friendly fascism lies deep in American society. There may even be a little bit of neofascism in those of us who are proudest of our antifascist credentials and commitments.

"You're either part of the solution," wrote Eldridge Cleaver in the 1960s, "or you're part of the problem." By now I think this statement must be both stood on its head and reformulated: "If you can't see that you're part of the problems, then you're standing in the way of attacks on them." It has taken me a long time to concede that I (and my colleagues) have often been a large part of the new Leviathan's entourage. In any case, I no longer am. I no longer regard decentralization or counterbalancing of power as either impossible or undesirable. I see Big Business and Big Government as a joint danger.

For the majority of the population, of course, this is common knowledge. What almost everybody really knows is that the fanfare of elections and "participatory" democracy usually disguises business-government control. Some years ago, a few students popularized this conjugation of the verb "participate":

I participate.	We participate.
You (singular) participate.	You (plural) participate.
He, she or it participates.	THEY decide.

In a world of concentrated, impersonal power, the important levers and wires are usually pulled by invisible hands. To no one is it given to look on many of the faces behind the hands. But everybody knows that THEY include both Big Business and Big Government. In a society dominated by mass media, world-spanning corporations, armies and intelligence agencies, and mysterious bureaucracies, THEY are getting stronger. Meanwhile, the majority of people have little part in the decisions that affect their families, workplaces, schools, neighborhoods, towns, cities, country, and the world. This is why there is declining confidence in the artificial images and rhetorical sales talks of corporate and political leaders and the many institutions which support them.

Some years ago Gunther Anders wrote a warning for the atomic age: "Frighten thy neighbor as thyself. This fear, of course, must be of a special kind: a fearless fear, since it excludes fearing those who would deride us as cowards; a stirring fear, since it would drive us into the streets instead of under the covers; a living fear, not *of* the danger ahead but *for* the generations to come."[6] If fear is to be fearless, stirring, and living, something else must be combined with it—in fact, envelop it.

That something is hope. I am not referring to any deterministic hope rooted in quasi-theological theories of inevitable emancipation through technological progress or proletarian revolution. I am referring to the kind of loving hope that is articulated in rising aspirations and actions toward a truly democratic America in a new world order.

In this hope I am encouraged by many visions of a future participatory democracy. I go along wholly with Alvin Toffler's objective in *Future Shock* of "the transcendence of technocracy and the substitution of more humane, more far-sighted, more democratic planning,"[7] and in *The Third Wave* of creating the "broadened democracy of a new civilization."

As a realistic futurist, however, I start with the past and the present. In part I, "The Roots of Friendly Fascism," I trace the sad logic of declining democracy in First World countries and of rising authoritarianism on the part of a few people at the Establishment's higher levels. For those who have been hiding their heads in the sand, this picture may be a present shock even more painful than Toffler's future shock.

A few years ago, William L. Shirer, whose monumental *The Rise and Fall of the Third Reich* certainly qualifies him as a penetrating observer, commented that America may be the first country in which fascism comes to power through democratic elections.[8] In part II, "The Specter of Friendly Fascism," I document this observation. These chapters provide chilling details on the despotic future that in the present already walks. Unlike Cassandra, I am not mad enough to prophesy what *will* happen. Looking at the future in the light of past trends and current tendencies, I warn against what *could* happen.

The main source of this new-style despotism, I show, is not the frenetics of the Extreme Right—the Know-Nothings, the private militias, the Ku Klux Klan, or the openly neofascist parties. Nor is it the crazies of the Extreme Left. True, either of these might play facilitating, tactical, or triggering roles. But the new order is likely to emerge rather as an outgrowth of powerful tendencies within the Establishment itself. It would come neither by accident nor as the product of any central conspiracy. It would emerge, rather, through the hidden logic of capitalist society's transnational growth and the groping responses to mounting crises in a dwindling capitalist world.

In tracing this situational logic, I try to see the changing crises in America and the world as they are viewed by the leaders of what is now a divided Establishment. I put myself in *their* position as they try to make the most of crises by unifying the Establishment's higher levels, enlarging its transnational outreach, and reducing popular aspirations at home. Without an analysis of this kind, preventive efforts will be myopic, if not blind.

There is an old adage that the cure for the weaknesses of democracy is more democracy. The reason it sounds hollow is that "democracy," like "fascism," is used in many entirely different—even contradictory—ways. When one uses the term to refer only to the formal machinery of representative government, the maxim is a meaningless cliché. Much tinkering with, and perhaps improvements in, democratic machinery might even be expected on the road to serfdom. But if democracy is seen in terms of the decentralization and counterbalancing of power, then the subject for analysis is the reconstructing of society itself.

In part III, "True Democracy," I discuss the endless processes of reconstruction. I show how the forces that have prevented friendly fascism from emerging already could be strengthened in the future. This, also, is not a prediction. It is a statement of what is possible, as well as desirable—and I concede at the start that it now seems less probable than a new despotism. But "in life," as Marvin Harris advises, "as in any game whose outcome depends on both luck and skill, the rational response to bad odds is to try harder." [9]

Fortunately, many people are already making the effort. In reviewing these warm currents, I show that they have an unfolding logic of their own—an alternative logic that includes and goes beyond the traditional American spirit of openness, willingness to experiment, "can do" optimism, and resistance to being pushed around. This is the long-term logic of democracy and of democratic response to crisis. This is a logic that helps define the endless agenda of things to be done and undone. It nurtures non-Utopian visions of true democracy. These are visions rooted in action to reduce the distances between THEM and US, and enlarge citizen activity and decentralized planning in our neighborhoods, cities, and counties. They are action-oriented visions of a country that no longer needs heroes and is led by large numbers of non-elitist leaders who recognize the ignorance of the wise as well as the wisdom of the ignorant.[10] And, above all, there is the vision of America as a true good neighbor in a new world order.

I have written parts of this book in other countries. There I have felt at first hand the fear in people's bones of renewed horrors stemming from American military force, economic penetration, or cultural domination. I have felt equally powerfully the hopes that people elsewhere have for those promises of American life that stand for peace, freedom, and progress. There is reason for these feelings.

As for America, I agree completely with Arnold Beichman that "This is a country in which one has the right to hope." [11] More than that, it is a place where millions of people exercise that right and have reason to do so. I hope that more people will gain the courage to raise their hopes still higher. In this context, and perhaps only thus, it is easier to escape the fear of fear and confront the serious dangers looming ahead. It takes ever-brimming hope—fused with realistic expectations, patience, impatience, anger, and love—to develop the courage to fear, and the sustained commitment to rekindle constantly our best promises.

ONE

The Roots of Friendly Fascism

Arturo Ui, referring to Adolf Hitler:
Let none of us exult too soon,
The womb is fruitful
From which this one crawled . . .

BERTOLT BRECHT,
The Resistible Rise of Arturo Ui

1

The Rise and Fall of Classic Fascism

BETWEEN THE TWO WORLD WARS fascist movements developed in many parts of the world.

In the most industrially advanced capitalist countries—the United States, Britain, France, Holland and Belgium—they made waves but did not engulf the constitutional regimes. In the most backward capitalist countries—Albania, Austria, Greece, Hungary, Poland, Portugal, Rumania, Spain, and Yugoslavia—there came to power authoritarian or dictatorial regimes that boastfully called themselves "fascist" or, as the term soon came to be an all-purpose nasty word, were branded "fascist" by their opponents. The most genuine and vigorous fascist movements arose in three countries—Italy, Germany and Japan—which, while trailing behind the capitalist leaders in industrialization and empire, were well ahead of the laggards.

ITALY, GERMANY, JAPAN

In Milan on March 23, 1919, in a hall offered by a businessmen's club, former socialist Benito Mussolini transformed a collection of black-shirted roughnecks into the Italian Fascist party. His word "fascism" came from the Latin *fasces* for a bundle of rods with an axe, the symbol of State power carried ahead of the consuls in ancient Rome. Mussolini and his comrades censured old-fashioned conservatives for not being more militant in opposing the socialist and communist movements that arose, in response to the depression, after World War I. At the same time, they borrowed rhetorical slogans from their socialist and communist foes, and strengthened their support among workers and peasants.

In their early days these groups had tough going. The more respectable elements in the Establishment tended to be shocked by their rowdy, untrustworthy nature. Campaign contributions from businessmen came in slowly and sporadically. When they entered electoral contests, the Fascists did badly. Thus, in their very first year of life the Italian Fascists suffered a staggering defeat by the Socialists.

In 1920 the left-wing power seemed to grow. Hundreds of factories were seized by striking workers in Milan, Turin, and other industrial areas. Peasant unrest became stronger, and many large estates were seized. The Socialists campaigned under the slogan of "all power to the proletariat."

For Mussolini, this situation was an opportunity to be exploited. He countered with a nationwide wave of terror that went far beyond ordinary strikebreaking. Mussolini directed his forces at destroying all sources of proletarian or peasant leadership. The Fascist *squadristi* raided the offices of Socialist or Communist mayors, trade unions, cooperatives and left-wing newspapers, beating up their occupants and burning down the buildings. They rounded up outspoken anti-Fascists, clubbed them, and forced them to drink large doses of castor oil. They enjoyed the passive acquiescence—and at times the direct support—of the police, the army, and the church. Above all, business groups supplied Mussolini with an increasing amount of funds. In turn, Mussolini responded by toning down the syndicalism and radical rhetoric of his followers, and, while still promising to "do something for the workers," began to extol the merits of private enterprise.

On October 26, 1922, as his Fascist columns started their so-called March on Rome, Mussolini met with a group of industrial leaders to assure them that "the aim of the impending Fascist movement was to reestablish discipline within the factories and that no outlandish experiments . . . would be carried out."[1] On October 28 and 29 he convinced the leaders of the Italian Association of Manufacturers "to use their influence to get him appointed premier."[2] In the evening of October 29 he received a telegram from the king inviting him to become premier. He took the sleeping train to Rome and by the end of the next day formed a coalition cabinet. In 1924, in an election characterized by open violence and intimidation, the Fascist-led coalition won a clear majority.

If Mussolini did not actually march on Rome in 1922, during the next seven years he did march into the hearts of important leaders in other countries. He won the friendship, support, or qualified approval of Richard Childs (the American ambassador), Cornelius Vanderbilt, Thomas Lamont, many newspaper and magazine publishers, the majority of business journals, and quite a sprinkling of liberals, including some associated with both *The Nation* and *The New Republic*. "Whatever the dangers of fascism," wrote Herbert Croly, in 1927, "it has at any rate substituted movement for stagnation, purposive behavior for drifting, and visions of great future for collective pettiness and discouragements." In these same years, as paeans of praise for Mussolini arose throughout Western capitalism, Mussolini consolidated his rule, purging anti-Fascists from the government service, winning decree power from the legislature, and passing election laws favorable to himself and his conservative, liberal, and Catholic allies.

> Only a few days after the march on Rome, a close associate of Hitler, Herman Esser, proclaimed in Munich among tumultuous applause: "What has been done in Italy by a handful of courageous men is not impossible here. In Bavaria too we have Italy's Mussolini. His name is Adolf Hitler. . . ."
>
> F. L. CARSTEN [3]

In January, 1919, in Munich, a small group of anti-Semitic crackpot extremists founded the German Workers Party. Later that year the German Army's district commander ordered one of his agents, a demobilized corporal, to investigate it. The Army's agent, Adolf Hitler, instead joined the party and became its most powerful orator against Slavs, Jews, Marxism, liberalism, and the Versailles treaty. A few months later, under Hitler's leadership, the party changed its name to the National Socialist German Workers' Party and organized a bunch of dislocated war veterans into brown-shirted strong-arm squads or storm troopers (in German, S.A. for *Sturmabteilung*). The party's symbol, designed by Hitler himself, became a black swastika in a white circle on a flag with a red background.

On November 8, 1923, in the garden of a large Munich beer hall, Adolf Hitler and his storm troopers started what he thought would be a quick march to Berlin. With the support of General Erich Ludendorff, he tried to take over the Bavarian government. But neither the police nor the army supported the *Putsch.* Instead of winning power in Munich, Hitler was arrested, tried for treason, and sentenced to five years' imprisonment, but confined in luxurious quarters and paroled after only nine months, the gestational period needed to produce the first volume of *Mein Kampf*. His release from prison coincided with an upward turn in the fortunes of the Weimar Republic, as the postwar inflation abated and an influx of British and American capital sparked a wave of prosperity from 1925 to 1929. "These, the relatively fat years of the Weimar Republic, were correspondingly lean years for the Nazis." [4]

Weimar's "fat years" ended in 1929. If postwar disruption and class conflict brought the Fascists to power in Italy and nurtured similar movements in Germany, Japan, and other nations, the Great Depression opened the second stage in the rise of the fascist powers.

In Germany, where all classes were demoralized by the crash, Hitler recruited jobless youth into the S.A., renewed his earlier promises to rebuild the German army, and expanded his attacks on Jews, Bolshevism, the Versailles treaty, liberalism, and constitutional government. In September 1930, to the surprise of most observers (and probably Hitler himself), the Nazis made an unprecedented electoral breakthrough, becoming the second largest party in the country. A coalition of conservative parties, without the Nazis, then took over under General Kurt von Schleicher, guiding genius of the army. With aged Field Marshal von

Hindenberg serving as figurehead president, three successive cabinets—headed by Heinrich Bruening, Franz von Papen, and then von Schleicher himself—cemented greater unity between big business and big government (both civilian and military), while stripping the Reichstag of considerable power. They nonetheless failed miserably in their efforts to liquidate the Depression. Meanwhile Adolf Hitler, the only right-wing nationalist with a mass following, was publicly promising full employment and prosperity. Privately meeting with the largest industrialists he warned, "Private enterprise cannot be maintained in a democracy." On January 30, 1933, he was invited to serve as chancellor of a coalition cabinet. "We've hired Hitler!" a conservative leader reported to a business magnate.[5]

A few weeks later, using the S.A. to terrorize left-wing opposition and the Reichstag fire to conjure up the specter of conspiratorial bolshevism, Hitler won 44 percent of the total vote in a national election. With the support of the Conservative and Center parties, he then pushed through legislation that abolished the independent functioning of both the Reichstag and the German states, liquidated all parties other than the Nazis, and established concentrated power in his own hands. He also purged the S.A. of its semisocialist leadership and vastly expanded the size and power of his personal army of blackshirts.

Through this rapid process of streamlining, Hitler was able to make immediate payments on his debts to big business by wiping out independent trade unions, abolishing overtime pay, decreasing compulsory cartelization decrees (like similar regulations promulgated earlier in Japan and Italy), and giving fat contracts for public works and fatter contracts for arms production. By initiating an official pogrom against the Jews, he gave Nazi activists a chance to loot Jewish shops and family possessions, take over Jewish enterprises, or occupy jobs previously held by German Jews.

Above all, he kept his promise to the unemployed; he put them back to work, while at the same time using price control to prevent a recurrence of inflation. As Shirer demonstrates in his masterful *The Rise and Fall of the Third Reich*, Hitler also won considerable support among German workers, who did not seem desperately concerned with the loss of political freedom and even of their trade unions as long as they were employed full time. "In the past, for so many, for as many as six million men and their families, such rights of free men in Germany had been overshadowed as he [Hitler] said, by the freedom to starve. In taking away that last freedom," Shirer reports, "Hitler assured himself of the support of the working class, probably the most skillful and industrious and disciplined in the Western world." [6]

Also in 1919, Kita Ikki, later known as "the ideological father of Japanese fascism," set up the "Society of Those Who Yet Remain."

His *General Outline of Measures for the Reconstruction of Japan*, the *Mein Kampf* of this association, set forth a program for the construction of a revolutionized Japan, the coordination of reform movements, and the emancipation of the Asian peoples under Japanese leadership.[7]

In Japan, where organized labor and proletarian movements had been smashed many years earlier and where an oligarchic structure was already firmly in control, the transition to full-fledged fascism was—paradoxically—both simpler than in Italy and Germany and stretched out over a longer period. In the mid-1920s hired bullies smashed labor unions and liberal newspapers as the government campaigned against "dangerous thoughts," and used a Peace Preservation Law to incarcerate anyone who joined any organization that tried to limit private property rights. The worldwide depression struck hard in Japan, particularly at the small landholders whose sons had tried to escape rural poverty through military careers. The secret military societies expanded their activities to establish a Japanese "Monroe Doctrine for Asia." In 1931 they provoked an incident, quickly seized all of Manchuria, and early in 1932 established the Japanese puppet state of Manchukuo.

At home, the Japanese premier was assassinated and replaced by an admiral, as the armed forces pressed forward for still more rapid expansion on the continent and support for armament industries. As the frontiers of Manchukuo were extended, a split developed between two rival military factions. In February 1936, the Imperial Way faction attempted a fascist coup from below. Crushing the rebels, the Control faction of higher-ranking officers ushered in fascism from above. "The interests of business groups and the military drew nearer, and a 'close embrace' structure of Japanese fascism came to completion," writes Masao Maruyama. "The fascist movement from below was completely absorbed into totalitarian transformation from above."[8] Into this respectable embrace came both the bureaucracy and the established political parties, absorbed into the Imperial Rule Assistance Association. And although there was no charismatic dictator or party leader, the Emperor was the supercharismatic symbol of Japanese society as a nation of families. By 1937, with well-shaped support at home, the Japanese army seized Nanking and started its long war with China.

BREEDING GROUNDS OF FASCISM

Before fascism, the establishments in Italy, Japan, and Germany each consisted of a loose working alliance between big business, the military, the older landed aristocracy, and various political leaders. The origin of these alliances could be traced to the consolidation of government and industry during World War I.

"Manufacturing and finance," writes Roland Sarti about World War I in Italy (but in terms applicable to many other countries also), "drew even closer than they had been before the war to form the giant combines necessary to sustain the war effort. Industrialists and government officials sat side by side in the same planning agencies, where they learned to appreciate the advantages of economic planning and cooperation. Never before had the industrustrialists been so close to the center of political power, so deeply involved in the decision-making process." [9]

United in the desire to renew the campaigns of conquest that had been dashed by the war and its aftermath, the establishments in these countries were nonetheless seriously divided by conflicting interests and divergent views on national policy. As Sarti points out, big-business leaders were confronted by "economically conservative and politically influential agricultural interests, aggressive labor unions, strong political parties ideologically committed to the liquidation of capitalism, and governments responsive to a variety of pressures." [10] Despite the development of capitalist planning, coping with inflation and depression demanded more operations through the Nation-State than many banking and industrial leaders could easily accept, more government planning than most governments were capable of undertaking, and more international cooperation among imperial interests than was conceivable in that period.

The establishment faced other grave difficulties in the form of widespread social discontent amidst the uncertain and eventually catastrophic economic conditions of the postwar world. One of the challenges came from the fascists, who seemed to attack every element in the existing regimes. They criticized businessmen for putting profits above patriotism and for lacking the dynamism needed for imperial expansion. They tore at those elements in the military forces who were reluctant to break with constitutional government. They vilified the aristocracy as snobbish remnants of a decadent past. They branded liberals as socialists, socialists as communists, communists as traitors to the country, and parliamentary operations in general as an outmoded system run by degenerate babblers. They criticized the bureaucrats for sloth and branded intellectuals as self-proclaimed "great minds" (in Hitler's phrasing) who knew nothing about the real world. They damned the Old Order as an oligarchy of tired old men, demanding a New Order of young people and new faces. In Japan, the young blood was represented mainly by junior officers in the armed forces. In Italy and Germany the hoped-for infusion of new dynamism was to come from the "little men," the "common people," the "lost generation," the "outsiders," and the "uprooted" or the "rootless." Although some of these were gangsters, thugs, and pimps, most were white-collar workers, lower-level civil servants, or declassed artisans and small-businessmen.

But the fascist challenge did not threaten the jugular vein. Unlike the communists, the fascists were not out to destroy the old power structure or to create an entirely new one. Rather, they were heretics seeking to revive the old faith by concentrating on the fundamentals of imperial expansion, militarism, repression, and racism. They had the courage of the old-time establishment's convictions. If they at times sounded like violent revolutionaries, the purpose was not merely to pick up popular support from among the discontented and alienated, but to mobilize and channel the violence-prone. If at the outset they tolerated anti-capitalist currents among their followers, the effect was to enlarge the following for policies that strengthened capitalism. Above all, the fascists "wanted in."

In turn, at a time of crisis, leaders in the old establishment wanted them in as junior partners. These leaders operated on the principle that "If we want things to stay as they are, things will have to change." Ultimately, the marriage of the fascist elements with the old order was one of convenience. In Italy and Japan, the fascists won substantial control of international and domestic politics, were the dominant ideological force, and controlled the police. The old upper-class structure remained in control of the armed forces and the economy. In Japan, the upper-class military was successfully converted to fascism, but there were difficulties in winning over Japan's family conglomerates, the *zaibatsu*.

Thus, while much of the old order was done away with, the genuinely anti-capitalist and socialist elements that provided much of the strength in the fascist rise to power were suppressed. The existing social system in each country was actually preserved, although in a changed form.

THE AXIS

From the start fascism had been nationalist and militarist, exploiting the bitterness felt in Italy, Germany, and Japan over the postwar settlements. Italians, denied territories secretly promised them as enticement for entering the war, felt cheated of the fruits of victory. Japanese leaders chafed at the rise of American and British resistance to Japanese expansion in China, and resented the Allies' refusal to include a statement of racial equality in the Covenant of the League of Nations. Germans were outraged by the Versailles treaty; in addition to depriving Germany of 13 percent of its European territories and population, the treaty split wide open two of Germany's three major industrial areas and gave French and Polish industrialists 19 percent of Germany's coke, 17 percent of its blast furnaces, 60 percent of its zinc foundries, and 75 percent of its iron ore.[11]

Furthermore, each of the fascist nations could ground their expansion in national tradition. As far back as 1898, Ito Hirobumi, one of the founders of the "new" Japan after the Meiji restoration of 1868, had gone into great detail on Japan's opportunities for exploiting China's vast resources. While the late-nineteenth-century Italians and Germans were pushing into Africa, the Japanese had seized Korea as a stepping-stone to China and started eyeing Manchuria for the same purpose. Mussolini's imperial expansion in Africa was rooted, if not in the Roman empire, then in late nineteenth-century experience and, more specifically, in the "ignominy" of the 1896 Italian defeat by ill-armed Ethiopian forces in Aduwa. Hitler's expansionism harked back to an imperialist drive nearly a century old—at least.

Now, while Japan was seizing Manchuria, Mussolini responded to the crash by moving toward armaments and war. He used foreign aid to establish economic control over Albania, consolidating this position through naval action in 1934. In 1935 he launched a larger military thrust into Ethiopia and Eritrea.

By that time, the Nazi-led establishment in Germany was ready to plunge into the European heartland itself. In 1935, Hitler took over the Saarland through a peaceful plebiscite, formally repudiating the Versailles treaty. In 1936 he occupied the Rhineland and announced the formation of a Berlin-Rome Axis and the signing of a German-Japanese Pact. Hitler and Mussolini then actively intervened in the Spanish Civil War, sending "volunteers" and equipment to support General Franco's rebellion against Spain's democratically-elected left-wing republic.

The timetable accelerated: in 1938, the occupation of Austria in March and of Czechoslovakia in September; in 1939, the swallowing up of more parts of Czechoslovakia and, after conclusion of the Nazi-Soviet Pact in August, the invasion of Poland. At this point, England and France declared war on Germany and World War II began. Japan joined Italy and Germany in a ten-year pact "for the creation of conditions which would promote the prosperity of their peoples." As a signal of its good intentions, Japan began to occupy Indochina as well as China. Germany did even better. By 1941 the Germans had conquered Poland, Denmark, Norway, the Netherlands, Belgium, and France. They had thrown the British army into the sea at Dunkirk and had invaded Rumania, Greece, and Yugoslavia. A new world order seemed to be in the making.

For Japan, it was the "Greater East Asia Co-Prosperity Sphere," and for Italy a new Roman Empire to include "the Mediterranean for the Mediterraneans." And, for Germany, the new order was the "Thousand-Year Reich" bestriding the Euro-Slavic-Asian land mass.

ANTI-FASCIST FAILURES

> Only one thing could have broken our movement: if the adversary had understood its principle and from the first day had smashed with extreme brutality the nucleus of our new movement.
>
> ADOLF HITLER[12]

Neither at home nor abroad did fascism's adversaries understand the potentials of the major fascist movements and counter them effectively.

For many years, Mussolini's regime had been supported by American bankers. From 1933 up to the outbreak of World War II Hitler received tremendous financial aid from private British banks and the Bank of England itself. Government appeasement of fascist aggression went back to Western flabbiness in the face of Japan's seizure of Manchuria in 1932, the British negotiation of a 1935 naval treaty with Germany (which recognized Germany's right to rearm), the League of Nation's futile gestures over Mussolini's conquest of Ethiopia, and the general acquiescence to Hitler's occupation and militarization of the Rhineland. In early 1938, the Western powers stood idly by as Hitler's armies, with the help of the local Nazis, swallowed up Austria. Later in the same year the leaders of Britain, France, Germany, and Italy signed the famous Munich agreement, which authorized Germany to absorb the Sudetenland, that part of Czechoslovakia with a significant German population. Neville Chamberlain, the British Prime Minister, returned home announcing "peace with honor" and "peace in our time." Hitler responded by taking over all of Czechoslovakia.

The Western appeasement of fascist aggression was rooted in an unequal balance between interventionists and noninterventionists. The most influential interventionists were those forces committed to continuing dominance by the leading capitalist powers. In Europe their most outstanding spokesman was Winston Churchill, whose main interest was in preservation of the British Empire. In the United States, where old-time statesmen like Henry Stimson had futilely called for sanction against Japan for the seizure of Manchuria, many northeastern corporate and banking groups gradually came around to Churchill's position. As members of a decades-old Anglo-American alliance, they gradually began to see American intervention against Axis aggression as reversing the relationship between the two countries and making this an "American Century" in the ultra-frank words of Henry Luce, editor of *Time, Life,* and *Fortune.* These interventionist forces were supported by anti-fascist refugees, the Jewish communities in democratic countries, many liberals and radicals, and—with the exception of the twenty-two months of the

Nazi-Soviet Pact between August 23, 1939 and June 22, 1941—all Communist parties and their sympathizers.

For many years the noninterventionists prevailed. Many British, French, and American leaders came to realize that there was a genuine logic in the fascist calls for a revision of the Versailles treaty; they hoped that with limited expansions, the Axis appetites would be satisfied and that with a few minor changes the old order could be maintained. Others were immobilized by the vaunted Nazi superiority in warfare. Still others were genuinely upset by the possibilities of mass destruction inherent in the new-style warfare. In Europe, memories of World War I were too vivid for many Europeans to risk death defending the Spanish Republic or Czechoslovakia, let alone the distant Africans in Ethiopia. In the United States, a March 1937 Gallup poll reported that 94 percent of Americans favored staying out of all wars instead of taking the risks involved in trying to prevent them from erupting or spreading.

One of the most powerful forces behind noninterventionism was widespread Western endorsement of the Axis powers' anti-Russian stance. The Japanese seizure of Manchuria seemed more acceptable if Japan would then be encouraged to continue north and west into Siberia. Germany's drive to the east was more plausible if the Germans would be satisfied with swallowing up the Soviet Union and leave the other powers alone. At best the fascists and communists would bleed themselves to death and the old order would be rescued from the twin specters of communism and fascist expansion. Or else the Soviet regime might be destroyed and Russia "regained." At least the Axis powers and the Soviet Union would both be greatly weakened, to the benefit of the Western democracies. Just as the French aristocrats and businessmen as far back as 1935 had sincerely believed "Better Hitler than Léon Blum," top business circles sincerely believed "Better Hitler than Stalin."

The leaders of the Soviet Union would also have preferred an isolationism of their own, standing by while the capitalist powers destroyed themselves in interimperialist warfare. Since this was unlikely, their major strategy was to try to divide the capitalist powers by linking up with one side or another. This was the logic of their Brest-Litovsk peace treaty of 1918, their Rapallo agreement with Germany in 1922, the winning of diplomatic recognition from Mussolini in 1924, the negotiation of trade agreements with the Weimar Republic, and the renewal of these agreements with Hitler in April 1933 (one of the first international acts of recognition of the Third Reich). At the same time, in an effort to develop a buffer zone against eastward German expansion, the Soviet union entered into a number of pacts with its Western neighbors. Nonaggression treaties with China, Poland, the Baltic states, Finland, and France became the prelude to a drive for "collective security against the aggressors" in the League of Nations, spearheaded by Foreign Commissar Maxim Litvinov. After Munich in 1938, as the prospects of collective security seemed dimmer, Stalin went back to the former Soviet policy of closer relations with Germany. Litvinov was replaced by Foreign Commissar Vyacheslav Molotov, who negotiated the Nazi-Soviet Pact of August 1939. A week later Hitler invaded Poland. By the next September, when the Axis of Germany, Italy, and Japan was finally cemented with ten-year pacts, he had conquered Norway, Denmark, Netherlands, Belgium, and France. The Battle of Britain was under way.

FASCIST EXPLOITS

The essence of the new fascist order was an exploitative combination of imperial expansion, domestic repression, militarism, and racism. Each of these elements had a logic of its own and a clear relation to the others.

Imperial expansion brought in the raw materials and markets needed for more profitable economic activity. By absorbing surplus energies as well as surplus capital, it diverted attention from domestic problems and brought in a flood of consumer goods that could—at least for a while—provide greater satisfactions for the masses.

Domestic repression in each of the three countries was essential to eliminate any serious opposition to imperialism, militarism, or racism. It was used to destroy the bargaining power of unions and the political power not only of communists, socialists, and liberals but of smaller enterprises. It helped hold down wages and social benefits and channel more money and power into the hands of big business and its political allies.

Militarism, in turn, helped each of the Axis countries escape from the depression, while also providing the indispensible power needed for both imperial ventures and domestic pacification.

All of the other elements were invigorated by racism, which served as a substitute for class struggle and a justification of any and all brutalities committed by members of the Master Race (whether Japanese, German, or Italian) against "inferior" beings. This may not have been the most efficient of all possible formulae for exploitation, but it was theirs.

No one of these elements, of course, was either new or unique. None of the "haves" among the capitalist powers, as the fascists pointed out again and again, had built their positions without imperialism, militarism, repression, and racism. The new leaders of the three "have nots," as the fascists pointed out, were merely expanding on the same methods. "Let these 'well-bred' gentry learn," proclaimed Hitler, "that we do with a clear conscience the things they secretly do with a guilty one." [13] There was nothing particularly new in Mussolini's imperialism and militarism.

His critics at the League of Nations in 1935, when a weak anti-Italian embargo was voted on, may have seemed shocked by his use of poison gas against Ethiopian troops, but he did nothing that French, British, English, and Dutch forces had not done earlier in many other countries. The Japanese and Germans, however, were a little more original. In China and other parts of Asia, the Japanese invaders used against Koreans, Chinese, Burmese, Malayans, and other Asians even harsher methods than those previously used by white invaders. Similarly, up to a certain point, the Nazi war crimes consisted largely of inflicting on white Europeans levels of brutality that had previously been reserved only for Asians, Africans, and the native populations of North, Central, and South America.

In open violation of the so-called "laws of war," German, Japanese, and Italian officials—to the consternation of old-style officers from the upper class "gentry"—ordered the massacre of prisoners. All three regimes engaged in large-scale plunder and looting.

Since German-occupied Europe was richer than any of the areas invaded by the Japanese or Italians, the Nazi record of exploitation is more impressive. "Whenever you come across anything that may be needed by the German people," ordered *Reichsmarschall* Goering, "you must be after it like a bloodhound. . . ." [14] The Nazi bloodhounds snatched all gold and foreign holdings from the national banks of seized countries, levied huge occupation costs, fines and forced loans, and snatched away tons of raw materials, finished goods, art treasures, machines, and factory installations.

In addition to this unprecedented volume of looting, the Nazis revived the ancient practice of using conquered people as slaves. In doing so, they went far beyond most previous practices of imperial exploitation. By 1944, "some seven and a half million civilian foreigners were toiling for the Third Reich. . . . In addition, two million prisoners of war were added to the foreign labor force." Under these conditions German industrialists competed for their fair share of slaves. As key contributors to the "Hitler Fund," the Krupps did very well. "Besides obtaining thousands of slave laborers, both civilians and prisoners of war, for its factories in Germany, the Krupp firm also built a large fuse factory at the extermination camp at Auschwitz, where Jews were worked to exhaustion and then gassed to death." [15]

Domestic repression by the fascists was directed at both working-class movements and any other sources of potential opposition. In all three countries the fascists destroyed the very liberties which industrialization had brought into being; if more was destroyed in Germany than in Italy and more in Italy than in Japan, it was because there was more there to destroy.

All three regimes succeeded in reducing real wages (except for the significant increments which the unemployed attained when put to work by the armaments boom), shifting resources from private consumption to private and public investment and from smaller enterprises to organized big business, and channeling income from wages to profits. As these activities tended to "de-class" small entrepreneurs and small landowners, this added to the pool of uprooted people available for repressive activities, if not for the armed services directly. Moreover, each of the three regimes attained substantial control over education at all levels, cultural and scientific activities, and the media of communication.

In Germany, however, domestic repression probably exceeded that of any other dictatorial regime in world history. An interesting, although little known, example is provided by Aktion t 4. In this personally signed decree, Hitler ordered mercy killing for hospital patients judged incurable, insane, or otherwise useless to the war effort, thereby freeing hospital beds for wounded soldiers. At first the patients were "herded into prisons and abandoned castles and allowed to die of starvation." Since this was too slow, the Nazis then used "a primitive gas chamber fed by exhaust fumes from internal combustion engines." Later they used larger gas chambers where "ducts shaped like shower nozzles fed coal gas through the ceiling . . . Afterward the gold teeth were torn out and the bodies cremated." Two years later, after about ten thousand Germans were killed in this manner, a Catholic bishop made a public protest and the extermination campaign was called off.[16]

By this time, however, Aktion t 4 had been replaced by Aktion f 14, "an adaptation of the same principles to the concentration camps, where the secret police kept their prisoners—socialists, communists, Jews and antistate elements." By the time he declared war on the United States in December 1941, Hitler extended Aktion f 14 to all conquered territories in his "Night and Fog" (*Nacht und Nebel*) decree, through which millions of people were spirited away with no information given their families or friends. This was an expansion of the *lettres de cachet* system previously used by French monarchs and the tsar's police against important state prisoners. Under this method untold thousands vanished into the night and fog never to be heard of again.[17]

Each of the three regimes, moreover, developed an extra-virulent form of racism to justify its aggressive drive for more and more "living space" (in German, the infamous *Lebensraum*). Italian racism was directed mainly against the Africans—although by the time Italy became a virtual satellite of Nazi Germany, Mussolini started a massive anti-Jewish campaign. Japanese racism was directed mainly against the Chinese, the Indochinese, and in fact, all other Asiatic people and served to justify, in Japanese eyes, the arrogance and brutality of the Japanese troops. The largest target of Nazi racism was the Slavs, who inhabited all of the Eastern regions destined to provide *Lebensraum* for the Master Race.

And during World War II more Slavs were killed than any other group of war victims in previous history.

But Nazi racism went still deeper in its fanatical anti-Semitism. Hitler, of course, did not invent anti-Semitism, which ran as a strand through most significant ideologies of the previous century. While a strong strain of anti-Semitism has usually characterized the Catholic church, Martin Luther, the founder of Protestantism, went further in urging that Jewish "synagogues or schools be set on fire, that their houses be broken up and destroyed."[18] Nazi anti-Semitism brought all these strands together into a concentrated form of racism that started with looting, deprived the German Jews (about a quarter of a million at that time) of their citizenship and economic rights under the Nuremberg Laws of 1935, and then—following Martin Luther's advice with a vengeance—led to the arson, widespread looting, and violence of the *Kristolnacht* ("The Night of the Broken Glass") of November 1938. Early in 1939 Hitler declared, in a Reichstag speech, that if a world war should ensue, "the result will be . . . the annihilation of the Jewish race throughout Europe," a threat and near-prophecy that he kept on repeating in his public statements. A few weeks after the Nazi invasion of Russia he started to make it a reality with a decree calling for a "total solution" (*Gesamtlosung*) or "final solution" (*Endlosung*) of the Jewish question in all the territories of Europe which were under German influence. The "final solution" went through various stages: at first simply working Jews to death, then gassing them in the old-style chambers used under Aktion t 4, then using still larger gas chambers capable of gassing six thousand prisoners a day—to the lilting music of *The Merry Widow*—through the use of hydrogen cyanide.

While business firms competed for the privilege of building the gas chambers and crematoria and supplying the cyanide, recycling enterprises also developed. The gold teeth were "melted down and shipped along with other valuables snatched from the condemned Jews to the Reichsbank. . . . With its vaults filled to overflowing as early as 1942, the bank's profit-minded directors sought to turn the holdings into cold cash by disposing of them through the municipal pawnshops." Other recycling operations included using the hair for furniture stuffing, human fat for making soap, and ashes from the crematoria for fertilzer. While a small number of cadavers were used for anatomical research or skeleton collections, a much larger number of live persons—including Slavs as well as Jews—were used in experimental medical research for the German Air Force on the effects on the human body of simulated high-altitude conditions and immersion in freezing water. All in all, of an estimated 11 million Jews in Europe, between 5 and 6 million were killed in the destruction chambers (and work gangs or medical laboratories) at Auschwitz, Treblinka, Belsen, Sibibor and Chelmna, as well as minor camps that used such old-fashioned methods as mere shooting.[19]

FASCIST IDEOLOGIES

The motivating vigor of German, Japanese, and Italian fascism transcended ordinary versions of the carrot (whether in the form of increased profits, power, prestige, or loot) and the stick (whether in the form of ostracism, torture, or sheer terror). Both the leaders of the fascist establishment and the many millions who did their bidding were impelled by sentiments and convictions. Any conflicting values were for many Germans, Japanese, and Italians consigned to the inner depths of conscience, to return only in the face of military defeat and postwar reprisals.

Centrally controlled propaganda was a major instrument for winning the hearts of the German, Japanese, and Italian people. The growth of the control apparatus coincided with the flowering during the 1920s and 1930s of new instruments of propagandistic technology, particularly the radio and the cinema, with major forward steps in the arts of capitalist advertising. "Hitler's dictatorship," according to Albert Speer, "was the first dictatorship of an industrial state in this age of technology, a dictatorship which employed to perfection the instruments of technology to dominate its own people." [20] Apart from technology, each of the Axis powers used marching as an instrument of dominating minds. In discussing this method of domination, one of Hitler's early colleagues, Hermann Rauschning, has given us this explanation: "Marching diverts men's thoughts. Marching kills thought. Marching makes an end of individuality. Marching is the indispensable magic stroke performed in order to accustom the people to a mechanic, quasi-ritualistic activity until it becomes second nature." [21]

The content of fascist propaganda, however, was more significant than its forms or methodology. In essence, this content was a justification of imperial conquest, rampant militarism, brutal repression, and unmitigated racism. Many fascist theorists and intellectuals spun high-flown ideologies to present each of these elements in fascist exploitation in the garb of glory, honor, justice, and scientific necessity. The mass propagandists, however (including not only Hitler, Mussolini, and their closest associates, but also the flaming "radicals" of the Japanese ultra-right), wove all these glittering abstractions into the superpageantry of a cosmic struggle between Good and Evil, between the Master Race which is the fount of all culture, art, beauty, and genius and the inferior beings (non-Aryans, non-Romans, non-Japanese) who were the enemies of all civilization. As the stars and the planets gazed down upon this apocalyptic struggle, the true defenders of civilization against bolshevism and racial impurity must descend to the level of the enemies of culture and for the sake of mankind's future, do whatever may be necessary in the grim struggle for survival. Thus, bloodletting and blood sacrifice became a spiritual imperative for the people, an imperative transcending mere materialism.

This holy-war psychology was backed up by the indiscriminate use of any concept, any idea, theory, or antitheory that was useful at a particular time or place. Liberalism and monarchism, individualism and collectivism, hierarchic leadership and egalitarianism, scientific management and organic spontaneity, private enterprise and socialism, religion and atheism—all were drawn upon as the condition warranted—to polish the image of the nation's leader and play upon the emotions of both establishment and masses. No human interest, drivė, or aspiration was safe from exploitation. To help in organizing support of specific groups, promises were made to workers as well as businessmen, peasants as well as landowners, rural folk as well as urbanites, the old nobility as well as the "common man," the old as well as the young, women as well as men. Once, in a Berlin speech before becoming chancellor, Hitler even promised, "In the Third Reich every German girl will find a husband." [22]

DESTRUCTION OF THE AXIS

While Nazi bombs were raining down on England, Colonel Charles A. Lindbergh, the American aviation hero, predicted that England would quickly collapse before Germany's superior equipment and spirit. His author-wife, Anne Morrow Lindbergh, proclaimed that the fascist leaders "have felt the wave of the future and they have leapt upon it . . ." [23]

And yet, as we now know, the wave was weaker than it seemed and was at last to be fiercely fought.

The first weakness was overextension by each Axis country. From the very beginning Mussolini went further in foreign adventures than the Italians—even those in uniform—were willing to accept. The Japanese leaders also suffered from dreams of easy glory. American researchers working for the War Crimes Trials in Tokyo were astounded to find that Japan's warlords had made no serious assessment of their capabilities for an extended war in the Pacific. The Nazis had the greatest blind spot of all. As Lawrence Dennis, America's most articulate fascist, put it, "Hitler and his top inner circle neither took the United States seriously as a possible armed foe in the future nor could they believe that the highly capitalistic United States ever could or would, line up with Communist Russia against Nazi Germany." [24] When the Nazis invaded the Soviet Union, they thought that the Americans would cheer them on or else simply stand by and let the Germans and Russians bleed each other white. By this mistaken position, they created a situation in which they themselves were soon to be bled white by a war on two fronts.

In comparison with the Americans, the Nazis were technologically backward. They did not lack for good scientists. Despite the loss of Jewish physicists who fled the country, the physicists who remained were among the best in the world. What they lacked—in terms that came into usage after the war—was a mature technostructure closely linked with top political and military leadership. In the autumn of 1942, outstanding Allied scientists had the ear of Roosevelt, Churchill, and their generals. The Hitler-Goering-Speer approach to technology was more circumscribed. Actually, it was Albert Speer himself, Hitler's chief aide on armament production, who scuttled the German atom bomb project at the very time the Americans and British were charging ahead at full speed.

Both overextension and technological backwardness, however, were relative matters. They would have hardly been decisive if the adversaries of the Axis had remained aloof or disunited. 1941 was a year of change. As American conservatives began to grasp the possibilities of the American Century and liberals to enthuse over the Century of the Common Man, noninterventionism began to ebb. The Lend-Lease Act gave President Roosevelt complete freedom to provide war material to any country whose defense he deemed vital to the United States. When the Germans invaded the Soviet Union in June, 1941, communists and their sympathizers all over the world switched to full-fledged interventionism. Almost as promptly, Churchill and Roosevelt pledged their support. By December 6, 1941, with help through Lend-Lease, Stalin was able—despite enormous reverses during the previous months—to mount the first Soviet counteroffensive against the German troops. On the following day, December 7, 1941, American noninterventionism was destroyed by the Japanese attack on the American navy at Pearl Harbor. From then, the U.S.-British-Soviet alliance became stronger.

This anti-Axis coalition lasted for fifty months. Its strength derived from the fact that it was grounded on certain limited common interests of the dominant groups in each of the three countries and wholehearted support by almost the entire population of each country. In both the Soviet Union and in Britain the war against the Axis soon became a struggle for national existence. In the United States, where national existence was not threatened, the war brought the Great Depression to an end and united the country in a high fever of activity that led the United States to become the dominant power of the world by 1945.

Thus the coalition was not an alliance against fascism as such. It was a temporary military alliance which, after knocking out the "new Roman Empire," shattered Hitler's "Thousand-Year Reich" (which lasted only twelve years) and destroyed the "Greater East Asia Co-Prosperity Sphere." In so doing, the coalition also destroyed its own reason for being.

INDESTRUCTIBLE MYTHS

One of the great successes of the classic fascists was to concoct misleading pronouncements on their purposes and practices. Anti-fascists have often accepted some of these self-descriptions or added part-truths of their own. The result has been a vast structure of apparently indestructible myths. Today, these myths still obscure the nature of classic fascism and of present tendencies toward new forms of the old horror.

Although the classic fascists openly subverted constitutional democracy and flaunted their militarism, they took great pains to conceal the Big Capital-Big Government partnership. One device for doing this was the myth of "corporatism" or the "corporate state." In place of geographically elected parliaments, the Italians and the Germans set up elaborate systems whereby every interest in the country—including labor —was to be "functionally" represented. In fact, the main function was to provide facades behind which the decisions were made by intricate networks of business cartels working closely with military officers and their own people in civilian government. In Japan, the corporate conglomerates called *zaibatsu* (wealth or money cliques) had already handled affairs along these lines; they merely tightened up.

A still more powerful device was the myth of the great leader who represents all the people and who makes all the decisions. Mussolini called the state a "violin in the hands of a maestro," namely, himself. The tune, however, was developed by the orchestra—namely, the Fascist establishment that unceremoniously dumped him shortly after the allied invasion of Italy. Although Hitler was much more of a top decision-maker, his personal power was won at the price of concentrating on certain matters and leaving huge realms of decision making to others—the well-developed style of today's corporate managers. Hugh R. Trevor-Roper reports on the Nazi establishment this way: "The structure of German politics and administration instead of being as the Nazis claimed, 'pyramidal' and 'monolithic,' was, in fact, a confusion of private empires, private armies and private intelligence services."[25]

In this situation of oligarchic in-fighting, the cartels did very well indeed—just so long as they "paid their dues" to the Nazis and supported Hitler's foreign adventures on their behalf. In Japan, of course, the Emperor was the source of all authority and the fountainhead of all virtue—but at the same time largely a figurehead. In all three countries, with their varying degrees of control imposed on capital, corporate accumulation expanded enormously during the war and by war's end (despite the physical damage inflicted on their properties), was more highly developed and productive than ever before.

Since the end of the war, the role of big capital in classic fascism had been obscured by the myth of fascism as a revolt of "little people." This myth confuses an important source of support with the centers of power. There is no doubt that in all three countries the consolidation of the fascist establishment was supported by a psychological malaise that had hit the lower middle classes harder than anyone else. But if one examines the support base of classic fascism, it is hard to avoid the conclusion that the fascists had *multiclass support.* Many workers joined the fascist ranks—even former socialist and communist leaders. To the unemployed workers not represented by trade unions or the socialist movement, fascism offered jobs and security and delivered on this promise. Although the older aristocrats were somewhat divided on the subject, many highly respectable members of the landed aristocracy and nobility joined the fascist ranks. The great bulk of civil service bureaucrats was won over. Most leaders of organized religion (despite some heroic exceptions in Germany and some foot-dragging in Italy) either tacitly or openly supported the new regimes. Leading academicians, intellectuals, writers, and artists toed the line; the dissident minority who broke away or left the country made the articulation of support by the majority all the more important. Hitler enjoyed intellectual support, if not adulation, from the leading academicians in German universities. In Japan, the Showa Research Association brought many of the country's leading intellectuals together to help the imperial leaders formulate the detailed justifications for the New Asian Order. In Italy, fascism was supported not only by Giovanni Gentile, but also by such world-renowned figures as Vilfredo Pareto, Gaetano Mosca, Roberto Marinetti, Curzio Malaparte and Luigi Pirandello. No *Lumpenproletariat* nor rootless little men these!

Attention to the full structure of the fascist establishments has also been diverted by many observers who, as in the old Hindu story about the blind men trying to describe an elephant, have concentrated on separate parts of the beast.

Psychologists have found the essence of fascism in the "authoritarian personality" or the consequences of sexual repression. Ernst Nolte discovers the hidden wellsprings of fascism as a metapolitical outlook, which he terms "resistance to transcendence . . . a lurking, subterranean fear . . . of the inevitable disintegration of national communities, races and cultures." Peter Drucker argues that in revolt against the view of man as an economic unit, people turned toward "new sorcerers" like Hitler and Mussolini who could offer the values of heroism, self-sacrifice, discipline, and comradeship. Hannah Arendt carries this idea further by describing fascism as an extreme form of irrationality produced by man's isolation, alienation, and loss of class identity. She sees anti-Semitism as basic to fascist irrationality, while also maintaining that anti-Semitism was narrowly rational as a part of a conservative struggle to end the threat of liberalism and radicalism. No big capitalist body for these observers! They prefer to concentrate—and often do so brilliantly—on trunk, tail, legs, or ears.

Many communists, in contrast, have seized directly on the "private parts" (if that Victorian euphemism can be used for an elephant) by defining bourgeois democracy as a fig leaf. By an easy step, this leads to a vivid definition of fascism: capitalism in full nudity. Once the fig leaf is removed, the argument has gone, the workers can then see—in the words of the Communist International in 1928—fascism as "a system of direct dictatorship—a terrorist dictatorship of big capital."

This analysis contains at least five oversimplifications. First of all, instead of operating directly, big capital under fascism operated indirectly through an uneasy partnership with the fascist politicos, the military leaders, and the large landowners. If the privileged classes won many advantages as a result of the indispensable support they gave to the fascist regimes in Italy, Japan, and Germany, they also paid a high price. In addition to being subjected to various forms of political plunder, they lost control of many essential elements of policy, particularly the direction and tempo of imperial expansion. Second, the shift from constitutional to fascist capitalism meant structural changes, not merely the removal of a fig leaf. The fascists suppressed independent trade unions and working-class parties and consolidated big capital at the expense of small business. They destroyed the democratic institutions that capitalism had itself brought into being. They wiped out pro-capitalist liberation and old-fashioned conservatism as vital political forces. Third, while classic fascism was terroristic, it was also beneficient. The fascists provided jobs for the unemployed and upward mobility for large numbers of lower and middle class people. Although real wage rates were held down, these two factors alone—in addition to domestic political plunder and war booty—improved the material standard of living for a substantial number, until the whole picture was changed by wartime losses.

Fourth, instead of moving to full nudity, fascism decked itself up in a full-dress costume which obscured all its many obscenities, under the guise of "revolutionary" dynamism and the myths of fascist idealism, spirituality, populist (in German *volkisch*) sentiment, and the omnipotence of the fascist state, party or leader.

Finally, no member of the fascist Axis was reactionary in the traditional sense of "turning back the clock of history" or restoring some form of old regime. Each separately and all three together were engaged in the displacement of old-time reactionaries, as well as of the conservative defenders of the status quo at home or abroad. Through imperialism, militarism, repression, and racism, they aimed at a new order of capitalist exploitation.

The most widespread myth of all, however, is the simple equation "fascism equals brutality." In a masochistic poem about her father, Sylvia

Plath wrote, "Every woman loves a fascist—the boot in the face." Although I refuse to think she was really speaking for every woman, her words illustrate the popular identification of fascism with sadism in any form—from war and murder to torture, rape, pillage, and terrorism. In this sense a brutal foreman, a violent cop, or even a teacher who rides roughshod over his or her students may be called a "fascist pig."

One difficulty with this metaphor is that for thousands of years hundreds of governments have been fiercely brutal—sometimes on conquered people only, often on their own people also. If we stick by this terminology, then many of the ancient Greeks and Hebrews, the old Roman, Persian, Byzantine, Indian, and Chinese empires, the Huns, the Aztecs, and the tsars who ruled Russia were also fascist. Some of these, let me add, also exercised total control over almost all aspects of human life. Indeed, "force, fraud and violence," as Carl Friedrich and Zbigniew Brzezinski have pointed out, "have always been features of organized government and they do not constitute by themselves the distinctively totalitarian operation." [26] But concentrated capital, modern-style government, and constitutional democracy are relatively new features of human history—as is also the kind of Big Business-Big Government alliance that subverts constitutional democracy. Anyone has the constitutional right to pin the label "fascist" or "fascistic" on the brutalities of a Stalin or his heirs in various "Marxist-Leninist" countries, or on the bloodbath inflicted by American firepower on Indochina for a full decade, or even on the latest case of police brutality in a black or Latin ghetto of New York City. This may be a forceful way of protesting brutality. It is much less than a serious examination of the realities of classic fascism or the accumulating tendencies toward new forms of fascism toward the end of the twentieth century.

2

The Takeoff Toward a New Corporate Society

> The multinational corporations are unifying world capital and world labor into an interlocking system of cross penetration that completely changes the system of national economics that characterized world capitalism for the past three hundred years.
>
> STEPHEN HYMER [1]

> The United States cannot shape the world single-handed—even though it may be the only force capable of stimulating common efforts to do so.
>
> ZBIGNIEW BRZEZINSKI [2]

> As long as the economic system provides an acceptable degree of security, growing material wealth and opportunity for further increase for the next generation, the average American does not ask who is running things or what goals are being pursued.
>
> DANIEL R. FUSFELD [3]

AS WORLD WAR II drew to a close, the victories of the anti-Axis forces triggered one crisis after another.

The first was economic jitters. In Washington we all knew that it was only the war that pulled us out of the Great Depression of 1929–39. Might not the war's end bring back the Depression? When Mussolini fell in 1943, postwar planning became high fashion in Washington and London. A year later, when the second front was opened against Germany, politicians began to vie with each other in promising "jobs for all" after the war. When Berlin fell, the British voters threw Winston Churchill out of office, fearing that under Churchill's form of conservative capitalism mass unemployment would return. When the Japanese surrendered, postwar planning went into high gear. I remember being called back from a brief vacation to organize the congressional hearings on full-employment legislation.

The atom bomb detonated another crisis. When Churchill told Lord Moran, his secretary, of the decision to bomb Japan, Moran wrote in his diary with shivering hand:

> I was deeply shocked . . . It was not so much the morality of the thing, it was simply that the linchpin that has been under pinning the world had been half-wrenched out of its socket. [4]

The shock did not disappear. "Every man, woman and child," warned President John F. Kennedy some years later, "lives under a nuclear sword of Damocles, hanging by the slenderest of threads, capable of being cut at any moment by accident, miscalculation or madness."

A more immediate crisis was the loss of one country after another to "Marxist-Leninist" regimes. Even before Hiroshima, Stalin's armies had taken over most of Eastern Europe. Immediately after Hiroshima, the Soviet armies rolled through Manchuria and North Korea. It was only the atomic explosions, which hastened the inevitable surrender of Japan, which kept them from descending into northern Japan. At Hanoi in September 1945 Ho Chi Minh proclaimed the Democratic Republic of Vietnam. In China, Mao Tse-tung's Red Army mobilized the peasants against Chiang Kai-shek, who was supported by the United States and Britain. By 1949 the People's Republic of China was set up and "we"—that is, the capitalist world—lost China. Amaury de Riencourt, the French historian, recorded that in the United States this was felt as "a personal insult" and "a stunning blow" more shocking than the Russian revolution of a generation earlier.[5] During this same period communist resistance movements were deployed in Laos, Cambodia, Thailand, Malaya, Indonesia, the Philippines, Burma, and Northern Iran. And in Italy and France, the capitalism of Western Europe's heartland was threatened by socialist and communist movements, which had won enormous prestige in the struggle against Mussolini and Hitler.

Finally, as though by an uncontrollable chain reaction, the old colonial empires were unravelled. Japan and Italy lost all their colonies promptly. But decolonization—often supported by the United States—also struck the French, Dutch, and Belgians. And after India's independence in 1947, the British Empire—without Churchill to preside over the process—was rapidly liquidated. It was obvious to all observers that by the 1960s political independence would be given to—or won by—almost all the colonies in Asia, the Middle East, Latin America, and the Caribbean.

With old empires breaking into pieces, economic collapse lurking around the corner, and anticapitalist movements gaining power, capitalist leaders faced an unprecedented challenge.

This challenge could not have been met merely by cold, warm, or hot wars against communism and socialism. Nor could it have been coped with by reviving the classic fascist regimes or returning to old-style conservatism, liberalism, or reformism. The logic of the situation called for something much more positive. Under American leadership it was supplied.

During the war thousands of businessmen, political leaders, military officers, and their professional, scientific, and technical aides had grown accustomed to working together on national and world affairs. Some of them were consciously preparing for the "American Century." As the war ended, they won the quick support of major elites in Western Europe and Japan in reconciling the contradictions among capitalist countries, fighting communism and socialism in a more unified manner, and moderating the capitalist business cycle. This is how it happened that they converted a bleak and squalid system from a cataclysmic failure in the 1930s into a formidable, if faulty, "engine of prosperity." [6] Without returning to classic fascism, they developed a new, expanding, and remarkably flexible—even to the point of sharp internal conflicts—structure of business-government partnership. If in the process constitutional rights had been thoroughly suppressed in many dependent countries, civil rights and civil liberties (although not all) were at the same time considerably expanded not only in America, but also in America's newfound allies, the former Axis powers.

THE SUN NEVER SETS ON AMERICA'S "FREE WORLD"

> In the realities of the capitalist system . . . "inter-imperialist or ultra-imperialist" alliances are inevitably nothing more than a truce between wars.
>
> V. I. LENIN [7]

Before World War II the idea of a single leader of world capitalism was a new one. For almost two centuries the dominant pattern had been bitter rivalry and recurring warfare among the capitalist powers. Nor did the business and political leaders of the other capitalist powers respond to the challenge of socialism and communism by trying to thrust leadership into the hands of the United States. They simply sought help in warding off the communist specter at home (and received it) and in trying to keep control of former colonies (which, generally, they did not receive).

For most communist leaders, the idea of an integrated world capitalist bloc was a theoretical impossibility. Even Lenin's close associate Nikolai Bukharin, who first referred to "the formation of a golden international," pointed out that the tendencies towards integration were opposed by fierce capitalist nationalism that would lead to "the greatest convulsions and catastrophes." [8] Lenin was even more vehement on the subject. He argued that before any ultra-imperialism is reached, "imperialism will inevitably explode" and "capitalism will turn into its opposite."[9] After Lenin died and Bukharin was liquidated, Stalin continuously restated the dictum that it was impossible for the major capitalist powers to get together. By the time his message was fully absorbed by loyal followers in many countries, the "impossible"—spurred on by the spread of communism itself—was already taking place.

As American leaders—political, economic, military, and cultural—were preparing for the American Century, they rushed in to extend a protecting arm over the major capitalist countries, fill the vacuums left by their departure from former colonies, and seek decisive influence over all parts of the globe up to (or even across) communist boundaries. In response to each extension of communism, American leadership strove to integrate the noncommunist world into a loose network of constitutional democracies, authoritarian regimes, and military dictatorships described as the "Free World."

For conservative commentators, the word "empire" is more descriptive. It emphasizes the responsibilities of imperial leadership with respect to protectorates, dependencies, client states, and satellites, without suggesting the Marxist connotations of "imperialism." Thus Richard Van Alstyne, George Liska, Amaury de Riencourt, and Raymond Aron have written insightful books, respectively, about *The Rising American Empire* (1960), *Imperial America* (1967), *The American Empire* (1968), and *The Imperial Republic* (1974).

If this be empire, it is very different from—as well as much larger than—any previous empire. First of all, the "imperium" (to use another word favored by conservative observers) is not limited to preindustrial countries. It also includes the other major countries of industrial capitalism: Canada, Japan, the countries of the North Atlantic Treaty Alliance (including Belgium, Britain, Denmark, France, Greece, Iceland, Italy, Luxembourg, the Netherlands, Portugal, Turkey, and West Germany), Spain, Australia, New Zealand, and Israel. In turn, instead of being excluded from America's preindustrial protectorates, the largest corporations in most of these countries share with American corporations the raw material, commodity, labor, and capital markets of the third world.

Then, too, U.S. imperial control is exercised not by American governors and colonists, but by less direct methods (sometimes described as "neocolonialism"). This has involved the development of at least a dozen channels of influence operating within subordinate countries of the "Free World":

- The local subsidiaries or branches of transnational businesses, including banks
- U.S. foreign military bases, which reached a peak of more than 400 major bases (and 3,000 minor ones) in 30 countries

- The C.I.A. and other intelligence agencies
- U.S. agencies providing economic and military aid through loans, grants, and technical assistance
- U.S. embassies, legations, and consulates
- The local operations of U.S. media (radio, TV, magazines, cinema) and public relations and consulting firms
- The local operations of U.S. foundations, universities, and research and cultural institutions
- Local power centers and influential individuals, friendly or beholden to U.S. interests
- Local armed forces, including police, equipped or trained in whole or part by U.S. agencies
- Subordinate governments—like Brazil, the Philippines, and Iran under the Shah—capable of wielding strong influence in their regions
- Transnational regional agencies such as NATO, the European Economic Community and the Organization of American States
- Agencies of the United Nations, particularly the World Bank and the International Monetary Fund

While these channels of influence have frustrated the efforts of any U.S. ambassador to establish personal control and have pushed final coordinating responsibilities to the level of the White House and the president's National Security Council, the net result has been a remarkably flexible control system in which competing views on strategy and tactics make themselves felt and are resolved through mutual adjustment. When serious mistakes are made, they can be corrected without injury to the dominant forces of a system that can adjust, however painfully, to the loss of any single leader, no matter how prominent. During the Korean War, when General Douglas MacArthur erred in driving through North Korea toward the Chinese border (which brought the Chinese into the war and lost the U.S.-occupied portion of North Korea to the capitalist world), he was promptly replaced. When President Lyndon Johnson erred in overcommitting U.S. troops and resources to the Indochinese war, he was pressured into retiring from the 1968 presidential campaign. Moreover, when new conditions call for new policies, the leaders of transnational corporations may move flexibly where political and military leaders fear to tread—as with corporate initiatives in commercial relations with the Soviet Union, China, and Cuba.

Moreover, the economic functions of subordinate countries now go far beyond those described many decades ago by Hobson and Lenin. Many Third World countries have become, or are about to become:

- Markets for raw materials, particularly wheat produced in the United States, Canada, and Australia
- Sources of trained technicians and professionals who may then move

through the so-called "brain drain" into the skilled-labor markets of the major capitalist countries

- Channels for mobilizing local capital which may then be invested locally under foreign control or repatriated to finance investment in the industrialized countries
- Sources of low-cost labor for transnational subsidiaries which then manufacture industrial goods that are marketed in the major capitalist countries as well as locally.

This last point bears special attention. There used to be a time when industrialization—often referred to by the magic word "development"—was seen as the road to economic independence. As it has emerged, however, industrial development has usually been a process of converting preindustrial dependencies into industrial dependencies. Previously, many left-wing revolutionary movements aimed to throw off the yoke of imperialism by joining with the native capitalists in "national revolutions." What has often happened, however, is that the local capitalists have supplanted the old landowning oligarchs in trying to cooperate with, rather than break with, foreign capital. Instead of "ugly Americans" or Europeans meddling in their affairs, many Third World regimes are increasingly manned by Americanized Brazilians, Anglicized Indians and Nigerians, and Westernized Saudi Arabians and Egyptians. As dependent industrialism grows, moreover, its roots spread deeply into the state bureaucracies, in the universities and among the managerial, technical, professional, and intellectual elites. As this happens, military control or the threat of a military takeover becomes somewhat less essential and the military themselves became more civilianized, if not even subordinate to corporate economic interests. Thus a huge infrastructure of dependency is developed which Susanne Bodenheimer sees as "the functional equivalent of a formal colonial apparatus." [10] In fact, external controls are now internalized in domestic institutions, and the new infrastructure may be more powerful than any previous colonial apparatus.

Thus, with the old oligarchies pushed aside by industrial development, the sons and grandsons of the preindustrial chieftains and feudal aristocrats leap from landowning to stockholding, from the protection of ancient privileges to the glory of new privileges as the local agents—at times, even junior partners—of the new industrial oligarchs of the "New World" empire. The lands they still own allow them to keep one foot in the past, thus easing the transition, or better yet, allowing them to move into the new world of chemically fertilized, supermechanized, and superseeded agribusiness.

Moderate nationalization is also being absorbed into the structure of dependent industrialism. On the one hand, in countries where sweeping nationalization had been undertaken earlier—as in Nasser's Egypt, Sukarno's Indonesia, Vargas's and Goulart's Brazil, and the first Peron regime in Argentina—national undertakings are being either placed into private ownership or else run like private firms. On the other hand, nationalization is also being used to directly aid private and foreign capital. The monetary policies of a government-owned central bank, as in India, and the credit policies of investment promotion corporations, as in Mexico and Indonesia, have long served to promote capitalist enterprises. Socialized enterprises in utilities, transportation, communication, and water are being used to subsidize private firms by providing them with essential services at nonprofit or below-cost prices. More nationalization of this type is under way—particularly in basic mineral, forest, and land resources.

Oil, of course, is the biggest issue. In Venezuela, nationalization of currently developed oil reserves, previously scheduled to come into effect by 1983, was completed in 1975—under terms that proved a bonanza to the foreign companies. Similarly, nationalization moved steadily forward in the Middle East, with Libya and Iraq taking the lead and Saudi Arabia and the smaller sheikhdoms trailing behind. But there is little prospect that the nationalization of oil would promote socialization in other sectors, any more than it did during the decades after Mexico's expropriation of foreign oil companies. On the contrary, it seems likely that the bulk of any additional money obtained from the larger share of oil profits will be plowed into private enterprise at home and abroad. This is one of the strange lessons of the oil embargo and price increases of 1973–74 and the spectacular rise since then in the oil income of the oil-exporting countries. Although the embargo was widely regarded as an anti-Western move inspired by the Russians, its long-range effect has been to bring the Arab countries more fully than before into the world capitalist market as well as to foster dependent industrialism in the entire Arab world. More extensive (albeit limited) nationalization will probably have a similar effect, with American and European oil companies beating a slow retreat from extraction, organizing joint private-government refineries and petrochemical complexes, trying to maintain their monopoly on worldwide distribution, and at the same time expanding their operations in natural gas, coal, atomic energy, and any other energy sources that may become profitable.

In some countries of dependent industrialism where capitalist expansion has proceeded most rapidly, the degree of dependence on the First World has lessened somewhat and the native capitalist and political leaders have developed the capability to define themselves as something slightly above the level of mere pawns or clients. Thus the military junta of Brazil has for many years held full status as a "subimperial power," influencing events in Paraguay, Uruguay, Bolivia, and other Latin American countries. "We too can invoke a Manifest Destiny," one of its leaders stated in the early 1970s, "even more so because it does not clash in the Caribbean with that of our older brothers to the North."[11]

Brazil's worldwide position is buttressed not only by its formidable growth rate but also by its purchase of nuclear reactor facilities from West Germany and its ill-concealed intentions of becoming a nuclear power. For all these reasons it was natural for Secretary of State Kissinger in 1976 to reach an agreement to consult with Brazil on all major events of international importance. This agreement has not been abrogated by the Carter administration.

But Brazil is not the only Third World country to seek subimperial status. In Latin America, oil-rich Venezuela may become a close rival. In West Asia, the largest subimperial drive was attempted by Iran under the Shah. Other major aspirants, provided they can achieve greater domestic stability, are Indonesia, the Philippines, and Zaire. In all of these countries, government tends to play a more central economic role than in the First World. From a longer-range view, India has the greatest subimperial potential. Although weakened by the poverty of its vast population and its lack (thus far) of domestic petroleum, India nonetheless possesses an industrial establishment and a science-technology elite far beyond that of Brazil or any other Third World country.

Some of the countries I have just referred to are frequently attacked as "fascist." This attack has also been levied against the regimes of other countries that have little ground for subimperial aspirations—such as Argentina, Bolivia, Chile, Haiti, and Paraguay.

Most of the governments in these countries are crude military dictatorships with few compunctions about wiping out most domestic freedoms in defense of the freedoms of domestic oligarchies and First World interests. Sheer brutality, however, as I have pointed out earlier, does not qualify a regime as fascist; its regime must also be interlocked with concentrated capital. Yet big capital is growing in these countries—albeit in forms that are mainly dependent on First World support and initiatives. Hence these can best be seen as countries of "dependent fascism." In some of the countries, as the domestic oligarchies become more closely linked with transnational capital, the regimes tend to become more sophisticated in drawing velvet gloves over iron fists and in assuming a "friendlier" visage.

THE GOLDEN INTERNATIONAL

Long before World War II, the larger capitalist corporations spread around the world in their efforts to obtain raw materials and sell manufactured products; a few developed manufacturing facilities in other countries. But they did these things in the context of deadly struggle among capitalist nations. After World War II, they reached an entirely new stage of international development by transcending the old limits on the location of activity. They learned how to do almost anything, any place—to engage in manufacturing and service enterprises in former colonies, to use foreign subsidiaries to vault over or under trade and credit barriers, to mobilize both equity and loan capital in other countries. The modern transnational corporation not only internationalized production, it became the only organization with resources and scope to think, to plan, and to act in developing global sources of raw materials. This wider scope of planning has given the transnationals the advantage of escaping whatever inhibitions might be imposed by national policies on currency, credit, trade, and taxes, and of allowing them to play national currencies and governments against each other. It has also put them in the strategic position of encouraging and profiting from the larger markets made available through the European Economic Community and other regional arrangements. Within these larger markets the transnationals have worked together (while also competing) to contain left-wing movements, subvert left-wing regimes, and maintain the integrity of the "Free World" empire.

The flexibility of the larger transnationals is enhanced by the fact that most of them have become conglomerates. No longer limited to specific sectors, their business is to get money and power, not make specific products. Competence in producing this or that specific product need no longer be built up over generations; it can be bought. Thus the giant Western oil companies have bought into coal, natural gas, uranium, atomic energy, and solar energy. Some have gone still wider, entering computers, retailing, and engine manufacture. Wide-spectrum transnational conglomerates like ITT and Gulf & Western have brought together scores of subsidiaries in such diverse fields as telephones, mining, sugar plantations, insurance, transportation, hotels, TV, radio, book publishing, movies, and professional athletics. This broad scope of business activities helps insulate them from collective bargaining by labor unions, which traditionally operate within one sector only. As many unionists have lamented, "How can workers strike a conglomerate transnational?" Host countries face similar difficulties. How can a government plug tax loopholes and enforce local regulations when the accounting wizards of the transnational corporations usually provide information only on a consolidated basis and refuse to provide data on specific products?

But no transnational operates as an island unto itself. The legal entity is merely the central node at the heart of a far-flung cluster of supporting organizations. These include subsidiaries, suppliers, distributors, research organizations, and firms (or occasionally individuals) providing banking, legal, accounting, managerial, advertising, and public relations services.

Each large cluster, in turn, usually operates as part of what we may call a constellation, a still larger group of organizations. The typical constellation (of which the cartel is one form) works out policies that become the framework for oligarchic cooperation and competition or—through secret consultations by subordinates, legal counsel, or otherwise—sets output quotas, divides markets, or fixes minimum prices. Many a transnational operates not only within its own cluster but within one or more constellations. In banking, which has usally taken the leading role in transnational expansion, the formal name for a constellation is "consortium" or "group." Sometimes competing constellations that are dependent on each other work together in a duopoly—as in the case of OPEC and the giant Western oil companies through which OPEC enforces its decisions.

In turn, the most dynamic clusters and constellations have learned how to imbed their activities within loose, flexible networks or "complexes" of private and public organizations, institutions, foundations, research institutes, law and accounting firms, and strategically placed individuals. The so-called "military-industrial complex" is no unique institutional form; the "complex" has become the standard mode of structuring the planning and control activities of corporate banking, agribusiness, and mass communications. One of the most important examples is the huge automobile-highway-petroleum-trucking complex. With the help of the Highway Trust Fund set up under the Eisenhower administration, this huge complex has become the major force in undermining mass transportation in American cities, promoting suburban expansion and attaining the "automobilization" of the U.S. economy.

In all the complexes or networks, the older forms of integration—financial groups, cartels, trade associations, interlocking directorates, and interlocking stock ownership—still exist. Indeed, they seem to have expanded. But the new interlocks are wider (covering more sectors and territorial space), deeper (covering more levels of activity) and more flexible. And decision making within the network is far more complex than in the old-style cartel or *zaibatsu*. The older practices of centralized hierarchy (still adhered to by some components) have been incorporated in a more flexible polyarchic system of mutual accommodation. The request "Take me to your leader" cannot be honored. In this new-style, faceless system no one knows his name; he does not exist. The web is spidery, but there is no single spider.

Some of these capitalist complexes are tightly organized, some remarkably loose. Most find ways of using public funds, contracts, or guarantees as an essential part of their operations. All of them have blurred older distinctions between "public" and "private". All have developed increased power by co-opting, or incorporating as valuable appendages, regulatory agencies presumably established to control them, and by influencing research institutions that might otherwise subject them to embarrassing scrutiny. Large transnationals like General Motors, it has often been pointed out, have total annual sales volumes larger than the annual GNP of medium-sized countries. What has been less noted or understood is that the multinational automobile-highway-petroleum complex (within which General Motors plays a vital role) controls far more money, scientists, and technicians than provided for in the entire budget of *any* capitalist country's national government, including the United States itself.

The emerging reality of the Golden International is concretized in a myriad of private, public, and international organizations. The growth of the European Economic Community and its many offshoots has triggered the parallel creation of such powerful business organizations as UNICE (the Union of Industries of the European Economic Community) and FBEEC (the Banking Federation of the European Economic Community). These operations, in turn, have necessitated more active cooperation among First World governments. Thus, in the field of international currency, the Group of Ten finance ministers—representing the United States, Canada, Japan, Britain, West Germany, France, Sweden, Italy, the Netherlands, and Belgium—has been negotiating to establish a new monetary system in which, as Sylvia Porter put it quite a while ago, "our proud but overburdened dollar will remain a key currency of the world—a first among equals—but . . . will not longer be the sole pivot money around which all other currencies revolve."[12] To those who mistakenly see the international value of the dollar as an unmistakable indicator of American capitalism's strength, this may look like an American retreat. For the American transnational corporations, however, who operate in all the world's media of exchange (including the International Monetary Fund's special drawing rights), this is an advance. Together with their European and Japanese brethren, they provide solid support (and more than occasional guidance) for the complex efforts of the IMF in setting up the new multicurrency, and also aid the World Bank in promoting conditions for profitable capitalist investment in the Third World.

As more transnational organizations of this type are set up, they tend to create more confusion, and the need is greater for strategic coordination. For a while it seemed that this need could be met by intergovernmental organizations such as the Organization for Economic Cooperation and Development (OECD) and the North Atlantic Treaty Organization (NATO). These were informally tied together by small and more secretive informal groups such as the G-5 group of finance or treasury officials from the "top five" countries, or by the annual Bilderberg conferences created "to preserve the Western way of life."[13] But by 1970, it became evident, as first pointed out in public by Zbigniew Brzezinski, that OECD was too narrowly limited to official government representatives. Neither provided a flexible enough framework for complex policy discussions among corporate and business leaders, or even a basis for legitimating the senior-partner status that Japanese and

Western European interests demanded, and which the leaders of the U.S. establishment have been willing to confer. Brzezinski succinctly defined the situation as requiring a new formal structure through which the Americans will "involve Western Europe and Japan" and the new holy trinity could "weave a new fabric of international relations."[14]

Anthony Eden followed up a little later in an article declaring that "The free world now needs its own organization where its leading nations can meet, discuss and deal with political problems which are worthwhile." With a rather clumsy lack of diplomatic skill, he nominated for membership in this working club "the four Western European powers, the United States and Canada, Brazil, Japan and Australia."[15] With much greater finesse, David Rockefeller and other banking leaders designed an organization of "prominent citizens" rather than governments, and limited the geographical scope to what they called the "trilateral world" embracing North America (the United States and Canada), Japan, and Western Europe. Thus the Trilateral Commission came into being in 1973. The commission's membership is mainly high-level bankers and industrialists supported by a sprinkling of enlightened and reliable politicians, public officials, intellectuals, and even union leaders—sixty people apiece from each of the three parts of the trinity. A smaller executive committee has been hard at work organizing task forces and behind-the-scenes discussions by top corporate and government leaders. Its basic task has been to formulate top-level strategy for the leaders of the First World's establishments on such intricate matters as monetary policy, energy, control of the high seas, trade, development, and relations with both communist nations and the Third World. It can do this because, as a *Newsweek* journalist pointed out, it is not "merely a rich man's club" but rather a "remarkable cross-section of the interlocking establishments of the world's leading industrialized nations."[16]

BIG WELFARE FOR BIG BUSINESS

The federal government is replete with supportive programs—subsidies, research, promotional, contracts, tax privileges, protections from competition—which flow regularly into the corporate mission of profit and sales maximization.

RALPH NADER[17]

Both welfare spending and warfare spending have a two-fold nature: the welfare system not only politically contains the surplus population but also expands demand and domestic markets. And the warfare system not only keeps foreign rivals at bay and inhibits the development of world revolution (thus keeping labor power, raw materials and markets in the capitalist orbit) but also helps to stave off economic stagnation at home.

JAMES O'CONNOR[18]

Although industrial capitalism has always enjoyed government support, the scale and pervasiveness of such support became immeasurably greater after World War II. Indeed, as Ralph Miliband has pointed out, in no previous epoch in the history of capitalism has the capitalist order been more fully accepted by the political leadership and government bureaucracy. In Western Europe and Japan, this acceptance has included socialist parties willing to take on the burdens and honors of trying to manage capitalist societies. In the United States it has extended to the many socialists and crypto-socialists operating under the banner of the Democratic party. Throughout the "Free World," moreover, many communists and revolutionaries often seek popular support as champions of immediate gains for workers through new forms of state intervention. As in the past, this tends to strengthen the hands of more moderate reformers in pushing backward capitalists into grudging acceptance of the larger government help required for a more perfect capitalism.

This state-supported capitalism has been imperfectly labeled by many popular terms which, while containing particles of truth, conceal the genuine nature of the new business-government relationships: "state capitalism," "welfare state," "warfare-welfare state," and "mixed economy." The power of the concept "state capitalism" (or "state monopoly capitalism") is that it stresses the alliance of powerful capitalist forces with the state. But it greatly underestimates the extent to which big business operates on its own, both without the state and beyond the reach of the state. In no country of advanced capitalism is business completely controlled by the state; the state, rather, is subject to business control, although not completely. The relationship is more that of a business-government partnership, with business often serving as the senior, although sometimes silent, partner.

The term "welfare state" also contains a germ of truth. Under pressure from communist regimes and movements, the governments of all major capitalist countries have out-Bismarcked Bismarck in taking over socialist demands and enacting a host of programs to provide state-ordained floors under living and working standards. In a broader sense, however, the "welfare state" idea is fundamentally misleading. The welfare provided is not the general well-being of the people. It is welfare, rather, in the narrow and restrictive sense of public assistance to the poor and other programs (usually financed by the lower and middle classes themselves) to take the rough edge off capitalist exploitation, promote docility among the exploited, and thereby help form a more perfect capitalism. If this be the general welfare it is "subwelfare," the level of which has been grudgingly attuned to the amount of domestic pacification required in a particular country or at a particular time.

Thus, in Britain and Western Europe, with stronger left-wing movements to be contained, the levels of subwelfare have been higher than in the United States, where the productive capacity itself could have supported the highest levels of welfare in the capitalist world. Under President Truman's Fair Deal (1946–52) dramatic proposals for raising the low U.S. levels, although never approved by Congress, helped placate the many liberal leaders who had been less than enthusiastic about the "cold war" and the Korean War. John F. Kennedy's pleas to "get the country moving again" linked a more interventionist attitude at home with one abroad. Although President Johnson's Great Society programs were stunted as money and energy went to the war in Asia, the various initiatives in social security, public assistance, health care, education, housing, job-training, and local uplift were cited by administration spokesmen as they begged for liberal and minority tolerance of intervention overseas. Many of these welfare programs, in fact, subsidized banks and other corporations under the banner of providing them with incentives for "doing good" for the poor. Indeed, in most countries of modern capitalism, big business makes at least as much money from welfare as from warfare. Hence there is some logic in using James O'Connor's term "warfare-welfare state."

But to focus attention on warfare-welfare spending alone would be to lose track of the Big Welfare handouts that big business gets or extracts from the normal peacetime activities of the capitalist state. Although it is perfectly true, as conservative economists insist, that "there are no free lunches," there are scores of corporate "free lunchers" who manage to get other people—via government intervention—to pick up all or part of the bill. Although new forms of this fine-tuned intervention are created every year, some of the more conspicuous examples in the United States are:

- The Federal Reserve system, which supports bankers by maintaining high interest rates and bailing out bank failures.
- The nominally progressive federal tax system, which has become a labyrinth of special loopholes that provide many billions of "tax expenditures" (indirect subsidies) for specific companies or groups. For fiscal year 1980 these tax expenditures amounted to over $150 billion—more than 20 percent of direct budget outlays for the same year.
- The Treasury Department, which maintains huge interest-free deposits in large banks while at the same time paying the bank's interest on money lent to the government.
- Billions in direct subsidies that are paid to airlines, the merchant marine, agribusiness and others.

- Federal expenditures for scientific research and development, which have subsidized the growth of capitalism's technological reserve.
- Government guarantees that protect many billions of bank mortgages and foreign investments against losses.
- Government regulations that give the large banks control over the investment of the pension funds of most labor unions.
- So-called regulatory commissions, which help maintain the oligarchic power of the communication media, public utilities, and major transportation interests.
- Government forays into wage-price controls, or "incomes policy," which are used to keep wages down or squeeze out business competitors.

A large amount of corporate planning involves intricate tussles to keep other people's hands out of this bustling free-lunch bazaar while getting as much as possible for one's own "crowd". Sometimes juicy scraps are snatched away by small-time operators whose proclivities for improperly covered lawbreaking may produce enough public scandal to distract attention from those quietly walking away with the lion's share.

There are two other forms of government intervention that tend to give the false impression that the modern capitalist economy is "mixed" in the sense of being less capitalistic than before: central government planning and government ownership. Since World War II, the government of every major capitalist country has engaged in some form of economic planning, albeit sometimes under the label of policy coordination or program integration. The central function of these planning efforts is to strengthen capitalist performance by (1) helping maintain market demand; (2) extending welfare-state programs as a means of doing this while also pacifying protest; (3) designing fiscal, monetary, and regulatory policies to support more profitable corporate operations in specific sectors; and (4) mediating conflicts among various interests in the corporate world. At the local level, this kind of planning has been backed up by zoning regulations, land-use plans, and public improvement programs that have helped subsidize both suburban growth and astronomical increases in urban and suburban land values.

In turn, government ownership and "mixed enterprises" in certain sectors of capitalist society have tended to (1) help corporate capital pull out of less profitable activities and move to greener fields; (2) promote technological rationalization of backward industries; (3) provide government capital for use by private corporate interests; (4) tax the lower classes by selling government-monopolized products at higher prices, or (5) subsidize private business by giving them government goods and services at low prices. In addition, both government planning and government ownership perform the invaluable service of mobilizing liberals, and socialists—and sometimes communist revolutionaries also—behind the policies needed for a more perfect capitalism.

MORE RATIONAL CORPORATE MANAGEMENT

> With the coming of science and technology, it is fair to say that we can get ten dollars out of nature for every dollar that we can squeeze out of man.
>
> KENNETH BOULDING[19]

Capitalists have never needed theorists to explain the connection between money and power. It has taken theorists at least a century, to develop the pretense that they are separate.

It has also taken businessmen more than a century to learn how to accumulate capital and power on the largest possible scale over the longest period of time. The older aristocratic traditions of aristocratic life had to be abandoned. The two oldest business commandments—"buy cheap, sell dear" and "let the buyer [or borrower] beware"—had to be expanded to a full decalagogue which included the following: (3) risk other people's money, (4) make money out of shortages, (5) use only those new technologies that are more profitable, (6) shift social costs to others, (7) conceal assets and income, (8) squeeze workers as much as possible, (9) buy political influence, and (10) help build a powerful establishment. Each of these maxims, of course, operated under the umbrella of "anything goes if you can get away with it."

During World War II many corporate planners learned how to get away with much more than had previously been imagined. After the war, corporate planning and control became the central focus of attention for hundreds of colleges or departments of business administration, thousands of management articles and books published every year, and hundreds of thousands of students participating in undergraduate and graduate programs and "management development" or "advanced management" seminars, conferences, and discussion groups. With or without the direct help of such formalities, the leaders of the largest corporate institutions became not inert organization men but adaptive innovators in the more rational and unconstrained pursuit of money and power for the owners and managers of large-scale private property. In this pursuit, they now for the first time had the help of a vast array of professional experts in such new technical fields as business policy, organization, finance, production, personnel, and marketing. Many of these subjects correspond to the majo. departments of course offerings in business schools, as well as to the functional division of labor within the typical corporation structure. Some are rooted in scientific research or advanced theoretical analysis, others in the careful *ad hoc* accumulation of experience. In each, there is a technical jargon that facilitates communication among the technicians in the same field and hinders communication with anyone else; this babel of many tongues becomes still more complicated whenever, as often happens, one specialty is subdivided into many subspecialties. In each area, particularly those allied with the various information sciences, the more creative experts often claim to be *the* management experts capable of either integrating or displacing the work of all the others.

Between the lines of these suitably arcane disciplines a modern Machiavelli can discern a blunter set of "tacit guidelines," as listed in the table, "Elements of Rational Corporate Management." The technical experts take those for granted, dress them up in fancy rationalizations, but openly discuss them only at their peril. Expanding on the older Ten Commandments, these unstated imperatives do not exhaust management techniques. It would be overly cynical to suggest that "managerial economics" or "cash-flow budgeting" or "product design and engineering" amount to nothing more than "make money from shortages," "speculate in international currency," or "plan accelerated obsolescence."

ELEMENTS OF RATIONAL CORPORATE MANAGEMENT

Technical Specialties	*Between-the-Lines: Tacit Guidelines*
Business Policy	
Business-government relations	Mobilize state support, public funds, and political influence
Investment and product-line planning	Extend structure of corporate power
Managerial economics	Make money from shortages
Management information systems	Shift social costs to others
Public relations	Build benevolent image and support the establishment
Organization	
Organizational development	Promote "profit consciousness"
Reorganization	Weed out "undesirables"
Decentralization of operations	Provide "cover" for top-level decision makers
Subcontractor-supplier relations	Maintain subcontractor-supplier dependency, build flexible clusters and constellations

Technical Specialties	*Between-the-Lines: Tacit Guidelines*
	Finance
Securities flotation	Risk other people's money
Accounting	Conceal assets, income, bribes, and political contributions
Capital budgeting	Shift costs to external accounts
Cash-flow budgeting	Speculate in international currency
	Production
Product design and engineering	Plan accelerated obsolescence
Research and development	Promote labor-saving technologies
Production scheduling	Minimize costs that cannot be shifted
	Personnel
Labor relations	Maintain work discipline, through "independent" unions where necessary
Human relations	Keep workers docile
Recruitment	Select "dociles," reject "undesirables"
Job analysis	Develop competitive, low-cost stratification
	Marketing
Market research	Manufacture consumer needs
Distribution	Keep prices as high as possible
Advertising	Conceal product defects

But the latter do represent crucial realities that are rarely publicly unacknowledged. Often, I am sure, these tacit guidelines are refined far beyond the rough-and-ready rules here listed and enter the infinite series of well-shrouded mysteries in the realms of high finance and high *politique.* They are the special province not of technicians but of the top-level overseers and executives whose task it is to nurture, guide, and coordinate the many technicians needed to help in the accumulation of concentrated power and wealth.

TECHNOLOGY: STARTING, STOPPING, SUPPRESSING

The pressures of World War II unleashed a new burst of technological creativity. The Nazis succeeded in fueling planes and tanks through gasoline made from coal and in developing advanced rocket technology.

The U.S. success with the atom bomb was matched by a whole spectrum of less spectacular achievements, including radar, jet propulsion, computers, and operations research. Instead of subsiding with the war's end, technological inventiveness thrived in the ebullient atmosphere of "Free World" integration and corporate expansiveness. With massive support from military and civilian agencies of government, Big Business once again devoted itself to what Karl Marx has called "revolutionizing the means of production." As had already happened in nuclear physics, theoretical and applied scientists were caught up within a complex network of technological research and development. They became valuable resources to be funded, nurtured, and honored by those who saw the possibility of distilling new power or capital from their findings.

The result was "a new technological revolution" in the methods of collecting, transforming, storing and moving almost all forms of energy, matter and information. There has been a veritable chain reaction in atomic energy: hydrogen bombs, nuclear-powered submarines and icebreakers, electricity production through nuclear fission. Important research is underway on electricity production through nuclear fusion and through the more direct use of solar energy through photovoltaic cells that convert sunlight into electricity, tapping the geothermal heat of the earth itself, and, above all, converting grains and other agricultural products into alcohol and other substitutes for gasoline. Also, as Alvin Toffler reports, "scientists are now studying the idea of utilizing bacteria capable of converting sunlight into electrochemical energy."[20] There have been continuing advances in production of energy from fossil fuels and its instantaneous transmission over vast distances through electrical grids, superconductors and the more spectacular means of lasers and microwaves.

Materials are no longer limited to those found in nature. They are now being created *de novo* either to substitute for such traditional materials as textiles, rubber, steel, aluminum, or paper, or to create entirely new materials, both inorganic and organic. "Just as we have manipulated plastics and metals," reports Lord Ritchie Calder, an eminent science commentator, "we are now manufacturing living materials."[21] Medical technology has been developing new capabilities for eradicating contagious diseases; for facilitating or preventing childbirth; for replacing parts of the body. The new "genetic engineers" have been discovering how to reprogram DNA molecules.

Still more revolutionary changes have been taking place in successive generations of information technologies. The collection of information is now possible through increasingly sophisticated systems, including the more ominous forms of remote electronic surveillance. The processing of information through fantastically rapid computers now facilitates the kind and quantities of calculations never before possible. The transmission, storage and retrieval of information is accomplished in new ways by the widespread advances in telecommunications and electronic coding. Finally, and most disturbingly, the means of control over this great mass has been developed to such a degree that centralized systems can keep tabs on incredible amounts of information over long sequences of widely dispersed and decentralized activities.*

This technological revolution is embodied in the plans and actions of industrial, military and political leaders. It is institutionally orchestrated and financed. One strategic objective has been to maintain the military and economic superiority of the United States and its "Free World" allies. Another has been to nurture the economic health of the largest "Free World" conglomerates, clusters, constellations and complexes by staving off the stagnation that always threatens in the event of a decline in innovation. Whether intended or not, a major result has been to help knit together the leading corporations of the technologically advanced countries and buttress their domination of technologically inferior countries.

The scientists and technologists have become an informal "techno-international" whose members (funded from establishment sources) keep in constant touch with each other and hold frequent international meetings. Having more common interests than the managers and owners of corporate wealth, they play a vanguard role in transcending national boundaries and helping make all corporate kings kin. They draw the new generations of Third World scientists and technologists into the First World culture, thereby fostering a Third World brain drain that turns out to be a continuing brain gain for the Golden International.

These activities are helped immeasurably by a euphoric vision—widely shared among the "knowledge elites", as Daniel Bell calls them—that any problems or crises created by new technologies can be coped with, if not solved, by some new technology.** The euphoria is nourished by technological thrusts and feints in myriad directions, with thousands of technologists or scientists plunging far beyond the realm of what may be immediately feasible. There is thus built up a huge stockpile or reserve of embryonic, nascent, semi-developed techniques, devices, inventions, theories and methodologies—a sort of reserve army of available but unused technologies.

Although the technology reserve is huge and growing, it is no cornucopia from which benefits quickly or automatically flow to meet the needs of humankind. The great bulk of the new innovations are those fostered by the Establishment's "master magicians"—namely, innovations responding to demands for more destructive weapons, more profitable

* In "Managing Information and Media" (chapter 12) I discuss how these many technologies may be used in personal surveillance and dossier-building.

** I touch on this subject again in "New Ideologies of Control" in "The Friendly Fascist Establishment" (chapter 9).

products and more labor-saving processes. In these areas, there is some relevance in Goethe's fable of the sorcerer's apprentice, in which the brooms and water pails take off on their own and run wild. In Pentagon-supported innovation, almost anything goes. For the first time in history, military leaders have escaped the traditional fixation on armaments used in past wars and are creatively at work on the weapons of the future. Side by side with this perverse form of creativity, untold billions are still spent on increasingly obsolete weapons of the past—such as tanks and aircraft carriers, both of which are sitting ducks for the new anti-tank and anti-carrier missiles.

In contrast, however, there is only a small amount of research on nutrition, health promotion (as contrasted with disease treatment), physical exercise, home building, mass transportation, the recycling of waste products, energy conservation, total energy systems, and the full use of agricultural products, including wood, in the production of alcohol and other fuels. When protests are made against the neglect of research in such areas, the response is "technological tokenism." Thus, early in 1980 the National Science Foundation proudly announced a new program to promote "approximate technologies." These were excellently defined as follows:

> Appropriate technologies are . . . those which possess many of the following qualities: they are decentralized, require low capital investment, are amenable to management by their users, result in solutions that conserve natural resources, and are in harmony with the environment; they are small or intermediate in scale, take into account site-available natural and human resources and are more labor than capital-intensive.[22]

These qualities, however, are clearly *in*appropriate for the maintenance, let alone the promotion, of large-scale, centrally controlled, labor-saving, energy-intensive operations. They were therefore put on a starvation diet of $1.8 million for fiscal year 1980—that is, about $300,000 apiece for each of six appropriate technology areas. The total budget allotment, it should be noted, was far less than one one-hundredth of one percent of the $47 billion in total spending on scientific research and development.

In covering up the Establishment's unyielding thrust toward inappropriate technology, statisticians have laboriously developed a narrow concept of "productivity" which measures the amount of labor used to yield a given quantity of output, but excludes inputs of capital, energy and materials. If the input of labor goes down relative to output, that demonstrates the forward march of productivity, which has become a fashionable indicator of economic progress. Accordingly, most efforts to measure capital productivity, energy productivity, materials productivity, or "total productivity" (which would take into account capital, energy, and materials as well as labor) have been shunted aside.[23]

In turn, the narrow concept of labor productivity has become the touchstone for a new "supply side" economics, oriented toward more government incentives for business investment and profitability. To the extent that any energy conservation measures replace machinery and fossil-fuel energy with people, this is registered on the "productivity" index as a backward step. The "remedy" is to freeze or suppress any conservation technologies and thereby restore the desired rate of increase in labor productivity. If this results in shortages of energy and capital * and a larger supply of wasted labor, no matter. The net result is continuing progress in the accumulation of capital and power under the control of an immensely sophisticated, albeit divided, Establishment. This progress, as described in the next chapter, is one of the miraculous achievements of modern capitalism.

* I discuss these shortages at greater length in the section on "An Abundance of Shortages" in "Friendly Fascist Economics" (chapter 10).

3

The Mysterious Establishment

The good old rule
Sufficeth them, the simple plan
That they should take who have the power
And they should keep who can.

WILLIAM WORDSWORTH

There are no stories or magazine sections [in CBS Evening News, NBC Nightly News, Newsweek, or Time] about what the sociologists call the Social Structure . . . nor about more easily grasped complexes such as the Class Hierarchy or the Power Structure.

HERBERT GANS [1]

MYSTERY HAS ALWAYS HOVERED around the masters of power and wealth.

The oligarchs of agricultural kingdoms wrapped themselves in witchcraft and divinity to conceal their weaknesses and magnify their strengths. They were helped by priests, scribes, courtiers, royal chamberlains, and old-style bureaucrats.

As industrial capitalism accumulated power and wealth, the old mysteries were replaced and dwarfed by the new mysteries of high finance, market manipulations, convoluted and lucrative legalisms, pressure-group politics, and a labyrinth of new bureaucracies. In 1918, Franz Kafka, unhappily embedded in an insurance company job in Prague, pictured the new order as a castle, "hidden, veiled in mist and darkness," a baffling symbol of the industrial establishment as it dominated the life of pre-industrial villagers. The socialist industrialists in Russia used the myths of monolithic omnipotence on the part of Party or leader to hide the new mysteries of struggle among powerful forces in the central oligarchy. During the short-lived fascism of Italy, Japan, and Germany, the myths of nationalism and divine or quasi-divine leadership cloaked the fierce tensions within the big business-military-political-bureaucratic establishments.

The building of the "Free World" empire after World War II has resulted in First World establishments that dwarf Kafka's unfathomable castle. Indeed, the Establishment in any of the leading capitalist societies is like a network of many castles—often a few hundred—spread across each country and linked with similar power structures in other countries.

THE CASTLES OF POWER

> *Establishment:* An exclusive group of powerful people who rule a government or society by means of private agreements or decisions.
>
> *American Heritage Dictionary*

The American Establishment is not an organization. Nor is it a simple coalition or network. Like the industrial-military complex, it has no chairman or executive committees.

Like the Golden International, the Establishment is more complicated than any complex. It is a complex of complexes, a far-flung network of power centers, including institutional hierarchies. These are held together less by hierarchical control and more by mutual interests, shared ideologies, and accepted procedures for mediating their endless conflicts.

Like the establishments in other First World countries, the American Establishment is not just a network of State leaders. Nor is it merely a coalition of private governments. It is an interweaving of two structures—polity and economy—that under industrial capitalism have never been independent of each other. It is the modern partnership of big business and big government. As such, it is much looser and more flexible than the establishments of classic fascism. And in contrast with them, above all, it operates in part through—and is to an important extent constrained by—the democratic machinery of constitutional government. Private agreements and decisions—even well-protected secrecy—play a large role in its operations; this adds to the Establishment's inherent mystery. It is why people often refer to it as the "invisible government." Yet many of its agreements and decisions are open to public view. Indeed, so much information is available in public reports, congressional hearings, and the specialized press that anyone trying to make sense of it all runs the danger of being drowned in a sea of excessive information. This, of course, is the problem faced by all intelligence agencies, which usually feed on a diet of 95 percent public data spiced with 5 percent obtained through espionage. Also, as with intelligence and counterintelligence, there are huge information gaps side by side with huge amounts of deliberately deceptive misinformation.

Thus the analysts of national establishments and power structures must bring to available data the same skepticism and creative imagination that Sherlock Holmes or Hercule Poirot brought to the clues left at the scenes of fictional murders. Since the truth of accumulated wealth and power is much stranger than fiction, any analyst must leave many riddles —and murders—unsolved. Besides, there are not many people who try to unravel these mysteries.

Social scientists receive research grants not to study power structures in any comprehensive sense. Those who make the effort—like G. William Domhoff, C. Wright Mills, and Gabriel Kolko—have had to operate on the fringes of scientific respectability, with more academic obstruction than support. Fortunately, their work has been aided by an equally small number of investigative journalists such as Ferdinand Lundberg and Morton Mintz, and lawyers like Jerry S. Cohen, and Arthur S. Miller, as well as a few other social scientists or journalists who have also helped tear away one or another of the veils that shroud the Establishment.[2]

From all this work, a few points stand forth clearly.

The Establishment has many levels. As shown in the chart, "The National Establishment, USA", these levels may be divided functionally. At the apex of strategic guidance are the "top dogs" of the Ultra-Rich and the Corporate Overseers. Among these are the president of the United States and those who assist him as commander in chief of the armed forces and in other roles. But these people cannot run things by themselves. They have the help of a larger group of "executive managers" who are, in turn, assisted by a much larger number of "junior and contingent members." Below these levels are the rest of the country's social structure—the middle and lower classes of the population in their roles as employees, self-employed, consumers, taxpayers, homeowners, and tenants.

The number of people actively involved—even at the very top—is too large for any meeting or convention hall. Robert Townsend, who headed Avis before it was swallowed by ITT, has made this estimate: "America is run largely by and for about 5,000 people who are actively supported by 50,000 beavers eager to take their places. I arrive at this figure this way: maybe 2,500 megacorporation executives, 500 politicians, lobbyists and Congressional committee chairmen, 500 investment bankers, 500 partners in major accounting firms, 500 labor brokers. If you don't like my figures, make up you own . . ."[3]

I am convinced his figures are far too small. If there are 4,000–6,000 at the top, they are probably able to deploy at least five times as many in executive management; who in turn operate through at least ten times as many junior and contingent members. My total ranges between a quarter and a third of a million. Even without adding their dependents,

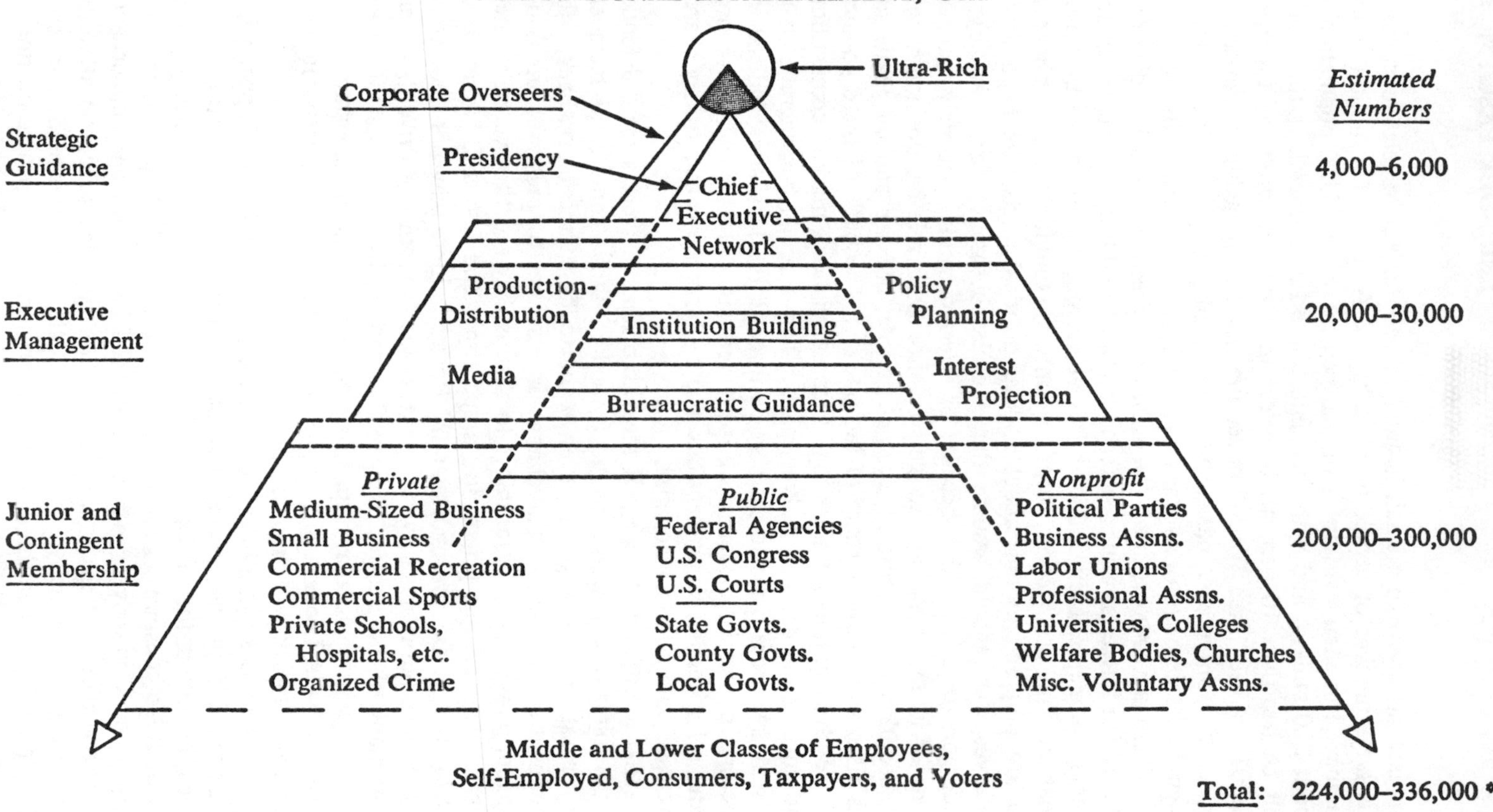

* Less than two tenths of one percent (.002) of the U.S. population and less than two hundredths of one percent (.0002) of the non-communist "free world" under the leadership of the U.S. Establishment.

this is a far cry from a small handful of people. Yet in relative numbers this large number of people is still a "few." A third of a million people numbers less than two tenths of one percent of the U.S. population of about 220 million; and with their immediate family members this would still be less than 10 percent. It is less than one hundreth of 1 percent (.0001) of the "Free World" under the shared leadership of the United States. Seldom, if ever, has such a small number of people done so much to guide the destinies of so many over such vast expanses of the planet.

There are conflicts at all levels. Most of these are rooted in divergent or clashing interests, values, perceptions, and traditions. Some are minor, others are major. Many minor crises at various points in the Establishment are daily occurrences, surprising only the uninitiated. But "whenever we are prepared to talk about a deep political crisis," as Papandreou observes, "we should assume that the Establishment (as a whole) is undergoing a crisis, either because of *internal* trouble—namely, because some of its members have seen fit to alter their relative position within the coalition—or because of *external* trouble, because another challenger has risen who wants a share of the power." The bulk of these conflicts are resolved through bargaining, accommodation, market competition, and government decision making, particularly through bureaucratic channels. A few more come to the surface through the legislative, judicial, or electoral processes. Coherence is provided not only through these procedures for conflict adjustment but also by large areas of partially shared interests, values, and ideologies.

It is constantly changing. If the Establishment were a mere defender of the status quo, it would be much weaker. While some of its members may resist many changes or even want to "turn the clock back," the dominant leaders know that change is essential to preserve, let alone, expand, power. "If we want things to stay as they are," the young nephew said to his uncle, the prince, in Lampedusa's *The Leopard*, "things have got to change. Do you understand?" Power holders may not understand this at once, but events drive the point home to them—or drive them out. Thus many of the changes occur in the membership of the Establishment which, at any point, may expand or contract. If the Establishment is a target, it is—in Leonard Silk's apt words for the "overall corporate government complex"—a "moving target." [4]

There is no single central conspiracy. I agree with Karl Popper when he says: "Conspiracies occur, it must be admitted. But the striking fact which, in spite of their occurrence, disproves the conspiracy theory is that few of these conspiracies are ultimately successful." Many of them have consequences entirely or partly unintended or unforeseen. Popper adds the observation that the successful ones rarely come to public attention and that there is usually a "situational logic" that transcends any conscious planning. When there is a fire in an auditorium, people do not get together to plan what to do. The logical response to the situation is "Get out." Some will do it in an orderly fashion; others might be rather rough toward people who get in their way. The Establishment often operates this way. Some of its most historic achievements have been forced on it by "fires" that break out suddenly, often unanticipated. The major advances in the welfare state, for example, have historically been opposed by most elements in capitalist establishments who were usually too stupid or nearsighted to realize that these measures would put a floor (or elevator) under market demand, thereby promoting the accumulation of corporate capital and taking the sting out of anticapitalist movements.

THE ULTRA-RICH

> Let me tell you about the very rich. They are different from you and me. . . . Even when they enter into our world or sink below us, they still think that they are better than we are. They are different.
>
> F. Scott Fitzgerald

> If we made an income pyramid out of a child's blocks, with each layer portraying $1,000 of income, the peak would be far higher than the Eiffel Tower, but almost all of us would be within a yard of the ground.
>
> Paul Samuelson[5]

The greatest difference between the Ultra-Rich and the rest of us is that most of them are addicted to sensory gratification on a grand scale. In part, as Ferdinand Lundberg has documented, this gratification takes the form of palatial estates, fabulously furnished town houses, private art collections, exclusive clubs, summer and winter resorts on many continents, membership in social registers, birth and burial under distinctive conditions, etc.[6] It also involves an array of services going far beyond the ordinary housekeepers, cooks, gardeners, masseurs, valets, chauffeurs, yacht captains, and pilots of the large fleet of rich people's private aircraft. But above all, the valets of the ultra-rich also include expert executives, managers, advisers, braintrusters, ghostwriters, entertainers, lawyers, accountants, and consultants. Most of their services are more expensive (and far more sophisticated) than those enjoyed by the emperors, emirs, and moguls of past centuries. Some are freely given in exchange for the privilege of approaching the throne and basking in the effulgent glory of accumulated wealth. Most are paid for by others—either being written off as tax deductions or appearing as expenses on accounts of various corporations, banks, foundations, universities, research institutes, or government agencies. These payments for modern valet service can be unbelievably high. Indeed, one of the earmarks of the Ultra-Rich in America is that they even have millionaires—most of them involved in big business—working for them.

Among the Ultra-Rich, of course, there are the so-called "beautiful people" who nourish their addiction merely by using a little of what accrues to them from fortunes managed by others. These are the "idle rich," the *rentiers* whose hardest work, beyond clipping coupons, is flitting from one form of entertainment to another. There are also a few deviants who betray their class by renouncing their addiction, getting along with small doses only, or actively using some of their money to finance liberal or left-wing causes. The great majority, however, seem to be stalwart conservatives who abstain from idleness by some form of "public service"—that is, by holding the top posts in the most prestigious institutions of philanthropy, higher education, health, culture, and art.

There are also those whose addiction is more powerful; they can satisfy it only by larger and larger doses of money or power. This can be done only by exercising directly or indirectly their roles as overseers, roles legitimized by their personal participation in the management of corporate property. As suggested by overlapping area (shared jointly by the Ultra-Rich and the Corporate Overseers on page 57), this probably comprises a large minority of the Ultra-Rich, in contrast with those lotus-eaters, deviants and "do-gooders" who do not take part in the guidance of national and international affairs.

If you ask how much a yacht costs, J. Pierpont Morgan once said, you're not rich enough to afford one. To this old principle, another may now be added: If you really know how much money you have, then you're not rich. The really rich cannot possibly calculate the present market value of their real estate, stocks, art or jewelry collections, bonds, trust funds, notes, or cash-surrender value of life insurance—and may even have trouble keeping track of many bank deposits in various countries. If a member of the Ultra-Rich is asked a question on total assets or net worth, as Nelson Rockefeller was asked in the congressional hearings before ascending (in reality, "descending") to the vice-presidency, he must use the services of experts on financial statements. For such services, any ultra-rich person or family spends hundreds of thousands of dollars a year (more than the annual income of the ordinary rich) in tax-deductible payments to hide both income and wealth from tax collectors or inquisitive reporters. In particular, corporate lawyers and accountants have made remarkable progress since World War II in the intricate arts of tax avoidance and evasion. Like an old-fashioned lady's hoop skirt, the corporation's annual financial statement conceals far more than it reveals and directly touches no sensitive parts. Reported assets are mere "book values." One set of books is prepared to ward off tax collectors, a second to attract investors, a third to help management decision making. Hidden reserves, slush funds, and political contributions never appear in the first two and are often kept secret from all but a few decision makers who really "need to know." Family accounts are even trickier. Hence, what observers can know about the money of the ultra-rich is unavoidably a combination of the demonstrable and the undemonstrable, the obvious and the conjectural, the known and the unknown.

In 1968 Arthur M. Louis attempted such a combination for *Fortune* magazine.[7] Putting together many combinations of "inside" and public information, he tried to calculate the "centimillionaires," those with a net worth of at least $100 million. The result was an Eiffel Tower like this:

	Number	
	By Level	*Cumulative*
$1 billion to $1.5 billion	2	2
$500 million to $1 billion	6	8
$300 million to $500 million	5	13
$200 million to $300 million	27	40
$150 million to $200 million	26	66
$100 million to $150 million	87	150

Louis readily acknowledges the incompleteness of the list and the downward bias in his estimates: "Some forms of wealth—and some of the Super-Rich themselves—absolutely defy detection." He also gives the names, ages, and some identifying data on the 66 above the $150 million level. Here we see many names associated with America's older fortunes: Rockefellers, du Ponts, Mellons, and Fords. Each of these appear with a few entries for each family: six Rockefellers, five Mellons, three du Ponts, and two Fords. The Kennedy family appears only under the name of the father, Joseph P. Kennedy. Many of the names are relatively obscure, such as Leon Hess of New York, Peter Kiewit of Omaha, William L. McKnight of St. Paul, and E. Clairborne Robins of Richmond. Some of the obscurity seekers have failed in their efforts and—as with the two billionaires at the top of the list, J. Paul Getty and Howard Hughes—have at times become conspicuously notorious.

Although one can only guess how many more people are now at the peak of the Eiffel Tower, there has been a remarkable increase in the number of mere millionaires a little closer to the ground:

1953	1963	1969	1979
27,000	67,000	121,000	520,000[8]

Part of this steep rise, of course, is the result of inflation—particularly the rising market value of real estate and other fixed assets. But from 1969 to 1979 prices as a whole went up only about 100 percent, as contrasted with a 300 percent increase in the number of millionaires.

For the same period, my guess is that the number of centimillionaires probably rose from 150 to 250 or so. If we could compensate for the downward bias in all these estimates, the total proportion of wealth at these heights would rise. And if we brought together into family units the various persons among whom familial wealth has been distributed to avoid taxes, the number of wealth hoards would decrease and a better picture would be provided on the concentration of money power. The billionaires, let me point out, have a thousand times more money than mere millionaires. It is this difference, I suppose, that let Paul Samuelson, himself a millionaire from the sales of his best-selling textbook *Economics*, to say that "almost all of us" are much nearer the ground. Like most economists, however, Samuelson prefers to write about income, which is less concentrated and a little more difficult to hide than wealth.

Many of the ultra-rich and the rich, of course, report no income whatsoever to the government, since they can escape U.S. income taxes by holding tax-exempt bonds and various foreign investments. What is more, many of the rich pay no taxes at all—or little more taxes than the run-of-the-mill office worker whose taxes are deducted at the source. Yet of those who paid taxes on reported income 1,779 persons reported to the Internal Revenue Service in 1978 that during 1977 they received incomes of $1 million or more. The average of this group was $2 million apiece.

"Wherever there is great property," wrote Adam Smith two centuries ago, "there is great inequality. For one very rich man, there must be at least five hundred poor, and the affluence of the few supposes the indigence of the many." Although totally excluded from establishment texts on economics, including Samuelson's, Smith's observation has become even more relevant in today's "more perfect" capitalism. If I consider the poor in Third World countries as well as in America, the ratio may be even higher than Smith's off-the-cuff estimate. If one concentrates on America, one finds a growing gap between the rich and the poor. Thus Herman Miller of the U.S. Census Bureau has calculated that the dollar gap between the average income of the "officially poor" (those below the government's poverty line) and the "rich" grew from $27,300 in 1959 to $37,700 in 1972. In 1959 the "ratio of rich to poor" was 12.5 to 1.[9] By 1972 it rose, according to Miller's calculations, to 16.3 to 1. But "rich" in this calculation referred to the entire top 20 percent of all the people in Samuelson's Eiffel Tower; this includes millions of people far nearer the ground than Samuelson. If Miller had defined "rich," rather, in terms of millionaires (less than two fifths of one percent) the ratio for 1972 would surely have been much more than 100 to 1 rather than the paltry 16 to 1. If he had focused on the ultra-rich, the ratio would have been far higher than 1,000 to 1. It is this higher group which probably owns over 80 percent of all corporate stock, 90 percent of all tax-exempt state and local bonds, and accounts for about a quarter of America's national wealth and income. If we compare any of these groups with the poor and the indigent, the ratios for income are astronomically high. As for wealth, ordinary arithmetic is not relevant—for large numbers of the lowest income groups have more debts than assets. The only way to picture their position is to dig deep underground cellars beneath the tower.

Apologists for concentrated income and wealth often defend the present structure by claiming that perfectly equal distribution—which nobody has ever seriously proposed—would bring everybody down to a dull level of gray austerity. Thus in 1972 Henry Wallich wrote a guest column for *The New York Times* in which he claimed that the average family income in America was only about $10,000. What he called "average," however, was the median. In other words, half the families got less than $10,000 and half more. But when income is inequitably distributed, the mean average is always much higher than the median average. In 1972, for a family of four, as I pointed out a few days later in the same paper's letter column, it was not $10,000 but almost $17,000.[10] By 1979, the mean income for a family of four was well over $33,000—and for the average family of 3.37 family members over $28,000 before taxes and about $24,000 after taxes. Similarly, if all personal wealth were to be divided by the total population, a family of four would have about $100,000. The reason these figures are so high, of course, is the tremendous amount of income and wealth at the very top. If the money of Henry Ford II, who has received as much as $5 million in one year, is added to that of a Ford assembly-line worker and then divided by two, the average comes out at the millionaire level. The high average does not suggest that the mythical average person is well off. On the contrary, it reveals the enormous amount of money available to gratify the self-indulgent whims and power lusts of the Ultra-Rich.

THE CORPORATE OVERSEERS

> No one can be truly powerful unless he has access to the command of major institutions, for it is over these institutional means of power that the truly powerful are, in the first instance, truly powerful . . .
>
> C. WRIGHT MILLS [11]

> Their [a few immense corporations] incredible absolute size and commanding market positions make them the most exceptional man-made creatures of the twentieth century. . . . In terms of the

size of their constituency, volume of receipts and expenditures, effective power, and prestige, they are more akin to nation-states than business enterprises of the classic variety.

RICHARD J. BARBER [12]

If better means more powerful, then the rich and the ultra-rich are truly better than most people. While you and I may work for major institutions, they are part of or close to (sometimes on top of) the cliques that control them. Their family life is also different. For ordinary people, family planning has something to do with control over the number and spacing of children. For the rich, family planning involves spawning trust funds and family foundations that hide wealth and augment control of corporate clusters and complexes. As a result of brilliant family planning, the formal institutions of corporate bureaucracy and high finance have not led to a withering away of the Morgans, Rockefellers, Harrimans, du Ponts, Weyerhausers, Mellons, and other oligarchic families of an earlier era. Nor have they prevented the rise of newer family networks such as the Kennedys. Rather, the nature of family wealth and operations has changed. "Rather than an Irénée du Pont exercising absolute domination, now the [du Pont] family fortune has been passed on to a number of heirs, even as the family's *total* wealth continues to grow. This splitting up of family stock blocks does not mean that capital no longer tends to accumulate. Just the opposite . . . du Pont wealth, and the power of their business class as a whole, is not diminishing, but growing." [13]

The growth of familial power, paradoxically, has been made possible by the sharing of that power with nonfamily members who handle their affairs professionally and mediate inevitable intrafamily disputes. Many of the corporate institutions, moreover, have been built and are guided by people who are merely rich and are ultra-rich only in intent. Whether the heirs of old wealth or the creators of new wealth, they mingle with the ultra-rich in clubs and boardrooms and play an indispensable role in overseeing corporate affairs.

The role of overseer no longer requires total ownership—or even owning a majority of a company's stock. Most corporations are controlled by only a small minority of corporate stockholders. By usual Wall Street calculations, 5 percent stock ownership is enough to give total control; in a few cases, the figure may rise to 10 percent. The larger the number of stockholders, the smaller this percentage. This "internal pyramiding" is carried still further through chains of subsidiaries and holding companies. Thus, strategic control of a small block of holding company stock yields power over a vast network of accumulated power and capital. Many of these networks include both financial corporations and corporations in industry, utilities, communications, distribution, and transportation. Most of the overseers are what Herbert Gans called Unknowns. "How many well-informed people," asks Robert Heilbroner, "can name even one of the chief executive officers—with the exception of Henry Ford II—of the top ten industrial companies: General Motors, Standard Oil (N.J.), Ford, General Electric, Socony, U.S. Steel, Chrysler, Texaco, Gulf, Western Electric? How many can name the top figures in the ten top utilities or banks—perhaps with the exception of David Rockefeller?" [14]

While the names of chief executive officers are a matter of public record, the names of the top stockholders are not. Most wealthy individuals, as Richard Barber has shown, "are tending to withdraw from direct stock ownership to companies and to funnel their investments through institutions, especially pension funds and mutual funds. This latter development has substantially increased the power of institutions—pension funds, banks, insurance companies and mutual funds—in the affairs of even the largest companies." [15] These institutions, in turn, manage their operations through the use of "nominees," otherwise known as "straws" or "street names." Thus, such "street names" as Aftco, Byeco and Cadco are some of the code words used by the Prudential Insurance Company, which tends to hide its interests from the general public.[16]

The major companies controlled by the corporate overseers are the largest concentration of capital in industrial capitalism's two-hundred-year history. An important part of this picture is seen by looking at the 500 largest industrial corporations listed every year in *Fortune* magazine. In 1954, when *Fortune* started this listing, these 500 accounted for half the sales and two thirds of the profits of all industrial corporations. By the mid-1970s these figures rose, respectively, to two thirds of the sales and three quarters of the profits. They have been rising since.

With all the attention given to the 500 industrials, most analysts have tended to neglect *Fortune's* annual listing of 300 additional corporations: 50 each in the six areas of commercial banking, life insurance, diversified financial companies, retailing, transportation, and utilities. If one looks at the entire 800 and selects the top 20, as I have done in the following table "The Apex of the Corporate Apex," one finds that by asset size only five industrials—Exxon, General Motors, Mobil, Ford, and IBM—are in this topmost group. At the very top stands American Telephone and Telegraph, while the remaining 16 are all financial corporations.

Since *Fortune* also lists the world's largest industrial corporations (outside of the communist countries), it is also interesting to look at the 20 largest as ranked by annual sales volume. Of these 20, 15 are American. While all 20 companies are huge employers, 13 have more than 100,000 employees apiece scattered all around the world. Of these 13, let it be noted, 9 are American. And only General Motors and Ford employ more than 400,000 people. None of the industrial giants, of course, could operate without support and assistance from the financial giants and the corporations in the other sectors.

THE APEX OF THE CORPORATE APEX

The 20 Largest U.S. Corporations, 1978 *
(Ranked by billions of dollars in assets)

	Assets
1. American Telephone and Telegraph (N.Y.)	103
2. BankAmerica Corp. (San Francisco)	95
3. Citicorp (N.Y.)	87
4. Chase Manhattan Corp. (N.Y.)	61
5. Prudential (Newark)	50
6. Metropolitan (N.Y.)	42
7. Exxon (N.Y.)	42
8. Manufacturer's Hanover Corp. (N.Y.)	41
9. J. P. Morgan & Co. (N.Y.)	39
10. Chemical New York Corp.	33
11. General Motors (Detroit)	31
12. Continental Illinois (Chicago)	31
13. Equitable Life Assurance (N.Y.)	28
14. Bankers Trust N.Y. Corp.	26
15. Western Bancorp (L.A.)	26
16. First Chicago Corp.	24
17. Aetna Life and Casualty (Hartford)	24
18. Mobil Oil (N.Y.)	23
19. Ford Motor (Dearborn, MI.)	22
20. IBM (Armonk, N.Y.)	21

* The 1979 Fortune Double 500 Directory

When one looks at the entire apex, whether defined in terms of 800 corporations or a somewhat larger group, it becomes apparent that a few thousand corporate overseers make strategic decisions on the volume and location of investment, the changing pattern of employment in many countries, the kinds of products that are produced, the level of prices and interest rates, and the content of mass advertising. "Instead of government planning," as Andrew Hacker puts it, "there is boardroom planning that is accountable to no outside agency: and these plans set the order of priorities on national growth, technological innovation, and, ultimately, the values and behaviors of human beings." [17] Boardroom planning is just that; its strategic outlines are never publicly proclaimed nor bureaucratically reported to any central control agency or clearing house outside the boardroom. Specific decisions—such as announced increases in prices or interest rates—may come sharply to the attention of buyers and borrowers, but usually after the fact and in isolation from other aspects of flexible corporate planning. Even in such highly concentrated areas as oil, automobiles, food, and commercial banking, the canny outsider can only learn bits and pieces of what is really going on.

THE APEX OF THE CORPORATE APEX

The World's 20 Largest Industrial Corporations, 1978 *
(Ranked by billions of dollars in sales)

	Sales	# Employees
1. General Motors (Detroit)	63	839,000
2. Exxon (N.Y.)	60	130,000
3. Royal Dutch/Shell Group (England/Netherlands)	44	158,000
4. Ford Motor (Dearborn, MI.)	42	507,300
5. Mobil Oil (N.Y.)	35	207,000
6. Texaco (N.Y.)	29	67,841
7. British Petroleum	27	109,000
8. National Iranian Oil	23	67,000
9. Standard Oil of Ca.	23	37,575
10. IBM (Armonk, N.Y.)	21	325,516
11. General Electric (Fairfield, CT.)	20	401,000
12. Unilever (Brit-Neth)	19	318,000
13. Gulf Oil (Pittsburgh)	18	58,300
14. Chrysler (MI.)	16	157,958
15. ITT (N.Y.)	15	379,000
16. Standard Oil (IN., Chi.)	15	47,601
17. Philips (Netherlands)	15	387,000
18. Atlantic Richfield (L.A.)	12	50,716
19. Shell Oil (Houston)	11	34,974
20. U.S. Steel (Pitts.)	11	166,848

* Fortune World Business Directory, 1979

THE CHIEF EXECUTIVE NETWORK

The most visible actors in modern capitalist establishments are the chief executives of national governments—whether presidents or prime ministers—and a few of their aides. Unlike the Ultra-Rich or the Corporate Overseers, the chief executives—and often their family members also—live in a blaze of publicity. They also wear many hats. In the United States the president is not only commander in chief of the armed forces, chief diplomat, high legislator with prerogatives of both initiative and veto, but also boss of covert operations, party leader, tribune of the people, manager of prosperity, symbol (for better or worse) of public morality, and "leader of the Free World." And wherever he goes, he carries with him the control box whose buttons, when properly pushed, would unleash again the fury of nuclear bombs.

Despite all the glare of spotlights on the presidency, however, no other institution in the country is so thoroughly obscured by carefully prepared clouds of mystery and darkness. During the presidential campaigns, in Nicholas Johnson's somewhat whimsical words, the contest is "waged between two television consultants nobody knows." Afterwards, the public image of the victor—including his face, words, and publicized actions—is a public relations product. But it is not quite correct to say that presidents are sold to the public like soap. In this case the product itself is remarkably active. At the risk of *lèse majesté* one might suggest that all recent presidents have shown the combined talents of huckster and actor.

The focus on the president himself obscures the fact that, in the words of an old-time White House correspondent, "the President is many men." In other words, he is a critical node in a Chief Executive Network of staggering complexity. The more formal elements in the network are the many agencies in the White House Office and the Executive Office of the president: particularly, the National Security Council, the National Security Agency, the Office of Management and Budget, the Council of Economic Advisers, and the various cabinet committees or groups supervised by members of the White House staff. Then there is a large number of official aides and advisers, both military and civilian, and a still larger number of unofficial agents and close associates. From this large mass of people—some of them never appearing on the payroll of the White House, the Executive Office or even the federal government—the president selects the members of the various "inner circles" with whom he consults from time to time or to whom he assigns specific missions. Many of these presidential aides enjoy the protection of well-maintained anonymity. Others are known somewhat in Washington circles or even—as in the case of Henry Kissinger before he became secretary of state—to the broader public. They are then given the special protection of the president's "executive privilege," in accordance with which quaint custom they may make statements to the press but may not be interrogated by congressional committees.

As linchpin of the entire capitalist Establishment, the Chief Executive Network plays a role somewhat similar to that of the Communist party structure in a Marxist-Leninist country. But it holds the Establishment together not by party discipline but through a rather flexible set of linkages with other parts of the system. Each of these linkages is wrapped in extra-special mystery. As a former official involved in the daily workings of the presidency during the Fair Deal and the Korean War, I can attest to my own inability to know what was really going on—or perhaps I should say my ability to appreciate the limits of what I could fathom. This same ability was shared not only by my immediate associates in the President's Council of Economic Advisers and budget office but also, I truly believe, by the president himself.

One part of the mystery is the linkage between the presidency and the Ultra-Rich and the Corporate Overseers. Formally, certain links are provided by such groups as the "President's Club" (executives who contributed $1,000 a year to Lyndon Johnson's campaign chest) or the various business advisory committees that mobilized large sums for the reelection campaigns of Presidents Nixon, Ford, and Carter. On his desk in the Oval Office, President Truman used to have a sign reading "The buck stops here." Another sign at the door of the Oval Office, never written but known to anybody aware of the president's central role in raising money for his party, reads "The buck comes here."

Apart from party financing, there has been increasing interpenetration between the Chief Executive Network and the informal circles at the pinnacles of business wealth and power. During the Johnson administration, special advisory groups from the financial community could be quickly brought into being at the suggestion of any top financial leader or top presidential adviser. The operations of the special Vietnam Advisory Group in 1968 were facilitated by the previous experience of Clark Clifford, then secretary of defense, as both counsel to President Truman many years earlier and then special attorney for Du Pont, General Electric, Standard Oil, TWA and RCA. Under Presidents Nixon, Ford, and Carter, two mutually supporting trends developed: the multiplication of advice-or-action groups in such areas as the promotion of multinational corporations, foreign currency manipulations, the protection of U.S. foreign investments, and the imposition of wage controls or wage guidelines; and increasing interaction between the financial community and presidential staff (many of whom have been "on leave" from business positions). Together, these trends have led to more integration than ever before in American history between top business leaders and the prime movers in the federal government. During the Carter administration, this process of integration was illustrated by acceptance through his executive network of the idea that higher business profits are the central purpose of domestic public policy. Thus at the very moment during the first half of 1979, when commentators were criticizing Carter for ineffectiveness, his administration proved remarkably effective for well-synchronized support of corporate profit making. In an article titled "The Secret Success of Jimmy Carter: Profits Without Honor," I came to Carter's defense by pointing out this achievement, while commenting on the paradox that for political reasons he could not take public credit for it.[18]

An equally challenging mystery is the president's involvement in other countries. This is an arcane world of high and low intrigue, far removed from one's customary picture of government bureaucracy, far closer to the world of adventure fiction, rarely unveiled in the diaries, memoirs, or files of participants. Although ambassadors and consular officials are presidential appointees, they often do little more than provide help to special emissaries (sometimes corporate overlords or their representatives) or "cover" for the chief CIA operative or military officer who organizes a coup d'etat. Indeed, under instructions from President Johnson during the 1960s, the CIA carried on a secret vest-pocket presidential war in Laos. Through its so-called "department of dirty tricks," the CIA provides a vehicle for direct or indirect cloak-and-dagger intervention by the presidency in almost any country of the globe. There is good reason to believe—although I cannot prove—that such intervention continued under President Carter in such diverse countries as, for example, Afghanistan, Pakistan, Bangladesh, India, Angola, Somalia, Italy, Portugal, and Spain.

Less dramatic, but more complicated, is the network of relations between the presidency and the rest of government—the courts, the Congress, the cabinet departments and independent agencies, and the state, local, and county governments, which receive in transfer payments almost $100 billion a year as a result of legislation, judicial decisions, and executive regulations and interpretations. Looking back through history, one may easily find dramatic confrontations between president and the courts and between president and members, committees, or houses of Congress. But the most grueling, the most baffling, the most endless and the most mysterious confrontations are between the president and his aides, on one side, and the labyrinth of intertwined executive bureaucracies stretching from national agencies through all levels of government down to every county, city, town, and neighborhood in the country. At any point in this labyrinth the president or his aides have some sort of potential influence. At a few points they can dominate—but only for a while. A president is like an oriental potentate with a harem of a thousand wives; the harems of his assistants probably scale down to one hundred and then to a measly ten. While the top man is theoretically free to do anything he wants with any harem member, he has only too few days and nights and too little energy in comparison to the opportunities lying before him. If the metaphor breaks down, it is mainly because in this case the underlings organize alliances of their own and can often outwit the president and his aides—particularly if they can win some support from a few entities in Congress, the external lobbies, and particularly the Corporate Overseers and the Ultra-Rich.

One way in which a president can help influence many government agencies at the same time is to pursue the role of "tribune to the people," a role which is best calculated to succeed when the president is doing what is needed by the Ultra-Rich and the Corporate Overlords. Although this role was anticipated many decades earlier by Andrew Jackson, its first exponent in the twentieth century was Theodore Roosevelt, who seemed at times to brandish his "big stick" on behalf of an aroused populace against the "malefactors of great wealth." The same stick—in weight more like an orchestra conductor's baton—was waved vigorously by Woodrow Wilson, Franklin Roosevelt, Harry Truman, John Kennedy, and Lyndon Johnson. But the chorus they led was not composed of popular masses who at last found a leader. It was made up, rather, of sophisticated upper-class corporate leaders and liberal intellectuals, lawyers, and scholars who favored continuous reforms designed to maintain and strengthen the capitalist order and its imperial structure. Often indeed, it seemed that only a president's voice could speak out loudly and clearly on such reforms as income taxes, antitrust legislation, workmen's compensation, regulatory commissions, social security, labor legislation, and expanded public works. But while the voice was that of the president (and broad assent was often obtained throughout the lower and middle classes), the hands that shaped the creaky machinery of government and usually reaped the longest-run benefits from it were those of the upper-class minorities.

These activities by the Chief Executive Network have been successful only to the extent that presidents have identified themselves with certain values or aspirations of the middle and lower classes. By so doing, Democratic presidents won more support from the "Common Man" in the lower classes, Republican presidents from "Middle America" on Main Street. Still more significant, each president uses his Chief Executive Network as a means of keeping in touch with all of the major institutions and organized groups of American society—particularly those at the middle and lower levels of the establishment. For every geographic, income, ethnic, and religious grouping there is some federal agency, some government policy, some direct or remote tie to some part of the Chief Executive Network. In this symbolic manner there are no longer any Forgotten Men or Forgotten Women in America. Some kind of attention to *all* interests is a prerequisite for adequate servicing of upper-class interests.

As linchpin of the Establishment, the Chief Executive Network often operates at a level of high policy in which apparently unconnected policies help solidify both the Establishment and its popular support. Thus in the early days of the "Free World" empire, President Truman's cold war and military expansion pleased the conservatives, while his Fair Deal proposals (blocked by the conservatives in Congress) placated the liberals. Similarly, as he expanded American military intervention in Vietnam, President Johnson won substantial liberal support by reviving much of the Fair Deal, improving a few of its elements and getting congressional action on them. Under President Carter two apparently contradictory policies—arms control for the liberals and military expansion for the conservatives—were wrapped together in one bundle. Similarly, President Carter's stress on human rights, in addition to restoring some moral tone to U.S. foreign policy, gave ammunition to conservatives for attacking all socialist countries and to liberals for campaigns against U.S.-supported dictatorships in Iran, Nicaragua, Argentina, Chile, and South Korea.

EXECUTIVE MANAGERS

I don't care what the management is so long as it is successful.
MARRINER ECCLES [19]

Karl Marx was one of the first to focus on the expanding role of industrial managers—as distinct from owners—in capitalist enterprise. In every generation since then, observers have rediscovered the same trend. While Marx underestimated the managers, James Burnham and John Kenneth Galbraith went to the other extreme by proclaiming a "managerial revolution" and rule by the "technostructure." But in a complex system the growing importance of some component—like radar instruments in an airplane—does not mean it is in charge. Executive managers are, of course, steering instruments, are used as such, and are particularly valued to the extent that they are self-starting and, subject to vague clues from above, self-steering. Despite some personal stockholdings, the higher executives are "hired executives." Their power and glory derive from service, and subservience, to superiors—above all, from their ability to provide this service most of the time without explicit tutelage. They can be ruthlessly fired if they fail to accumulate the capital that their overseers deem possible.

The most obvious function of executive management is the production and marketing of goods and services for profits. This is the mighty engine that keeps the wheels of capitalism turning, and provides jobs for the great majority of the wage-earning population, the worldly goods for man's consumption or use, and the money and power so essential to satisfy the acquisitive drives of the Ultra-Rich Corporate Overseers. In a still larger sense, moreover, the high executives who manage the domestic and foreign aspects of banking, agribusiness, mining, manufacture, construction, transportation, wholesaling, and retailing also oversee the systematized rewards and punishments embodied in the wages, salaries, and other emoluments received or sought by 70 million private-sector employees. This is a bonding element in the structure of power, one that helps bind the Establishment as a whole to the population's pockets.

To a large extent the mass media are subsidized through the advertising divisions of the larger corporations. Some of the advertising is frankly institutional, associating one or another big-business institution with socially approved values of integrity and public service. But most of it is directly aimed at "soft" or "hard" selling, with "puffery" triumphing over integrity and public manipulation over public service. The entertainment subsidized by advertising provides escape from the strains of the real world or entry into an imaginary world peopled by dramatic symbols of high consumption, excitement, and sexual fulfillment.

The news and commentaries subsidized by advertising provide a more varied agenda, highlighting the rich diversity of views within the public consensus as defined by the Establishment and sharply defining—if not often creating—those subjects generally recognized as public issues. The elite media, in turn, provide the technical, cultural, and recreational materials needed or desired by all the various groupings, currents, and cross currents within the Establishment itself.*

Another executive-management function of vital importance is developing the new or stronger institutions required by any powerful and flexible establishment. This is the major task—rarely recognized—of such superfoundations as Ford, Rockefeller, Duke, Johnson, Lilly, Pew, Carnegie, and Mellon. The avowed purpose and legal justification of these foundations is "philanthropy," the giving of charity to the poor and the helpless; hence their executives are sometimes called "philanthropoids." Before the welfare state, some of the foundations were actually engaged in direct charitable activities. More recently, this function has faded into the background. Most analysts of the growth of American foundations seem agreed on a variety of narrow functions: the avoidance of inheritance taxes; perpetuation of personal or family control over corporate activities through indirect means; extension of power and control into such areas as education, science, technology, the arts, and welfare programs; and creation of a public relations image of "doing good" to help cover up the crudity, violence, lawbreaking, or corruption often associated with the making of the donors' fortunes. All of these are indeed a part of the picture—particularly tax avoidance, without which most of the foundations would immediately crumble and wither away. But emphasis on these points tends to distract attention from the specific ways in which the philanthropoids of the superfoundations have used tax-exempt money in immortalizing corporate control and creating personal and family images: They have financed many of the most prestigious universities, hospitals, scientific laboratories, museums, and social service institutions. During the quarter century after World War II they sparked new initiatives in technical assistance to underdeveloped countries, the development of new government programs at all levels, and the immense expansion of the social and behavioral sciences. While often operating under the guidance of the Corporate Overseers or Ultra-Rich, they contribute to almost all of the institutions of executive management. Also, a major thrust is to promote the still greater expansion of institutions and personnel at the lower levels of junior and contingent membership. They are thus a positive force in promoting the system-strengthening reforms so essential for the sustained growth of a more sophisticated capitalism.

---

* The media deserve much more attention—and they get it in chapter 12, "Managing Information and Minds."

Institution building, in turn, verges over into the closely related function of broad policy planning. It is more diffusely oriented, rather, to the germination, crystalization, and clarification of the wide variety of competing policy options (many of them to be hailed, or adopted, as "reforms" or "revolutions") that may best serve the interests of dominant establishment forces. Hence, there is a wide diversity of emphasis in the conduct of policy planning functions. The values of conservative business and wealth are translated into policy specifics through such groups as the National Association of Manufacturers, the Conference Board, the Chamber of Commerce of the United States, the Business Council, the American Farm Bureau Federation, their sectoral affiliates in areas ranging from automobiles and cotton through machine tools and zinc, and their state and local branches. Still more conservative views are articulated by the American Enterprise Institute and the American Security Council. Policy formulation for the more liberal businessmen and plutocrats is handled by such groups as the Committee for Economic Development, the National Planning Association, the Twentieth Century Fund, and The Brookings Institution, and—in foreign policy—the Council on Foreign Relations and the Foreign Policy Association.

Cutting across both sets of interests are a long succession of *ad hoc* task forces and blue-ribbon commissions (some requested by presidents, to prepare the groundwork for shifts in presidential policy) and a far-flung array of "think tanks" and research institutions. Many of the latter —like RAND, the Systems Development Corporation, the Institute for Defense Analysis, the Centre for Research on Institutions and Social Policy, the Hudson Institute, and the Urban Institute—are wholly or in large part financed by government contracts. Most new policy departures —including the U.S. switch on the admission of China into the United Nations, the use of armed forces in Vietnam, the institution of systems budgeting, federal revenue sharing, and President Carter's cautious "opening" toward Cuba—are initiated only after careful sifting, formulation, and reformulation by one or more of such groups. Sometimes these departures are prepared for by special commissions set up by the president, foundations, or both together.

Throughout this process opportunities are created for people from the junior and contingent level (particularly experts and academics) to make contacts with Corporate Overseers, their aides and the advisers of the chief executive. Executive managers, in turn, meet many people from vastly different ethnic and class backgrounds. These contacts facilitate the selective recruitment of sound "upward-mobiles" into the high-energy staffs at executive levels. With the participation of elected and appointed government officials, they also help crystallize government policy options before they are crystallized within government in operational form.

The nature of this advance preparation—as well as the complexity of the process—is partially suggested in Domhoff's chart "The Policy

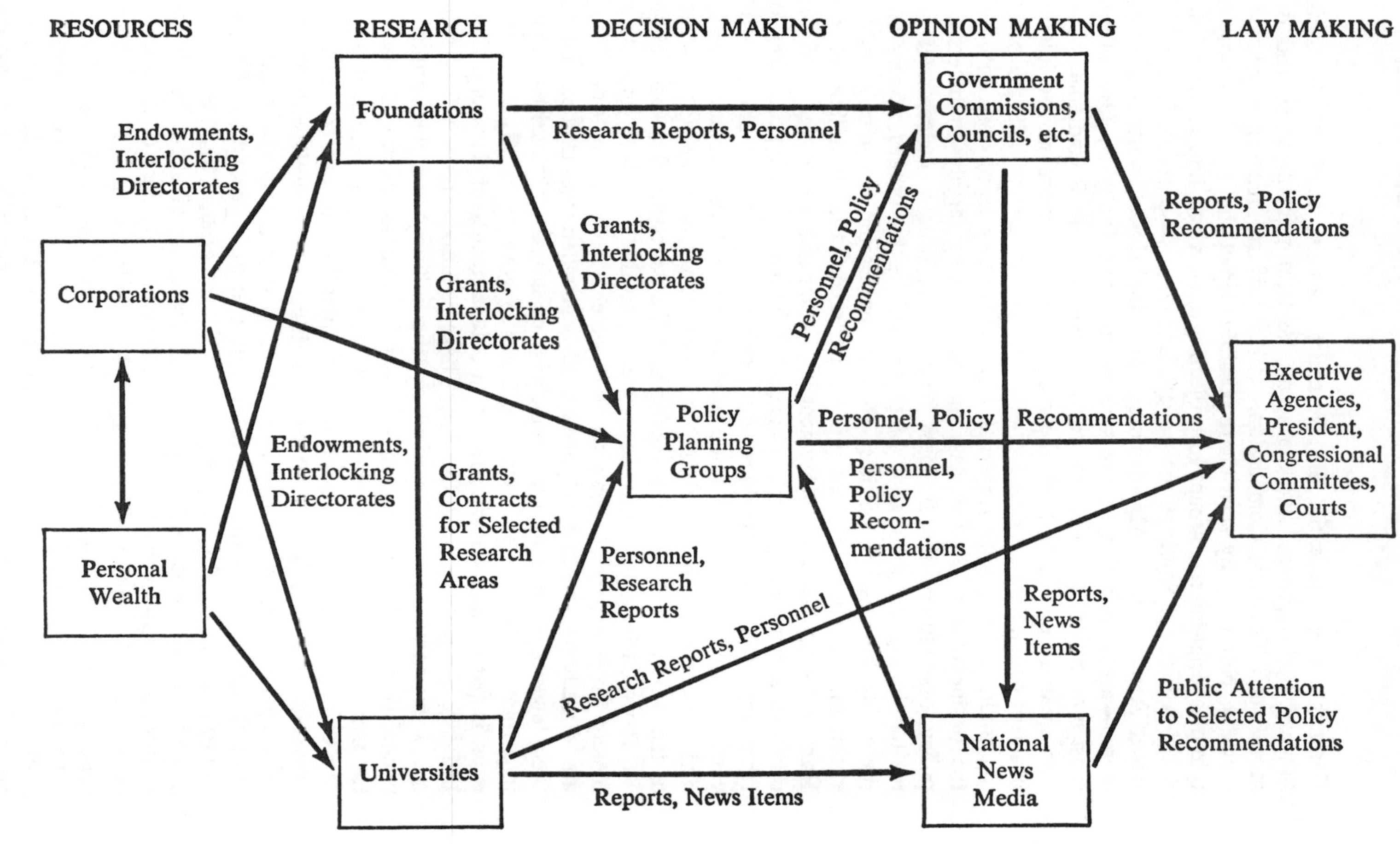
THE POLICY FORMULATORS
RESOURCES
RESEARCH
DECISION MAKING
OPINION MAKING
LAW MAKING
Corporations
Personal Wealth
Endowments, Interlocking Directorates
Foundations
Universities
Endowments, Interlocking Directorates
Grants, Interlocking Directorates
Grants, Contracts for Selected Research Areas
Research Reports, Personnel
Grants, Interlocking Directorates
Policy Planning Groups
Personnel, Research Reports
Research Reports, Personnel
Reports, News Items
Government Commissions, Councils, etc.
Personnel, Policy Recommendations
Personnel, Policy Recommendations
Personnel, Policy Recom-mendations
Reports, News Items
National News Media
Reports, Policy Recommendations
Executive Agencies, President, Congressional Committees, Courts
Public Attention to Selected Policy Recommendations

Formulators"[20] (table 6). But the chart does not touch on the transnational policy groups, like the secret Bilderburg conferences and the more open Trilateral Commission, which perform the same functions globally. Nor can any such chart possibly depict the equally important role of special-interest groups in projecting their views into governmental decision making. Some of the policy formulators—particularly the National Association of Manufacturers and the U.S. Chamber of Commerce—are also active as pressure groups and lobbyists. One of the most powerful of the pressure groups is the Business Roundtable, which was created in 1973 through the merger of three more narrow-interest business committees originally organized, respectively, to fight the building trades unions, work for more restrictive labor legislation, and "tell the business story" in the mass media. Drawing largely on others for policy orientations, the Business Roundtable usually concentrates on masterminding the application of these policies by propagandizing and pressuring government officials. During the Carter administration, for example, the group chalked up to its credit the castration of the Humphrey-Hawkins full employment legislation and the murder of bills to establish a consumer protection agency and provide more protection for labor unions. Thousands of less spectacular campaigns are always being carried out by specialized trade associations, *ad hoc* committees, individual corporations, law firms, and such powerful professional bodies as the American Medical Association and the American Bar Association.

It would be a great mistake, however, to think of these interests as merely projecting their views on government from the outside. Many are directly represented in government—as when business executives, their lawyers or their expert technicians, or advisers themselves occupy important positions at the executive levels of government. This phenomenon is particularly conspicuous in the departments of Treasury, State, Defense, Agriculture, and Interior. There is also a reverse flow from many executive agencies—particularly the military and the regulatory commissions—whereby thousands of expert officials prepare themselves for more lucrative private employment through their government work. More formal representation of private interests, mainly corporate, is provided by hundreds of advisory committees that consult with government agencies on proposed policies at early stages, originate many new policies, or veto initiatives that run counter to their perception of Establishment interests. The most powerful of these groups was the Defense Department Industrial Advisory Council consisting of about twenty-five high-level executives from major war contractors. Because of its work in obtaining higher profit rates on cost-plus contracts and promoting the sale of arms abroad, a former Pentagon cost analyst, A. Ernest Fitzgerald, called the IAC "the board of directors of the military-industrial complex." This was an exaggeration, of course. A complex does not have any single board of directors any more than a capitalist ruling class can have a single executive committee. The institutional basis of coherence is much more delicate and complex. Actually, the IAC was dissolved in 1974. It was replaced by a network composed of the Aerospace Industries Association, the National Security Industry Association, and more specialized groups that work closely with the military on a daily basis. The power of the military-industrial complex has not been adversely affected by this change.[21]

On a broader scale, there are also many continuing efforts to bring together the dominant interests in the private, public, and nonprofit sectors. "Every year since 1950, it has been discovered, major business groups join with the American Farm Bureau Federation, the American Bar Association and the American Medical Association for an annual Greenbrier Conference—named after the plush hotel in the resort town of White Sulphur Springs, West Virginia, where they meet—to map out their lobbying strategy for the coming year." [22] Through these and other less formal or more secret processes big business, corporate law, and the biggest farm organizations work out common views on major issues. Ever since World War II these views are projected on to a much wider public through the lavishly funded advertising campaigns of the Advertising Council.

An equally essential but still more complicated function of executive management is provided by the higher-level bureaucrats who guide the operations of the intertwined bureaucratic hierarchies in the private, public, and nonprofit sectors. According to the fairy tales of official sociology or public administration, a top-level bureaucrat is an organization man who takes orders, obeys rules, and competes jealously with all other organizations. As a former bureaucrat of this type in President Truman's office, I reject this stereotype. Many top-level bureaucrats—whether advisers or administrators—are innovative persons who, like Edward Gibbon's "masters of the Roman world," humbly profess themselves the accountable servants of their superiors whose decrees they dictate and obey. Most of them can survive or be successful only by being "wheelers and dealers" who continuously forge and reforge alliances with varied bedfellows—above, alongside and below—in the Establishment. Because many of these officials resist pressures from the Chief Executive Network, the president's aides often see them as being "in business for themselves." Actually, it is this free-wheeling operation that has often done wonders to energize the Chief Executive Network itself and contribute to the more successful performance of the Establishment's business.

This function is probably best illustrated by the rather tough-minded and "independent" bureaucracy in the military services. The Department of Defense and the Joint Chiefs of Staff are the largest employers and spenders in the United States. They must supervise over a million civilian employees, over two million military people, large reserve contingents, and hundreds of huge military contracts, installations, and movements across fifty states, scores of other countries, and on, over and under the high seas. Quite a large number of "high brass" and civilian executives are required to impose some degree of managerial control. But this does not mean that this country's highest-ranking military notables may be ranked (as C. Wright Mills once suggested) alongside the Ultra-Rich, the Corporate Overseers, or the presidency. On all major issues they are subordinate to civilian superiors whose militaristic *machismo* is sometimes bloodthirstier than that of people with battlefield experience; and their eagerness for postretirement jobs with the corporations guarantees an appropriate subservience to civilian overlords.

JUNIOR AND CONTINGENT MEMBERS

> It [the Establishment] may even include leadership or pressure groups of organizations antagonistic or potentially antagonistic to the dominant class and the social order. . . . Their continued participation is dependent upon their continued good behavior.
>
> ANDREAS PAPANDREOU [23]

The lowest levels of the Establishment include the leaders of all the many institutions that directly employ, govern, or feast upon the vast middle and lower classes of workers, consumers, taxpayers, and voters. These private, public, and nonprofit institutions provide the solid foundation for, and operating arms of, Establishment power. As such, they have proliferated enormously in the decades since World War II. As one looks back upon the 1960s especially, one recalls how frequently it was said, in popular and activist parlance, that in one or another of these areas, "That's where the action is." And that is where it continues to be: not action to decide the course of national policy at home or abroad, but action to implement it, to absorb the shock of attacks on the Establishment, and to suck upward into the higher ranks those few members of the middle and lower classes capable of proving their usefulness and reliability. Many people suffer from the illusion that the "They" of the Establishment are those juniors closest to them and most visible—namely, immediate employers, officials of schools, hospitals, welfare agencies, and police, and leaders of trade unions, political parties, and churches. Only when they get closer to the action (particularly when they prepare to move upward themselves) do they realize that meaningful participation at this level is contingent, in Papandreou's words, "upon their continued good behavior."

According to the myths of old-fashioned political science, the "separation of powers" endows the Supreme Court and the Congress with power equal to the president's while the federal system reserves for the fifty states all the "powers not delegated to the United States by the Constitution, nor prohibited by it to the States." Beyond the constitutional niceties, political parties are supposed to bring separated parts of government together in organic unity, while also providing the electorate a clear choice among alternative directions. That things do not happen exactly this way under conditions of escalating presidential power is illustrated by continuing outcries for the restoration of congressional authority, the exercise of judicial restraints on executive usurpation, the revival of states' (or local governments') rights, and the building of a responsible party system. The hard-fact content underlying the litany of plaintive calling for this or that reform is that all government below the Chief Executive Network operates most of the time at the junior level. If there is a real, rather than an illusory, tripartite separation among counterbalancing powers, it is not to be found in the formal structure of government. It lies, rather, in the divisions among the Corporate Overseers, the Ultra-Rich, and the Chief Executive network. And to a smaller degree a certain hierarchical separation may be found: between the new Lords at the Establishment's apex, the Lords Temporal of executive management, and the junior and contingent members who comprise the new Commons of the modern capitalist Establishment. Moreover, the old saying "You can't beat City Hall" needs substantial revision. Those who have "beaten" City Hall, the police department, the welfare agency, the university, or any of the junior-level institutions find out that they have captured an empty citadel and end up serving as instruments of, or transmission belts for, higher business and political power.

Another myth elaborately nourished by the more conservative business and political leaders of macrobusiness is the great power of labor unions. Business outcries against the tyranny of Big Labor were particularly strong during the many decades before the New Deal and the government-protected rise of industrial unionism. In recent years, the myth has lingered on—although in a somewhat ethereal rather than full-bodied form. Behind the earthy image of cigar-chomping George Meany lies the power to get a few paltry patches on the sub-welfare state, a few vetoes on issues of marginal importance, a few dedicated friends in elected posts, and many ringing campaign promises that are largely forgotten after elections. Andreas Papandreou's comment about contingent status in the Establishment is particularly relevant to organized labor. While "responsible" trade unions can be immense forces for maintaining the discipline of the work force and nipping socialist movements in the bud, there is always a potentiality for antagonism to "the dominant class and the dominant social order." This potentiality expresses itself whenever a union goes too far in pressing its demands on profits or directly involving itself in matters assumed to be the special prerogatives of management. More broadly, there is also the risk of more widespread unionization. If the proportion of unionized workers in America should rise from 25 percent to the British level of 40 percent, the Swedish of 60 percent, or the Israeli of 75 percent, the payoff in terms of benefits and shared power might be somewhat uncomfortable. These are the reasons, rather than their uncouth manners or backgrounds, why labor leaders' participation in higher affairs is usually "contingent upon their continued good behavior."

There seems to be a general rule that the power of any junior-level group or institution is widely exaggerated during any period in its expansion. Before World War II, the growth of professional management was clearly documented by such astute observers as Walter Rathenau, Adolf Berle, and James Burnham, each of whom then dizzily proceeded to suggest the success of a "managerial revolution" that divorced managers from control by the wealthiest property owners. The rising role of engineers in the processes of production and distribution led Thorstein Veblen to envision an economy in which the engineers became the top managers, replacing both capitalists and politicians. This vision was later embodied in Technocracy, Inc., a movement led by engineers and economists in the 1930s. After the atomic explosions at Hiroshima and Nagasaki, atomic physicists were often hailed as "the new men of power," or attacked as a new satanic priesthood capable of taking society by the scruff of the neck. They were soon outclassed, however, by the economists, who have received much of the credit for the "sophisticated judgments" responsible for taming the capitalist business cycle. The hegemony of the economists, in turn, was challenged during the 1960s by increasing numbers of behavioral or social scientists from sociology, psychology, political science, anthropology, and the newer fields of "computer science" and "systems analysis." After "cracking the genetic code" through their work on DNA and RNA, biologists began to compete with atomic physicists. The only professional groups that have not aspired to more limelight have been the lawyers and accountants; this is possibly to be explained less by inherent professional modesty than by the movement of their most able spokesmen into executive management roles where power, like sex, is best enjoyed when least exhibited in public.

All these many professional specializations have been transcended, however, in magnificent claims for new-style technocrats. Thus Daniel Bell has hailed the broad new class of "knowledge elites," the vast array of experts who are pragmatically empirical in specifying *where* one wants to go, *how* to get there, the costs of the enterprise, and some realization of, and justification for, the determination of *who* is to pay.[24]

In a similar spirit of magnification, John K. Galbraith has acclaimed the role of "the technostructure"—all who bring specialized knowledge, talent, or experience to group-decision making—in providing the "guiding intelligence" or "brain" of large-scale corporate and federal action.[25] Daniel P. Moynihan has pointed out that America has arrived at a "type of decision-making that is suited to the techniques of modern organizations, and which ends up in hands of persons who make a profession of it. . . . They are decisions that can be reached by consensus rather than conflict." [26] Clearly, this style of exaggeration does not discuss the processes of decision making on *which* brains to hire, *what* to do with their products, or *where* the consensus begins and ends. But it does serve the function of morale building throughout the junior levels.

The competition among competing specialties is unnerving, to say the least. Hardly does one group of experts carve out an "ecological niche" for itself than some other group arises to challenge its competence or—as the case with much of systems theory and computer science—to assert general hegemony over all specialized areas. Moreover, the incessant multiplication of expertly defined options for either selection or rejection by those at higher levels inevitably means more of the latter than the former. To this situation must be added the tendency of all junior-level institutions to compete bitterly among themselves for larger shares of scarce resources and, wherever possible to veto the claims of competitors. This is why there is so much empirical backing to the lower levels of the Establishment for David Riesman's view of society as an aggregation of conflicting "veto groups." Also relevant is Daniel Bell's story of the social scientist who runs from his office into the streets shouting "I have a solution! Who has a problem?" When there are more offered solutions than takers, the expert tends to resemble the call girl who stands by the telephone but is seldom called. Perhaps in John Milton's words, "they also serve who only stand and wait."

The very process of waiting or actively seeking to serve, however, has implications. Intellectuals are brought out of the ivory tower and lined up for foundation grants, government contracts, corporate consultancies, or luscious lecture fees. The fallout, or spinoff, from such emoluments helps convert erstwhile intellectuals into technicians no longer interested in ideas for their own sake. "Independent merchants and lawyers, once noted for their forthright views on public affairs," comments Ferdinand Lundberg, "spoke out as the occasion seemed to require. Now that they are gone down the corporate drain, theirs and other voices are frozen in corporate silence." [27] University presidents also once used to speak out with a measure of independence. Under modern capitalism, their voices are "frozen in corporate silence" or else carry the burden of technocratic argumentation within the boundaries of Establishment consensus. Such circumstances help fashion a younger generation of pragmatic mercenaries eager to enter the brains-for-hire market.

At the junior and contingent level, however, the boundaries of Establishment consensus are broad enough to allow generous room for debate not only on minor details but also on established departures from the middle of the road. Heretics on both the Left and the Right are encouraged. Indeed, one minority of the Ultra-Rich has continuously subsidized various left-liberal and radical groups, parties, and publications, while another minority (sometimes larger) has supported various right-wing extremists. One can truly wonder how any institution can long continue to function *outside* of the Establishment. Fundamental dissent is not impossible, but there is no point in denying its difficulty. The very act of institutionalizing—whether in a John Birch Society or a Communist party—tends to bring it into or close to the system, even if only on a contingency basis. Heretics and infidels operating at the Establishment's border only make it easier for the middle-of-the road institutions to put into effect the continuing reforms required for the maintenance and strengthening of modern capitalism.

CONFLICTS AMONG THE FEW

Neither the government nor the Establishment as a whole act unitedly on many fronts. Even the broad general agreements that are often tacitly accepted are usually flawed by clashing interpretations and shifting blocs and coalitions. These divergencies are partly rooted in the sharp rivalries between the producers of military and civilian goods and services; between consumption and investment goods producers; among manufacturers, wholesalers, and retailers; between financial institutions and their creditors; between owners with many interests and executives with narrower interests; among large, medium, and small enterprises; among regional and family groupings; among trade associations with different constituencies; and between self-seeking business interests and presidents (and their staffs) seeking to represent what they presume to be the interests of business as a whole. Above all, when the Ultra-Rich and Corporate Overseers enter the charmed circles of chief-executive power and compete for positions of either open or hidden influence on the high issues of national policy, deep personal drives, propensities and peculiarities—always a part of normal business conflict—become accentuated. Differences over strategy and tactics become inseparably linked with personal ambitions, thereby adding a distinctly human flavor to the changing conflicts among the Establishment's leaders.

These conflicts among the few are not mere imperfections in ruling-class power, imperfections to be ironed out in the course of increased centralization and concentration. Rather, they are an integral part of the process whereby a ruling coalition comes to power and expands its power. Often, as I have shown in chapter 1 on classic fascism, the more powerful a ruling oligarchy, the sharper—and rougher—the conflicts among the oligarchs may become. So long as unity is somehow attained on the most basic matters, internal conflicts may bring new options into the open, thereby avoiding routinization and serving as a vital source of strength. Moreover, there is a vast difference in the nature of conflicts at the lower levels of the American power structure and those at its highest levels. At the lower levels, conflicts are more numerous, intricate, and unresolved. They often constitute what C. Wright Mills described as a "semi-organized stalemate, a way of hampering the more direct expression of popular aspiration," and a form of "divide and rule" through which the few at the very top gain immensely through the divisions among their subordinates. In contrast, conflicts among the very few at the top of the Establishment determine the major public issues in American life—not only when there is a "deep political crisis," as Papandreou suggests, but also in normal times.

Before World War II, the ultra-rich, top business leaders, and the leading contenders for the U.S. presidency were divided on three major issues. During the three decades following World War II, as these issues were partly resolved, they changed their form.

The first issue was the geographical orientation of American economic and political involvement abroad. On the one side stood those who cherished ties with Britain and Europe. Seeing Britain and Europe as the former center of the British Empire and the world, they called themselves "internationalists." Pitted against them were those who favored more aggressive U.S. intervention in Asia and the entire Pacific basin. To the Europe-oriented elites, they were "isolationists" from European affairs or "noninterventionists" in European wars. By the end of World War II, both groups became more world-oriented and the old divisions slowly (and sometimes painfully) faded into the background. The present divisions are among different styles and emphases in the preservation or expansion of the "Free World" empire.

The second issue was the extent of the federal government's intervention into the economy. The basic division has been between the "business conservatives," who favor large-scale help to big business directly, with carefully restricted social welfare programs, and the "big-business liberals," who favor both direct and indirect help to big business, with more central government planning and larger social welfare programs to maintain market demand and dampen class conflict. The New Deal, Fair Deal, and Great Society reform measures were, in large part, a victory for the business liberals. By the mid-1970s most of the business conservatives accepted many of these reforms and the entire struggle started all over again with respect to new expansions in government intervention. The most fundamental of these relate to alternative ways of coping with (and benefiting from) stagflation and attaining higher rates of profitability and capital accumulation.

The third issue has been the conflict over which groups shall be more influential among the Ultra-Rich, the Corporate Overseers and the key personnel of the Chief Executive Network. Before and during World War II the dominant element in national affairs was the complex network often referred to as the "Eastern Establishment," and was often attacked by rival financial groups as "*the* Establishment." The dominance of this network over both the Republican party and the Republican presidency was dramatized in the nomination of Wendell L. Willkie (against Senator Robert Taft) in 1940 and of New York Governor Thomas E. Dewey (against Taft) in 1948 and in the election of General Dwight D. Eisenhower in 1952 and 1956. But the huge economic expansion in the postwar period—particularly in oil and defense contracts—brought new business moguls to greater heights of economic and political power. Thus, the presidential nomination of Senator Barry Goldwater in 1964 was a defeat for the northeast liberal corporate wing of the Establishment. But in 1968, with the nomination and election of Richard Nixon, who succeeded in planting one foot firmly in each camp, a new synthesis was achieved. By admitting the new challengers from the West, Southwest and South, the northeastern wing succeeded in maintaining its power. By the 1970s it slowly began to dawn on political commentators that there is no longer any northeastern liberal corporate faction clearly identified with the "Atlantic Alliance" and mild social reform. The top financial, business, and political oligarchs are now increasingly global in their orientations. But they are still divided on how to cope with the expansion of socialism and communism, the crises of stagflation and class conflict, and the side effects of their success in accumulating capital and power. As for the heretical deviations that recurringly crop up within the Establishment itself, they are divided on tactics, but unified on the central necessity of maintaining the Establishment's central values.

PURGES AND CONVERSIONS

> At least 8,000,000 Americans are always under shadow of having to prove their loyalty, if any anonymous, protected informer questions it. Including the families of 8,000,000, about 20,000,000 American citizens are subject to investigative procedures at any time. As people enter and leave investigated employment, the vast total of people who have secret police dossiers compiled about them increases every year.
>
> D. F. FLEMING [28]

After the fall of Japan in 1945, the wartime American Establishment was not yet up to the task of overseeing the reconstruction of war-torn capitalist countries, unifying the noncommunist world, and coping with the old crises of capitalism. At one and the same time, it was necessary to demobilize America's far-flung armies in response to war weariness at home and then to expand and restructure the Establishment as a whole, while infusing large amounts of loyal brainpower into its many levels.

But there were serious obstacles to doing this effectively. Old-time pacifists and noninterventionists—some in important positions of power—began to voice their opposition to the Truman Doctrine, Greek-Turkish aid, the Marshall Plan, universal military training, and other cold-war programs. Moreover, "a war which was defined as a struggle against Fascism . . . tended to reinforce the political predominance of leftist liberal sentiments." Throughout the lower levels of the establishment, there were many thousands of officials, professionals, experts, intellectuals, and artists who, if they had not adopted certain aspects of Communist ideology, were at least sympathetic with America's recent allies, the communists in Russia, China, and Indochina. Among these, there were undoubtedly underground members of various left-wing parties and a larger number of "crypto-socialists" who could no longer accept corporate entitlements to power, privilege, and property and who saw the Democratic party as a vehicle for bringing some form of socialism to America. In 1944, according to one informed estimate, Communist leaders were in control of trade unions with 20 percent of union membership. Leaders with socialist leanings probably accounted for at least another 20 percent.

If these impurities in the establishment had not been eliminated, the unity of the "Free World" might have been undermined at its vital center. Socialism and communism might have expanded more rapidly, and many corporate plans for the accumulation of power and capital would probably have been impaired. Above all, the conflicts at the higher levels of the Establishment might have erupted into differences on fundamental values rather than on tactics and techniques.

In communist countries disloyalty and dissidence within the power structure are usually fought by purges and ideological campaigns led by the Party's dominant faction. In the postwar United States there was no single group with the vision or power to attempt such a cleansing operation. Instead, there developed a veritable orgy of competing purification efforts in which many of the most effective purifiers were themselves branded as traitors or "pinkos" and impelled into still greater demonstrations of their loyalty to the new capitalist order. In this process, immeasurable help was provided by Stalinism in the Soviet Union, which helped convert many noninterventionists and "Asia-firsters" into cold warriors on a global scale and served to disillusion American liberals and radicals concerning the potentialities of any serious alternative to welfare-state capitalism.

The least remembered story on the postwar purification of the American Establishment is the story of what happened to the conservative noninterventionists who objected vigorously to the global expansion of American empire under a military umbrella. As far back as 1943, after the Germans had been defeated at Stalingrad and Allied troops had landed in Italy, influential Senators—backed up by various forces in the business community and the press—were already looking forward to an American withdrawal from Europe at the war's end. Instead of waiting for their blows to fall, President Roosevelt took the initiative. Rather than directly attacking such men as Senators Vandenberg, Taft, Wheeler and Nye, he prodded Attorney General Francis Biddle into a mass indictment of what James McGregor Burns has called "a grand rally of all the fanatic Roosevelt haters."[29] The defendants were charged under the Smith Act of 1940 which (originally aimed at the Communists) prohibited groups from conspiring to advocate the violent overthrow of the government or insubordination and mutiny in the armed forces. With huge amounts of publicity, the great "sedition trial" got under way in the spring of 1944. As a judicial undertaking it was a colossal failure; after seven and a half months, the judge died, and the Justice Department—battered from pillar to post by the civil libertarian counterattacks of the defendants—dropped the case completely. As propaganda, however, it was a great success; it suggested that the real opponents of the administration's policies were—like many of the defendants—anti-Semites, Nazi sympathizers, and fascist fellow travellers. It was thus a factor in preventing unity between right-wing and left-wing opponents of the administration. As suggested by Ronald Radosh, it helped isolate—and push to the right—such liberal critics as Charles Beard, the historian, Oswald Garrison Villard, former editor of *The Nation*, and John T. Flynn, columnist for the *New Republic*, all of whom attacked the drift toward American empire.[30]

Still greater success was attained in converting former "isolationists," some of whom were justifiably afraid of the attacks leveled against them, others of whom were amply rewarded for their switch by being acclaimed as towering statesmen. Thus Senator Arthur Vandenberg of Michigan, one of the most forthright among the earlier noninterventionists, was brought into the counsels of the Roosevelt and Truman administrations and became the widely acclaimed leader of the bipartisan foreign policy consensus on U.S. leadership of the "Free World." At a later date, the same happened with many other conservative leaders, including Senator Everett Dirksen of Illinois. In neither the Vandenberg nor the Dirksen case could this change of heart be separated from the new global orientations of the largest midwest corporations in industry and banking. All such shifts, whether among political leaders or business leaders, were part of a painful process that did not end until the Eisenhower administration. Thus, with the outbreak of the Korean War in 1950, Senator Robert A. Taft of Ohio reluctantly supported Truman's military policies but not his failure to seek a declaration of war by Congress. A year later he rallied the isolationist forces to pass a Senate resolution to keep the President from sending troops to Western Europe without congressional authorization. But the authorization was given. And in 1952, as the Eisenhower forces on the floor of the Republican National Convention shattered Taft's bid for the presidential nomination, the right-wing opponents of "cold war" imperialism went down to their final defeat.

Left wing opposition to the Establishment's global orientation was demolished by a long-drawn-out process of so-called "witch hunting" or "red baiting." The history of these activities has often been associated with the name of Senator Joseph McCarthy of Wisconsin, who from 1950 to 1954—luridly supported by the attention of press, television, and radio—conducted a rabid campaign against "traitors in high places," "egg-sucking phoney liberals," "prancing mimics of the Moscow party line," "top Russian espionage agents" in government departments, and "dilettante diplomats" who "cringed" in the face of communism. Although never supported by evidence, McCarthy's sensational charges helped defeat many Democratic liberals and middle-of-the-roaders in the congressional elections of 1950 and 1952. As a reward, the Senate Republican leadership gave him the chairmanship of the Senate's Permanent Investigations Subcommittee, an ideal springboard for another two years of flamboyant witch-hunting.

Anyone who gives too much attention, however, to the "McCarthyism" of the early 1950s may underestimate the wide-ranging purges that took place in earlier years. Back in 1934, Representative Samuel Dickstein of New York proposed a special House Committee to investigate "Nazi activities in the U.S. and other forms of subversive propaganda." As a result, a House committee under the chairmanship of John McCormack of Massachusetts (with Dickstein as vice-chairman) conducted some investigations of Nazi-American and anti-Semitic organizations. When the committee's authority expired, Dickstein tried again, this time teaming up with Representative Martin Dies of Texas, who wanted an investigation of all "un-American" activities. The Dies-Dickstein resolution—with the support of many liberal groups—was passed. This time Dickstein was shoved aside even more completely, not even getting a place on the committee. Under Dies's chairmanship, the new House Committee on Un-American Activities forgot almost completely about pro-Nazis and anti-Semites and launched a vigorous attack on alleged radicals in government, on the more liberal members of President Roosevelt's cabinet, and on the more liberal and radical trade unions then represented by the newly organized CIO.[31] The committee received powerful support from a special "un-American activities" group set up by the U.S. Chamber of Commerce. During the period of the Nazi-Soviet pact (August 1939 to June 1941), as many American communists opposed the Administration's policies of aid to Britain, the Dies Committee stepped up its attack on radicals in government. Although Dies himself was not a conspicuous anti-Hitlerite, he made brilliant political capital out of embarrassing people who had been vigorously anti-Hitler until the Nazi-Soviet pact and then promptly changed their minds. By the time the pact was itself destroyed by Hitler's invasion of the Soviet Union and the American communists had switched their position again, pressure from the business-backed "un-American activities" groups had forced FDR's administration to initiate an Attorney General's list of "subversive organizations" and a new system of "loyalty checks." As the war drew to a close and the Soviet Union changed almost overnight from ally to cold-war adversary, the anti-communist campaign was renewed. In January 1945, the House Un-American Activities Committee—through a surprise move by the House conservatives—was made a standing, rather than merely a special, committee. It conducted a free-swinging investigation of Hollywood, the Communist Party, and various "communist front" organizations. During this period, many innocents were smeared, many careers were wrecked, and some ended up in jail. At the same time, the entire radical movement in America was weakened, as the communists dwindled in number and activity and the left-liberals were increasingly co-opted into cold-war programs. With its left-liberal wing demoralized, the Democratic party lost its congressional majority in the 1946 elections. Many conservative Republicans won their seats by attacking their opponents as "soft on communism." Of these, the most vigorous was Richard Nixon, who won election by unscrupulous smearing of the New Deal Democrat Jerry Voorhis, who himself had been a member of the House Committee on Un-American Activities.

The anti-communist movement, of course, was much broader than Richard Nixon. In 1947 the liberals and socialists in the CIO, conceding the correctness of many of the right-wing charges, started a campaign to de-communize the CIO. Many union leaders who had attained their power through communist support suddenly switched. Where this did not happen, purges were initiated. "By March 1950, every C.P.-dominated union in the C.I.O. was expelled . . . By the mid-fifties the Communists had been reduced to marginal status in the unions—a clump of harried party members here, a scattering of frightened sympathizers there." [32] In the radio and television industries, Hollywood, and many universities, many people with radical connections or leanings (or even relatives) were fired or blacklisted. In the federal government President Truman signed an executive order requiring 2.5 million government employees to undergo security checks. This was soon extended to include 3 million members of the armed forces and 3 million employees of defense contractors.[83] At first, the loyalty boards were obligated to have "reasonable grounds" for dismissing an employee suspected of disloyalty. By 1950, only a "reasonable doubt" was necessary. The cultural impact of this operation was enormous. If only 212 employees were fired, and only 2,000 left voluntarily, one may presume that hundreds of thousands were taught a clear lesson by the clearance experience: namely, to abandon any reservations they had about the Establishment's basic policies and demonstrate at all possible opportunities their dedication to the new "Free World" strategy. On a broader front, this lesson was drummed into actual or potential dissidents by the indictment in 1948 (shortly before the 1948 elections) of Communist party leaders under the Smith Act. This time, in contrast with the earlier trial of the right-wingers, the government won its case. Harry Truman also won the 1948 election. One reason was that he demonstrated his administration's ability to conduct purification operations more efficiently than the various congressional committees on "un-American activities" and "internal security." More important, in presenting his Fair Deal proposals for mild domestic reform, he placated the many liberals and radicals who feared that a combination of cold-war foreign policy and anti-communism at home would mean a halt to the growth of the welfare state. Many former communists became avid Fair Dealers.

During the next few years the purge-conversion processes were accelerated by the loss of China, the first atomic bomb explosion by the Soviet Union, and the exposé of various spy rings in Canada and the United States. Many important second-level experts in the executive branch—among them Lauchlin Currie, Harry Dexter White, and Alger Hiss—were accused of directly or indirectly helping the communists. Of these, Alger Hiss was finally convicted of perjury and jailed. Others were convicted of spying; Julius and Ethel Rosenberg were executed. By 1950, riding the wave of success in their "un-American activities" programs, Richard Nixon and Karl Mundt were able to rise from the House to the Senate. In this election Nixon distinguished himself by using smear tactics even more effectively than in his first House victory four years earlier. He also endeared himself to the right-wing extremists in the Republican party, including many of the "Asia Firsters" who were apoplectic over the loss of China and suspicious of, if not antagonistic toward, those Republicans who favored the Marshall Plan and NATO. Hence, in backing Nixon as Dwight Eisenhower's running mate in 1952, the anti-Taft Republicans in the top corporate levels of the Establishment did something more than bring into the vice-presidency the most vigorous of the anti-communists. They also helped accelerate the conversion of the isolationists and noninterventionists to the globalism of the new "Free World" empire.

PURIFYING IDEOLOGIES

Those who take the most from the table
Teach contentment
Those for whom the taxes are destined
Demand sacrifice
Those who eat their fill speak to the hungry
Of wonderful times to come
Those who lead the country into the abyss
Call ruling difficult
For ordinary folk.

BERTOLT BRECHT

As the takeoff toward a more perfect capitalism began after World War II, popular support of the system was assured in large part by the system's performance—more striking than ever before—in providing material payoffs and physical security. The record of over a third of a century has included the avoidance of mass depression or runaway inflation in any advanced capitalist country, expanded mass consumption, the maintenance or expansion of personal options, no near-war between any advanced capitalist countries and, above all, no world war.

Yet these achievements have depended upon a level of commitment among the elites at the Establishment's lower and middle levels that could scarcely have been forthcoming if either had seriously doubted the legitimacy of the evolving order. This legitimacy was fostered by a three-pronged ideological thrust.

The first prong has consisted of a sophisticated and passionate reiteration in a thousand variations of the simple proposition: *communism and socialism are bad.*

Before World War II there were many small, right-wing movements whose members were driven by nightmares of evil conspirators—usually communists, Jews, Catholics, "niggers" or "nigger lovers"—bent on destroying the "American way of life." During the immediate prewar period, their fears were expressed directly in the Dies Committee's crusade against "pinkos" in the Roosevelt administration. After World War II, these witch-hunting nightmares were transformed into dominant ideology. Professional antiradicalism became entrenched during the brief period of atomic monopoly. It grew stronger in the more frenetic period of nuclear confrontation after Russia acquired atomic bombs. With some toning down and fine tuning, it has maintained itself during the present and more complex period of conflict with socialism and communism. During each of these stages it meshed rather well with anti-capitalist ideology in the Soviet Union, China, Cuba, and other communist countries, thereby providing an ideological balance to parallel the delicate balance of nuclear terror. More specifically, it has given the overall rationale for the extension of America's multicontinental frontiers. It has helped link together the many disparate elements in America's quasi-empire. In large measure, the unity of the NATO countries in Europe had depended on their fear of Soviet communism, and the allegiance of Japan to the United States on the fear of either Soviet or Chinese communism. American aid to "have-not" countries, in turn, has often varied with their ability to produce—or invent—a communist threat on or within their borders. At home, anti-communism has provided the justification needed by the ambitious leaders of the massive military establishment. As Colonel James A. Donovan wrote after retirement from the U.S. Marine Corps, "If there were no Communist bloc . . . , the defense establishment would have to invent one." [34]

Above all, anti-communism has been a valuable instrument in containing pressures for a more rapid expansion of welfare-state measures as opposed to more generous forms of aid to business. In this sense, the ideology of anti-communism has also been anti-socialistic. Although favoring corporate and military socialism for the benefit of businessmen and military officers, the anti-communists have bitterly attacked the "creeping socialism" that aims to benefit the poor, the underorganized, and the ethnic minorities.

The power and the imaginative vigor of anti-communist and anti-socialist ideology has stemmed from its many interlacing currents. At one extreme, there have been those like Senator Joseph McCarthy and Robert Welch of the John Birch Society, both of whom charged that Secretaries of State Dean Acheson and George Marshall were communist agents or dupes. In the middle, people like Acheson and Marshall themselves developed the more influential, mainstream version of anti-communist ideology. By deeds as well as words, they attempted to prove they were more anti-communist than their detractors. Toward the left, many brilliant intellectuals have done their own thing less stridently, demonstrating the inefficiency of communist and socialist practice and the stodginess of communist and socialist doctrine. Each of these currents have been invigorated by significant numbers of former communists and socialists, who have atoned for their former sins by capitalizing on their special knowledge of communist inequity or socialist futility. Each helped publicize many of the Soviet Union's hidden horrors—although the tendency has been less to understand the deformation of Soviet socialism (and its roots) and more to warn against the horrors that would result from any tinkering with the American system.

Thus, like a restaurant with a large and varied menu, anti-communist and anti-socialist ideology has been able to offer something for almost any taste. Each dish, moreover, is extremely cheap. A high price is paid only by those who refuse to select any variety, thus opening themselves to the charge of being "soft on communism." For over a quarter of a century there has been only a small minority—particularly in the realm of government service and academia—willing to pay the price. The result has been a rather widespread conformity with ritualistic anti-communism and anti-socialism and a powerful consensus on the virtues of the established order.

The second prong of the ideological thrust consists of even more sophisticated variations on an equally simple proposition: *the capitalist order is good.* Before World War II one of the weakest links in the established order was the image of the corporation. For its consumers, the corporation said, "The public be damned!" On matters of broad public policy—particularly during the depths of the Great Depression—corporate leaders often distinguished themselves by ignorance and incompetence. There was blantant evidence to support President Roosevelt's epithet "economic bourbons." Even during the 1950s Charles Wilson, a former General Motors president, as secretary of defense, was able to suggest that what's good for General Motors is good for the United States. In short, the large corporation—as the central symbol of capitalism—was selfish, venal, and mean.

To cope with this situation, huge investments were made in public relations campaigns. Some of these campaigns concentrated on the corporate image. Many of them set forth in excruciating detail the infinite blessings of private ownership and free, competitive private enterprise. An exhaustive analysis of the material appears in *The American Business Creed*, by a group of Harvard economists.[35] The essence of this so-called creed (to which no serious corporate executives could possibly have given credence) was the ridiculous assumption that the market was mainly composed of small, powerless firms and that large, powerful corporations were controlled by huge numbers of small stockholders instead of a small minority of large stockholders, managers, or investment institutions.

During the same period, however, a more influential ideology for postwar capitalism was formulated by various groups of pragmatic intellectuals. Their problem was that many corporate managers and their truly conservative economists were traditionally rather blunt in stating that their job was moneymaking, period—no nonsense about social responsibility. Besides, even the most dedicated corporate lawyers often remembered Justice Oliver Wendell Holmes's dictum on the subject: "The notion that a business is clothed with a public interest and has been devoted to the public use is little more than a fiction intended to beautify what is disagreeable to others." Nonetheless, the Advertising Council spent billions over the decades in creating fictional images of business "clothed with public interest." In this they were helped by uninhibited academics like Carl Kaysen, who stated that in the corporate world of Standard Oil, American Telephone and Telegraph, Du Pont, General Electric, and General Motors "there is no display of greed or graspiness:

there is no attempt to push off onto the workers or the community at large part of the social costs of the enterprise. The modern corporation is a soulful corporation." [36] Others have pursued the soulful theme even further by suggesting that the executives of transnational corporations are the real "world citizens" whose efforts may soon usher in a new era of permanent peace.

The third prong in the ideological package is the tacit—but breathtaking—assertion or premise that *capitalism no longer exists.* "A research report of the United States Information Agency," C. L. Sulzberger revealed in a typically incisive column back in 1964, "has ruefully discovered that the more our propaganda advertises the virtues of 'capitalism' and attacks 'socialism' the less the world likes us . . . Most foreigners don't regard 'capitalism' as descriptive of an efficient economy or a safeguard of individual rights. To them it means little concern for the poor, unfair distribution of wealth, and undue influence of the rich." [37] But what the USIA allegedly needed a research report to discover concerning capitalism's image in other countries was already well understood by capitalism's major publicists and spokesmen at home. As far back as 1941, in his "American Century" editorial, Henry Luce used the well-established term "free economic system" instead of "capitalism." The international capitalist market protected by American hegemony became the "free world" and "freedom" became the code word for both domestic capitalism and capitalist empire. In Carl Kaysen's article on the soulful corporation, the nasty word "capitalism" makes not a single entry. Its use would have introduced a jarring note. It would also have violated a powerful norm among economists—namely, that instead of trying to analyze the workings of modern capitalism, capitalism should be discussed mainly in the framework of criticizing Marxian economics or making passing references to the imperfections in Adam Smith's model of perfect competition. When Governor George Romney of Michigan announced that "Americans buried capitalism long ago, and moved on to consumerism," what was really being buried was the old-time conservative defense of capitalism as unadulterated self-interest as superior to socialistic altruism. True believers like Ayn Rand were of no avail in charging that "if the 'conservatives' do not stand for capitalism, they stand for and are nothing" and in proclaiming (like one of her characters in *Atlas Shrugged*) "We choose to wear the name 'Capitalism' printed on our foreheads boldly, as our badge of nobility." [38] The most intelligent spokesmen for the changing capitalist order wear a variety of names on their foreheads.

The first term—and still the most appealing—has been "mixed economy." The persuasive power of this concept stems mainly from lip service to the perfect-competition model as defined in classical or neoclassical ideologies. If capitalism used to be what Adam Smith advocated, the reasoning goes, then capitalism has been replaced by a mixture of private and public enterprise—or even of capitalism and socialism. This mixture blends the (alleged) productive efficiency of the former with the social justice sought by the latter. At the same time, it preserves the beautiful equilibrium of the classical model by providing opportunities for all interests in society to organize in their own behalf. From this competition in both the political and economic marketplaces comes a peaceful resolution of conflicts through the negotiation, bargaining, pressure and counter-pressure, propaganda and counterpropaganda that underlie electoral campaigns and executive, legislative, and judicial decision making. From this confused but peaceful process of political competition among selfish interests there emerges—as though by some invisible guiding hand—the best possible satisfaction of the public interest. Granted, there may be some imperfections in this political marketplace, too much strength at some points and too much weakness at others. But then enlightened government, with the help of Ivy League professors, can come in as a balancing factor and restore the equilibrium.

This pluralistic myth is often reinforced by statistical exercises suggesting that the unfair distribution of wealth and influence was on its way out and the majority of the population had attained "affluence." Thus the mere contemplation of the "objective data" carefully selected under his direction induced the usually self-contained Arthur Burns (later named chairman of the Council of Economic Advisers and the Federal Reserve Board) into the following orgasmic spasm of economic hyperbole: "The transformation in the distribution of our national income . . . may already be counted as one of the great social revolutions in history." [39] With such well-certified "evidence" coming across their desks, former Marxists or revolutionaries were able to explain their conversion to the existing order with something more convincing than diatribes (which often appeared in the form of Trotskyism) against Stalinism and more self-satisfying than the attacks on former comrades made by the former communists who converted to professional anticommunism. By 1960, Seymour Martin Lipset was able to proclaim that "the fundamental political problems of the industrial revolution have been solved." [40] This viewpoint was enlarged by Daniel Bell's sadly joyous funeral oration over the end of socialist or communist ideology in the Western world: "For the radical intelligentsia, the old ideologies have lost their 'truth' and their power to persuade . . . there is a rough consensus among intellectuals on political issues: the acceptance of the Welfare State; the desirability of decentralized power; a system of mixed economy and political pluralism. In that sense, too, the ideological age has ended." [41]

In continuation of the same argument, Bell has moved to replace the old ideologies of competing systems with a new end-of-ideology ideology celebrating the new power of theory, theoreticians, and his best friends. With more wit, passion, and inventiveness than most competing sociologists, Bell has capitalized on the fact that both Western capitalism and Russian socialism have been forms of industrialism. In so doing he defines industrialism loosely as something that has to do with machines, almost completely glossing over the organizational and imperial aspects of industrial capitalism.

This allows him to proclaim the coming of something called "post-industrialism," which is characterized by the increasing relative importance of services as contrasted with goods, of white-collar employment, and of more technical and professional elites. The essence of this allegedly "post" industrialism is "the preeminence of the professional and technical class." This preeminence, in turn, is based on "the primacy of theoretical knowledge—the primacy of theory over empiricism and the codification of knowledge into abstract systems of symbols." The masters of the new theory and symbols are the "knowledge elites" and their domicile is the university, "the central institution of post-industrial society." [42]

With equal wit and a larger audience, Galbraith propounded a similar theme when, in 1968, he claimed that power in the new industrial state has shifted from capital to the "organized intelligence" of the managerial and bureaucratic "technostructure." [43]

For Bell, if the new knowledge elites do not make the ultimate decisions, it is because of a combination of old-fashioned politics and new cultural styles, particularly among younger people who tend to revolt against the rule of reason itself. If these obstacles can be overcome and if enough resources are channeled into R & D and the universities, then man's reason shall at last prevail and rational calculation and control will lead to stable progress. For Galbraith, the remedy was similar, since the system of industrial oligarchy "brings into existence, to serve its intellectual and scientific needs, the community that, hopefully, will reject its monopoly on social purpose." Galbraith's hope lay (at that time) in the wistful presumption that "the educational and scientific estate, with its allies in the larger intellectual community" might operate as a political force in its own right.

Although both Bell and Galbraith have been willing to concede the existence of capitalism (and Galbraith has more recently revealed himself as an advocate of public ownership of the one thousand corporate giants whom he describes as the "planning system," [44] most Establishment social scientists in both the Ivy League and the minor leagues seem to have adopted methodological premises that rule capitalism out of existence. Without the wit, wisdom, or vision of a Bell or Galbraith, they have busied themselves in efforts to provide technical solutions to political, moral and socio-economic problems. The problems they presume to solve—or in Daniel P. Moynihan's more modest terms, to cope with—are defined at the higher or middle levels of the Establishment where decisions are made on which research grants or contracts are to be approved and which professors are to be hired. They are carefully subdivided into categories that reflect the division of labor within the foundations and government contracting agencies.

In turn, the presumably independent "knowledge elites" of the educational, scientific, and intellectual estates—having usually abjured efforts to analyze the morality and political economy of the so-called "market system"—are now rated on their performance in the grant-contract market. The badges of achievement are the research proposals accepted by the Establishment, with the rank order determined by the amount of funds obtained. Alongside the older motto "Publish or perish" (which puts the fate of many younger people in the hands of establishment faithfuls on editorial boards), has risen an additional imperative: "Get a grant or contract and prosper." This imperative also applies to department heads, deans, and college presidents who—like professors—are expected to bring in the "soft money" to supplement the "hard money" in the regular college and university budgets. During the early 1960s the largest amounts of "soft money," came from the government agencies involved in the "hardware" and "software" needed by the military and outer-space agencies, and including the many programs of "area studies" focused on Asia, Africa, the Middle East, and Latin America. Later, with the civil rights and antiwar movements, a minor avalanche of "soft money" was let loose for research, field work, and demonstration projects in the so-called "anti-poverty" and "model cities" programs. The word went quickly around among the new generation of academic hustlers that "Poverty is where the money is." Under these new circumstances, the serious applicant for funds was well advised to steer clear of root causes or systemic analysis. There was no prohibition against proposing research work or field organization designed to challenge the capitalist system, but no applicant has ever been known to openly propose anything so patently "unsound." Moreover, many of the wisest heads in the academic community—whether from profound inner disillusionment or in the heat of professional arrogance—openly advocated the treatment of symptoms only and inveighed against wasting time with the examination of systemic roots of poverty, unemployment, inflation, crime, or environmental degradation.[45]

On a broader scale, methodology became the "name of the game." A new generation of methodologists learned that with unspoken constraints upon the purpose and content of research and theory, greater importance must be attached to means and form. Younger people who scorned the catch-as-catch-can methodologies of a Bell, Galbraith, or Moynihan—and were embarrassed by their unseemly interest in turning a good phrase—became the new ideologues of scientific methods. On the one hand, "abstracted empiricists" (as C. Wright Mills called them) became frenetic data-chasers eager to produce reams of computer printouts. On the other hand, enthusiastic model-builders erected pretty paradigms from which hypotheses might be deduced. Both sought verification through the application of methods long proven useful in the natural sciences. In this process, they had the aid and participation of many natural scientists perfectly willing to accept admiration from those naive enough to think that their skills in physics, biology, engineering or mathematics were readily transferable to the analysis of social problems. They also enjoyed the guidance or blessings of old-time radicals who—scorched by the heat of the purges or disillusioned by Stalinism—were eager to build a new God in the image of so-called scientific method. These activities became intensely competitive, with ever-changing cliques and currents providing endless opportunities for innovative nuances in the production of iconoclastic conformity and irrelevant relevance.

Occasionally, the existence of capitalist society has been allowed to enter into the frame of reference—but only marginally. Thus, it has become fashionable for many social science departments to have a well-behaved "Marxist" in residence: an element of good behavior, of course, is to accept the subdivision of mental labor and be a "Marxist" economist, socialist, or political scientist rather than dealing with capitalist society as a whole. A more widespread form of marginal acceptance of capitalist reality is the idea of "putting the profit motive to use in achieving social purposes." The reiteration of this imperative in every area from narcotics control to education has become one of the most effective methods of pledging allegiance to the undescribed and unexamined capitalist order.

Although these many establishment ideologies have not produced any dedicated loyalty or deep commitment to modern capitalism, they have nonetheless been a major factor in the purification process. They have made it possible for purges and induced conversions of dissidents to be reduced in relative significance and conducted on a low-key, routine basis. They have helped absorb some of the activists of the old "New Left" of the 1960s into the Establishment, purify thoughts and behavior during the 1970s, and channel into harmless—if not profitable—ways the resentments and grievances fed by the many crises and traumas of a more perfect capitalism.

4

The Side Effects of Success

So bye bye Miss American Pie
Drove my Chevy to the levy but the levy was dry,
And them good old boys were drinking whiskey and rye,
Singing this'll be the day that I die,
This'll be the day that I die . . .

DON MCLEAN

EVEN IN ITS MORE EXPANSIVE and successful moments a deep malaise corrodes the atmosphere of every advanced capitalist society.

"We are very rich," mused Walter Lippmann a little before his death. "But our life is empty of the kind of purpose and effort that gives to life its flavor and meaning." [1] I am always suspicious of statements that throw the word "we" around to cover different kinds of people. For Nelson Rockefeller, up to the moment of his death, life was far from empty. It was full of the hidden flavor and meaning gained by the relentless pursuit of money, power, and sexual gratification. But if Lippmann was referring only to those values of which a person can be openly proud, I am willing to include Rockefeller along with the ordinary rich and the much larger number of un-rich and poor, both young and old, who suffer from the lack of meaning in life.

"If we just enlarge the pie, everyone will get more." This has been the imagery of capitalist growthmanship since the end of World War II—and I once did my share in propagating it. But the growth of the pie did not change the way slices were distributed except to enlarge the absolute gap between the lion's share and the ant's. And whether the pie grows, or stops growing, or shrinks, there are always people who suffer from the behavior of the cooks, the effluents from the oven, the junkiness of the pie, and the fact that they needed something more nutritious than pie anyway.

If this be a failure of "piemanship," it is a special kind—one that illustrates the saying "Nothing fails like success." In all its many forms, both spiritual and material, the malaise of modern capitalism appears side by side with the gains and benefits of capitalist growth and accumulation. None of these forms is often part of central or conscious aims at the Establishment's apex, where dedication to new exploits in a dwindling capitalist world tends to distract attention from—or else, justify—the use of unpleasant or regrettable means, and unpleasant or unintended consequences. Yet these side effects are very real. They spread out in long, interweaving, mutually reinforcing, and incredibly complex sequences of injuries or costs to individuals, families, small groups, organizations, and the entire structure of society.

AN ABUNDANCE OF FRUSTRATIONS

From its very beginnings capitalism has been a dream factory. Since World War II, this factory has produced successive waves of rising aspirations. Its old men have dreamed dreams. Its young men have seen visions. Its political and economic leaders have made promises. No sector of society is immune to the festering sore of a dream deferred or, when it comes true, converted into a nightmare.

A major side effect of increased mass consumption over the years has been to raise aspirations for additional consumption by those who had previously been satisfied with less. As millions of poor people have made more material gains, they have learned to want more—particularly as they see that the gains of other sectors of the population have exceeded theirs. Among blacks, Latins, and Native Americans—some of whom are hopelessly submerged in the underclass—this contrast becomes desperately painful. The pain is not displaced by the humiliations imposed by the welfare system, food stamps, training programs, public housing, and other "uplift" programs. The pain reverberates among the lower- and middle-income workers who are taxed to provide support for people described to them as "loafers" and "spongers." In turn, many people at the middle and higher levels find that skyrocketing prices for highly desired services—household help, good restaurants, taxis, good theatre, a nice cottage at a quiet beach—deny them the affluence to which they think themselves entitled.

At the same time, paradoxically, other aspirations have gone far beyond either the ancient struggle for subsistence or current struggles for more equity in the distribution of material goods. As material needs are met, other values come to the surface. Large sections of the population now aspire to freedom from historic forms of institutionalized injustice. Few black Americans are now willing to tolerate being regarded as subhuman or biologically inferior; many reject jobs that they now see as humiliating and demeaning. Other ethnic groups, stirred out of melting-pot somnolence by the example of blacks, are reasserting ancient traditions and making new demands on the polity. Women increasingly demand liberation from centuries of imprisonment in social roles that presume biological inferiority, physical inability, and mental incapacity. Older people are rejecting the "ageism" that dumps men and women into forced retirement, segregated communities, or nursing-home warehouses without reference to their capabilities for productive work and service.

Moreover, people in all walks of life are becoming interested in satisfactions that transcend the dominant materialisms of the past. They want employment that is fulfilling—not merely full or fair. They want education that liberates the imagination instead of merely giving a certificate. They want to commit themselves to purposes beyond careerism and institutional aggrandizement. They seek new forms of community with others. These higher aspirations have been encouraged by "quality of life" promises by political leaders. At the same time the hard realities continue: racism, ethnic discrimination, male chauvinism, the treatment of young people as children, and older people as waste products. On these cruel rocks, the waves of higher aspirations are repeatedly shattered.

The most dramatic expression of the new hopes was embodied in the counterculture and the New Left of the 1960s. The counterculture touched all forms of artistic expression. It included the theatre of the absurd; pop paintings; rock, acid-rock and folk-rock music; dramatic "happenings," guerilla theatre; psychedelic multimedia dance scenes; "underground" papers; and explicit sexuality in all of the foregoing. But it went much further than previous cultural protest in affecting actual life-styles—from the superficialities of obscene language, hippy or mod clothing, and organic foods to the more fundamental life-style changes of communal living arrangements, liberation from traditional sexual restraints, drug use, and experimentation with mystic experiences and new religious fads. For younger people it provided a "youth culture" that presumed to rebel against the System. For the older people who joined the rebellion, it provided an intimation of regained youthfulness. For both, it provided the illusion that somehow or other—in the euphoric words of Charles Reich—the flower power of a new consciousness would push up through the concrete pavements, through the metal and the plastic, and bring about "a veritable greening of America." [2]

A common element in both the counterculture and the New Left is that some leaders of each became media heroes. In this way they had an impact on American life—the former in changing the nature of mass culture, art, recreation, and sexual mores; the latter in shaking up the administrators and faculties of American universities, awakening American opinion to the horrors of the American war in Indochina, and encouraging black militancy. In so doing, the counterculture became absorbed into the Establishment, functioning more and more as an arm of business operations in entertainment, clothing, foods, and foreign cars, while the

New Left and the many organizations of white and black revolution collapsed into sawdust.

If modern capitalism nurtured new values and aspirations, it has by no means displaced the traditional values of Western civilization and constitutional capitalism. Indeed, under the pressure of social change, many people have gone back to older values, clinging to them more desperately under the threat of confusing new outlooks.

On the one hand, a large part of the lower and middle classes, particularly the many people fighting their way into the lower strata of the Establishment, saw the counterculture or the New Left as perversions of American values and a personal affront. They had grown up and eked their way ahead in rather full acceptance of patriotism, self-discipline, conformity, future preference, and material acquisition. But the counterculture, the New Left and—still more offensive—often their own sons and daughters would desecrate the flag, behave in an undisciplined fashion, violate established norms of clothing, personal appearance, and speech, live for the pleasures of the moment, and turn their backs on many of the established symbols of material well-being. Their neighborhoods and schools were invaded by unfamiliar, low-income blacks—with the invasion often backed up by court order, government action, and high-sounding policy statements by Establishment leaders who themselves lived in exclusive neighborhoods and sent their children to private schools. The permissiveness of the younger generation somehow or other became equivalent to the spread of mugging, burglary, rape, and homicide. This reaction has not been limited to whites alone. Many black parents and grandparents have viewed the revolt of their children and grandchildren as a direct attack on their own values and middle-class aspirations.

On the other hand, the power of the counterculture and the New Left was largely based on the fact that their younger adherents went back to some of the oldest values of Western civilization and American tradition. In many of their actions, they have taken seriously the precepts of the Ten Commandments, the Sermon on the Mount, the Declaration of Independence, and the Bill of Rights. By these standards, they tend to condemn the Establishment, the formalistic traditionalists, and many of their parents as corrupt and complacent hypocrites.

Other older values are common to both of these groups: the ethos of personal autonomy and independence, the desire to participate in decisions affecting one's life, and—to a lesser degree—the dignity of ordinary work. And for both groups these values tend to be perverted by the manipulative nature of large-scale bureaucracy and concentrated wealth and power. The sense of powerlessness and helplessness affects both those industrial and construction workers still indignant against opposition to large military budgets and those still indignant against racism, male chauvinism, militarism, and imperial intervention in other countries. Divided on many specifics, each side clings to certain unspoken common values.

An important source of frustration has always been the Faustian driving force among those committed to the pursuit of money and power. As this pursuit becomes more rational, it feeds upon itself. "The acceptance of wealth (or power for that matter) as the source of self-esteem," Stanislas Andreski has written, "enhances the feeling of insecurity because they are transient possessions which can easily be lost—which may be the reason why people who have acquired them never cease to want more . . ." [3] More is never enough; it becomes ashes in the mouth. The yardstick of money and power does not add much to one's essential self-esteem—especially when one suspects that most of one's closest friends (if the word "friends" can be at all used in this context) are interested mainly in handouts, favors, and deals. Abroad, the top capitalists of other countries are not so eager to go along with American penetration, even in the form of friendly partnerships. At home, as James Reston observes, the leaders in business and the professions "seem unhappy in a system they cannot quite understand or reconcile with their private ideals." [4]

FALLING APART: WORK, COMMUNITY, FAMILY

Turning and turning in the widening gyre
The falcon cannot hear the falconer;
Things fall apart; the centre cannot hold . . .

WILLIAM BUTLER YEATS

In its earlier years industrial capitalism shattered the ancient skills of artisans and craftsmen by fostering an ever more specialized division of labor; this reduced production costs and increased the power of managers. The concentration of production in urban areas and the building of national labor markets went far toward severing human ties to the land; it helped convert the extended family of many interacting relatives into the nuclear family limited to parents and children. These changes, in turn, went so far toward fragmenting human relations that some observers warned that people might be converted—in the words of Emile Durkheim—into "anonymous specks in a cloud of dust."

During the first decades of transnational capitalism, these processes of social fragmentation have undergone a qualitative change. With the new technological revolution, not only physical labor but mental labor as well is being broken down into smaller and smaller parts. As much of the labor force becomes migratory both community and family life decline.

The upsurge of technological innovations after World War II gave rise to many rosy predictions on the nature of work. There would be an end to back-breaking, dangerous, or routine labor. The energies of employees at all levels would be released for leisure and more fulfilling jobs.

It is now possible to see the results. A few million workers are still engaged in labor requiring huge muscular effort, as in mines, foundries, and coke works. This kind of work has been described in a *Wall Street Journal* headline: "Brutal, Mindless Labor Remains a Daily Reality for Millions in the U.S. Mining Coal, Shoveling Slag, Gutting Hogs Pays Bills, But Can Drain Spirit, Hope." [5] But the great majority of modern workers now face the newer hardships of routinized work consisting of minute repetitive fragments. In previous decades, the fragmentation had been done largely by studying the work movements of the best craftsmen and allocating these various movements among less skilled and lower-paid workers; the simplest of these movements were then mechanized. Under the new technological revolution, machines are now designed to do what people could never have done, and people are needed not so much to operate the machines as to serve them.

In this respect there is little difference between factory work and office work, between so-called "blue collar" workers and "white collar" workers. "The office today, where work is segmented and authoritarian, is often a factory," a government report tells us. "Computer key-punch operations and typing pools share much in common with the automobile assembly line." [6]

In the service occupations and retail trade, there are the same tendencies toward specialization and job dilution, whether or not associated with increased mechanization. The basic differences among all these types of work now relate to dangers and pay. In many industrial and construction activities the new technologies have brought new dangers to health, if not to life and limb—through speedier operations, air and noise pollution at the workplace, and the handling of dangerous chemicals and other substances. In contrast, clerical employees and workers in service occupations and retail trade tend to make even less money than laborers.

The basic similarity is the ongoing process of fragmenting work and coordinating the many parts through rules, regulations and hierarchical stratification. Under the impact of this process, employees become increasingly disconnected from the end products to which they contribute and the needs or responses of the consumers who use them. They have only the vaguest idea about the total operations of the organization that employs them or the ongoing dilemmas faced by its managers. As a result, according to Robert Dubin, "the classical distinction between managers and workers has been hardened by the growing gulf of education and knowledge that separates these two classes." [7] This gulf is hardened by widespread hostility and resentment toward management "ripoffs."

But this does not automatically produce the "working class consciousness" which, according to some Marxists, would lead the workers to become the "gravediggers of capitalism." Rather, it leads to the isolation of employees from one another. "The 'large socialized workplaces' which were supposed to generate the 'gravediggers of capitalism,'" John and Barbara Ehrenreich argue, "themselves become the graveyards for human energy and aspirations. The overwhelming response of working people is to withdraw their energy and hopes from the work world and invest them in the only other sphere provided by contemporary capitalism —*private life*." [8]

The work of experts, scientists, and professionals is a major exception. Here, as in the managerial classes, large numbers of men—and, increasingly, women—throw themselves into their work with passionate commitment. Many become work addicts (or "workaholics") capable of giving but grudging attention to private life. In contrast with moonlighters, who take on additional jobs to make money, some of them become what might be called "starlighters," that is, people who extend their regular hours of work beyond any definable limits in order to satisfy their needs for self-expression and creative activity. Needless to say, starlighters may also find that their work addiction pays off in enlarged income and perhaps in diminished frustrations.

But here also the fragmentation process is continuously at work. Every lawyer, physician, engineer, architect, or accountant tends to become a specialist in a small part of the profession—and the number of specializations and subspecializations steadily increases. The same is true of each area of the natural and social sciences, as disciplinary subdivision continuously advances. The decline of the general practitioner in medicine is paralleled by the decline of the generalist in all these fields. These declines are accelerated by the information overload created by the growing volume of publications and research findings in every specialized field. The simplest way to cope with the impossible problem of "keeping up" is to burrow even more deeply into a smaller specialization and ignore relevant information in allied fields. Thus, in the professional and scientific "rat races" the specialized experts may build tight little islands of security, protected against more intruders by a Maginot Line of almost impenetrable jargon. Instead of trying to see the whole woods, he or she focuses on an individual tree, or else a branch, twig or leaf thereof. As with employees at lower levels of the totem pole of status and prestige, the specialists become increasingly isolated from each other, little capable of working together to use their expertise for the common good, and more susceptible to regimentation. The narrow focus of their preoccupations also provides them with an excellent opportunity to ignore —or push deep into the subconscious—the extent to which they consciously or unwittingly help concentrate increased power in the Establishment's leaders.

In changing the nature of work, modern capitalism has uprooted both workers and their managers. With the mechanization of agriculture, the farm population has declined drastically. As former family farmers, tenant farmers, and farm workers have moved to urban areas, the factories of older industrial cities have migrated to rural areas (or other countries) where labor is cheaper and less organized. As black and Latin poor people pour into the central cities, middle-level and upper-level families move to the suburbs—one ring after another. This suburban migration—one of the greatest population movements in history—has burst the boundaries of most cities and created huge metropolitan regions. These, in turn, tend to cluster into megapolitan regions—in the Northeast, the midwest Great Lakes area, and the West Coast. Here are found the headquarters and major regional offices of the huge corporate and government agencies whose operations transcend the boundaries of both urban regions and nations.

While the headquarters tend to stay in the same places, people are on the move. Many Americans have become modern nomads, ever willing to pull up stakes and move elsewhere in search of better jobs, living conditions, or schooling for children. In the brief period of 1975–77, more than one of every four Americans moved from one dwelling to another—half within the same metropolitan area, half elsewhere. Within an area, many are pushed from apartment to apartment or house to house by tidal waves of blight and decay often at their heels. Many poor people are pushed out by redevelopment programs that convert former central-city slums into high-profit real estate developments. These, in turn, bring more well-to-do people back into the "gentrified" central areas. Previously, the perpetual transients were migratory farm workers and derelicts, traditionally referred to as "bums." Today's transients also include technicians, experts, managers, scientists, and academics. For those who stubbornly remain put, in Vance Packard's words "the turnover of people around them is so great that they can no longer enjoy a sense of place."[9] Apart from the embellishments of nostalgic memory, the old neighborhoods (like many old friendships) are rarely what they used to be.

Moving is more than changing one's home. It is also a matter of getting to work. Less than 8 percent of all workers walk to work or work at home. All the rest use some form of transportation other than their feet—and in most cases this is the private automobile. The vast extent of commuting to work is partly shown in the following table:

PERCENT OF WORKERS COMMUTING, 1970 *

	Out of City	Into City	Total
New York City	5.7	18.6	24.3
Chicago	16.8	28.1	44.9
Los Angeles	29.5	38.0	67.5
Philadelphia	12.7	29.1	41.8
Detroit	32.9	41.8	74.7
Houston	9.8	24.1	33.9
Washington, D.C.	19.1	57.5	76.6
Dallas	13.4	34.3	47.7
San Francisco	10.3	39.8	40.1
Boston	23.1	56.7	79.8
Cleveland	25.2	54.7	79.9
Baltimore	25.4	38.1	63.5

* Statistical Abstract of the United States, 1979

What is not shown is the vast amount of time consumed by all this movement, time that might otherwise be available for more enjoyable or productive purposes. Official language tells us that a person "lives" where he or she resides—and "resides" usually means sleeps. But as Richard Goodwin has written in words that apply to women also, "A man works in one place, sleeps in another, shops somewhere else, finds pleasure or companionship where he can and cares about none of these places." [10] The so-called dwelling is merely a "base from which the individual reaches out to the scattered components of his existence." This is what Vance Packard has in mind when he says that America is "becoming a nation of strangers."

The crumbling of community ties is always easier to bear when solace and satisfaction are found in the warmth of family life. Yet the nuclear family seems to be crumbling also. Part of this is evidenced by the dramatic increases that have been taking place in divorce rates since the mid-1960s and the more recent decline in marriage rates. These statistics are buttressed by shakier information on informal separations, illegitimacy, and single-headed families—particularly in lower-income groups.

As with neighborhoods, however, the basic story on fragmentation is told by information not on outright dissolution but on the weakening of human ties. Edward Shorter, an historian of family life, suggests that "Three different aspects of family life today are evolving in directions that have no historical precendent: the definitive cutting of the lines leading from younger generations to older . . . the new instability in the life of the couple . . . [and] the systematic demolition of the 'nest notion' of nuclear family life . . ." [11] Natural "generation gaps" are accentuated by the attenuation of relations with grandparents. Indeed, by consigning their own parents to the cold comfort of retirement communities and nursing homes, many mothers and fathers have denied their children the warmth and shock-absorbing potentials of three-generational contact. They have also prepared the way for their own inevitable classification—in Suzanne Gordon's words—as "unwanted, helpless, ugly and unpleasant" [12]—and burial, before death, in "golden age" warehouses.

In turn, couples who remain married until death does them part tend to become psychologically uncoupled. On the one hand, there is still a tendency for husbands to become rather fully involved in activities outside the house, with only superficial or fluctuating attention to family management and child raising. On the other hand, in a society where monetary values are important, the wife's unpaid activities in procreation, household work, and family management are seriously unappreciated or depreciated. Under these conditions the home, despite its heavy investment in consumer durables, is less of a protective nest than a small-scale motel with an unpaid, unhonored, overworked and increasingly rebellious female manager tending transient guests who may eat or watch TV together but have—as the years go by—less and less in common.

LONELINESS AND ALIENATION

What makes loneliness so unbearable is the loss of one's self.
HANNAH ARENDT [13]

To break or loosen one's bonds with community or family is to gain freedom from the restraints of older values and traditions, from inquisitive neighbors, and from domineering relatives. In the anonymous privacy of the metropolis, one may choose—within the limits of available income—between this or that life style, this or that mate, and this or that form of self-gratification. To "do one's own thing" in this way is an exalted height in the individualistic ideology of capitalism.

But here, as though by invisible hands, anyone may easily be led to break down the very self which was supposed to be liberated. "Detachment from others, from shared existence, is diminution of the self," writes Richard Goodwin, "just as if one were deprived of perceptual capacities or outlets for sexual instinct." [14] With the loss of intimacy, personal commitment and close bonds, the ideal of "I am the master of my fate, I am the captain of my soul" is fatuous. One is in danger of becoming, instead, a soulless victim of fate.

Early industrialism, it was charged by almost all of its critics, tended to reduce individuals to cogs in an imperial system and undermine one's personal sense of identity. Reduced to a set of formal roles, individuals became alienated from other people and from themselves. The same criticism is made more tellingly today. On the more liberal side, Hans Morgenthau writes that people feel they live in "something approaching a Kafkaesque world, insignificant and at the mercy of unchallengeable and invisible forces . . . a world of make-believe, a gigantic hoax." [15] On the more conservative side, George Charles Roche writes that "on every hand he [the individual] meets a denial that the individual is genuinely significant; on every hand he is confronted with vast constitutional amassments that seem beyond his control and his comprehension. He truly lives in 'The Age of Bewilderment!' " [16]

The bewilderment touches almost everything. Throughout the middle and lower classes, people learn that there are mysterious powers that bring about higher taxes, higher prices, diminished job opportunities, and abundant shortages. The promises of politicians—whether liberal, conservative, or radical—to *do something* are discounted. The members of the so-called "silent majority" feel isolated, self-estranged, and powerless—out of touch with themselves, with most other people, with the dominant institutions of society, unsure who "They" are but sure that "They" will somehow or other always manipulate things to their own advantage and "the people be damned!"

The bewilderment is made more painful by its sense of personal helplessness. A government report on work in America describes middle Americans as "alienated from their society, aggressive against people unlike themselves, distrusting of others and harboring an inadequate sense of personal or political efficacy." [17] Among people interviewed by Studs Terkel, the white-collar moan is as bitter as the blue-collar blues: "I'm a machine," says the spot welder. "I'm caged," says the bank teller, and echoes the bank clerk. "I'm a mule," says the steelworker. "A monkey can do what I do," says the receptionist. "I'm less than a farm implement," says the migrant worker. "I'm an object," says the high-fashion model. Blue collar and white collar call upon the identical phrase: "I'm a robot." "There is nothing to talk about," the young accountant despairingly enunciates.[18]

If the young middle manager finds nothing to talk about, the root of his despair may be that he sees useless make-work in executive suites, has too much to complain about, and finds no one to listen. Where can the young corporate accountant bring into the open what he suspects or knows about the use of what Abraham Briloff calls "accounting game plans" [19] to prepare fraudulent balance sheets to hide profits, fleece investors, and camouflage lawbreaking?

"When people begin to feel worthless, abandoned and lonely for the world to which they had grown accustomed," writes Suzanne Gordon, "they understandably begin to withdraw from social contacts." [20] The same withdrawal has been found on the part of other kinds of people who, in a society where people are valued by the price they get for their labor, find that their labor is worthless: those in their thirties or forties who are laid off and then told at employment offices that people over thirty (or forty as the case may be) need not apply; women who after the hard work of raising children try to find paid work outside the home and cannot; young people with high school or college or graduate diplomas who can find no work at all or else nothing faintly approaching what they had been educated to expect. Any serious comparison of steadily employed people with the unemployed shows—as in the survey of the three authors of *The Unemployed*—that the latter "see themselves as undesirable, doubt their own worth, often feel anxious, depressed or unhappy, and have little faith or confidence in themselves." [21] It is no cause for surprise, therefore, when one notes the results of Harvey Brenner's masterful study of the relation between economic instability and admission to mental hospitals. "Instabilities in the economy have been the single most important source of fluctuation in mental hospital admissions or admission rates . . . and there is considerable evidence that it has had greater impact in the last two decades." [22] Other observers have found that the impact is greatest on the poorest people. Poverty means weakness not merely in purchasing power but in other forms of power over the course of one's life. "All weakness tends to corrupt," writes Edgar Z. Friedenberg, "and impotence tends to corrupt absolutely." [23]

But mental hospitalization, like suicide, is an end point on a long, causal chain of breakdowns in social relationships. Whenever one of these points is reached for one person, many others—whether relatives, associates or friends—have already been damaged along the way, and perhaps just as deeply.

For the bulk of the population, breakdown comes in less extreme forms that defy statistical capture. Anxieties and tensions break out in vindictiveness, distemper, child abuse, increased susceptibility to physical illness, alcoholism, addiction, or crime. Still more pervasive is the simple withdrawal of commitment. "Is There Life Before Death?" ran the headline in a student newspaper. "With rising insistence and anguish," writes Margaret Mead, "there is now a new note: Can I commit my life to anything? Is there anything in human cultures worth saving, worth committing myself to?" [24] As those who ask it stay not for an answer, the question hangs ominously in the air. For many, I fear, the answer is, "Very little" or "Nothing."

CRIME: THE DIRTY SECRETS

The law locks up the hapless felon
Who steals the goose from off the common,
But lets the greater felon loose
Who steals the common from the goose . . .

ANCIENT JINGLE

. . . While law enforcers quake in awe
Of felons who transcend the law . . .

AUTHOR'S ADDENDUM

We are not letting the public in on our era's dirty little secret: that those who commit the crime which worries citizens most—violent street crime—are, for the most part, products of poverty, unemployment, broken homes, rotten education, drug addiction, alcoholism and other social and economic ills about which the police can do little if anything.

ROBERT D. DIGRAZIA,
Boston police commissioner [25]

The subject of crime and corruption in the United States is a tangle of dirty secrets: facts that informed insiders know but rarely mention in public.

A dirty little secret is that the police can do very little, if anything, about crime in the streets, which is a side effect of poverty and social fragmentation. Another is that it is the poor more than anybody else who have the most to fear from lower-class crime. The burglary rate in central-city slums, where there is less to be stolen, is at least three times higher than in the suburbs. All victimization rates are higher among blacks than among whites; for murder, the victimization rate is about seven times higher for black women and ten times higher for black men. Outside the area of official statistics, similar differentials are obvious. Vandalism, mugging, rape, and sheer terror have reached scandalous proportions in lower-class schools. In slum and ghetto areas vast numbers of people are victimized by the so-called "victimless crimes" —young men by narcotics addiction, young women by prostitution, and people of all ages by gambling rackets and loans on terms even more extortionate than those of the banks. An important part of this victimization enters the public schools. "Every Monday to Friday," a former high school principal has written, "somewhere in our schools, some students are molested, mugged, assaulted, shaken down or shaken up. Known and unknown drug pushers ply their trade within the school's once-inviolate halls." [26]

This brings us back to the dirty secrets about crime. One of the best kept secrets is the relation between crime and unemployment. Most larceny, burglary, and robbery is a form of self-employment that fills the vacuum created by the lack of jobs. For the young unemployed, "street crime" has the attraction of flexible hours, challenge on the job (instead of routine), fairly good income depending on skill and luck, high prestige among peer groups, no taxes, and the availability of welfare payments, food stamps, and unemployment compensation even while earning criminal income. Despite some risks, this form of self-employment offers possible upward mobility (from small stuff to the bigger rackets). High-class vocational training is provided free, along with board, for those passing through detention homes, jails, and other public institutions.

Another dirty little secret is that the largest proporition of "street criminals" are young blacks. To discuss this fact openly is to make some black people uncomfortable and to underscore the closer relation between street crime and the endemic massive unemployment and underemployment that have confronted young black people for over two decades. A *middle-sized* secret is that most blacks are deeply law-abiding and are much more terrorized by crime in the streets than anyone else. This is also true—although to a somewhat lesser degree—of young blacks, who are themselves terrorized by the active and repetitive law-breaking of a statistical minority among their ranks.

Legitimate concern with crime at the lower depths has other less legitimate functions. It contributes to social fragmentation by creating huge waves of fear and suspicion among people of different ethnic backgrounds. It provides opportunities for the cry of "law and order" to be used by various Establishment forces to justify either illegal or disorderly means of repressing lawful activities by trade unions, minority political parties, and other groups engaged in active resistance to exploitation. Above all, it distracts attention from crime and corruption in higher levels of society.

"Money is the name of the game. Without it you're dead," Gerald Ford is reported to have said while Republican leader in the House of Representatives.[27] Politics is fueled by money and the biggest source of money is business, particularly when business has a pipeline into public treasuries. Some of this money is obtained by elected officials or appointees who "go into business for themselves." The larger part, however, is probably channeled through new-style political machines that have replaced the smaller, tighter machines run by old-fashioned bosses. Although not yet dissected by political scientists, the new machine is an intricate network of government officials, law firms, bankers, and businessmen. It has much more government funds at its disposal and many more favors to dispense than the tighter political machine of a previous era. But like the business complex, it is fluid, hard to pin down, and much harder to bust up or replace.

This combination of private and public corruption spills over into all the many institutions at the junior and contingent levels of the Establishment. Much of this is well-known but rarely commented on in public: the friendship cliques and favoritism in voluntary associations and social service agencies; the foundation officials who give huge sums to universities and then move into cushy jobs thus created; the fee splitting by lawyers and doctors; the padding of bills by hospitals submitting their accounts to insurance funds; the fraudulent claims made by educational institutions, consultants, and research hustlers. Much greater publicity is usually given to corruption in trade unions and the petty frauds perpetrated by recipients of public assistance and unemployment compensation. At a convention session of the Mass Retailing Institute Herbert Robinson charged that bribery runs rampant in retailing: "Ten billion dollars is a conservative estimate . . . The great growth of the economy in recent years has been paralleled by a growth in corrupt business behavior." [28]

Businessmen loudly complain of the money they lose from pilfering by their employees. At the same time, they sanction widespread bribery—and sometimes illegal espionage—in the conduct of their own business. In radio, when disc jockeys are "put on the pad" by record companies, the industry term is "payola." When building contractors win inflated appraisals from the Federal Housing Administration, the best term is "fraud." But, as a Justice Department investigator told the press, it is difficult to trace such frauds because they are "intertwined with the morals of the marketplace." [29] The same "morals" guide the stores that gouge their buyers with high interest rates on credit; the banks with major investments in slum housing that violates local building codes; the contractors and building and financial institutions that manipulate zoning ordinances and land-use plans in order to squeeze maximum profit from land speculation, high-income building, and adroitly designed tax havens. The law is even more brazenly flouted by the so-called law enforcers in the FBI and other branches of the Justice Department who organize burglaries and illegal wiretapping against leaders and participants in dissident movements. The fact that they regard themselves as above the law is not disproved by their claims that illegal action is necessary to protect the national security or fight "organized crime."

The racketeering groups called "organized crime" are not nearly as well organized as any medium-sized corporation. They are merely small or medium-sized networks of businessmen who provide a wide range of illegal services: drugs not readily available from doctors and pharmacies; gambling more exciting or accessible than church benefits, Wall Street, or government betting systems; any form of sexual service other than marriage; and high-interest loans. They are also prone to use considerable violence in controlling competitors and employees. The high demand for their illegal services depends entirely on laws that make certain forms of drugs, gambling, and purchases of sex illegal. Their ability to supply this demand, in turn, depends largely upon the undercover permissiveness, if not enthusiastic cooperation, of legitimate businessmen and government officials at all levels. Despite recurring exposés, thousands of policemen in all the larger cities are "on the pad" of the racketeers. Beyond this, many policemen go very far in expecting money, favors, merchandise, or services from local businessmen. "We wanted to serve others," writes David Durk, a former police officer, "but the department was a home for the drug dealers and thieves . . . Like it or not, the policeman is convinced that he lives and works in the middle of a corrupt society, that everybody is getting theirs, and why shouldn't he . . ." [30]

Police susceptibility to graft is closely connected with morale breakdowns created by "war against crime" rhetoric. To get more funds, police chiefs almost invariably pretend that the main job of the police is to catch criminals and deter lawbreaking. But apart from their illegal cooperation with criminals and lawbreakers, most of the time of the police is dedicated to traffic control, automobile accidents, municipal inspection activities, and internal red tape. Those policemen directly involved in coping with crime are caught in the infuriating bind that even while concentrating on petty crime, they are, by and large, trapped in operations whose failures are always greater than successes. Even petty criminals are rarely obliging enough to be caught in the act. Only a small percentage is arrested after the act, and most of those arrested are never found guilty. Of those who are sentenced, well-to-do people who can afford to hire clever lawyers or subservient judges usually get off with suspended sentences or quick releases through good behavior—or even presidential pardons. Overflowing with poor people (particularly blacks and Hispanics), the jails become training grounds for petty recidivists. Thus even the public records themselves, doctored though they may be to make the picture look less grim, reveal sustained defeat in the so-called "war against crime." The defeated foot soldiers in this phoney war are hemmed in between a criminal-justice system which is criminally corrupt or inefficient, radicals who brand them as pigs or fascists, and intellectuals who see them as incompetent or stupid. Their typical reaction is one of furious resentment, which often finds its expression in the abuse of their duties.

But all the dirty *little* secrets fade into insignificance in comparison with one dirty *big* secret: *Law enforcement officials, judges as well as prosecutors and investigators, are soft on corporate crime.* Modern capitalism requires a legal system to protect private property, enforce contracts, and promote confidence in corporate institutions. On the other hand, the more perfect pursuit of capital and power often requires widespread evasion of the same legal system, let alone of ordinary moral codes. This deep contradiction has worked out in such a way as to tarnish the reputation of government even more than of big business, thereby strengthening corporate defenses against any threat of widespread public ownership.

In his classic *White Collar Crime*, Edwin H. Sutherland reviewed the lawbreaking record of seventy large corporations. He found that the courts or federal administrative agencies had made a total of 980 adverse decisions against them. Their crimes ranged over these areas: restraint of trade; infringement or manipulation of patents, copyrights, and trademarks; misrepresentation in advertising; unfair labor practices; financial manipulation; war crimes; and such miscellaneous activities as unhealthy working conditions, pollution, bribery, fraud, libel, and assault. These crimes had been committed against "consumers, competitors, stockholders and other investors, inventors and employees, as well as against the State."[31]

In analyzing these 980 crimes, Sutherland found these points of similarity with crimes committed by lower-class thieves:

1. Most of the crimes were deliberate rather than inadvertent violations of technical regulations.
2. Most of the offenders were repeaters; there was no effective rehabilitation or deterrence.
3. Illegal behavior by corporations was "much more extensive than the prosecutions and complaints indicate."
4. The businessman-lawbreaker "does not customarily lose status among his business associates."
5. Businessmen customarily feel and express contempt for law and for government "snoopers" charged with law enforcement.
6. Corporate crime is organized informally and formally, through an unwritten consensus on "business ethics," secret agreements and cartels, and formal reward systems for officials who maximize profits and conceal unsavory means.
7. Corporate lawbreaking is shrouded in secrecy, with secrecy facilitated by juggling corporate personalities and brand names and by smokescreens of favorable advertising.

Sutherland also found that muggers, burglars, and racketeers see themselves as criminals and are so defined in the public conception. But corporate lawbreakers do not regard themselves as criminals, and do not customarily associate with "common" criminals. They occupy superior status in society, admired by investigators, prosecutors, judges, and jury members as well as by the media and the public at large. This status is protected by special procedures—such as administrative hearings, consent decrees, and cease and desist orders—that protect them from being treated like ordinary criminals. Another difference is that "the corporate form of business organization also has the advantage of increased rationality" in the use of whatever illegal or unethical means may help maximize pecuniary gain. The corporation "selects crimes which involve the smallest amount of detection and identification . . . [and] in which proof is difficult." Above all, the corporation engages in "fixing" on a scale "much more inclusive than the fixing of professional theft." The corporation's "mouthpieces" and "fixers" include lawyers, accountants, public relations experts, and public officials who negotiate loopholes and special procedures in the laws, prevent most illegal activities from ever being disclosed, and undermine or sidetrack "over-zealous" law enforcers. In the few cases ever brought to court, they usually negotiate penalties amounting to "gentle taps on the wrist." [32]

Although Sutherland covered many decades up to 1944, he merely scratched the surface. Confining himself to manufacturing, mining, and merchandising, he did not try to track down the corporate record in banking, insurance, commmunication, transportation, or construction. Dipping lightly into public utilities, he found that fifteen power and light companies had been found guilty of defrauding consumers or investors in thirty-eight cases. But he withdrew quickly after finding that the perpetrators of fraud in this area were so politically powerful that few cases were ever brought against them. He barely hinted at the massive black marketeering and falsification engaged in during World War II in violation of emergency controls over prices and scarce materials. He stayed away completely from the still larger vast area of criminal profiteering by corporations with large war contracts.

Since 1944, there have been two major changes. On the one hand, there has been a vast increase in the laws needed to provide the business system with larger financial support and protect it against the dangerous consequences that might result from no controls whatsoever over the injuries inflicted on employees, consumers, small investors, and the physical environment. On the other hand, although no one has yet attempted to update Sutherland, it is clear that the scale of corporate crime has risen enormously. From 1945 through 1965 the Federal Trade Commission issued cease and desist orders in almost four thousand cases of business fraud and misleading advertising, and the Food and Drug Administration initiated a much larger number of criminal prosecutions.[33] In 1975 alone Exxon, one of the largest corporations in the world, was defending itself against antitrust charges brought by Connecticut, Florida, Kansas, and the Federal Trade Commission and was charged with three air-quality violations, forty-five environmental violations and fifty-three oil discharge violations.[34] In the wake of the Watergate prosecutions, 150 American corporations admitted having made illegal political contributions from secret slush funds. Lockheed Aircraft and other corporations have confessed to large-scale bribery of officials of foreign governments. For those who study the situation carefully, it is now clear that, in Ralph Nader's words, "corporate economic, product and environmental crimes dwarf other crimes in damage to health, safety and property, in confiscation or theft of other people's monies, and in control of the agencies which are supposed to stop this crime and fraud." [35]

Some things, however, remain unchanged. The few executives ever punished—no matter how lightly—for illegal behavior still complain that they had no choice: they were merely following "standard business ethics." The courts still rule, and the wealthiest stockholders still insist, that the executive's highest responsibility is to maximize long-term corporate profits. "A sudden submission to Christian ethics by businessmen," as one executive has been quoted, "would bring about the greatest economic upheaval in history."[36] Even a slow submission to the much lower level of conduct required by laws and regulations would disrupt the processes of efficient accumulation. More widespread lawbreaking, in turn, disrupts very little. While a few people are punished by wrist slaps—or, as one observer has put it, by "eyewinks"—most of the executive criminals are unscathed, while their multimillionaire superiors operate through remote-control techniques that provide them with full and complete cover, if not mantles of impeccable respectability.

I am convinced that among the great majority of the people below the Establishment only a small minority break the law. Perhaps this reflects not only ordinary morality but also a scarcity of opportunities. But as we look at the Establishment, the higher we go the more do marketplace norms take over and the greater the opportunities for illegal gain become—from the padding of expense accounts and the inflation of tax deductions to favoritism and corruption in the dispensation of employment and promotions, the awarding of contracts, and the interpretation of rules and regulations. But to find offense ratios of truly staggering proportions one must try to look, as Sutherland did, at corporate crime. Of the seventy corporations he studied, not a single one had a clean record. Half had been found guilty more than ten times. One wonders how much larger this figure would have been if Sutherland could have included the much larger amount of illegal behavior that was never brought formally before the courts or regulatory agencies. One is also entitled to ask how many of the thousand largest corporations today could have a perfectly clean record. The probability of a large corporation's having violated no laws on pollution, product debasement, tax evasion, political contributions, or misrepresentation in advertising may be compared—in the words of Matthew—to the likelihood "for a camel to pass through the eye of a needle" or "for a rich man to enter the kingdom of God." It is still harder to find any case of a millionaire lawbreaker who is sent to jail or kept there as long as someone who has stolen a loaf of bread.

THE EROSION OF AUTHORITY

There aren't any heroes anymore.

WARD JUST[37]

Opinion polls in the United States have repeatedly documented a growing lack of confidence in, if not contempt for, the major institutions of American society.

To some extent this is a youth phenomenon. Young people lose confidence when they sense the contrast between the ideals and the behavior of their elders. But hypocrisy is not perceived only by younger people. Men and women of all ages, colors, and income levels hear cries for "law and order" raised by respectable lawbreakers; by slumlords who violate local building codes; by police departments in collusion with organized crime; by self-proclaimed defenders of morality who regard sex as something evil or dirty and incidentally assist organized crime in maintaining its market monopoly through the present laws on prostitution, gambling, drugs, and pornography; by land developers and speculators who undermine the Supreme Court's rulings on segregation, local government officials who wink at such lawbreaking, and high-minded bankers who finance it; and by the new Suburban Bourbons who talk "liberalese" but have built the lily-white suburbs that encircle our Northern cities; by corporate and public executives who speak unctuously about the environment and accelerate its pollution.

Another dimension of erosion is the decline of authority figures. The titans of big business have retreated into anonymity. Nor are there many trappings of high authority surrounding the "littler giants" of church, school, office or home: minister, priest, rabbi, teacher, professor, the "boss," or Mother and Father. No national heroes have come into being from the ranks of organized labor, educators, students, blacks, or women's liberation. If some Senators become nationally known while investigating Watergate, multinational corporations, the CIA or the FBI, this has been part of a trend toward superficial debunking. It has not brought to national or international attention any genuine leaders with charisma. Roosevelt, Churchill, de Gaulle rise in retrospective stature in comparison with such pigmy-like heirs as Nixon, Ford, Carter, Callahan, Thatcher, Schmidt, or Giscard d'Estaing.

Established doctrines are also faring badly. Even the most ardent reformers are less than enthusiastic with the heritage of past liberal reforms. They are forced to concede the conservative and radical critique that the New Deal, Fair Deal, New Frontier and Great Society overpromised and underdelivered. But neither conservatism nor radicalism have done much better. Conservatives have been increasingly split three ways between free-market, almost anarchist libertarians, strong authoritarians, and the uncouth extremists of the "radical right." Radicals have long since lost confidence in the Soviet Union, which once was accepted as the beacon light of world socialism. Instead, a "thousand flowers" of Marxism and Marxist doctrines come and go, leaving behind them too little serious analysis of the realities of either modern capitalism or the many varieties of socialism now being attempted. A similar decline of confidence may be observed in the promises of science, technology, or expertise. Scientists are increasingly blamed (with something less than full justification) for the destructive uses to which science has been put.

New technologies are increasingly blamed (with more justification) for the plagues of pollution. Although this may be the age of Keynes, the authority of Keynesians and of all economists who promised endless prosperity without inflation has waned. The flamboyant promises made by operations researchers, systems analysts, futurists, and experts in social indicators—all have been punctured. While each of these doctrines or methodologies has certain assets at its disposal and enjoys a coterie of supporters and a broader area of goodwill, each has the greatest of difficulty in meeting the obligations it has previously accepted, even sought to assume. In the accounting sense, therefore, despite their accumulated assets, they tend toward insolvency.

The erosion of authority also affects the institutional structure of the Establishment. Opinion polls tend to show steadily falling public confidence in major corporations, banks and financial institutions, business executives, building contractors, and advertising executives. Higher education, science, and organized religion do not fare much better. The executive branch, the Congress, and even the Supreme Court tend to fare worse.

Although election victories confer formal authority upon the victors, this authority is tarnished by the fact that large numbers of people fail to vote. Thus in 1964 and 1972, respectively, Presidents Johnson and Nixon each won about 60 percent of the votes cast. But of the total voting age population, Johnson won only 38 percent and Nixon only 34 percent; in 1976 Carter's percentage was less than 27 percent. In the nonpresidential election years voter turnout is always lower, and in recent years has been declining. In 1974 elections of the House of Representatives voting participation fell to 36 percent, the lowest since 1944. In many state and local elections it is generally lower, and participation is still lower in primary elections. When nonvoters are asked why they do not vote, the most frequent answer is simply that they do not see candidates worth voting for. Accordingly, as a group of political observers concluded in *Society*, the political system "has forfeited its one high level of diffuse support—the sustaining belief that even if a particular election is deemed unfavorable, at least the system is fair, open and likely to produce favorable outcomes in the future."[38] In 1979, 79 percent of Louis Harris's respondents said that "the rich get richer and the poor get poorer," up from 45 percent in 1966 and 48 percent in 1972. Comments by Harris and other pollsters indicate that most people see the candidates of both parties as contributing to this process of progressive enrichment and impoverishment.

5

The Challenge of a Shrinking Capitalistic World

> There are clear signs that America is being displaced as the paramount country, or that there will be a breaking up, in the next few decades, of any single-power hegemony in the world .
> The American Century lasted 30 years.
>
> DANIEL BELL [1]

THE MALAISE IN FIRST WORLD countries has global roots.

Many top Establishment leaders—particularly in the United States—are frustrated by new events in the world order they helped create and brilliantly led. Having successfully coped with the huge postwar losses of Eastern Europe, China and North Korea, they have more recently been shaken by smaller losses that might augur the continuing shrinkage of the "Free World" and perhaps even its falling apart. They see clear signs, in Daniel Bell's words, that "America is being displaced as the paramount country." Their institutional authority is eroded. They are less able to use tried and tested means of continuing in operation the great engine of prosperity of the postwar Western world.

In 1960, when Daniel Bell first proclaimed the end of ideology, I was inclined to go along with him. It took me many years to realize that the funeral oration came from one of the builders of a new Establishment ideology. In 1975, when Bell announced the end of the American Century, I desperately wanted to believe him. I now see that the American Century is still alive, although unwell. To call it dead is like saying that the Catholic Church was killed by the Reformation.

But when I say it still lives, I am not suggesting it could survive as long as the Catholic Church. Its life expectancy, along with transnational capitalism as a whole, depends not only on the power of the forces against it but also on its adaptation to the unintentional consequences of its own successes.

NEW LOSSES TO COMMUNISM

By 1950, as shown in the table "Growth of National Communism," the "Free World" had shrunk from over 90 to less than 70 percent of the world's population. But concurrently it gained some things that industrial capitalism had never before enjoyed. As stated in "The Takeoff Toward a New Corporate Society" (chapter 2), the "Free World" attained a totally unprecedented unity among the leading capitalist powers. This unity was based not only on American political leadership but also on a multicontinental market exploited by giant transnational complexes. Above all, faced by the challenge of communist regimes that had sidestepped the capitalist business cycle, the "Free World" overcame the catastrophic depressions that in the past had always been part and parcel of industrial capitalism. With these new capabilities, under American guidance, it was possible to contain the rising tides of communism and socialism not only in such decisive spots as Western Europe, Japan, and India, but also in many other countries where capitalism was on the defensive.

But only for a while. Wherever military power and right-wing dictatorships became the major instruments of containment, with little or no reforms to improve the living conditions of the people, the barriers proved very shaky and at times unbelievably fragile.

The longest and bloodiest of all containment struggles was in Indochina. It began in 1945 when Ho Chi Minh set up the Democratic Republic of Vietnam. If there had been no containment effort, communist regimes would have probably followed promptly in the rest of Indochina; this could have had important repercussions in such nearby countries as Thailand, Malaysia, Indonesia, and the Philippines. But in 1946 French forces intervened, fighting the communists until decisively defeated eight years later at Dien Bien Phu. The U.S. government quickly moved in to fill the vacuum by supporting an anticommunist state in South Vietnam. Under Presidents Eisenhower and Kennedy, U.S. help gradually increased. As this involvement became massive under President Johnson and was extended to Cambodia under President Nixon, "national honor" and presidential prestige began to hang in the balance. By 1972, when it was already clear that a U.S. victory was no longer possible, Nixon guaranteed his election to a second term by toning down the U.S. conflict with the Soviet Union and China and beginning the long-drawn-out process of withdrawing American forces from South Vietnam and liquidating the military draft. In early 1975, communist regimes won control in all of Vietnam, Cambodia, and Laos. The United States had to accept what Richard Nixon had in 1970 called unacceptable—namely, the "first defeat in its proud one hundred and ninety-year history."

In the meantime, lots of things had been happening in other countries.

One of the most important was in Cuba. In January 1959 the American-supported Cuban dictator, Fulgencio Batista, was overthrown by guerrilla forces under Fidel Castro. There then started a long process toward nationalization of major business enterprises and full socialization of Cuban society. But small though this island of nine million people was in the world arena, the "Castro shock" to the U.S. Establishment was enormous. There was never any doubt as to whether or not "we had Cuba." The Castro example might be followed, it was feared, in other Caribbean or Latin American countries, undermining the sphere of influence so laboriously established in more than a century of the Monroe Doctrine and many decades of economic investment. The island itself could even become a base for Soviet forces or missiles. The United States responded to this challenge by a series of limited actions: an attempted invasion by anti-Castro refugees, a trade embargo, a naval quarantine to force the removal of launching pads, infiltration of Cuba to disrupt the economy and assassinate its leaders, and many steps to prevent or suppress similar socialist or communist tendencies in the rest of the Western Hemisphere. Although some of this effort was successful, it failed on three scores: the invasion was defeated at the Bay of Pigs; Castro and his associates escaped assassination; and by the mid-1970s Cuba was firmly established as a viable communist nation ninety miles off the coast of world capitalism's proudest citadel.

In 1974, on the eve of the American defeat in Vietnam, another communist wave started in Africa. In Portugal, the old Salazar dictatorship was overthrown by military officers radicalized by years of failure in fighting liberation movements in Portugal's African colonies. By 1976 communist regimes took power in these colonies—Mozambique, Guinea-Bissau, and Angola. Similar regimes had previously been established in the Congo and Benin. Shortly thereafter, the old feudal monarchy in Ethiopia, the second largest country of Africa, was replaced by a Marxist-Leninist government. Nor were West Asia and Asia immune to these trends. By the late 1970s communist-style regimes were in power in both South Yemen and Afghanistan.

Thus by 1980, the total number of communist regimes reached twenty-five, almost twice the number that had existed in 1950. Their share of the world's population was about a billion and a half. If this was not a large percentage rise (from 31 percent in 1950 to 36 percent in 1980), it nonetheless suggests the possibility of continuing increases during the 1980s. There is reason to suppose that the rate of communist expansion may accelerate during the 1980s. In Africa, for example, where the conflicts with white-dominated South Africa, Southwest Africa, and Rhodesia are becoming much hotter, the major liberation movements are all led by outspoken foes of capitalism. If and when these countries become (to use their African names) Azania, Namibia, and Zimbabwe, they will probably be governed by Marxist regimes. Similar specters of

GROWTH OF NATIONAL COMMUNISM
TABLE 8

	Population[a] (Millions) 1920	1950	1980	Land Area[b] (Thousands of square kilometers) 1978
Soviet Union	143	193	259	22,402
Europe				
Albania	—	1	3	29
Bulgaria	—	7	9	111
Czechoslovakia	—	12	15	128
East Germany	—	17	17	108
Hungary	—	9	11	93
Poland	—	25	35	313
Rumania	—	16	22	238
Yugoslavia	—	16	22	256
	—	103	134	1,276
Asia				
Afghanistan	—	—	17	647
Cambodia	—	—	9	181
China	—	463	958[c]	9,597
Laos	—	—	3	237
Mongolia	—	1	2	1,565
North Korea	—	9	17	121
Vietnam				
North	—	13	—	
All	—	—	47	332
	—	486	1,053	12,680
Western Asia				
South Yemen	—	—	2	333

	Population [a] (Millions) 1920	1950	1980		Land Area [b] (Thousands of square kilometers) 1978
Africa					
Angola	—	—	6 [d]		1,247
Benin	—	—	3		113
Congo	—	—	1		342
Ethiopia	—	—	29		1,222
Guinea	—	—	5		246
Guinea-Bissau	—	—	1		36
Mozambique	—	—	10		783
	—	—	55		3,989
Western Hemisphere					
Cuba	—	—	10		115
Oceania	—	—	—		—
Total Population	143	782	1,515	Total Land Area	40,795
Total Countries	1	13	25		
[c] World Population	1,813	2,501 [e]	4,208	World Land Area	135,830
Communist Nations as Percent of World	8%	31%	36%		30%

Notes:

[a] Estimates under "1980" are for midyear 1978 (or, where this is not available, mid-1977) and are taken from the *Monthly Bulletin of Statistics,* April 1979, United Nations: New York.

[b] Land area estimates refer to total surface area, including inland waters. Taken from *Statistical Yearbook, 1977,* New York: United Nations 1978.

[c] *New York Times,* 12 July 1979, p. A-12.

[d] For 1972.

[e] *Statistical Yearbook, 1975.*

social revolution loom ahead in other parts of the world. Before the year 2000—if current tendencies continue—the ratio between capitalism and communism may well shrink from 65:35 to 50:50. The implications of such a shift are enormous.

But if the shrinkage of the capitalist world has thus far been accompanied by its unification, the expansion of the communist world has been characterized by multipolarity and divisiveness. The myth of a communist monolith headed by the Kremlin or of a Moscow-Peking Axis (as fostered by the secretaries of state under Eisenhower, Kennedy, and Johnson) was nonsense from the beginning. Communist unity was badly shaken as far back as 1948, when Tito first proclaimed Yugoslavia's independence from Moscow. It was weakened as well as strengthened by the Russian troops sent into Hungary in 1956 and Czechoslovakia in 1968. It was shaken still further as strains developed between the two communist giants, the Soviet Union and China, in the 1950s and 1960s, and eventually broke out into both mutual name-calling and border conflicts in the 1970s. The idea that all communist countries would live in loving peace with each other was itself laid to rest during the more recent wars between Vietnam and Cambodia, China and Vietnam, and Ethiopia and the Eritrean Liberation Front.

If unity among the communist nations, particularly between China and the Soviet Union, should somehow be restored, the threat to capitalism would be much stronger. In fact, it might be decisive in strengthening the extremely divided radical forces in India, which itself accounts for at least one sixth of the world's population.

But strangely enough, disunity has by no means eliminated the communist challenge. While communist movements may be encouraged by international support, their basic power stems from their nationalist roots in countries where people have long suffered from oppression and exploitation. They are thereby far stronger than they would be if they were—or even appeared to be—mere pawns on a chessboard whose pieces were moved by a distant communist power. Thus all of the newest communist regimes—whether in Angola, Ethiopia, or Mozambique—must strongly assert their independence from Moscow, even though, without exception each has been dependent on Soviet arms and military and economic aid in order to take power, survive, and consolidate itself. My personal guess is that before the end of the 1980s, Communist China, strengthened by the new aid pouring in from the leading capitalist powers, will itself become a new source of aid to communist movements in many parts of the world.

The most threatening of all the new spectres of communism, however appear not in the Third World but on the southern flank of European capitalism itself—namely, in Portugal, Spain, France, and Italy. In Portugal, a complex social upheaval was touched off when its armed forces, disillusioned by years of fruitless efforts against the guerrilla independence movements in the African colonies, overthrew the Caetano government in April 1974. In March 1975 the Armed Forces Movement instituted a more radical regime, which, although deeply divided into many shifting factions, seemed agreed on the desirabliity of building some kind of socialist society. In Spain, after the demise of Franco, Socialist and Communist groupings have come to the forefront after many years of repression. In France, strong Communist and Socialist parties, although still divided on many issues and engaged in electoral jockeying, did unite in a popular front movement that in the late 1970s came a hair's breadth from winning the presidency in a national election. In Italy, a still more powerful Communist party has achieved important footholds in major cities and provinces and has been moving toward an "historic compromise" through which they might enter the Italian government along with the Christian Democrats. In each of these four countries, the official Communist party is dynamic, well-organized, rooted in national culture and traditions, and capable of working with many other anticapitalist groupings. The Portuguese Party is the only one to be embarrassed by close adherence to Soviet policies and strategies. The others have demonstrated independence from Soviet positions and disagreement with the approach of the Portuguese Communists. The "loss" of Portugal to the "Free World" would be a much greater blow than the loss of Portugal's former colonies; this would be a crack near the heartland itself. The loss of either Spain or France or Italy would be more than a crack. And the loss of all four countries together with their strategic geopolitical positions and their combined populations of almost 150 million people would mean an historical change in the entire structure of world capitalism.

CREEPING SOCIALISM

While "capitalism" is regarded as an unpleasant term in the United States, where "free enterprise" and other euphemisms are used to describe the system, many Americans fail to realize that "socialism"—also unpopular in the United States—is one of the most popular political catchwords in the rest of the world. The leaders of communist regimes say that their task is to build socialism as a transitional stage before their countries can enter into true communism, when the "dictatorship of the proletariat" will no longer be necessary. The leaders of many Third World countries, such as India, join in waving the banner of socialism as they expand the physical and corporate infrastructure of industrial capitalism. In Western Europe, as Michael Harrington has brilliantly demonstrated, there has been a long tradition of socialist parties taking the responsibility of "running capitalism." [2] Indeed, after World War II the takeoff toward transitional capitalism in all of Western Europe was facilitated by welfare-state programs that helped maintain market demand and submerge class struggles and nationalization programs, and in turn helped subsidize the private corporate sectors. Both socialist ideals and socialist parties have helped strengthen capitalism.

But the popularity of socialist ideals and the appeal of socialist parties has other implications also, implications that may prove dominant over the long run. The first implication is that the short-range steps that may stave off social revolution may also constitute major (albeit confusing) breaks with the capitalist world. Conservatives and reactionaries have long argued that any socialist parties, even such mild reformists as the West German Social Democrats and the British Laborites, are a "camel's nose under the tent." Just a litle socialism, they argue, will lead to a lot of socialism and the end of capitalism. There is some genuine merit in this view.

In the Third World, for example, as shown in the table, "Socialistically Inclined Third World Countries," there are at least a dozen countries whose regimes embody not only the nose and head but at least one hump of the camel. Their total population adds up to over 138 million people. At least four of these countries (Iran, Libya, Algeria, and Iraq) have strategic importance because of their petroleum resources. Jamaica and Guyana contain important bauxite deposits. Somalia is strategically located in geopolitical terms, while Tanzania and Zambia exercise strategic politico-economic influence. Other observers would probably add four or five countries to this list.

None of these regimes is communist in the sense of being "Marxist-Leninist" or pledging themselves to "scientific socialism." Yet the first nine on the list—those in Asia, Western Asia, and Africa—share certain features with communist regimes, particularly one-party politics and tight control of the press and other media. In contrast, the three small countries in the Western Hemisphere—Guyana, Jamaica, and Nicaragua—are politically more similar to Western democracies.

They are also countries whose leadership and people have been among those most influenced by Fidel Castro's advice, Cuban technical assistance, and above all, Cuban example in combating destitution, illiteracy, ill health, and the American "Colossus of the North." In turn, the influence of these three countries, particularly Nicaragua, has been felt among the people in the neighboring Central American dictatorships of Guatemala, El Salvador, and Honduras, and in the Caribbean dictatorship in Haiti. There is a strong possibility that the 1980s will sooner or later see the Caribbean as a socialist sea and Central America as a socialist isthmus. This would not mean Cuban or other Marxist-Leninist style of socialism. It would, however, mean a new series of "losses" to capitalism.

Another implication—or aspect—of socialism's popularity in the world is that it is related to the narrowing of the historic breach between evolutionary and revolutionary socialism. In many parts of the world

SOCIALISTICALLY INCLINED THIRD WORLD COUNTRIES

	Population in 1980 (millions)	Land Area (thousands of square kilometers)
Asia		
Burma	32	676
Western Asia		
Algeria	19	2,382
Iran	35	1,648
Iraq	12	435
Libya	2	111
Syria	8	185
Africa		
Somalia	3	638
Tanzania	17	945
Zambia	5	753
Western Hemisphere		
Guyana	1	215
Jamaica	2	11
Nicaragua	2	130
12	138	8,129
Percent of world's total:	3.3%	6.0%

communist parties previously dedicated to revolution as *the* path to socialism have both accepted the possibility of a peaceful path to socialism and rejected one-party dictatorship as the necessary foundation for building socialism in societies long operating within the framework of constitutional capitalist democracy. This change of position has allowed them to take the position that their socialism would be quite different from that of all communist regimes thus far established. It has also brought them much closer to the socialist and social-democratic parties. Thus the strength of what has been called "Eurocommunism" also adds to the strength of "Eurosocialism." And insofar as Western Europe is concerned, whatever probability there is for communist party regimes, the probability is much greater that socialist governments may not merely run capitalism but may in actuality run or walk away from it.

THIRD WORLD DEMANDS

The First World's difficulties with expanding communism and socialism are increasingly augmented by the rising demands of Third World countries.

The term "Third World," of course, has no meaning except by reference to the "First World" of developed capitalism and the "Second World" of communism. By my classification, as shown in the table, "An Overview of the Three Worlds," it refers to almost eighty countries embracing about half of the world's population. But if one wants to include in this category the seventeen pre-industrial countries of the divided communist world, including China, the number of countries rises higher and the proportion of the population moves from 50 to 75 percent. This broader definition, however, blurs the vital distinction between countries with communist and noncommunist regimes. The larger number can better be described, by the terminology of development, which has given us a sequence of labels from "underdeveloped" (regarded as objectionable by many), "developing" (regarded as an exaggeration by others) to "less developed countries" or LDCs—the last now the United Nations' official label for the majority of its members.

No matter what definition one uses, however, the variety of countries referred to is enormous. Some are still largely primitive, tribal societies like Mali and Oman. Traditional feudal hierarchies—among them Saudi Arabia, Pakistan, and Paraguay—comprise the majority. Then there are those, like India and Brazil, that are well advanced in the transition to modern industrialism although still containing feudal or even tribal elements. They also vary considerably on the extent of democratic constitutionalism. Even when one excludes (as in my table) the "people's democracies" of communism, only a minority operate along the lines of capitalist democracy. The great majority are authoritarian or dictatorial in nature, often with central power openly exercised by a military junta. Economic variations are even more striking. Some are oil-rich countries with a relatively high level of national income per capita (usually enjoyed by a small entrenched minority). Others are in the middle range of national income. A third group is desperately poor.

Despite these vast differences, however, the Third World countries have been remarkably united in making three demands on the First World: an end to colonialism, neocolonialism, and imperialism; more economic and technical aid on better terms; and improved trade relations with the developed countries.

The first demand arose in the immediate years after World War II, in the effort to accelerate decolonization and eliminate the dwindling minority of surviving colonies. The native leaders of former colonies then attacked neocolonialism. By this, they meant either the maintenance of colonial traditions and procedures after liberation or the indirect economic and political pressures exerted by the former colonial power, the United States, or transnational corporations. In many cases, this attack was made by the very leaders who themselves were the people responsible for preserving colonial mentality or serving as submissive, if not servile, cooperators with First World powers. Anti-imperialism became a form of rhetoric available to both its opponents and its friends. The general adoption of this rhetoric, however, has had political implications. Many of the most reactionary collaborators with neocolonialism or imperialism often joined with other Third World countries in attacking American intervention in Vietnam and Cuba and supporting the liberation movements against the Portuguese and in such countries as South Africa, Namibia, and Rhodesia.

The demand for more aid, an even more powerful unifying force, was associated with the growth of the "nonaligned" movement. During the 1950s and the early 1960s, when the confrontation between the United States and the Soviet Union became extremely sharp, a group of Asian leaders started to organize a "third force" to act as a buffer zone between capitalism and socialism. Their successive conferences on the subject (Colombo in 1954, Bandung in 1956, Belgrade in 1961) were sharply denounced as a betrayal of the "Free World" by the American Secretary of State, John Foster Dulles. "If you are not *with* us," Dulles proclaimed in essence, "you are *against* us." What Dulles failed to realize (apart from the fact that his attack helped unify them) was that many of the nonaligned countries were very much *for* capitalism and the "Free World." In India, for example, socialist rhetoric was helpful in placating left-wing parties and getting them to go along with the massive public-sector assistance to the Birlas, Tatas, and other large capitalist conglomerates. But much more was needed: a large infusion of foreign capital and technology. This was obtained under Nehru's inspired leadership by an adroit playing of the Soviet Union against the capitalist countries. The more help they received from the Soviet Union (in return for which small favors were given on the world political arena), the easier it was to raise more funds from First World countries, the World Bank, and the International Monetary Fund. The more help from these, the easier it was to get arms, a huge steel plant, and public sector assistance from the Soviet Union. As many other countries operated according to the same logic (or were inspired by Nehru's example), "Third Worldism" became a tried and trusted method of mobilizing resources in the form of loans, grants, military aid, and technical assistance. To help legitimate India's and other Third World demands for resources, Nehru developed the questionable idea that war is caused by poverty. This idea was warmly embraced by the richer countries who were themselves both the ammunitions makers for the world and the stockpilers of atomic weapons. In return, many Third World countries went through the motions of going along with the still more questionable idea that poverty is caused by overpopulation, despite the evidence that high birthrates and large families are often the only way that poor people can fight poverty. Thus First and Third World countries often found themselves collaborating in antipoverty programs that, like most development programs, enriched Third World elites, and in population-control

AN OVERVIEW OF THE THREE WORLDS
TABLE 10

		Population Millions	%	GNP %	Establishment Structure	International Context
THIRD WORLD	Primitive				Localized tribal/clan domination	Many clients, satellites or junior partners of First World capitalism; some genuinely "nonaligned"; some strongly socialist or socialistically inclined; most capitalist with feudal vestiges and socialist rhetoric
	Traditional				Feudal hierarchies, military juntas	
	Transitional (including socialist and capitalist)				Shifting business-landowning coalitions, with powerful military forces and large bureaucracies	
	Total	2,063	49	10–15		
SECOND WORLD	Pre-industrial Communist				Party leaders, state functionaries, military	Nationalist oriented, polycentric; established with USSR aid but in some cases opposing USSR leadership
	Industrial Communist				Same as above, but with more professionals and technocrats	Associated with COMECOM and Warsaw Pact, under varying forms of USSR leadership
	Total	**1,519**	**36**	**20–25**		

FIRST WORLD	High-technology capitalist				Loose but tightening business-government partnerships served by competing parties, military, professionals, technocrats.	Cooperating through OECD and NATO, with support of IMF and World Bank, in promoting transnational capitalist expansion under U.S. leadership
	Transnational capitalist				Same, with "trilateral" interlocking among national establishments and with Third World partners, satellites, and clients.	
	Total	630	15	60–70		
	Grand Total	4,212	100	100		

programs that had little or no effect in reducing family size. These programs, however, were doubly helpful to the richer people in the poor countries. In addition to getting better and more subsidized birth-control help for themselves, they have received ideological protection against any charge that it was they themselves, by exploiting and repressing the lower classes, who helped cause poverty among the wretched of the earth.

From the earliest days of the Third World's campaign for more aid, it was clear that trade and aid were closely connected. Better trading relations with the First World would be just as helpful as aid and, insofar as aid was directed toward increasing Third World exports, would bring such aid to successful fruition. But it soon became apparent that the terms of trade were often weighted against Third World countries, while First World tariffs and quotas would often deny the Third World access to the huge First World Markets. After years of agitation, the United Nations Conference on Trade and Development was established to help rectify matters through international agreements. A more effective means of changing the terms of trade was found in the early 1970s as the Organization of Petroleum Exporting Countries, OPEC, began to force steady increases in the price of petroleum. In 1974, shortly after OPEC's success in raising crude-oil prices, the president of Algeria, Colonel Houari Boumedienne, delivered a stirring address at the United Nations in which he asked all "Third World" countries to take control of their own resources and work together to change the international terms of trade in their favor. The result was a United Nations declaration calling for a "new international economic order" (NIEO) that would end the exploitation of the "Third World" by Western capitalism. A subsequent declaration by the UN General Assembly, by then often dominated by Third World countries, put it this way:

> The new international economic order should be founded on full respect for the following principles:
>
> —Full permanent sovereignty of every state over its natural resources and all economic activities . . .
>
> —Just and equitable relationship between the prices of raw materials, primary commodities, manufactured and semi-manufactured goods exported by developing countries and the prices of raw materials, primary commodities, manufactures, capital goods and equipment imported by them.[3]

The newness behind these euphemisms boils down mainly to two matters: Third World demands to nationalize foreign companies and to get higher prices for their exports while paying less for their imports. Neither of these demands are in themselves either socialist or Marxist-Leninist. For the most part they express the long-term interests of the richest native capitalists and those political leaders and feudal aristocrats who—like the Japanese rulers of a previous era—see public enterprise and enlarged trade as instruments in the transition to industrial capitalism. Nonetheless, these demands have usually won the enthusiastic support of both communists and socialists. The reasons for this, rarely stated in public, are important. For many anticapitalists, as for Marx, Engels, and Lenin in earlier periods of history, the growth of industrial capitalism, its technological capabilities, and its proletariat is a precondition for genuine socialism. Equally important, a major communist and socialist strategy in fighting imperialism or neocolonialism has long been to unite with native capitalists against foreign domination—even at the risk of building the power of the native capitalists who are then to be fought. And from a more global perspective, support for the NIEO can help play LDC capitalists against First World capitalists, thereby diminishing "Free World" unity. Both the Soviet Union and China, each in its own way, have tried to do this.

For First World capitalism, the sum total of these three demands represents a complicated challenge. The complication has been compounded by the growth of the nonaligned movement to include over ninety countries by the time of its Havana conference in 1979. Although many of its newer members include resolutely capitalist countries like Venezuela or right-wing dictatorships, as in Pakistan, communist Cuba and the new communist countries among the LDCs have played a major role in shifting the definition of "nonalignment" to anti-imperialism. It should be noted that the most outspoken conflict at the Havana conference was between two communist leaders: Castro of Cuba, who wanted more open acknowledgment of Soviet support for Third World demands, and Tito of Yugoslavia, whose political *raison d'être* had for thirty years been opposing Soviet interventon in the affairs of other communist countries. The resolution of the conflict, of course, was greater emphasis on struggles against imperialism. To the extent that this struggle is carried out more effectively, the result will be some further advances of communism and socialism and greater independence from First World hegemony on the part of the more vigorous regimes of Third World capitalism.

DETENTE: A COOLER COLD WAR

I am repeatedly amazed by the way in which the catchwords "cold war" and "détente" have served to confuse, rather than illuminate, the long history of capitalist-communist conflict. First of all, cold war was no invention of the 1950s. As Henry L. Roberts has pointed out, it has marked the major capitalist powers' relations with the Soviet Union ever since the early 1920s when hot intervention by American, British, French, and Japanese forces was ended.[4] At that moment the cold war was launched through Western arms and money for anti-bolshevik rebellions and covert sabotage, followed by protracted economic blockade. The Russians responded for a while by unsuccessful support for revolutionary movements in Europe and by more successful efforts to break the economic blockade. During World War II the cold war was put into cold storage, to be brought out again after the communist expansion in Eastern Europe and China. Détente—that is, the cooling down of the cold war—was originally a communist invention. Once in power, the leaders of every communist revolution—from Lenin to Ho Chi Minh, Mao Tse-tung, and Castro—wanted peace on their borders, freedom from subversion and sabotage, and a chance to import capitalist technology. The first formal calls for détente came after Stalin's death with Krushchev's suggestions for "peaceful coexistence" or "peaceful competition." These calls struck a responsive chord in the boardrooms of many large corporations—more in Western Europe than in the United States—which were more interested in profitable undertakings than in conformity with the cold war slogan "you can't do business with the communists." By the late 1960s, as the sources of dynamic growth in the "Free World" became weaker, more and more corporations began to explore the expanding communist markets. Many American corporations moved in to "leapfrog" their Western European competitors and associaates. This effort was buttressed by President Nixon's highly dramatized visits to Moscow and Peking, visits that despite the Vietnam War cast him in the role of world peacemaker and guaranteed his reelection in 1972.

As interpreted by Brezhnev on the Soviet side and Presidents Nixon, Ford, and Carter, détente has never meant an end to conflict or competition between capitalism and communism. Its essential element has been the avoiding of nuclear warfare, which would mean untold destruction for both the United States and the Soviet Union, as well as other countries. This is a mutual interest of vast importance. But it is not inconsistent with ideological conflict and reciprocal strategies of covert intervention, containment, rollback, or the use of business ventures, diplomatic offices, and cultural interchanges as covers for espionage. Nor is it inconsistent with economic, military, or technical assistance to various governments, movements, and parties throughout the world. In the real sense of the idea that détente is a two-way street, each side does all of these.

Who gains the most is a question that thus far can have no answer. Insofar as the avoidance of nuclear war is concerned, there is a sense in which the capitalist powers have more to gain. A third World War would unquestionably mean an end to capitalism. Although the survivors of such a war might well envy the dead, as Krushchev once said, I tend to agree with Mao Tse-tung's view that only communist or other thoroughly collectivist regimes of some type could possibly survive the wreckage of nuclear conflict. Also, in a paradoxical sense that would certainly be a surprise to either Marx or Lenin, the communist countries have come to the rescue of First World countries by supplying large new markets to supplement declining Free World demand. More efficient exploitation of these markets also provides opportunities for capitalizing on the many divisions in the communist world.

On the communist side, détente could be a decisive force for economic progress if it should be accompanied by reduced military expenditures. This would facilitate more rapid progress in overcoming shortages of consumer goods and moving toward the long-promised and long-postponed age of socialist abundance. Progress toward this goal would also be advanced by fuller access to capitalist technology. In a still larger sense, any cooling of the cold war renders less effective the formidable capitalist ideologies depicting communism as a totalitarian horror and socialism as the road to either communism or bureaucratic inefficiency and stultification. Finally, wherever capitalist-communist tensions lessen the greater the likelihood that First World unity—which came into being in a high-tension period—will be impaired.

INSTABILITY AT THE TOP

> I sometimes wonder what use there is in trying to protect the West against fancied external threats when the signs of disintegration within are so striking.
>
> GEORGE KENNAN [5]

During the more immediate aftermath of World War II the normal tensions among the world's major capitalist forces were contained both by the exigencies of internal reconstruction and by the vast business opportunities created by U.S. leadership in building multicontinental markets. Although some vigorous competition began to reappear among Western European countries, and between Japan and Western Europe, and resentment began to develop against American efforts to penetrate both, the competition and the resentment were powerfully contained by the dynamics of American hegemony in military power, trade, technology, and control of transnational institutions and world finance. Increasingly, this hegemony was symbolized less in America's surplus of atomic overkill and more in the "gold-dollar" system whereby for all members of the International Monetary Fund the U.S. dollar was "as good as gold."

Gradually, however, the tensions reasserted themselves. Western Germany and Japan both made huge advances in exports. British, Swiss, and Dutch multinational corporations picked up steam. With the United States giving major attention to military and space technologies, European and Japanese companies surged ahead impressively in many areas of civilian technology. With this resurgence of competition, the barriers to international trade and investment became somewhat higher. In many cases, the strengthening was directly aimed at reducing American dominance.

Paradoxically, America's financial dominance was reduced most significantly by American efforts to maintain military invincibility. During the 1960s the costs of "policing the free world" rose significantly, with American expenditures on the prolonged Vietnam War added to the "normal" expenditures on American military bases around the world and military aid to junior partners and client states. The foreign costs of this policing were met by a huge outflow of American dollars, which in due course converted Europe's postwar "dollar shortage" into a "dollar surplus." The central banks of Japan and Western European countries accumulated far more dollars than their countries or companies wanted to use. Under these circumstances the suspicion arose that the United States was getting real goods and services, plus ownership of industrial facilities in every European country, in exchange for pieces of green paper that were no longer "as good as gold." First France and then other countries started to cash in their paper for gold, thus contributing further to the shakiness of the dollar. By 1971, under the influence of rising imports and the disappearance of the U.S. trade surplus, the outflow of dollars—as measured in all the various indices on the balance of international payments—became enormous. Of such materials, the so-called "international monetary crisis" was born.

In formal terms, the essence of the crisis has been the replacement of controlled exchange rates by "floating currencies." This has meant the devaluation of the dollar, upward revaluation of other currencies (particularly the Japanese yen and the West German mark), a flight to gold that sent the price of gold up to hitherto unknown heights, and recurring speculative attacks upon the dethroned dollar by American transnationals and other wolfpack speculators in the First World. The American government's response to this crisis has been threefold: (1) to withdraw from Indochina and seek greater European armaments to supplement America's military burden in Europe; (2) to seek more foreign income by encouraging more foreign investment by American transnationals; and (3) to reestablish a surplus in foreign trade. Among the weapons in the last two of these steps have been a variety of protectionist measures—import charges, tariffs, preferential measures, quotas, etc.—that threaten the access of other capitalist countries to America's huge domestic markets. The power of these weapons has resided in the fact that for all First World competitors of the United States in the world trade struggle, access to the U.S. market is of vital importance. Beyond this, while no longer exercising financial, trade, or even technological supremacy, the U.S. lion is still the most powerful single force in the world market. A whole series of "Nixon shocks" have been given to many countries—particularly to Japan, whose government had been stubbornly resisting American efforts to buy into (let alone swallow up) Japanese firms or establish Japanese subsidiaries of American transnationals. In turn, other countries have responded with their own forms of protectionism wielded against the United States or each other. Although it would be farfetched, in my judgment, to assert that a full-fledged trade war has begun, there is no doubt that initial skirmishes have been fought. The possibility of sharper conflicts in the future clearly exists.

Moreover, along with détente—and to some extent as an objective factor supporting détente—an important change has been taking place in the composition of First World trade. This is highlighted in the following estimates from *The Wall Street Journal*: [6]

Regions of Europe	European Market Shares (by %)			
	1970		1990	
Capitalist				
Northwest	49		33	
South	6		12	
Total		55		45
Communist				
Soviet Union	32		39	
Eastern Europe	13		16	
Total		45		45

By these estimates, the communist sector of Europe is expected to attain by 1990 the 55 percent level of the capitalist sector in 1970. This means that capitalists in the Northwest countries (mainly West Germany, France, Britain, and Italy) would seek to expand their business in the growing markets of the Soviet Union and Eastern Europe. It also suggests greater market importance for the southern region (defined as Spain, Portugal, Greece, and Turkey), which is politically less stable than the North and more apt to move directly toward socialism, communism, or some intermediate stage presaging the replacement of capitalism at a later date. The future of Japan in the First World alliance raises even more complex questions. Suffering more than any other major capitalist country from the energy crisis, Japan can most easily find the oil it needs from the two neighboring communist giants, China and the Soviet Union. Beyond this, Japan is in a remarkably favorable situation not only to supply both with "advanced" technologies but also to exploit their gigantic markets. While this means competition with all First World countries, it may mean above all a loosening of ties with the United States and less dependence on American markets.

Thus, while the first postwar wave of communist and socialist expansion helped unify the First World, the more recent shrinkage of the capitalist world has tended to create internal tensions. It also promotes a wave of speculations about the future. Thus, without going along with Bell's funeral oration for the American Century, Mary Kaldor in *The Disintegrating West* places her bets on a complete breakup of the "Free World." She even goes so far as to suggest that Europe might be politically unified and that a European supergovernment could—as Germany, France, and England did in the past—be ready to go to war with other capitalist powers.[7] I think this is highly improbable. In any case, to approach such questions, I suggest, it is imperative to look again at the older crises of capitalism—world war, class conflict, and the business cycle—as they are reappearing in new forms. That is my task in the next chapter.

6

Old Crises in New Forms

> The calm is on the surface. Underneath, crisis-laden tendencies and contradictions not only continue to exist but to multiply and are sure to erupt into the open in the historically near future.
>
> PAUL M. SWEEZY [1]

BY THE END OF WORLD WAR II, the armed forces of America and Britain, with Russian help, smashed the Italian, German, and Japanese regimes of classic fascism. After the war, the leaders of America, Western Europe, and Japan made giant strides in coping with the business cycle, class conflict, war among capitalist powers, and the domestic threats of socialism and communism—that is, with the old crises of capitalism which were at the root of classic fascism.

Nowhere was morale higher than among Establishment economists in the United States. In protracted orgies of self-congratulation they praised their capabilities in fine-tuning the economy—some through fiscal policy, others by trying to control the money supply. By 1970, hailing the National Bureau of Economic Research for its diligence in collecting figures on economic fluctuations, Paul Samuelson joyously proclaimed that the bureau "had worked itself out of one of its first jobs, namely, the business cycle." [2] Most of Samuelson's less eminent colleagues supported his judgment that neither unemployment nor inflation presented serious dangers. Thus along with ideology and the American Century, the business cycle also was given a premature burial. In turn, the very idea of class conflict was beyond the pale of serious discussion. As for war, the ancient enmities among Western European nations subsided. And despite the cold war, fears of World War III slowly faded and military spending as a percent of the GNP began to decline.

Paul Sweezy, a neo-Marxist, was one of the first to see that old problems were boiling beneath the surface. Unlike more orthodox Marxists, often ready to predict the system's imminent collapse, Sweezy noted both the decline of the "New Left" of the 1960s and the new combination of "cyclical boom and secular stagnation." But no economists—liberal, radical, or conservative—were prepared for the more disconcerting events of the 1970s, particularly the full emergence of stagflation—the two-misery mixture of stagnation and inflation—and its interconnection with OPEC, the energy crisis, and war dangers in Western Asia. On their part, corporate and military leaders were better prepared respectively, for the threats of class conflict and nuclear war. Yet these preparations have in large part helped intensify the problems they were designed to solve.

By the beginning of the 1980s it became clear that a dangerous beast does not vanish when caged—nor a storm disappear when people find shelter, nor dynamite when defused. The return of old crises in new forms seemed to suggest that the cage door was being pried open, the shelters being slowly flooded, and the fuse in danger of being reignited. Thus the leaders of "free world" capitalism—in Western Europe, Japan, and Oceania as well as North America—now face challenges at home that add immeasurably to the perils of social fragmentation, eroded authority, and a shrinking capitalist world.

UNTAMED RECESSION

> No sane political figure is going to say a kind word for recession—but the universally avoided truth is that there is at present no better way to increase productivity in plants, to turn impulse buyers into careful shoppers at supermarkets, and to cut seriously into rising living costs.
>
> WILLIAM SAFIRE [3]

During the first thirty-five years after World War II, the United States witnessed eight minor economic contractions: two under Truman (beginning in 1946 and 1949), three under Eisenhower (1953, 1957, and 1960), one under Nixon (1970), one under Ford (1974), and one under Carter (1979–80). To explain their brief and relatively mild nature, people invented one new word and two new theories. The word was *recession,* which replaced *depression* and stressed the limited nature of the evil. The first theory was the Keynesian "fine tuning," through which professionally advised governments would manage fiscal and monetary affairs in such a way as to promote rising (albeit mildly undulating) total demand and avoid any serious decline in jobs and output. The attractiveness of the theory was based on much more than Lord Keynes, who was probably rolling over sadly in his grave as his name was bandied about by upstarts who selected from his writings a few things out of context. The neo-Keynesians also—for the most part—performed the service of understating the contributions to market demand of the Korean and Vietnamese wars. Their learned memos helped conceal the enormous expansion of labor reserves behind the official figures on unemployment and "labor force." Above all, they distracted attention from the large body of government and corporate policies rather finely tuned toward the accelerated accumulation of corporate capital through more full-bodied support for corporate profitability at home and abroad. All this helped inflate the egos and career opportunities of certified Keynesians.

By the early 1970s the reputation (but not the egos or job openings) of the Keynesians was punctured by recurring recession and continuing inflation. Into the vacuum rushed a new group of self-styled "post-Keynesians" who tried to shift attention from the "demand" side to the "supply" side. The supply-side policy advisers advocate action on such a variety of issues as productivity, capital formation, technology, labor supply, bottlenecks, and government regulation. Underlying this large menu, however, is a common theme that does not differentiate them too much from the pre-post Keynesians: namely, the promotion of corporate profitability. But like the Keynesians, most of them prefer to discuss surrogates of profits rather than coming into the open on a politically delicate subject. Only the true-blue conservatives wear the badge of capitalism on their foreheads and openly stress the role of profitability in accumulating capital and power.

Another common element uniting most Keynesians and post-Keynesians is the ridiculous but politically powerful idea that a recession coming at the time of a Nixon, Ford, or Carter administration is created by it. All that is needed, it is thereby hinted, is a smarter crowd in the White House. Only the Marxists and the dyed-in-the-wool conservatives accept the business cycle as alive and operating. Although Establishment leaders can spin this wheel faster or slower, they cannot justly be given the blame or credit for inventing it.

Corporate leaders, of course, take the cycle for granted and incorporate it into their longer-range plans, which often cover two, three, or more full cyclical swings. In so doing, I believe they often recognize one of the basic contradictions of capitalism, long ago noted by Karl Marx: *Trying to maximize profits tends to undermine profitability.*[4] This undesired (although sometimes anticipated) consequence takes place to the extent that ebullient profitmaking (1) undermines mass purchasing power, thereby lowering the capacity to consume relative to expanded productive capacity, (2) nurtures overexpansion in some areas and neglect of others, thereby creating bottlenecks, (3) provides opportunities for organized workers to raise some wages to the point where they squeeze some profits, or (4) nurtures speculative activities that cannot be maintained. Although competing theorists make a big to-do about one or the other of these, all these factors—and sometimes a few more—are usually at work at the same time.

Since economic downturns have long been regarded as inevitable as sleep or winter, it is only natural that the smartest capitalists long ago learned how to make a virtue of necessity by "riding the business cycle." A corporation did not have to be very smart to make money in boom periods. With depressions, a minority of ultra-clever operators long ago learned how to force competitors to the wall, pick up depression bargains in stocks, land, and companies, and put wages through the wringer. Since World War II, as deep depression was converted into moderate recession, this one-time cleverness became standard operating procedure. "It's not that we look favorably upon depressions or recessions," states Walter Grinder in *Business Week*. "It's just that they are necessary after a bout of antisocial overinvestment in capital, engendered by expansionary monetary policies."[5] Like sleep, recessions now tend to serve as a period of recuperation from, if not cure for, previous excesses. During this refreshing pause, plants are closed, unprofitable products dropped, and employees fired. As conditions for renewed profitability are created, the larger corporations move ahead with their long-range plans. If winter has come, can spring be far behind?

The answer is "perhaps." There is no dearth of new technologies in modern capitalism's vast technology reserve, nor any lack of new tricks whereby government can subsidize profits. But the new world environment is not as favorable as it used to be. The spread of communism, socialism, and crude-oil capitalism—as well as the instabilities in the First World—have created new difficulties for transnational expansion. Under these conditions a First World return to ebullient growth might require putting the majority of its home population through a tighter wringer than any capitalist establishment has thus far been able to operate.

THE HIDDEN UNEMPLOYED

The current definition of unemployment captures only the tip of the iceberg of potential workers; it is itself part of a grand cover-up of the shortage of jobs.

FRANK FURSTENBERG, JR.
AND CHARLES A. THRALL [6]

During a recession, many things—like GNP, income, profits, wages, or even oil imports—go down temporarily. But one thing goes up: unemployment. The height of these unpleasant upswings in various periods, as officially measured in the United States, has been reported like this:

PERCENTAGES OF "LABOR FORCE"

Prewar Depression		Postwar Recessions					
1933	1939	1949	1954	1958	1961	1971	1974
24.9	17.2	5.9	5.5	6.8	6.7	5.9	8.5

These reports are limited to those actively seeking work; they do not include the much larger number of unemployed people who are able and willing to work for pay but are not at the moment seeking jobs—some of them because they already know there are none to be found. Nonetheless, by some mysterious magic, these numbers—routinely publicized every month—have assumed great importance. In Establishment politics, the number of officially estimated job seekers has become enshrined as the measure of full employment. It is as though the number of unmarried men and women over 18—now around 50 million people—should be reduced to those who actively sought a mate during the last four weeks.

It was not always thus. During World War II, full employment was first defined as a shortage of labor—a situation when more employers were seeking workers than there were workers seeking jobs. Toward the end of the war, the Roosevelt administration set a full employment goal: 60 million peacetime jobs. With less attention to numbers, the original full-employment bills drafted in 1944 defined full employment in terms of Roosevelt's Economic Bill of Rights "the right to a useful and remunerative job in the industries or shops or farms or mines of the Nation." This right was to be guaranteed by federal action which, after promoting private employment, would provide "last resort jobs" for anyone the private sector could not or would not hire.

Thirty years later, through Rep. Augustus Hawkins and the Congresional Black Caucus, this principle was restated more strongly in the first versions of the Humphrey-Hawkins Full Employment and Balanced Growth Bill. In this measure full employment was defined as "a situation under which there are useful employment opportunities for all adult Americans willing and able to work." Once again, this desirable goal was to be attained by a government guarantee. In addition, as a guide for government planning, specific quantitative numbers were to be set forth every year for the total number of full-time and part-time jobs. Thus, if the legislation had been enacted in its original form, the full-employment goal for 1984 might be—for example—around 125 million jobs: perhaps 20 million full-time or part-time jobs that might not otherwise be available.

In both 1944 and 1974 the supporters of this far-reaching approach argued that it would go far toward reducing poverty and social tensions and would also assure business of stable markets and more stable profits. In both periods big business and conservative opponents opposed it on the ground that it would require more government intervention into economic affairs, which was undoubtedly correct. What really rubbed them the wrong way, however, was that this kind of intervention threatened the rate of profit by curtailing low-wage employment and creating conditions under which individual employees and unionized workers would have more bargaining power to increase wages, improve working conditions, or even enter the sacred precincts of managerial decision making.

Thus the idea of guaranteeing human rights was ruthlessly stricken from the bills finally enacted as the Employment Act of 1946 and the Full Employment and Balanced Growth Act of 1978. In place of human rights to useful paid employment came a whole series of ceremonial rites in which the operational definition of full employment soon became "whatever level of official unemployment is politically tolerable." Over the years this level constantly rose:

ESTABLISHMENT DEFINITIONS OF FULL EMPLOYMENT: UNEMPLOYMENT AS PERCENT OF LABOR FORCE

1940s	1950s	1960s	1970s	1980s
2–3%	2–4%	3–4.5%	4–5.5%	6–?%

The apologists for this continuing redefinition were quick with justifications. Many of the new job-seekers, they argued, were women seeking paid work outside the home, or young people with little or no work experience. Others were black, Hispanic, or members of other minorities. In contrast with prime-age, white males, these no-account people, they argued, should not be taken into account. Subtract them from today's overall figure of 6 or 7 percent and one gets right back to an old-time 3 to 4. The explanation, however, as distinct from the apologetics, is that the higher levels have thus far proved to be politically tolerable. Thus in many of the largest cities of the country official unemployment often reached 9, 10, or 11 percent without political explosions. One basic reason has been the growth of huge government transfer payments to the unemployed and the poor: unemployment compensation, public assistance, food stamps, rent subsidies, and training programs. These payments helped make unemployment tolerable both to business, by helping maintain market demand, and to the unemployed, by helping them get along at minimal levels of subsistence. Without this money, shopkeepers and landlords would have long ago protested the bite of recession, and the unemployed would have been loudly protesting, if not rioting, in the streets, banks, and government offices.

The handling of the transfers, moreover, often helped establish the idea that certain groups of people were not entitled to jobs. Thus the recipients of public assistance have been officially classified as "unemployable"—even though field surveys have proved that most mothers receiving "aid for dependent children" are able to work and would prefer decent jobs if they were available. Indeed, as Furstenberg and Thall have demonstrated, the official unemployment definition itself has helped bolster a "job rationing ideology" which helps indoctrinate older people, women, and younger people with the idea that they are not entitled to a job. This ideology is supported by the grim fact that in a job-scarcity anyone who gets or holds onto a job might feel that he or she is taking it away from someone else.

By massaging the official figures, one can learn a lot more about what different people can tolerate. Black job seekers in America usually outnumber others by two to one; their official unemployment rate is always at a serious recession level. For teenagers as a whole, the figure is much higher. For black and Hispanic teenagers it bursts the confines of recession and hits levels which, by any standard, are those of catastrophic depression.

When one goes beyond the officially reported job seekers, hard facts are harder to get, but the situation is obviously grimmer. Literally, countless millions of people are no longer looking for what experience has proved cannot be found; these are often termed "dropouts from the labor force." Some of them are older people with many years of work experience who are "pushed out" by the motto "No applications accepted from people over 40." Others—mainly women and minorities—are impeded by institutionalized bias; they are in fact "kept outs." A vague idea of how much all this adds up to is provided when a few job openings are advertised—whether for street cleaners, construction workers, or even assistant professors—and the applicants outnumber the openings by astronomical ratios. If ever directed to do so, the U.S. Employment Service could get a complete unemployment index covering everyone able and willing to work by simple expedient of advertising that such-and-such jobs were really available (part time as well as full time) for such-and-such types of people. This, of course, is what the government would have been obliged to do if either of the original full-employment bills of 1944 or 1974 had been enacted without prior castration. In the absence of such a job guarantee policy, a statistical estimator faces as much difficulty as getting an index on nasal congestion, middle-age loneliness, or teenage orgasm.

My own estimate is that the total number of people not working for pay but able and willing to work has generally been at least three times the number of reported job seekers—even between recessions. For 1978 that gives us a figure of about 18 million people. In recessions, of course, the number rises. If Karl Marx were alive today, he would call this "the relative surplus population" or "the reserve army of the unemployed." To this surplus, he would have to add the dependent family members of the unemployed, those who work for a while and then are laid off, those who suffer from permanent insecurity in their jobs, and those whose job insecurities are rooted in their provision of illegal services. But no matter how the surplus is estimated, I doubt whether he would still use the army metaphor. Here there are no commanding officers, no guiding strategy or tactics, no discipline—merely casualties, and most of these come from battle among the nonemployed over who will get a scarce job first or be fired last.

THE NEW INFLATION: HYENA'S DELIGHT

> There is neither system nor justice in the expropriation and redistribution of property resulting from inflation. A cynical "each man for himself" becomes the rule of life. But only the most powerful, the most resourceful and unscrupulous, the hyenas of economic life, can come through unscathed . . . Inflation is a tragedy that makes a whole people cynical, hardhearted and indifferent.
>
> THOMAS MANN [7]

> A spectre is haunting the major industrial nation of the free world . . . That spectre is the grim visage of inflation.
>
> GENE KORETZ [8]

Before World War II, inflation in capitalist societies tended to be violent and temporary. For wartime governments, inflation of the money supply was the quickest way to mobilize resources for war by taxing the masses. In Germany during the 1920s, as Franz Neumann has shown, the creation of runaway inflation "permitted unscrupulous entrepreneurs to build up giant economic empires at the expense of the middle and working classes." In other countries, unplanned speculative booms—whether in boom towns or times—facilitated the sudden growth of great fortunes in the hands of Thomas Mann's "economic hyenas." But sooner or later the inflationary bubbles always burst, with most prices falling sharply and the general price level drifting downwards before any "reflation." During any periods of actual contraction, business and government leaders sought ways and means of preventing prices from falling or "reflating" enough to encourage recovery.

After World War II, modern capitalism entered a new era of the sustained use of mildly inflationary stimulants. Among these were military expenditures, particularly those connected with the Korean and Vietnam wars. These, in turn, were major sources of federal deficits, which pumped additional purchasing power into the economy. The same support for demand was obtained by increasing civilian expenditures (favored by more of the liberals) and reducing taxes (favored by most conservatives). In either case the rising national debt became a valued source of direct profits by the banks holding government securities. Rapidly rising municipal and state debt, also an effective stimulant, became an invaluable form of tax evasion by the wealthy. Corporate debt rose still more rapidly. But the most massive debt increases have been in home mortgages, installment loans, and other forms of consumer credit; together they went rather far in filling the large gap between the actual income of the middle and lower classes and the incomes that would have been necessary to buy the goods and services that could be produced through the expanded productive capacity of private business.

During the first twenty-five years after World War II, except for a brief price splurge when war price controls were suddenly removed, all these measures never pushed prices up as high as 6 percent a year. Most Establishment leaders felt that mild price increases of 2 or 3 percent a year were a good tonic. In this sense, they were all inflationists—both the conservatives who inveighed against inflation and the liberals who regarded anti-inflation talk as an indirect attack on social spending, wage increases, and high employment.

But in the 1970s something new burst onto the scene. Before then, the rate of price increases had always slowed down during a recession. But in 1974–75 and again in 1979, the general price level misbehaved: *it rose during recession*. These figures show how:

Percent Changes from Previous Year	1974	1975	1979 (2nd quarter)
Decline in GNP, constant dollars	−1.4	−1.3	−2.3
Increase in GNP price measure	9.7	9.6	9.3
Increase in consumer prices	12.2	7.0	12–13 (est.)

Economic Indicators, December 1979

This misbehavior proved immensely embarrassing to all varieties of Establishment economists. "The economy is not working the way it's supposed to," they complained. Not being able to tame it, they tried to name it. One name was *slumpflation,* which hinted that after the slump was over ebullient growth would be restored. The name that has stuck—without yet entering the dictionaries—is *stagflation.* More realistically, this word suggests a stagnant economy in which, when recession passes, inflation will continue, and perhaps accelerate, but growth will be sluggish despite inflationary stimulants.

Most people in America—especially those whose heads have not been shrunken or brainwashed by immersion in Establishment economics—know intuitively that the new inflation is a *profit inflation.* They have seen the price of oil pushed up by OPEC, have cringed under the impact of rising prices for gasoline, heating oil, and natural gas, and have accurately sensed the fact that the American oil companies have worked hand in glove with OPEC and made huge profits from well-designed, well-exploited—and therefore real—shortages. They know that the burgeoning prices of food, medical care, and housing have similar roots, being nurtured by government policies to curtail agricultural output, put floors under prices, subsidize the doctor–drug-company–hospital complex, raise interest rates, and encourage land speculation.

The Establishment notables know all this. Indeed, they have a term for it—administered prices (or oligopolistic price setting)—which is not to be uttered in polite society. Publicly, they offer two explanations: demand pull and cost push. In discussing demand, they level their fire at the purchasing power created by wage increases, government's social programs, the federal deficit, and the money supply. They leave out the insatiable demand for profits by transnational corporations with long-term expansion plans they prefer to finance through the larger cash flows won by higher prices. They also tend to exclude the higher demand created by military spending and inflated consumer credit. They define the money supply in terms of current prices alone, studiously avoiding even the barest hint that during inflation the value of money goes down and that the *real* money supply contracts. In complaining about higher costs, they concentrate their fire on rising wages (which in real terms have been declining and by 1979 fell below those paid in West Germany, the Netherlands, Sweden, and Belgium) and falling labor productivity (which always falls when there is a decline in the volume of production). They carefully avoid the costs of capital embodied in higher profits, interest rates, and rents—and in the rising emoluments of the corporate overseers and executive managers.

While both of these explanations avoid direct attention to profits, the explainers are usually united in their less publicly expressed conviction that a central objective of public and private policy under capitalism should be the promotion of higher profits. This is very close to the historical driving force of industrial capitalism since its beginnings about two hundred years ago. But there is a difference: the growing ability of powerful sellers, usually with open or covert government support, to increase profits by raising prices and get away with it even when demand is falling. There is also a difficulty: *making more money by pushing prices up reduces the value of the money made.*[9] This adds an additional twist to the old contradiction that profit maximization tends to undermine profitability. It gives the producers of inflation an interest in trying to modulate the inflation they produce.

One way to do this is to put a lid on wages. This is done through wage-price policies that—in the words of an associate of President Nixon—"zap labor" while being soft on business. This is being done throughout the First World, not only in the United States. As a result, wage increases in general lag behind prices during stagflation, indirectly contributing to corporate profitability. When some militant and well-organized unions succeed in catching up with prices, or even getting a little ahead, the employers usually succeed in passing the additional labor costs on to the consumer in the form of higher prices. This usually accelerates the drive to squeeze wages still more in the unorganized sectors.

Another way to modulate inflation is to play the business cycle by bringing recession sooner and trying to make it a little deeper and longer. This is the celebrated "tradeoff" policy which, although sometimes disavowed, dominates the White House, corporate boardrooms, Wall Street, the OECD, and the International Monetary Fund. This policy rests on the long-observed fact that under present-day capitalism prices are pushed up when employment is high and an economy is racing along and that a truly serious economic decline will tend to push many, if not all, prices down. The policy dictates that recession and unemployment are the easiest way to prevent runaway inflation. Although this policy would require a deep depression to bring inflation down to the old-time levels of 2 to 4 percent a year, it does dampen inflationary surges a little. Accordingly, never have so many bankers, business leaders, and even sane political leaders said so many kind words for recession.

The kindest words of all come from the bankers who, with the help of the Federal Reserve Board, have been raising interest rates—that is, the prices they charge for credit. This is probably even more inflationary than raising the price of oil; higher interest rates enter into the costs of all economic activities relying on credit. One of the bankers' justifications is that they are merely adjusting to inflation. Yet the spread between the interest rates they pay and those they charge has steadily been increasing. Moreover, as the following figures show, as prices rose four times between 1945 and 1979, various interest rates rose by multiples of 12, 17 and 32:

Prices	1945	1979	Increase, in multiples
Consumer price index (1967 = 100)	51.3	227.5 (Nov.)	4.43
GNP price measure (1972 = 100)	37.92	167.2 (3rd Quart.)	4.41
Selected Interest Rates			
Federal Reserve Bank discount rate (N.Y.)	1.0	12 (Dec.)	12
Prime commercial paper, 4–6 months	.75	13.01 (Dec.)	17.34
3-month Treasury bills	.38	12.2 (Dec.)	32.1

Economic Report of the President, January 1979
Economic Indicators, December 1979

If rising interest rates and other factors should push inflation still higher, the hyenas of economic life—to use Thomas Mann's words—can come through unscathed. During the long-lived virulent inflation in Latin America, the First World's transnational corporations have long ago learned the mysterious arts of appreciating capital under conditions of depreciating currencies and massive unemployment. This capability can readily be transferred to the home country. And if the consequence—whether sought or unanticipated—is more unemployment, the side effect will be to enhance the hyenas' future profitability by dampening wage increases, undermining union power, and engulfing many islands of small-business competition.

"Sweet are the uses of adversity," says the Duke in Shakespeare's *As You Like It*, putting the best possible face on his misfortune in being banished to the Forest of Arden. In today's capitalist jungles the uses of adversity are still sweeter when other people, not the corporate elites, suffer the misfortunes of recession and inflation.

THE DYNAMITE OF CLASS CONFLICT

> In the United States resistance to work seems to reach acute proportions from capital's point of view.
>
> STEPHEN HYMER [10]

> Socialism Is No Longer a Dirty Word to Labor
>
> HEADLINE,
> *Business Week* [11]

Class conflicts since World War II would certainly have been more open, bitter, and prolonged if not for the successes of American-led capitalism in maintaining "First World" leadership, limiting war, moderating the business cycle, and achieving substantial economic growth through more efficient exploitation of people and resources on a global scale.

As it is, class conflict has tended to be submerged, unclear, and sporadic—indeed, even more under control than empire, war, or the business cycle. The greatly enlarged working classes have been divided into five different labor markets: capital intensive, labor intensive, public, nonprofit, and underclass. They are also divided along racial, religious, national, sectional, and regional lines. Since the nineteenth century conceptions of the working class can no longer be automatically applied to late twentieth-century realities, many observers seem to have concluded that the obvious absence of sharp class-consciousness means that there are no underlying class interests and, in fact, no working class at all. Many unions or union leaders see their role in narrow and parochial terms, with little or no interest in organizing all classes of workers, combating the many forms of exploitation outside wage-and-salary bargaining, or seeking any significant changes (other than securing their own positions at the junior and contingent level) in the Establishment. Outside the Marxian minority in America, Daniel P. Moynihan was one of the few people to point out—as he did at the time of the 1967 riots in Detroit—that class interests are still influential in America.

Nonetheless, the perception of exploitation exists. It is expressed in the popular language of complaint by blue-collar, white-collar, and technical workers who feel they have been "ripped off," "shafted," or "screwed" by employers, banks, landlords, supermarkets, and politicians. With more job insecurity, more inflation, more onerous taxation, more military adventurism, the resentment against ripoffs deepens. It reveals itself in many forms of alienation and resistance that are promptly seen by the more farsighted leaders of corporate capital as serious obstacles to efficient accumulation.

In the early nineteenth century organized workers often fought the domination of industrial capitalism's new machinery by wrecking the machines. The new Luddites in the modern working classes often fight mechanization by informal or formal efforts to prevent the introduction of labor-displacing machinery or work routines. In some industries this has been rather successful. In others, the unions have cooperated with corporate mechanization programs in return for somewhat higher positions for a privileged, well-protected, and declining union membership.

The most insidious form of resistance is simple individual withdrawal from efficient work. This withdrawal takes the form of tardiness, early leaving, prolonged coffee breaks, or lavatory visits. Still more serious are high—and often rising—rates of absenteeism and turnover. Thus Harry Braverman reports that "The Fiat Motor Company, Italy's largest private employer with more than 180,000 employees, 147,000 of whom are factory workers, [has] had 21,000 employees missing on a Monday and a daily average absenteeism of 14,000." [12] Throughout the 1970s these conditions became more acute in almost all First World countries. As for the United States, he reports: "At the Chrysler Corporation's Jefferson Avenue plant in Detroit, a daily average absentee rate of 6 percent was reported in mid-1971, and an annual overall turnover of almost 30 percent . . ." Many companies that have fared better than Chrysler in maintaining profitability have been plagued by equally serious absenteeism and turnover.

Somewhat less measurable are the many negative forms of slowdown or "featherbedding" on the job—although a 1972 Gallup poll reported that 57 percent of their respondents thought "they could produce more each day if they tried" and that this figure rose to 70 percent for professionals and businessmen and 72 percent for 18–29-year-olds. Still less measurable—and more disruptive—are such deliberate acts as defective work, pilfering, and sabotage.

The strike, or work stoppage, of course, is the most direct form of resistance to exploitation on the job, and the classic form of class conflict. But the outbreak of many strikes does not necessarily mean that class struggle is coming into the open. Strikes may be precipitated by *agents provocateurs* working for the employers, may be timed in such a way as to coincide with corporate desires to slow down production, or may be "won" by union leadership which then sells out its members. Successful strikes by workers in capital-intensive industries may provide employers with excuses for raising prices to levels that go far beyond what may be needed to cover increased labor costs and thereby impose new burdens of price exploitation on all workers. "Strikes conducted in the state sector by state workers," as James O'Connor points out, "lead either to increases in prices or higher taxes or to lower real wages for the tax-paying working class—or both . . . [They] therefore always hold a potential for dividing the working class . . ." [13]

Nonetheless, the strike threat is always taken seriously by the leaders of corporate capital—and, from their viewpoint, properly so. Despite the cooperative spirit of old-style union management, rank-and-file workers—particularly younger ones or those who come from agricultural backgrounds and have not yet been fully socialized into the acceptance of company or trade-union discipline—are often extremely aggressive. Throughout the First World, O'Connor reports, "there has been a noticeable shift from national, official and centrally directed and controlled strikes to short, local, unofficial slowdowns and strikes." In the state sector, moreover, union militancy—whether by official leadership or rank-and-file pressure—"clearly has the potential for radicalizing both state employees and their organization." This radicalization has even extended to police forces and the uniformed armed services themselves, the very instrumentalities of traditional control over radicals. Sometimes, these forms of resistance—although rooted in antagonism created by the Establishment—serve Establishment interests by being redirected against ethnic minorities, women, younger people, the unemployed, and other exploited people, including the clients or recipients of state services. As countervailing forces (and a threat to the upper levels of the Establishment), there are tendencies toward what O'Connor calls "the developing relationship between state workers and state dependents . . . between teachers, students, and office and maintenance personnel, between welfare workers and welfare recipients, between public health workers and people who use public health and medical facilities, and between transport workers and the public served by public transit."

But the largest steps toward more open and bitter class conflict in the United States have been taken by corporate leaders. In the South and the Southwest—particularly in textiles—they have fought bitterly against the spread of unionism. In the West, they have spared no efforts in preventing the unionization of agricultural workers. Throughout the country they have been successful in slowing down unionization drives among white-collar and service workers. Above all, they have gone in for union busting in a big way—even in areas where previously unions had been formally accepted by management.* In response, some of the most old-time and most conservative leaders of the American trade unions have been accusing corporate leaders of "waging class warfare."

In response to employers, proclaims the *Business Week* headline referred to earlier, "Unions That Used to Bait 'Commies' and 'Kooks' Now Join Forces with Socialists." More and more union leaders—particularly among the machinists, government employees, auto workers, textile workers, and steelworkers—publicly identify themselves as socialists. In 1979 the building trades workers, long regarded as the most conservative element in organized labor, took a full-page advertisement in the newsletter of the Democratic Socialist Organizing Committee. In one of his last public statements before resigning from leadership of the AFL-CIO, George Meany called for the nationalization of the oil industry if "the monopoly fails to adequately serve the public interest." Many more unions now call for government controls over prices (and other forms of income) and investment, and more worker participation in management decision making. Above all, militancy seems to be rising in union relations with employers. If stagflation continues to undercut real wages and working conditions, the class consciousness of employers may be met by more class cohesiveness among employees. In this way, the dynamite of class conflict may be ignited.

LIMITED WAR

> Every man, woman and child lives under a nuclear sword of Damocles, hanging by the slenderest of threads, capable of being cut at any moment by accident, miscalculation or madness.
>
> PRESIDENT JOHN F. KENNEDY,
> September 1961

During the so-called "Hundred Years' Peace" (1815–1914), all wars among the Great Powers were minor, short, or localized. General peace was preserved in an environment of unending limited war.

---

* I discuss this more fully in "The Friendly Fascist Establishment" (Chapter 9).

The period since 1945 has also been one of limited war. Whatever military action has taken place—whether in Korea, Indochina, the Middle East, Africa, or Latin America—has been geographically limited. Although the devastation has been ghastly, no nuclear weapons have been used.

But limited war has created a baffling problem for the leading capitalist powers, particularly the United States: A reduction in military stimulants to economic expansion and capital accumulation. The present condition of the American industrial establishment, writes David Bazelon, "is unthinkable without the benefit of the capacity-building expenditures of the past twenty years induced by war and preparedness measures."[14] The U.S. Arms Control and Disarmament Agency has thought about this in terms that are themselves unthinkable to most Establishment economists: "It is generally agreed that the great expanded public sector since World War II, resulting from heavy defense expenditures, has provided additional protection against depression, since this sector is not responsible to contraction in the private sector and has provided a sort of buffer or balance wheel in the economy."[15]

Strangely enough, the use of military-growth stimulants in the United States also served to stimulate growth in the two major capitalist societies with relatively small military budgets: Japan and West Germany. An important part of U.S. military expenditures spilled over into both Japan and West Germany in the form of both procurement of supplies and payments for the maintenance of U.S. installments. More indirectly, the U.S. concentration of war-related technology (which includes advanced computerization, communication systems, and electronic controls) gave the largest corporations in other leading countries of the "Free World," particularly Japan and West Germany, an opportunity to catch up with, or plunge ahead of, the United States in civilian technologies and thereby make spectacular advances in world trade.

As the United States began its slow withdrawal from Indochina in 1969, military expenditures began to level off and then—while prices for military goods were still rising—to fall by almost $4 billion from 1969 to 1972. As a proportion of total GNP, military spending fell even more drastically—from 9.1 percent in 1967 and 1968 to around 6 percent in 1979. Expenditures for "international affairs" (closely related to military expenditures) also declined. The size of the U.S. armed forces fell from over 3.5 million in 1968 to 2.1 million in 1979. In other words, the military slowdown under conditions of deescalation and détente deprived the American economy of a defense against recession that had been provided during the 1960s. This was one of the factors in the recessions that began in 1970, 1974, and 1979. In each case unemployment rose. In 1975, the total end to the hugely destructive war in Indochina was a retrogressive economic force, as unemployment in the United States and other capitalist countries rose to the highest levels since the Great Depression.

The response of the industrial-military portion of the Establishment has been prompt, publicly warning against the great perils of becoming weaker than the communist enemy and privately warning against the disastrous economic effects of the slowdown. The positive action has been in two directions: the expansion of new and costly weapons systems and the sale of arms to other countries. Under conditions of détente, however, the two of these together were insufficient to restore defense spending to the proportions of GNP reached during Indochinese wars. Thus the American industrial establishment was subjected to a slow withdrawal of the stimulus to which it had become accustomed. The NATO countries were subjected to a sharp decline in the vigor of the Soviet "threat," which was the official *raison d'être* for NATO's existence. The capitalist world was subjected for a while to the "threat" of a peaceful coexistence in which the economic stimulus of war and preparedness would no longer be available at the level to which it had become accustomed. With any decline in détente, of course, these conditions change.

UNLIMITED OVERKILL

The dominant logic of "Free World" militarism in a period of limited warfare has been slowly developing during the 1970s. If unlimited warfare is "dysfunctional," then two lines of operation are indicated.

The first has been to channel a larger portion of military resources into weapons systems produced by the largest military contractors, even though this means a dwindling number of people in the armed services. The result has been a continuous increase in "overkill" capabilities whose actual use would surely destroy capitalism itself, but whose production and deployment contribute to the maintenance of a capital accumulation. Overkill itself is matched by various forms of "overdelivery": globe-circling missiles in addition to bombers; multiple warheads on a single missile (MIRVs); launchings from roving submarines, ocean-floor emplacements and eventually satellite space stations; ocean explosions to produce *tsunamis* (tidal waves); antiballistic missiles that would themselves emit vast radiation dosages over the territory presumably defended; and, more recently, cruise missiles that could be launched from submarines, planes, or ships, fly at radar-eluding altitudes, and maneuver around defensive fire. Less publicized, and often excluded from official estimates of nuclear megatonnage, is the armory of "tactical" nuclear weapons. These include huge numbers of air-to-ground, ground-to-air, and ground-to-ground missiles, of which over seven-thousand are stationed in Europe for use by NATO forces. The average yield of these weapons, according to Robert McNamara as far back as 1964, was about 100 kilotons, about five times greater than the strength of Hiroshima's Little Boy. Moreover, considerable "progress" has been made in developing the biological, chemical, physiological, and nuclear instrumentalities that could offer the prospect, in the words of a high U.S. Navy official, of attaining "victory without shattering cities, industries and other physical assets." [16] The extent of this progress was revealed by the announcement in 1977 of the "neutron bomb" and its promotion for NATO use.

The second has been a massive escalation of arms sales and government-subsidized arms gifts to Third World countries. In the United States, this program—which represents a huge stimulus to American industry—reached $11.2 billion in fiscal year 1977, and then, under the Carter administration rose to $13.5 billion in fiscal 1979. This activity has been paralleled by similar arms exports from other "First World" countries. A large part of these exports has gone to the Middle East, thereby recycling "petrodollars" for such countries as Iran and Saudi Arabia. A considerable part of the U.S. exports, in contrast to those from most other First World countries, have gone to Israel, as well as to Third World regimes threatened by domestic upheaval. Moreover, a large number of countries have received indirect arms aid in the form of nuclear plants producing the plutonium that could be used for atomic bombs. This implies a widening nuclear capability that is bound to be translated into the wider stockpiling of nuclear weapons and the development of smaller-scale balances of nuclear terror as counterparts to the primary balance of nuclear terror existing between the United States and the Soviet Union. The logic for such counterparts has been vigorously set forth by Robert Tucker in an article in which he argues that "a nuclear balance between Israel and the major Arab states would have a stabilizing effect." [17] Without the help of Tucker's advice, similar "stabilizing balances" have already been developing between China and the Soviet Union and India and China; with the help of expanded export of arms and nucelar plants, they might well develop between many other much smaller nations. Back in 1969 Hasan Ozbekhan of the Systems Development Corporation predicted that "within the next 20 years all the main underdeveloped nations will be in possession of [nuclear] weapons, and of limited, but perhaps sufficient, delivery capabilities." [18] It now seems that Ozbekhan overestimated the time it would take; he also was not able in 1969 to predict more recent developments in the manufacture of "suitcase bombs," small nuclear weapons that could be "delivered" by simply leaving a suitcase in a building, a street, or a reservoir. Thus, by the late 1970s even more than in 1961, when President Kennedy used the quaintly old-fashioned "sword of Damocles" metaphor, men, women, and children in many parts of the world have lived under the threat of some kind of war—perhaps even of the colossal blasts, raging firestorms, and devastating radiation of nuclear war or the less-known evils of bacteriological warfare.

Moreover, since President Kennedy's warning, there have been many mini-accidents. Some of them have involved the leakage of nerve gas from proving grounds, storage tanks, or disposal facilities. Since 1958 there have been over sixteen American accidents with nuclear weapons. Known as *Broken Arrow*, these have involved fires, collisions, and crash landings of nuclear-equipped planes—as well as accidental release from bomb bays.[19] In the realm of accident prevention, several missile crewmen have been arrested on narcotics charges, including the use of LSD. Although no catastrophe has yet occurred, the "accidental explosion of one or more nuclear weapons in the next 10 years," as reported by a research team at Ohio State University, "is not improbable." [20] If this is the American record, it is reasonable to assume that similar mini-accidents —whether smaller or larger—have occurred in other countries also. Nor are miscalculations impossible. An accident may be seen as an act of sabotage or aggression. In the case of actual attack, the wrong country may be perceived as the attacker. Retaliatory strikes may go astray and hit at unintended spots. Tactical moves could logically ascend the escalation ladder and lead to all-out war as an involved series of rational moves and equally rational countermoves add up to collective madness.

The freedom from general warfare that the world has enjoyed since 1945 is sometimes attributed to the delicate balance of terror widely known as MAD, the acronym for Mutual Assured Destruction. Since this term was invented in the 1960s, the escalation of both the arms race and the arms trade has unquestionably moved from MAD to MADDER. The direction of this movement unquestionably suggests that some involved series of supposedly rational moves and equally rational countermoves might well add up before the century's end to the collective madness of MADDEST.

TWO

The Specter of Friendly Fascism

Cassandra:
Cry, Trojans, cry! lend me ten thousand eyes
And I will fill them with prophetic tears . . .
Troilus:
Cassandra's mad . . .

WILLIAM SHAKESPEARE,
Troilus and Cressida

Often do the spirits
Of great events stride on before the event
And in today already walks tomorrow.

JOHANN VON SCHILLER,
Wallenstein

7

The Unfolding Logic

> The logic of events is driving [the rulers of the Third World] toward more modern and more efficient forms of dictatorship and all modern dictatorships are bound to have fascist features to some extent.
>
> WALTER LAQUEUR [1]

HOW ARE THE LEADERS of the "Free World," the Golden International, and the U.S. Establishment responding to the challenges that face them?

If one looks at any particular area, the prompt reply may be: "With cautious confusion." When one looks at this or that part of the U.S. Establishment, one can see reactionaries trying to "turn back the clock of history," conservatives who seem to favor the status quo and liberals who seek some system-strengthening reforms.

But as I survey the entire panorama of contending forces, I can readily detect something more important: *the outline of a powerful logic of events.* This logic points toward tighter integration of every First World Establishment. In the United States it points toward more concentrated, unscrupulous, repressive, and militaristic control by a Big Business-Big Government partnership that—to preserve the privileges of the ultra-rich, the corporate overseers, and the brass in the military and civilian order—squelches the rights and liberties of other people both at home and abroad. That is friendly fascism.

There is, of course, no master plan, no coordinated conspiracy. There is no predestined path, leading step by step to a sudden seizure of power by friendly fascists. I emphasize these points, if only because it is easy for a confusion to arise. By trying to make my *analysis* systematic and explicit, I may give the impression that the *reality* will be equally systematic and explicit.

On the contrary, the powerful leaders of the capitalist world have no single secret flight plan. In fact, the major navigators are in constant dispute among themselves about both the direction and the speed of flight, while their most redoubtable experts display their expertise by nitpicking at each other over an infinity of potentially significant details.

At any particular moment First World leaders may respond to crisis like people in a crowded night club when smoke and flames suddenly billow forth. They do not set up a committee to plan their response. Neither do they act in a random or haphazard fashion. Rather, the logic of the situation prevails. Everyone runs to where they think the exits are. In the ensuing melee some may be trampled to death. Those who know where the exits really are, who are most favorably situated, and have the most strength will save themselves.

Thus it was in Italy, Japan, and Germany when the classic fascists came to power. The crisis of depression, inflation, and class conflict provided an ideal opportunity for the cartels, warmongers, right-wing extremists, and rowdy street fighters to rush toward power. The fascist response was not worked out by some central cabal of secret conspirators. Nor was it a random or accidental development. The dominant logic of the situation prevailed.

Thus too it was after World War II. Neither First World unity nor the Golden International was the product of any central planners in the banking, industrial, political, or military community. Indeed, there was then—as there still is—considerable conflict among competing groups at the pinnacle of the major capitalist establishments. But there was a broad unfolding logic about the way these conflicts were adjusted and the "Free World" empire came into being. This logic involved hundreds of separate plans and planning committees—some highly visible, some less so, some secret. It encompassed the values and pressures of reactionaries, conservatives, and liberals. In some cases, it was a logic of response to anticapitalist movements and offensives that forced them into certain measures—like the expanded welfare state—which helped themselves despite themselves.

Although the friendly fascists are subversive elements, they rarely see themselves as such. Some are merely out to make money under conditions of stagflation. Some are merely concerned with keeping or expanding their power and privileges. Many use the rhetoric of freedom, liberty, democracy, human values, or even human rights. In pursuing their mutual interests through a new coalition of concentrated oligarchic power, people may be hurt—whether through pollution, shortages, unemployment, inflation, or war. But that is not part of their central purpose. It is the product of invisible hands that are not theirs.

For every dominant logic, there is an alternative or subordinate logic. Indeed, a dominant logic may even contribute to its own undoing. This has certainly been the case with many strong anticommunist drives —as in both China and Indochina—that tended to accelerate the triumph of communism. If friendly fascism emerges on a full scale in the United

States, or even if the tendencies in that direction become still stronger, countervailing forces may here too be created. Thus may the unfolding logic of friendly fascism—to borrow a term from Marx—sow the seeds of its destruction or prevention. But before turning to this more hopeful subject in Part Three, it is first imperative to look carefully at the unfolding logic itself.

MAKING THE MOST OF CRISES

> The symbol for "crisis" in Chinese is made up of two characters whose meanings are "danger" and "opportunity." To me, that precisely describes the present situation.
>
> JOHN D. ROCKEFELLER III [2]

A few years before his death, John D. Rockefeller III glimpsed—although through a glass darkly—the logic of capitalist response to crisis. In *The Second American Revolution* (1973) he defined the crises of the 1960s and early 1970s as a humanistic revolution based mainly on the black and student "revolts," women's liberation, consumerism, environmentalism, and the yearnings for nonmaterialistic values. He saw these crises as an opportunity to develop a *humanistic* capitalism. If the Establishment should repress these humanistic urges, he wrote, "the result could be chaos and anarchy, or it could be authoritarianism, either of a despotic mold or the 'friendly fascism' described by urban affairs professor Bertram Gross."

Before his book was completed, one of Rockefeller's consultants visited with me at Hunter College. We discussed tendencies toward friendly fascism, not humanistic capitalism.* I made my case that friendly fascism would be a despotic order backed up by naked coercion as well as sophisticated manipulation. Above all, I warned that the various crises in American society provided opportunities for Establishment leaders to do things that would accelerate—often unintentionally—the tendencies toward a repressive corporate society. This warning was not reflected in Rockefeller's book.

The better schools of business management train their students not merely to adapt to the stresses of corporate life but to anticipate challenges before they materialize. The best ones stress the shaping of the crises that may open up new horizons. In national politics, crisis management and crisis exploitation have become well-established modes of leadership.

---

* In "The Democratic Logic in Action," (chapter 20) I discuss the possibility of humanistic capitalism, but in terms that are quite different from Rockefeller's.

At the higher levels of transnational capitalism, therefore, it is only logical for many corporate and political leaders to respond to challenges by creative efforts to perfect their accumulation of capital and privilege.

If *you* were a billionaire, a corporate overseer, or a top executive and dedicated entirely toward advancing your own interests and those of your family members and associates, how would you respond to specific crises of the kind outlined in the previous three chapters? If *you* were a behind-the-scenes adviser to one of the above, what would you propose? I can answer this question by simply observing the behavior (not the public pronouncements) of Establishment notables as they try to make a virtue of necessity or enjoy the sweet adversity of other people's misfortunes. But one can get almost identical answers to putting one's self in their position. Performed as a mental exercise (however unpleasant), the logical result of this is a series of general recipes like the following.

Responding to the Side Effects of Success. Consider a certain amount of frustration as contributing to a stabilizing cynicism and apathy. Nonetheless, tone down overly high aspirations, especially among the lower levels of the Establishment. In turn, provide for tighter integration and higher expectations at the Establishment's top levels. Publicly lament restlessness, family breakdown, alienation, and other forms of social fragmentation. But recognize that these powerful tendencies deepen the apathy that represents mass consent to governance by the Establishment's upper levels. Remedy any resulting absenteeism, turnover, and low productivity with human relations programs conveying a sense of employee "participation." Resist regulations that shift to the polluters and makers the cost of antipollution and consumer protection measures; instead, use pressures for protecting people and nature as an excuse for higher prices and more public subsidy. Respond to crime and corruption by expanding "law and order" drives against street-level and middle-level lawbreaking. Direct attention away from the crimes of corporate and government elites; sanitize these activities by legislative and judicial action exempting the elites from scrutiny and prosecution. If necessary, substitute coercion and new forms of authoritarianism for declining public confidence in the authority of leaders, institutions and doctrines.

Responding to the Challenge of a Shrinking Capitalist World. Try to prevent formation of new socialist or communist regimes, overthrow those that are formed, and do profitable business with those that cannot be overthrown. Extend efforts to absorb communist regimes into the world capitalist economy. Undertake the delicate task of absorbing the new crude-oil capitalists and the more powerful Third World regimes into the middle levels of the Golden International. Try to integrate the strategies and policies of the governments and larger corporations of the Trilateral World and the many international agencies that serve them, particularly the World Bank and the International Monetary Fund.

Responding to New Forms of the Old Crises. In the name of "full employment," job creation, and "supply side" economics, promote new forms of open or hidden payments to big business. In the name of combating inflation, cut social expenditures and promote recessions that lower real wages and weaken labor unions. Hold forth the promise of greater profitability in the future. Dampen class conflicts by sharing the spoils of Third World exploitation with parts of the home population. If exploitation of the Third World is less successful, resort to firmer treatment at home. In either case, "divide and conquer" by co-opting the leaders of potential opposition and nurturing class fragmentation and ethnic conflicts. Try to keep actual warfare limited to small geographical areas and non-nuclear weapons. While calling for a balanced budget, expand arms exports (including the nuclear power plants that enable the proliferation of nuclear war capabilities) and the stockpiling of overkill while striving for "first strike" superiority. Reap the benefits from arms production as a factor in overcoming economic stagnation and a guarantee of profitable growth in the industrial-scientific-military complex. Seek larger armed forces, draft registration and conscription as instruments of military intervention, relief of unemployment, and promotion of militarist discipline in society.

CONSOLIDATING POWER

> *Lippmann:* The breakdown of forms of authority is a much deeper and wider process in modern history than the Vietnam War . . . The destruction of that threatens to produce the chaos of modern times.
>
> *Steel:* You see this as leading to authoritarianism or fascism?
>
> *Lippmann:* It's absolutely one of the things that will occur . . .
>
> RONALD STEEL [3]

Back during the early days of World War I, Robert Michels, the German sociologist who later supported Mussolini's fascism, formulated his famous "iron law of oligarchy." [4] As any organization grows, he held, the more dominant force will be a small minority at the top. Today's crises and future threats, genuine or conjured, only promise to accelerate what—in deference to the superior technologies of the present—might be renamed the "steel and plastic law of oligarchy." The word "law," of course, is always deceptive. It promises a regularity, a uniformity, an inescapability, which I do not accept. Even within the logic of the passage to friendly fascism there is room for surprises, reverses, and variations.

Behind all the varied and conflicting responses to different crises, however, there is a broad and almost all-encompassing unity: the effort to consolidate oligarchic power. A new round of miraculous exploits would be incompatible with too much conflict, chaos, or anarchy within or among the national Establishments. These Establishments must be reshaped and redeployed. This is what President Nixon had in mind when he told C. L. Sulzberger that the trouble with the country was the weakness and division among "the leaders of industry, the bankers, the newspapers . . . The people as a whole can be led back to some kind of consensus if only the leaders can take hold of themselves."[5]

This, of course, is the fundamental insight underlying the creation and the operations of the Trilateral Commission. Where this logic is heading is suggested in *The Crisis of Democracy*, a sophisticated call for oligarchic integration. This study was prepared for the commission by three social scientists. Samuel Huntington of the United States finds a "democratic distemper" in the United States caused by an upsurge of egalitarian values and an "excess of democracy." Michel Crozier of France holds that "European political systems are overloaded with participants and demands," while the Communist parties of the area "are the only institution left in Western Europe where authority is not questioned . . ." Joji Watanuki of Japan finds that "in comparison with the United States, where the 'democratic surge' can be regarded as already having passed the peak, in Japan there is no sign of decline in the increasing tide of popular demands, while at the same time the financial resources of the government are showing signs of stagnation." Together, the three seem to agree that "the principal strains on the governability of democracy may be receding in the United States, cresting in Europe, and pending in the future for Japan." Huntington argues that the challenge of communist threats, inflation, unemployment, commodity shortages, and frustrated aspirations can best be met by *less,* not *more,* democracy. "Democracy will have a longer life," suggests Huntington, "if it has a more balanced existence."[6] The essence of such balance is to respond to the erosion of authority by more authoritarian government.

This unusual bluntness, as Alan Wolfe points out, shattered "a taboo of American society, which is that no matter how much one may detest democracy, one should never violate its rhetoric in public."[7] As a result, when the report was formally discussed at a Trilateral Commission conference at Kyoto, Japan, in May 1975, various commission members denounced the report as too pessimistic. While some of this disagreement may have been for the public record only, some of it undoubtedly reflected the sincere attachment of old-fashioned conservatives to the liberal proprieties. Also, some top- and middle-level members of First World establishments may have trembled at what might happen to them with a tightening of oligarchic concentration and control. Even the dissenters, however, did not contradict the trilateral report's assumption of a need for greater consolidation and coordination within and among national establishments.

To discard the remaining liberal checks on growing oligarchies may be a difficult and heart-rending decision for many such individuals. It may be facilitated by a deepened sense of impending threats to the system, like those that appeared to loom up during the 1960s. Writing in the *National Review* toward the end of that decade, Donald Zoll provided an example of the possible rationalizations. Responding to the turmoil of the antiwar and civil rights movements, Zoll argued in a spirit of rueful advocacy that in the face of truly serious crisis, conservatives must consider *expediential fascism*. They should contemplate abandoning the "traditional rules of the game" by "candidly facing the necessity of employing techniques generally ignored or rejected by contemporary Western conservatives." He therefore urged "political approaches that are totalitarian in nature [though] not quite in the original fascist sense that puts all aspects of life under political authority, at least in the general sense that political theory can no longer restrict itself to general conditions and procedural rules." His alternative to "totalitarian radicalism" would be a totalitarian conservatism uninhibited by "liberal proprieties as to method." Zoll confessed that this "might imply common cause with the Radical Right or even some form of expediential fascism—hardly an appealing association." [8] But if the alternative to expediential fascism is to "let America die," then—according to Zoll's logic—better fascist than dead.

A similar note of urgency is trumpeted by General Maxwell Taylor who, in contrast with Zoll's response to internal dangers, warns mainly against external dangers. "How can a democracy such as ours," he asks, "defend its interests at acceptable costs and continue to enjoy the freedom of speech and behavior to which we are accustomed in time of peace?" Although his answer is not as candid as Zoll's, he replies that such traditional and liberal properties must be dispensed with: "We must advance concurrently on both foreign and domestic fronts by means of *integrated national power responsive to a unified national will*" [9] (my italics). Here is a distressing echo of Adolf Hilter's pleas for "integration" (*Gleichschaltung*) and unified national will.

THE CAT FEET OF TYRANNY

> I believe there are more instances of the abridgement of the freedom of the people by gradual and silent encroachments of those in power than by violent and sudden usurpations.
>
> JAMES MADISON [10]

It is hard to grasp the unfolding logic of modern capitalism if one's head is addled by nightmares of spectacular seizures of power. The combined influence of institutional rigidities, traditional concepts of constitutional democracy, and rifts among powerful elites is so great that friendly fascism could hardly emerge other than by gradual and silent encroachments. Like the tyranny referred to in a *New York Times* editorial, it "can come silently, slowly, like fog creeping in 'on little cat feet.'"[11] Many of the most important changes would be subtle shifts imperceptible to the majority of the population. Even those most alert to the dangers would be able to see clearly, and document neatly, only a few of these changes. Indeed, some important social and economic innovations in manipulation or exploitation (coming in response to liberal or radical demands) might well be hailed as "progress." In other cases, dramatic exposure, attack, and hullabaloo could have smokescreen consequences, blurring and sidetracking any effort to uncover root evils.

Hence I deliberately avoid the high-charged attention-attracting drama of predicting the decade, year or circumstances of a sudden seizure of power by the friendly fascists. Like Oliver Wendell Holmes, I have almost no faith in "sudden ruin." Although friendly fascism would mean total ruin of the American dream, it could hardly come suddenly—let alone in any precisely predictable year. This is one of the reasons I cannot go along with the old-fashioned Marxist picture of capitalism or imperialism dropping the fig leaf or the mask. This imagery suggests a process not much longer than a striptease. It reinforces the apocalyptic vision of a quick collapse of capitalist democracy—whether "not with a bang but a whimper," as T. S. Eliot put it, or with "dancing to a frenzied drum" as in the words of William Butler Yeats. In my judgment, rather, one of the greatest dangers is the slow process through which friendly fascism would come into being. For a large part of the population the changes would be unnoticed. Even those most alive to the danger may see only part of the picture—until it is too late. For most people, as with historians and social scientists, 20–20 vision on fundamental change comes only with hindsight. And by that time, with the evidence at last clearly visible, the new serfdom might have long since arrived.

MANY PATHS

When the experts of the Rand Corporation or the Hudson Institute prepare step-by-step scripts for future events, the effect is to heighten the drama—and perhaps the saleability—of their work. But the single-track scenario is a highly misleading device. It violently oversimplifies the immense complexity of historical change. It obscures the vast possibilities for accident, spontaneity, and the unpredictable conjuncture of simultaneous action on many apparently different fronts. The logic of events cannot be explained by any simple-minded syllogism or simplistic assumption of unified action along one clear path.

It would be easier to grasp the unfolding logic of modern capitalism if the most powerful leaders in capitalist society could readily agree on the flight plan toward a still more perfect capitalism. As it is, the major navigators are in constant dispute among themselves about both the direction and speed of flight, while their most redoubtable experts prove their expertise by nitpicking at each other on an infinity of potentially significant details. Besides, with weather conditions often turbulent and changing, forward motion sometimes creates more turbulence, and these are situations in which delays or even crashes may occur. Thus, in the movement toward friendly fascism, any sudden forward thrust at one level could be followed by a consolidating pause or temporary withdrawal at another level. Every step toward greater repression might be accompanied by some superficial reform, every expansionist step abroad by some new payoff at home, every well-publicized shocker (like the massacres at Jackson State, Kent State, and Attica, the Watergate scandals or the revelations of illegal deals by the FBI or CIA) by other steps of less visibility but equal or possibly greater significance, such as large welfare payments to multinational banks and industrial conglomerates. At all stages the fundamental directions of change would be obscured by a series of Hobson's choices, of public issues defined in terms of clear-cut crossroads—one leading to the frying pan and the other to the fire. Opportunities would thus be provided for learned debate and earnest conflict over the choice among alternative roads to serfdom . . .

The unifying element in this unfolding logic is the capital-accumulation imperative of the world's leading capitalist forces, creatively adjusted to meet the challenges of the many crises I have outlined. This is quite different from the catch-up imperatives of the Italian, German, and Japanese leaders after World War I. Nor would its working out necessarily require a charismatic dictator, one-party rule, glorification of the State, dissolution of legislatures, termination of multiparty elections, ultranationalism, or attacks on rationality.

As illustrated in the following oversimplified outline, which also points up the difference between classic fascism and friendly fascism, the following eight chapters summarize the many levels of change at which the trends toward friendly fascism are already visible.

Despite the sharp differences from classic fascism, there are also some basic similarities. In each, a powerful oligarchy operates outside of, as well as through, the state. Each subverts constitutional government. Each suppresses rising demands for wider participation in decision making, the enforcement and enlargement of human rights, and genuine democracy. Each uses informational control and ideological flimflam to get lower- and middle-class support for plans to expand the capital and power of the oligarchy and provide suitable rewards for political, professional, scientific, and cultural supporters.

A major difference is that under friendly fascism Big Government would do less pillaging *of*, and more pillaging *for*, Big Business. With

CLASSIC FASCISM	FRIENDLY FASCISM, U.S.A.
Drives by capitalist laggards to build new empires at the expense of leading capitalist powers.	Drive to maintain unity of Free World empire, contain or absorb communist regimes, or else retreat to Fortress America.
A tight Government-Big Business oligarchy with charismatic dictator or figurehead, and expansionist, scapegoating, and nationalistic ideologies.	An integrated Big Business- Big Government power structure with new technocratic ideologies and more advanced arts of ruling and fooling the public.
Liquidation or minimization of multiparty conflict and open subversion, with little use of democratic machinery and human rights.	Subtle subversion, through manipulative use and control of democratic machinery, parties, and human rights.
Negative sanctions through ruthless, widespread, and high-cost terror; direct action against selected scapegoats.	Direct terror applied through low-level violence and professionalized, low-cost escalation, with indirect terror through ethnic conflicts, multiple scapegoats, and organized disorder.
Ceaseless propaganda, backed up by spies and informers, to consolidate elite support and mobilize masses.	Informational offensives backed by high-technology monitoring, to manage minds of elites and immobilize masses.
Widespread benefits through more jobs, stabilized prices, domestic spoils, foreign booty, and upward mobility for the most faithful.	Rationed rewards of power and money for elites, extended professionalism, accelerated consumerism for some, and social services conditional on the recipients' good behavior.
Anxiety relief through participatory spectacles, mass action, and genuine bloodletting.	More varied relief through sex, drugs, madness, and cults, as well as alcoholism, gambling, sports, and ultraviolent drama.
Internal viability based on sustained, frantic, and eventually self-destructive expansion.	Internal viability based on careful expansion, system-strengthening reforms, multilevel co-optation, and mass apathy.

much more integration than ever before among transnational corporations, Big Business would run less risk of control by any one state and enjoy more subservience by many states. In turn, stronger government support of transnational corporations, such as the large group of American companies with major holdings in South Africa, requires the active fostering of all latent conflicts among those segments of the American population that may object to this kind of foreign venture. It requires an Establishment with lower levels so extensive that few people or groups can attain significant power outside it, so flexible that many (perhaps most) dissenters and would-be revolutionaries can be incorporated within it. Above all, friendly fascism in any First World country today would use sophisticated control technologies far beyond the ken of the classic fascists.

While the term "friendly" is useful (indeed invaluable) in distinguishing between the old-fashioned and the modern forms of repressive Big Business-Big Government partnerships, the word should not be stretched too far. The total picture provided by the following eight chapters may be thought of as a cinematic holograph of horror—all the more horrifying if the reader finds himself or herself entranced, if not captured, by its compelling logic.

Despite my emphasis on the United States, this unfolding logic is not strictly American. It may be discerned in the other "Trilateral" countries (Canada, Western Europe, and Japan) and in the closely related capitalist societies of South Africa, Australia, New Zealand, and Israel. In all the more developed capitalist societies, corporate oligarchies tend to transcend the nation-state, while in the less developed ones—often with the rhetoric of socialism—State control plays a more decisive role in fostering the growth of big capital and its entry into the larger world of the Golden International. Moreover, the emergence of neofascism in the First World will often continue to be blurred by denunciation of old-style autocracies and military dictatorships as "fascist" in accordance with the colloquial identification of fascism with simple brutality or oppression. Often, the germ of truth in such denunciations is that under dependent fascism old-style dictatorship may often serve to nurture the growth of big capital. On the other hand, when genuine neofascism emerges it may be associated with a relaxation of crude terror and the maturation of more sophisticated, effective, and ruthless controls.

A major factor, of course, is the historic pattern of relationships within the big-business community and between big business and government. Thus, in Japan, the logic of oligarchic integration in response to economic adversity is much more compelling and feasible than in the United States—so much so that many American business leaders look longingly at the pattern of what they like to call "Japan, Inc." On the other hand, it is distinctly possible that the Japanese may plunge far ahead of the Americans in the creation of a tighter power structure. In Japan, *Business*

Week has reported, "vast empires are growing, embracing scores of companies in a dozen or more businesses, each company nominally independent, but with increasingly centralized management, and often bound together by ties that go back a century to the original zaibatsu. . . . All the groups are drawing more tightly together today in the face of economic diversity—consolidating resources and integrating management." [12] Similar tendencies may also be found in Germany; there the resurgence of Nazi-style parties, fashions, and cults must also be taken into consideration. The United States, in turn, may outpace all the others in exploiting ethnic conflicts and organized disorder. Also, big capital in America, already more transnational than the Japanese, has a flying head start in making the leap towards an international capitalist Establishment with de-Americanized Americans as the first among the senior partners. This possibility is underscored by the Americans' low-key leadership through the Trilateral Commission in articulating—as Richard Falk has put it—the "general recognition by the elites in the most powerful states that there is an emergent crisis of unprecedented proportions that involves, in particular, the capacity of capitalism to adapt to the future." Americans on the commission have vigorously insisted "that national governments are not necessarily capable on their own of working out the adaptations that are necessary to sustain the existing elites in power in these three centers of global wealth." Thus, as Falk has explained, the Trilateral Commission operates "as a geo-economic search for a managerial formula that will keep this concentration of wealth intact, given its nonterritorial character and in the light of the multiple challenges to it." [13]

As an American traces the many paths to friendly fascism, he or she may find—as Theodore Draper did in commenting on my first article on the subject many years ago—an "uncanny resemblance to present-day America." [14] Those from Canada, Japan or Western Europe may find distressing similarities with their own countries. The reason is that I offer facts on a present "in which already walks tomorrow" and judgments concerning a possible future clearly suggested by present trends.

In so doing, I may have underestimated the evils of friendly fascism and overstated the present facts and tendencies relating to America's world orientation, establishment, informational management, rewards and punishments, and modes of system maintenance. These are empirical questions; I stand ready to be corrected by any superior presentation of the indicators. Also subject to an empirical challenge is my analysis in the following eight chapters of the various paths toward repression and exploitation by a new corporate society. Speculation and conjecture have their place, of course, and I have used both. But so do informed judgments on demonstrable—albeit controversial—indicators and trends. I should be more than delighted if someone can demonstrate that there is little or no motion along any or most of the paths through which I trace the unfolding logic of friendly fascism.

8

Trilateral Empire or Fortress America?

THE UNFOLDING LOGIC of friendly fascism is reasonably clear. But the specific manner in which it takes place will be greatly affected by the changing nature of the Golden International.

Indeed, the future of the Golden International itself may prove open to serious question. Not only have the crises and traumas of Western capitalism, old and new, created considerable uncertainty; the outlook is further clouded by obscure conflicts within the ruling circles of the major powers—and among the various movements that challenge the capitalist empire. These uncertainties suggest that even the most logical policies may often give rise to totally unintended consequences.

Nonetheless, I see two broad alternatives: (1) a breakup of the "Free World" empire or (2) its reconstruction in more mature form. During the 1970s it was possible to see tendencies in both directions at once. This apparently contradictory situation takes each tendency out of the realm of pure speculation. It suggests that either may be a viable alternative under circumstances that may arise.

As for the 1980s, the two tendencies will continue to coexist for a while. But either could become dominant. My own judgment is that the latter is more likely. Indeed, any contraction of world capitalism (unless it becomes cataclysmic) would seem to reinforce transnational integration and the resilience of the Golden International—exactly as the loss of Eastern Europe and China after World War II was a factor in the birth of the "Free World" itself. Remodeled under pressure, the "Free World" might then, conceivably, be capable of reexpansion, effectively absorbing various communist regimes back into the capitalist world order.

AMERICAN RETRENCHMENT

> Dr. Kissinger has, of course, been wringing his hands at the prospect of a Marxist take-over of Europe . . . His nightmare scenario envisions a European domino effect, with one country aping another, with cuts in military budgets, with participation in

NATO a mockery, until the United States, disgusted, distrustful, disillusioned, withdraws to "Fortress America" leaving Europe to the Russians.

VICTOR ZORZA [1]

The relation between anticapitalist advance and intercapitalist conflict is a splendid example of circular causation.

On the one hand, communist or socialist advance promotes various conflicts among the major capitalist countries. When a communist or semicommunist regime is established, the political and corporate leaders of various First World countries compete with each other in the effort to establish themselves in the communist markets. This undermines the unity of those very First World efforts to undermine or overthrow new anticapitalist regimes. On the other hand, conflict among capitalist interests in the First World facilitates the use of divide-and-conquer strategies by anticapitalist regimes and movements.

Moreover, the internationalization of capital itself promotes new forms of intercapitalist conflict. In a penetrating study for the Soviet Union's institute of World Economics, Margarita Maximova, while quietly burying the old Lenin-Stalin thesis of inevitable war among the capitalist powers, has carefully described the many conflicts (much short of war) that are promoted by the very process of the internationalization of capital. "The chief means and methods of cooperation between monopolies of different capitalist countries and groups of countries," she writes, "are simultaneously the forms of inter-imperialist rivalry and struggle." [2] Maximova meticulously ticks off the many conflicts among the corporations, the dominant political leaders, the smaller and larger capitalist powers, the West German and French rivals for European leadership and, above all, between the Americans, West Europeans, and the Japanese. The smaller the scope of capitalist operations in the world and the more concentrated the world capitalist oligarchy, the less room there is at the top and the more there is to fight about.

One of the strongest tussles of all has been described by Sankar Ray, an expert Indian observer: "A new polarization between international corporations of European origin and those of American and Japanese domination is the most noticeable financial element in the investment situation in Europe." [3] This polarization has led to new mergers by corporations from different European countries: Dunlop-Pirelli (UK and Italy), Philips-Ignis (Netherlands and Italy), Fiat-Citroen (Italy and France), and others. As a result, the share of European corporations in European markets has increased, although the U.S.-based corporations have maintained their lead in the appropriation of profits from their operations in Europe. This conflict spills over into corporate strategies for dealing with both Third World countries and communist regimes.

And as I have already pointed out in "The Challenge of a Shrinking Capitalist World" (chapter 5), much of the confrontation between the First and Third worlds is a polarization between the entrenched capitalist forces of North America, Western Europe, and Japan and their new capitalist challengers—particularly the crude-oil capitalists—from Western Asia, Asia, Latin America, and Africa. Although the capitalist aspects of this conflict are obscured by anticapitalist or semisocialist rhetoric, it is likely that this form of polarization may become much more significant than any of the conflicts within the First World itself.

If, during the 1980s, American leadership should be strengthened, socialist and communist advances will unquestionably be opposed—in one form or another—by a more united First World. Yet the entire nature of this conflict has already been altered by a certain amount of retrenchment.

From a radical viewpoint, Gabriel Kolko finds the source of this retrenchment in America's military defeat in Vietnam: "The essential problem for the U.S. is . . . its lack of a military equivalent that can stop healthy Third World forces that have defeated American interests and power repeatedly in the postwar era."[4] A middle-of-the-roader like Robert W. Tucker advocates a "new isolationism," pointing out that for U.S. security there is no longer any need for the vast system of alliances and commitments built up during the cold war era. Our difficulty in the past, says Tucker, is that the U.S. wanted "paramount influence," not mere security; today paramount influence simply costs too much and should no longer be sought. On the more extreme right, James Burnham and many others lament the collapse of the American will. The refusal to send troops to Angola was a signal that in the face of communist liberation movements, "the West will remain as inert as putty."[5] With the overthrow of the Shah of Iran and the Somoza regime in Nicaragua, these laments have mounted. Irving Kristol complains that "Congressional neo-isolationist liberals have no compunction about cutting the military budget, restricting the government's freedom of action in foreign affairs, and generally following a course of mindless appeasement . . ."[6]

Peter Berger explains this unwillingness by suggesting that there is an unconscious convergence between intellectuals favoring a more modest American posture in the world and corporate elites who like to do business with stable dictatorships. The corporations, he suggests, are impressed not only by the stability of communist regimes but also by the fact that communist markets are untroubled by coups, terrorism, aggressive trade unions, inflation, or complex tax regulations. "A sovietization of Western Europe," he argues, "is becoming less unthinkable to the American business elite."[7] Accordingly, it is becoming less self-evident to the economic elite that American economic interests necessitate the preservation of democracy in Western Europe and the expensive deployment of American military power to that end. This corporate "flabbiness" ties in with and supports "wide-spread weariness with foreign commitments, a fear of Vietnam-like episodes in the future and considerable disillusionment with patriotic rhetoric about America's mission in the world." Thus, Daniel P. Moynihan's 1976 departure from his post as U.S. ambassador to the United Nations was interpreted by some—and presented by Moynihan himself—as an illustration of the U.S. government's unwillingness to maintain the burden of Free World leadership and speak out bluntly against any form of communist advance. With left-wing delight, middle-of-the-road sorrow, and right-wing horror, America's retrenchment has been widely seen as steady, if not headlong, retreat.

But when Victor Zorza writes about a withdrawal to "Fortress America," he knows that he is not referring to any headlong retreat, let alone the complete dissolution, of empire. The idea of "Fortress America" was first originated just before World War II. At that time the so-called isolationists opposed American military intervention in Europe by insisting that the United States should be content with dominion over the Americas—then defined to include Canada, Latin America, and the Caribbean as well as the continental United States itself. Since then, with the admission of Alaska and Hawaii as states, American boundaries were extended far into the Pacific. Also, the islands of Guam, Wake, and Midway and the vast Micronesian trust territory include a chunk of Oceania as large as the continental United States. According to C. L. Sulzberger, the withdrawal of military forces from Vietnam makes this "haphazard empire" off the coasts of Asia all the more important to the United States.[8] If dominion can be maintained over Canada, Latin America, and the Caribbean, this enlarged and well-fortified fortress would be no small potatoes.

A "TRUE EMPIRE"

> The Vietnam war . . . may well come to rank on a par with the two world wars as a conflict that marked an epoch in America's progress toward definition of her role as a world power . . . If the United States comes out of the military confrontation in Europe with a sharpened sense of how to differentiate its role and distribute the various components of national power in the different areas of the world, it will have transcended to the crucial and perhaps last step toward the plateau of maturity. It will then have fulfilled the early hopes of its spiritual or actual founders and will have become a true empire.
>
> GEORGE LISKA[9]

Although American hegemony can scarcely return in its Truman-Eisenhower-Kennedy-Johnson form, this does not necessarily signify the end of the American Century. Nor does communist and socialist advance on some fronts mark American and capitalist retreat on all fronts. There are unmistakable tendencies toward a rather thoroughgoing reconstruction of the entire "Free World." Robert Osgood sees a transitional period of "limited readjustment" and "retrenchment without disengagement," after which America could establish a "more enduring rationale of global influence."[10] Looking at foreign policy under the Nixon administration, Robert W. Tucker sees no intention to "dismantle the empire" but rather a continued commitment to the view that "America must still remain the principal guarantor of a global order now openly and without equivocation identified with the status quo." He describes America as a "settled imperial power shorn of much of the former exuberance."[11] George Liska looks forward to a future in which Americans, having become more mature in the handling of global affairs, will at last be the leaders of a *true empire.*

The current tendencies toward the recreation of American hegemony in new forms once more illustrate the motto "If we want things to stay as they are, things will have to change." A new world situation has been created by the growing economic and military strength of the communist nations, the new militancy of many Third World countries, the rather successful reconstruction—with American help—of capitalism in Western Europe, and the slow but steady internationalization of capital.

Under these new conditions the breakup of the "Free World" empire would be a virtual certainty without sustained leadership by the American establishment. "For better or worse," as Zbigniew Brzezinski puts it, "the United States is saddled with major responsibility for shaping" the future of the world order.[12] For George Liska, this means that the United States must become the active center of a dynamic "global equilibrium."[13] For both, as for all recent U.S. presidents, America must never become a "pitiful, helpless giant." Rather, it must try to remain economically and militarily Number One in the world. "With Kennedy," Brzezinski has written, "came a sense that every people had the right to expect leadership and inspiration from America, and that America owed an almost equal involvement to every continent and every people."[14]

But America's "debt" to the rest of the world, by this line of thought, cannot be paid by routinized maintenance of the kind of American leadership symbolized by Kennedy or his immediate successors. If the capitalist world is to be held together, some things will have to change. The most significant is that the American-led empire must be less American. If the United States cannot shape the world single-handed, other hands must be found and strengthened. The American-led structure of power must be remodeled by converting some clients, satellites, and pawns into allies in a multi-tiered alliance that has room for many junior and senior partners.

In the past, America's role in the world has often been defined as model for the world, as missionary bringing salvation to the heathen, as crusader, and as world policeman. The newly emerging role is that of "Free World Manager." This new role is a far cry from the old-fashioned style of the highly visible, domineering robber-baron or tycoon. It conforms, rather, with the more modern style of the behind-the-scene guidance system attuned to the realities of flexible oligarchy and vast, decentralized operations.

As the new role grows, it does not rule out (and might even reinforce) the old roles of model, missionary, crusader, or policeman. More hands and brains are mobilized to do the manager's bidding and take his advice on what and how to bid. American levels of consumption and American affluence become the model for elites in other capitalist countries, and American styles of large-scale business management become the model for their plutocrats, big-business leaders, executives, and technicians. America's media are the new missionaries of the modern world, with TV shows, films, magazines, and popular music bringing "culture" to the heathen who might otherwise have eked out their lives minus "Kojak," "Bonanza" or "The Incredible Hulk." American corporations —backed up by universities, research institutes, foundations, and political action committees—have been mounting a technological crusade that does much more than win markets, raw materials, and accumulated capital; it also sucks the best and brightest of other countries into the American brain drain or else employs them in their local subsidiaries. Police functions are vastly enlarged through the sound business principle of combining U.S. strategic guidance with decentralized operations by the military and paramilitary forces of many nations.

The greatest impediment to true empire is that the capitalist drive for boundless acquisition is geographically bounded by the continuing expansion of socialist or communist regimes. Under these circumstances the expansive drives of the Golden International must be confined within a dwindling capitalist world—unless something can be done about the boundaries themselves.

The most obvious "something"—which has largely determined the nature of the cold war since the early 1920s—has been the twofold strategy of trying, on the one hand, to "roll back" communist regimes by intervention and subversion of economic blockades and, on the other hand, to contain communist expansion beyond the existing boundaries. Since these strategies have not proved sufficient, the logic of the situation increasingly calls for a new strategy of penetrating, or vaulting over, established boundaries and absorbing the people and resources of communist nations into the capitalist world economy. This logic breaks down into four closely related parts.

The first part focuses on capitalizing on and widening, if possible, the conflicts among the many regimes of national communism. The biggest threat to the capitalist world would be not a worldwide communist conspiracy directed from Peking or Moscow but a loose alliance of nationally rooted anticapitalist regimes and movements capable of integrating their economic and political resources to strengthen existing communist and socialist regimes and support anticapitalist movements in both the First and Third Worlds. The obvious capitalist counterstrategy, therefore, has been to forestall this kind of alliance by providing various kinds of support for "dissident" communist regimes. This has been attempted with varying degrees of success through First World economic support for Yugoslavia, through broader Western efforts to "build bridges" to Eastern Europe, and—more recently—through closer economic relations with China. Whatever successes have thus far been attained have been facilitated by Soviet insistence upon a primordial Russian hegemony in the entire communist world. As a result, the possibilities exist for a capitalist divide-and-conquer strategy to counter the divide-and-conquer strategy used by communist regimes and movements in the Third World. Indeed, in the many years since Kissinger first stated that the primary task of American leaders was "dividing the USSR and China," [15] these possibilities have been growing. The most dramatic, of course, is highlighted by references in the American media to "playing the China card." In a less dramatic sense, there has already been a lot of playing with the Yugoslavia card—and possibilities exist for finding and exploiting many other such cards by the end of the 1980s, in Africa, West Asia, and Latin America, as well as Asia.

The second motion toward integration attempts to do more business with most communist regimes. Naturally, this means setting aside the cold war doctrine of "You can't do business with the communists," and limiting economic blockades to a few regimes that might still be regarded as shaky or to a few products that are regarded as "military secrets." Of course, even during the hottest of the cold-war years, many corporate giants of the West were doing the kind of business with the communists that official doctrine held should not be done. With the official split between the Soviet Union and China, it became increasingly apparent that by expanding this business Western corporations ran much less risk of being branded "traitors to the capitalist class." Nonetheless, a doctrinal revision protected their political flanks: capitalist business with Communist countries would contribute to the liberalization of the communist regimes. Behind this rationalization there glimmered the tough-minded doctrine of seeking more liberal communist attitudes toward capitalist penetration of communist markets, capitalist use of raw materials from communist countries, and long-term agreements to assure long-term capitalist profit-making.

During the next decade, at least, this kind of communist liberalization can play a role in helping the First World manage the capitalist business cycle. It is one of the supreme ironies of world history that the very communist regimes that represent the greatest threat to Western capitalism are already beginning to provide the markets and raw materials necessary for capitalist survival. Or to put it another way, the same capitalist forces that have consistently tried to overthrow or undermine communist regimes are now forced by the logic of events to develop business with the communists in a way that helps ease the capitalist crisis, reverse capitalist trade deficits, and moderate the capitalist business cycle. From this point of view, the drift of economic activity from the capitalist to the communist regions of the world can be seen not merely as a danger but—in Rockefeller's term—as an opportunity to be exploited.

The third movement in this logic promotes capitalist hegemony over communist economies or, to put it another way, fosters, if possible, dependent communist industrialism. In an address to U.S. ambassadors in Europe in December 1975, the State Department's counsellor, Helmut Sonnenfeldt, formulated this logic with semi-straight-talk bluntness by urging that the West use commercial sales to the Soviet Union and Eastern Europe "to draw them into a series of *dependencies and ties with the West.*"[16] The opportunity to do this is provided in the first instance by communist eagerness—first evident in the Soviet bloc and now still more evident in China—to import Western capitalist technologies, particularly in the area of mining, manufacturing, computers, and automatic control systems. Thus, in their long-term planning, the communist leaders give increasingly high priority to the "scientific-technological revolution" which requires long-term help from the transnational corporations of the First World. This dependence on the West goes beyond mere hard-goods technology. With the aid of Western management and accounting firms, such as Arthur Anderson and Co. of Chicago, Soviet enterprises have been plunging furiously into the use of the most advanced techniques of corporate planning and control. Computerized systems of automated control are being rapidly developed wherever feasible. American computer languages are being installed—COBOL for the economists, ALGOL for the engineers, and FORTRAN for the scientists. While old timers warn against the import of capitalism under the guise of neutral management technologies, the majority of the higher party leaders maintain that their dependence on capitalism will be a temporary expedient only and that in due course, a more advanced communist industrialism will catch up to the West in all areas where it now lags and plunge ahead into the worldwide scientific and technological superiority.

Could the further integration of communist economies into the world capitalist market mean "creeping capitalism" within the communist world? The Chinese Communist leaders have no hesitation in answering this question with a resounding "yes." They excoriate the Soviet leaders as

State-capitalist revisionists who have deserted socialist ideals and are using the Soviet Union's superpower status as a means of building "social imperialism" in the Third World. In turn, the Soviet leaders pillory both Mao and his less-Maoist successors for abandoning the proper style of building socialism and creeping back to capitalism.

From the First World's viewpoint, however, a fully successful creeping capitalism throughout the communist world—no matter how much it might be temporarily acclaimed in such spots as Yugoslavia—would be a mixed blessing. The emergence of a vigorous and well-integrated capitalist society within the present boundaries of communism would present new and formidable rivals to the now dominant capitalist societies; it could well destroy even the most mature American hegemony and bring back the era of deadly intercapitalist rivalry. The exploitative interests of First World capitalism would be better served by a dependent communist industrialism whose leaders would not compete with the West in the bitter struggle for superprofits but who would, instead, serve as intermediaries for the more effective, albeit limited, exploitation of their resources and people by transnational corporations of the First World.

Finally, the fourth step toward integration has more to do with socialist movements and socialistically inclined regimes. Here the logical strategy is rather obvious: to maintain or promote the long-standing dissensions among the two major wings of anti-capitalism, socialism and communism. This presents some difficulties at a time when many official communist parties have given up their revolutionary heritage or convictions and come very close to the principles of evolutionary socialism. This phenomenon is found not only within the so-called Eurocommunist parties of Spain, Italy, and France but also in the communist parties of Japan, England, and various other countries. It has led to growing calls for a reuniting of socialists and communists. If this should happen, the result might be that socialist-communist coalitions would take on the mixed responsibility, as I suggested earlier, of both running capitalism and running—or walking—away from it and toward socialism. The obvious antidote is for strong support of those self-styled socialist (or social democratic) regimes, as in West Germany, will have nothing to do with communists and are dedicated to the managing of capitalism. In the case of such other socialistically inclined regimes—as with the last Labor party government in England and the Manley regime in Jamaica—the antidote is to give them the kind of support, through the International Monetary Fund and other agencies, that promotes unemployment and austerity, and gives "socialism" a bad name. In the case of Jamaica, Manley's rhetorical tilts toward Cuba and revolutionary socialism do little to maintain popular support. If the socialistically included governments of Jamaica or Nicaragua should take the quantum leap toward full socialism (no matter how different they might do it in comparison with the Cuban style), then the immediate First World reaction, I presume, could be a return to the good old strategy of economic squeeze and open or covert subversion.

ALTERNATIVE OUTCOMES

Debate over domestic policies in the United States often takes place with sublime remoteness from the conflicting tendencies I have just been discussing. And when the broad alternatives are touched upon, the discussion is often couched in a cloudy meta-language limited to high ideals and timeless abstractions.

Thus those who favor the withdrawal of U.S. support from South Africa or Chile, to take but two examples, often suggest that this would be a victory for black people, working class people, socialists, and Third World supporters in the United States. Those who favor the restoration of American hegemony in the Third World often argue that American retrenchment would mean an end to everything of value in the country—even to the point of its being conquered by the advancing communist or socialist world. A sophisticated consultant to the Department of Defense, Professor Robert L. Pfaltgraff, Jr., concedes that even with a retreat to Fortress America, "American military power, at substantially lower levels than that of the Soviet Union, may be adequate to *deter* an attack against the United States and would enable the United States to survive in a largely hostile world." But this survival would not take place, he insists, "without major changes in its living standards and in its political institutions—at a cost unacceptable to most Americans." [17] The implication, of course, is that with a unified "Free World" under more mature American leadership, there need be no major changes in living standards and institutions, and no unacceptable costs.

Although one can only speculate on these alternatives, this is an unavoidable kind of speculation; it enters into all serious debates on foreign political and economic policies, and on military budgets, the deployment of armed forces, and the nature of the controlled or uncontrolled arms race.

I shall make a few brief observations only.

First of all, a major additional shrinkage of the capitalist world means in the first instance less opportunities for the Golden International to exploit the resources of other countries, less resources for easing difficulties at home, and an intensification of stagflation and all the internal conflicts associated with it. This would accelerate tendencies toward a less friendly, indeed, an unfriendly fascism.

Second, if movement toward a true trilateral empire takes place without large-scale military involvements, then enough resources could be extracted from the rest of the world to maintain U.S. living standards and perhaps even return to a somewhat higher level of growth for another decade or more. This movement could take place, as I have already suggested, even with a certain amount of additional shrinkage in the capitalist world. It is one of the premises for my suggesting the greater probability of friendly, rather than unfriendly, fascism.

Neither alternative, however, can be regarded as an end point. From a long-range viewpoint, each could trigger new coalitions of power that might change the outlook substantially. Under certain political conditions, the very withdrawal of American military power, which is branded "the new isolationism" by militarists, might be accomplished in the context of a new, and true, internationalism. One can even conceive of a "Free World" coalition which, with different coalitions in power in Western Europe, Japan, and America, would work toward a major easing of tensions with the Second World, a serious deescalation of the arms race, and a degree of tolerance concerning the drives for national capitalism or pre-industrial socialism in Third World countries. But these possibilities relate to the alternative logic (itself promoted by the unfolding logic of friendly fascism) set forth briefly in Part Three. Most specifically, they relate to the potentialities for a fundamental restructuring of friendly fascism's emerging power structure.

9

The Friendly Fascist Establishment

Caesarism can come to America constitutionally without having to break down any existing institution.

AMAURY DE RIENCOURT [1]

Oceania has no capital and its titular head is a person whose whereabouts nobody knows.

GEORGE ORWELL, *1984*

THE UNFOLDING LOGIC OF FRIENDLY FASCISM, as I have shown, is responding to crises by actions that consolidate power. But what kind of power structure would emerge?

This question would be easy to answer *if* the processes of transition from the present Establishment were entirely new, *if* they eliminated all conflicts at the Establishment's higher levels, *if* they led to a static state, *if* they concentrated power in the hands of a single transcendent person or group, or *if* they led to more visibility and less mystery.

None of these "ifs" apply. The processes of Big Business-Big Government integration have been going on for some time despite (or even because of) the divisions stemming from government-supported expansion. Their acceleration takes place unevenly, with detailed changes that are unforeseeable at any particular point and with broad international orientations that are even more unpredictable. Movement toward greater oligarchic unity on broad policy is accompanied (as with the classic fascists of Germany, Italy, and Japan) by deep internal infighting among the oligarchs. As it emerges, oligarchic integration is dynamically changing. It is rooted in institutional networks of increasing mystery and declining visibility. If it should ever fully emerge, everyone—even those in high positions—would be hard put even to start answering the question "Who are THEY really?"

As I have already stressed, a friendly fascist power structure in the United States, Canada, Western Europe, or today's Japan would be far more sophisticated than the "caesarism" of fascist Germany, Italy, and Japan. It would need no charismatic dictator nor even a titular head. As I have already suggested, it would require no one-party rule, no mass fascist party, no glorification of the State, no dissolution of legislatures, no denial of reason. Rather, it would come slowly as an outgrowth of present trends in the Establishment.

From the viewpoint of their capability to maintain or strengthen the accumulation of capital and power, the present capitalist Establishments have all shared—in varying degrees—certain institutional weaknesses:

Insufficient cohesion
A discredited or flabby chief executive
Dampened militarism
Discredited right-wing extremism
The erosion of older Establishment ideologies
Linguistic foul-ups

In the United States these weaknesses can be met and Establishment power enhanced without any wholesale purges or profound restructuring of institutions. The takeoff toward a new corporate society began some time ago. All that is now needed is acceleration of the retooling processes already under way.

FROM FLOUNDERING ESTABLISHMENT TO SUPER-AMERICA, INC.

A great empire and little minds go ill together.
EDMUND BURKE

The transition to a remodeled "free world" or to the smaller empire of a "Fortress America" involves much more than learning the lessons of Vietnam "errors" and post-Watergate morality. It requires great minds, as Edmund Burke thundered while the small minds of King George III's court were losing the American colonies. It requires leaders who are not only well selected and well socialized, but also are constantly growing rather than frozenly servile to technical models or temporarily useful ideologies.

Many years ago the Japanese made technological headway by copying American gadgets and technologies. More recently, American leaders have been looking to Japan as a model for the U.S. Establishment. In 1972 the U.S. Department of Commerce published a best-selling "guide for the American businessman," *Japan, the Government-Business Relationship*. Eugene J. Kaplan, the report's author, spells out how Japan's "rolling consensus" restructured the computer, auto, and steel industries. "Japan, Incorporated," he explains, "is not a monolithic system in which government leads and business follows blindly. It is rather more of a participatory partnership . . . Economic decision-making is dominated by the political leadership, the business community, and the administrative bureaucracy." [2]

Some observers have claimed that America, Inc. already exists. This is the view of Morton Mintz and Jerry S. Cohen in their well-documented book under that title. The same view has been set forth by the noted constitutional lawyer, Arthur S. Miller, in his *The Modern Corporate State: Private Governments and the American Constitution.* Both books reveal many facts and trends in which "already walks tomorrow." If one really believes that "America, Inc." and the "modern corporate state" have *already* arrived, then what is slowly emerging might deserve the label "Super-America, Inc." Many critical changes have not yet occurred. They are still around the corner or even on a farther-off horizon. When and if they materialize, it is likely that the Japanese—as well as the Germans and the Italians—may once again look to America as a model.

John B. Connally has long been one of the most outspoken proponents of America, Inc. In discussing the matter with a reporter from the *Wall Street Journal,* he once said that although nobody can foresee the exact changes that "are going to have to take place in American society," there will have to be a "transformation of traditional business-labor-government relationships." According to Richard F. Janssen, the reporter, these changes would include:

> Turning antitrust policy inside out so that in many cases the government would encourage mergers instead of discourage them. More long-range government planning for the economy. Much more federal assistance to key industries—along with much more influence over them. Diverting many young people away from the universities and into vocational training. Convincing—or compelling—unions to abandon lengthy strikes.[3]

But Super-America, Inc. would have to be much broader in scope than the Connally model, with its tilt toward protectionism and rough treatment of First World allies. More thoroughgoing integration of First World Establishments, while playing Second World regimes against each other and co-opting Third World regimes, would be the strategic principles. Only on this basis could the Golden International be strengthened and, in turn, provide reciprocal strength to the American Establishment. The new rolling consensus, in short, must roll over national boundaries.

But global reach requires a firm domestic base. In a simpler world, as Henry Kissinger has pointed out, the foreign ministers of the Austrian and British empires were always frustrated, and at times undone, by domestic opposition. In commenting on empires as diverse as those of Rome, Spain, the Ottoman, and Britain, George Liska finds that "a precondition of success [was] to insulate the internal consumer economy from the cost of external activities by supporting the latter from extraordinary sources." Whether or not this could be done during the remaining years of the century, a number of institutional changes would be necessary at the higher levels of the Establishment.

First, there is still progress to be made in integrating various regionally based interests into the American Establishment and integrating the American Ultra-Rich, Corporate Overseers, and executive managers into the Golden International. These orientations would also have to be shared by a somewhat larger number of well-selected scientists, researchers, intellectuals, and labor leaders.

Another change—and this might be somewhat extraordinary—would be the development of a rolling consensus that could operate successfully without too many calls for heads to roll. I suppose this means a Japanese (or German) style of ego-integration or ego-shrinking, which would make it possible for such remarkably able people as, for example, John Connally, Henry Kissinger, Zbigniew Brzezinski, and Daniel P. Moynihan to work together in constructive harmony with more retiring folk like Cyrus Vance and Harold Brown. To the extent that this can be done, the upper-level bureaucrats will get the signals and work more cooperatively to adjust their competing views. There would still be a need for what Kissinger calls "black channels." No bureaucracy, cluster, constellation, complex, or Establishment could operate without strange labyrinths of unofficial communication. But it is exactly these many informal channels that carry much of the blood through the arteries of the Japanese system. The same is true of the transnational complexes that animate the Golden Internatonal. Above all, on the Big Business side of the emerging partnership, decreased visibility is one of the prices of power; and this has generally been true in the bureaucracy as well. From my own experience in the federal government, I can reliably report that I was never so influential on vital matters as when I operated strictly behind the scenes, with my face known only to insiders and my name never appearing on the multitudinous official documents I wrote. As for higher-ups, it is not enough that they enjoy the protection of shock absorbers in the form of aides who can be thrown to the dogs when doing so may be useful. Decreased visibility is also required—so that there will be less risk of losing face or head. With but few exceptions, the new rulers must be faceless oligarchs.

Third, the new rolling consensus could scarcely take place without an interim period of executive turbulence. Greater cohesion among the leaders of Big Business, the Ultra-Rich, and the Chief Executive network requires executive managers with unprecedented abilities in attaining and maintaining greater profitability in the face of—and often by means of—recurring crises. With the vast banking expansion of the 1960s and early 1970s, according to *Business Week*, "a new generation of bankers was taking over, and where the men they had succeeded had been pussy-cats, they were tigers: bold, aggressive, and not only willing but literally obliged to seek out profit opportunities." [4] But that was merely a transitional period during which state-chartered banks "went national" and transnational, moved into every variety of financial services, and then through new-style holding companies plunged into the leasing of industrial equipment. For the most part the bankers of that period were merely tiger cubs, not yet fully at home in global operations or in the formulation of the financial policies to guide the operations of the mergers they presided over or the use of the equipment they owned. Under mature oligarchy the bank executives would no longer be cubs. Friendly fascism would see a new generation of management "tigers" handling the top executive problems not only of finance but of production and distribution, communication, policy planning, institutional building, and national security as well. Neither long experience nor high-class education and executive development exercises, nor even the proper family connections would be enough to prepare managers for these tasks. The most basic requirement would be success in surviving recurring shakeups and fighting the battle of the executive suites in a manner that wins the confidence of the Ultra-Rich.

The turbulence of these battles is an essential part of the processes of integration at the very top; it helps separate the tigers from the mere men. While turbulence also reflects some of the continuing cleavages within competing circles of the Ultra-Rich, at a lower level it serves to prevent direct confrontation at the top—just as the world's superpowers may often conduct a conflict indirectly through war between satellite or client states. In this way the owners and top political leaders may reap the considerable benefits of trial-and-error learning, while the costs of the errors are levied against their hired help. The top executives are the "fall guys," always susceptible to summary dismissal when "guilty" of mistaken policies designed to serve (or even dictated to them by) their chiefs. Under such circumstances, executive emoluments become more enormous than ever before. The cost of high-class help—even if it brings top executives into the millionaire class—is a pittance compared to the enormous monetary gains accruing to the Ultra-Rich. Under friendly fascism, could top executives escape control by their controllers, or even seize power from them? There is little danger of it. Precisely because they would operate on longer leashes than before, they could have enough rope to hang themselves or prove themselves; in this basic sense, they would be better controlled than ever. And as before, only a tiny minority could ever "make it" into the rarefied heights of the plutocratic stratosphere.

Fourth, a basic path for the training and selection of management "tigers" in broad policy planning is what Alvin Toffler calls "ad-hocracy." Such great national associations as the U.S. Chamber of Commerce, the National Association of Manufacturers, and the American Bankers Association adjust too slowly to the transition from semi- to mature oligarchy. The same is true of the Committee for Economic Development, the Council on Foreign Relations and "think tanks" like the Rand Corporation and the Hudson Institute. "Throwaway organizations," *ad hoc* teams, and informal, often secret committees, are increasingly needed to withdraw people from institutional slots and give them broader perspectives. As Toffler points out, "this process, repeated often enough, alters the loyalties of the people involved; shakes up lines of authority; and accelerates the rate at which individuals are forced to adapt to organizational change." [5] In this manner, the established policy organizations are given new guidelines. Indeed, some of them—like the famed Council on Foreign Relations—remain as hollow shells of their former selves. By the time the political science textbooks get around to identifying them as agencies of high-policy formulation, they have little more to do than acquaint middle-level executives and technicians with the essentials of policies formulated elsewhere.

A RIGHTEOUS PRESIDENCY

> I cannot lay too great stress upon the high ethical righteousness of the whole oligarchic class. This has been the strength of the Iron Heel.
>
> JACK LONDON, *The Iron Heel*

> The corporate state, American style, exemplifies a politico-legal form of syzygy.
>
> ARTHUR S. MILLER [6]

The word "syzygy" has long been a winning ploy in word games like Scrabble or Ghosts. Few people know its major meaning: the conjunction of two organisms without either of them losing its identity. When Arthur S. Miller uses the term to refer to the American-style corporate state, he helps us remember that both Big Business and Big Government—despite their fusion in operations—retain certain special identities.

For the Chief Executive, a conspicuous exception to the general principle of facelessness, this is particularly vital. Under the full-fledged oligarchy of friendly fascism, the Chief Executive network would become much more powerful than ever before. And the top executive—in America, the president—would in a certain sense become more important than before. But not in the sense of a personal despotism like Hitler's.

Indeed, the president under friendly fascism would be as far from personal caesarism as from being a Hirohito-type figurehead. Nor would a president and his political associates extort as much "protection money" from big-business interests as was extracted under Mussolini and Hilter. The Chief Executive would neither ride the tiger nor try to steal its food; rather, he would be part of the tiger from the outset. The White House and the entire Chief Executive network would become the heart (and one of the brain centers) of the new business-government symbiosis. Under these circumstances the normal practices of the Ultra-Rich and the Corporate Overlords would be followed: personal participation in high-level business deals and lavish subsidization of political campaigns, both expertly hidden from public view. What would be "abnormal" is a qualitative forward leap—as previsioned by John Connally back in 1972—toward a business-government relationship that breaks all precedent in promoting mergers, supporting American-based transnationals abroad, and preventing any serious losses that businesses might sustain through expropriation abroad, rising wage demands or prolonged strikes at home, changing conditions in markets and technology, recession, inflation, or even managerial errors.

This transformation would require a new concept of presidential leadership, one emphasizing legitimacy and righteousness above all else. As the linchpin of an oligarchic establishment, the White House would continue to be the living and breathing symbol of legitimate government. "Reigning" would become the first principle of "ruling". Only by wrapping himself and all his agents in the trappings of constitutionality could the President succeed in subverting the spirit of the Constitution and the Bill of Rights. The Chief Executive Network, Big Business, and the Ultra-Rich could remain far above and beyond legal and moral law only through the widely accepted image that all of them, and particularly the president, were fully subservient to law and morality. In part, this is a matter of public relations—but not the old Madison Avenue game of selling perfume or deodorants to the masses. The most important nostrils are those of the multileveled elites in the establishment itself; if things smell well to them, then the working-buying classes can probably be handled effectively. In this context, it is not at all sure that the personal charisma of a president could ever be as important as it was in the days of Theodore or Franklin Roosevelt, Dwight Eisenhower, or John F. Kennedy.

It is no easy task to erect a shield of legitimacy to cloak the illegitimate. Doing so would require the kind of leadership that in emphasizing the long-term interests of Big Business and the Ultra-Rich would stand up strongly *against* any elements that are overly greedy for short-term windfalls. Thus in energy planning, foreign trade, labor relations, and wage-price controls, for example, the friendly fascist White House would from time to time engage in activities that could be publicly regarded as "cracking down on business." While a few recalcitrant corporate overseers might thus be reluctantly educated, the chief victims would usually be small or medium-sized enterprises, who would thus be driven more rapidly into bankruptcy or merger. In this sense, conspicuous public leadership would become a form of followership.

Another requirement would be the weaving of comprehensive linkages to all political currents and major interest groups in American society, including those still opposed to the oligarchy in principle or representing potential sources of future opposition. For every ethnic, religious, sectional, or geographic grouping, for every faction or fraction in conservative, liberal, reactionary, or radical movements, there must be direct or indirect liaison and, for many of their leaders, at least the illusion of access to the "top." This would be the kind of broad-minded totalitarianism that a Nixon, Ford, or Carter administration, and particularly such narrow-gauged assistants as H. R. Haldeman, John Ehrlichman, and Hamilton Jordan could never comprehend. It would provide an "open door" presidential leadership that in fact, makes the White House a more effective instrument on behalf of the "closed door" power of the Corporate Overseers and the Ultra-Rich.

REMOLDING MILITARISM

> Overgrown military establishments are under any form of government inauspicious to liberty, and are to be regarded as particularly hostile to republican liberty.
>
> GEORGE WASHINGTON

> The Institute [for Land Combat] has thus far identified almost 400 possible wars (385 to be exact) for the years 1990 and about 600 new weapons and other pieces of equipment with which to handle these conflicts.
>
> PAUL DICKSON [7]

During the 1970s, as its forces slowly retreated from the Asiatic mainland, the U.S. military establishment seemed to dwindle. Even with veterans' and outer-space expenditures included, war spending declined as a portion of the GNP. Conscription ended in 1973. All proposals for overt military intervention in the Third World—whether in Angola, West Asia, Afghanistan, the Horn of Africa, the Caribbean, or Central America—were sidetracked. From an earlier high of 3.5 million people in 1968, the active military fell to 2 million at the beginning of the 1980s.

But in real terms the military establishment is enormous, much more than most people know. To the 2 million on active duty must be added another 2 million in the reserves, and a million civilians in the defense department. This 5-million-figure total is merely the base for a much larger number of people in war industries, space exploration, war think-tanks and veterans' assistance. Behind this total group of more than 12 million—and profiting from intercourse with them—stands an elaborate network of war industry associations, veterans' organizations, special associations for each branch of the armed services, and general organizations such as the American Security Council and the Committee on the Present Danger. But there is something else that George Washington could never have dreamed of when he warned against an overgrown military establishment and that Dwight D. Eisenhower never mentioned in his warning against the military-industrial complex: namely, a *transnational military complex*. This American-led complex has five military components beyond the narrowly defined U.S. military-industrial complex itself:

1. The dozen or so countries formally allied with the United States through NATO
2. Other industrialized countries not formerly part of NATO, such as Spain, Israel, Japan, Australia, and New Zealand
3. A large portion of the Third World countries
4. Intelligence and police forces throughout the "Free World"
5. Irregular forces composed of primitive tribesmen, often operating behind the lines of the Second World countries.[8]

All these forces are backed up by a support infrastructure which includes training schools, research institutes, foreign aid, and complex systems of communication and logistics.

If there is one central fact about this transnational military complex at the start of the 1980s it is *growth*. Paradoxically, every arms-control agreement has been used as a device to allow growth up to certain ceilings, rather than prevent it. And since those ceilings apply only to selected weapons systems, growth tends to be totally uncontrolled in all other forms of destruction. In the United States, total military expenditure has started to move upward at a rate of about 5 percent annual growth in real terms—that is, after being corrected for the declining value of the dollar. A drive is under way to register young people for a draft, while also providing alternative forms of civilian service (at poverty wages) for people objecting to military service on moral, religious, or political grounds. New weapons systems are being initiated—particularly the MX missile, which holds forth the promise of a "first strike" capability against the Soviet Union. Major steps are being taken to increase the military strength of all the other components of the transnational complex—

particularly through the expansion of both tactical and strategic nuclear weapons in Western Europe and the beefing up of the defense forces and nuclear capabilities of the Japanese. Above all, despite some internal conflicts on when and where, the leaders of the U.S. Establishment have become more willing to use these forces. Richard Falk of Princeton University presents this thesis: "A new consensus among American political leaders favors intervention, whenever necessary, to protect the resource base of Trilateralistic nations'—Europe, the United States and Japan—prosperity and dominance." [9] This has required strenuous propaganda efforts to overcome the so-called "post-Vietnam syndrome," that is, popular resistance to the sending of U.S. troops into new military ventures abroad. Equally strenuous efforts are made to convince people in Western Europe that as East-West tensions have been relaxing and East-West trade rising, the West faces a greater threat than ever before of a Soviet invasion.

The logic of this growth involves a host of absurdities. First of all, statistical hocus-pocus hides the overwhelming military superiority of the "Free World." One trick is to compare the military spending of the United States with the Warsaw Pact countries but to exclude NATO. Another trick is to compare the NATO countries of Europe with the Warsaw Pact countries, but to exclude the United States. Still another is to exclude not merely Japan, but also the huge Chinese military forces lined up on China's border with the Soviet Union. Any truly global picture shows that while the geographical scope of the "Free World" has been shrinking, its military capability has been expanding. This expansion has been so rapid that there may even be good reason for the nervous old men in the Kremlin to feel threatened.

Second, much of this expanding military power involves nothing more than overkill. Thus just one Poseidon submarine carries 160 nuclear warheads, each four times more powerful than the Hiroshima bomb. These warheads are enough, as President Carter stated in 1979, "to destroy every large and medium-sized city in the Soviet Union." Pointing out that the total U.S. force at that time could inflict more than fifty times as much damage on the Soviet Union, President Carter then went on to raise the level of overkill still higher.

Third, the advocates of new interventionism foster the delusion that military force can solve a host of intertwined political, economic, social, and moral problems. This delusion was evidenced in the long-term and highly expensive U.S. support for the Shah of Iran and the Somoza dictatorship in Nicaragua. As U.S. strike forces are being prepared for intervention in West Asia (whether in Saudi Arabia, Libya, or elsewhere) the presumption is that military action of this type would preserve the availability of petroleum for the West. What is blindly lost sight of is the high probability—and in the judgment of many, the certainty—that any such intervention would precipitate the blowing up of the very oil fields from which the deep thinkers in the White House, Wall Street, and the Pentagon want to get assured supplies.

Yet in the words of Shakespeare's Polonius, "If this be madness, yet there is method in it." It is the not-so-stupid madness of the growing militarism which is an inherent part of friendly fascism's unfolding logic. "Militarism," Woodrow Wilson once pointed out at West Point in 1916, "does not consist of any army, nor even in the existence of a very great army. Militarism is a spirit. It is a point of view."[10] That spirit is the use of violence as a solution to problems. The point of view is something that spills over into every field of life—even into the school and the family.

Under the militarism of German, Italian, and Japanese fascism violence was openly glorified. It was applied regionally—by the Germans in Europe and England, the Italians in the Mediterranean, the Japanese in Asia. In battle, it was administered by professional militarists who, despite many conflicts with politicians, were guided by old-fashioned standards of duty, honor, country, and willingness to risk their own lives.

The emerging militarism of friendly fascism is somewhat different. It is global in scope. It involves weapons of doomsday proportions, something that Hitler could dream of but never achieve. It is based on an integration between industry, science, and the military that the old-fashioned fascists could never even barely approximate. It points toward equally close integration among military, paramilitary, and civilian elements. Many of the civilian leaders—such as Zbigniew Brzezinski or Paul Nitze—tend to be much more bloodthirsty than any top brass. In turn, the new-style military professionals tend to become corporate-style entrepreneurs who tend to operate—as Major Richard A. Gabriel and Lieutenant Colonel Paul L. Savage have disclosed—in accordance with the ethics of the marketplace.[11] The old buzzwords of duty, honor, and patriotism are mainly used to justify officer subservience to the interests of transnational corporations and the continuing presentation of threats to some corporate investments as threats to the interest of the American people as a whole. Above all, in sharp contrast with classic fascism's glorification of violence, the friendly fascist orientation is to sanitize, even hide, the greater violence of modern warfare behind such "value-free" terms as "nuclear exchange," "counterforce" and "flexible response," behind the huge geographical distances between the senders and receivers of destruction through missiles or even on the "automated battlefield," and the even greater psychological distances between the First World elites and the ordinary people who might be consigned to quick or slow death.

Some people see the drift from MAD to MADDEST exclusively in terms of hard-goods technology. By this reasoning, the ultimate logic of expanding militarism would be a doomsday machine brought into operation by the spiraling arms race. I see the trend in broader terms. The spirit and viewpoint of militarism spreads a subtle poison that can permeate every aspect of life, erode civil liberties, and promote not only police repression but also private terrorism in areas of tension among ethnic groups. They enable establishment leaders to deflect attention from social injustice and racism at home by stirring up hostility toward imagined enemies abroad. When I use the term MADDEST, it is not just to warn against nuclear, bacteriological, or chemical holocaust, it is to pinpoint the effectiveness of the new militarism as a whole and its deadly nature as an emerging part of the friendly fascist power structure.

THE RESTRUCTURING OF THE RADICAL RIGHT

> Leadership in the right has fallen to new organizations with lower profiles and better access to power . . . What is characteristic of this right is its closeness to government power and the ability this closeness gives to hide its political extremism under the cloak of respectability.
>
> WILLIAM W. TURNER [12]

> By 1976 the New Right had helped to elect almost 25 percent of the U.S. House of Representatives.
>
> SASHA LEWIS [13]

With stagflation, alienation, and frustration a growing part of life in Western Europe, many neofascist groups are openly rearing their heads. A so-called "World Union of National Socialists" boasts branches in many countries. The members of its British branch wear Nazi uniforms and distribute Nazi literature. The German neo-Nazis specialize in desecrating Jewish cemeteries. Its French members vow to "exterminate all Jews and generalize the system of apartheid throughout the world." The Italian neo-fascists practice open terrorism.

In the United States, there is also a resurgence of what might be called—in the American tradition—"Know Nothing nut power." Small groups of Nazis parade in public. The Ku Klux Klan organizes in the North as well as the South, and has units among American soldiers and policemen. Secret groups throughout the country launch attacks against both blacks and Jews. "The vision of a fascist future may seem idle," write two reporters, Joseph Trento and Joseph Spear, "but Willis Carto, now in his mid-forties, is working every day to make it come true. And more frightening than the remote possibility Carto will realize his dream is the current power of the (Liberty Lobby) apparatus he has built to bring himself and his ideas into power."[14] The Falangist Party of America openly proposes "an authoritative, one-party government." Claiming that frustrations "need a channel," it argues that "the Falangist can cut the two-party system to ribbons with the inflation issue."[15]

Although most of these right-wing extremists avoid open identification with the classic fascists, the similarities with the early fascist movements of the 1920s are clear. Small clusters of highly strung, aggressive people think that if Hitler and Mussolini (both of whom started from tiny beginnings) could make it into the Big Time under conditions of widespread misfortune, fortune might someday smile on them too.

I doubt it. Their dreams of future power are illusory. To view them as the main danger is to assume that history is obliging enough to repeat itself in unchanged form. Indeed, their major impact—apart from their contribution to domestic violence, discussed in "The Ladder of Terror," (chapter 14)—is to make the more dangerous right-wing extremists seem moderate in comparison.

The greatest danger on the right is the rumbling thunder, no longer very distant, from a huge array of well-dressed, well-educated activists who hide their extremism under the cloak of educated respectability. Unlike the New Left of the 1960s, which reached its height during the civil rights and antiwar movements, the Radical Right rose rapidly during the 1970s on a much larger range of issues. By the beginning of the 1980s, they were able to look back on a long list of victories. Their domestic successes are impressive:

- Holding up ratification of the Equal Rights Amendment
- Defeating national legislation for consumer protection
- Defeating national legislation to strengthen employees' rights to organize and bargain collectively
- Undermining Medicare payments for abortions
- Bringing back capital punishment in many states
- Killing anti-gun legislation
- Promoting tax-cutting programs, such as the famous Proposition 13 in California, already followed by similar actions in other parts of the country
- Promoting limitations on state and local expenditures, which in effect (like the tax-cutting measures) mean a reduction in social programs for the poor and the lower middle-classes
- Undermining affirmative-action programs to provide better job opportunities for women, blacks and Hispanics
- Killing or delaying legislation to protect the rights of homosexuals

They have also succeeded in getting serious attention for a whole series of "nutty" proposals to amend the Constitution to require a balanced federal budget or set a limit on the growth of federal expenditures. By the beginning of 1980, about 30 State legislatures had already petitioned the Congress for a Constitutional convention to propose such an amendment; only 34 are needed to force such a convention, the first since 1787. The major purpose of this drive, however, was not to get a Constitutional amendment. Rather, it was to force the president and Congress to go along with budget cutting on domestic programs.[10] By this standard it has been remarkably successful.

On foreign issues, the Radical Right came within a hair's breadth of defeating the Panama Canal Treaty and the enabling legislation needed to carry it out. They have been more successful, however, on these matters:

- Reacting to the Iranian and Afghanistan crises of 1979 with a frenetic escalation of cold war
- Helping push the Carter administration toward more war spending and more militarist policies
- Making any ratification of the SALT II treaty dependent on continued escalation in armaments
- Preventing Senate consideration, let alone ratification, of the pending UN covenants against genocide, on civil and political rights, and on economic, social, and cultural rights.

In a vital area bridging domestic and foreign policy, they provide a major portion of support for the drive to register young people for possible military service and then, somewhat later, reinstitute conscription.

Almost all of these issues are "gut issues." They can be presented in a manner that appeals to deep-seated frustrations and moves inactive people into action. Yet the New Right leaders are not, as the Americans for Democratic Action point out in *A Citizen's Guide to the Right Wing,* "rabid crackpots or raving zealots." The movement they are building is "not a lunatic fringe but the programmed product of right wing passion, plus corporate wealth, plus 20th century technology—and its strength is increasing daily."[17]

This strength has been embodied in a large number of fast-moving organizations:

American Legislative Exchange Council (ALEC)
American Security Council
Americans Against Union Control of Government
Citizens for the Republic
Committee for Responsible Youth Politics
Committee for the Survival of a Free Congress
Committee on the Present Danger
Conservative Victory Fund
Consumer Alert Council

Fund for a Conservative Majority
Gun Owners of America
Heritage Foundation
National Conservative Political Action Committee
National Rifle Association Political Action Committee (PAC)
Our PAC
Public Service PAC
Right To Keep and Bear Arms Political Victory Fund
Tax Reform Immediately (TRIM)
The Conservative Caucus (TCC)
Young Americans for Freedom/The Fund for a Conservative Majority

Many of these groups, it must be understood, include nonrabid crackpots and nonraving zealots. They are often backed up—particularly on fiscal matters—by the National Taxpayers Union and many libertarian groups which may part company from them on such issues as the escalation of war spending or the return of military conscription.

All of them, it should be added, seem to be the recipients of far more funds than were ever available to the less respectable extremists. Much of this money unquestionably seeps down, as the ADA insists, from corporate coffers. Some of it unquestionably comes from massive mail solicitations by Richard Viguerie, who has been aptly christened the "Direct Mail Wizard of the New Right." Since 1964, when he was working on Senator Goldwater's campaign for the presidency, Viguerie has been developing a mailing list operation which puts the New Right into touch with millions upon millions of Americans.

Today, the momentum of the Radical Right is impressive. It has defeated many well-known liberal candidates for reelection to national, state, and local offices. Having helped elect a quarter of the members of the House of Representatives in 1976, it looks forward to much greater influence by the mid-1980s. Like the American labor movement, which has always supported some Republicans as well as many Democrats, the Radical Right has no firm commitment to any one party. Its strength among Democrats is much larger than that of labor among Republicans. It supports candidates of the two major parties and is closely associated with small-party movements, which sometimes have a decisive impact on electoral or legislative campaigns. Its biggest success, however, is that many of its positions which first sounded outrageous when voiced during the Goldwater campaign of 1964 are now regarded as part of the mainstream. This is not the result of Radical Right shifts toward the center. On the contrary, it is the result of a decisive movement toward the right by the Ultra-Rich and the Corporate Overseers.

The unfolding logic of the Radical Right, however, is neither to remain static or to become more openly reactionary. "We are no longer working to preserve the status quo," says Paul Weyrich, one of its ablest leaders. "We are radicals working to overturn the present power structure." [18] To understand what Weyrich means, we must heed Arno J. Mayer's warning—based on his study of classic fascism—that in a time of rapid change "even reactionary, conservative and counter-revolutionary movements project a populist, reformist and emancipatory image of their purpose." [19] More populism of this type can be expected: in a word, more attacks on the existing Establishment by people who want to strengthen it by making it much more authoritarian and winning for themselves more influential positions in it.

There is also a role in all this for left-wing extremists. Bombings, assassinations, or kidnappings by purported revolutionaries can serve as valuable triggering mechanisms for repressive action. Under such circumstances, official violence can take the garb of antiviolence, even though it may be far more extensive than required for the simple squashing of terrorists. With good luck, the friendly fascists can rely on the spontaneous initiatives of "revolutionary" wild men. If this is not forthcoming, they may not hesitate to spark such violence through the use of *agents provocateurs.**

NEW IDEOLOGIES OF CENTRAL POWER

> For any imperial policy to work effectively . . . it needs moral and intellectual guidance . . . It is much to be doubted that the United States can continue to play an imperial role without the endorsement of its intellectual class . . . It is always possible to hope that this intellectual class will . . . help formulate a new set of more specific principles that will relate the ideals which sustain American democracy to the harsh and nasty imperatives of imperial power.
>
> IRVING KRISTOL [20]

During the late 1960s and early 1970s Kristol clearly saw that "a small section of the American intellectual class has become a permanent brain trust to the political, the military, the economic authorities." These are the men, he reported, who "commute regularly to Washington, who help draw up programs for reorganizing the bureaucracy, who evaluate proposed weapons systems, who figure out ways to improve our cities and assist our poor, who analyze the course of economic growth, who reckon the cost and effectiveness of foreign aid programs, who dream up new approaches to such old social problems as the mental health of

---

* See discussion in "The Ladder of Terror," chapter 14.

the aged, etc., etc." But unfortunately, he lamented, the majority of the intellectuals refused to accept these responsibilities. A new class had arisen—mostly pseudo-intellectuals—composed of people alienated from an established order that refused to provide them with enough power or recognition.

Kristol's lament was picked up by a brilliant group of neoconservatives who, clustering around such magazines as *Commentary* and *The Public Interest* and the Basic Books publishing house, levied fierce and unrelenting attacks on this new class of irresponsibles. At the same time an equally brilliant group of somewhat more old-fashioned conservatives developed around William Buckley's *The National Review*, *The American Spectator*, the Arlington publishing house, and the Conservative Book Club. Together, these two new streams of intellectual activity have many elements in common. Some of their most brilliant practitioners are former Marxists, communists, or left-leaning liberals. Having seen the error of their own ways, they are particularly scornful of those bemused intellectuals who have not yet seen the light and—in Norman Podhoretz's term—"broken ranks." They have remarkable access to corporate funds, large and small foundations, and a host of new prosperous research centers and institutes. They have strong footholds in colleges and universities. Indeed, as *Newsweek* pointed out in 1979, "major corporations ...now underwrite at least 30 academic centers and chairs of free enterprise."[21]

Peter Steinfels has pointed out in *The Neoconservatives* that the Kristol-Podhoretz-Moynihan-Bell intellectuals consistently ignore the realities of corporate power.[22] So do the new intellectuals among the more old-fashioned conservatives. By so doing, whether consciously or not, both groups contribute to its increased concentration at the higher levels of both the U.S. Establishment and the Golden International.

One way of doing this is merely to reinforce the older ideologies concerning the badness of socialism and communism and the goodness—or nonexistence—of capitalism. This has led to oft-repeated odes on the pristine beauty of automatic market forces in comparison with the deadly hand of inefficient and corrupt government bureaucracy. The invisible hands of corporate bureaucracies—as well as the multitudinous assists they get from government—are kept invisible.

The routinized reiteration of this older conservative doctrine, however, is buttressed by a new ideological reformaton that emphasizes the excellence of hierarchy, the wonders of technology, and the goodness of hard times. In *The Twilight of Authority*, Robert Nisbet makes an eloquent call for a return to the old aristocratic principle of hierarchy: "It is important that rank, class and estate in all spheres become once again honored rather than, as is now the case, despised or feared by intellectuals."[23] If democracy is to be diminished and if rank, class, and estate are once again to be honored, the intellectuals at the middle and lower levels of the establishment must be brought into line on many points. Those who advocate a somewhat more egalitarian society must be pilloried as "levellers" who would reduce everybody to a dull, gray uniformity. They must be convinced that the ungrateful lower classes whom they hope to raise up are, in fact, genetically and culturally inferior. They must be flattered into seeing themselves as part of a society in which true merit, as defined by the powerful, is usually recognized and rewarded. The power of the Ultra-Rich and the Corporate Overlords must be publicly minimized and the endless plutocratic search for personal gratification must be obscured by lamenting the self-gratifying hedonism of the masses.

Arguments along these lines by Arthur R. Jensen, Edward Banfield, R. J. Hernstein, and Daniel Bell have not yet won the day—not by any means. Indeed, the Watergate debacle of the Nixon administration proved rather embarrassing to those who had hinted that the America of 1973 was led by its best men. But the devotees of meritocratic hierarchy have nonetheless commanded a remarkable degree of attention, often staking out the territory for intellectual combat. The largest battles on this front still lie ahead. A sweeping victory for the advocates of hierarchy would be one of the conditions marking the advent of friendly fascism.

In the face of so many unhappy complications with nuclear energy and pollution, the earlier glorification of "knowledge elites" and science-based technology is losing much of its vigor. The existing order must be justified by more convincing affirmation of the wondrous benefits attainable through the ongoing technological revolution. Just what form these may take is not entirely clear. Three hints are provided by current developments in technology assessment, systems analysis of social problems, and *avant garde* techniques of social control.

Technology assessment itself has been invented as a new "soft" technology. It promises to cope with the second-order and third-order consequences of new technologies that threaten environmental degradation and resource depletion. "None of this has to be," Daniel Bell tells us. "The mechanism of control are available as well." [24] These mechanisms are to be found in the scientific assessment of all possible impacts of new technologies before they are introduced. It was more or less assumed that this assessment could be done "neutrally"—apart from considerations of basic values, economic interests, or political power. But this very emphasis on neutrality is in fact part of a "technological" ideology. It evades realities like those revealed in Philip Boffey's study, *The Brain Bank of America* (and not mentioned by Bell)—for example, that the National Academy of Engineering (an authoritative source for both the theory and practice of technology assessment) is packed with industry-paid assessors who have persistently "parroted the line of corporate interests." [25]

While faith in technology assessment provides a front-line of defense against any attack on the financial oligarchy's use of destructive "hard" techniques, systems analysis—also hailed by Bell as an historic advance—suggests the possibility of technical solutions to almost any social problem. Ida Hoos paraphrases the sales talk of the systems analysts: "Do you want to launch a rocket, run a bank, catch a crook? Do you want to improve the efficiency of a fire department, a library, a hospital? The 'scientific methods' of operations research, systems analysis and the like provide the tools whereby you can proceed 'rationally.'"[26] Although these claims are essentially irrational, credibility is given by elaborate kowtowing to the mythology of presumed success in outer-space technology and military systems and the magic-laden symbolism of computer-based mathematical models. According to Ida Hoos, the boom in systems analysis can be explained this way: "Merchandised as a Space Age speciality, a precise and sophisticated set of tools, systems analysis has become the stock-in-trade of practically any individual or organization seeking a government grant or contract or engaged in a project. Its language is the life line of everyone who aspires to make his work appear systematic or technically sophisticated . . . Contrary to being an instrument of innovation, the system approach is essentially reactionary."[27]

Technology assessment, systems analysis, and similar developments serve to restore the public's wavering confidence in technology. They promise to solve technology's problems by more technology. At the same time, old-fashioned innovation continues unabated: breakthroughs in biology and new developments in medicine keep alive humanity's hope of escaping its most basic ills, if not death itself, through science. A society moving toward friendly fascism would be particularly taken with *avant garde* technologies of social control. B. F. Skinner has provided a vivid preview, attracting a national audience for his vision of utopia through a "science of behavior" and a centralized program of conditioning.[28] José Delgado has proposed widespread "behavior control" through electrical stimulation of the brain.[29] And a host of more modest proposals employing drugs, behavior therapy, and screening have been taken quite seriously. It is hard to discern the real promise, or threat, of these lines of research. Ideologically, they distract attention from the political or economic dimensions of social problems. The emphasis on the technological wonders to be gained from the natural or social sciences depoliticizes the establishment's technicians and facilitates stigmatization of social critics as "Luddites." All these tendencies would be exacerbated under friendly fascism, while the long-run possibility of actually adding new instruments of control to the establishment's armamentarium would be carefully pursued.

A successful transition to friendly fascism would clearly require a lowering of popular aspirations and demands. Only then can freer rein be given to the corporate drives for boundless acquisition. Since it is difficult to tell ordinary people that unemployment, inflation, and urban filth are good for them, it is more productive to get middle-class leaders on the austerity bandwagon and provide them with opportunities for increased prestige by doing what they can to lower levels of aspirations. Indeed, the ideology of mass sacrifice had advanced so far by the end of the 1970s that the most serious and best-advertised debate among New York liberals on the New York City fiscal crisis rested on the assumption that the level of municipal employment and services *had* to be cut. The only questions open for debate were "Which ones?" and "How much?" This ideology—although best articulated in general form by political scientists like Samuel Huntington and sociologists like Daniel Bell—also receives decisive support from Establishment economists.

Religious doctrines on the goodness of personal sacrifice in this world have invariably been associated with promises of eternal bliss in the next world. Similarly, the emerging ideologies on the virtues of austerity are bound to be supplemented by visions of "pie in the sky by and by." In their most vulgar form these ideologies may simply reiterate the economistic notion that reduced consumption now will mean more profitability, which will mean more capital investment that in turn will mean increased consumption later. In more sophisticated form, these ideologies take the form of a misty-eyed humanism. While moving toward friendly fascism we might hear much talk like Jean-Francois Revel's proclamation that "The revolution of the twentieth century will take place in the United States" or Charles Reich's view that the counterculture of the young will, by itself, break through the "metal and plastic and sterile stone" and bring about "a veritable greening of America." Indeed, work at such "think-tanks" as the Rand Corporation and Hudson Institute increasingly foregoes its old base in economics and related "dismal" disciplines for straight and unadulterated "humanism," the rhetorical promotion of which seems directly related to their involvement in dehumanized and dehumanizing technologies.

As with the ideologies of classic fascism, there is no need for thematic consistency in the new ideologies. An ideological menu is most useful when it provides enough variety to meet divergent needs and endless variations on interwoven melodic lines. Unlike the ideologies of classic fascism, however, these new ideologies on market virtue, hierarchic excellence, wondrous technology, and the goodness of hard times are not needed to mobilize masses to high peaks of emotional fervor. In contrast, they help prevent mass mobilization. Yet their growing function is to maintain the loyalty of intellectuals, scientists, and technicians at the Establishment's middle and lower ranks, thereby minimizing the need for systemic purges. On this score the two streams of conservative ideology have been remarkably effective. They have taken over the most commanding heights on the intellectual fronts, reducing to a "small section" those anti-Establishment intellectuals who try to swim against the main currents. Indeed, through a remarkable dialectic, the opponents of the so-called "new class" have themselves become a dominant new class of intellectuals who provide the moral and intellectual guidance on the harsh and nasty imperatives of imperial survival in the era of the stagflation-power tradeoff and the movement toward Super-America, Inc.

TRIPLESPEAK

During the take-off toward a more perfect capitalism, the debasement of the language moved no slower than the abasement of the currency through creeping inflation. The myths of the cold war gave us the imagery of a "free world" that included many tyrannical regimes on one side and the "worldwide communist conspiracy" to describe the other. The "end of ideology" ideologies gave us the myth of all-powerful knowledge elites to flatter the egos of intellectuals and scientists in the service of a divided Establishment. The accelerating rise of scientific and pseudoscientific jargon fragmented social and natural scientists into small in-groups that concentrated more and more on small slices of reality, separating them more than ever before from the presumably unsophisticated (although functionally literate) working-buying classes.

In the early days of this process, George Orwell envisioned a future society in which the oligarchs of 1984 would use linguistic debasement as a conscious method of control. Hence the Party Leaders imposed *doublethink* on the population and set up a long-term program for developing *newspeak.* If Orwell were alive today, I think he would see that many of his ideas are now being incorporated in something just as sophisticated and equally fearful. I am referring to the new *triplespeak:* a three-tiered language of myth, jargon, and confidential straight talk.

Unlike Orwell's *doublethink* and *newspeak,* triplespeak is not part of any overall plan. It merely develops as a logical outcome of the Establishment's maturation, an essential element in the tightening of oligarchic control at the highest levels of the Golden International. Without myths, the rulers and their aides cannot maintain support at the lower levels of the major establishments, and the might itself—as well as the legitimacy of empire—may decay. Jargon is required to spell out the accumulating complexities of military, technological, economic, political, and cultural power. Straight talk is needed to illuminate the secret processes of high decision making and confidential bargaining and to escape the traps created by myth and jargon.

Herein lie many difficulties. With so much indirection and manipulation in the structure of transnational power, there is no longer any place for the pomp and ceremony that helped foster the effulgent myths surrounding past empires—no imperial purple, no unifying queen, king, or imperial council, no mass religion or ideology to fire the emotions of dependent masses. Hence the symbolic trappings of past empires must be replaced by smaller mystifications that at least have the merit of helping maintain the self-respect and motivations of the elites at the middle and lower levels of the national Establishments. Thus the operating rules of modern capitalist empire require ascending rhetoric about economic and social development, human rights, and the self-effacing role of transnational corporations in the promotion of progress and prosperity. The more lies are told, the more important it becomes for the liars to justify themselves by deep moral commitments to high-sounding objectives that mask the pursuit of money and power. The more a country like the United States imports its prosperity from the rest of the world, the more its leaders must dedicate themselves to the sacred ideal of exporting abundance, technology, and civilization to everyone else. The further this myth may be from reality, the more significant it becomes—and the greater the need for academic notables to document its validity by bold assertion and self-styled statistical demonstration. "The might that makes right must be a different right from that of the right arm," the political scientist, Charles Merriam, stated many years ago. "It must be a might deep rooted in emotion, embedded in feelings and aspirations, in morality, in sage maxims, in forms of rationalization . . ." [30]

Thus, in 1975 and 1976, while the long right arm of the American presidency was supporting bloody dictatorships in Chile, Brazil, Indochina, and Iran (to mention but a few), Daniel P. Moynihan, the U.S. ambassador at the United Nations, wrapped himself in the flag of liberty and human rights. His eloquent rhetoric—deeply rooted in emotion and embedded in feelings and aspirations—set a high standard of creative myth-making.[31] At that time, his superiors in Washington failed to realize that Moynihan's approach was, in Walter Laqueur's terms, "not a lofty and impractical endeavor, divorced from the harsh realities of world endeavor, but itself a kind of Realpolitik." [32] Within two years, however, the next president, Jimmy Carter, seized the torch from Moynihan's hand and, without thanks or attribution, set a still higher standard by clothing the might of his cruise missile and neutron bomb in human-rights rhetoric even more deeply rooted in morality, sage maxims, and forms of rationalization.

Domestic myths are the daily bread of the restructured Radical Right and the old-style and new-style conservatives. Many of the ideologies discussed in the last section of this chapter serve not only as cover-ups for concentrated oligarchic power. They provide code words for the more unspoken, mundane myths that define unemployed people as lazy or unemployable, women, blacks and Hispanics as congenitally inferior to other people. Presidential candidates invariably propagate the myth that Americans are innately superior to the people of other countries and that therefore they have a high destiny to fulfill in the leadership of the world's forces for peace, freedom, democracy, and—not to be forgotten—private corporate investment and profitability. Trying to flatter the voting public as a whole, they ascribe most of America's difficulties to foreign enemies or a few individuals at home—like Richard Nixon—who have betrayed the national goodness. Not so long ago, General Westmoreland went much further when, to reassure the more naive members of the American officer corps, he soberly declared that "Despite the final failure of the South Vietnamese, the record of the American military of never having lost a war is still intact." [33] With the arrival of friendly fascism, myths like these would no longer be greeted, at least not publicly, with the degree of skepticism they still provoke. Instead, the Establishment would agree that the domestic tranquility afforded by these convenient reassurances qualified them, in contrast to more critical, less comforting diagnoses, as "responsible." As old myths get worn out or new myths punctured, still newer ones (shall we call them "myths of the month"?) are brought into being.

The momentum of jargon would not abate in a friendly fascist society but move steadily ahead with the ever-increasing specialization and subspecialization in every field. New towers of Babel are, and would be, continuously erected throughout the middle and lower levels of the Establishment. Communication among the different towers, however, becomes increasingly difficult. One of the most interesting examples is the accumulation of complex, overlapping, and mystifying jargons devised by the experts in various subdivisions of communications itself (semiotics, semantics, linguistics, content analysis, information theory, telematics, computer programming, etc.), none of whom can communicate very well with all the others. In military affairs, jargon wraps otherwise unpleasant realities in a cloak of scientific objectivity. Thus, "surgical strike," "nuclear exchange," and even the colloquial "nukes" all hide the horrors of atomic warfare. The term "clean bomb" for the new neutron bomb hides the fact that although it may not send much radioactive material into the atmsophere it would kill all human life through radiation in a somewhat limited area; this makes it the dirtiest of all bombs. Similarly, in global economics the jargon of exchange rates and IMF conditions facilitates, while also concealing, the application of transnational corporate power on Third World countries. The jargon of domestic economics, as I have already shown, hides the crude realities of corporate aggrandizement, inflation, and unemployment behind a dazzling array of technical terms that develop an esprit de corps which unites the various sectors of Establishment economics.

Rising above the major portion of jargon and myth is *straight talk,* the blunt and unadorned language of who gets what, when and how. If money talks, as it is said, then power whispers. The language of both power and money is spoken in hushed whispers at tax-deductible luncheons or drinking hours at the plushest clubs and bars or in the well-shrouded secrecy of executive suites and boardrooms. Straight talk is never again to be recorded on Nixon-style tapes or in any memoranda that are not soon routed to the paper shredders.

As one myth succeeds another and as new forms of jargon are invented, straight talk becomes increasingly important. Particularly at the higher levels of the Establishment it is essential to deal frankly with the genuine nature of imperial alternatives and specific challenges. But the emerging precondition for imperial straight talk is secrecy. Back in 1955, Henry Kissinger might publicly refer to "our primary task of dividing the USSR and China." * By the time the American presidency was making progress in this task, not only Kissinger but the bulk of foreign affairs specialists had learned the virtues of prior restraint and had carefully refrained from dealing with the subject so openly. It may be presumed that after the publication of *The Crisis Democracy*, Samuel Huntington learned a similar lesson and that consultants to the Trilateral Commission will never again break the Establishment's taboos by publicly calling for less democracy. Nor is it likely that in discussing human rights the American president will talk openly on the rights and privileges of American-based transnationals in other countries. Nor am I at all sure that realists like Irving Kristol, Raymond Aron, George Liska, and James Burnham will continue to be appreciated if they persist in writing boldly about the new American empire and its responsibilities. Although their "empire" is diligently distinguished from "imperialism," it will never be allowed to enter official discourse.

For imperial straight talk to mature, communication must be thoroughly protected from public scrutiny. Top elites must not only meet together frequently; they must have opportunities to work, play, and relax together for long periods of time.

Also, people from other countries must be brought into this process; otherwise there is no way to avoid the obvious misunderstandings that develop when people from different cultural backgrounds engage in efforts at genuine communication. If the elites of other countries must learn English (as they have long been doing), it is also imperative for American elites to become much more fluent in other tongues than they have ever been in the past. In any language there are niceties of expression—particularly with respect to money and power—that are always

---

* Referred to in chapter 8, "Trilateral Empire or Fortress America."

lost or diluted if translated into another language. With or without the help of interpreters, it will be essential that serious analysis, confidential exchanges, and secret understandings be multilingual. Thus, whether American leadership matures or obsolesces, expands or contracts, English can no longer be the lingua franca of modern empire. The control of "Fortress America" would require reasonable fluency in Spanish by many top elites (although not necessarily by presidents and first ladies). Trilateral Empire, in turn, imposes more challenging—but not insuperable—linguistic burdens.

10

Friendly Fascist Economics

The worst is yet to come.

IRVING KRISTOL [1]

There is a subtle three-way trade-off between escalating unemployment together with other unresolved social problems, rising taxes, and inflation. In practice, the corporate state has bought all three.

DANIEL FUSFIELD [2]

WHAT WILL DAILY LIFE be like under friendly fascism?

In answering this question I think immediately of Robert Theobald's frog: "Frogs will permit themselves to be boiled to death. If the temperature of the water in which the frog is sitting is slowly raised, the frog does not become aware of its danger until it is too late to do anything about it." [3]

Although I am not sure it can ever be too late to fight oppression, the moral of the frog story is clear: as friendly fascism emerges, the conditions of daily life for most people move from bad to worse—and for many people all the way to Irving Kristol's "worst."

To Fusfeld's trio of more unemployment, taxes, and inflation, however, we must also add a decline in social services and a rise in shortages, waste and pollution, nuclear poison and junk. These are the consequences of corporate America's huge investment in the ideology of popular sacrifice and in the "hard times" policies that have US "pull in the belts" to help THEM in efforts to expand power, privilege, and wealth.

MORE STAGFLATION

Money to get power, power to protect money.
Slogan of the Medici family

Capital has always been a form of power. As physical wealth (whether land, machinery, buildings, materials, or energy resources), capital is *productive* power. As money, it is *purchasing* power, the ability to get whatever may be exchanged for it. The ownership of property is the power of *control* over its use. In turn, the power of wealth, money, and ownership has always required both protection and encouragment through many other forms of power. Businessmen have never needed theorists to tell them about the connection. It has taken economic theorists more than a century to develop the pretense that money and power are separate. Indeed, while Establishment militarists persistently exaggerate the real power of destructive violence, the same Establishment's economic policymakers increasingly present destructive economic policies as though they have no connection with power.

The vehicle for doing this is becoming the so-called "tradeoff" policy. The more conservative Establishment notables argue that the way to fight inflation is to curtail growth, even though the inescapable side effect is recession and higher unemployment. Their more liberal colleagues politely beg to differ, arguing that the way to cope with unemployment is to "reflate" the economy. For scientific support, both sides habitually refer to a curve developed by A. W. Phillips on the relation between unemployment and changing money rates in England from 1861 to 1957. Giving modern support to part of Karl Marx's theory on the "reserve army of the unemployed," Phillips showed that when more people were jobless, there was less chance of an increase in money wage rates. Phillips also made a sharp distinction between wages and prices, mentioning prices only to point out in passing that a wage increase does not by itself require a proportionate increase in prices.[4] On this side of the Atlantic, Paul Samuelson and various colleagues applied Phillips's curve to prices instead of wages, and hiding their biases behind Phillips's data, developed the current tradeoff theory.

In its more virulent form at the beginning of the 1980s, this theory means the following: Recession is needed to bring the rate of inflation down below the double-digit level—that is, to less than 10 percent. The most naive backers of the theory suggest that once this is done, the "back of inflation will be broken," inflationary expectations will be buried, never to rise again, and the country can return to the good old days of Lyndon Johnson and Richard Nixon.

Many liberal opponents of this theory, in turn, accept on good faith the credentials of the self-styled inflation fighters. Apparently operating on the premise that economic policymaking is a technical exercise in puzzlesolving, they argue that the conservatives are simply mistaken in their understanding of economic behavior, and in failing to see that untold millions may be injured by pro-recession policies. In my judgment, however, the liberals who take this view fail to understand or face up to the nature of Establishment power.

In a world of many divergent objectives that must be reconciled with each other, the leaders of any Establishment are continuously engaged in complex juggling acts. Whether developing global investment policies or apportioning economic or military aid around the world, everything cannot be done at the same time. Above all, in planning for corporate profitability, compromises must continuously be made. Profitability in one area is often accompanied by unavoidable losses in another. Short-term profits must often be sacrificed in the interest of the greater profitability that can come only from the fruition of long-term investment programs. Above all, the maintenance or strengthening of the power to protect future profitability often requires the sacrifice of some present, even future, profits. Neither market power nor the political power supporting it are free goods. They too cost money—and in periods of stagflation they tend to cost more money than before.

Toward the end of 1979, more than 100 corporate executives attended a meeting of the Business Council at Hot Springs, Virginia. Almost to a man, they enthusiastically supported the recessionary policies of the Federal Reserve Board and the Treasury. "The sooner we suffer the pain," stated Irving S. Shapiro, chairman of Du Pont, "the sooner we will be through. I'm quite prepared to endure whatever pain I have to in the short term." Steven Rattner, the reporter for *The New York Times*, pointed out that signs of suffering were nowhere in sight: "The long black limousines and private jet planes were still evident in abundance." Rattner also suggested that Shapiro was apparently referring not to any loss in his personal income but rather to the "pain" that might be inflicted on Du Pont's profits.[5]

How much profit a company like Du Pont might lose in the short run is a matter of conjecture. Unlike American workers, a giant corporation can engage in fancy tax-juggling that pushes its losses on to ordinary taxpayers. Unlike middle-class people, the Ultra-Rich billionaires and centimillionaires can shift the costs of recession or social expenditures to the lowly millionaires, who in turn can pass them along to the middle classes. Above all, the hyenas of economic life can get theirs from recession as well as inflation.

Any serious effort to control stagflation—either its recession side or its inflation side—would require serious limitations on both Big Business and the support given to it by Big Government. Any such limitations, in turn, would have to be backed up by a broad anti-Establishment coalition including, but not limited to, organized labor. The other side of this coin may now be seen in stark clarity: The price of preventing any such coalition and of preserving, if not expanding, Establishment power, is to choose continuing stagflation as the price that must be paid to protect future profitability. The real tradeoff by the big-time traders is not between price stability and high employment. Rather, it is the sacrifice of both in order to curtail union power, dampen rising aspirations among the population at large, and take advantage of both inflationary windfalls and recessionary bargains.

Indeed, not only the U.S. Establishment but the Golden International as a whole has in practice accepted the realities of continuing stagflation (with whatever ups and down may materialize in the proportions of combined inflation and unemployment) as the new economic order of the "Free World." This has long been the operating doctrine of the International Monetary Fund in Third World countries. It is now emerging as a doctrinal strategy for the 1980s in the entire First World.

In the 1960s and early 1970s no one ever dreamed that Americans could become accustomed to levels of either inflation or official unemployment as high as 6 or 7 percent a year. As the Big Business-Big Government partnership becomes closer, the levels previously regarded as unacceptable will—like the hot water to which a frog has become accustomed—be regarded not only as normal but as objectives of official policy. Indeed, 8 percent unemployment is already being regarded as full employment and 8 percent inflation as price stability. Under the emerging triplespeak—in a manner reminding us of "War Is Peace" and "Freedom Is Slavery" in Orwell's *1984*—the norm for unemployment could reach and the norm for inflation far exceed the double-digit level of ten apiece. When the two are added together, this provides what I call a "limited misery index"—limited because no similar arithmetic value can be given to such things as job insecurity, crime, pollution, alienation, and junk. The so-called "tradeoff" theory merely tells us that either of the two elements in the index may go down a little as the other one goes up. What the tradeoffers fail to point out is that despite fluctuations the long-term trend of the two together is upward. Thus in the opening months of the 1980s, even without correcting for the official underestimation of unemployment, the limited misery index approached 20. Under friendly fascism it would move toward 30. . . .

MORE MONEY MOVING UPWARD

As the limited misery index creeps or spurts ahead, a spiraling series of cure-alls are brought forth from the Establishment's medicine chest. Logically, each one leads toward the others. Together, apart from anyone's intentions, the medicines make the malady worse.

To cure inflation, interest rates are raised. This cannot be done by bankers alone. Intervention by central banks, acting on their behalf, is necessary. This results in a quick upward movement in prices and a further increase in government spending on new debt service. The companion step is to cut government spending on most social services—education, health, streetcleaning, fire and police protection, libraries, employment projects, etc. The deepest cuts are made in the lowest income areas, where the misery is the sharpest and political resistance tends to be less organized.

To cure stagnation or recession, there are two patent medicines. The first is more Big Welfare for Big Business—through more reductions in capital gains taxes, lower taxes on corporations and the rich, more tax shelters, and, locally, more tax abatement for luxury housing and office buildings. These generous welfare payments are justified in the name of growthmanship and productivity. Little attention is given to the fact that the major growth sought is in profitability, an objective mentioned only by a few ultra-Right conservatives who still believe in straight talk. Less attention is given to the fact that the productivity sought is defined essentially as resulting from investment in capital-intensive machinery and technology that displace labor and require more fossil fuels. The second patent medicine, justified in terms of national emergencies with only sotto voce reference to its implications for maintaining employment, is more spending on death machines and war forces. This, in turn, spurs the growth of the federal deficit.

To keep the deficit within limits and provide enough leeway for alleviation of the worst cuts in social services, higher taxes are required. This is done by a hidden national sales tax. The preparations for this have already been made by preliminary legislative action toward the imposition of the so-called Value Added Tax (VAT), already in force in France and England. VAT takes a bite out of every stage of production. At the end of the line, this means higher prices for consumers. . . . And so the dismal round continues—higher interest rates, cuts in social services, more tax subsidies for Big Business, and higher sales taxes hitting the middle- and lower-income groups.

Over the short run (which may be stretched out longer than some expect), the net effect of this cycle is to move purchasing power upward toward the most privileged people. This compensates in part for the paradox that making money by raising prices reduces the value of the money made. Over the longer run, however, it intensifies the older contradiction of capitalism, namely, that profit maximization undermines the mass purchasing power required for continued profitability.

AN ABUNDANCE OF SHORTAGES

Be not afraid of great shortages. Some benefit from shortages that are borne naturally. Some achieve shortages by cooperative work, and some have shortages thrust upon them.

An adaptation of Maria's letter to Malvolio in WILLIAM SHAKESPEARE'S *Twelfth Night*

Back in 1798, in his *Essay on the Principle of Population*, Thomas Malthus argued that population tends to grow faster than the food supply. Devastating shortages of food are inevitable, he argued, unless population growth is curbed. For Malthus the major curbs, in addition to sexual continence, were poverty, starvation, pestilence, and war. Today's neo-Malthusians have modernized his thesis. Conceding that food supply has been increased by modern technology, they argue that further growth of production and population will bring back the Malthusian nightmare. According to Herman Kahn, they claim that "the world is entering so severe a period of international scarcity of major agricultural goods that mankind may have to come to grips with the decision of who shall eat and who shall not (the triage decision)," a decision presumably to be made by the major grain-exporting nations.[6] The triage decision refers to the practice of overworked medical staffs in wartime who may divide the wounded into three groups: those who can no longer be helped (and must be allowed to die), those who can get along without help, and those who can be saved by quick help. The implication is that with growing shortages of food, the same grim choices will have to be made. With somewhat less grimness, the sons of Malthus now argue that desperate shortages of all nonrenewable minerals (bauxite, cobalt, copper, chromium, columbium, iron ore, lead, manganese, molybdenum, nickel, tin, tungsten, and uranium, etc.) are around the corner. The greatest fury of all surrounds fossil fuels (coal, natural gas, and petroleum) which, unlike metals, cannot be recycled after they are burned for fuel or transformed into such new products as fertilizer, plastics, textiles, dyes, or dynamite. Because these fossil-fuel deposits will eventually be depleted, the major energy reserves of modern civilization will disappear with them.

In rebuttal, anti-Malthusians argue convincingly that the limits of growth lie not only decades ahead but many centuries in the future. Herman Kahn and his associates at the Hudson Institute estimate that the resources of the planet, although limited, are enough to support a world population of 15 billion people by the year 2176 at a per capita national product of $20,000, or two and a half times the U.S. per capita product in 1976.[7] Barry Commoner estimates that "in round numbers, some 350 billion barrels of domestic crude oil are available to us . . . At the present rate of oil consumption (slightly more than six billion barrels per year), this amount would take care of *total* national demand for oil without any imports for a period of fifty to sixty years."[8] Herman Kahn makes a similar estimate for the entire world supply of oil and gas.

There are also vast proven reserves of coal in the United States. Herman Kahn cautiously estimates that "potential U.S. resources of oil, gas and coal are sufficient to supply the energy needs of this country for more than 150 years."[9] Both Commoner and Kahn point out that within the next fifty years it would be both technologically and economically feasible to replace nonrecoverable fossil fuels with alternative energy sources: nuclear fission (with all its attendant dangers), solar energy in many forms, geothermal energy and eventually, perhaps, nuclear fusion.

But most debates about resource depletion versus resource sufficiency tend to obscure one of the most fundamental facts of life: *Whenever things that many people want are in short supply, those who control the supply have important power over those who want some.* For many centuries this principle was used by feudal landlords, kings, merchant capitalists, and colonial exploiters. In India under the British, for example, crop failures that resulted in widespread famine were occasions for joyous profiteering by landlords and colonial officials, who were able to sell food at extortionate prices. Under modern industrial capitalism, this principle survives in a new form. The new technologies that make abundance possible have the potentiality of abolishing scarcity. From the viewpoint of many large corporations this has always been a great disadvantage: it can create a shortage of shortages. It is only logical, therefore, that corporate executives do everything possible to get into situations in which shortages are available. The established methods of doing this are (1) keeping production down, (2) restricting competition by other producers or substitute products, (3) using patent monopolies to keep out of production products or processes that would diminish the scarcity, and (4) throwing a tight mantle of secrecy over reserves that are kept off the market or out of production. In the case of many basic raw materials or food products—particularly uranium, tin, copper, coffee, wheat, sugar, milk, etc.—this is done through formally organized commodity agreements, marketing agreements, or cartels. In a still larger number of areas production is kept down and prices up by less formal arrangements. Under "price leadership," a dominant concern will set a certain pattern and the others will follow the leader. Over two hundred years ago Adam Smith described some of the informal ways of doing this: "People of the same trade seldom meet together, even for merriment or diversion, but the conversation ends in a conspiracy against the public, or in some contrivance to raise prices." Since then, conventions, conferences and clubs—all subsidized through tax deductions—provide much greater opportunities of this type. Trade associations make it possible for this kind of cooperation to be handled indirectly by experts who are not even on the direct payroll of the cooperating corporations. Hence it is that modern capitalism is moving toward a growing abundance of shortages.

These shortages appear in a huge variety of forms. Some come from the natural or historical disproportionality of productive forces. Soil, mineral, fuel, and climatic resources are distributed very unevenly among the countries of the world and within most countries. So are the technological and institutional capabilities of using these resources. Successful growth in any country invariably pushes it up to the limits of certain resources within its borders and makes it more dependent on imports. During the upward swing of the business cycle some sectors within any country hit the top of their capacity before others, thereby creating "bottleneck" shortages. Those who hold the neck of the bottle are seldom loath to take advantage of their opportunity; the result is inflationary price increases.

Some shortages stem from bad weather, droughts, earthquakes, or tidal waves. In 1972 and 1974 there were extensive droughts in many countries. One of these countries was the Soviet Union, which faced a serious shortage of feed stock for its farm animals and cattle. A massive Soviet purchase of American wheat sent the price of American grain skyrocketing. In a few weeks' time a handful of corporate traders (who were close to the Nixon administration) cashed in on advance information. "In those few weeks," according to Jim Hightower, "the grain oligopoly collected $300,000,000 in export payments from the taxpayers."[10] Although they did not share in this windfall at once, wheat farmers subsequently benefited from the high prices they were able to wrest from any other food-scarce countries. In what sense natural events are always "natural" is somewhat debatable. The extensive droughts in sub-Saharan North Africa have resulted in part from the pressure of fast-growing human and livestock population on food-producing ecosystems. "Denuding the semi-arid landscape by deforestation and overgrazing," two observers reported to the Club of Rome, "has enabled the desert to move southward, in some cases up to thirty miles a year, particularly in the years plagued by increasing droughts."[11]

Some shortages stem from conscious business decisions, usually supported by government action, to get higher prices by keeping the supply levels low. In periods of agricultural glut, this has often been done by destroying crops, pouring milk into the ground, and slaughtering livestock. The more modern tendency is toward keeping a lid on production —as has been done extensively in the United States—by maximum production quotas and by subsidies to farmers (usually in the name of conservation) for allowing fertile land to lie unused.

In energy, the maintenance of low supply levels has been an equally central—although less widely known—aspect of corporate policy. In the United States, as James Ridgeway reports "the Connally hot oil act, passed in the 1930s, first formally allowed the oil industry to set its own rate of production through creation of state 'conservation' agencies." [12] Under this legislation prices were kept at artificial levels by firm ceilings on domestic production. Later, as large amounts of oil became available in the Middle East, oil import quotas were set up to protect the American market from the threat of abundance. These were enforced by the co-operative relationships among the seven major Western companies: Exxon, Gulf, Texaco, Mobil, Socal, British Petroleum, and Shell. As revealed in the magisterial historical analyses by Robert Engler and John Blair, these companies have traditionally kept production down and prices up through price-fixing agreements, interlocking directorates, and banking ties.[13] The success of this Western cartel has led to its being referred to in the industry as the "Seven Sisters."

Early in the 1970s the Sisters were confronted by the fact that their junior partners in the major oil-exporting countries organized what they called "a cartel to confront the cartel," namely, the Organization of Oil Exporting Countries, or OPEC. Thus it was that the Western cartel suddenly had a new shortage thrust upon it. Its response to this opportunity has led to relations with OPEC that are best described in the remark of a rich Armenian oil speculator, Calouste Gulbenkian: "Oilmen are like cats; you can never tell from the sound of them whether they are fighting or making love." [14] Actually, it is the sound of making money. As OPEC has piled up petrodollars by continuously raising its prices while keeping output down, the Western oil cartel has made fabulous sums by operating as OPEC's distributors, raising the price of its non-OPEC petroleum toward OPEC levels and investing its huge profits in other energy sources (gas, coal, uranium, and solar energy). It has also achieved the semantic miracle of hiding its cooperative relationship with OPEC—which can be precisely described as a bilateral monopoly or duopoly—and creating the false impression that there is only one cartel, OPEC.

As prices rise, the Sisters and the Brothers are still faced by a short-range oil surplus that threatens prices and profits. They counter this threat with a combination of well-made shortages and expertly contrived warnings of imminent depletion. To support these warnings, they publicize oil-reserve figures that are limited to the "known recoverable" or "proven" reserves—in other words the inventories held underground. These artfully contrived statistics usually leave out or seriously underestimate the full amount of these inventories and the potentiality of newly discovered oil fields. Logically, therefore, one would expect that the companies would slow down the rate of new discovery, thereby reducing the burden of carrying overly large inventories and sharpening the illusion of impending doom. This is exactly what has happened: "The declining rate of oil discovery per year," Barry Commoner revealed in 1974, "is a result of company decisions to cut back on exploration efforts rather than of the depletion of accessible oil deposits. We are not so much running out of domestic oil as running out of the oil companies' interest in looking for it."[15]

As world oil prices have risen rapidly, there has been some recent increases in exploration, enough indeed to threaten the maintenance of well-designed shortages. Thus, in his first energy address to the nation, President Carter predicted a serious energy crunch in the 1980s. Since then, new oil fields in the North Sea, Alaska, Mexico, and many other countries have resulted in the oil industry itself now stating that no serious shortages are imminent until the 1990s. Even then, they maintain, if the price is right—that is, high enough—there will then be bountiful supplies. At the same time, however, they take vigorous action to prevent any tendency toward the expansions of supplies not under their control. In 1978, for example, the World Bank, reversing a long-standing policy, announced a plan to finance exploration by Third World countries. This plan was based on a study by the French Petroleum Institute, which reported that of seventy-one non-OPEC developing countries only ten had been adequately explored. Of these, as reported in *The New York Times*, twenty-three were "judged to have excellent prospects for finding oil or gas." At this point Exxon went to work on the U.S. Treasury Department and convinced it to force the World Bank not only to scale down its program but to put it in the hands of the Western oil companies rather than Third World public enterprises.[16]

In the case of almost all other minerals, known reserves are large and potential reserves still larger. But any individual country may face the prospect of imminent depletion of this or that resource. Hence a world-wide scramble for materials. The United States is extremely well situated, since its dependency on imports is limited mainly to cobalt, chromium, manganese, tin, bauxite, nickel, and zinc. In some of these fields, depletion of high-quality ores is just around the corner—and future needs could be met only by expanded imports, use of low-quality ores (which is expensive), or use of substitute materials. In any of these cases, depletion means substantial dislocation, as the populations of former mining areas are left stranded and the changeover costs of shifts to alternative sources are inflicted on the people in these areas and the general taxpayers.

Depletion of a specific resource—whether by destructive fishing methods, deforestation, soil depletion, or running down the supply of a given mineral—is indeed killing a goose that lays golden eggs. But goose killing is not necessarily bad for business. In the words of Daniel Fife and Barry Commoner, "the 'irresponsible' entrepreneur finds it profitable to kill the goose that lays the golden eggs, so long as the goose lives long enough to provide him with sufficient eggs to pay for the purchase of a new goose."[17] Ecological irresponisibility can pay—for the entrepreneur, but not for society as a whole. The fact must be faced however, that ecological irresponsibility is the other side of the capitalist coin. The major responsibility of corporate executives, so long as they are not constrained by enforced law, is to maximize their long-term accumulation of capital and power no matter what the cost may be to geese, people, or physical resources.

MORE WASTE AND POLLUTION

Hatcheck Girl: Goodness, what beautiful diamonds!
Mae West: Goodness had nothing to do with it, dearie.

The Wit and Wisdom of Mae West

To those who marvel at the alleged efficiency of American technology under a so-called "free market" system, one may accurately reply in the style of Mae West. This kind of efficiency, dearie, has nothing to do with the proper allocation of resources. The free market's efficiency relates to the piling up of capital and power—and that kind of efficiency depends on profit calculations that do not take into account the vast liquid, gaseous, solid, and bacteriological wastes produced by the processes of production and consumption, and the costs these wastes may impose on others. The accounts of the corporation, even if purged of all the mystifications designed to conceal profit from tax collectors and mistakes from shareholders, can never reveal the "external costs," the damages inflicted on air, water, land, and people. Often, indeed, the expansion of these unpaid costs becomes a side effect—and sometimes a prerequisite—of drives toward greater corporate profitability. Thus, in the broadest sense, a larger GNP may be partly attained by the growth of waste and inefficiency. "It is a well-established fact," states a Club of Rome article, "that in the world's developed, industrialized regions materials consumption has reached proportions of preposterous waste."

The waste is obvious to even the most generous-minded visitor. The garbage pails of the First World—particularly in America—contain more food than the average diet in many Third World countries. Junk and litter pile up in huge trash heaps. An earlier estimate for the United States tells us that "the annual discard of 7 million cars, 100 million tires, 20 million tons of paper, 28 billion bottles and 48 billion cans is just the beginning."[18] Less obvious to the naked eye but much larger in quantity and pervasive in consequences are the residues from the processes of production, consumption, transportation, and energy conversion. Agriculture is made more productive by chemical pesticides that also impair plant and animal life, and by fertilizers that become pollutants as they are washed into the rivers, lakes, and oceans. Strip mining destroys vast areas of land. Factories and mines spew tons of arsenic, lead, mercury, sulphur oxides, asbestos, and other poisons into the water and the air. Industrial sewage emissions alone "account for 31 trillion gallons of waste, while all municipal emissions total 14 million gallons." [19] Automobiles emit not only carbon monoxide (a deadly gas at very low concentrations) but also sulphur oxides, nitrogen oxides, hydrocarbons, carbon dioxide, and particulates. The internal combustion engine—while a brilliant device for guzzling gasoline—turns out to be remarkably inefficient in converting fuel into power. "In oil-fired electric power generation and transmission," Herman Kahn reports, "about 70 percent of the energy in the fuel is lost before the user receives the power. Autos generally deliver, as motive power, only about 10 percent of the energy in the original petroleum." [20]

More broadly, in the production of energy from fossil fuels, huge amounts of potential energy are wasted through incomplete combustion, the production of waste heat, and losses in transmission. Instead of focusing merely on the energy content of the fuel, physicists have started to measure waste by relating the energy actually needed for a particular task (say, warming a building) to the energy actually provided. They have found that the energy technically needed for space heating, water heating, and refrigeration is only a small fraction of the energy actually provided. By this calculation the efficiency of an oil burner, which uses 60 percent of the energy in the oil, may be as low as 8 percent. In other words, while 40 percent of the fuel may be wasted, over 90 percent of the energy produced is also wasted.

What happens to all the wastes? "In one sense they are never lost; their constituent atoms are rearranged and eventually disbursed in a diluted and unusable form into the air, soil, and the waters of our planet. The natural ecological systems can absorb many of the effluents of human activity and reprocess them into substances that are usable by, or at least harmless to, other forms of life." [21]

But when effluents are released on a large enough scale, they saturate the natural absorptive mechanisms and exceed the limits of compatibility with healthful living, or even with some form of life itself.

The injurious effects of pollution are augmented by long sequences of interacting side effects. Radiation, fertilizers, pesticides, and industrial or municipal sewage may come back in the fish or fowl one eats, the water one drinks, or the air one breathes—and may be given to babies in mothers' milk. Through what may be called "pernicious synergy" two or more pollutants may combine to do more damage than the sum of the separate pollutants. This is the essence of the pollution problem—a man-made plague that threatens to increase exponentially.

Many well-intended "cures" may spread the pollution plague more widely. The high smokestack deposits pollutants into the upper-air currents, which may carry them far and wide. The electricity that is "clean" at the point of consumption may come from generating plants that pollute the air at distant spots. Air pollution is reduced by filtering the chimney emissions and then flushing the pollutants into the nearest sewer. For this purpose, the planet's streams, rivers, seas, and oceans serve as the largest sewers available to flush away the effluents of capitalism. In turn, water purification programs may make the water even worse. Since untreated sewage tends to deplete the oxygen supply of surface waters, it is often converted through treatment plants into inorganic effluents. But these, in turn, often support the growth of algae, which bloom furiously, soon die, and release organic matter that uses up the oxygen supply. Thus may a body of water "die," that is, lose the oxygen that supports aquatic life. To avoid this, the effluents are often filtered out of the water and then dumped onto the land or, through burning, shot into the air. The air pollution of thermal power plants may be cured by nuclear energy plants that, in providing "clean" electricity, also produce thermal pollution through the discharge of heated water in huge quantities and—much more dangerous—long-lived radioactive wastes and (as with breeder reactors) large amounts of plutonium, one of the most dangerous substances in the world.

Looking into the future, some observers fear that the protective layer of ozone that surrounds the earth may be depleted by the freon emitted from aerosol spray cans in many countries, and by the water vapor produced by high-altitude aircraft, both regular and supersonic. If this should happen, humankind's protection from ultraviolet solar radiation would be impaired. Others predict that present rates of energy conversion would, if continued to the year 2000, double the carbon dioxide content of the air. Even if the increase is smaller, the effect—according to Herman Kahn—would be "the trapping of long-wave infra-red radiation from the surface of the earth, which tends to increase the temperature of the atmosphere." [22] This additional heat would combine with the thermal pollution resulting directly from more energy conversion. The resulting "greenhouse effect," Robert Heilbroner writes, might even melt the Arctic and Antarctic ice caps, raise the level of the oceans, and create tidal waves or permanent flooding in many areas that are now above water. The increased heat, itself, he feels, is a reason for "anticipating a fixed life span for capitalism." [23] Some observers combine these possibilities with the accidental or purposeful use of nuclear or bacteriological weapons, the blowing up of nuclear power plants, the escape into the atmosphere of laboratory-produced viruses, bacteria, genetic material, and other kinds of catastrophe. To dramatize the fact that such eventualities could be more destructive than old-time plagues of nature's own earthquakes, tidal waves and hurricanes, they use such terms as "biocide" or "ecocide." An easy scenario for eventual suicide is provided by imagining what would happen if the three fourths of mankind represented by underdeveloped countries were to squander natural resources at the same rate (in per capita terms) as, for example, the United States or the Western European countries. The answer of a Brazilian delegate at a United Nations conference on the environment: "There would be so much carbon, sulphur and nitrogen dioxide that mankind would be pushed toward extinction." [24]

In the meantime, the burdens of present pollution—as with the costs of unemployment and inflation—fall disproportionately upon the poor in all countries. For them there is rarely any escape to air-conditioned, water-filtered, soundproofed homes, or recreation areas of natural beauty and safety. For them, the ecocrises of filth in air, water, and land—often accompanied by congestion, noise, and insect and rodent infestation—are routinized parts of the environment to which they must try to adapt.

The most concentrated pollution, however, is felt in "modern" factories and mines. The Toxic Substances Strategy Committee, an inter-agency group set up by President Carter in 1977, reported in 1979 that "more than 100,000 workers were believed to die each year as a result of physical and chemical hazards at work and that the occupational exposure to cancer causing agents was a factor in an estimated 20 to 38 percent of all cancers." [25] In many cases, as with coal dust and asbestos, the physical cause of the trouble is well known to most people, but the companies involved have long succeeded in avoiding the extra costs—and diminished profits—involved in safety equipment. In other cases, where new chemical and other materials are introduced, little or no testing is done in advance and the first evidence of the damage done is the death of the workers. Thus the supermodern workplace may not only depress human energy and aspirations, as shown earlier in this chapter, but may also become a graveyard for the workers themselves.

MORE NUCLEAR POISON

> As a physician, I contend that nuclear technology threatens life on our planet with extinction. If present trends continue, the air we breathe, the food we eat, and the water we drink will soon be contaminated with enough radioactive pollutants to pose a potential health hazard far greater than any plague humanity has ever experienced.
>
> DR. HELEN CALDICOTT [26]

For the country as a whole nuclear radiation is the most poisonous pollutant.

It comes in three forms: *alpha particles,* which can penetrate only short distances into matter, but when coming into contact with a living body cell, can burst through the cell wall and do very serious damage; *beta particles,* which can penetrate much further than alphas; and *gamma rays,* which are like X rays and have very deep penetrating power. Any of these entities injures people by ionizing—that is, altering the electrical charge of the atoms and molecules in body cells. As at Hiroshima and Nagasaki, these particles can cause almost instant death. Even very small doses can produce cell changes that produce cancer after a latency period of twelve to forty years, or effect genetic mutations that may not be manifested for a few generations. But in recent decades this natural radiation has faded into insignificance in comparison with the flood levels brought about by so-called "advanced" technology.

A small amount of natural radiation reaches the earth in the form of ultraviolet rays from the sun and cosmic rays from outer space (most of which is filtered out by the outer atmosphere's ozone layer) and radioactive substances in some soils.

For a long time many people used to think that the only nuclear danger stemmed from atomic explosions, whether for testing purposes or actual war. From this viewpoint, there was no peril in the "peaceful uses of atomic energy." More recently, with growing popular education on the subject, it has become increasingly clear that in both the production of nuclear bombs and in the use of atomic energy to produce electricity, dangerous amounts of radiation are emitted at every stage:

1. *Mining.* The mining of uranium produces radioactive dust and radon, a still more dangerous radioactive gas.

2. *Milling.* The grinding, crushing, and chemical treatment of uranium ore produces waste ore called "tailings," which contain radioactive materials that last for thousands of years. In the last thirty years about 100 million tons have accumulated in the American Southwest alone.

3. *Enrichment.* To get fissionable uranium 235, enrichment plants must further refine the uranium ore. This also leaves radioactive tailings.

4. *Fuel fabrication.* The enriched uranium is then converted into small pellets, which are placed in long fuel rods. At this stage workers are exposed to gamma radiation from the enriched fuel.

5. *Nuclear reactors.* When operating properly, the reactors throw off large amounts of radioactive isotopes that may last thousands of years. Ordinary repairs subject workers to serious radiation dangers; for this purpose transient employees willing to expose themselves to high risks are customarily hired. Beyond ordinary repairs, major breakdowns have been frequent. The risks are so great that private companies in the United States refused to operate reactors until the government agreed to assume the major financial responsibilities for compensating people hurt by accidents.

6. *Nuclear waste.* Both nuclear reactors and the building of atomic bombs produce intensely radioactive spent fuels in liquid or solid form, in such "low level" wastes as contaminated articles of clothing, decommissioned plant components, and by-products given off through "routine emissions" of diluted liquids and gases. By 1979 there were 74

million gallons of high-level liquid wastes from military reactors in storage tanks. Many of these wastes boil spontaneously and continuously and will continue doing this for thousands of years. Leakages have already occurred in many places. No scientists, political leaders, or corporation executives have developed any foolproof plan for handling these indestructible wastes. I suspect it might be impossible to do so.

7. *Decommissioning.* After twenty to thirty years, every nuclear reactor becomes too radioactive to repair or maintain. It must then be "decommissioned" by disassembly, through remote control or burial under tons of earth or concrete to become a radioactive mausoleum for thousands of years.

Over the years, various government agencies interested in promoting nuclear power invented the idea of a "safe" level of radiation. But when investigations of low-dose ionizing radiation revealed that levels of radiation lower than those permitted were causing cancer, government agencies attempted to suppress the findings. Scientists are now coming to realize that there is no such thing as a "safe" level. One reason is that a single radioactive atom may initiate damage to a cell or gene. More important, *the effects of radiation are cumulative.* "If all Americans," observes two experts, "were annually exposed to the officially allowable dose of 170 millirems of radiation (the equivalent of about six chest X rays a year) over and above the background levels, there would be an increase of 32,000 to 300,000 deaths from cancer each year."[27] Indeed, the effects of any long series of exposures—whether from mining, milling, enrichment, fuel fabrication, nuclear reactors, nuclear waste, or decommissioning—can be the same as a very large dose all at once.

Then there is the military connection. In visiting India during the mid- and late 1970s, I learned that India's plans for nuclear energy plants were clearly based—despite official denials—on the fact that such plants would provide the Indian military with the materials for enlarging their nuclear bomb capability. The same motive, I found, inspired many other Third World countries to build nuclear energy plants, usually with equipment lacking many of the safety devices used in the First World countries of their origin. But at that time I failed to note the equally intimate connection in the United States between nuclear energy and the growing stockpile of atomic bombs. I operated on the impression that only "breeder reactors" produced the plutonium used in atomic bombs.

More recently, however, the American Electric Power Institute and Britain's Atomic Energy Authority have admitted for the first time that the spent fuel rods from the currently operating nuclear reactors are "plutonium mines."[28] This means that all the many countries building nuclear reactors can rather quickly follow India's example; and Pakistan seems to be already doing so. Even if not used for this purpose, plutonium is extremely deadly; if uniformly distributed, one pound could produce lung cancer in every person on earth. A by-product of plutonium is a still more deadly chemical with the strange name "americum," which is now used industrially in smoke detectors. If one of these is burned or, when defective, thrown on a dump, the radiation will quickly migrate into the air or the soil and enter human bodies through breath or food. When the new "fast breeder reactors" (now being planned in many countries) come into operation, the stockpiles of plutonium and americum will grow much larger.

The breakdown at Three Mile Island in 1979 gave the impression that the greatest threat in nuclear power plants is the possibility of a "meltdown" or "melt-through-to-China syndrome." Another equally terrifying possibility seems to have been overlooked—that *all reactors, both civilian and military, are potential neutron bombs.* To detonate any of them, terrorist groups or enemy agents would need nothing more than a conventional bomb. Thus, if there were a non-nuclear war in those parts of Western Europe now using nuclear-based electricity, the conventional bombing of power plants would release catastrophic nuclear devastation. As for the United States, it looks as though the Pentagon and the nuclear power industry together have built a veritable archipelago of potential enemy bases across the country.

As the antinuclear movement slows down the construction of nuclear power plants, the Establishment's reaction is to use such tactical defeats as an opportunity for forward marching on three fronts: getting huge Federal subsidies for a "synfuel" program for the 1980s, which itself would be a new source of large-scale pollution; shifting to coal for electricity generation on the condition that antipollution controls on coal burning and mining are relaxed; and sponsoring an Energy Mobilization Board which—in the words of Anthony Lewis—would have the power to "pre-empt the functions of local zoning or health or safety boards from Maine to Texas."[29] Such a board, of course, would be able to override local objections to new nuclear power plants and dumping grounds for radioactive waste. Thus, a friendly fascist federalism would come through new concentrations of regulatory (or de-regulatory) power as well as through the use of federal aid as a club.

MORE JUNK AND DISSERVICES

Since the GNP measures the total output of goods and services (and this terminology seems inescapable), one may be forgiven if he or she assumes that all goods are good and all services useful.

Nonetheless, a major side effect of capitalism's spectacular increase in the quantity of output has been a widespread degradation of quality that renders many goods into junk. The General Motors policy of "planned obsolescence" (also referred to as "dynamic," "progressive," "built-in" or "artificial" obsolescence) has been widely followed by the major manufacturers not only of automobiles but also of furniture, household equipment, housing, television, and radio. In their internal communications engineers and business people speak of "product death dates," the "time to failure" and "the point of required utility." [30] The overriding principle is to promote replacement markets by producing products designed for the junk heap. For one GM chairman, who calculated the profits obtained from this principle, planned obsolescence was "another word for progress." The other American motor companies, unfortunately, have been equally addicted to this type of progress.

Death-dating of products and their parts, unfortunately, is not the only form of quality degradation. Many household goods are fire hazards, shock hazards, or sources of dangerous radiation. Almost any automobile is an instrument of potential destruction, while many are death traps. The annual death toll from automobile accidents in the United States exceeds fifty thousand, while the number of people injured ranges between four and five million. Some of this carnage, of course, is due to bad driving, drunken driving, or sheer accident, if not even attempted suicide or homicide. Yet, much of this could be avoided through better braking systems, bumpers, body construction, and safety devices. The resulting economic loss, little of which hits the auto makers, was estimated at over $30 billion for 1974 alone.

Quality is also degraded by what modern market researchers call "psychological obsolescence"—that is, wearing the product out in the owner's mind. The pioneers in doing this have been the producers of women's clothes. It has become embedded in the industrial designing and redesigning of most automobiles, and the entire gamut of home furnishings, appliances, and communication equipment.

"Functional obsolescence" degrades existing products by producing new ones that do the same job differently, more quickly, or in a manner that appears to be better. Much of this appears to be genuine progress—as with safe, swift and quiet jet planes, easy-to-see television, high-fidelity recordings, and stereophonic equipment. Yet much of this is carried to excess—as in the case of supersonic civil aircraft, three-channel stereo, and kitchen equipment with huge control boards connecting to a variety of gadgets that are prone to breakdown and have doubtful utility. In the fields of producers' durable equipment and machinery, where performance standards and physical durability are strictly monitored by powerful producers' organizations, functional obsolescence is a major driving force. Indeed, according to Schumpeter and other economists, it provides the central dynamics of capitalism. It affords more profitability and productive capacity to boost the makers and users of the new equipment. The side effects are something else. In addition to shifting the balance between human labor and fossil fuels and contributing to the wastes of both, some of the new productive capacity is dangerous to life, limb, lung, eyes, and brain. This is particularly true not only of high-speed cutting and stamping equipment, but even more so of the toxic liquids, gases, and solids ushered in by the new technological revolution. A 1968 report by the U.S. Surgeon General revealed that 65 percent of industrial workers are exposed to toxic materials or harmful levels of noise or vibration. Only 25 percent of these workers were safeguarded in any way from these hazards.[31] Since 1968, with the uncontrolled introduction of new materials and machinery, the situation has not improved.

As durable goods have become more transient, such "non-durables" as meat, vegetables, and fruit have been made more durable by processing that gives them long "shelf life" in cans, bottles, jars, plastic wrappers, and freezers. "Even raw food products today are engineered commodities, designed to meet the steel grip of harvesting machinery or survive the long haul from Texas, California and Florida fields to eastern cities. Using genetics to harden fruits and vegetables, chemicals to ripen them artificially, and treated waxes and glosses to give them longer life in grocery bins, taste has been lost along the way." Dozens of natural varieties have disappeared from ordinary food stores, along with many natural nutrients that are not, or cannot be, replaced by injecting artificial nutrients. Food processors claim it is up to the consumers to prove that one or another of the many new chemical additives are dangerous. If the Food and Drug Administration had as much political courage as was exhibited by the Surgeon General on the health hazards of cigarette smoking, many food packages, and not only saccharin-saturated diet foods, would have to include a sentence: "The FDA warns that eating this stuff may be dangerous to your health." Jim Hightower, a political activist and campaigner against the food conglomerates, explains the situation this way: "Nutrition has not been deliberately trimmed by the food firms that dominate the market, but it has been inadvertently lost . . . It leaves you eating the image advertising, the synthetic nutrients, the chemical preservatives, the artificial flavors and the high price of manufactured foods—the inevitable results of oligopoly." [32]

In the pharmaceutical industry, FDA approval is required *before* many new drugs can be marketed. Yet such approval is often given on the basis of tests made by the manufacturers themselves or testing labs hired by them. Under these circumstances information on dangerous side effects may be suppressed. Thus in the case of MER/29, an anticholesterol drug, both laboratory tests and negative reports from doctors indicated such side effects as hair loss, cataracts, and blindness. Only after the drug had been in use for some time was it finally revealed that, under instructions from the company's vice-president, the laboratory directors had deliberately falsified the test results. One thing the drug companies also get away with is extensive manipulation of doctors. Dr. A. Dale Console, former medical director of E.R. Squibb and Sons, has testified that they do this through such promotional techniques as:

1. A "barrage of irrelevant facts [which the physician] has neither the time, inclination, nor frequently the expert knowledge to examine critically . . ."
2. The hard-sell tactics of detail men who follow the maxim "If you can't convince them, confuse them . . . "
3. Testimonials "used not only to give apparent substance to the advertising and promotion of apparently worthless products, but also to extend the indications of effective drugs beyond the range of their reality." [33]

These techniques succeed. In "serving" their patients, many doctors prescribe brand-name drugs that may cost ten to thirty times as much as identical drugs ordered by their chemical name. But medicine is only an outstanding case of private and public services where "more" may not be better—and may even be wasteful or dangerous. According to Dr. Richard Kunnes, at least one hundred thousand unnecessary hysterectomies (around 40 percent of the total) are performed every year.[34] Similar ratios have been estimated for tonsillectomies, mastectomies and thyroidectomies. In terms of genuine social accounting the unnecessary removal of a part of one's body is clearly a "disservice."

11

Subverting Democratic Machinery

No truly sophisticated proponent of repression would be stupid enough to shatter the facade of democratic institutions.

MURRAY B. LEVIN [1]

It is the irony of democracy that the responsibility for the survival of liberal democratic values depends on elites, not masses.

THOMAS R. DYE AND
HARMON ZIEGLER [2]

IN *THE COMMUNIST MANIFESTO OF 1848* Karl Marx paid tribute to the "colossal productive forces" created by the industrial capitalists. He paid less attention to the greatest social invention of all time: the democratic machinery of constitutional government.

During the twentieth century, the improvement of democratic machinery has provided new opportunities for ordinary people to take part in the processes of government. Through democratic institutions people can hope to combat exploitation and discrimination, make government and business more responsive to popular interests, and win expanded, albeit grudging, recognition of human rights. In the United States, the largest and richest of the First World democracies, these institutions include:

A central government in which power is disbursed among three separate branches (President, Congress and Supreme Court)
A federal system of fifty separately elected state governments
Strong traditions of local government in over 80,000 cities, counties, and school boards
Competitive political parties
A Bill of Rights that protects freedoms of speech, press, assembly, and other civil liberties, together with legislation to recognize or enforce civil rights
Military and police forces subject to civilian control.

In the constitutional democracies, capitalist establishments have tended to use the democratic machinery as a device for sidetracking opposition, incorporating serious opponents into the junior and contingent ranks, and providing the information—the "feedback"—on the trouble spots that required quick attention. As pressures were exerted from below, the leaders of these establishments consistently—in the words of Yvonne Karp's commentary on the British ruling elites—"allowed concessions to be wrung from them, ostensibly against their will but clearly in their own long term interests." Eleanor Marx, Karl Marx's youngest daughter, described their strategy (often opposed by the more backward corporate types) in these pungent words: "to give a little in order to gain a lot." [3] Throughout the First World the Ultra-Rich and the Corporate Overseers have been in a better position than anyone else to use the democratic machinery. They have the money that is required for electoral campaigns, legislative lobbying, and judicial suits. They have enormous technical expertise at their beck and call. They have staying power.

Hence it is—as Dye, Ziegler, and a host of political scientists have demonstrated—that the upper-class elites of America have the greatest attachment to constitutional democracy. They are the abiding activists in the use of electoral, legislative, and judicial machinery at all levels of government. It is their baby. Ordinary people—called the masses by Dye and Ziegler—tend to share this perception. The democratic machinery belongs to them, "the powers that be," not to ordinary people. It is not their baby.

What will happen if more ordinary people should try to take over this baby and actually begin to make it their own? How would the elites respond if the masses began to ask the elites to give much more and gain much less—particularly when, under conditions of capitalist stagflation and shrinking world power, the elites have less to give. Some radical commentators claim that the powers that be would use their power to follow the example of the classic fascists and destroy the democratic machinery. I agree with Murray Levin that this would be stupid. I see it also as highly unlikely. No First World Establishment is going to shatter machinery that, with a certain amount of tinkering and a little bit of luck, can be profitably converted into a sophisticated instrument of repression.

Indeed, the tinkering has already started. Some of it is being undertaken by people for whom the Constitution is merely a scrap of paper, a set of judicial decisions, and a repository of rhetoric and precedents to be used by their high-paid lawyers and public relations people. Some of it is being perpetrated by presidents and others who have taken formal oaths to "preserve, protect and defend the Constitution of the United States." Sometimes knowingly, often unwittingly, both types of people will spare no pains in preserving those parts of the written or unwritten constitution that protect the rights of "corporate persons" while undermining, attacking, or perverting those parts of the Constitution that promote the welfare and liberties of the great majority of all other persons.

Some may call this the normal operations of modern capitalism. I call it subversion—and set forth the logic of this subversion in the following pages.

INTEGRATING THE SEPARATE BRANCHES

Integration of governmental agencies and coordination of authority may be called the keystone principle of fascist administration.

LAWRENCE DENNIS [4]

Although there have always been ups and downs in the relationship between the president, the Congress and the Supreme Court, the general tendency has been toward a strengthening of the presidential network. This is particularly true in foreign affairs.

Strangely, the first step toward greater domination of the Congress and the courts is to achieve greater mastery of the bureaucracy. This means tighter control of all appointments, including the review by White House staff of subordinate-level appointments in the various departments. It means tighter control of the federal budget, with traditional budgetary control expanded to include both policy review and efficiency analysis. In his effort to master the bureaucracy, President Nixon and his aides went very far in subjecting various officials to quasilegal wiretaps. President Carter broke new ground by having his economic advisers review the decisions of regulatory agencies that impose on corporations the small additional costs of environmental or consumer protection. Both presidents used their close associations with big-business lobbyists to bring recalcitrant bureaucrats into line and to see to it that they follow the "president's program" in dealing with the Congress or the courts.

Throughout American history wags have suggested that the U.S. Congress has been the best that money could buy. This joke expresses popular wisdom on how far big money can go in "owning" or "renting" members of the House and the Senate. In the present era of megabuck money, however, the old wisdom is out of date. With enough attention to "congressional reform" and the cost-effectiveness of campaign and lobbying expenditures, the top elites of the modern Establishment could buy a "much better" Congress.

Back during the New Deal and Fair Deal periods, a major impetus to congressional reform came from those who felt that a reorganized Congress would be more amenable to the leadership of a progressive

President. In those days and by those standards, congressional streamlining was seen as a major step toward more rational economic and social planning.

Today, the more prominent proposals for congressional streamlining are based on the bureaucratic principles of a highly specialized division of labor and hierarchic control of the specialized units. Thus Professor Robert L. Peabody of Johns Hopkins University suggests that—like the Chase Manhattan Bank or General Motors—the committees of the House of Representatives be unified by a two-tiered structure. The top tier is to be shared by two special leadership committees, one on budget and one on agenda. Beneath them, on the second tier, there would be eight standing committees to take the place of twenty-one at present. And beneath these, there would be a maximum of fifty to seventy subcommittees—much less than the current 128. Above all, the work of each committee member would be more narrowly circumscribed than ever before, since no member would be allowed to serve on more than one committee and two subcommittees of that committee. With a structure of this type the party leadership of the House could become a more powerful force than ever before in subordinating the entire body to the interests of the Establishment's higher levels.[5] Indeed, the proposal is very close to the reorganization plan imposed by General deGaulle on the French Chamber of Deputies during the transition from the Fourth to the Fifth Republic.

A major part of the Peabody plan has already come into being. Some years ago President Nixon signed the Congressional Budget and Impoundment Control Act, which established a budget committee in both the House and the Senate and a joint House-Senate budget office. Setting up an assembly-line procedure on budgetary matters, the new law "tilts" the appropriations and revenue process toward more conservatively defined balanced budgets. The most significant aspect of the "reform"—although far from obvious to casual observers—was that it concentrated budgetary power in the hands of the members of Congress most sensitive to the needs and desires of the country's most powerful business interests. With such arrangements, presidential impounding of appropriations for social programs could be carried out with the prior approval of a cooperative Congress. More important, prior restraint on such appropriations could now be exercised through the instrumentality of a "budget ceiling" set forth in a concurrent resolution to be formulated by the budget committees of each house with the help of the Congressional Budget Office. Thus far budget ceilings have invariably been set at a level consistent with the maintenance of high official unemployment, thus squeezing many social programs that might otherwise have reduced unemployment and tilted toward higher wages and somewhat smaller profit margins.

But it is not the White House alone, however, that wields the rubber stamp or controls the transmission belt. Business interests may be equally important—particularly when they choose to operate directly, rather than through the Chief Executive Network. Indeed, the streamlined rubber-stamp machinery of Congress is susceptible to being used either to force certain actions on a reluctant White House (as occasionally happens with expanded military expenditures) or to unravel executive decisions regarded as insufficiently responsive to macrobusiness interests, as when congressional opposition was mobilized in the Senate to force the Nixon administration to back down on its earlier proposals for a guaranteed minimum income under Daniel P. Moynihan's Family Assistance Program. The extension of these tendencies as part of the processes of oligarchic integration certifies that the major gatekeepers of a more coordinated Congress may become important members of the Establishment in their own right.

But in neither corporation nor complex is a subordinate unit—whether subsidiary or regional office—expected to be merely a rubber stamp. Within certain flexible restraints, it is supposed to exercise initiative of its own. This is the kind of initiative that Albert Speer enjoyed—and promoted—as Hitler's minister of armaments and war production. Similarly, integration at the Establishment's higher levels requires a certain amount of free-wheeling initiative within the House and Senate. Every major group at the Establishment's highest levels already has *avant garde* representatives, proponents, and defenders among the members, committees and subcommittees of Congress. Thus at some date, earlier or later, we may expect new investigatory committees of Congress working closely with the major intelligence and police networks and handling their blacklists more professionally than those developed during the days of Joseph McCarthy.* We may expect special investigations of monopoly, transnational corporations, international trade, education, science and technology, civil liberties, and freedom of the press. But instead of being controlled by unreliable liberal reformers, they would be initiated and dominated by a new breed of professional "technopols" dedicated to the strengthening of oligarchic corporations, providing greater subsidization of the supranationals, strengthening the international capitalist market, filling "gaps" in military science and technology, extending the conformist aspects of the educational system, routinizing police-state restraints on civil liberties, and engineering the restraint of the press by judicial action. A small idea of what is involved here is provided by Professor Alexander Bickel's 1971 brief before the Supreme Court in the case of the Justice Department's effort to prevent publication of the

* See "Precision Purging" in "The Ladder of Terror" (chapter 14).

famous "Pentagon Papers." The Yale University law professor proposed the establishment of clear guidelines for prior restraint of the press by the executive branch. Here is a challenging task for imaginative lawyers—particularly if they work for strategically placed members of Congress eager to find a loophole in the old Constitutional proviso against the making of laws that abridge the freedom of the press.

In the winter of 1936, "the most liberal four members of the Supreme Court resigned and were replaced by surprisingly unknown lawyers who called President Windrip by his first name." This is part of how Sinclair Lewis—in his book *It Can't Happen Here*—projected his vision of how "it" *could* suddenly happen here.

Though a new "it" would happen more slowly, a decisive group of four or more justices can still be placed on the Court by sequential appointment during the slow trip down the road to serfdom. During this trip the black-robed defenders of the Constitution would promote the toughening of federal criminal law. They would offer judicial support for electronic surveillance, "no-knock entry," preventive detention, the suspension of *habeas corpus,* the validation of mass arrests, the protection of the country against "criminals and foreign agents," and the maintenance of "law and order." The Court would at first be activist, aggressively reversing previous Court decisions and legitimating vastly greater discretion by the expanding national police complex. Subsequently, it would probably revert to the older tradition of *stare decisis*—that is, standing by precedents. The result would be the elimination of opportunities for juridical self-defense by individuals and dissident organizations while maintaining orderly judicial review of major conflicts among components of the oligarchy and the technostructure.

If this slow process of subverting constitutional freedoms should engender protest, the Men in Black may well respond with judicial *jiujitsu.* The administrative reform and reorganization of the judicial system, for example, is needed to overcome backlogs of cases and provide speedier trials. It would require the consolidation of the judicial system, the development of merit systems for judicial employees, the raising of judicial salaries, and stricter standards for outlawing "objectionable" lawyers, all of which poses ample opportunity for undermining legal protection in the name of reform or efficiency.

Judicial approval of new functions for grand juries serves as another example. Historically, federal grand juries were created as a bulwark against the misuse of executive authority. The Fifth Amendment states that a person should not be tried for a serious crime without first being indicted by a grand jury. Thus, a prosecuting attorney's charges would not be sufficient—at least not until upheld by a specially selected jury operating in secret sessions. Historically, grand juries have been widely used to investigate charges of corruption in local government. More recently, they have been set up to investigate political cases under federal criminal laws dealing with subversion and the draft. There have been times when at least twelve federal grand juries were operating simultaneously and using their subpoena power vigorously. Collectively, these may be regarded as "trial runs" which a Supreme Court on the road to friendly fascism would perfect with decisions upholding the wide use of subpoena power by the grand juries and the denial of transcripts to witnesses.

The strong point of a friendly fascist grand jury system is the "Star Chamber" secrecy that could be made operational throughout the fifty states. But this should not obscure the contrapuntal value of a few highly publicized trials. A grand jury indictment can do more than merely set the stage for a showcase trial. It can sort out conflicting evidence in such a way as to induce a self-defeating defense. This can be much more effective than the elaborately contrived "confessions" developed by the Russian secret police in the many purges of Old Bolsheviks. Shrewd and technically expert legal strategies could crucify opponents without allowing them—dead or alive—to be converted into martyrs.

FRIENDLY FASCIST FEDERALISM

> In the name of fiscal survival the entire political base of this city [New York City] has been emasculated and constitutional privileges abridged. Conservative fiscal reform has a clear road.
>
> L. D. SOLOMON [6]

> The suspension of democratic rule in New York City was a fair price to pay for the good wishes of the investment community . . .
>
> ROGER ALCALY [7]

In the holy name of economy and efficiency, the separate existence of the states is ended. The whole country is divided into eight provinces with natural boundaries. One of the most logical of these is the "Metropolitan Province" including Greater New York, Westchester County up to Ossining; Long Island; the strip of Connecticut dependent on New York City; New Jersey, North Delaware, and Pennsylvania as far as Reading and Scranton. Each province is divided into districts, each district into counties and each county into cities and townships.

This is how Sinclair Lewis outlined the new structure of state and local government in *It Can't Happen Here.* In so doing he gave expression to some of the fondest dreams of American political scientists and public administration experts. In one bold stroke he provided both for metropolitan government on a truly large scale and a kind of state government that could facilitate rather than impede efficient federal administration. Doremus Jessup, Lewis's antifascist hero, living in the Vermont hills of District 3 in the Northeastern Province, looked upon all this and conceded that it was "a natural and homogeneous Division" of the country.

But this was before the era of federal aid, truly large-scale urban sprawl, and successive fashions in federalism. In the many decades since Lewis wrote his many novels on American life, the institutions of state and local government have changed substantially. At the same time, new techniques of decentralized administration have grown up as indisposable instruments of central control. In the corporations and the complex, the primary instrument is financial control through budgets, investments, and lines of credit. In the American government the primary instrument is federal aid, loans and guarantees, some given to state governments, some sidestepping the states and given directly to cities.

The new road to serfdom would unquestionably involve a strengthening of federal controls over state and local government. This would involve basic changes in the labyrinth of categorical federal aid programs which expanded during the "creative federalism" of Presidents Kennedy and Johnson. The very multiplicity of aid channels and strings tended to weaken the strength of any one string. The first steps toward overcoming this weakness were taken by the move toward block grants under the "new federalism" of President Nixon. Federal revenue sharing could go still further in this direction. If the federal government is to give a few huge sums to each state and to many cities, this would provide a stick-and-carrot of unprecedented political power. This new form of concentrated power would not be diminished by rhetoric concerning the return of "power to the people." It would probably be augmented by the inclusion in the new federalism of well-selected grants and contracts to private corporations for the conduct of local public functions.

Several institutional changes may also be expected. More vigorous councils of government in metropolitan areas, with greater power to approve aid to central cities, could help to repress any disturbing tendencies on the part of black-controlled central-city governments. Thus would the "white noose around the black ghetto," feared by many black leaders, be applied and tightened. Major federal agencies, moreover, would be expected to "get with it" by delegating greater authority to their regional and local offices. This kind of decentralization for Washington bureaus, already pioneered by the Internal Revenue Service and the Federal Aviation Administration, would provide stronger control at the local level. At the same time managerial logic would call for the expansion of the coordination councils already being set up by the president's Office of Management and Budget to bring together the top officials of federal agencies in each metropolitan area.

As a result of the impact of the 1974–76 recession on New York

City, an entirely new pattern emerged for the suspension of democratic rule at the local level. During the preceding decade or so, the New York City government had financed an expanding volume of local public works and social services by the large-scale flotation of city securities. In this effort, the elected city officials were encouraged and supported by the commercial banks and investment banking firms, which succeeded in steadily raising the interest rates they received on their tax-exempt securities. By 1975, with inflation pushing municipal costs upward and recession pushing municipal revenue downward, the city faced default on its current obligations. After a temporary period of uncertainty, the assets of the largest bondholders were saved by the State's creation of a Municipal Assistance Corporation ("Big Mac") to refinance the securities, and a Financial Emergency Control Board to seek balance in the city's budget through large-scale reductions in municipal services and employment. On the basis of these two steps, which in effect replaced local officials with top officials of the banking and business community, the Ford administration extended a three-year loan to the city under conditions that reinforced the bankers' insistence on an enforced policy of "hard times" for the middle and lower classes and possible prospects for higher profit rates for big business.

"If New York is able to offer reduced social services without disorder," observed a local publisher, L. D. Solomon, "it would prove that it can be done on the most difficult environment in the nation."[8] The "it," of course, is not merely the shifting of income from the majority of the people to a small minority, but the subversion of locally elected government: New York today; Boston, Chicago, Detroit, and Los Angeles a little later. The "later" may well arrive by the time that, with the next dip in the business cycle, federal guarantees are provided for municipal bonds on the basis of federally monitored state supervision of all major municipal activities. By that time the popularly elected mayors of America's major cities—many of them black—would be little more than figureheads, pawns, and "fall guys" for the faceless oligarchs controlling municipal finance.

Let it not be thought, however, that a new fascist federalism would be tightly organized. That would hamper the development of local initiative. We might expect, rather, that at the crabgrass roots of suburb-dominated state legislatures, many state governments would assume their old role of serving as laboratories for advanced ideas. One can see many home-grown Hitlers and mute, inglorious Mussolinis developing the arts of police state repression in California and Ohio, in Philadelphia, Minneapolis, and New Orleans. One can see some of the largest and most prestigious state-supported universities among the first victims. One can see state and local grand juries indicting the victims rather than the instigators of brutality and repression.

Walter Lippmann was recently asked whether he saw a danger of fascism in America. "There will be a danger," he responded. "I don't think there will be fascism on a national scale—the country's too big for national fascism. But I think there will be local fascism. In local communities, majorities or strong minorities will rise up if they think they're threatened. And they'll use violence ruthlessly." [9] It is clear that Lippmann was thinking of unfriendly fascism at the local level. This could serve as an important ingredient of *friendly* fascism for the country as a whole.

COMMUNITY CARNIVALS

The medieval carnival was a festivity before Lent when, with unrestrained dancing and gaiety, Catholic villagers said farewell to the eating of meat (in Latin: *carne vale*). In Brazil the minifascist militarists have exploited the carnival as an instrument of social control. All year long, the poor blacks in the *flavellas* surrounding Rio expend tremendous energies preparing their special costumes, songs, and dances. During carnival week they vie with each other for the honor of a few paltry prizes. The merchants and hotel owners cash in on the money spent by tourists who come to enjoy the splendid spectacle. In the ardors of festival preparation and then in the dancing itself, the poor people expend more energies than would be needed for a social revolution. This is the major benefit to the junta.

During the centuries of the Tokugawa *shogunate* in Japan all-year-round control of villagers was facilitated by five-man groups among the peasantry. Under Japanese fascism this system was restored in stronger form. Starting in 1930, a network of neighborhood groups enabled the central government to reach every household through a face-to-face hierarchy of command.[10]

During the 1960s the Democratic administration developed a unique combination of local participation and carnival. The avowed aim was to abolish poverty and raise the quality of life in slum and ghetto neighborhoods. The real objective, as Francis Fox Piven and Richard A. Cloward have shown, was to integrate into the Democratic party the large numbers of black people who had been streaming into the nation's central cities. This was accomplished by a new kind of pork barrel—a miscellaneous set of projects to be developed in poor communities "with the maximum feasible participation of residents of the areas and members of the groups served." Thousands of jobs were involved—a small number of high-paying jobs for "poverty professionals" and a larger number of low-paying jobs for the poor. The participation machinery led to neighborhood elections, advisory committees, frantic debate, demonstrations, confrontations.

As in the more traditional style of carnival, the frantic activity always bordered on violence—sometimes crossing the border. Unlike the traditional carnival, the festivities took place all year. And instead of preceding meatless months, they celebrated the ceaseless apportioning of federal pork.

For a truly successful friendly fascism, a revival of such programs would seem essential. Otherwise, the establishment would lack roots among the underclass. Aggressive organizers in the black ghettos might lead attacks on the faceless oligarchy itself. Better to invest some small change in neighborhood-uplift activities that will co-opt the more vigorous leaders of neighborhood organizations, divert the attention of their followers, and incidentally provide good jobs for certified professionals at the junior and contingent levels of the Establishment. The next round, however, could scarcely repeat the "war against poverty" in accordance with the model of the 1960s. More likely, it would come in the form of picayune public employment programs established under the banner of "full employment" but designed, rather, to take the edge off sustained unemployment in the central cities.

CONTRAPUNTAL PARTY HARMONY

> If a nation wishes, it can have both free elections and slavery.
>
> GARRY WILLS [11]

> The average American is just like the child in the family.
>
> PRESIDENT RICHARD M. NIXON [12]

If friendly fascism arrives in America, the faceless oligarchy would have little or nothing to gain from a single-party system. Neither an elitist party along Bolshevik lines nor a larger mass party like the Nazis would be necessary. With certain adjustments the existing "two party plus" system could be adapted to perform the necessary functions.

The first function would be to legitimate the new system. With all increases in domestic repression, no matter how slow or indirect, reassurance would be needed for both middle classes and masses. Even in the past, national elections have provided what Murray Edelman has described as "symbolic reassurance." According to Edelman, elections serve to "quiet resentments and doubts about particular political acts, reaffirm belief in the fundamental rationality and democratic character of the system, and thus fix conforming habits of future behavior." [13]

Second, political-party competition would serve as a buffer protecting faceless oligarchs from direct attack. This would not merely be a matter of politics—as when the slogan of "ballots not bullets" is used to encourage the alienated to take part in electoral processes. It would be a question of objectives. The more that people are encouraged to "throw the rascals out," the more their attention is diverted from other rascals that are not up for election: the leaders of macrobusiness, the ultra-rich, and the industrial-military-police-communications-health-welfare complex. Protests channeled completely into electoral processes tend to be narrowed down, filtered, sterilized, and simplified so that they challenge neither empire nor oligarchy.

Last but not least, the competing political parties would play a distinctive role in the complex processes of policy formulation by the ruling elites. The old-fashioned radical or Marxist is apt to say that the Republican and Democratic parties have always been the same. Under fascism, by this line of reasoning, if they are not liquidated altogether they would survive as Tweedledom and Tweedledee, with no difference between them.

This viewpoint, however, misjudges the nature of large-scale oligarchy and the necessity for creative policymaking. As I see it, competing parties that are *really* different *in certain respects* are essential for both the transition to a friendly fascist regime and the maintenance of its power. This goes beyond the provision of symbolic reassurance and a buffer zone, the two points already covered. It goes right to the heart of oligarchic policymaking.

According to Ferdinand Lundberg, the United States has a single party, the Property Party, with two subdivisions, the Republicans and the Democrats.[14] Picking this idea up, G. William Domhoff declares that "a Property Party with two branches is one of the neatest devices ever stumbled upon by rich men determined to stay on top." This view underestimates the factionalism within the "two branches." It also ignores the smaller discords created by minor parties and by nonparty political movements.

There have been many long-standing differences between the Republicans and the Democrats. The Republican party has long been the favorite party of big business; the Democratic party the haven of millionaires without full acceptance in the "upper crust." The farmer's appeal has been stronger among the large numbers of small-town, old-style businessmen and get-rich-quick professionals. The latter has provided more leadership opportunities for activists among ethnic and religious minorities, trade unions, and the lowest income groups. Each has enjoyed substantial sectional monopolies—the former in certain rock-ribbed Republican sectors of the Midwest and New England, the latter in the formerly "Solid South" and equally solid central-city districts. In terms of specific policies, there have been discernible (although partially blurred) tendencies toward these kinds of policy differences:

Republicans	Democrats
Higher interest rates and "tight" money	Lower interest rates and "loose" money
Protectionism and commodity agreements in foreign trade	Freer trade and commodity agreements
Higher levels of tolerated unemployment	Lower levels of tolerated unemployment
Less expansion in economic policy	More expansion policies of economic growth
Slow growth of welfare state	More rapid growth of welfare state
Modulated military expenditures	Larger military expenditures

The blurring of these tendencies is largely due to the power of the subdivisions or branches *within* each party. The Republicans have traditionally been the home of the so-called "northeastern corporate liberals," who join with liberal Democrats in developing policies of corporate state planning and welfare expansion. The Democrats have been the home of conservative Southerners who join with Republican conservative in holding up welfare-state reforms, and with Democratic and Republican liberals in advancing internationalist foreign policies. Republicans in the White House concentrate on trying to unify their own party. Because of Southern recalcitrance on racial issues, Democrats in the White House have a harder task in doing this: they go further in developing bipartisan foreign policies.

Despite these complex blurrings, the basic underlying difference relates to *the overhead costs of maintaining state-supported capitalism.* The Republicans express more clearly the views of business interests that see no reason to have the state assume greater obligations than those that are gradually forced upon it. The Democrats give better expression to the farsighted minority of businessmen who favor more rapid increases in welfare, military expenditures, and imperial commitments. The Republicans can be stubbornly stingy, because they know they can rely on the Democrats to pull them forward more rapidly. The latter can make more expansive gestures because they know they can rely on the former to modulate the pace of expansion.

During the early period of transition from national to international capitalism, Democratic leadership built up the "free world empire" and conducted two Asiatic wars. In turn, Republican leadership withdrew American troops from both Korea and Vietnam, cooled down the cold war and organized the politics-and-business-based détente and rapprochment with the Soviet Union and China. This alternation has expressed a clear political logic: neither party could have performed so well the task undertaken by the other. By the same token, the logic of the new authoritarianism points to a new role for a Democratic White House during much of the 1980s: leadership in rebuilding the "Free World" through closer cooperation with the socialist parties of Western Europe and Japan and the creation of an American-led complex with many junior and senior partners in the Third World. The crises and traumas of this transition period can be surmounted only through more stringent national and international controls than most Republican leaders by themselves are likely to negotiate, and higher overhead costs of system maintenance than the more old-fashioned Republicans may willingly accept. Thus, in their international achievements the Nixon and Ford administrations left behind a void that has beckoned invitingly to Democratic successors. On the other hand, absorbing stable communist regimes into the world capitalist economy may require the kind of "doing business with the communists" and business-based détente that might be more feasible under a Republican return to power.

In this strange dialectic of discord, minor political movements also have roles to play. The political supporters of George Wallace of Alabama—whether operating as a minority within the Democratic party or moving outside into third-party status—forced both parties to pay more attention to alienated white workers and the lower-middle classes. Ironically, they also served to counterbalance the more progressive forces within the democratic party and force stricter conformity with big-business interests. A still more pungent irony is provided by the role of left-wing splinter parties. As in the past, they provide feedback on mass discontents and formulate reforms and *avant garde* proposals that will be picked up in modified form by the Democrats. This function, in turn, can be fulfilled only if there are enough protests and resistance movements, like the peace movement of the late 1960s, or popular demonstrations, like the black riots and the welfare-rights agitations, to convince the Establishment of the political wisdom in paying slightly higher overhead costs for system maintenance.

UNION-BUSTING AND THE SLOW MELTDOWN

I believe leaders of the business community, with few exceptions, have chosen to wage a one-sided class war today in this country.

DOUGLAS FRASER [15]

> Gone are the not-so-good days of blackjack and machine guns . . . Enter the slick smiling lawyer, armed with the latest strategies to subvert workers' legal rights to collective bargaining.
>
> NANCY STIEFEL [16]

In their march to power in Germany, Italy, and Japan, the classic fascists were not stupid enough to concentrate on subverting democratic machinery alone. They aimed their main attack, rather, against the non-government organizations most active in using and improving that machinery; namely, the labor movement and the political parties rooted in it. In Germany, where these organizations seemed immensely powerful, many German leaders thought that even with Adolf Hitler as chancellor, fascism could make little headway. They underestimated the Nazis and their Big Business backers. "All at once," observed Karl Polanyi, the historian, "the tremendous industrial and political organizations of labor and other devoted upholders of constitutional freedom would melt away, and minute fascist forces would brush aside what seemed until then the overwhelming strength of democratic governments, parties and trade unions." [17]

In most First World democracies a slow meltdown has already started. As I pointed out in "The Take-Off toward a New Corporate Society" (chapter 2), conglomerate or transnational corporations expand beyond the scope of any labor unions yet invented. In the more narrow spheres where labor organization is well established, the unions have usually been absorbed into the Establishment's junior and contingent levels, often becoming instruments for disciplining workers. As the work force has become more educated, sophisticated, and professionalized, many labor leaders have become stuffy bureaucrats, unable to communicate with their members, and terrified at the thought of widespread worker participation in the conduct of union affairs. Some of them have been open practitioners of racism, sexism, and ageism. The media have done their bit by exaggerating the power of organized labor and the extent of labor union racketeering and corruption. The new class of conservative intellectuals, in turn, has launched devastating attacks on labor unions as interferences with the "free market" and as the real villains behind high prices and low productivity. All these factors have contributed to a major loosening of the ties between organized labor and the intellectuals, ties that are quickly replaced by grants, contracts, and favors from foundations and government agencies.

In the Third World countries of dependent fascism, antilabor activity has become much more blatant. There the response to trade unions is vigorous resort to the old-time methods used in Western Europe and America during the nineteenth century: armed union-busters, police and military intervention, machine guns, large-scale arrests, torture, even assassination. In countries like Argentina, Chile, Brazil, South Korea, Taiwan, the Philippines, Zaire, and many others, these measures have proved decisive in attracting transnational investment and keeping wages down. They have also helped beat back the forces of socialism and communism in these countries.

Although First World establishments have generally supported (and often braintrusted) this kind of action in the Third World, I do not foresee them resorting to the same strategies at home. The logic of friendly fascism calls, rather, for a slow and gradual melting away of organized labor and its political influence.

At the outset of the 1980s, major steps in this direction are already under way in the United States. They are being worked out by an impressive array of in-house labor relations staffs in the larger corporations and of out-house consulting firms made up of superslick lawyers, personnel psychologists, and specialists in the conduct of anti-union campaigns. The efforts of these groups are backed up by sectoral, regional, and national trade associations, the U.S. Chamber of Commerce, the National Association of Manufacturers, the Business Roundtable, and a long series of "objective" studies commissioned either by these groups or the new "think tanks" of the Radical Right.

The heat for the meltdown is applied on four major fronts. First, the union-busters operate on the principle of containing labor organization to those places where unions already exist. This requires strenuous efforts to preserve a "union-free environment" in the South, in small towns, and among white-collar, technical, and migratory workers. When efforts are made to extend unionism into one of these areas, the union-busters come in to help the managers conduct psychological warfare. Often, the core of such a campaign is "the mobilization of supervisors as an anti-union organizing committee." Each supervisor may be asked to report back to a consultant, often daily, about the reactions of employees. There may be as many as twenty to twenty-five meetings with each employee during a union campaign. In one successful campaign at Saint Elizabeth's hospital outside of Boston, according to Debra Hauser, the methods used included the discriminatory suspension or firing of five union activists; surveillance, isolation, interrogation and harassment of other pro-union employees; and misrepresentation of the collective bargaining process by top management. "This resulted in the creation of an atmosphere of hysteria in the hospital."[18]

A second front is the dissolution of unions already in operation. Construction companies have found that this can be done by "double-breasting"—that is, by dividing into two parts, one operating under an existing union contract and the other part employing nonunion labor. The unions themselves can be dissolved through "decertification," a legal process whereby the workers can oust a union that already represents them. Under the National Labor Relations Law, management cannot directly initiate a decertification petition. But managers have learned how to circumvent the law and have such petitions filed "spontaneously" by employees. They have also learned how to set the stage for deunionization by forcing unions out on strikes that turn out to be destructively costly to both the unions and their members.[19]

The third front is labor legislation. In many states the business lobbies have obtained legislation which—under the label of "right-to-work" laws—make union shops or closed shops illegal. Nationally, they are trying to repeal the Davis-Bacon Act (which maintains prevailing union wage rates on government-sponsored construction) and impose greater restrictions on peaceful picketing.

Fourth, the most generalized heat is that which is applied by the austerity squeeze of general economic policies. This heat is hottest in the public employment area, particularly among teachers and other municipal or state workers where unionization has tended to increase during recent years.

As a result of all these measures, the labor movement in America has failed to keep up with population growth. Union membership in 1980 covered about 22 million employees. Although this figure is larger than that of any past year, it represents a 3 percent decline from 1970, when union members accounted for 25 percent of nonfarm employment.

This slow melting away of labor's organized force has not been a free lunch. It has cost money—lots of it.

But the consequences have also been large: a reduction in the relative power of organized labor vis-à-vis organized business. Anybody who thinks this reduction is felt only at the bargaining table would be making a serious error. Its consequences have been extremely widespread.

For one thing, the morale, crusading spirit, and reformist fervor has itself tended to dissipate within many, if not most, branches of the labor movement. Dedication toward the extension of democracy has often been replaced by cynical inactivism. This has been felt by all the many agencies of government that have traditionally looked to labor for support in the extension and improvement of government services in health, education, welfare, housing, environmental protection, and mass transporation. It has been felt by all candidates for public office, for whom labor support now means much less than in previous years. Above all, the weakening of the labor movement has been one of the many factors in the sharp conservative drift within the Democratic party. This drift reinforces the widespread idea that there is little likelihood of serious disagreement on major issues of policy between the two major parties. The continuation of this drift would be one of the most important factors in brushing aside what might still seem to some as the overwhelming strength of America's democratic machinery.

LESSONS OF THE WATERGATE CONSPIRACY

Watergate shows what comes from using cheap help.

JOHN SHAHEEN,
businessman[20]

One popular "lesson" of the Watergate conspiracy under the Nixon administration was that America had escaped by just a hair's breadth from becoming a police state. Had it not been for the taped lock discovered at the Democratic party's headquarters, had it not been for Judge John J. Sirica's persistent toughness, had it not been for James W. McCord's belated confession concerning the break-in at the Democratic headquarters, and so on . . . Another was that the uncovering of the White House's attempted cover-up proved the strength and resilience of both the courts and the Congress, thereby affirming the future viability of constitutional democracy. A more piquant "lesson," offered by Irving Kristol, is that "Watergate has endowed the businessman-in-politics with an aura of corruption and irresponsibility." As a result, laments Kristol, "this [the business] sector is now much feebler and more vulnerable than it was." A common element in many of these "lessons" is a neglect of the growing strength of big-business networks both inside and outside the formal structure of national government, both during and after the Watergate period.

But all lessons imply the existence of people trying to learn how to do something better. In this case, I suggest that the most active students have been the same people who, during the quarter century after World War II, learned how to unify the "Free World" and bring about the economic miracles of the postwar period. If, as I fear, the logic of large-scale organization, capital accumulation, and the need to cope with current crises and side effects presses toward an American *Gleichschaltung,* these are the lessons I believe they have learned from the failures and successes of the Watergate conspirators.

For Presidents and the key members of the Chief Executive network:

1. Don't let political amateurs like H.R. Haldeman and John Erlichman into top positions in the White House; provide a larger piece of action for cooperative members of Congress.
2. Where nonpolitical personnel are given top positions, use true experts with proven flair and flexibility, individuals like Henry Kissinger, Daniel Patrick Moynihan, Peter Flanagan, George Schultz, and Arthur Burns.
3. Be much more effective and unscrupulous in "plugging the leaks"

in all parts of the Chief Executive Network and critical agencies of government.

4. Make fuller use of established bureaucracies (like the FBI and CIA) rather than running the risks of alienating them by setting up parallel "plumbers' groups."
5. Don't ever get caught—prepare two or three layers of cover ahead of time, so that "cover-ups" will not have to be improvised on the spot. Naturally this requires periodic housecleanings and cover-building for both the CIA and the FBI.
6. Be prepared with a reserve supply of plausible diversions to divert attention from major scandals that may possibly touch the White House—including White House leadership of attacks on state, local, and business corruption. The Nixon administration's sacrifice of Vice-President Agnew, while temporarily distracting attention and deflating the dump-Nixon approach of some Agnew supporters, was far less effective than it would have been to bring indictments against a number of Democratic senators, governors, and mayors.

And for the Ultra-Rich and the Corporate Overlords, I believe the lessons have been these:

1. For the "cowboys" or roughneck billionaires who have just arrived: Pick up some of the finesse of the old-timers and learn the grand arts of smoother manipulation.
2. For the managers of "old wealth": Bring more of the defense-space-reality *arrivistes* into the charmed inner circles.
3. Take your time both abroad and at home, as with the slow, careful, meticulous, and highly secret groundwork that led to the military-police coup of September 1973 against the Allende government of Chile.
4. Be much more circumspect and indirect in the manner of providing support for election campaigns.
5. Pay more attention to ideological justifications for concentrated power.
6. Be prepared with the alternatives that make it possible to throw any president or vice-president to the dogs.
7. Don't rely on cheap help.

UNHINGING AN ANTI-ESTABLISHMENT WHITE HOUSE

Suppose that despite everything a truly anti-Establishment president is elected and installed in office. Further suppose that, like Senator George McGovern or former Senator Fred Harris, his program is not only to provide greater opportunities for women, racial minorities, and young people, but also to reverse the trend toward concentrated income, wealth, and power. Unlike McGovern and Harris, he succeeds in winning a huge popular following including blue-collar workers, white ethnics, lower and middle classes, scientists, artists, professionals, rebellious establishment technicians, and maverick millionaires. Finally, suppose that in the course of the campaign his program becomes more militant and coherent and that he sweeps into office a resounding majority in both houses of Congress. In his inaugural address, he pledges to cut the military budget, restore détente, strengthen the United Nations, recognize Cuba and Vietnam, impose price controls on the largest corporations, provide jobs at fair wages for everyone able and willing to work, conserve energy through a massive expansion of mass transport, set up one federal corporation to develop the government's oil reserves and another to break up the alliance between OPEC and the Seven Sisters by monopolizing the importation of petroleum.

To subvert such a government, some people might think that some kind of coup d'etat might be needed. Although this could conceivably happen, it need not. The prerogatives of the Corporate Overseers and the Ultra-Rich could be protected by a combination of legal means so effective that within a few years' time the president would be thoroughly discredited and the trend toward integrated oligarchy and imperial reconstruction could be resumed by the time of—or even before—the next presidential election.

There are at least three reasons why I believe that indirect methods of subversion could do the job.

First of all, the very strength of the new president would be a source of weakness. Willy-nilly, his successful campaign would raise hopes and expectations beyond the possibility of immediate fulfillment. (This was true even in the case of Jimmy Carter's anti-Establishment rhetoric throughout the 1976 presidential campaign year, rhetoric which was quickly reversed in his Inaugural Address and first State of the Union Message.) His broad, multihued coalition of supporters would include many elements that can more easily be unraveled than held together. Senator George McGovern's activities in 1972 clearly demonstrated the profound difference between a movement capable of winning the Democratic nomination and one capable of winning a presidential election. The very first months of a populist "McGovernment" would reveal the still greater difference between winning a presidential election and affecting the direction of change in American institutions.

Second, the American Establishment—divided though it is—has tremendous resources, staying power, and resiliency. The mere election of a popular populist as president would not by itself undo its institutionalized strength. Years of experience in constitutional manipulation and the orchestration of contrapuntal party harmony would provide a solid foundation for the Establishment's confrontation with a populist president.

Third, the thoroughgoing unhinging of an anti-Establishment White House would not require a tightly planned conspiracy. It would develop, rather, through the normal establishment processes of "rolling consensus." Many disparate elements at the higher and middle levels of the Establishment would "do their own thing" to disrupt the new regime from within, shatter its coalition of supporters, and create unsettling conditions in the country.

To present any specific scenario on how this might be accomplished would be to oversimplify the immense number of possible permutations and the linkage of any very specific situation with the events immediately preceding it. Nonetheless, since the processes of internal disruption are not very mysterious, a few major possibilities may be mentioned.

It may be presumed that even from the beginning of the drive to electoral victory, some of the president's closest supporters were Establishment figures who did not take seriously his anti-Establishment pledges. Some of them will automatically move into critical positions in the Chief Executive Network. To these must be added enough old-time "new blood" to make a critical mass. This would be supplied by members of the "liberal" wing of Big Business who extend a warm hand of cooperation to the new president—an offer that no new president can refuse, for even if he suspects that their strategy is to "divide and conquer," his own strategy is to do the same. Thus he would bring into critical positions of his administration (in the departments of Defense, Treasury, and State as well as the White House staff, the Office of Management and Budget, and other executive office agencies) a whole string of "double agents." In short order this would lead to a chain reaction of internecine squabbles, slowdowns, and explosions on every basic policy issue—and inevitable resignations, firings, and reorganizations. The president's closest supporters would be personally attacked as incompetent, parochial, corrupt, sinister, socialistic, or communistic. In due course, after his coalition starts to fall apart and the conditions in the country become unsettled, the processes of character assassination would reach the president himself. He would be pilloried (in some sequential order that cannot be predicted in advance) as a snob, a loner, a novice, a fool, an incompetent, and a moral degenerate who vacillates between recklessness and inability to make decisions.

A big step toward breaking up the president's coalition might be taken by trade-union allies demanding major wage increases. Pleas for patience and moderation would go unheeded, and he would finally give his support in a grudging manner that would lose him part of their support. In some sectors the immediate results would be wage increases that business leaders compensate for by both price increases and unemployment. This would move the burden onto the shoulders of lower- and middle-class consumers. It would also enrage the leaders of black, Hispanic, and Native American minorities, who would demand an immediate end to discriminatory employment barriers imposed by white ethnic and Protestant union leaders. To prevent new outbreaks of interracial and interethnic conflict, the president would move rapidly on public-job creation. But his emergency employment agencies themselves would become a battleground among minority activists fiercely competing for larger slices of an overly small pie. The pie would be kept small by old-line members of Congress dominating the budget committees of the House and the Senate and soon reconstructing the old two-party conservative coalition in Congress. In these efforts they would be directly helped by holdover conservatives in the federal bureaucracy, many of who oppose the new president from much deeper convictions than the earlier opposition to President Nixon by holdover liberals. The president's congressional opponents would be indirectly helped by the president's appointees in the emergency job program, many of them not only offensive to powerful members of Congress but given to emphasizing quick results rather than the niceties of financial control, civil service regulations, and other legal procedures. The Controller General's staff and a growing number of congressional committees would undertake detailed evaluations and investigations of executive incompetence, wastefulness, malfeasance, and misfeasance. Under the banner of restoring the usurped prerogatives of the Congress, these activities would broaden to cover every aspect of the administration's activities; by the end of the president's first year in office, a thorough logjam would obstruct all the president's legislative proposals. This logjam could be broken only by his acceptance of emasculating amendments—or by the conversion of his proposals into measures that restore, or even improve upon, the old tradition of promoting more extensive and intensive exploitation by the Corporate Overseers and the Ultra-Rich.

Finally, the breakup of the president's team and coalition would be facilitated by the still broader processes of economic disruption. As already shown, these would include business decisions to raise prices and curtail employment. As in previous historical periods, the business community would be divided on price-wage controls. But once they are used by the new president, these divisions would fade. Businessmen would manipulate the control system to keep wages lagging behind prices and establish price ceilings that either place an umbrella over the highest-cost producers or force weaker competitors out of business. Both large and small business concerns would cash in on the inevitable opportunities, created by controls themselves, for lush profits through speculation, hoarding, and black marketeering. Still larger speculative activities would be initiated by the largest transnational corporations, which can shift massive amounts of capital abroad, provoking seemingly anarchic fluctuations of both the dollar and stock-market prices. Every presidential effort to counteract this situation would be doomed to failure—with the single exception of moves dictated to him by the leadership of the banking community. But these, in turn, would help demoralize his administration, divide his coalition, and finally present the image of a president uncertain of whether he is coming or going. This image would be reinforced by his administration's declining prestige in other countries and the humiliating snubs of the president himself by leaders of Western, Communist and Third World countries.

Thus, at low overhead costs to themselves and perhaps even with huge financial gains, the top leaders of the American Establishment could convert the populist president's promises into worthless rhetoric and render the president's closest supporters and the president himself helpless, discredited, disillusioned, and pathetic fragments of political junk to be easily swept aside by the next administration.

COUP D'ETAT AMERICAN STYLE

> If the new military elite is anything like the old one, it would, in any great crisis, tend to side with the Old Order and defend the *status quo,* if necessary, by force. In the words of the standard police bulletin known to all radio listeners, "These men are armed —and they may be dangerous."
>
> FERDINAND LUNDBERG [21]

> A coup consists of the infiltration of a small but critical segment of the state apparatus, which is then used to displace the government from its control of the remainder.
>
> EDWARD LUTTWAK [22]

Capitalist democracy has often been described as a poker game in which the wealthiest players usually win most of the pots and the poor players pick up some occasional spare change. The assumption underlying the preceding pages of this chapter is that this cruel game will continue for quite a while in the United States.

But suppose the losers find out that the deck has been "stacked" and the rules manipulated against them. Suppose they organize enough power to offset totally any effort to unhinge their regime by peaceful means.

Under such conditions, many of the old dealers might well consider calling off the game. As in many Third World countries, might they not unseat their opponents through military force and rule through some kind of junta until they create the conditions for restoring constitutionalism in more well-behaved form?

I think this highly unlikely. Nonetheless, people close to Presidents

Kennedy, Johnson, and Nixon have occasionally voiced fears of military-CIA reprisals against sudden changes in presidential foreign policies. And in any case, I think it worthwhile to consider exactly how such a coup might be undertaken.

One view of this possibility was vividly presented some years ago by Fletcher Knebel and Charles W. Bailey II in their novel *Seven Days in May*. An unpopular president, according to their story, negotiates a disarmament treaty with the Russians over the vehement opposition of the Joint Chiefs of Staff. The chairman of the Joint Chiefs responds to this presidential "betrayal" by organizing ECOMCON, a secret assault force to take over the White House. He has the support of a powerful Senate committee chairman and an influential TV newscaster. But before the coup can be attempted, it is exposed by a loyal marine colonel in the Joint Chiefs' office. Although the moral is not spelled out by the authors, it is rather obvious: A much broader basis of support is needed (particularly among top Corporate Overseers), and that the organizers of a replacement coup must plan in advance to immobilize or liquidate any possible source of opposition within the armed or para-military forces.

Moreover, a first principle of any replacement coup in the First World is that the replacers operate in the name of "law and order" and appear as the defenders of the Constitution against others eager to use force against it. Something along these lines happened in Japan back in 1936 when a section of the army staged a short-lived revolt against the "old ruling cliques." The defeat of this "fascism from below," as Japanese historian Masao Maruyama points out, facilitated "fascism from above," respectable fascism on the part of the old ruling cliques. In modern America, much more than in Japan of the 1930s, the cloak of respectability is indispensable. Thus a "feint" coup by Know Nothing rightists or a wild outburst of violence by left-wing extremists could be effectively countered by the military establishment itself, which, in defending the Constitution, could take the White House itself under protective custody.

A preventive coup is more sophisticated; it avoids the replacement coup's inherent difficulties by keeping an undesirable regime—after it has been elected—from taking power. Edward Luttwak, author of the first general handbook on how to carry out a coup, has himself published an excruciatingly specific application: "Scenario for a Military Coup d'Etat in the United States." He portrays a seven-year period—1970 through 1976—in which as a result of mounting fragmentation and alienation, America's middle classes become increasingly indifferent to the preservation of the formal Constitution. Under these circumstances two new organizations for restoring order are formed. With blue-ribbon financial support, the Council for an Honorable Peace (CHOP) forms branches in every state. The Urban Security Command (USECO) is set up in the Pentagon. CHOP prepares two nationwide plans: Hard Surface, to organize right-wing extremists, and Plan R for Reconstruction, based on the principle that "within the present rules of the political game, *no* solution to the country's predicament can be found." Then, during the 1976 election campaign the Republican candidate is exposed by a former employee as having used his previous senatorial position for personal gain. With a very low turnout at the polls, the Democratic candidate easily wins. Thus "an essentially right-of-center country is now about to acquire a basically left-of-center administration." Immediately after election day, CHOP and USECO put into effect Plan Yellow, the military side of Plan R. By January 4, 1977, the new regime is in power.

A still more sophisticated form of preventive coup would be one designed to prevent the formal election of a left-of-center administration. In the event that the normal nominating processes fail to do this, any number of scenarios are possible before election day: character defamation, sickness, accidental injury, assassination. If none of these are feasible, the election itself can be constitutionally prevented. Urban riots in a few large central cities such as New York, Newark, and Detroit could lead to patrolling of these areas by the National Guard and Army. Under conditions of martial law and curfews during the last week of October and the first week of November large numbers of black voters would be sure to be kept from the polls. With this prospect before them many black leaders, liberals, and Democratic officials would ask for a temporary postponement of elections in order to protect the constitutional right to vote. Since there is no constitutional requirement that voting in national elections be held on the same day throughout the country, there might well be a temporary postponement in New York, New Jersey, and Michigan. The political leaders of these states, in fact, would soon see that postponement puts them in a remarkably influential bargaining position. After voting results are already in from all other states, the voting in their states would probably determine the election's outcome. Party leaders in Illinois and California would then seek postponement also. To restore equilibrium, elections could then be postponed in many other states, perhaps all of them. Tremendous confusion would thus be created, with many appeals in both state and federal courts—and various appeals to the Supreme Court anticipated. In short order Article II, Section 3 of the Constitution would come into effect. Under this provision the Congress itself declares "who shall then act as President" until new provisions for election are worked out by the Congress. If major differences prevent the Congress from making all these decisions, the stage is then set for the kind of regime described by Luttwak under a name such as The Emergency Administration for Constitutional Health (TEACH). In treating Americans like children in the family, the "Teachers" would not spoil the child by sparing the rod.

The best form of prevention, however, is a consolidation coup, using illegal and unconstitutional means of strengthening oligarchic control of society. This is the essence of the nightmares in *The Iron Heel* and *It*

Can't Happen Here. Both Jack London's Oligarchy and Sinclair Lewis' President Windrip, after reaching power through constitutional procedures, used unconstitutional means in consolidating their power. This is rather close to the successful scenarios followed by both Mussolini and Hitler.

If something like this should happen under—or on the road to—friendly fascism, I think it would be much slower. The subversion of constitutional democracy is more likely to occur not through violent and sudden usurpation but rather through the gradual and silent encroachments that would accustom the American people to the destruction of their freedoms.

12

Managing Information and Minds

> There is no subjugation so perfect as that which keeps the appearance of freedom, for in that way one captures volition itself.
>
> JEAN-JACQUES ROUSSEAU, *Emile*

INFORMATION HAS ALWAYS BEEN a strategic source of power. From time immemorial the Teacher, the Priest, the Censor, and the Spy have helped despots control subject populations. Under the old-fashioned fascist dictatorships, the Party Propagandist replaced the Priest, and the control of minds through managed information became as important as terrorism, torture, and concentration camps.

With the maturing of a modern capitalism, the managing of information has become a fine art and advancing science. More powerful institutions use world-spanning technologies to collect, store, process, and disseminate information. Some analysts see a countervailing equilibrium among these institutions. While computerized science and technology produce shattering changes, it is felt that the schools and the media tend to preserve the status quo. Actually, all these institutions have been involved in changing the world. Each has played a major role in easing the difficult transition from national to transnational capitalism by winning greater acceptance of manipulation or exploitation—even as it becomes more extensive and intensive—by those subjected to them. Only through managed information can volition itself be captured and, as Rousseau recognized, can minds be so perfectly subjugated as to keep "the appearance of freedom."

Indeed, friendly fascism in the United States is unthinkable without the thorough integration of knowledge, information, and communication complexes into the Establishment. At that point, however, the faceless oligarchy could enjoy unprecedented power over the minds, beliefs, personalities, and behavior of men, women, and children in America and elsewhere. The information overlords, intellectuals, and technicians —sometimes unwillingly, more often unwittingly—would be invaluable change agents in subverting (without any law of Congress doing it openly) the constitutitional freedoms of speech and press.

So much "progress" has already been made in the management of minds that it is hard to distinguish between current accomplishments and future possibilities. The difficulty is compounded by the fact that the best critics of the information industry (like the best analysis of the American power structure) have often exaggerated the damage already done. This is a risk that I too must run, although I should prefer, rather, to understate what has already occurred and—for the sake of warning—overstate the greater terrors that may lie ahead.

INFORMATION AS THE MARCH

> The content and forms of American communications—the myths and the means of transmitting them—are devoted to manipulation. When successfully employed, as they invariably are, the result is individual passivity, a state of inertia that precludes action.
>
> HERBERT SCHILLER [1]

For Hitler, according to Hermann Rauschning, marching was a technique of mobilizing people in order to immobilize them. Apart from the manifest purpose of any specific march (whether to attack domestic enemies or occupy other countries) Hitler's marchers became passive, powerless, non-thinking, non-individuals. The entire information complex—which includes education, research, information services, and information machines as well as communications—has the potential of becoming the functional equivalent of Hitler's march. As I reflect on Hermann Rauschning's analysis of Hitler's use of marching as a means of diverting or killing thought, I feel that it would be no great exaggeration to rewrite one of these sentences with the word "TV" replacing "marching." That gives us this: "TV is the indispensable magic stroke performed in order to accustom the people to a mechanical, quasi-ritualistic activity until it becomes second nature." *

As a technique of immobilizing people, marching requires organization and, apart from the outlay costs involved, organized groups are a potential danger. They might march to a different drum or in the wrong direction . . . TV is more effective. It captures many more people than would ever fill the streets by marching—and without interfering with automobile traffic. It includes the very young and the very old, the sick

* In "The Rise and Fall of Classic Fascism," chapter 1.

and the insomniac. Above all, while marching brings people together, TV tends to separate them. Even if sitting together in front of the TV, the viewers take part in no cooperative activity. Entirely apart from the content of the messages transmitted, TV tends to fragment still further an already fragmented population. Its hypnotic effect accustoms "the people to a mechanical, quasi-ritualistic activity until it becomes second nature." And TV training may start as early as toilet training.

Unlike marching, TV viewing can fill huge numbers of hours during both day and night. According to the *Statistical Abstract*, the average TV set in America is turned on, and viewed, for more than six hours a day, which amounts to over forty-two hours a week. This is much more than the average work week of less than thirty-six hours and still more than the hours anyone spends in school classrooms. Among women, blacks, and poor people generally, the average figure rises to over fifty-five hours a week. Televised sports events attract huge numbers of spectators. Widely touted educational programs for children help "hook" children at an early age, thereby legitimating their grooming to become passive viewers all their lives. But it should not be assumed that the more adult, educated, and privileged elements in the population are immune to TV narcosis. The extension of educational TV in general—like "public interest" or "alternative" radio—caters mainly to elite viewers. If this trend continues, even intellectuals and scientists, as pointed out to me by Oliver Gray, a former Hunter College student, may well be trapped into hours upon hours of viewing the cultural heritages of the past, both artistic and scientific.

Many parts of the information complex also serve a custodial function that separate people from the rest of society. This is a form of immobilization that goes far beyond the march.

The hypnotizing effect of TV, both mass and elite, can also be augmented by allied developments in modern information processing and dissemination. For example, the fuller use of cable and satellite technology could do much more than bring TV to areas outside the reach of ordinary broadcasting facilities. It could also provide for a much larger number of channels and a larger variety of programming. This could facilitate the kind of sophisticated, pluralistic programming which appeals to every group in the population. The danger is that an additional layer of "cultural ghettoization" might then be superimposed on residential ghettoization. With extensive control "banks" of TV tapes that can be reached by home dialing and with widespread facilities for taping in the home, almost every individual would get a personalized sequence of information injections at any time of the day or night.

TV fixes people in front of the tube in their own houses, without a marginal cent of additional social overhead to cover the cost of special buildings. The young people who walk the streets with transistor radios in their hands, or even with earphones on their heads, are imprisoned in their own bodies. During the 1967–74 period of the Greek junta, the number of TV receivers and viewers in Greece steadily rose—much more rapidly than the number of people released from jails in recurring amnesties. By the time the junta was replaced by a conservative civilian government and all the political prisoners were let free, TV sets were already being installed in the bars of Athens and the coffee houses of village Greece. In America meanwhile TV sets have been installed, as a reinforcement of the custodial functions, not only in jails and hospitals but also in nursing homes for the aged. One of the reasons why nursing homes are an important growth industry for the 1980s is the fact that TV, radio, and tapes provide the "indispensable magic stroke" needed to accustom older people to acceptance of life in a segregated warehouse.

According to Arthur R. Miller, TV teaching programs, entirely apart from their content, "anesthetize the sensitivity and awareness" of students, no matter what their age. This paraphrase of Arthur Miller's comment on electronic teaching devices is particularly relevant when techniques are provided for audience reaction. With teaching machines, the programmed students are given the feeling of participation by their having to provide answers to carefully administered questions. "Students often seem dominated by the machines," reports Miller. "They don't seem to realize that they are boss and can push a button, turn the thing off and walk away." [2]

With the participatory cable-TV programs of the future, as illustrated in the MINERVA project studied by Professor Amitai Etzioni of Columbia University, the members of the audience could immediately "vote" their choice and a well-controlled local or national plebiscite could readily be staged. A trial run along these lines was conducted by the New York Regional Plan Association in 1973. Six one-hour films purporting to define *the* issues in housing, transportation, the environment, poverty, urban growth, and government—in that order—were shown on practically all of the TV stations in the tri-state (New York, New Jersey, and Connecticut) metropolitan area of New York City. The visual presentation of issues was backed up by a paperback modestly titled *How to Save Urban America.*[3] Through church, civic, and business organizations, a few hundred thousand viewers were gathered in small groups to watch the films and "vote" on the issues by responding to the multiple-choice questions formulated by the staff. Their "ballots" were then processed by George Gallup's National Institute of Public Opinion, which promptly reported how "the people had voted." The functional significance of this $1.5 million experiment (whose prime corporate sponsors were Chase Manhattan, the Bell System, IBM, and Coca-Cola) is that it provided valuable experience in the combined arts of official issue-definition, collective TV viewing, and illusionary participation by TV viewers. Many similar experiments may be expected in the future, as a prelude to larger-scale and more firmly controlled operations.

THE SYMBOLIC ENVIRONMENT

> Through clever and constant application of propaganda, people can be made to see paradise as hell, and also the other way around to consider the most wretched sort of life as paradise.
>
> ADOLF HITLER [4]

"You may fool all of the people some of the time; you can even fool some of the people all of the time," said Abraham Lincoln, "but you can't fool all of the people all of the time." Yet Lincoln's famous statement antedates the modern-day information complex and its potentialities for service to modern capitalism. Hitler's boast about what he could do with "the clever and constant application of propaganda" is also outdated—so too, his more quoted statements that big lies are more easily believed than small ones. Improvements in the art of lying have kept up with advances in communication hardware. The mass-consumption economy of transnational capitalism requires the ingenious invention of impressively (sometimes even artistically) presented myths to disguise the realities of capitalist exploitation. In the misleading advertisements of consumers goods the arts of professional lying are technically referred to as "puffery . . . the dramatic extension of a claim area." With the rapid extension of puffery to include all aspects of politics and institutional advertising, it is not too hard to visualize the faceless oligarchs as managing to fool most of the people (including some of themselves and more of their professional aides) most of the time.

The size of lies varies immensely with the directness or indirectness of propaganda. Thus advertising in the mass media deals mainly with small lies projected into the minds of millions of viewers, listeners, and readers. The truly big lies are those that create the myths of what George Gerbner calls the "symbolic environment." [5] These myths penetrate the innermost recesses of consciousness and effect the basic values, attitudes, and beliefs—and eventually volition and action themselves—of viewers, listeners, and readers. Herbert Schiller analyzes five of the myths, which in his judgment have represented the media's greatest manipulative triumphs of the past: (1) the myth of individualism and personal choice; (2) the myth that key social institutions are neutral instead of serving concentrated wealth and power; (3) the myth that human nature does not change, despite the mythmakers' successes in helping to change it; (4) the myth of the absence of serious social conflict; and (5) the myth of media pluralism.[6]

Of making myths there is no end. In an era of friendly fascist "triple-speak," as I pointed out in chapter 9, the imagery of major myths must constantly be updated, and one obvious technique in both mass and elite media is "take over the symbols of all opposition groups." Peace, equality, black power, women's rights, the Constitution, for example, may become prominent in the sloganry justifying increased armament, oligarchic wealth, institutionalized white and male supremacy, and the subversion of constitutional rights. The thin veneer of Charles Reich's Consciousness Three could become a useful facade to adorn the evolution of his Consciousness Two into a more highly developed technocratic ideology. Under friendly fascism, one could expect the shameless acceptance of a principle already cynically tolerated in advertising: "Exploit the most basic symbols of human needs, human kindness, and human feeling." For those hardened to such appeals, there would be a complementary principle: "Make plentiful use of scientific and technical jargon."

Of course, not even the most skillful of media messengers can juggle their imagery so as to avoid all credibility gaps. In this sense, Lincoln was right: at least some of the people some of the time will be aware that someone is trying—very hard—to fool them. But it is wishful thinking to assume that these failures in mind management will necessarily have a positive outcome. Unfortunately even credibility gaps can be functional in the maintenance of a nondemocratic system. They may deepen the sense of cynicism, hopelessness, and alienation. A barrage of myth-making can create a world of both passive acquiescence and of little real belief or trust. In such a world, serious opponents of friendly fascism would have but a slight chance of winning a hearing or keeping anyone's allegiance.

IMAGE AS THE REALITY

> Hitler's vast propaganda successes were accomplished with little more than the radio and loudspeaker, and without TV and tape and video recording . . . Today the art of mind control is in the process of becoming a science.
>
> ALDOUS HUXLEY[7]

In looking back on his previous writings on science-based totalitarianism, Aldous Huxley in 1958 maintained that since Hitler's day vast progress had been made in applied psychology and neurology, fields which he regarded as the special province of "the propagandist, the indoctrinator and the brainwasher." But even Huxley failed to appreciate the tremendous progress since Hitler's day in advertising and the other mind-managing arts of the information complex.

References to Hitler and Mussolini are unfortunate, however, if they give the impression that mind control under friendly fascism would be characterized by the wild demagogy and frantic emotionalism of old-fashioned fascism. The logic of the emerging corporate society and the new informational institutions themselves point toward more modulated and sophisticated approaches.

No totalitarian regime is possible without censorship. But in the age of the modern information complex there is much less of a role for the old-fashioned censor as an outsider who clamps down on the mass and elite media against their will. Today, far more information is available than can be possibly used by the mass media in their present form. The filtering-out process by itself represents suppression on a mammoth scale. The editors of *The New York Times,* for example, confront a world in which "all the news that's fit to print" probably comes to about 100 million words a day, a very small proportion of all potential news. About one tenth of this—or 10 million words—gets written up every day. But of all the news that is actually written there is never space to print more than 10 percent. Thus, the printed news is probably no more than 1 percent of the available possibilities. It is the editors of course, who select what in their best judgment is "fit to print," just as in the preparation of a movie, most shots may end up on the cutting-room floor. TV and radio newscasting is still more selective. Occasionally, the nature of this selectivity comes to the public attention, as when Fred Friendly quit his job as head of CBS news because he was not allowed to cover the Senate's Vietnam War hearings complete and alive. In terms that relate to newspaper and magazines as well as TV and radio, Friendly pointed out that CBS was in business to make money and that informing the public was secondary to keeping on good terms with advertisers. "I must confess that in my almost two years as the head of CBS News I tempered my news judgment and tailored my conscience more than once." [8]

In a certain sense, events exist only if they are recorded or reported by the media. Thus, every month there are many scores of detailed congressional hearings that are recorded only in the recondite and largely unread committee hearings, most of which are not even accorded the honor of being listed in the publications of the Government Printing Office or in library catalogues. "When people exercise their constitutional right to petition Congress," Theodore J. Gross has suggested, "the members of Congress then petition the media for attention. But most of their petitions are turned down. For this, there is no redress." [9] Thus can the bulk of congressional hearings become "non-events." When a petition is granted, certain unwritten conditions may be imposed—namely, that the event be staged in order to be titillatingly "newsworthy" or that none of the content be directly offensive to major advertisers or other powerful interests. There thus originates what Daniel Boorstin has called the "pseudo-event," [10] something that has been "planned, planted, or incited." A special kind of pseudo-event is the "actuality," a tape-recorded pronouncement or interview available to any radio station that dials the correct number. The tapes of televised actualities may, like old-fashioned press releases, be mailed to TV stations.

In George Orwell's *1984* Winston Smith and his fellow bureaucrats in the Ministry of Truth labored diligently to rewrite past history. Under friendly fascism, in contrast, skillful technicians and artists at scattered points in the information complex will create current history through highly selective and slanted reporting of current events. Like self-regulation of business, self-censorship is the first line of defense. "Prior restraint" is more effective when part of volition itself, rather than when imposed by courts or other outside agencies.

Under friendly fascism the biggest secrets would no longer be in the thriller-story areas of old-fashioned espionage, military technology, and battle plans. Nor would there be little if any censorship—even among America's more prudish partners in the dependent fascist regimes of Brazil, Chile, Pakistan or Indonesia—of visual or written portrayals of frontal nudity and sexual intercourse. The primary blackout would be on any frontal scrutiny of the faceless oligarchs themselves and their exploitative intercourse with the rest of the world. It would not be enough to divert attention toward celebrities, scandals, and exposés at lower and middle levels of power, or new theories exaggerating the influence of knowledge elites, technicians, labor unions, and other minor pressure groups. Neither scholars, reporters, congressional committees, nor government statisticians would be allowed access to the internal accounts of conglomerates and transnationals. Whenever such information would be compiled, it would be done on the basis of misleading definitions that underestimate wealth, profit, and all the intricate operations necessary for serious capital accumulation. As already indicated, "straight talk" must never be recorded in any form, and, if recorded, must be promptly destroyed. Recurring clampdowns by "plumbers' groups" would also enforce established procedures for official leaks to favorite reporters or scholars. At present, information on corporate corruption at the higher levels is played down in both the mass and elite media. Under friendly fascism, while the same activities would take place on a larger scale, they would be protected by double cover—on the one hand, their legalization by a more acquiescent and cooperative state, and, on the other hand, the suppression of news on any such operations that have not yet been legalized.

The whole process would be facilitated by the integration of the media into the broader structure of big business. Thanks to the recurrent shake-ups, quasi-independent newspapers and publishing houses would become parts of transnational conglomerates, a trend already well under way. To make a little more money by exposing how the system works, bringing its secrets to light, or criticizing basic policies (as in the case of this book's publication) would no longer be tolerated. Dissident commentators would be eased out, kicked upstairs, or channeled into harmless activities. "Prior restraint" would be exercised through the mutual adjustments among executives who know how to "go along and get along."

Although "actualities" have thus far been used mainly in political campaigns, it seems likely that in the transition to a new corporate society they will become a standard means of making current history.

Whenever necessary, moreover, residual use would be made of direct, old-fashioned censorship: some matters cannot be left to decentralized judgment. Thus, where official violence leads to shooting people down in jails, hospitals or factories, or on the street or campus, there would be a blackout on bloodshed. If a My Lai should occur in Muncie, Indiana, the news would simply not be transmited by the media. A combination of legal restraints, justified by "national security" or "responsibility," would assure that the episode would simply be a non-event.

NARROWING THE SCOPE OF CONTROVERSY

> While the Constitution is what the judges say it is, a public issue is something that Walter Cronkite or John Chancellor recognizes as such. The media by themselves do not make the decisions, but on behalf of themselves and larger interests they certify what is or is not on the nation's agenda.
>
> LARRY P. GROSS [11]

A problem usually becomes a "public issue," as pointed out in an earlier chapter, when open disputes break out within the Establishment. But even then, there is a selection process. Many vital disputes—particularly those among financial groups—are never aired at all. Sometimes the airing is only in the elite media—business publications, academic journals, or the liberal or radical press. Those who seek to create a "public issue" must often first submit their petitions to the elite media, hoping that they may then break through to the mass media. Issues that are finally "certified" by a Walter Cronkite or John Chancellor are, in the words of Larry P. Gross, thereby placed on the "nation's agenda." But this privileged position cannot last any longer than a popular song on the "hit parade." Civil rights, busing, women's lib, pollution, energy shortages—such issues are quickly created and then unceremoniously even cast into the shadows of the elite media. Under such circumstances, the time available in the hit parade of vital issues is not enough for serious presentation, let alone sustained analysis, of alternative views. This kind of issue creation helps nourish the drift toward a new corporate society in which the range of public issues would be narrowed much more rigorously and the nation's agenda rendered much more remote from the real decision making behind the curtains of a more integrated establishment.

In *Don't Blame the People,* a well-documented study of bias in the mass media, Robert Cirino shows in detail how "money buys and operates the media" and how this fact "works to the advantage of those with conservative viewpoints," namely, the radical right, the solid conservatives, and the moderate conservatives. The radical left and the solid liberals are outside the limits, thus leaving the moderate liberals to "compete alone against the combined mass media power of the conservative camp."

But to have their petitions recognized by the mass media, the moderate liberals usually have to accept or operate within the unwritten rules of the game. Thus their tendency, I would argue, is increasingly to press upon moderate conservatives the kind of reforms which, although usually opposed by solid conservatives, are required to strengthen Establishment conservatism. Similarly, the tendency is among the solid liberals and the radical left to win some slight hearing for their own voices by accepting as a fact of life (what choice is there?) the agenda as certified by the media. The middle ground is moved still further to the right as conservative or moderate-liberal money subsidizes the radical left and the more militant liberals.

Such shifts are supported by the growth of highly sophisticated conservatism, as illustrated by the *National Review, Commentary,* and *The Public Interest.* Within these elite circles the spirit of conservative controversy flourishes, both dominating the agendas of nonconservatives and giving the appearance of broader freedom. How much further a friendly fascist regime would go in narrowing still further the limits of elite opinion among solid liberals and the radical left is impossible to predict. The important point is that the basic trends in the information complex could render dissenting or critical opinions increasingly isolated and impotent.

MANUFACTURING OPINION BY POLLING

> The poll, though a scientifically shaped instrument, cannot be a neutral construct . . . The (opinion) survey is invariably a mechanism of manipulative control.
>
> HERBERT SCHILLER [12]

Many social scientists have dreamed wistfully of opinion polls that might provide a truly unbiased reflection of what various groups of people are really thinking. But the requirements for translating this dream into reality are many. They include efforts to estimate the intensity and salience of opinions as well as their direction. They include depth interviews that get beyond the rigid limitations of getting brief responses to a fixed set of prefabricated questions. And since any set of questions implies some bias in the very selection and presentation of the subject matter, another requirement would be the conduct of opinion surveys by a wide variety of different groups, including those that reject the basic premises and value orientations of the more powerful elements in society. The hope of some day living up to such requirements has nourished the belief that opinion polls, by conveying the people's will more pointedly and frequently than elections, might lead at last to the attainment of true citizen sovereignty.

But the basic thrust of opinion measurement has been to assist in the manipulation of opinion by large corporations, government agencies, and well-financed political candidates. A major part of the corporate effort has been in market research. With the growth of advertising on radio, and then on TV, audience surveys became the analogue of the statistics on the circulation of newspapers and magazines. There was no other way to estimate the size of the audience. The surveyors went further: they provided information not only on audience size but also on audience make-up reaction and preferences. This information is particularly useful to business when it is tied in with specific marketing and public relations efforts. Probably the largest and stablest flow of funds to opinion research companies comes from executives in search of help on changes in products, packaging, or advertising techniques. Some of these companies have been brilliantly successful in helping public relations men project fountain pens as body images, automobiles as wives, mistresses, or mothers, cigarettes as symbols of masculinity and sexual potency, and ladies' underwear as reassurance of femininity to working women who have taken over functions traditionally limited to men. In all such cases, the more scientifically valid the survey, the more it can do to help manipulate consumer opinion and guide consumer behavior.

The same principle applies to opinion polling by government agencies and political candidates. The highly professional survey can be immensely helpful in packaging either a policy or a candidate. The impact on political campaigns is particularly powerful when, as with selling soap or cigarettes, polling is combined with image creation through TV. "The real combined effects of polls and television," write two observers, "have been to make obsolete the traditional style of American politics, and to substitute a 'cool' corporate-executive style. This is the 'new politics' as it actually is today—purposefully analytic, empirically opportunistic, and administratively manipulative." [13] In this new politics, as in the most advanced market-research surveys, polling rises to the realm of "straight talk" and by that token is highly confidential. Only through leaks or exposés do we learn of studies like the Semantic Differential Test conducted by John Maddox as preparation for the creation of Nixon's TV image in the 1968 campaign. By asking people all over the country what qualities the best possible chief executive should have, Maddox created an Ideal President Curve and uncovered a Personality Gap—particularly on the "cold-warm continuum"—between Nixon and Humphrey. "If the real personality warmth of Mr. Nixon could be more adequately exposed, it would release a flood of other inhibitions about him—and make him more tangible as a person to large numbers of Humphrey leaners." [14] The term "real personality warmth," to describe Nixon was, of course, a departure from the frankness of pure straight talk, but nevertheless conveyed the message to Nixon's campaign managers: their task was to wrap a cold candidate in a package of apparent warmth.

On the other hand, instead of being a confidential guide to mind managers, opinion polls and surveys can themselves be constructed for direct propagandistic purposes. For example, when the TV industry was being criticized for gulling little boys and girls into the bliss of mass consumption (without reference to the quality of the products sold), the Television Information Office (the public relations unit of the National Association of Broadcasters) commissioned the Roper Organization to conduct a poll. In due course they were able to issue a press release to the effect that "seventy four per cent of adult Americans approve the principle of commercial sponsorship and support of children's television programs." But the questions asked by Roper were cleverly slanted. Thus: "How do you feel—that there should be no commercials on any children's program or that it is all right to have them if they don't take advantage of children?" The editors of *Transaction* made this comment: "The saving beauty of that last clause!" [15] A poll-taker's masterpieces may be found regularly in the many polls on current policy issues and in those political polls designed to celebrate the virtues of the candidate financing the poll. In 1972, one of the Nixon campaign organizations put this question to the voters: "Do you think President Nixon has gone far enough in combating crime or should he go still further?" This is a clever variant of the old question "Have you stopped beating your wife?" Any answer forces the respondent to accept the premise behind the question.

In the past few years, Herbert Schiller points out, "the best-known polling companies have either become weighty economic units in their own right, or have been incorporated into business conglomerate empires." Louis Harris and Associates, Yankelovich, Daniel Starch, the Roper Organization, and at least sixteen others have all been bought up by big business. This trend to consolidation is associated with the transnational extension of the larger polling companies and their intimate working relationships with the transnational public relations firms. These trends seem likely to continue. If they do, whatever looseness that now exists between polling practices and the needs of the powerful is bound to diminish. The truly scientific polls would become confidential aids to manipulation and the trickier polls (which themselves may be prepared on scientific lines) increasingly used in the managing of minds and the packaging of consciousness. With TV and education as a new form of lockstep, the image as reality and monitoring as the message, the final touches could be added to the new realities of citizen, consumer, and employee serfdom.

THE ELECTRONIC THRONE

The White House is now essentially a TV performance.
EDMUND CARPENTER [16]

No mighty king, no ambitious emperor, no pope, or prophet ever dreamt of such an awesome pulpit, so potent a magic wand.
FRED W. FRIENDLY [17]

In capitalist countries the business of all the private mass media is making money from advertising revenue. Their product is the seeing, listening, or reading audience—or more specifically the opportunity to influence the audience. Although the members of the TV and radio audience seem to be getting something for nothing, in reality they pay for the nominally free service through the prices they pay for advertised products. The larger the estimated audience, the more money the media receive from advertisers.

The biggest exception is the provision of free time—usually prime time—to the chief executive. In return, the media feel they maintain the goodwill of a government which has granted them without any substantial charge the highly profitable right to use the airwaves. This indirect cash nexus is customarily smothered in a thick gravy of rhetoric about "public service." But no equivalent services are provided for the chief executive's political opposition, or for lesser politicians. And in the United States, as distinct from some other capitalist countries, the media extort enormous fees from all candidates for political office, a practice that heightens the dependence of all elected officeholders (including the president) upon financial contributions from more or less the same corporations who give the media their advertising revenue.

Friendly fascism in the United States would not need a charismatic, apparently all-powerful leader such as Mussolini or Hitler—so I have argued throughout this book. The chief executive, rather, becomes the nominal head of a network that not only serves as a linchpin to help hold the Establishment together but also provides it with a sanctimonious aura of legitimacy through the imagery of the presidential person, his family, his associates, and their doings. The chief executive is already a TV performer, and his official residence is indeed "an awesome pulpit" from which he and his entire production staff can wield a potent "magic wand."

If historical analogies to old-fashioned fascism are needed, then the Japanese Emperor is a little closer than Hitler or Mussolini. The further integration of the Establishment's top levels would not remove power from the chief executive, but it would accentuate the need for at least one fully presented face, to help counterbalance the facelessness of the oligarchy and legitimate the regime as a whole. What is more, liberal commentators can be relied upon to exaggerate the power of the throne, thereby distracting attention from the powers operating behind and through it. This phenomenon itself is vivid testimony to the power of presidential imagery as a substitute for reality.

MONITORING AS THE MESSAGE

No one shall feel alone, ignored
As unrecorded blanks,
Take heart, your vital selves are stored,
In giant data banks.

Author's adaptation from
FELICIA LAMPERT [18]

Although all the novelists of totalitarian futures foresaw monitoring by despotic rulers, they generally failed to appreciate the potentialities of advanced technology. The Oligarchs of Jack London's *The Iron Heel* and the Minute Men in Sinclair Lewis's *It Can't Happen Here* rely on spies. In Eugene Zamyatin's *We* everyone lives in apartments with transparent glass walls (with permission curtains that can be pulled during sexual intercourse) and an agent of the Well-Doer checking entrances and exits. Modern monitoring methods appear only in George Orwell's *1984,* Big Brother's spies watch people through two-way TV screens and listen to them through microphones. In the Garrison State of political scientist Harold Lasswell, the Elites do not even get this far. Their use of modern technology is limited to coercion, propaganda, and drugs.

This collective underestimation has special meaning. If farsighted people in earlier decades could go wrong at a time when informational technologies were moving along very slowly, estimates prepared in the 1970s and 1980s, when these technologies are progressing at startling speed, might be even more off base.

Nonetheless, my own guess is that in the new era of international capitalism societal monitoring has important consequences entirely apart from the content or quality of the information obtained. To revert to McLuhan's style of discourse, the message is that "they" are watching.

Although Big Brothers of friendly fascism in the United States might not use two-way screens, their instruments of personal surveillance would be highly advanced. On the basis of present technologies alone, we may assume the availability of the following options:

1. The tapping of any telephone wires or cables
2. The use of any wires in the "wired society" as listening devices, even when the receiver is on the hook or the dial at "off"
3. The tapping of computer tapes and computer communication lines
4. Listening in through remote auditory devices independent of wires or plants
5. The major extension of visual surveillance and optical scanning through TV monitoring and taping in public places, work places, and (with telescopic TV operating through windows) homes
6. Recording individual peculiarities through fingerprints, voice-prints, and polygraphs (sometimes called "lie detectors")
7. Checking on human movement and activity through remote sensing devices such as infrared cameras and heat-radiation detectors
8. The extension of "mail cover" techniques, which record the names and addresses of senders and receivers, to include scanning of contents
9. Sensing and reporting devices embodied in credit cards and automobile tags
10. Transponders (miniature electronic devices) implanted in the brains of arrestees released on bail, criminals on parole or probation, and patients leaving mental institutions [19]

Rather than replacing old-fashioned undercover agents, the new techniques would require more and better trained personnel. During the 1970s an estimated two hundred thousand people were working for America's foreign intelligence apparatus. While some of these were involved in the surveillance of people involved at home in antiwar and ecology movements, the full growth of high-technology, professionalized domestic monitoring would probably require another two hundred thousand positions. With this kind of staffing it would no longer be necessary for policemen to masquerade as newspapermen at demonstrations and press conferences. Qualified newspapermen—along with editors and administrative personnel—would handle the task more efficiently through a form of "on-the-job moonlighting." Students with special scholarships would be able to record professors' lectures and classroom discussions. Both medical personnel and actual patients would monitor confessions on the psychoanalyst's couch and uninhibited activities at encounter groups. A large professional core, moreover, would be able to handle a still larger number of volunteers. Thus the use of Boy Scouts as informers, as initiated some years ago by the FBI in Rochester, suggests untold opportunities for similar use of school children, 4-H clubs, and other youth groups. Under Operation SAFE (Scout Awareness for Emergencies) Boy Scouts were instructed among other things to report on unusual activity or lack of activity in neighbors' homes.

Covert monitoring, however, would probably be dwarfed by the overt collection of information from acquiescent respondents. The decennial census, as required by the Constitution, would become a ceaseless census—with occasional head-counting supplemented by annual, quarterly, monthly, weekly, and, at times even daily reports and sample surveys. Market surveys and opinion polling would cover the entire population—and special target areas—more thoroughly than ever before. Sophisticated research projects and evaluation studies would multiply, with priority given to actual or potential disaffection. Educational institutions and large employers would explore new frontiers in the testing of intelligence, skills, emotional stability, and personal values.

In foreign intelligence activities, the justification for collecting mountains of data has traditionally been the resulting molehill of secret information on military capabilities, intentions, or movements. In corporate espionage the object has been to uncover technological or marketing secrets. Under friendly fascism, however, surveillance would have a broader objective: the promotion of conformist behavior. The details of monitored behavior might be less important than the influence on behavior of the fear that one's words or actions are being recorded.

It must not be thought, however, that personal privacy would be entirely destroyed. Rather, it would become a special privilege enjoyed by the highest level of the Establishment and its organizations. This privilege would not be costless. It would require protective work by experts in uncovering or jamming all monitoring devices, in responding evasively to all official questionnaires, in keeping serious researchers busy on other projects, and in feeding "inside dopesters" with titillating information on the middle levels of decision making.

WOMB-TO-TOMB DOSSIERS

All monitoring, no matter what the primary purpose may be, provides informaton that can be used in compiling dossiers on individuals. As a Rand Corporation computer expert has put it, "You can extract intelligence information from a statistical system and get statistics from an intelligence system."[20]

But to extract high-grade intelligence on individuals, three requirements must be met.

The first is the recording of all information received. With the expanding use of electronic recording devices, this requirement is already being met.

The second is the pooling of all available information. At first, it seemed that the way to do this was through a Federal Data Center to collect and computerize all machine readable data from all federal agencies. In the name of better statistical information, this was first proposed in 1965 by a committee of the Social Science Research Council, headed by Richard Ruggles, a Yale economist. The idea was further articulated and defended in reports by Edgar S. Dunn, Jr., of Resources of the Future, and Carl Kaysen, head of Princeton's Institute for Advanced Study. The proposal was publicly attacked by a few members of Congress as a threat to individual privacy. Less publicly, it was criticized as a naive and old-fashioned form of overcentralization ill-suited to modern organizational forms. In its place there developed the more advanced concept of a data complex—that is, a network of specialized data banks. Parts of this network are already in operation: the new National Crime Information Bureau; the files of the various civilian and military agencies; the millions of personal files held by the Social Security Administration, Internal Revenue Service, Department of Defense, Veterans Administration, Civil Service Commission, Passport Office, National Science Foundation, Census Bureau, and the revived Selective Service System; the new statistical data banks being set up in the fields of education, health, and mental health; and the more than 100 million personal files in the hands of credit-rating bureaus and banks. Major progress is being made in the facilitating of data interchange through standardization of coding, remote access facilities, and procedures for the release of presumably confidential information. As of early in 1980 detailed plans were worked out to register the country's young people without their knowing through what is known as "passive" or "faceless" registration. This would be done by compiling a computerized list of names and addresses by assembling the information from school records, the Internal Revenue Service, the Social Security systems, and state driver's license bureaus.

The third requirement is the capability to sift or synthesize available raw data. A complete womb-to-tomb dossier on any individual—even if expressed in wholly intelligible English—would be a series of volumes more difficult to comprehend than James Joyce's *Finnegan's Wake*. To be useful, a dossier must represent refined—that is, highly filtered—data, not raw indigestible data bits. This requirement is also being met through a combination of computerized scanning facilities and the growth of personal expertise in data selection.

The most significant factors, however, are the uses to which dossiers may be put. Under friendly fascism, I suggest, these uses would be a combination of the well known and the novel.

The most well-known use would be witch-hunting. This would come in slow stages, and could include: the updating (or revival) of the Attorney General's list of subversive organizations, already attempted by former President Nixon; [21] new legislation and Supreme Court decisions to remove what former Assistant Attorney General Robert C. Mardian called "the recent tidal wave of legalisms which has clouded all personal security programs"; [22] the extension of witch hunts and blacklists to all government contractors and enterprises, such as TV stations, operating under government franchise; the broadening of grounds for dismissal (or refusal to hire) from loyalty and security to simple efficiency. The old principle of guilt by association, developed by Senator Joseph McCarthy during the late 1940s and early 1950s would be more powerful, inasmuch as with modern monitoring and retrieval much more information would be more powerful, inasmuch as with modern monitoring and retrieval much more would be known about any person's associations. "Second order associations," that is, the associations of a person's relatives and direct associates would also be tracked down. "I have in my hand a computer printout proving that . . ." etc., could be the classic opening statement of the new Grand Inquisitors. But this would rarely be done—as in the McCarthy era—by a lone wolf on the floor of the Congress. Rather, it would be done by faceless men behind the closed doors of bureaucratic committees or grand juries.

A similar use would be direct character assassination and defamation. Here the womb-to-tomb dossier can be invaluable. On the one hand, it can reveal embarrassing personal facts on practically everyone. Seen in context, these facts may indeed demonstrate past personal wrongdoing or even proclivities for future behavior of the same sort. On the other hand, if the dossier is complete enough, it can provide the basis for pulling facts out of context and holding them over a person's head as a weapon against him. For many years J. Edgar Hoover, as head of the Federal Bureau of Investigation, provided such a serivce to presidents. With the new technologies, this service could be supplied as a matter of course to all top members of the oligarchy.

In the McCarthy era Senator Millard Tydings of Maryland was publicly pilloried through use of a photograph showing him in close conversation with Earl Browder, the then Communist leader in the United States. The photograph was a phony one—prepared by putting two unrelated photographs together. The creative assembly of unrelated sounds is now possible through electronic means. A person's words, as recorded on electronic tape, may now be easily edited by dropping out key words. If enough care is exercised, nobody can detect the elision. Beyond that, if the vocal part of a person's dossier is large and varied enough, the phonemes—separate sounds—can be completely rearranged. Thus through "tape-recoding," a person's own voice may be used to say anything that the tape recorders want him to say. With much greater difficulty the same principle is applicable to the editing of film and video tapes. Here the problem is one of whether the visual record is large enough. If so, the use of new RAVE methods (Random Access Video Editing) would allow preparation of the Tydings-Browder type of picture in cinematic form. There would be few limitations other than the imagination or the conscience of the editors.

A more novel, and widespread, use would be the application to people—called personnel or "human resources"—of the inventory-control methods developed during the 1960s with respect to goods and machinery. The first problem in inventory control has always been that of managing huge amounts of records. With computerization, this task has at long last become manageable. In the personnel field, however, even such simple tasks as compiling rosters of scientific and technological personnel have been bungled. With the growth of a computerized dossier network, however, and enough R & D investment in its perfection, it will be possible to keep up-to-date inventories on all employees in America. As with industrial inventory management, this new system will facilitate efforts to find the right people for specific slots and arrange for whatever retooling might be necessary for a smooth fit.

Here also *jiujitsu* techniques could be used, by seizing the attackers of the dossier system and using their arguments in strengthening it. Outcries against misinformation in the files could be met by procedures for providing fuller information. Protests against military surveillance of civilians could be met by extended civilian surveillance. Complaints against duplicating and uncoordinated work by monitoring agencies could be met by more coordination and cooperative interchange. The central thrust of those demanding protection of individual rights to privacy and due process could be deflected by developing complicated devices for the purging or destruction of incriminating files—devices that the oligarchs themselves could easily utilize for their own protection and that of their most trustworthy managerial and technical aides.

ECONOMIC AND SOCIAL VINDICATORS

The tacit messages of personal surveillance and dossier compiling are: "*They* are watching you," and "*They* know all about you." Whether or not they really watch and know much about you may be less important than the fear created by the very existence of surveillance and dossier activities.

The monitoring of economic and social trends, in contrast, tends to counteract any fear that *They* don't know what is going on in the world.

In economic and social intelligence the tacit message is: "*They* are getting all the best information needed to guide the ship of state." Confidence in this message is built up by an accelerating expansion of far-flung data collection. The Census Bureau and other government agencies operate expanding archives of economic, social, environmental, and political information. Monitoring is done through an increasingly sophisticated battery of instruments—from the direct head-count and comprehensively administered questionaire to the sample survey and satellite scanning. The largest corporations are increasingly active in the design of these instruments, through which they obtain essential data for market research and business analysis in general.

Within the government sphere of the establishment, public programs are increasingly subject to a bewildering variety of cost-benefit analyses, evaluation surveys, and economic-impact or environmental-impact studies. The technical support for this immense activity comes from a "statistocracy" of experts in archival collection, a network of professional analysts who convert the raw data into presumably objective analyses, and from many thousands of experts who make their living—whether in universities, research institutions, or consulting firms—by processing the data and the analyses. Much of the processed data flows through narrow channels, officially or unofficially removed from public scrutiny. The portions that are made public are ever more complex, adding considerably to the information overload on the knowledge elites. But the very existence of this rising flood of data tends to give the impression that the leaders of government have the best possible information at their fingertips. This impression is reinforced by the elaborate rituals of ceremonial meetings with experts and advisers. It is strengthened still further by the technocratic promise that improved economic and social intelligence will provide the data base for better policymaking or, in Kenyon B. DeGreene's more explicit words, the improved "management of society."[23]

Some decades ago public reporting of economic and social information by corporations and governments was seen as an instrument of democratic accountability, of rendering an open accounting to the public. There were two weaknesses in this view. First, the assembly and initial interpretation of the information was left entirely to the reporting agency. In the case of corporate financial accounting, it is the corporation itself that hires the certified public accountants and—as Professor Abraham Briloff has demonstrated—calls the tune.[24] In the case of government, it is the agency head or Chief Executive Network that organizes the information. In both cases, the reports are mainly designed to show a favorable record. Second, both corporations and governments usually enjoy enough of a privileged position in the information complex to prevent or swamp any countervailing interpretations by others. There is little doubt that the officials of a friendly fascism could go much further in suppressing unfavorable data, shaping its interpretations, or generally turning statistical sows' ears into silk purses. A number of current practices and recent episodes illustrate the pattern, which friendly fascism would surely intensify.

- During the Nixon administration, as the official statistics on unemployment, prices, and crime became rather unpleasant, the president's men often took the task of releasing such data away from the professional statisticians. The impact of "bad news" was eased by having it released by higher officials who invariably gave it a more favorable interpretation.
- Professional statisticians themselves may police the definitions and concepts used in the basic-data collection, so that the product gives the "appropriate" impression without the intervening services of a fancy interpretation. Definitions worked out in past periods are frozen, thus keeping hidden unemployment out of official employment data, hidden price rises out of price indices, hidden profits out of reported profits, corporate crime out of reported crime statistics. The justification for this hardening of the statistical categories is the need to make present data comparable with past data. This justification can readily be forgotten, however, when—without reference to comparability with the past—conceptual reformation is needed to give a more favorable picture. With unemployment, the basis for such reformulations is already being developed. A few years ago the Council of Economic Advisers concocted "variable unemployment," a new definition that succeeded in cutting the official unemployment figure by at least a million. A prominent economist has gone still further in this direction by inventing an "unemployment severity index," which reduces the perceived volume of unemployment still more. Others concentrate on male household heads out of work for a long period of time. By excluding the hardships of many others, including women, unmarried males, and male household heads not included in the narrow "labor force" concept, they almost define unemployment out of existence.
- The older rhetoric of democratic accountability through public reporting can reinforce the armor of establishment power. We can expect many more public reports on the state of the city, metropolis, state, and union, and the social achievements of large corporations. One of the most ambitious efforts in this direction is the spadework now being done on the so-called "periodic social audit of the corporation." [25] This idea originated with the American Institute of Certified Public Accountants, some of whose members saw a new "product line" that could help their corporate customers ward off attacks by "Nader's Raiders" and other corporate critics. By the late 1970s trial runs on this new form of corporate audit were completed and big business was able to drape its activities with the help of better tailored data than ever before available.

While the certified public accountants have not yet solved the technical problem of how to best present public reports on the social achievements of their corporate clients, the national-income economists have done much better. Strongly attacked during the 1960s on the ground that GNP is not an adequate all-purpose indicator of welfare or utility, they have moved forward creatively to fabricate such an all-purpose indicator by making a few adjustments in GNP. William Nordhaus and James Tobin have added to GNP various estimates on the value of leisure, unpaid household work, and the services provided by consumers' durable equipment. Then they have subtracted the estimated costs of pollution and other "disamenities and urbanization." [26] They baptized the resulting figure MEW, a "measure of economic welfare," modestly claiming that it allows for "the more obvious discrepancies between GNP and economic welfare." Professor Paul Samuelson proceeded to pick up the Nordhaus-Tobin MEW, rename it NEW (meaning "net economic welfare") and formally present it—minus most of the Nordhaus-Tobin qualifications—in the next edition (the ninth) of his widely used introductory textbook, *Economics*.[27]

But what about the essential inappropriateness of regarding *any* measure of output quantity (no matter how much adjusted or refined) as an indicator of social welfare? Raising this point in 1966, I proposed a system of social or societal accounting to provide an ordered array of not only economic data but also "cultural, technological, biophysical, institutional and political information," much of which would be qualitative instead of quantitative and, if quantitative, noncommersurable and nonaggregative.[28] I developed these proposals during a period of overexuberant acceptance of President Johnson's "Great Society" rhetoric for shifting national policy goals from the quantity of output to the "quality of life." But as President Johnson vastly expanded U.S. involvement in the Vietnam War, the enthusiasm of social scientists for such an approach rapidly waned. The economists were the only social scientists who did not allow the horrors of U.S. military activities in Southeast Asia to distract them from buckling down to serious work. In response to charges like mine of "economic philistinism," they developed, as already shown, the more subtle economic philistinism of GNP in NEW clothes. But NEW also is due for multisided attack—particularly by all those who look beyond the scrubbed-up Samuelson version and take seriously the limitations more frankly stated by Nordhaus and Tobin. And in response to these, a broader "social philistinism" is being developed through composite statistical aggregates that presume to rank cities or nations in accordance with their so-called "quality of life." When these are increasingly criticized for leaving out "cultural, technological, biophysical, institutional, and political information," flexible technicians are sure to come up with broader-gauged measures. It is virtually inevitable that most of these indicators will help vindicate the goals and exploits of an increasingly powerful Establishment, thus becoming social vindicators more than indicators. Indeed, my own proposals could be misused in this fashion. This potentiality is inherent not so much in the nature of the proposals themselves as in the fact that any truly multidimensional effort to develop a systematic array of qualitative and quantitative information on the "state of the nation" is an immense undertaking. Like the uses of atomic energy for peaceful purposes, it requires a vast commitment of resources that only the Establishment itself can provide.

EDUCATIONAL AUTHORITARIANISM

> Students are carefully channeled, processed, manipulated, tested, inspected, indoctrinated, programmed and eventually packaged. . . .
>
> RICHARD GREEMAN [29]

To find powerful instruments for managing minds, however, one need not look only to fancy new technologies. The entire educational system itself may be seen as a mammoth set of disciplined activities that—irrespective of any specific indoctrination of knowledge or programming of skills—can help produce docile, accepting personalities.

Almost every component of America's mammoth school system serves as a training ground in the submission to authoritative rules and procedures. By being given meaningless assignments and subjected to large-scale, uniform testing, students are trained in the acceptance of meaningless work, mindless rules and mind-numbing orders from superiors. Rebellion itself often leads to little more than different forms of passivity—the passivity of those who drop out completely, of those who idly go through the motions, or of those who, by trying to "beat the system," tacitly accept the system as the springboard or framework of thought and action. Whenever student rebellion erupts more violently, a typical reaction is to pacify the rebels and their supporters by trotting out some new variation of "student government," thereby sidetracking the energy of activists and paving the way for a quick return to passivity. When rebellion is directed against restrictive entry to the sytem, the system's doors may be opened a little more (to women and to minorities, for example), so that new groups may have "equal opportunities" for personal pacification. This, in turn, tends not only to enlarge the system as a whole but also promotes more sophisticated stratification. At the level of so-called "higher education" the clear tendency is toward a sharp ranking along such lines as these:

The elite schools	For future elites at the Establishment's higher levels
The small bohemian colleges	For activist dissenters
The State (and city) colleges and universities	For middle level white-collar workers and middle-class professionals and technicians
The junior and community colleges	For the sons and daughters of lower class people.

It is hard to think of a new corporate authoritarianism in America without an increase in the student population at the bottom level and without still sharper stratification within the entire structure.

It would be a mistake, however, to think of passivity as a consequence manifested only at the lower levels. College undergraduates tend to be more docile than high school students, graduate students more "processed" than undergraduates, the recipients of higher degrees more channeled and packaged. At all levels teachers themselves are rendered passive by the pacifying operations they perform on others. It is their volition also which is captured, even though they may openly scoff at bureaucratic rules and themselves exhibit the appearance of freedom.

This appearance is usually most impressive among those who are most fully captured—namely, the most trusted processors and channelers in the professoriat of the Ivy League and other elite schools. From these home bases come the scientists, consultants and advisers who roam the corridors of the Establishment's middle and higher levels. In a certain sense their freedom is real—but just so long as they passively accept the Establishment's basic values and strategic policy orientation.

Within these confines, they—and their lower-caste brethren in the State universities and private research institutions—are inordinately active. Those who are less successful may be constrained by the rules of modern positivism, which channel creative thought and research toward technical questions subject to presumably "value free" empirical or semi-empirical testing. The furious controversies that may rage within these limits distract attention from the systemic processes that provide the real-life framework for the technical debates. No better examples can be found than the current controversies concerning energy and inflation. Many fine scientific minds are doing impressive work on energy conservation and—what is more interesting to physical scientists—atomic fusion, solar energy and other sources of energy that escape over-reliance on fossil fuels. Often, the missing element is the connection between these proposals and the profit-power position of the energy cartels and conglomerates. This subject verges on "straight talk" and must be left for the privacy of the corporate boardrooms. Similarly, the debates on double digit inflation swing mindlessly back and forth between "cost push" or "demand pull," indirect controls or direct controls, monetary policy or fiscal policy, and political courage or political cowardice. Although these debates lead nowhere, they are well reported by the media. But "profit grabs" are outside the pale of polite discourse and anyone who mentions the role of transnational corporations in raising capital by "taxing" consumers is *ipso facto* unsound. He or she may be tolerated as an instructor who befuddles the minds of young students in nonelite colleges—but serious debate on an issue of this type will not be joined, nor will such undocile thoughts be given serious attention in the elite media of learned journals.

CUSTODIAL FUNCTIONS

Many parts of the information complex also serve a custodial function that separates people from the rest of society. This is a form of immobilization that goes far beyond the march.

With such closed institutions as prisons and asylums, the custodial function is clear, albeit often hidden under the facade of manifest functions: rehabilitation or therapy. In schools, colleges, universities and research institutions, there is more reality to the manifest functions of providing certified knowledge, skills and values. But the custodial function always lurks in the background—usually unmentioned, always highly prized. Nurseries, kindergartens and elementary schools are a form of collectively-organized daytime baby sitting. High schools keep the "kids" off the streets, out of the home and apart from the labor market. The vast expansion of higher education has proved an indispensable part of modern capitalism's answer to the problem of how to enjoy a large supply of unemployed labor without the embarrassment of a large increase in open unemployment. Undergraduate and graduate "make work" seems less costly than the expansion of public service employment at fair wages. Research assistants and doctoral candidates accept minor pittances for their labors, grateful that they are protected from the horrors of the primary, secondary and tertiary job markets and hopeful for the day they may be vouchsafed entrance into the elite job categories. Overwhelmed by the information overload, thousands upon thousands of professionals and scientists are confined in libraries or behind ever higher piles of books, journals and reprints, immobilized by the no-win, sure-fail urge to "keep up." Many of the most intelligent, creative and brilliant people of the country are imprisoned within the walls of the narrowly defined discipline, laboratory or professorial chair, amply rewarded by respect and emoluments so long as they never (or rarely) venture forth beyond the imprisoning walls into the undisciplined area of genuine controversy. "Shoemaker, stick to your last," is the unwritten rule, "or you may not last . . ."

13

Incentives for System Acceptance

> It should be possible to design a world in which behavior likely to be punished seldom or never occurs. We try to design such a world for those who cannot solve the problems of punishment for themselves, such as babies, retardates and psychotics, and if it could be done for everyone, much time and energy would be saved . . .
>
> B. F. SKINNER [1]

> "And that," put in the Director sententiously, "that is the secret of happiness and virtue—liking what you've *got* to do. All conditioning aims at that: making people like their unescapable social destiny."
>
> ALDOUS HUXLEY [2]

THE OPEN BRUTALITY of the old-fashioned fascist regimes has misled many observers into equating fascism with official violence—as though official violence were something new under the sun. This oversimplified equation of fascism with brutality obscures the very real and widespread "positive reinforcements" that the German, Italian, and Japanese fascists provided for large parts of their populations through somewhat better living standards—at least until the tides of war engulfed and substantially destroyed these valued rewards.

This brings us up against one of the difficulties in understanding tendencies toward friendly fascism in the First World. On the one hand, the emerging logic of corporate authoritarianism requires a complex blend of rewards and punishments. On the other hand, the myths of old-style fascism lead many observers to look for overt terror and neglect positive incentives that result in "liking what you've got to do." Or else, appreciating the present power of positive incentives, they may—like Reimut Reiche, the West German Marxist—feel that "the techniques of manipulative rule used today are a necessary condition for the functioning of the capitalist system without fascism."[3] Having one-sided images of old-fashioned fascism in the back of their minds, people like Reiche fail to see the expanded use of these manipulative techniques as a necessary condition of the capitalist system *with friendly fascism.* Or else, overly influenced by Orwell's nightmare, they are unprepared for a strange new blend of Huxley's *Brave New World* with Orwell's *1984.* One of the many achievements in the new era of more perfect capitalism has been the proliferation of widespread incentives far more meaningful than any older forms of bread and circuses. While some people may have to be "knocked off" in the slow processes of integrating the Establishment's top levels, consolidating empire, and subverting constitutional machinery, it is cheaper to maintain control by a large amount of small but carefully distributed payoffs.

EXTENDED PROFESSIONALISM

To understand the growth of professionalism, we must think of the employers' need not only for skills but also for docility. With the emergence of a more educated and highly trained population, there are many rough challenges to the corporate elites. Trade unions can engage in more sophisticated bargaining, capitalizing on informal slowdowns, wildcat strikes, and expert knowledge of corporate and bureaucratic operations. Among unorganized workers, incentives for loyal and efficient work decline. Blacks, other minorities, and women demand larger proportions of high-level positions. Some experts and technicians "blow the whistle" by leaking inside information or linking themselves with outside groups trying to attack their organizations. And bubbling upward from all levels are aspirations for fulfilling employment disconnected from consumer exploitation, environment degradation, or militarism.

Control of this situation could not be won by any return to old-fashioned methods: not the iron law of subsistence wages, nor union-busting, nor bread-and-butter trade unions, nor the simple replacement of troublesome workers by machinery. The logic of oligarchic management, rather, requires an employee reward system that helps buttress market demand without interfering with the increased concentration of wealth, gives all workers unmistakable stakes in the regime, and contributes to the future fragmentation of both masses and technicians. This can best be done by a vast extension of bureaucratized professionalism to all kinds of work. The governing principle would be controlled mobility through many levels of conditional satisfactions.

Many elements of such a system are already at hand. Finely graded positions and ladders of advancement are provided by civil service arrangements. The advanced techniques of personnel management provide for job specification, job analysis, performance rating, seniority, within-grade increases, promotions, and career counseling. Mechanization and new technology require a wide variety of specialized positions, some linked closely to the machinery, others involved in functions not worth assigning to machines. People become "personnel," a special form of "materiel." As "human resources" or "human capital," they can be as valuable and as manipulable as money in building wealth and power.

In a loose but immensely impressive manner, social scientists, personnel managers, and assorted experts in investment of human capital are working assiduously to achieve one of the conditions that Aldous Huxley (writing his 1947 foreword to *Brave New World*) felt essential if people are to be induced to love their servitude: "a fully developed science of human differences, enabling government managers to assign any given individual to his or her proper place in the social and economic hierarchy." [4]

Many critics of present-day America—including William H. Whyte, Lewis Mumford, and Charles Reich—have bewailed these elements. But by concentrating on the present and often exaggerating their case in order to attract necessary attention to hidden evils, they have tended to obscure the greater dangers that lie ahead. If America is already dominated by Whyte's Organization Man, Reich's Corporate State and Mumford's Megamachine, what could be worse?

My answer is another version of the distinction between cold water and ice. Under friendly fascism, the water would be much colder. The chunks of ice, now floating around conspicuously, would disappear as separate phenomena. With everything frozen, the change would be qualitative. The vast hierarchy of professionalized roles would extend in all directions. Sideways, it would cover every field of employment. Upwards, it would provide special status, emoluments, and rituals governing the life of the full professionals—and some superprofessionals or stars—among managers, militarists, scientists, writers, and entertainers. Downwards, it would provide niches, if not careers, for sub-, para- and quasi-professionals. There would even be sub-professional roles (and informal training facilities) for deviants, dropouts, dole-receivers, criminals, and resisters, with higher status groups serving as professional pacifiers for each of these categories. In Huxley's *Brave New World,* where all people are born in test tubes, everyone belonged to one of five groups, ranging down from Alpha and Beta at the top to Gamma, Delta, and Epsilon. Although less advanced in eugenic control, the United States would be more advanced in personnel policy. Its status graduations would run from Alpha to Omega, with many fine subdivisions among the Alphans and Omegans. And the ever-present incentive of rising a little higher would serve as a major force for systemic stability within the many corridors of the new Tower of Babel.

JOB, PROMETHEUS, FAUST

In this vast Tower of Babel, people would not be herded together like sheep. Rather, every woman and man would be separated from everyone else, each with her or his own personal niche, number, and furnishings. While growing like Topsy in confused response to crisis and demands, this labyrinthine social structure would, in function, be exquisitely designed—like the natural-habitat zoos with unpassable ditches instead of bars—to give the illusion of freedom. Within the system's constraints, there would also be options. With seniority, sweat, or manipulation, people can get a better cell. With good behavior, indentured experts can move from the boredom of routinized work into a sunny prison courtyard where they may enjoy expense accounts, professional mobility and mutual back-scratching, and select their own forms of dehumanized and dehumanizing labor. While rewards are distributed in accordance with each one's power and service to the system, the illusion of meritocratic justice is provided by computerized rating systems that, by purporting to report on intelligence and effort, strongly suggest the stupidity and immorality of the weak.

In this new form of status slavery, there can be no single style of servitude. The life-styles of Modern Man and Woman in Captivity under the United States would, despite their newness, be little more than updated forms of ancient legends expressing mankind's deepest fears. Thus, some would be Job, some Prometheus, some Faust.

The average worker would be the Job of the future. Suffering from boredom, apathy, alienation, and the erosion of any earlier dreams of rising in the world, he is prepared to hibernate forever. He takes out his aggressions on others, particularly those beneath him. With harmless words, unlike the Job of the Bible, he curses his gods, his family and the "powers that be." But, in action, he goes along passively and accepts his fate.

The Prometheus of the future would be the technician who brings to the system the essential fires of technological or scientific skill. But he is bound by a narrow and specialized role that prevents him from using this skill for the liberation of humankind. No eagle, but his own unending doubts gnaw at his liver. He feeds on others also and, by his example, teaches them to consume themselves.

The Faust of the future sells his soul in exchange for the opportunity to engage in an endless rat race for ephemeral satisfactions. By an updated version of Parkinson's Law, his work expands to take over all his time, even his dreams, leaving little if any available for anything else. He soars high and frantic, tasting prestige here and power there, condemned to constant movement. If he slows down, he may be destroyed.

His pact with today's devil is very close to the "brutal bargain" brilliantly described in Norman Podhoretz's biographical account of how he rose from the Brooklyn slums: "It appalls me to think of what an immense transformation I had to work on myself in order to become what I have become; if I had known what I was doing I would surely not have been able to do it . . . In matters having to do with "art" and "culture" (the "life of the mind," as I learned to call it at Columbia), I was being offered the very same brutal bargain and accepting it with the wildest enthusiasm."[5]

The neo-Faustian bargain, as Podhoretz describes it, is that in matters of dress, speech, and social contacts he had to "transform" himself. Only by accepting the superiority of the intellectual class he was entering and the inferiority of those among whom he had been born and raised was he able to become a successful editor and conspicuous member of the New York intellectual establishment. "That was the bargain—take it or leave it." Whether or not there was some fine print in the Podhoretz bargain, whether or not there were other and less explicit "brutal bargains" that he accepted later in order to continue "making it," is a question that might take another decade or two for Podhoretz—penetrating self-analyst though he is—to explore. In my own upward movement through both government and academia, I have made many bargains covering "the life of the mind," although I invariably tended to enter into them willingly without being aware at the time of any hidden "brutality." Thus it is easy for me to understand how most of the Faust-like intellectuals, scientists, and artists of the United States would eagerly accept the superiority of the system that provides their opportunities for service, if not the ultimate benevolence of the higher powers they serve.

For all three—Job, Prometheus, and Faust—anxiety runs deep concerning the security they do not really believe in, the rewards that come ever so slowly, the decline of bodily and sexual powers. At times, family and friends may be a refuge. But increasingly they are things to be used—and then, when they lose their usefulness, to be thrown away like toilet paper or no-return bottles.

This anxiety is sharpened by both unemployment and inflation. Hidden unemployment at all levels, while unreflected in official statistics, is nonetheless widely sensed by the employed. The unemployment of the underclass, while never large enough to threaten the system, is large enough to enhance the lower and middle-income employees' appreciation of their own stake in the system. The unemployment of technicians results in employed technicans tightening their grip on their own positions. The recurring rise and fall in the job outlook hones the fine edge of anxiety. It is sharpened still further by the hidden taxes levied through creeping or walking inflation. Neither one's current income nor one's savings can be relied upon any more for security. The system itself becomes one's rock and one's deliverance; the chains of servitude, one's salvation.

As yet the educational system does not go nearly as far as it might in conditioning people to accept Alpha-to-Omega professionalism. Basic education "for its own sake"—whether called "liberal," "academic," or "general"—is still a valued objective in some parts of the educational complex. Vocational education to prepare people for specific slots is still only *a part* of the system. Under the Nixon, Ford, and Carter administrations, however, with the active participation of many experts who never regarded themselves as Nixon, Ford, or Carter admirers, "career education" was developed as a new doctrine to expand old-time vocational education until it permeates and tends to dominate the entire educational system.

FOR CONSUMERS: KIDNAPPER CANDY

> Now megatechnics offers, in return for its unquestioning acceptance, the gift of an effortless life: a plethora of prefabricated goods, achieved with a minimum of physical activity . . . life on the installment plan, as it were, yet with an unlimited credit card, and with the final reckoning—existential nausea and despair—readable only in fine print . . . The "Big Bribe" turns out to be little better than kidnapper's candy.
>
> LEWIS MUMFORD [6]

> Oh Lord, won't you buy me a color TV?
> I'll wait for delivery each day until three.
>
> JANIS JOPLIN,
> "Mercedes Benz"

Extended professionalism, of course, implies accelerated consumption. On the one hand, money (along with status) is the major payoff to everyone from Alpha to Omega and the major source of psychic income. This money, and the increments obtainable through credit, is useful only if it can be spent on consumers' goods and services. On the other hand the output of every stratified complex—particularly with new technologies—is an ever larger volume of goods or services. The investment of part of this output increases capabilities of producing for consumption. Neither foreign markets nor expanded militarism can go far enough, by themselves, in absorbing the enlarged output. To keep the system going, everyone must be induced to absorb more and more goods and services.

At first blush, accelerating consumption might appear as a redeeming—or at least unobjectionable—feature of friendly fascism. Isn't consumption the ultimate goal of economic activity? If underconsumption was one of the evils of older-style capitalism, wouldn't ever-rising consumption be a constant virtue? Wasn't Aldous Huxley going a little too far in lampooning the compulsion upon the citizens of his *Brave New World* to consume so much a year? If poverty means too few goods and services, would not even higher levels of consumption be the long-sought realization of one of humanity's dreams, the elimination of poverty?

Then there are the interrelated questions of product debasement and the neglect of public services. Here again, by emphasizing current evils, social critics have tended to give the impression that the situation could not become worse and—in accordance with the tacit assumption of inevitable progress—will probably improve. If consumers have been defrauded by misleading advertising, bad merchandise, and price-gouging, cannot substantial reforms be expected? If the public sector has been unduly constrained (leading to what Galbraith describes as the contrast between private opulence and public squalor) can we not expect an expansion of the public sector? The optimism in such rhetorical questions is supportable by two unquestionable trends—the relentless rise in public-service expenditures and the inclusion within the public-service sphere of new or expanded forms of consumer protection and consumer advisory services.

On the other hand, I foresee the possibility of exploitative abundance—abundance which enslaves consumers through a destructive combination of genuine and pseudo-satisfactions. There are already many tendencies in this direction, tendencies that could be accelerated during the transition from semi-oligarchy to full oligarchy.

One of these—the tendency toward more throwaways—is regarded as inevitable by Alvin Toffler. In *Future Shock* he predicts that the well-oiled machinery for the creation and diffusion of fads—now entrenched in automobiles and clothing—will be adopted throughout the economy. In this new economy of impermanence we will "face a rising flood of throwaway items, impermanent architecture, mobile and modular products, rented goods and commodities designed for almost instant death." [7] Toffler hints that in the throwaway society, consumption might really be designed to meet human needs. But he fails to stress that these would be less the needs of consumers, more those of businessmen seeking additional capital and power. Toward these ends, much more could be accomplished than in the past—particularly with the new pinpoint propaganda capabilities of cable TV—in educating consumers to seek sexual surrogates, higher status, and ego inflation by overeating, overreducing, and building up stocks of short-lived, wasteful, unused, or time-consuming durables. After more than a decade of soaps; deodorants, and washes to overcome odors of mouth, armpits, feet, navel, or vagina, we can look forward to the promotion of new perfumes to bring back "that good old natural body odor" with higher-price sprays hailed as "body bouquet" or "sex scent." A new industry of psychogratification, staffed with artists and environmental entrepreneurs, would provide people with both simulated and real experiences.

They would go much further than the orgies and "feelies" of *Brave New World*, using electronic stimulation of the brain, mixed-media assaults on the senses, and efficiently staged group therapy and communal massage experiences. Past achievements in the creation of fictitious consumer needs may be as nothing in comparison with Toffler's titillating future.

SERVITUDE'S SERVICES

One of the many illusions of the modern world has been that economic growth gives people more leisure or free time. And this despite the encroachment of work and work's anxieties far beyond the hours of recorded physical presence at the workplace! But, as Swedish economist Staffan B. Linder has pointed out, high-level consumption also eats up time. The choice among varied goods and products takes times. Rational procurement becomes so time consuming that it is more rational—according to Linder—to save time by buying wastefully.[8] The goods you buy require valuable maintenance or repair time—services decreasingly available on the market. If they are not thrown away, that may be because of the lack of time to throw them away. The services you are expected to want consume so much time that time-efficiency methods must be applied: either do a lot of things simultaneously or cut down on the time for each. Eating, lovemaking, exercising, meditation, reading, contemplation, relaxation—all are compressed into ever-shorter quantities of time. Under the accelerated consumption of techno-urban fascism, this trend would be accentuated. Charlie Chaplin's *Modern Times* would be reenacted in new form, with Charlie spending less time at the conveyor belt and much more of his time in high speed, semiautomated running through the enlarged spectrum of required consumption. If *Readers' Digest* was one of the great commercial successes of the mid-twentieth century, I can see a still greater future for quick-eating food, quick-scanning drills to replace quick-reading courses, a two-year Bachelor of Arts degree, a twelve-minute version of *Hamlet* for cable TV and Beethoven's Ninth Symphony on a six-minute cassette. As for completely free time, the only genuine form of leisure, the Job of the future would have little, Prometheus less, and Faust none.

During the decades since the end of World War II, as John K. Galbraith has pointed out, the growth of mass consumption has imposed vast burdens on women.[9] Far more than men, they have had to spend large amounts of time in both shopping for consumer goods and managing household equipment. During the next decade or so, it may be expected that some of this burden will be shifted onto male shoulders. If this by itself be female liberation, it is the kind of liberation that allows more women to escape from the frying pan of accelerated consumption to the fire of extended professionalism. For men, this means more equality in sharing the burdens of servitude. For the purveyors of goods and services, both private and public, it means a broader and more secure base for consumer exploitation.

Much has been made of the transition from a goods to a service economy. Yet a growing part of the services rendered by professionals may turn out to be "disservices," as I have suggested in "The Side Effects of Success" (chapter 4). Most of the professionalized service systems assume that service is a unilateral process, like waiting on tables. According to John McKnight of Northwestern University, these systems tend to communicate three propositions:

You are deficient.
You have a problem.
You have a collection of problems.

The professionals, in turn, are the "loving" or "caring" problem solvers, who use these deficiencies of their clients to feather their own nests. Thus, McKnight suggests, people are "prepared for anti-democratic leaders who can capitalize upon the dependencies created by unilateral, expert, professionalized helpers who teach people that 'they will be better helped because I know better.' "

CONDITIONAL BENEFACTIONS

For people who earn their own income, consumer control through accelerated consumption is indirect. For those receiving an open dole from the state—in welfare payments, food stamps, or rent subsidies—it is much more direct. As Piven and Cloward have repeatedly pointed out, these payments serve as cyclical instruments for "regulating the poor." [10] On the upswing they reinforce the system by allaying social discontent. On the downswing, actual or threatened withdrawal forces people into low-wage humiliating work. Another function (only touched on by Piven and Cloward) is to supplement emerging tendencies toward both extended professionalism and accelerated consumption. In addition to building up many cadres of relief-giving professionals, the relief system tends to encourage demands for paraprofessional opportunities. On the consumption side, the recipients—like Pavlov's dogs—are kept salivating in sustained hunger for both necessities and luxuries. In any transition to friendly fascism, these salivary anxieties would be exacerbated by the conversion of any rights won in the past into conditional benefactions. Thus relief would be given, maintained, or withdrawn on the basis of individual tests—an open means test and various hidden tests concerning loyalty, dissent, and political activity. Indeed, new forms of "conditionalism"—essential to the use of benefactions as positive reinforcements—would be developed for last-resort public employment, scholarship aid, health insurance, pensions, and other expanding forms of welfare state "goodies."

The accelerated use of computers to record and investigate the "character" or "good behavior" of recipients gives "conditional benefaction" the potential of becoming a much more precise operation.

The process may also be extended beyond what is normally considered the welfare population. Under mature oligarchy, a somewhat larger proportion of employees enjoy limited benefits of job tenure and pensions. These rights—to use the words of William H. Whyte *The Organization Man*—imprison the thus-honored employees in the beneficence of the organization. They create in addition a barrier of hostility between the beneficiaries and the larger number of workers who envy these petty privileges. All lower-income workers may be drawn further into "conditionalism" by the imposition of user charges on services that had previously been available gratis. In the case of publicly supported community colleges, for example, tuition fees replace previous rights to free education, with the result that lower-income students, if not eliminated altogether, are offered scholarships or partial tuition waivers on the basis of means tests and attestation of their worthiness for public largesse.

RATIONED PAYOFFS

It has long been thought that networks of upward mobility might democratize a power structure and that higher levels of consumption might equalize wealth and income. The exploits of modern capitalism have proved that "it ain't necessarily so." The expansion of bureaucratic careerism, while providing new opportunities for many people of lower birth, has been perfectly consistent with semi-oligarchic deveolpments. Mass consumption has come about through a huge enlargement of the total pie, with no redistribution of shares in favor of the poor. Only by keeping these points in mind can one appreciate the much greater change that would take place under friendly fascism: a much larger concentration of wealth, income, and all the other attributes of power.

There is a sense in which a little wealth tends to produce large wealth, large wealth much greater wealth, and great wealth immense wealth. In the monetary world, this is the inexorable law of compound interest. A similar law applies to power. Large concentrations of power tend to grow still larger through an integration and compounding of the many sources of power. This can provide continuing incentives for the wealthy and powerful to keep up the effort and "get themselves together." With sustained thrusts of economic growthmanship, it is possible for top-power holders to ride the modified business cycle and accumulate more money and power during recessions, inflationary splurges, and prolonged stagflation. More important, they can ride recurring cycles of dissent and consensus, enhancing their wealth during each. The technological growthmanship of the Golden International provides much larger shares of income, wealth, and power for the faceless oligarchs themselves—a process facilitated by the selective rationing of income, consumption, and departmentalized privilege throughout the Establishment's middle levels.

The name of the game is "incentive," the long-hallowed term used by economists to describe the positive reinforcements that government provides for private business. The transition to a new corporate society requires new bursts of innovation in providing more "tax expenditures" for business, more subsidies for banks and transnational corporations, more extensive use of private contractors to handle public functions, and more of all the other aids to business reviewed in "Big Welfare for Big Business" (chapter 2).

New vistas are available through the development of public and mixed-public enterprises. Still greater vistas are possible through the proliferation of direct federal controls over wages and prices. These can provide government agencies and private interest with powerful new instruments for directing the flow of income. Politically, these can be used to bring recalcitrant enterprises into line and encourage the channeling of political funds and influence in desired directions. Automatically, without any conscious effort, they penalize smaller or more rambunctious enterprises and promote an integration of orientation and effort, if not of formal consolidation.

All of these devices, it may be noted, can readily be formulated as "solutions" to pressing economic and social problems, even though increased concentration of income and wealth is seen as part of the problem to be solved. Yet no one has ever come up with money incentives for reducing the inequities in income and wealth distribution. The essence of business incentive systems—even those which purport to help "small" business—is to socialize the risk in business risk-taking and reward the wealthy for success in becoming wealthier.

From the viewpoint of the population at large, this is an extension of the filtering-down philosophy expressed in the motto: "The way to feed pigeons is to give hay to horses." The weakness of this motto is that it ignores pigeon droppings. In the managed society, these would be assiduously mopped up and filtered down to lower species.

In the other direction, I foresee an equally powerful extractive process that would siphon income, wealth, and power upward. Established instruments for doing this are tax devices that place the greatest burden of government services upon the lowest income groups. Some of these—such as sales, excise and value-added taxes—are openly regressive.

Others, like taxes on personal income and corporate profits, may be nominally progressive but—when conditions allow them to be passed on to the bulk of consumers—are little more than sophisticated ways of siphoning income away from the majority of the population. Cleverly administered price and wage regulations can help create such conditions. The extensions of metropolitan operations may have a similar effect, as the central-city poor are taxed to subsidize services for middle-level elites in the more affluent suburbs. In the case of cable TV, this can happen merely by a uniform installation charge, with ghetto residents—where installations are cheaper—paying the same fee as high-income suburbanites with huge distances and much more expensive wiring between dwelling units.

Similarly, most—but not necessarily all—reform measures provide a means of siphoning up political power. Where they involve new benefactions or new regulations, this can happen whenever their provision involves the setting up of a new or stronger bureaucracy. Any concrete benefits for people at the middle and lower levels of the social pyramid are balanced off by additional power or prestige at the top. This is why many reforms that may indeed be great victories for the organizers of the poorer or weaker elements of society may turn out also to be a form of payola. Under German and Italian fascism the top industrialist and miiltarists "paid off" in a rather uncontrolled manner to the semi-gangster types in the fascist parties. Under friendly fascism the payoffs would be more orderly and better distributed among political and technical functionaries, without the Ultra-Rich, the Corporate Overseers, or their executive managers running the risk of building up unreliable political forces.

Moreover, both the filtering-down and siphoning-up processes would probably be handled with fastidious care for legality or ex post facto legalization. Naturally, this would necessitate considerable changes in the legal structure. A model for this exists in the many tax loopholes developed in past decades, most of which convert (illegal) tax evasion into (within the law) avoidance. On the road to friendly fascism there would be massive changes of this type—through both statutes and judicial decisions—in the various laws governing taxation, foundations, banking, industry, utilities, public contracts, pollution, consumer protection, and natural resources. In purely legal—as distinguished from moral—terms, the blatant "corporate crime" or "crime in the suites" exposed by the muckrakers would diminish. Under friendly fascism, with the faceless oligarchs fully in charge of and above the law, they might even vanish.

Even under such a regime, however, there would be work for muckrakers. At the middle levels of the various hierarchies and complexes, the expansion of welfare-state benefactions and regulations opens up the doors for a new Age of Corruption. A new generation of business bribers, small-time land speculators, urban hustlers, and mafiosi-type racketeers (with multi-ethnic backgrounds) crowds through these doors, viciously clawing at one another. For them, law avoidance is less available, law evasion more normal. Recurring anticorruption campaigns and crackdowns serve valuable functions. At times, they lead to "reform legislation" strengthening oligarchic controls. More generally, as sophisticated forms of dramatic circus, they distract attention from the more legalized corruption at higher levels.

THE EFFULGENT AURA

While the greater concentration of both power and wealth would be largely hidden, let us not think it would be totally invisible. Although Kafka's K could never understand what was really going on in the Castle, he could nevertheless see it in the distance—even through the heavy snows. Similarly, many castles of the modern Establishment are visible from the distance. No matter how much the Rich and the Super-Rich may shun conspicuous consumption, glimmering of hidden oppulence—in the form of manorial estates, lordly offices, *haute cuisine* executive dining rooms, art treasures, jewelry, dog and horse shows, and sea and air yachts—would undoubtedly filter through public relations screening. Tidbits of baronial caprice and whimsy, of superprivleged gratifications, would find their way downward through the labyrinthine mazes of every complex, thereby testifying to the power of "They." The word would probably get around that "They"—more than anybody else in society—have availed themselves of the latest advances in geriatrics and gerontology. In *Future Shock*, Toffler suggests that "advanced fusions of man and machine—called 'Cyborgs'—are closer than most people suggest." Dr. Leon R. Kass of the National Academy of Sciences has already warned that "an extended life span, made possible by such techniques of modern medicine as organ transplants and artificial pacemakers for the heart, would become a privilege of the rich."[11] In a new corporate authoritarianism we may expect that after sufficient experimentation on lower-status people the faceless oligarchs will go further than anyone else in availing themselves of the heart pacemakers, artificial organs, and other mechanical extensions that will prolong their life span at high levels of activity and gratification.

Would such perceptions of "Life in the Castle" breed resentment? Undoubtedly. But hardly to the extent of threatening the regime.

Under extended professionalism, there would be a sense of justice concerning the distribution of rewards. With accelerated consumerism, the immediately perceived face of a person's increased consumption could counterbalance any vague sense of relative deprivation in contrast with the dimly perceived living standards of distant oligarchs.

Above all, great aggregations of wealth and power, as always, would emanate an effulgent and magnetic aura. They would attract thousands upon thousands of seekers after patronage, favors, tidbits, legacies, grants, contracts, access, or even benign glances. Under friendly fascism in the United States, the aggregate efforts of all such camp followers—from university presidents, middle-level businessmen, and foundation executives to free-floating writers, scholars, artists, and technocrats—would go much further in accelerating and justifying the processes of more exploitative accumulation.

14

The Ladder of Terror

The very first essential for success is a perpetually constant and regular employment of violence.

ADOLF HITLER, *Mein Kampf*

America has always been a relatively violent nation.

National Commision on the Causes and Prevention of Violence.[1]

THERE IS NOTHING DISTINCTIVELY FASCISTIC about violence and brutality. Force, fraud and violence, "have always been features of organized government." To recognize that "America has always been a violent nation" is to correct a false self-image among many Americans and to identify a characteristic that helps make the whole world kin. It does not put the finger on the essence of the drift toward friendly fascism. Indeed, the apparent ebbing of overt domestic violence after the 1970 outbursts has coincided with the slow but steady processes of integration at the highest levels of the Establishment and of more effective manipulation of government machinery by big business, increased management of information and minds, and more extensive use of incentives for system acceptance.

Punishments by themselves can never be a sufficient method of control. As B. F. Skinner has repeatedly insisted, they are essentially negative in character; they condition people *not* to do certain things without training them for what *should* be done. Even Hitler, with all his frankness about the use of violence, supplemented violence with a perpetually constant and regular employment of mind management and positive incentives. Moreover, the withholding or withdrawal of positive rewards can itself be a positive form of terror. This is particularly true of the deep fears spread by inflation, unemployment, job insecurity, career anxieties, and conditional benefactions. For at least half the population, the inexorable operations of the business cycle keep these fears alive in the back (or front) of the mind.

On the other hand, there are serious weaknesses in control through positive reinforcements alone. Positive rewards are expensive, even when carefully rationed. If enough resources are used to reward the middle-level elites, then there are less resources available for the rest of the population. To keep the lower-level masses under control—in effect, to keep them from demanding the same incentives that the higher elites require—aversive sanctions are required. A new corporate society could not be managed by velvet gloves alone.

THE RUNGS OF VIOLENCE

Force is never more operative than when it is known to exist but is not brandished.

ALFRED THAYER MAHAN [2]

Though in many of its aspects this visible world seems formed in love, the invisible spheres were formed in fright.

HERMAN MELVILLE,
Moby Dick

Some years ago Herman Kahn bewailed the existence of "two traditionally American biases" toward the use of force in international affairs. On the one hand, there was "an unwillingness to initiate the use of moderate levels of force for limited objectives" and, on the other hand, "a too great willingness, once committed, to use extravagant and uncontrolled force." To promote a more deliberate approach to the use of force, he set forth an "Escalation Ladder" with forty-four rungs, leading from low-level international crises met by threats and ultimata through the use of conventional weapons up to various kinds of nuclear war, and finally all the way up to "spasm or insensate war—all the buttons are pressed and the decision-makers and their staffs go home—if they still have homes . . ." [3]

Kahn's analysis is also applicable, with certain variations, to the Establishment's use of force at home. Police operations during the 1960s and early 1970s often swung between "too little" and "too much." Since then, the military and paramilitary services have worked together intensively, with the support of various academic research institutions, to develop professional capabilities to make the punishment fit the perceived situation.

To help bring into the open some of the tacit premises underlying the more advanced planning, training, and practice by military and police professionals, I have prepared the table "The Ladder of Domestic Violence." As with Kahn's Escalation Ladder, this table helps explain the

THE LADDER OF DOMESTIC VIOLENCE
Available for Use by . . .

Level	Establishment	Both Sides	Opposition	Level
HIGH	14. Counterrevolution	14. Civil War	14. Revolution	HIGH
HIGH		13. Coup d'Etat		HIGH
HIGH	12. Counterinsurgency		12. Insurgency Rebellion Mutiny	HIGH
HIGH		11. Execution Mass, group, individual		HIGH
HIGH	10. Pacification Sabotage		10. Disruptive Sabotage	HIGH
HIGH		9. Personal Injury Mutilation, drugging, torture, rape, assault, incapacitation		HIGH
HIGH		8. Riot Looting, physical destruction		HIGH
		Injury Threshold		
MEDIUM	7. Legal Confinement Concentration camp Cordon sanitaire, curfew Jails, hospitals, etc. Exile House confinement		7. Kidnapping	MEDIUM
MEDIUM	6. Court Trial		6. Citizens' Tribunal	MEDIUM
MEDIUM	5. Arrest Mass Individual		5. Sit-Down or Sit-In	MEDIUM

Forceful Confrontation Threshold

LOW				LOW
	4. Job Action Purge, blacklists Reorganization Isolation		4. Strike General or partial Regular or wildcat Slowdown, "working to rule"	
		3. Harassment Threats Invective		
	2. Dossier-building		2. Peaceful demonstrations, hunger strikes, suicides, marches, assemblies	
	1. Surveillance		1. Noncooperation Law evasion or avoidance, withdrawal, nonfraternization	

unfolding logic with respect to the use of domestic force. Naturally, in any specific situation, a combination of various modes may be used at one and the same time—such as harassment, arrests, and assaults, with the relative proportions of the various modes determined by the nature of a particular crisis and the interaction among competing control agencies.

As in Kahn's analysis, the primary emphasis is on the development of capabilities to operate at any or all levels depending on the specifics of any situation. To be credible, most of these capabilities must be used from time to time, or at least displayed to be fully effective. At the same time, as Mahan has advised, the more forceful measures should not be overly used or explicitly threatened. An atmosphere of fear is itself a powerful force. Present fears, to recall Macbeth's words, are even "less than horrible imaginings." With but slight expenditures of force, an all-pervasive sense of fright may be produced in the "invisible spheres" of life. An ounce of actual violence can yield a pound of terror.

PRECISION PURGING

> We're faced with an unprecedented problem. Not only are revolutionary terrorists finding it easier to infiltrate the bureaucracy but we're getting more people in government who feel they should be ruled by a sense of conscience. . . .
>
> ROBERT MARDIAN [4]

Since surveillance and dossier building have already been discussed in "Managing Information and Minds" (chapter 12), we may now proceed up the ladder to "job actions." To be sure, unemployment and job insecurity are the most pervasive forms of job action: in an environment of genuine full employment, more precisely punitive job actions would not be very threatening; one could always walk away from one position and find another, perhaps better, one elsewhere. This is one of the many reasons for Establishment opposition to genuine full employment—particularly at a time when the bonds of ideology seem weak and purges are needed to help purify the Establishment's middle and lower ranks.

During the "nightmare decade" of the 1950s, congressional hearings and long, tortuous "loyalty" and "security" investigations became the tools of a modern-day Inquisition. Under the whiplash of the House Un-American Activities Committee, Senator Joseph McCarthy, J. Edgar Hoover, and various right-wing extremist groups, purges and blacklisting hampered dissent in general, stifled liberal or radical ideas in government, academia, and the media, and promoted the large-scale conversion of dissenters into loyal establishment supporters.

Many of those who fear a return to old-style "McCarthyism" probably are due for a double surprise, one pleasant, one unpleasant. The pleasant surprise is that old-time red-baiting—particularly the kind that identifies opponents as the conscious or unconscious agents of Moscow or Peking—may prove difficult to bring back in full-blooded form. It is not easy to attack American radicals as recipients of Russian or Chinese financial aid at a time when government subsidies are given to large capitalist enterprises doing business with this or that Communist regime.

In contrast, the unpleasant surprise would be the emergence of a new-style McCarthyism, rooted in the Establishment's inner core rather than its extremist fringes and operating much more subtly, not against "reds" and "pinkoes" alone, but rather against people on the ground of mental instability, technical unfitness (as determined by allegedly objective tests), or unemployability. New methods of doing this are being developed. Various congressmen have already proposed legislation requiring full field investigations of the one million or more persons who apply for U.S. jobs each year. Administrative officers are devising new "probationary periods" after which any employee may be terminated on efficiency grounds. This form of "preventive purge" avoids any costly appeal procedures that may be invoked when a probationary employee is stigmatized as disloyal or a security risk.

Older employees, in contrast, may be subjected to the "silent purge" sanctions of reorganization. The logic is clear. Whenever reorganization occurs, opportunities are created for terminating unfavored personnel by abolishing various divisions and units, while at the same time creating new positions for favored individuals through new divisions and units. In the drift toward friendly fascism, reorganizations of this type are inevitable at all levels. A continuous rhetoric of attack against "deadwood" facilitates the replacement of organizational dissenters or freethinkers by individuals whose loyalty to the system is greater than their personal sense of conscience.

Those dissenters who remain—or suddenly crop up—may be given assignments that isolate them from the organization or force them either to make their peace or resign. This might be called the "Herbert treatment," after Colonel Anthony B. Herbert, who exposed war crimes against civilians in South Vietnam and was promptly sent back home to take charge of kitchens and laundries in an army training camp. In the ITT merger case, something similar seems to have happened with the lawyers in the Justice Department's Antitrust Division, while the head of the division, Richard McLaren, was "kicked upstairs" by an appointment to the bench. In reporting on such cases in private business, the *Wall Street Journal* ran this headline: "Spilling the Beans: Disclosing Misdeeds of Corporations Can Backfire on Tattler—Whistle Blowers Lose Jobs, Face Ostracism, Threats." [5]

During the period of the first Watergate exposures, many middle-level employees were encouraged to "blow the whistle" on wrongdoing in the corporations for which they worked. One of the longer-term effects of these disclosures, as revealed by Joann S. Lublin, staff reporter for the *Wall Street Journal*, was to establish object lessons on what may happen to individuals who uncover and publicly reveal "fraudulent, harmful or wasteful activities on the part of their employers." Ronald Secrist, the man who "spilled the beans" about bogus insurance policies written by the Equity Funding Corporation, came to the conclusion that his years of work in the insurance industry "gained me nothing but the option of being crooked to survive." After informing the Securities and Exchange Commission about inventory mistatements and inflated sales in Cenco's financial reports, Thomas M. Howard was turned down by about 150 firms when looking for his next job. Henry Durham, an ex-marine who informed a Senate committee about mismanagement, false documentation, and waste in the Lockheed Company's production of military aircraft, was "ostracized, fired, criticized and virtually abandoned [by former friends]." Although it is impossible to assess the extent to which such sanctions are currently being used in either business or government, it is clear that every such action has resonant reverberations among other employees who hear about it.[6]

FORCEFUL CONFRONTATION

Above the "Forceful Confrontation Threshold," the next three rungs in the escalation ladder consist of arrest, trial, and confinement. In using these sanctions, police and military forces may also escalate beyond the "injury threshold" by assaulting people while arresting them, torturing them in preparation for trial, and mutilating them while in confinement. There have been enough examples of such behavior in the United States —particularly with the arrest of blacks, Hispanics, Native Americans, and poor people generally—to give the impression that a more repressive America would provide more of the same.

This impression is at least partly buttressed by some of the plans developed by military and police authorities on the use of domestic force. Thus, the following table "Riot Control Pyramid Phasing System" summarizes materials from an FBI police instructor's bulletin. Bulletins of this type suggest rather quick escalation from the use of local police to a complete takeover by federal troops.

In my judgment, this is a false impression. The major thrust of police professionalism in a new corporate society is to overcome what Herman Kahn referred to in the international arena as "an unwillingness to initiate the use of moderate levels of force for limited objectives." Negatively, this means giving up the use of immoderate force that might, by arousing too great a reaction or even radicalizing middle-of-the-roaders,

RIOT CONTROL PYRAMID PHASING SYSTEM *
TABLE 19

	Phase	What Events Occur	Who Keeps Order?	Who is Notified	Who Decides to move to Next Phase
	IV	Disturbance continues to spread, serious domestic violence is in progress	Federal troops		
MAY BE	III		National Guard County and state forces Whole police department	Federal troops alerted	The Governor
BY	II	More arrests are made Arrests are made	Sniper squad Helicopters	Local and state intelligence officers; through Military Intelligence, the Pentagon	The Mayor
PASSED			Additional on-duty police	Local emergency headquarters	
	I	A peaceful demonstration involving any number of people	The police who are on duty	FBI Mayor Fire Chief Police Chief	The police commander on duty

* FBI Police Instructor's Bulletin, as published by National Association for Research in Military-Industrial Complex (NARMIC), May 1971.

prove counterproductive. Positively, this means the development of more subtle methods of—in Brigadier Frank Kilson's phrase—"divorcing extremist elements from the population which they are trying to subvert." Some of the available methods are listed in "Innovative Police Action." All of these have already been used—with moderate amounts of accompanying personal injury—in various parts of the United States. A good part of the experimentation has developed in the District of Columbia, with its unusually large proportion of black residents, under an "anti-crime" law enacted during the early years of the Nixon administration.

INNOVATIVE POLICE ACTIONS

1. No-knock police entry on private premises.
2. Preventive detention.
3. Arrest on illegal or unconstitutional grounds.
4. Large-scale arrest with "field arrest forms." *
5. Mass arrest without "field arrest forms."
6. Denial of bail, or setting of bail beyond reach.
7. Failure to inform arrested people of their Constitutional rights.
8. Denial of access to lawyers.
9. Harassment of civil liberties lawyers.
10. Trumped-up charges, often through falsified arrest records.
11. Replacement of total immunity rights by "use immunity." **
12. Optimal show trials.
13. Extra-heavy sentencing, particularly of "multiple offenders."
14. Punitive forms of jail confinement.
15. Restrictive controls over people released on probation.

In reviewing the flowering of these various methods in the past, Richard Harris points up an interesting paradox. On the one hand, the popular justification for these measures has been to maintain law and order by punitive action against criminals and dissidents. In doing so, on the other hand, officials of the Justice Department themselves flagrantly violated many laws of due process. The paradox may be resolved, Harris points out, by retroactive legalization of the illegal: "The danger today is not only that the Constitution will continue to be violated by the Government, as it has been repeatedly in the past couple of years, but that the present Administration will rewrite the essential protections contained in

---

* Field arrest forms may provide for a Polaroid photograph of arrested person with arresting officer together with the officer's statement on the circumstances of arrest.

** Older federal immunity laws under the Fifth Amendment provide that no person may be compelled to testify against himself unless granted *total* immunity. Under *use* immunity, such a person may be prosecuted on the basis of other evidence.

that document, with the consent of the governed, and the agreement of Congress and the Supreme Court, in the name of private and public security." [7]

PERSONAL INJURY

If it takes a bloodbath . . . let's get it over with.

RONALD REAGAN,
when governor of California [8]

Research is under way on non-lethal weapons [for the National Guard]: wooden or rubber projectiles that could temporarily immobilize; high-pressure water streams; piercing noises; blinding lights.

ALAN L. OTEN [9]

Above the personal injury level the more obvious punishments that come to mind are assault, torture, mutilation, and murder (or "executive action" in the strange language of the CIA). None of these measures are unknown in present-day America, whether in the isolated form of police brutality behind prison walls, the alleged murder of Fred Hampton by the Chicago police, the killings by STRESS police units in Detroit and other cities, or larger-scale, more publicized form of assassinations as at Kent State, Jackson State, and Attica prison. None of these measures would be foreseen under friendly fascism. Indeed, with the war in Vietnam over, the well-developed capabilities of the "eliminating with prejudice" or "wasting" have been transferred to the domestic scene. *If* a bloodbath is needed, the paramilitary and military forces are prepared to act on Macbeth's maxim: "If it were done when 'tis done, then 'twere well it were done quickly."

A lot hangs, however, on how the wielders of deadly force decide whether or not "it takes a bloodbath." Too many criminals or corpses can create widespread resentment or disillusionment, perhaps even within the paramilitary forces themselves. To be thoroughly effective, one of two things are needed: convincing justification or a thorough blackout on what actually happens. In the absence of these conditions, it may be doubtful that bloodshed is really needed if other fearful, but less deadly, sanctions are available.

An early approach to this problem was the equipping of police forces with tear gas and rubber truncheons. The more advanced approaches include many varieties of chemical gases, blinding lights, deafening noises, and drug pellets or darts that can be shot from guns. These methods require greater restraint in the use of traditional firearms. Thus the pattern of the Attica massacre could be avoided; in future prison riots, prisoners could be incapacitated through the use of drug-tipped darts from the kind of guns now used on grizzly or polar bears. Vigorous crowd dispersal need not be handled in the style of the killings at Kent State. The more probable example to be followed is the style of the Chicago "police riot" during the 1968 Democratic National Convention. Considering the provocations the Chicago police regarded themselves as subjected to, and considering the police force's potential for greater destructiveness, this "riot" was a model of modulated self-control: hundreds of beatings without a single death. A facilitating circumstance was the fact that most of the demonstrators were white middle-class students. To achieve similar restraint in the handling of lower-class blacks, Puerto Ricans, or Chicanos, (who tend to fight back more vigorously), considerable training will be required. This will necessarily involve greater emphasis on rifle and revolver marksmanship, so that "shoot to disable" may compete with "shoot to kill."

Another advanced method of punishment is commitment to a mental institution. Nominally, this is merely a form of legal confinement that sidetracks most of the procedural restraints on incarceration in jails. Actually, it is often a brutal form of degradation and incapacitation. The purely physical injuries often inflicted on mental patients—straitjacketing, beatings, withdrawal of the simplest amenities—are often much less damaging than the psychological injuries. The person stigmatized as "mentally ill," "insane" or "mad" is automatically defined as someone who is "less than human" and no longer entitled to human rights or constitutional protection. Some people accept this definition, thereby relinquishing their humanity. If one disputes this definition, a new version of the "Catch 22" principle comes into being. If an alleged madman insists that he is not sick and that he wants to leave, as Dr. Thomas Szasz has charged, "his inability to recognize that he is, is regarded as a hallmark of his illness."[10]

The Soviet Union has led the way in employing psychiatric authority and commitment to asylums as a means of disciplining dissenting intellectuals. In the United States, where asylums have long been dumping grounds for the poor, the helpless, and the aged as well as the genuinely insane, new legal limitations have been put on the more arbitrary forms of commitment, and the rights of the mentally ill have been at least theoretically affirmed in a number of court decisions. The right climate of opinion, however, or a determined effort by the Establishment could easily reverse this direction. The weapon of "normality," wielded by the prestigious discipline of psychiatry, could be an extremely powerful one for friendly fascism.

Exactly how powerful is demonstrated by the history of lobotomy, an operation that involves a surgical incision into the frontal lobe of the brain. After more than fifty thousand people were lobotomized in the 1940s and 1950s, most of them in mental institutions and women and old people in particular, the technique was abandoned. As the U.S. Public Health Service said in 1948, lobotomized people tended to "lose their values, their interest in everyday life and their feelings for themselves and others." Lobotomy was rejected only partially because of questions about its effectiveness, its consequences on the personality, and its potential for abuse. In fact, a better treatment had been developed—doctors turned to massive use of tranquilizers, and hundreds of thousands of people on drug therapy were released from institutions. More recently lobotomy has started a major comeback—but in far more modern form. It is now called psychosurgery. Instead of relying on the knife alone, psychosurgeons now use ultrasonic waves and irradiation. The various areas of the brain and their functions have been mapped far more extensively. Simple incisions and separations can be supplemented by planting electrodes in the brain for the administration of electric stimulus. Complicated control mechanisms, using the panoply of computer technology, are in the offing. For a short period, vast claims were being advanced for these new techniques, and in a few cases they may have actually been tried out on experimental subjects like children and prisoners.

Reports of psychosurgery, indeed of lobotomy before it, have frequently been exaggerated. Even without exaggeration, the public is apt to be squeamish enough about intervention in the brain to react negatively. Nonetheless, it is testimony to psychiatry's power, its clients' powerlessness, and public acquiescence that lobotomies were so widely employed without sufficient investigation or safeguards. The new psychosurgery has likewise been slowed by hostile publicity, but the limitations placed on its application largely derive from its unknown or uncertain effects. What will happen when these techniques are in fact perfected, and unpleasant side effects better controlled? When will it become far more effective to put the jail inside the deviant's head rather than put the deviant inside the jail? When, instead of an eerie, emotionless "zombie" the result of these procedures is a cheerful, lively, hard-working, but docile "good citizen"?

COVERT ACTION

> A society in which people are already isolated and atomized, divided by suspicions and destructive rivalry, would support a system of terror better than a society without much chronic antagonism.
>
> EUGENE V. WALKER [11]

Covert action is the most obvious form of indirect punishment. Its widespread use abroad by the CIA has helped develop the personnel and methodology for domestic application. It has also provoked hot rivalry (as well as tense cooperation) between the CIA and other agencies involved in clandestine operations: the FBI, the various arms of the Department of Defense, the Secret Service and the larger state and local police departments. Among those secret activities already partially revealed to the public have been the following:

Operation CHAOS	CIA
COINTELPRO	FBI
GARDENPLOT	Department of Defense
SWAT (Strategic Weapons And Tactics) teams	Police Departments

In addition, as reported by R. Harris Smith, scores of large transnational corporations "have their own covert branches and very often recruit out of the CIA." [12] Recent congressional investigations in this area have concentrated on the CIA and the FBI, giving very little attention to other agencies of the federal government, and none to the covert operations of state and local police forces or large corporations. Even within this narrow focus, the investigators could not penetrate very far. Members of the investigatorical committees had reason to fear that if they went too far, they themselves—as objects of covert surveillance—would be subjected to retaliation. CIA and FBI officials, as "loyal Americans," eager to protect their patriotic activities from prying politicians, lied like troopers to congressional interrogators, with no danger of ever being charged with perjury. Miles Copeland, a former CIA official, reports on the views of his former colleagues this way: "Almost all the [CIA] people I talked to assured me unashamedly, almost proudly, 'Of *course,* we are going to lie to the congressional committees.' They felt that as loyal Americans they cannot do otherwise." [13] Looking back on his own behavior, Walter Sullivan, former deputy director of the FBI, has been still franker: "Never once did I hear anybody, including myself, raise the question: is this course of action which we have agreed on lawful . . . We were just naturally pragmatic." [14]

Nonetheless, a few interesting tidbits have been brought to light. Thus the FBI's COINTELPRO program included:

- Anonymously attacking the political beliefs of targets in order to induce their employers to fire them.
- Anonymously mailing letters to the spouses of intelligence targets for the purpose of destroying their marriages.
- Falsely and anonymously labeling as government informants members of groups known to be violent, thereby exposing the falsely labeled member to expulsion or physical attack.
- Sending an anonymous letter to the leader of a Chicago street gang . . . saying that the Black Panthers were supposed to have "a hit for

you." The letter was suggested because it may "intensify . . . animosity" and cause the street gang leader to "take retaliatory action." [15]

Although COINTELPRO was alleged to have been discontinued in 1971, in 1975 a former FBI operative, Joseph A. Burton, publicly revealed the continuation of the same kind of tricks, in subsequent years.[16] Other former agents have disclosed how, under instructions from the FBI, they operated as provocateurs, suggesting illegal activities to antiwar groups, in one case even supplying them with explosives.[17]

All these tidbits, however, merely illustrate the logic of Walter Sullivan's pungent comment about being "naturally pragmatic." The pragmatics of covert action require more effective cover, better coordination among federal, state, local, and private operations, and—above all—a higher level of professionalism. One can envision an informal civil service network, with CIA and Green Beret types of various nationalities moving back and forth throughout the United States and the entire "Free World," with promotions and family security benefits based on professional skill in covert action. Under these circumstances one can look forward to improved capabilities not only for harassment but also for the use of deadlier force through induced heart failure, deep lobotomy (surgical, electrical, or pharmaceutical), induced suicide (as attempted with Dr. Martin Luther King), and "accidental" automobile fatalities. One may expect much greater ingenuity in providing the kind of advice and material with which supermilitant opponents of the Establishment may act out revolutionary fantasies by moving upward on the ladder of terror, thereby providing police agencies with the justification needed for the application of overt force.

CONFLICT AMONG THE "SLOBS"

I can hire one half of the working class to kill the other half.

JAY GOULD,
In reference to Knights of Labor strike, 1886

Jay Gould's boast that he could hire half the working class to kill the other half should be regarded less as a report on his employment practices than as an affirmation of confidence in the strategy of indirect violence. The mere act of bringing different ethnic groups to the same city or factory was often far more effective than extra expenses for hiring strikebreakers or financing the political campaigns of officials who sent the police or National Guard in to break heads.

After World War II, largely as an unforeseen consequence of the mechanization of Southern agriculture, millions of black people from the rural South moved into America's central cities. Here they came into many forms of conflict with other ethnic groups who had "made it" on the lower or middle range of the social ladder. In turn, blacks were followed by people from Puerto Rico, Mexico, Central America, and the Caribbean.

For the higher powerholders, still predominantly White Anglo-Saxon Protestant (WASP), this passage of hatred has been a godsend—what people of French ancestry in Louisiana call *lagniappe,* an unexpected dividend. The "slobs" could be expected to fight among themselves almost endlessly—for jobs, for admission into unions or civil service positions, for entry into this or that neighborhood, for acceptance into higher status schools, even colleges and universities.

During the 1960s and the early 1970s, conflicts among the "slobs" (much more vulnerable than others to business downturns) were fanned by a wide variety of factors. In New York City, as Nathan Glazer and Daniel Patrick Moynihan have pointed out, "The Protestants and better-off Jews determined that the Negroes and Puerto Ricans were deserving and in need and, on these grounds, further determined that these needs would be met by concessions of various kinds from the Italians and the Irish (or, generally speaking, from the Catholics[s] . . . and worse-off Jews."[18]

Blacks themselves were caught between two conflicting tendencies: assimilation (or integration) and separatism. The assimilationists asked for acceptance on equal terms by white employers, neighbors, landlords, and trade unions. Their demands, often based on the self-demeaning assumption that black students could not get a proper education unless sitting alongside whites in a classroom, often met with stubborn resistance and sometimes with a condescending acquiesence that offered quick "plums" to token blacks. The separatists and nationalists, in turn, sometimes sought to unify their followers by raising the level of ethnic invective against "Whitey" and occasionally descending to the level of countering white racism with black racism and anti-Semitism. This conflict was exacerbated by deep tensions between upwardly mobile black professionals, business people, technicians and the majority of stable working-class elements, and the members of the highly unstable "underclass."

With the stagflation of the late 1970s, the potentials for more acute group conflicts have grown. More and more people compete with each other for fewer and fewer job opportunities. Moreover, so-called "affirmative action" programs, which sought to provide more openings for black and Latin job-seekers have been converted into what Representative Augustus Hawkins once called "negative action"—namely, the firing of a large proportion of minority people (and women) who previously benefited from preferential hiring. Ghetto crime increases. In the public schools, there are more beatings, thefts, rapes, riots, and murders. In white communities the result is fear—deep fear of the "Black Terror" that may strike in the streets (unless properly cordoned and patrolled), in their homes (unless properly guarded or armed), and in the public schools (unless segregated). This is what Andrew Hacker had in mind in his analysis of white fears some years ago when the unemployment-inflation outlook was less foreboding: "Those who preoccupy themselves with the immorality and irresponsibility found in slum society would do well to turn their attention to the new generations of youngsters being spawned in our ghettoes at this very moment . . . In the process of creation right now are rioters and rapists, murderers and marauders, who will despoil society's landscape before this country has run its course . . . Violence will mark relations between the races. Whites will live in increasing fear of depredations against their persons and property ...If a single word characterizes white attitudes, it is *fear*."[19]

By the end of the 1970s and the beginning of the 1980s this fear was exacerbated by new outbreaks of cross-burnings in front of the homes of black families in the North and hate-ridden attacks on blacks moving into formerly lily-white suburbs. Nazi-style swastikas have been painted on synagogues and on the graves in Jewish cemeteries. Jay Gould would clap his hands in glee at the coming prospect of new waves of conflict among ethnic and religious minorities.

A VIOLENCE-VIGILANTE CULTURE

Well, what is a vigilante man?
Tell me, what is a vigilante man?
Has he got a gun and a club in his han'?
Is that a vigilante man? . . .
Would he shoot his brother and sister down?

WOODIE GUTHRIE

Under "advanced" capitalism, Woodie Guthrie's old question might be asked again—not to probe the motives of someone who might "shoot his brother and sister down" but to establish his identity. One answer to the question is given by Kanti C. Kotecha and James L. Walker in their article "Police Vigilantes": "Police vigilantism can be defined as acts or threats by police which are intended to protect the established socio-political order from subversion, but which violate some generally perceived norms for police behavior." [20] Unlawful police violence is usually covert. Beatings and torture may be hidden by the doors of the police van or jailhouse. The police may form off-duty groups—like the terrorist "death squads" in Brazil or "The Band" in the Dominican Republic—that dispense with legal formalities in "disposing" of dissenters or petty criminals who fail to buy protection. Another answer leads straight to the door of the chief executive, whose personal network usually includes various groups of illegal operators. In this way, in Alan Wolfe's pungent words, "vigilantism may be turned on its head: instead of a private group using illegal violence for public ends, a public group uses illegal violence for private ends." [21] Also, as in the case of President Ford's indirect encouragement of the antibusing rioters in Boston, a chief "law enforcer" may promote conflict among the "slobs" by condoning illegal violence by private groups.

But the central domain of terror continues to be the "symbolic environment." While the myths and fantasies of popular culture are replete with opiate-like images of virtue or cleverness rewarded, boy-getting-girl, girl-getting riches, and everyone getting pie in Pollyanna's sky, more "realistic" imagery is used to sell movies to audiences and TV audiences to advertisers. Symbolic violence gets and keeps attention. And despite sporadic gestures toward "cooling it," the long-term tendency seems to be toward escalation. "The world of television drama is, above all, a violent one," report George Gerbner and Larry P. Gross, the two most assiduous monitors of American TV. "More than half of all characters are involved in some violence, at least one tenth in some killing, and three fourths of prime time hours contain some violence." [22] The net effect of this tendency, as Gerbner and Gross point out, may be "a demonstration of power and an instrument of social serving, on the whole, to reinforce and preserve the existing social order." Although their emphasis is on the preservation of the status quo, their analysis clearly suggests that an increase in symbolic violence could help usher in a new serfdom of fear, anxiety, and simultaneous identification with the unconstrained and violent forces of "law."

15

Sex, Drugs, Madness, Cults

HOW DOES A SOCIETY blow off steam: Where are the escape valves that offer relief from tension and anxiety?

A powerful head of steam is an inescapable by-product of trends toward friendly fascism. The rewards of extended professionalism, accelerated consumerism, and elite power work *if*—and *only if*—they create anxiety. Much of this anxiety (and even terror) is free floating and, like explosive gases, might be touched off by stray sparks—unless dissipated by channeling into available escape valves.

Four of these escape valves—sex, drugs, mental illness, and cults—merit special attention. Although each is usually seen from entirely different perspectives, in each we find a phenomenon already uncovered in other spheres—that actions hailed as hallmarks of progress may turn out to be major steps down the new roads to serfdom. As I shall now proceed to suggest, friendly fascism, American style, might well be described as a sex-driven, drugged, mad (or Therapeutic), and cult-ridden society.

SEX: THROUGH LIBERATION TO REPRESSION

Since World War II the so-called "sexual revolution" has started to demolish old-fashioned sexual repression. This has evidenced itself in a significant lifting of taboos on premarital sexual intercourse, marital infidelity, male and female homosexuality, masturbation, prostitution, and even incest. Explicit representation of nude bodies and a wide variety of sex acts are now much more acceptable not only in "how-to-do-it" sex manuals but also on TV and the stage, and in movies, dance, poetry, and novels.

If Wilhelm Reich were alive today (and should stick by his guns), he would probably hail the sexual revolution as destroying the basis of any future fascism. Indeed, he said just about that back in 1933: "The biologic rigidity of the present generation can no longer be eliminated

. . . However new human beings are born every day, and in the course of thirty years the human race will have been biologically renewed; it will come into the world without any trace of fascist distortion." Liberation from sexual repression, Reich insisted, would bring human freedom. And Reich hammered this point home with the assertion that "Sexually awakened women, affirmed and recognized as such, would mean the complete collapse of the authoritarian ideology." [1] Although Reich died in jail in 1957 (after being convicted for fraud in the sale of his "orgone box"), his spirit has carried on. For more than a decade after his death, many "counterculture" enthusiasts thought that the possibility of political repression would somehow or other be destroyed by the lifting of sexual repression. This, indeed, is part of Charles Reich's optimistic prediction that liberated lifestyles will undermine the Corporate State. Others have seen the sexual revolution as freeing both men and women from the commercialization of sex and as opening up new horizons of freedom and equality.

Yet, there are at least three elements in the sexual revolution that might contribute to, rather than reverse, present trends toward technology based authoritarianism.

First of all, the sexual revolution has helped make more women available to more men on easier terms. A "liberated" woman, as Anselma Dell' Olio has put it, is often regarded as one who "puts out" sexually at the drop of a suggestive command, doesn't demand marriage, and "takes care of herself" with contraceptives. This type of liberation has little to do with the kind of love that is based on the two-way communication and respect and that only exists between equals. It has little to do with the changing of sex roles in family, school, workplace, or economic politics. In her "The Sexual Revolution Wasn't Our War" in *Ms.* magazine, Dell' Olio has put it this way: "We have come to see that the so-called Sexual Revolution is merely a link in the chain of abuse laid on women through patriarchal history. While purporting to restructure the unequal basis for sexual relationships between men and women, our beneficent male liberators werc in fact continuing their control of feminine sexuality." [2]

Second, there seem to be growing tendencies toward engineered routinization of sex. A new "sex technology"—backed up by expanded R & D—propagates techniques not only of birth control and abortion but also of body massages, foreplay, intercourse, and afterplay. As with other forms of social engineering, the sex technologists suggest a technical solution for almost every sexual probelm. Over the short run, emotions remain in the picture—because their excitement contributes to the consumer expenditures essential for the income and profits of *Playboy-Penthouse-Hustler*-style magazines, more explicit pornography, rent-a-girl enterprises, and the new corporate brothels. Over the longer run, to the extent that sex drives are more thoroughly separated from truly deep emotions and warm interpersonal relations among mutually respecting individuals, the emotional content could be largely drained out. This is the friendly fascist perspective: sex as a quick impersonal activity that contributes to individual alienation and social fragmentation. "As political and economic freedom diminishes," Aldous Huxley once wrote in an introduction to his *Brave New World,* "sexual freedom tends compensatingly to increase." It helps reconcile people to "the servitude which is their fate."

Finally, the sexual revolution could possibly have a dual effect on human energies. For the majority of people, it could drain off, along with violent sports, alcohol, and drugs, energies from any dedicated efforts to oppose oligarchy, empire, and the subversion of formal democracy. This would be classic escapism—well garbed, perfumed, self-induced, and beefed up with smooth commercialism and technological gadgetry. For the oligarchs and their professional aides in the technostructure, however, it could build up a new form of manipulative *machismo.* Their difficulties in coping with the fathomless bafflements of the Establishment, their frustrations at not receiving respect and honor from subordinates, associates, mates, and children, their self-doubts concerning the meaning of the rat race and rewards of manipulative power—all these can be compensated for by the synthetic potency of orgasm-cum-flattery bought cheap and worth every dollar on the corporate expense account. With this kind of bedroom support, the banker, executive, general, admiral, and professional can go back to the fray with renewed energies.

DRUGS: RELIGION OF SOME PEOPLE

In today's First World, oppression takes many different forms. It is rooted in the frustration of rising aspirations, in the anguish of old crises in new forms, in the new environmental crises, and in the erosion of authority. Above all, the impact of tendencies toward extended professionalism is to accentuate fragmentation, anxiety, and alienation. The by-products of accelerated consumption are boredom, apathy, and tension. The slow growth of concentrated elite power builds up repressed aggressiveness and despair at all levels. Throughout the population, including the top elites, an eagerness for escape could lead to a Drug Age in which—in the words of Harrison Pope, Jr., "drug use ranges from simple fun—a transient relief from boredom—to an entire way of life, an identity which buffers against apathy." Hallucination, he adds, "can become a means for a psychological or philosophical quest, a search for meaning in a society perceived as unloving, lonely, and meaningless." [3]

The power of drug relief is the huge range of demands fulfillable by modern industrialism's expanding pharmacopeia. A. E. Housman referred only to traditional alcoholic drinks when he wrote his famous lines to the effect that ". . . malt does more than Milton can/To justify God's ways to man." Conviviality and good cheer can be promoted by marijuana, hashish, and amphetamines. LSD and its many rivals can open up new vistas of fanciful and other-worldly sensation. Some of these provide indescribable heights of pleasure. As Dr. Marshall Dumont puts it, the "abdominal orgasm that follows the 'opiate flash' is better than sex." "Uppers" provide temporary *fun,* or relief from boredom, apathy, or alienation. They may be followed by "downers" that may "ease the crash" and put one at blissful ease or into a light or deep slumber. Both uppers and downers allow people to sidestep the pressures of competition, aggression, and loneliness.[4]

Market demand for these various forms of drug relief is already far more widespread than indicated by public distress about "junkies" among black and Puerto Rican minorities. Heroin and methadone are increasingly used among the rat racers in the technostructure and the upper elites. As for age, the great majority of the "pillheads" are to be found among the adult population. The 25–64 age group outnumbers the 14–24 group by more than 2 to 1. It also has much more money to back up its demands. This is where the future market potential lies. If you are lonely, nervous, unattractive, overweight or underweight, if you have difficulty in sleeping or waking up, if you have upset this or clogged that, mass advertising tells you that the answer is a pill or a drink. But telling you is only half the story. The most strategic messages are found in these drug company advertisements in psychiatric and medical journals:

> WHAT MAKES A WOMAN CRY? A man? Another woman? Three kids? No kids at all? Wrinkles? You name it . . . if she is depressed, consider Portofane.
>
> SCHOOL, THE DARK, SEPARATION, DENTAL VISITS, MONSTERS—THE EVERYDAY ANXIETY OF CHILDREN SOMETIMES GETS OUT OF HAND. A child can usually deal with his anxieties. But sometimes the anxieties overpower the child. Then he needs your help. Your help may include Visatril.[5]

The aim of the drug industry seems to be much more than getting people to define human and social problems as open to medical remedies; it includes enrolling all levels of so-called "health personnel" as pushers. Already, the mass use of tranquilizers is spreading from mental institutions and hospitals to out-patient clinics and treatment in doctors' offices.

Other professions are getting into the swim. "Well-adjusted" behavior can also be produced in the classroom—without any changes in the apathetic or stultifying, often implicitly racist atmosphere of many schools —by administering Ritalin to "hyperactive" children. "Two hundred thousand children in the United States, it has been estimated, are now being given amphetamine and stimulant therapy, with probably another hundred thousand receiving tranquilizers and antidepressants."[6] Looking into the future, two professors of education have hopefully seen this number rising into the many millions: Biochemical and psychological mediation of learning is likely to increase," they assert; "new dramas will play on the educational stage as drugs are introduced experimentally to improve in the learner such qualities as personality, concentration and memory."

Some psychologists envision still greater dramas in other stages. In his presidential address at the American Psychological Assocation, Professor Kenneth Clark announced that, as a result of "many provocative and suggestive findings from neurophysiological, biochemical and psychopharmacological research . . . it is now possible—indeed imperative—to reduce human anxieties, tensions, hostilities, violence, cruelty and the destructive power irrationalities of man, which are the basis of wars."[7] He then made a formal proposal: "Given these contemporary facts, it would seem logical that a requirement imposed upon all power-controlling leaders and those who aspire to such leadership would be that they accept and use the earliest perfected form of psychotechnical, biochemical intervention which would assure their positive use of power and reduce or block the possibility of their using power destructively . . ."[8]

It is in the sphere of direct rehabilitation that drug relief is most vigorously spread by alleged cures. The most heavily financed rehabilitation efforts, instead of dealing primarily with a person's need and demand for drugs, involve counter-drugs. Thus, back in the 1890s, many physicians joined with Dr. J. R. Black when, in a medical journal article, he concluded that "I would urge morphine instead of alcohol for all to whom such a craving is an incurable propensity."[9] Heroin, in turn, was originally invented and introduced by physicians as a cure for morphine addiction. Methadone—also addictive and capable of producing a "high"—is now used to block heroin addiction. In rehabilitation circles, major hopes are being placed on even newer counter-drugs: cyclazone, naloxone, M5050, and many others.

The inner logic of all these tendencies, I suspect, is to produce eventually a qualitative change in public controls: the removal of the major legal restrictions not only on marijuana but also on heroin and amphetamines. Under such conditions the repressive controls on addicts would be lifted. Mainliners would be as free to induce their own tastes as winos, alcoholics and "pill heads." As in England, where low-cost heroin has been widely available under the National Health Service, robbery and larceny would no longer be necessary to support a hundred-dollar-a-day habit. With less costs imposed on others, more people would be free to injure themselves. If and when such a reform comes, it would be presented as a triumph for more humanism in the handling of lower-class addiction. In a broader sense, however, it could be a major step toward friendly fascism.

"Each one of us," mused the Controller in *Brave New World,* "goes through life in a bottle. But if we happen to be Alphas, our bottles are, relatively speaking, enormous. We should suffer acutely if we were confined in a narrower space." Under friendly fascism also, each person would live in his or her own bottle, and everyone—even the Alphas—would complain about the confinement. But in this fully Bottled Society, everyone, instead of being limited to a dose of standardized *soma,* would be able to win relief from frustrations through the intake of pills, drinks, injections, and sniffs from an enormous variety of smaller bottles.

MADNESS: ESCAPE FROM MADNESS

> Would not the diagnosis be justified that many systems of civilization—or epochs of it—possibly even the whole of humanity—have become "neurotic" under the pressure of the civilizing trends?
>
> SIGMUND FREUD [10]

The old-fashioned madhouse—often referred to as "Bedlam," "looney bin" or simply "insane asylum"—was one of the earlier blights of civilization. An element of progress may be found in its replacement by modern practices of psychiatry, psychoanalysis, psychiatric social work, and similar forms of social engineering. On the other hand, the usual criticism of modern psychotherapy is that there is still too much of the filth, ignorance, degradation, and cruelty of Bedlam in the present-day asylum. In practically every state of the union, any crusading journalist for a TV station or newspaper can make instant headlines by exposing shocking conditions in the nearest public institutions to which the "mentally ill" are committed. The immediate impact was previously to suggest the need for larger budgets and more professional care; more recently, "deinstitutionalization" became the common goal of reformers, civil libertarians, and budget cutters. Only slowly do the other defects of modern psychiatric care emerge as starkly as those of asylum.

One of these is the tendency of modern psychotherapy to become a new instrument of direct repression. This is most evident, as Dr. Thomas Szasz has pointed out in a long series of powerfully argued books, in "institutional psychiatry." Rather than dedicating themselves to a confidential and unique relation with each client, institutional psychiatrists tend to become agents of the state and, in that capacity, are responsible for certifying various people as mad (by a variety of unbelievably elastic quasidiagnostic terms) and thereby commiting them to incarceration. Whether they want it or not, those who are thus imprisoned escape from the stresses and strains of the "real world" outside the locked doors and barred windows of the mental hospital. Instead of the harsh competition, fragmentation, and materialism of the outside world, they enter a strange new world of dull and (for some) soothing routines, of the constrained anxieties relating to the small rewards and punishments administered by staff and other inmates, and of unrestricted opportunities for illusions and delusions. For some—perhaps the majority—the real delusion is that they are essentially different from the staff, the physicians, and the nondeviants in the outside world.

"Because the concept of mental illness is infinitely elastic," argues Dr. Szasz, "almost any moral, political or social problem can be cast into a psychiatric mold." He then drives his point home by discussing the possibility of a new fascism: "Unlike political fascism, which sought its justification in the value of the "good of the state," and subordinated everything else to it, the moral fascism we have been cultivating subordinates all to the value of the 'welfare of the people.' "[11]

A far more widespread tendency, however, is the authentication by most forms of psychotherapy of widespread escape from the anxieties of the real world. As opposed to the over two million in-patients and out-patients receiving formal "mental health" treatment in 1976, one may estimate that there were four to five times as many—from eight to ten million people—rather fully involved in various forms of more informal varieties of "therapy." These forms, and the labels affixed thereto, vary from traditional psychoanalysis to group therapy, encounter groups, marathon groups, family therapy, and behavioral therapy. Some are intimately associated with drug therapy.

Like drugs, this kind of help can become powerfully addictive; the people who are hooked experience painful withdrawal systems. But unlike drug addicts, the people "in treatment" can readily switch from one form to another. This leads to considerable shopping around. Only rarely do therapists allow attention to be focused on the many sources of anxiety and misery that lie in the political, economic, and social sphere. To do so would require not only dealing with social fragmentation and exploitation but encouraging the kind of resistance and counterattack that could only be handled by a political movement that may not yet exist. So willy-nilly the therapists, sometimes consciously and with the immediate interests of their individual patients at heart, accept the realities of a mad society—and provide the escape valves required for its acceptance by their patients.

This is a consumer-service area of considerable potential. Dr. Gerald Klerman, professor of psychiatry at Harvard University, estimates that one out of eight Americans—about 28 million people—"can expect to experience depression during his life." [12] In a report for the National

Institute of Mental Health, Dr. David Rosenthal projects a larger market: "possibly 60 million Americans are borderline schizophrenics or exhibit other deviant mental behavior in the schizophrenic category." If friendly-fascist tendencies continue, the number of people getting "help" could well be somewhere between Dr. Klerman's 28 million and Dr. Rosenthal's 60 million.

For this expansion to take place, two technical conditions will probably have to be met: (1) a large expansion of subprofessional helpers and (2) tacit assurance that most of the "helpees," so long as they behave themselves according to dominant values, will face little risk of compulsory commitment.

The social sciences have never been lacking in delusions. Delusions are nourished by grant applications that exaggerate the results to be attained, by grants and contracts that legitimate these ebullient claims, and by recognition from political leaders desperately in need of the legitimation obtainable only from recognized "authorities." Each social science discipline seems to produce its specialized delusions—the economist's vision of an econometric model guiding the behavior of oligarchic capitalists, Carl Kaysen's "corporation with a soul," Daniel Bell's university as the central institution of modern capitalism, or B. F. Skinner's world of autonomous B. F. Skinners administering the postive reinforcements that will bring people "beyond freedom and disunity" to beneficial adjustment. Oddly enough, the psychiatrist—the self-avowed specialists in diagnosing and treating the delusions of others—seem most susceptible to delusions of grandeur. Few others have gone as far as Dr. Howard P. Rome in calling the entire world their "catchment area." Dr. G. Brock Chisholm has gone still further by urging that psychiatrists "must now decide what is to be the immediate future of the human race. No one else can. And this is the prime responsibility of psychiatry." [14]

CULTS: BELONGING THROUGH SUBMISSION

As we have seen already, greater cohesion at the peak of a capitalist establishment is perfectly consistent with social fragmentation among the population at large. Accordingly, there comes into being a huge and desperate demand for something to belong to and believe in.

Such a demand could be met in the 1980s by a popular anti-establishment movement. One could visualize large numbers of lower- and middle-income people working together to transform capitalist society into a democratic, pluralistic socialism or a truly humanistic capitalism. In the struggles of such a movement, people could find not only a new spirit of community but a new or restored faith in the future of family, community, and country. They could find the best possible protection against environmental degradation, unemployment and inflation, and the ever-present dangers of limited or unlimited warfare. If such a movement came into being, of course, it would face the danger of being shattered into pieces by a combination of minor concessions, the co-opting of key leaders, penetration, provocation, and direct repression. The possibility that such a movement might come into being and overcome this danger is one of the reasons why friendly fascism is not inevitable.

More probable, however, is the absorption of many potential leaders or devoted followers of such a movement into one or another religious or quasi-religious cult. In 1976, according to *U.S. News & World Report,* anywhere from one to three million Americans, mostly in their twenties or late teens, are active in hundreds of these new cults.[15] One of these is the Unification Church, led by Sun Myung Moon, the millionaire Korean industrialist. The Moon church offers thousands of young Americans the security of perennial childhood. "To lonely young people drifting through cold, impersonal cities and schools," one observer reports "it offers instant friendship and communion . . . a life of love, joy and inner peace, with no hassles, no doubts and no decisions." [16] Other young people are absorbed into the Divine Light Mission led by the young Indian, Guru Maharaj Ji; the International Society for Krishna Consciousness, whose flowing robed "Krishna chanters" may be seen dancing on the streets of many American cities; the Church of Scientology; Jews for Jesus; and the Children of God, sometimes called "Jesus freaks." In turn, EST (Erhard Seminars Training), like most of its competitors in the packaging of encounter groups and group therapy, appeals mainly to people in their late twenties, thirties, and early forties. Erhard's message is simple but powerful: "There is nothing out there. No one cares. Do you get it? You can change nothing. Accept what is." [17]

And for those who are older, have already "made it," and fear that they have "had it," there are the beginnings of a new fundamentalism made up of "evangelicals" who, by the late 1970s, according to Carey McWilliams, attracted up to 40 million followers in the mainline Protestant denominations alone.[18] Others may turn to astrology, transcendental meditation, or belief in extrasensory perception.

Although some of the going enterprises in this area have already become financially successful, I do not see many elements of this sector being absorbed into the capital-rich world of the transnational conglomerate. The outlook, rather, is for a highly competitive market in which a few cults may remain and many will disappear to be replaced by new ones. Some will stress retreat from the world, while others will seek to bring God back into the classroom. Some will offer personal salvation by getting in touch with one's body or inner self, while others will offer it by closer contact with God or the universe as a whole.

Underlying all this diversity, however, I see two common elements: acceptance of the existing social structure and the submission to an authoritarian doctrine or leader. The satisfaction thereby provided can go far in narcotizing the dissatisfactions of those who feel they are being "ripped off" by a heartless world. On the road to friendly fascism, the new cults can provide exploited people not only with a sigh (to use Karl Marx's old phrase) but with those "uppers" and "downers" that channel tensions into harmless activities and thereby promote submission to the growing powers of the faceless oligarchy and the Golden International.

16

The Adaptive Hydra

If we want things to stay as they are, things will have to change. Do you know?

GIUSEPPE DI LAMPEDUSA,
The Leopard

THE MYTHICAL HYDRA of Greek antiquity was a remarkable animal. If an attacker cut off one of its many heads, it would function through the others. And then a new head would sprout to replace the lost one.

The modern complex outdoes the ancient Hydra. It has many more heads, and each of them enjoys less visibility. It has greater regenerative powers; for each head springs from a managerial reservoir full of upwardly mobile men (and a few women), breathlessly awaiting more room at the top. This modern Hyrda is also *adaptive*—both in the passive sense of responding to change and in the active sense of anticipating or guiding it.

During the period between the years 1984 and 2000, the generations coming into the Establishment's positions of higher power will be those born during World War II and the decade thereafter. Of these, the oldest will be those who were of college age at the time of the various "rebellions" of the 1960s. They will be people who, while probably passive onlookers at that time, nonetheless jumped into the counterculture by the time it became respectable. They will probably still maintain longish hair and mod clothes, and inhale or ingest whatever drug becomes the latest fad. Just as Charles Reich's corporate planners were more sophisticated than the Consciousness One individualists, the faceless oligarchs of the Berkeley-Columbia generation would probably be far more advanced than the corporate-military planners of today. Some of them may indeed be former militants—like Eldridge Cleaver—who have "got religion" and changed their spots. "One who pays some attention to history," Noam Chomsky warns, "will not be surprised if those who cry most loudly that we must smash and destroy are later found among the administrators of some new system of repression."[1] In any case, having already adapted themselves to changing conditions and opportunities, these new leaders will probably show remarkable adaptivity in facing up to changing challenges to the Establishment's power.

FRYING PAN–FIRE CONFLICTS

Many years ago Frank Stockton wrote a short story about a semi-barbaric king who used to try accused criminals in a public arena. The defendant was forced to open one of a pair of doors in the arena wall. Behind one there was usually a hungry tiger. If the man chose that door, he was killed immediately and declared guilty. Behind the other door was supposed to be a slave girl who, if that door was opened, became his wife as a reward for his innocence. When the king's daughter took a lover from the peasant class, the king decided to punish the man by placing him in the arena. After asking her father which door was which, the princess signaled her lover to choose the right-hand door. He did so. At this point Stockton ends the story: "And so I leave it with all of you: Which came out of the opened door—the lady or the tiger?"

When I first heard this story discussed in a high school class, the question seemed to be one of female psychology. Did the princess direct her lover to the tiger, sparing herself the pain of seeing him married to another? Or rather, being unable to face the spectacle of seeing him torn to pieces, did she direct him to the lady?

Even in high school, I was never able to accept the question entirely as it was put. Knowing already that everything a father says is not necessarily so, I wondered whether perhaps in this very special case, the king had placed a tiger behind *each* door. More recently, reflecting on the behavior of leaders who preserved their power for long periods, it has occurred to me that the king probably put a tiger behind one door and a pack of wolves behind the other. In either case the daughter did not really know what the options were and her lover faced a classic choice between a frying pan and a fire.

As I peer down the road to friendly fascism, I see many choices of this type. From the viewpoint of the Establishment, the logic is absurdly simple: any grievance that ordinary people suffer may be cured by measures that consolidate the repressive power of the Big Business-Big Government partnership. Nor is this an entirely new logic; rather, it is merely the fruition of a long sequence of reforms—often first articulated by socialists or communists—that have strengthened the structure of concentrated power. Debates over these reforms have usually included few if any references to the power elites that would ultimately run them or benefit from them. Indeed, as is often the case with welfare-state reforms, the most vocal opposition has sometimes come from conservatives or reactionaries who were not prescient enough to know on which side their bread was buttered.

If one looks quickly back at the preceding eight chapters, he or she will find copious examples of such system-strengthening reforms. Among them are centralized economic planning, executive agency reorganization, streamlining Congress, more integrated data collection, and, above all, government control of prices and wages. Any one of these can be hailed in advance as a forward step toward a more humanist, enlightened, egalitarian, or democratic society—and have often so been hailed by liberal or radical reformers. Yet any one could turn out to be another step down one of the many roads to serfdom.

A crucial example is the debate over the mode of recruiting people into the American army: voluntary enlistment or a return to conscription. As formulated within the Establishment's higher circles, the issue has been *how* to maintain or enlarge an already huge war force. When Presidents Nixon and Ford liquidated the draft, their purpose was to reduce the opposition to American intervention in Vietnam. The shift to a volunteer army helped achieve this purpose. It also tied in with a reduction in the size of the war force and a massive expansion in weapons that needed very little manpower for their use. In 1979 and 1980 the campaign to register American youth for a subsequent draft has been part of resurgent militarism based on a rapid expansion in both missile systems and armed forces. In this context, the most important question is not voluntary recruitment versus registration for a draft; it is the pace of the arms race, the future of detente, and the preparations for "new Vietnams." If these larger issues are obscured, then the method of recruiting people into the army is a frying-pan-versus-fire question. Militarism can be remolded either way. There are dozens of false micro-alternatives of this type. These are crossroads where either road can lead in the direction of friendly fascism. On the macro-level there are such broader issues as deflationary stagnation or inflationary recession, polarization versus consensus, standardized liberalism versus conservatism—each pair of which may be nothing other than alternative roads to serfdom.

Actually, none of these alternatives turns out to be a simple pair. In the real world, there are more ways to be killed than suggested by the limited options of being fried in a pan, being directly burned, or being attacked by tigers or wolves. When I was very young—even before reading Stockton's "The Lady or the Tiger"—the nice, well-behaved boys on my block used to propound a difficult question: How would you prefer to be killed—by being shot, poisoned, drowned, hung, stabbed through the heart, or thrown off a roof? Today, the scientists, "security managers," and military contractors offer a still more bewildering variety of destructive options: at least a dozen different varieties each of new intercontinental missiles, large or small submarines, manned or unmanned aircraft, and chemical and bacteriological warfare. Less frank than the boys on my block, however, they usually fail to indicate that in any future war in which some of these options are chosen the senders as well as the receivers may also be annihilated.

If all these bright ideas were to originate in one spot, the spectrum of choice would be much more narrow. But adaptivity on the road to friendly fascism depends on "oligarchic democracy" within an establishment's top and middle levels. In his own rather limited way, Albert Speer recognized the necessity of working this way as Hitler's minister of armaments and war production. Instead of sending out authoritarian orders from his office, he tried to develop a spirit of so-called "parliamentarianism" in accordance with which arguments and counter-arguments were heard on all sides before decisions were made. He preferred "uncomfortable associates to compliant tools." [2] He thus exploited the creative energies and spontaneity of many technocrats who, lacking or stifling all moral scruples, dedicated themselves to solving the technical problems assigned to them or originated by them. What Speer nurtured in the context of the more rigid bureaucracies of Germany has already been fully developed in the modern Establishments of the First World. Coordination already takes place in accordance with what Charles E. Lindblom of Yale University once called "partisan mutual adjustment." Without stating it directly, Lindblom put his finger on the nature of system strengthening in a power structure undergoing transformation into Super-America, Inc.

If this kind of power structure is to come into being and maintain itself, redundancy is essential. Errors made at one point can thus be corrected at other points. Naturally, in the process of eliminating some internal conflicts, the Establishment's leaders knowingly or unwittingly create others. As the partnership between Big Business and Big Government becomes much closer, personal infighting becomes more intense. Some plutocrats remain wedded to the old order, preferring the established ways and fearing the leap into global operations. Tactical conflicts arise about who gets how much of the pie and, more broadly, about the shape of empire; the pace of oligarchic integration; the timing of constitutional subversion; the degree of informational management; the delicate balance between positive reinforcements and the use of violence; the uses of sex, drugs, madness, and cults; and the scope of system-strengthening reforms and adaptation.

On all these points, the oligarchs need conflicting proposals and pressures from executive managers and junior-contingent members. From time to time, indeed, the intensity of such conflicts might stymie the processes of mutual-adjustment decision making, or even threaten the oligarchy's viability. Yet, its internal tensions would be much less fierce than those that raged violently in fascist Germany, Japan, and Italy. There, the business oligarchs often found themselves uncomfortably pressed by the political leaders and military overlords, or both. In contrast, the Corporate Overseers and Ultra-Rich of the United States would enjoy a much larger degree of hegemony and the possibility of enlarged empire without the unsettling horrors of openly initiating a large-scale war to extend their frontiers—an option never available to Hitler, Mussolini, or the Japanese leaders.

The price of oligarchic democracy is sustained controversy in the executive suites—mostly behind closed doors, some spilling over into arenas of more public visibility. The minimum benefit is the prevention of top-level stagnation. The optimum outcome—from the viewpoint of the friendly fascists—is an oligarchy capable of creative dynamism.

MULTILEVEL CO-OPTATION

Just for a handful of silver he left us,
Just for a riband to stick in his coat.

ROBERT BROWNING,
The Lost Leader

Co-optation, according to Phillip Selznick in a study of organizational behavior, is "the process of absorbing new elements into the leadership or policymaking structure of an organization as a means of averting threats to its stability or existence." [3] From the viewpoint of a country's establishment, co-optation has historically gone far beyond averting threats; it has served the more positive function of strengthening the system. In some cases co-optation has been associated with system-strengthening reforms. Michael Harrington points out that in adopting various welfare-state programs that originated in the German socialist movement, "it was the Junker Bismarck who came up with the truly bold scheme: he proposed to co-opt socialism itself." [4] But a system can also be strengthened by absorbing elements into minor roles far below the leadership or policy-making level. Some of these roles may be purely symbolic, some technical, some administrative. When William Wordsworth "left us" (in Robert Browning's words) to become poet laureate, he did not enter the inner councils of the expanding British empire. When Daniel P. Moynihan spent the first two years of the Nixon administration as counsellor to the president, his role was both symbolic and technical. As a former high Democratic official and an officer of the left-liberal Americans for Democratic Action, he was a living symbol of the Nixon administration's adaptability. He also did a superb technical job in formulating Nixon's welfare reforms. The late Chapman James, the Air Force's top-ranking black general, performed all three functions. It was he whom the Secretary of Defense Melvin Laird, according to Mary McGrory, always sent out to prove to dissenters that the military, like the war in Vietnam, was not racist.[5]

In most cases, the "handful of silver" is far less generous and the "riband" smaller than in the cases of Wordsworth, Moynihan, or James. In Robert Browning's poem, "They with the gold to give, doled him out silver/So much was theirs who so little allowed." The key word in Browning's poem is "doled." By being short-changed on the silver, by receiving more copper pennies and "ribands," the salivary glands of actual and would-be co-optees are kept working more energetically. In return, high benefits may be received by the Establishment: the weakening of opposing groups, administrative linkages with such groups, symbolic substitutes for reform, or the rhetorical trappings for reform proposals not meant to be acted upon. Less obvious, but probably just as significant, is what might be called "preventive co-optation"—namely, keeping internal dissidents working within the system instead of openly expressing their opposition.

At times, it is very difficult to tell the difference between co-optees, on the one hand, and those who see themselves as "boring from within," that is, as activists who seek to improve the system by working within it. The person who does this, to use Joseph S. Clark's phrase "gets along by going along."[6] But the more he goes along, the more the hope of being an effective-change agent may fade into the background and become little more than a personal rationalization for being a full-fledged co-optee.

The processes of moving toward friendly fascism in America would rather automatically—without any conscious planning—provide thousands of lower-level plums for dissidents and rebels demanding "a piece of the action." Some of these would go in advancc preemptively to those showing exceptional promise; others would be held out as prizes. In either case, choices would be available. Positions close to the leadership or policy-making structure, however, would probably be available only after considerable effort and intrasystem coalition-building and politicking. Often, entire organizations or subsystems might be co-opted. In what could be called "subsystem co-optation," liberal and purportedly radical organizations could be used to provide young people with opportunities to "work off their steam" harmlessly or to provide the backdrop for the system's normal compromising in the resolution of routine conflicts. Conspicuous advisory or public relations positions could probably be provided for oppositionists, including former left-wingers of a previous generation.

Multi-ethnic co-optation can also be taken for granted. Particularly conspicuous roles would undoubtedly be assigned to both blacks and Jews. According to Samuel F. Yette, the selection of black appointees to administrative posts in government has already shown the way toward attaining three goals: "(1) to provide color credibility wherever such credibility was crucial to selling an otherwise invalid product; (2) to neutralize such talent by taking it from potentially radical stations (the hiring off of militants) and placing it officially on the side of the establishment . . . ; and (3) to have a black person in position to take responsibility for antiblack policies and decisions, usually made exclusively by whites—without the black appointee's knowledge, consent or ability." [7] These practices can be used in foreign-policy areas also. Alphonso Pinkney, the Hunter college sociologist, sees the possibility of "American troops, with many Black soldiers, airlifted to South Africa to help the White government conduct an anti-insurgency operation against the rebellious African majority." [8] In early 1976, with the help of Floyd McKissick, something similar—but limited to black mercenaries—was briefly attempted in Angola.

While a much smaller minority of the population than blacks, Jews have been conspicuous in the past for their progressive and liberal tendencies. As some Jewish businessmen and professionals have shifted to conservatism, major opportunities naturally develop for a minority of Jews to achieve strategic positions at the establishment's upper levels, particularly in the Chief Executive Network. Before the Nixon-Ford-Carter administrations there were occasional Jewish members of both the Supreme Court and cabinet, and a small sprinkling of Jews in the White House staff and in Executive Office positions. Under Nixon, Ford, and Carter an unprecedented number of Jews reached significant positions at the highest levels of government—namely, secretaries of state, defense, and treasury, chairman of the Federal Reserve Board and members of the Council of Economic Advisers. In American society, personnel actions of this type, which represent considered political judgments, are entirely consistent with the development of an authoritarian oligarchy, although starkly inconsistent with historic Jewish ideals and the progressive tendencies of most Jewish Americans.

No matter which way America goes during the remainder of this century, more women will undoubtedly reach positions of higher prestige and visibility. Whether or not we get a woman president eventually, the time is not far off when there will be a woman Supreme Court justice, women astronauts, and more women as corporation executives, generals, police officers, legislators, politicians, professionals, and middle- and top-level bureaucrats. Such a development is not at all inconsistent with the crystallization of a full-fledged oligarchy. Indeed, it could help. By bringing more women into well-established masculine roles, it could undermine system-transforming tendencies in the women's liberation movement and maintain, if not strengthen, the manipulatory *machismo* that seems inherent in many of the tendencies toward friendly fascism.

CREATIVE COUNTERRESISTANCE

In general, there are two kinds of counter-resistence: one is *reactive,* the other *preventive.*

EUGENE V. WALTER [9]

Many of the previous chapters deal with the counterresistance operations of genuine capitalism. These operations—both preventive and reactive, both suave and rough—have been so successful in preventing a revolutionary movement in America that the very use of the term "counter-revolution" instead of "counterresistance" is little more than obeisance to the fantasy-life of radical idealists nursing memories of revolutionary glories in other countries or a bygone era. Their continued use in the years that lie ahead—particularly in manipulating democratic machinery, managing information, and providing incentives, punishments, and escape valves—could pave the way to friendly fascism. The adaptive use of system-strengthening reforms and multilevel co-optation could stave off the kind of reforms that might weaken or transform the system.

But beyond the subjects already discussed there are at least three other types of creative counterresistance that might be anticipated.

Under the ancient Hebrew kings there were always cities of refuge, sanctuaries to which people could flee. In other cultures this often became the function of religious buildings. Under the fascist and communist dictatorships of the past, according to Carl J. Friedrich and Zbigniew Brzezinski, the church, the family, the universities, and the military forces themselves often provided "islands of separateness" in which individuals could withdraw from the regime's oppressiveness and nurse hopes for a better day.[10] What Friedrich and Brzezinski fail to point out is the possibility that these islands of separateness may also serve to strengthen the regime by providing dissidents with a mechanism for withdrawal. In 1961, Paul Goodman spelled out this possibility in an imaginative essay entitled *1984:*

> There were two main movements toward rural reconstruction in the early '70's. The first was the social decision to stop harassing the radical young, and rather to treat them kindly like Indians and underwrite their reservations . . . The second wave of ruralism was the amazing multiplication of hermits and monks who began to set up places in the depopulated areas for their meditations and services to mankind.[11]

What Goodman leaves out is the likelihood of such reservations in urban ghettoes and in various suburban communities—and not only for youth, but also dissidents from all age, ethnic, and income groups. Many of these could be financed by benevolent foundations, if not by police and intelligence agencies themselves.

The second type of creative counterresistance goes a step beyond the islands of separateness: the direct sponsorship of indirectly controlled opposition. There are many precedents for this style of actions. In the early 1960s the technocrats in the French planning office got some of the socialist leaders to propose a more liberal "Counter-Plan." This style of opposition helped make the official plan more acceptable. In similar fashion the dominant Mexican political party has often subsidized opposition parties merely to liven up the rather fully controlled electoral process and thereby strengthen its own position. In the Soviet Union, according to Leopold Tyrmand, the Stalinist Establishment often showed greater ingenuity. It gave certain conspicuous positions to two categories of recognized dissent: professional non-Party people and professional oppositionists. The division of labor was significant. On the one hand, the non-Party person—often one with established prestige in the arts or sciences—conspicuously followed the Party's position. He thereby demonstrated its broad appeal. On the other hand, the professional oppositionist made a big to-do about disagreeing with the Party on inconsequential matters. This dramatized the Party's broadmindedness.[12]

The third type of creative counterresistance is entrapment. Islands of separateness and controlled oppositions can do more than sidetrack energies into harmless channels. They can also bring potentially dangerous people together into situations in which they can be decisively handled. The most obvious methods are co-optation, reform, or a combination of the two. The more these methods are used the easier it would be, in a minority of cases, to use brutal suppression. This ties up, of course, with the ever-present potentialities for using agents provocateurs—amply supplied with funds, equipment, and technical know-how—to provoke acts of violence that can be used as a triggering mechanism for a bloodbath.

INNOVATIVE APATHETICS

The tyranny of a prince in an oligarchy is not so dangerous to public welfare as the apathy of a citizen in a democracy.

BARON DE MONTESQUIEU,
The Spirit of the Laws

"Apathetics," the nourishment of apathy, is more a by-product of semi-oligarchic and oligarchic power than a conscious pursuit. Apathy is fostered by both the triumphs of the System and the labyrinthine complexity that protects individuals and groups from accountability for its failures. It is promoted by the information, rewards, and escape valves that make the system tolerable, and by the direct or indirect punishments that make serious opposition intolerable. It is deepened by the perception that reforms may strengthen the System, reformers be co-opted, and resistance be prevented, sanitized, or suppressed.

The present processes of transition from capitalism to friendly fascism almost automatically produce additional attitudes that accelerate these tendencies. On the one hand, there are those who predict that a more repressive society (whether or not defined in terms of fascism) is inevitable. On the other hand, there are those who assert that such a contingency is impossible. But all of these contradictory views—impossiblity, inevitability, irreversibility—have one element in common: They rationalize or promote the apathetic stance.

It would be a great mistake to think of apathy strictly in terms of inaction. Doing so would focus on action—as distinct from analysis—as the only alternative to apathy. There is also such a phenomenon as *intellectual apathy*. In part, this is already being promoted by channeling off intellectual actvities into relatively harmless areas, remote from the System's power structure, by the subtle anti-intellectualism of vocational training and career-oriented education, and still more by the way in which the mass media, particularly TV, determine the shifting agenda of "public issues." There is a widespread anti-intellectualism among the Etablishment's opponents. This is what Herbert Marcuse once called "a handout to the establishment, one of the fifth columns of the establishment in the new left." An obvious by-product of disillusionment with the kind of absurd intellectualism embodied in traditional liberalism and dogmatic Marxism, this kind of intellectual apathy can protect incipient friendly fascism against the kind of serious analysis that might help lay the basis for preventive or remedial action.

17

The Myths of Determinism

"Nonsense! Nonsense!" snorted Tasbrough. "That couldn't happen here in America, not possibly! We're a country of freedom."

SINCLAIR LEWIS,
It Can't Happen Here

"It cannot happen here" is always wrong: a dictatorship can happen anywhere.

KARL POPPER[1]

IMPOSSIBILITY: IT COULDN'T HAPPEN

THE THOUGHT that some form of new fascism might possibly—or even probably—emerge in America is more than unpleasant. For many people in other countries, it is profoundly disturbing; for Americans, it is a source of stabbing anguish. For those who still see America as a source of inspiration or leadership, it would mean the destruction of the last best hope on earth. Even for those who regard America as the center of world reaction, it suggests that things can become still worse than they are.

An immediate—and all too human—reaction among Americans, and friends of America, is to deny the possibility. In other countries it might happen—but not here. In the Communist world, dictatorships of the proletariat or the Party . . . Military juntas in Argentina, Brazil, Chile, Nigeria, and many other places . . . Other dictatorial styles in India, Pakistan, Iran, Saudi Arabia, and the Philippines . . . But nothing like this in the prosperous, enlightened nations of Western civilization and the Judeo-Christian tradition. Above all, not in the United States of America, not in the land of the free and the home of the brave . . .

But why not? Why is it impossible?

Many of the arguments purporting to demonstrate impossibility actually demonstrate little more than an unwillingness to "think the unthinkable." Some people try to protect their sensibilities behind a tangle of terminological disputation. The word "fascism," they say, is an emotion-laden term of abuse, as though the brutal, inhuman realities behind other terms—whether "manipulatory authoritarianism," "bureaucratic collectivism," or "military junta"—do not also evoke deep human emotions. Some people argue that the future threat in America is socialist collectivism, not fascism, implying that those who detect a fascist danger are spreading leftist propaganda for the purpose of bringing on a different form of despotism. Others merely react to exaggerated claims that fascism is already here or is inevitable.

Nonetheless, there are at least three serious arguments used by those who think that it could not happen here.

One of the most subtle arguments is *"American capitalism does not need fascism."*

On this point, let me quote from Corliss Lamont, who grew up as a member of one of the families most closely associated with the Morgans and other titans of American banking:

> The capitalist class in the United States does not need a fascist regime in order to maintain its dominance. The radical and revolutionary movements are weak and disunited. A large majority of the trade unions are conservative, and are actually part of the establishment . . . I do not see in the offing any constellation of forces that could put fascism across here.[2]

To buttress his case, Lamont points out that the threat to American civil liberties was much greater during the periods of the notorious Palmer raids after World War I and of McCarthyism after World War II. He also cites various judicial victories in recent civil liberties cases. Unfortunately, he does not deal directly with the structure of the "capitalist class" and the Establishment, nor with any of the domestic and international challenges to American capitalism. Moreover, his thesis on the weakness of "radical and revolutionary movements" and the conservatism of trade unions is a double-edged argument. True, these factors are no serious challenge to capitalist dominance. By the same token, they could not be regarded as serious obstacles to creeping fascism. On this matter, Lamont leaves himself an escape clause to the effect that he does not see the necessary constellation of forces "in the offing."

A similar escape clause has been carved out by Theodore Draper. In a scholarly critique of an earlier article of mine on the subject, he added as an afterthought that he did not intend to give "assurances that we will not follow the German pattern of history into some form of fascism." And then he added that although the Republic is not *"im-*

mediately (my italics) in danger, if worse comes to worse, we may yet get some form of fascism."[3]

A more widespread argument is *"American democracy is too strong."*

It is true, of course, that old-fashioned fascism never took root in a country with a solid tradition and history of constitutional democracy. The kind of democracy that grew up in both England and the United States was too much of a barrier to the Oswald Mosleys, the Huey Longs, and the Father Coughlins of a past generation. Even in France, the rise of the French fascists under Pétain occurred only after military conquest by the Nazis.

But this kind of argument boils down to nothing less than the identification of obstacles. It provides no evidence to suggest that these obstacles are immovable objects that cannot be overcome or circumvented in the future.

In the early 1970s this argument took a more exhilirating—albeit occasionally flatulent—form. *The democratic forces are becoming stronger.*

In *The Greening of America,* Charles Reich predicted a "revolution of the new generation." He saw in the counterculture of youth a movement that would break through the metal and plastic forms of the Corporate State (which he held was already here) and bring forth a new flowering of the human spirit. This optimistic spirit was repeated in global terms by Jean Francois Revel a year later. In *Without Marx and Jesus,* Revel pointed out that dissent has always thrived in America and that the new dissenters are building not merely a counterculture but a countersociety that rejects nationalism, inequality, racial and sexual discrimination, and all forms of authoritarianism. As the first and best hope of the world, America will soon produce "a *homo novus,* a new man very different from other men."[4]

I have never laughed at these salvationist predictions. They are based on an honest perception of many of the things that are not merely good, but wonderful, in my country. In fact, as I demonstrate in "The Democratic Logic in Action" (chapter 20), neither Reich nor Revel, nor other celebrants of America's potentialities have done sufficient justice to the variety of these hopeful currents. But they have tended to exaggerate their strength, perhaps on the theory that a strongly presented prophecy might be self-fulfilling.

I think it imperative to articulate more fully hopeful visions and to ground them on the more hopeful parts of the present. But in doing so, it would be highly misleading to ignore the fact that the new democratic currents represent a threat to all those elements in the Establishment that look forward to a more integrated power structure. This means conflicts whose outcomes cannot be predicted. Revel himself writes that America is "composed of two antagonistic camps of equal size—the dissenters and the conservatives." Writing before the rise of the new Radical Right, he then hazarded the guess that "the odds are in favor of the dissenters." Nonetheless, he accepted the possibility of the authoritarian suppression, sidetracking, or co-opting of the dissenters. I think he would agree with me today that if this should happen there would be many subspecies of the new man—and new woman—faceless oligarchs, humanoid technocrats, and comatose addicts of loveless sex, drugs, madness, and cults.

A third argument is that *"While possible, a new form of fascism is too unlikely to be taken seriously."*

I see this view as a tribute that blindness pays to vision. It is merely a sophisticated way of conceding possibility while justifying inaction. The outside chance, after all, rarely deserves to be a focus of continuing attention. In terms of its implications, therefore, "unlikely" may be the equivalent of either "impossible" or "so what?"

In daily life, of course, people and groups do take precautionary action to protect themselves or others against some unlikely events. This is the basis of the vast insurance industry in the capitalist world, which provides protection for some people against some of the monetary losses resulting from ill health, accidents, theft, fires, earthquakes, or floods. In all these cases of unlikely "bads," not insurance but prevention is the best protection. In the case of friendly fascism, it is the only protection.

Yet prevention is always difficult and requires entry into many fields. The prevention of disease and the prolongation of life go far beyond mere medical services; they involve nutrition, exercise, housing, peace of mind, and the control of pollution. The prevention of theft and corruption goes far beyond anything that can be done by police, courts, and jailers; it involves employment opportunities, working conditions, the reduction of discrimination and alienation, and a cleaning of higher-level corruption. The record is also discouraging in the case of all the unlikely major calamities of the modern age: power blackouts, the disposal of radioactive wastes from nuclear power plants, the control of plutonium from fast-breeder reactors, the spread of nuclear weapons, and the escalation in ever-deadlier forms of nuclear, chemical, and bacteriological overkill. Here preventive action spreads into other fields, going far beyond anything that can be done by "fail-safe" mechanisms. It involves nothing less than alternative forms of energy, human as well as solar, and the destruction of the deadliest weapons, if not the elimination of war itself as a mode of resolving conflicts.

There are two natural reactions in the face of the difficulties of prevention. One is to push the possibility into the background by mathematically based arguments that the statistical probability is very low. The other is to exaggerate both the horror and the probability of the calamities to be avoided, justifying such exaggeration on the grounds that it alone can move people to action.

I cannot accept either. As in the following chapters, I prefer to deal with preventive action directly. I do so because in my considered judgment, the coming of some new form of fascism in the United States—and other First World countries—is not only more likely than the extreme catastrophe, but it would also contribute to conditions under which most of the others would become less unlikely. At times, I find myself saying that friendly fascism is a a two-to-one probability well before the end of the century. Then I stop and remind myself that in diagnosing broad historical trends no quantitative calculus is really possible. A more balanced statement is that friendly—or even unfriendly—fascism is *a truly significant, not an insignificant, possibility.* Perhaps it is even highly probable.

INEVITABILITY: IT WILL HAPPEN

When Herbert Marcuse writes about "incipient fascism," when Kenneth Lamott used "para-fascism" to describe California as the "distant warning system for the rest of the United States," when Michael Parenti talks about "creeping fascism," the main purpose is to identify present tendencies and future dangers. Similar use might be made of "proto-fascism" or—better yet—"pre-fascism." These are unwhispered words of warning, often engulfed by the vast silences on such subjects by the mass and elite media.

But the ambiguity of these words is often a weakness, one not to be overcome by stridency. They are wide open to anyone's interpretation that what creeps down the road will necessarily get to the road's end, that the latent must become full-blown. The "womb of history" metaphor used so vigorously by Marx tends to suggest that a little fascism is like a little pregnancy. With a strange innocence concerning the possibility of miscarriage or abortion, it can then be assumed that the pre- and the para- must eventually become the real thing itself.

But even without the use of such words I have found that any strong argument on the possibility of neofascism in America leads many people to conclude that it is inevitable. For some, both the logical case and the empirical evidence in present-day tendencies appear overwhelming. The fact that friendly fascism may come in a variety of forms and circumstances—rather than in some single guise and scenario—strengthens the sense of high probability. For others, perhaps, the judgment of inevitability heightens whatever masochistic pleasure people may get from premonitions of doom, or provides justification for personal escapism from any form of political activism or commitment. For still others, I suspect, the sense of inevitability is intensified by disenchantment with liberalism, socialism, and communism. Many of the very people who in previous periods were attacked as agents of "creeping socialism" or "creeping communism" now feel that if either were to arrive in America—unlikely though this possibility may be—the result might not be too much different from the fruition of "creeping fascism." Indeed the possible convergence of neofascist state-supported capitalism and high-technology state socialism tends to give the impression that there are few alternatives to some form of repressive collectivism as the profile of man's fate by the end of this century.

The power of modern determinism lies in its "if-then" formulation: "If one does A, then B will result." In truly scientific terms the "will result" is generally a probability statement. But in the real world of political or managerial control, there is always a strong tendency to let the probabilistic tone fade into the background and to exploit the propagandistic potentialities of a more deterministic mood. In the work of many self-styled Marxists, this has led to an interesting contradiction. On the one hand, the collapse of capitalism under the battering ram of a proletarian revolution is often seen as inevitable. On the other hand, the leaders of the working class must not merely ride the waves of an inevitable future. Rather, they must work strenuously to bring the inevitable into being. Expressing the essence of a long stream of philosophic thought from Kant through and past Hegel, Engels put this powerfully in his cryptic thesis that "freedom is the recognition of necessity." While anti-Marxists are always eager to attack the alleged determinism of Karl Marx, they are rarely unloath to voice their own form of determinism. Thus Friedrich Hayek vigorously argues that (1) it was the socialist trends in Germany that led to German fascism, (2) a little bit of socialism leads inevitably to large-scale collectivism, and (3) socialism inevitably leads to fascism.[5] In other words: "If s, then f."

Finally, in modern science there is a large strain of hope and faith in the eventual discovery and elucidation of deterministic laws of social control. B. F. Skinner has expressed this hope and faith more frankly than most of his colleagues in psychology and other disciplines. His critics have argued cogently that his views have a totalitarian bent—and I have already suggested how Skinnerian reinforcements could be used to help economize on terror and develop what Stephen Spender once called "fascism without tears." Another critical comment is in order, however. The very idea of deterministic control tends to spread inner feelings concerning the inevitability of some repressive form of collectivism—whether Skinner's type or some other. In turn, the sense of inevitability tends to undermine any serious efforts to develop alternatives or fight. The prediction that "It must happen"—particularly if the subjective feeling is more powerful than the rationalistic qualifications and "ifs" that most self-respecting intellectuals will automatically tack on to it—can contribute to a sense of hopelessness and the apathetic acceptance of the unfolding logic. It thus holds forth the potentiality of possibly—not inevitably—becoming a self-confirming prophecy.

IRREVERSIBILITY: ETERNAL SERVITUDE OR HOLOCAUST

Not mine own fears, nor the prophetic soul
Of the wide world dreaming on things to come
Can yet the lease of my true love control,
Suppos'd as forfeit to a confin'd doom.

WILLIAM SHAKESPEARE,
Sonnet 107

To shake people out of apathy toward some future danger, the self-destroying prophecy is often attempted. Its essence is the confident prediction of doom, either confined or unconfined. Thus the coming of neofascism to the United States may be seen as the maturation of an invincible oligarchy, or even as prelude to the global holocaust of all-out nuclear warfare.

I am peculiarly sensitive to this temptation. When a few of my students argued a decade ago that fascism would shake Americans from torpor and prepare the way for a more humanist society, I countered one irrationality with another by arguing that the "improbability of any effective internal resistance" to neofascism would doom all hopes of a humanist future. I drew an exaggerated parallel with the past by pointing out that after all serious internal resistance had been liquidated by the German, Japanese, and Italian fascists, "the only effective anti-fascism was defeat by external powers." Since the "only war that could defeat a neofascist America would be a nuclear war, a holocaust from which no anti-fascist victors would emerge," I concluded with the prophecy: "Once neofascism arrives, the only choice would be *fascist or dead.*" [6]

My phrasing at that time was an echo of Franklin D. Roosevelt's wartime rhetoric: "We, and all others who believe as deeply as we do, would rather die on our feet than live on our knees." [7]—itself borrowed from the exhortation of the communist leader, Dolores Ibarruri ("La Pasionaria") in rallying the Loyalist forces against the Franco uprising in Spain. It was an effort to suggest "better dead than fascist." The aim in each case, of course, was to stress the urgency of vigorous and dedicated opposition to tyranny—indeed, to give up one's life, if necessary, to prevent the victory of tyranny.

Today, while still agreeing with Roosevelt that there are things worth dying for, I would rephrase the ancient rhetoric this way: "Better alive and fighting tyranny in any form than dead and unable to fight." If neofascism should come to America, people may have to learn how to fight on their knees. The guiding rhetoric should be Churchill's statement that "We shall fight in the fields and in the streets; we shall fight in the hills; we shall never surrender." [8] To paraphrase: "We shall face the faceless oligarchs inside and outside the Establishment; we shall fight them openly when possible, secretly when necessary; we shall fight them legally and illegally; like the people of all oppressed countries from time immemorial, we shall fight on our feet, on our knees, on our bellies, on our backs; we shall never surrender."

Such an attitude is not mere bravado. The "Thousand Year Reich" lasted for only twelve years. More recently, the long-lived fascist or proto-fascist regimes of Franco in Spain and Salazar in Portugal were replaced by constitutional democracies. The junta of the Greek colonels, despite strong NATO support, proved to be rather short lived. The awesome power of the Shah's dictatorship in Iran was overthrown by a multiclass revolutionary uprising. One need not sing paeans of praise to the new regimes of Spain, Portugal, Greece, or Iran to realize that they have all been—at the very least—much lesser evils than the greater evils preceding them.

Similarly, I cannot conceive of a neofascist America—in the context of either a "Free World" remodeling or a "Fortress America"—as an immortal phenomenon. There is a limit to the destructiveness of any engine of exploitation and the further modern capitalism may move toward the perfection of exploitation, the more severe will become the internal conflicts among the oligarchs themselves, the more divisive the conflicts within various levels of the Establishment, and the less quiescent and more rebellious the large masses of exploited employees, consumers, taxpayers, and voters.

But what about a nuclear holocaust? Would not a neofascist America inevitably lead to a nuclear *Götterdämerung* that would destroy all of modern civilization, perhaps even all of human life on the planet?

Not necessarily. First of all, the nuclear dangers—as I have already shown—exist already. This sword of Damocles has long been hanging over our heads and, I am afraid, the threat will become greater in any event.

But just as nuclear war has been avoided in recent years, it might be avoided under neofascism also—whether the "Free World" empire shrinks or expands, whether it breaks up into quarreling blocs or, whatever its geographical coverage, it is held together under more mature American leadership. Big Capital knows one thing about Big War, namely, that another one would mean another giant forward step for communism and another historical contraction for capitalism, perhaps even capitalism's long-predicted demise.

In short, the terrors of neofascism—no matter what the balance between "friendly" rewards and "unfriendly" punishments—are so real that an effective warning does not require predictions of total and irreversible doom. The modern Paul Revere may not get his messages across if, when telling people that friendly fascism may be coming, he also suggests that the end of the world is around the corner.

THREE

True Democracy

The utterance of democracy is a way of saying *no* to inequality, injustice and coercion.

GIOVANNI SARTORI

It is better to allow our lives to speak for us than our words.

MAHATMA GANDHI

Even an ant can harm an elephant.

AFRICAN PROVERB

18

It Hasn't Happened Yet

> The Communist Party characterized Bruening's regime as already fascist, then Papen's regime, then Schleicher's regime, so that when the fascist Hitler came to power, theoretically, it was not prepared for the difference in political *quality* which the difference in political *degree* had brought about.
>
> SIDNEY HOOK [1]

FROM THE PRECEDING CHAPTERS some readers may have received the false impression that friendly fascism has already arrived in the United States.

If so, I believe they may have read something into the text that is not really there. I cannot prevent anyone with obsessions about America from projecting his or her beliefs into my pages. Nor can I prevent people who disagree with my analysis from caricaturing it in the effort to make a point.

At the same time there are real difficulties in distinguishing between the small changes of degree that may occur in the future. Cold water is rather similar to ice, particularly if some chunks of ice may be floating in it.

In any case, to say that a new fascism is already here could cut the ground from under serious efforts to consider "What is to be done?" It could be as dangerous as any of the myths of determinism.

As a brief preliminary to discussing preventive action, therefore, I feel obliged to attack the illusion that "it" has already happened, as well as to suggest the reasons that it has not.

THE USA TODAY VS. FRIENDLY FASCISM, USA

If friendly fascism had already arrived in the United States, a book like this could not be published—unless previously edited to make repression seem more acceptable and its reversal impossible. And if the dark age were just around the corner, the pressure from the typical publisher would be to picture the wave of the future as either impossible or desirable. In the latter case the message would be "Get with it..."

Under today's conditions of greater freedom, some cry "Fascism!" to voice anguished protest against current evils. For anyone who has been painfully and continuously repressed or persecuted, repression and persecution are *his* or *her* reality. This has not happened to most white people. But it has happened to many blacks, Hispanics, and Native Americans. This should be kept in mind when recalling that the president of a black college a few years ago charged that America has "come to embrace Hitlerism," or when one hears the term "fascist pigs" in attacks on racists and police brutality. Indeed, I could almost go along with the idea that neofascism will have arrived in America whenever most white people are subjected to the kind of treatment to which many black people have long become accustomed. But then I stop short. America has *not* embraced Hitlerism—nothing like it. To look only at police brutality in urban ghettoes, the murders at Jackson State, Kent State, and Attica prison, and the almost-genocidal war waged against the people of Indochina for over ten years, and *not* at the rest of American life, would be an exercise in obsessional perception. It would also mean a tragic underestimate of the length, breadth, and depth of the destructiveness of a new fascism in America. Thus to all those—black, white, Hispanic, Native Americans, or others—properly indignant against present evils, I am inclined to say, "Buddy, you ain't seen nothing yet."

Some people shout "Fascism!" or "Totalitarianism!" to arouse an apathetic public. This accords with a time-honored practice in American politics. Old-style businessmen and politicos lambasted Franklin D. Roosevelt's New Deal with the prediction that "grass will grow in the streets." They branded Harry S. Truman's Fair Deal as "creeping socialism." When Richard Nixon imposed wage-price controls, Murray Rothbard, America's leading libertarian economist, proclaimed that "On August 15, 1971, fascism came to America." During that same year, when radical students tried to break up one of his public addresses, Daniel Moynihan cried out "I am a political scientist and I smell fascism." Without the help of Moynihan's nose, many liberals and radicals have also smelled fascism just around the corner. To cry "Wolf! Wolf!" when wolves are on the prowl, however, is not as misleading as it was for

Aesop's shepherd to cry "Wolf!" just to see if his friends would come. In today's jungles there *are* wolves. But to imply that they can take over in one apocalyptic descent on the fold is to sow distrust. After too many calls of this type, few will respond.

Something like this happened during Hitler's rise to power in Germany. As I have shown in "The Rise and Fall of Classic Fascism" (chapter 1), while the Socialists welcomed Hitler's predecessors as "lesser evils," the Communists attacked them as fascists and branded the Socialists "social fascist." This stance has persisted in a form of perverted Marxism, which states that modern capitalism is merely a *masked* form of dictatorship. "Imperialism under challenge," writes Felix Greene," will drop the mask of 'liberalism,' of 'democracy,' and will openly identify itself with the violence and the repressive forces on which its power rests." [2] As another version of the "fig leaf" myth discussed in chapter 1, this imagery suggests that the power structure behind the mask does not really have to be consolidated; so steps toward strengthening need not be fought. It suggests that bourgeois democracy is of little or no consequence, perhaps not even worthy of trying to defend or extend.

Although it is easy to set aside the mask–fig-leaf imagery, it is much harder to compare the United States of today with some future friendly fascism. The present is a period in which change is rapid, multidimensional, and confusing; much of it is shrouded in mystery. A friendly fascist future could materialize in a variety of forms.

The present, moreover, is a mixture of Good and Evil, of some of the Best and some of the Worst in mankind's history. To glorify it as heaven on earth would be a ridiculous caricature, as it would also be to depict a neofascist future as a living hell for everyone. Even under Hitler, as Richard Grunberger has pointed out, "most Germans never knew the constant fear of the early-morning knock on the door." [3] Indeed, up to the outbreak of World War II, except for the increased prosperity brought on by public works and the arms boom, "Most people retained the impression that within their own four walls life remained appreciably unchanged." The imagery of water changing to ice can be preserved only by thinking of a vast stream in which some parts are frozen over sooner and other parts much later.

The most direct way to look at the freezing process is to contrast the realities of social control in the United States today with those to be expected in a friendly fascist future. In "The Unfolding Logic" (chapter 7) I used an abbreviated summarization to compare a future friendly fascism with classic fascism. Let us now use similar shorthand to compare it with present-day America:

USA, Early 1980s	Friendly Fascism, USA
"Free World" empire in process of slow shrinkage and confused adjustment to changing conditions	Drive to maintain unity of "Free World" empire, contain or absorb communist or socialist regimes, and perhaps retreat to "Fortress America"
A divided, semi-oligarchic Establishment facing deep difficulties in responding to changing crises	A more integrated Big-Business–Government power structure, backed up by remolded militarism, new technocratic ideologies, and more advanced arts of ruling and fooling the public
An economy oriented toward subsidizing concentrated profitability, despite the social and economic consequences	A more unbalanced economy, rooted in extended stagflation, manipulated shortages, more junk, and environmental degradation
Growing power of Chief Executive Network, together with chaotic conflicts at all levels of government	Subtle subversion, through manipulative use and control of democratic machinery, parties, and human rights
Semi-unified information management with beginnings of scientific monitoring and dossier-keeping	Informational offensives, backed up by high-technology monitoring, to manage minds of elites and immobilize masses
Major trends towards rewards based on credentialized professionalism, mass consumption, and elite power	Rationed rewards of power and money for elites, extended professionalism, accelerated consumerism for some, and social services conditional on recipients' good behavior
Tendencies toward both professional and unprofessional use of domestic violence, with outbursts of ethnic conflict and scapegoatery	Direct terror applied through low-level violence and professionalized, low-cost escalation, with indirect terror through ethnic conflicts, multiple scapegoats, and organized disorder
Anxiety relief through such traditional escape mechanisms as alcohol, gambling and sports, and ultra-violent drama	More varied and extensive anxiety relief through not only traditional escape mechanisms but also through sex, drugs, madness, and cults

USA, Early 1980s	Friendly Fascism, USA
With immature oligarchic control, little decisiveness and insufficient adaptability in coping with crises	Internal viability grounded on system-strengthening reforms, multilevel co-optation, creative counterresistance, and innovative apathetics

If the contrast between these two columns is not sharp enough, one reason is that "in today already walks tomorrow." In human affairs, as distinguished from the world of physics and chemistry, differences of both degree and quality are hard to judge. Let me now start to redress the balance.

First of all, the processes of imperial consolidation are moving slowly and tortuously. Open interventionism is more talked about than practiced. Judged by the size of the armed forces (as distinguished from the growth of overkill), militarism has not returned to its Vietnam levels.

Second, despite erosion of democratic machinery, the level of democratic openness and opportunity in the United States is still high, particularly in comparison with many other constitutional democracies. Although threatened, personal privacy exists. The thick clouds of government secrecy are often pierced. Civil liberties and civil rights are alive (although not in the best of health) and can be fought for openly. Labor unions can organize and strike. If "it" had already happened, these freedoms would be cherished memories or fraudulent facades.

WHY IT HAS NOT YET HAPPENED

In considering the rise of classic fascism during the 1930s, I hope that historians will some day explain the failure of the fascist movements in the United States and England. Consideration of the reasons why it did not happen either here or there *then,* may throw some light on the obstacles that have thus far kept any new fascism from dominating either country *now.*

In "The Rise and Fall of Classic Fascism," (chapter 1) I have already shown that the old fascist movements rose to power mainly in the "second place" countries whose dominant elites were eager to replace the "major powers." Also, Italy, Germany, and Japan were countries in which democratic institutions were relatively recent and had never taken root. In each, industrial cartelization was widespread and militaristic traditions—particularly in Germany and Japan—deeply embedded in history and culture.

Among the major powers, in contrast, and particularly in England and the United States, there was no similar dynamism aimed at winning more; they already had plenty. Democratic institutions and traditions were probably the strongest in the world. The liberties that existed had been fought for and slowly won for more than a century. Business life was much more competitive. Militarism was reserved for colonial expeditions or gunboat diplomacy; it was never a major force at home. The native fascists were extremists. Although they enjoyed some support from higher Establishment levels, their behavior (as well as the color of some of their shirts) suggested suspicious resemblances to political movements in adversary countries. And in the United States, where the Great Depression of 1929–39 was probably more of a shock than in Europe, the leadership of Franklin D. Roosevelt's New Deal inspired widespread hope for democratic solutions to the economic crisis.

In the early 1980s, I see various reasons why friendly fascism, while a serious threat and perhaps even a probability, has not yet arrived.

The first is that the combination of domestic and foreign crises has not yet become so serious that the unfolding logic completely unfolds. The United States is still the richest country in the world. If the belt of austerity is tightening, the girth is still large. The "Free World" is still led by the United States, even though in faltering fashion; it still encompasses the majority of the world's population. In other words, while it would be dangerous to project into the future Corliss Lamont's statement that American capitalism does not need fascism, his statement explains the faltering nature of those steps in that direction that were taken in the 1960s and the 1970s.

The second reason is that despite substantial erosion in constitutional democracy, there are still many people and groups who insist on using the freedoms and opportunities that are available. I am not referring only to the electoral, legislative, and judicial machinery of representative government. I am referring to union organization, neighborhood organization, and a host of spontaneous or only semi-organized movements of self-help or defense against resurgent militarism or corporate aggression. Although some people still seem to subscribe to the old adage that liberty is too precious to be used, its use helps explain its survival.

Equally important is the fact that the unfolding logic of oligarchic integration tends to intensify the confusions among the few at the Establishment's pinnacle. This is the practical—although immensely difficult—lesson to be learned from the concentration of oligarchic power in the classic fascism of Germany, Italy, and Japan: the tensions among the oligarchs become more intense. In the face of mounting challenges, the outcome can be either inaction or, as in the case of the Axis, overextension.

The ability to respond successfully to crisis may also be undermined by the very strategies of information management that help maintain the power of the Establishment. Expanding systems or economic, social, and political intelligence tend to flood Establishment leaders with more information than they can absorb. Additionally, "hard" statistics, usually based on concepts and premises of an earlier time, give greatly distorted images of reality, while "soft" facts are often concocted to please higher-ups and help the technical interpreters climb the ladder of career advancement. Also, emerging triplespeak, as discussed in chapter 9, serves to narrow the circles in which straight talk is practiced. Neither side can bring itself to openly discuss—or even have its experts seriously attempt to analyze—the basic contraditions involved in accumulating capital through enhanced profitability, which reduces mass purchasing power, and chronic inflation, which reduces the value of the money made. Both sides are loath to alert the middle levels of the Establishment to the inseparable connection between First World profitability and the conflicts with the Second and Third Worlds. No group or leader will take the risk of authorizing the extensive technical analyses needed to develop and carry out the policy of exploiting the conflicts between China and the Soviet Union, and of trying to absorb established communist regimes into the world of transnational capitalism; to do so would let too many people in on the realities of straight talk. The result is a swirling fog of jargon and myth which, while helpful in mystifying other educated people, may also addle the heads of the jargon experts, the mythmakers, and the economic and political overlords themselves.

There is another self-defeating aspect of advanced capitalism's unfolding logic: the production of an enormous potential for anti-Establishment action. In the world of pure physics, action provokes reaction; in the nineteenth-century world of Marx, capitalism was to produce its own gravediggers, the proletarians. In the last decades of the twentieth century, the reaction to the growth of the corporate-government complex defies any simple formulation. *But it is there:* embodied partly in alienation, anxiety, apathy, and self-hatred, expressed partly in free-floating discontent and resentment, and often taking the form of scattered acts of protest and resistance. The fact of concentrated power tends to promote an interest in deconcentration. Its excesses may enlarge that interest. By promoting false participation in decision making, the processes of concentration may have the unintended consequence of nurturing demands for genuine participation. To put it in a nutshell, the dominant logic tends to create a counter-logic that is more than a counter-logic: an alternative logic of true democracy, which is positive rather than merely reactive, and which transcends old distinctions between capitalism and socialism.

Before proceeding to the logic of democracy, a word on circular response. On the one hand, far-flung anti-Establishment action might tend to dispel the confusions within the Establishment's higher level and bring about the very unity whose absence Richard Nixon once bewailed.

On the other hand, the democratic logic itself—if more effectively practiced—would have the effect of splitting away from the Establishment many of its leaders and advisers who have lost faith in the marketplace as a legitimate entitlement to power, privilege, and property. This could mean great opportunities for those who use the alternative logic as a guide to social reconstruction.

19

The Long-Term Logic of Democracy

Democracy is a process, not a static condition. It is becoming, rather than being. It can easily be lost, but is never fully won. Its essence is eternal struggle.

WILLIAM H. HASTIE [1]

SOME PEOPLE RESPOND TO FEARS of creeping despotism with utopian visions of a delightful future—that is, with wish lists of all the good things they would like to see in America. The bad, in contrast, is waved into the shadows or wished out of existence.

But the top-down logic of transnational capitalism and the Golden International cannot be countered by mere wish lists. Inspiring visions of a truly civilized civilization in the West, although a tonic for their creators, are no antidote for creeping barbarism. Any serious opposition must be based on a logic of its own. Without an alternative logic, rooted in the changing conditions of life, there would be little hope of animating and bringing together the many forces needed to counter the power of oligarchy, empire, and manipulative repression. Friendly fascism might indeed be the inevitable wave of the future.

Fortunately, there is an alternative logic.

It is a logic grounded in humankind's long history of resistance to unjustified privilege. It is the logic which eventually led—after centuries of struggle and defeat—to the virtual end of slavery, serfdom, and colonial empire. It is the logic of all those who seek freedom from ripoffs, manipulation, and the other evils of concentrated power, of all those who seek true individualism through the kind of cooperative commitment that provides meaning and purpose throughout the life cycle. It is the logic of seeking *the opportunity for all persons to take part—directly and indirectly, both in large and small measure—in the decisions that affect themselves, others, and the larger communities of which they are a part.* It is the logic of true democracy.

Properly understood, this logic is rooted in the recognition that human beings will always be both good and evil. It is based on the premise that all future societies, like those in the past, will contain varying combinations of the two. In the past, however, the logic of democracy has always been shrouded in mystification, and all victories have been partial, with every democratic advance counterbalanced by some new form of concentrated power.

THE DEMOCRATIC MYSTIQUE

> The words men fight and die for are the coins of politics, where by much usage they are soiled and by much manipulation debased. That has evidently been the fate of the word "democracy." It has come to mean whatever anyone wants it to mean.
>
> BERNARD SMITH [2]

> For the first time in the history of the world . . . practical politicians and political theorists agree in stressing the democratic element in the institutions they defend and in the theories they advocate.
>
> United Nations Educational and Scientific Organization [3]

Since the destruction of Axis fascism in World War II, "democracy" has become an honorific label oratorically affixed to almost every national system in the world. Gone are the days when American conservatives parroted James Madison's contention that the Constitution established American government as a republic, not a democracy. We seldom hear any more that the only kind of democracy is direct democracy confined, in Madison's words, "to a small spot." There are still those who believe in their hearts that any moves toward more democracy would be a descent into the inferno of mobocracy, loutishness, vulgarity, ingnorance, inefficiency, anarchic breakdown, or despotic rule by swinish (and, in central cities, dark-skinned) multitudes. But the whisper of their hearts is rarely spoken aloud. Even the new conservatives, wracked by doubts and reservations, approach the subject as though walking on eggshells, content to preach hierarchy, meritocracy, and technocracy while avoiding a direct confrontation with democracy. In suggesting less democracy, the pundits of the Trilateral Commission take the position that they are saving it. Meanwhile, communist movements pledge allegiance to democracy. For them, a proletarian dictatorship is a democratic dictatorship, representing the majority of the people. It is merely a transitional stage to prevent the restoration of capitalism and prepare the way toward an eventual classless society in which the dictatorial state will have withered away.

"Sure, we'll have fascism, but it will come disguised as Americanism." This famous statement has been attributed in many forms to Senator Huey P. Long, the Louisiana populist with an affinity for the demagogues of classic European fascism. If he were alive today, I am positive he would add the words "and democracy." Indeed, to understand the difficulties facing the logic of true democracy, one must realize that the unfolding logic of friendly fascism leads directly to democratic disguises.

Nonetheless, many elements of true democracy have often existed—and exist today. But like traces of a precious metal scattered through vast ore deposits, they are not easy to find. Some are mixed with a "fool's gold" that glitters deceptively. Besides, as though in some great compression of geological time, the rock formations are constantly in flux and occasionally in upheaval. No simple task to bring together—even in one's mind—the many elements for a viable alternative to a system of concentrated power.

DEMOCRATIC STRUGGLES

Often, the logic of democracy is revealed simply in some reaction (other than flight or apathy) to concentrated power. If this reaction is merely one of saying "no" to inequality, injustice, or coercion, it is nonetheless positive. While "no-sayers" may be gagged, imprisoned, or murdered and their ties with each other shattered, the history of humankind is full of resounding "noes" and recurring efforts—spontaneous or planned—to win some freedoms.

Some of the more memorable efforts occurred in ancient times when despotic tribal chiefs or city-state tyrants were overthrown and replaced by assemblies of adult males (with the exception of slaves). Something similar developed a century or so ago in Swiss cantons and New England town meetings. These were all cases of so-called government *by* the people, self-government, or *direct* democracy. Qualified adult males all had a chance to take part in the processes of decision making—whether through majority vote or consensus. They were not representatives; they were the rulers themselves. However, the women, children and slaves, were not represented; they were ruled.

More frequently, though, a single tyrant shares powers with a few others; or as a few more burst (or are brought) into the select circle, a limited democracy comes into being. The barons at Runnymeade wrest a Magna Carta from a king. A council of elders, a more varied assembly, or a number of "estates" is set up to advise the ruler, share in rule, or choose the ruler. Among themselves, the aristocrats learn to treat each other as "peers," that is, as equals. Despite differences and conflicts among them each must get the respect, courtesy, information, and time required for participation in decision making. And each must give the same—at least formally—to others. This is the meaning of "noblesse oblige" (nobility obliges), which among peers is equivalent of "égalité oblige" (equality obliges).

With the industrial revolution, as the older aristocracy of the landed nobility merged with the new aristocracy of business and finance, the scope of this limited democracy was enlarged. It was broadened still more as this or that group of Establishment leaders sought to advance their own interests through alliances with tradesmen, artisans, laborers, and peasants. There thus came into being a *representative* democracy in which all men of property or substance could help choose representatives in government, have access to an array of specialized courts, and enjoy many personal rights. To protect themselves against a majority that might infringe on these rights, restraints were often provided in written or unwritten constitutions. This gave us *constitutional* democracy. Eventually, as suffrage was extended, representative constitutional democracy was extended still more until, like a pancake being almost infinitely flattened, it became all but transparently thin. As large corporations became "persons" before the law (and thereby entitled to personal rights), they tended to displace or diminish many direct personal relations among real people. They looked on most real people as atomized units with roles in mass production, mass consumption, mass education, mass communication, and mass culture. There thus came into being *mass* democracy, under which increasingly powerless people were given through voting a chance to exercise—in the words of Giovanni Sartori—"a powerless fraction of power." Paradoxically, the largest number of voters appear at the polls under *plebiscitary* or *totalitarian* democracy, where the function of voting is to elect a candidate who has no opposition, or to legitimate some other decision already made. In less extreme cases, despite a huge component of false democracy, mass democracy may contain some true elements of civil and political liberties and self-organization. But the relative proportions of false and true do not change very much if the "ins" show "compassion" for the masses by doing a little more for them, if former "outs" replace the "ins," or if either group reduces somewhat the height of the Establishment's pyramid. A larger proportion of true democracy is provided to the extent that there is a reduction of status distances and exclusionary barriers based on sex, color, race, religion, national origin, or age. Yet this kind of *social* democracy may also develop—to a certain extent—as a means of recruiting a few leaders from oppressed groups into a more representative oligarchy.

Nor can mass democracy suddenly become true democracy when a "dictatorship of the proletariat" provides *economic* (or *socialist* or *people's*) democracy by guaranteeing full employment, free medical care and education, low-cost housing, and more broadly available welfare-state services. In taking control of the major means of production, the dictatorship also abolishes basic civil and political liberties and concentrates enormous power in the hands of party leaders. One of the reasons there has as yet been no socialist takeover of corporate power in any First World country is the deep attachment that people have to the civil and political liberties that have always been sacrificed under Second World socialism. This attachment is among the reasons why, as I have pointed out in "Subverting Democratic Machinery" (chapter 11), friendly fascism would preserve most democratic formalisms.

The giant scale of modern organization is another reason for concentrated power in all parts of today's world. Persons, families, and neighborhood or village groups are pygmies (and labor unions and most political parties nothing but somewhat larger lightweights) in comparison with the huge private and public bureaucracies and the globe-spanning clusters, constellations, complexes, and establishments that dominate most of the planet. Here too there is a tendency for limited democracy to broaden, but too often in a manner that promotes a greater concentration of power. The manager of a large system can be successful only by becoming part of a management team. The system itself can become colossal only by administrative decentralization—that is, by delegating mountains of detailed decisions to area and functional specialists, and keeping for the few at the top the most critical functions of central guidance. This requires far-flung hierarchies of management teams. It is *managerial* democracy. Similarly, First World leaders can guide the policies of former colonies more efficiently through economic and political manipulation rather than by the more direct and costlier techniques of old colonialism. This is *imperial* democracy—sometimes referred to as neocolonialism, noncolonial empire, or indirect imperialism. In the United Nations almost all the countries of the world are represented; and in its General Assembly each nation has one vote. This is a limited *international* democracy.

Often, the logic of reaction to limited democracy is some form of broadening. To counter the power wielded over them by employers, workers form unions. This has often been called *industrial* democracy. Industrial democracy goes much further when workers participate in management at one or more levels of the managerial hierarchy, and workers' self-government or participatory management develops. Similarly, representatives of consumers, "the public," or government may sit on top management boards. But any form of broadened democracy can, in fact, become a facade for legitimating the narrowing of control. This happens when labor leaders become instruments of control by corporate overseers, racketeers, or the two together, or when consumer or public representatives on a board are manipulated by top financial interests. A still more flagrant facade is *marketplace* democracy. Government restriction or intervention is reduced in favor of the "impersonal" forces of the so-called "free market." But "free market" is mainly a euphemism for free-wheeling by faceless oligarchs whose invisible hands dominate most markets. A simliar facade is *chamber of commerce* democracy, under which national or state functions of government are turned over —under the banner of *grass roots* democracy—to local cabals of corrupting contractors, land speculators and corruptible officials. Another facade has at times been provided by *functional* democracy, under which business, labor, professions, and many other interests are formally organized in guilds, chambers, or corporations that exercise governmental powers. As I have pointed out in chapter 1, this was one of the myths that classic fascism employed to conceal repressive control by Big Business-Big Government partnerships. Today, as new-style partnerships develop in most First World societies, a new corporatism is emerging, a corporatism described by some observers—with sublime indifference to the implications for personal liberties—as *corporatist* (or *consociational*) democracy.[4] This brings us back to friendly fascism coming in the guise of democracy or even—if its savants are clever enough—of "true" democracy.

Despite the mystifications, the elements of true democracy are strewn throughout the world. How many? I cannot count them. The chemistry of society provides no fixed table of elements. Old ones change their form and news ones—invented as well as discovered—burst into being. In each country of the world the old and the new combine in unique and changing patterns. There is no country without "fool's gold" and the coarser elements of open despotism and manipulative tyranny. But there is no country without some portion (even if only minute traces) of those truly democratic elements that may be symbolized by such adjectives as direct, representative, constitutional, political, economic, social, or industrial. One or more of these may be crushed into dust and apparently obliterated. But somehow or other they always rise again. Indeed, the false rhetoric of the oligarchs often encourages those who attempt inroads into the structure of concentrated power.

The nature of these inroads—currently weak though they may be—is the subject of the next chapter.

20

The Democratic Logic in Action

O this is not Spring but in the air
There is a murmuring of new things.
This is the time of dark winter in the heart
but in me are green traitors.
KAY BOYLE

SOME YEARS AGO the turmoil of dramatic movements in America—civil rights, antiwar, students, woman's liberation—rang like shots around the world. From Yugoslavia in the early 1970s Vladimir Dedijer wrote to *The New York Times* that "The future of the world depends so much on the American New Left . . . Therefore it [America] is the greatest country in the world." [1]

By the end of the 1970s many observers had already jumped to the other extreme. The New Left had vanished, it was said. Many of its former leaders—having passed the magic age of thirty—had settled down to middle-class placidity or been co-opted into Establishment rat races. The counterculture had become a commodity sold at record stores and health-food counters. The euphoria faded, abroad and at home.

For those who still pose the question of where all the flowers have gone, and want to listen, there is an answer: Now, in the early 1980s, there are more flowers than there were a decade earlier. However, instead of being bunched together, they are widely scattered. True, there is now a New Left committed to varied forms (and labels) of socialism. But far beyond this, there are new currents and undercurrents of change swirling through all the strata of First World society. In part, these currents are responses to the crises of social disorganization, global disorder, stagflation, and environmental degradation. In part, they express evolving human needs for participation and commitment, needs that are not suppressed—but indeed are sometimes nurtured—by material deprivation or material accumulation. In either case they represent the long-term logic of democracy as expressed in a new awareness of human potentialities, in scattered action on a thousand fronts, and in challenging questions concerning positive alternatives to every aspect of concentrated power.

These currents are much more than knee-jerk reactions to stimulus; they also express the long-term historic human urge for truly democratic mixtures of freedom and responsibility. I see in these currents the possible beginnings of a new bottom and a new middle that may already, for all anyone knows, comprise a new—although largely silent and lamentably weak—majority. If so, it is a silent majority that has thus far spoken through minority actions only. Also, these actions are sporadic as well as scattered. Sometimes little or no ground is gained. Often, small Pyrrhic victories are followed by the disappearance of the victorious groups once a battle has been won. Often, victory is followed by the co-optation of successful leaders. Indeed, some of the most promising public-interest movements are financed by banks, corporations, and Establishment foundations as a way of "keeping their finger" on movements that might go too far if not subjected to the delicate controls of upper-class budgeting.

Thus, where a thousand buds may have blossomed, some are frozen before flowering or wilt prematurely after a brief opening. But still they appear and reappear.

A GOOD NEIGHBOR IN A NEW WORLD ORDER

> We are not wholly patriotic when we are working with all our heart for America merely; we are truly patriotic only when we are working also that America may take her place worthily and helpfully in the world of nations . . . Interdependence is the keynote of the relations of nations as it is the keynote of the relations of individuals within nations.
>
> MARY PARKER FOLLETT [2]

When confronted with the choice between Fortress America and a more mature Trilateral Empire, the democratic response begins with Mercutio's "A plague o' both your houses!" It continues with a search for the avenues leading toward a more civilized world.

Here, the logic of democracy (as on all other points) provides no detailed plan or formula. Like the unfolding logic of friendly fascism, it merely suggests broad objectives. The rest is left to necessary, indeed endless, debates on both "what?" and "how?"

As these debates develop, I see a few promising moves. Third World regimes push for a new international *economic order,* defined mainly as improved patterns of trade with, and investment in, the First World. In turn, this demand has led to similar calls for a new *information* order, to free Third World countries from domination by First World media, and a new *technological* order, to provide them with better access to the technologies for their appropriate development. Others add *cultural,* to recognize the rich values of diversity in national traditions and styles of life. If we then add *political,* the idea becomes so broad that limiting adjectives may as well be dropped. While the American Establishment may demur, those Americans who are more conscious of the interdependence among peoples and less addicted to superpower posturing are increasingly willing, I believe, to move toward a new order in general. Here, the difficulty is that many of the worst things in the world are new: more destructive weapons systems, new escalations of the same arms race, and new forms of domination by transnational corporations and cartels.

What kind of world order would be *both* new and more civilized?

One sign of progress in America, I believe, is declining attachment to the idea that—by grace of manifest destiny, innate superiority, or economic and military superiority—the American government and its close allies must answer this question by themselves. A modest coming of age, but not to be sneered at. Moreover, it is associated with a growing ability by many Americans to work with people from First, Second, and Third World countries in a spirit of interdependence rather than domination. At a time when Establishment leaders have skuttled the détente which Nixon and Brezhnev initiated in 1972, I see signs of hope in opposition to the new militarism and in support of some improved form of détente. It would be comforting to find some easy method of strengthening these positive currents and converting the American government from bully to good neighbor. All I can do at this point is insist that the logic of democracy requires much more open debate—and more straight talk—on such controversial issues as these:

1. *Should not preparations be made for a Detente II to replace Detente I?* As a cooling-off to the cold war, Detente I was a vague bilateral argreement expressing the mutual interest of the United States and the Soviet Union in avoiding any direct confrontation that might result in nuclear war. Neither NATO nor the Warsaw Pact countries were party to the agreement. Excluding the Third World as well, it left the door open to warmer, or even hot war by either party in most parts of the Third World. Is it not imperative to prepare for Detente II which would produce clearer, more multilateral bases for arms control and disarmament?
2. *Should the U.S. government more fully accept socialist measures or regimes in other countries?* In 1938, when Mexico expropriated

American oil companies, President Roosevelt turned his back on pressures from the companies and on U.S. traditions of military intervention in Mexico. A financial settlement (very favorable to Mexico) was eventually negotiated. This was one of the high points of Roosevelt's Good Neighbor Policy. Today, in a "world of neighbors" (to use a phrase from Roosevelt's first inaugural address), would not similar responses to socialist measures or regimes be more civilized than the repetition of old efforts at subversion or destabilization? More specifically, would not the international atmosphere be better if the U.S. government should extend more promptly to Cuba and Vietnam the same diplomatic and trading relations belatedly worked out with the Soviet Union and China?

3. *Are the vital interests of American corporations abroad identical with the vital interests of the American people?* The essence of rational public relations by any large corporation is to win acceptance of such an identity by the power centers of government. Thus, when Prime Minister Mossadegh of Iran nationalized British and American oil companies in 1953, the British and American governments organized a coup to overthrow Mossadegh and get agreement on the division of oil profits. This was quite different from the handling of the Mexican oil crisis some years earlier. Now, almost thirty later, with not only Iran but the entire Persian gulf facing a succession of crises, the issue is much broader. High American officials define the flow of Persian Gulf oil, distributed by Western companies, as so vital to the American people that any interference would justify U.S. use of military force. Representative Jim Weaver (D., Ore.) is not so sure. "We must all ask ourselves," he argued in March 1979, "if we believe it worthwhile to send our sons to die in the Persian Gulf so that we can continue to fuel our Winnebagoes. Is it worthwhile to go to war so that we don't have to wait in line at the gas station to buy gas we fritter away?" [3]

4. *How useful in world affairs is the use or threat of military force by the United States?* To the leaders of the military-industrial complex the value of military spending and stockpiling is clear; it is their special form of welfare handout from government. It also has the advantage of promoting the idea that force can be used to settle economic, social, and moral conflicts, thereby accelerating spending on instruments of force. But if conventional weapons were truly powerful, the British would still be ruling India, Somoza would still be in power in Nicaragua, the Shah of Iran would still sit astride his peacock throne and American preparations to use force in the Persian Gulf would tend to reduce—

rather than build—tensions in that area. As for nuclear weapons, what trust can one place in national leaders, military or civilian, who would take seriously the use of methods that would guarantee the death of most Americans in an effort to "defend" America?

DEMOCRATIZING THE ESTABLISHMENT

The vulgar charge that the tendency of democracies is to levelling, meaning to drag all down to the level of the lowest, is singularly untrue; its real tendency being to elevate the depressed to a condition not unworthy of their manhood.

JAMES FENIMORE COOPER [4]

We can have democracy in this country or we can have great wealth in a few hands, but we can't have both.

LOUIS D. BRANDEIS [5]

From the viewpoint of the Powers That Be, the democratic currents running throughout America are unquestionably disagreeable. Both Big Business and Big Government are increasingly unpopular. If their decisions tend to stick, this is not because of active consent by the majority of Americans; it is the product, rather, of passive acquiescence under conditions of felt helplessness. The consequence is increasingly widespread feelings that THEY are not to be trusted. At times, these feelings are expressed in open opposition to Establishment programs—particularly to the expansion of nuclear energy, the restoration of the draft, and preparations for renewed military intervention in Third World countries. They are articulated in citizen activism that runs the gamut of the entire political spectrum. They are expressed in the new vigor of minority political movements by both libertarians and radicals.

Moreover, as Robert L. Heilbroner has observed, America is "in the midst of an extraordinary outpouring of literature on, about, into, out of, and by Marx." [6] In the wake of the example set by the Union for Radical Political Economy, every discipline in the social sciences now has a Marxist, neo-Marxist, or anti-Establishment caucus with a regular publication. The number of openly socialist authors has grown still more rapidly. In 1975, under the auspices of the Democratic Socialist Organizing Committee (DSOC), seven Nobel Prize winners joined in a statement questioning the economic systems of "advanced industrial democracies," and calling for "the exploration of alternative economic systems." At least two dozen left-wing political organizations—many of them dividing, subdividing, submerging, and merging in intricate philosophical dance steps that even the FBI must have difficulty in following—are in open operation. Some of these are strict, down-the-line adherents of official (albeit often switching) party lines. Others are more open to, and may even welcome, internal discussion and dissent. Many have gone far beyond the old tradition of regarding Marx, Engels, Lenin, or Mao as gospel givers, often using Marx's methods to dissect the evils of concentrated bureaucratic power. I suspect that in no other capitalist country at any other time in history has there been such a varied, large, and growing literature challenging basic principles of its governing Establishment.

Disagreeable though they have been, the Establishment's many opponents have still not gone very far in discussing, as James Russell Lowell has characterized them, The Powers That Ought To Be. Some hope that the Establishment can be forced or cajoled into being more responsive, "compassionate," or "humanitarian." Some may think that they themselves, if only given the chance, would be much better than the present THEY. Others oppose in principle almost any form of power, authority, of leadership—less because of any utopian anarchism, more from sheer skepticism concerning the possibility of power, authority, and responsibility that are truly—rather than rhetorically—democratic. Although I too have some skepticism on this matter, I believe that the majority of the American people would welcome any progress in democratizing the American Establishment. But any such progress requires democratic controversy on all the difficult questions raised in this chapter. At this point I shall touch only on those that bear directly on the problem of concentrated power.

1. *Should not limits be set on the concentration of private wealth and income?* The owners and controllers of huge private fortunes have always had something in common with true democrats: they both have recognized the incompatibility of true democracy and "great wealth in a few hands." The long-term purpose of inheritance taxes and progressive income taxes, of course, was to put a reasonable ceiling on both wealth and income. To go back to this original purpose would require a reform of the tax laws that would remove the loopholes and tax shelters specially created for the Ultra-Rich. This need not bring their living levels down to "the level of the lowest." Indeed, even the most fervent egalitarians, I suspect, would be willing to allow people to accumulate as much as a few million dollars of assets (in 1980 currency) and keep, a few hundred thousand in income. This would be far from "levelling." All it would mean would be a reduction in a few thousand people's addiction to the thrills of irresponsible power and perpetual self-indulgence, and in their ability to bribe politicians and escape prosecution for violations of civil and criminal

law. Like many drunkards, they will resist any cure. But once cured, their lives might even be happier.

2. *Should not public control of the larger corporations be expanded?* Corporations are in business to make money; this involves getting and keeping whatever power is needed to maintain profitability and stay in business. As Milton Friedman has often pointed out, to expect them to exercise social responsibility entirely on their own is nonsense. Unfortunately, efforts to cope with this situation have usually been limited to single remedies. The two oldest remedies have been the break-up of giants into smaller (and presumably more competitive) organizations and the imposition of public interest standards by presumably "independent" regulatory agencies. In Western Europe and Scandinavia, much more use has been made of four other methods: public ownership at the national or local level; mixed public-private ownership; public or workers' representatives on boards of directors; and workers' ownership. Experience has tended to show that neither competition nor regulation can be very effective without a credible threat of some form of public or worker ownership. In the United States would not a combination of all six approaches be desirable?
3. *Should not government be both decentralized and deconcentrated?* Much progress made in the public control of private corporations —whether through regulation, breakup or public ownership— holds forth the danger of overly concentrated government power. This is one of the great contradictions of true democracy. It cannot be resolved merely by efforts to make government more responsible. It is also essential to decentralize government. This principle should be applied to the operations of almost all government agencies, just so long as it does not open the back door to takeovers by narrow vested interests. Also, much of the necessary public-sector expansion—in medicine and electricity generation as in public education—should take place locally and regionally.
4. *What about the alleged inefficiencies of public-sector activities?* Not the private, the public, or the nonprofit sector has a monopoly on inefficiency. It is nonsense to contend that one is necessarily more inefficient or efficient than the other. The major difference is that corporate inefficiencies (particularly the huge social costs they push onto others) are more hidden from view. The inefficiencies of public agencies are more open to public exposure. In any case, is not full exposure and accountability needed for all three sectors?

BALANCING THE ECONOMY

What I wish to emphasize is the *duality* of the human requirement when it comes to the question of size: there is no *single* answer. Man for his different purposes needs many different structures, both small ones and large ones, some exclusive and some comprehensive.

E. F. SCHUMACHER [7]

Among economists I see some awareness that economics has, in John Kenneth Galbraith's words, "an instrumental function—instrumental in that it serves not the understanding or improvement of the economic system but the goals of those who have power in the system." [8] But I am not sure that even those who share Galbraith's views on this matter have much faith in the possibility that economists will take the lead in evaluating alternative structures of economic power. They are more likely, I suggest, to follow in the wake of democratic currents.

Fortunately, there are such currents. Insofar as theory is concerned, they are rather weak—hence the general recognition that few economists have any useful answers to economic questions. Some people even blame economists for inflation, high taxes, unemployment, shortages, waste, pollution, junk, and other aspects of an unbalanced economy. This, of course, is unfair; economists merely serve the vested interests whose activities have these consequences. Insofar as economic statistics are concerned, most people take them with a huge grain of salt. Many have unlearned the false lesson, taught them over the first decade after World War II, that growth in the GNP is a touchstone of economic progress. Insofar as citizen action is concerned, the positive currents are somewhat stronger. This may be found in the organization of cooperatives, in self-help movements, and in the many neighborhood groups that have been developing what Karl Hess calls "community technology." The popularity of E. F. Schumacher's *Small Is Beautiful* attests to the existence of a widespread urge to create labor-intensive forms of production as a counterbalance to whatever giant, capital-intensive operations may be truly necessary. Above all, by the end of the 1970s progressives of all stripes belatedly realized that fighting inflation could not be left to the bankers and conservatives who try to send unemployment up as a way to keep prices down. Progressives now seek *both* full employment and price stability, rejecting the tradeoff argument that attaining either one requires sacrifice of the other.

But any further progress along these lines will be beset by enormous difficulties—and at least four key questions.

1. *How can stagflation best be fought?* Any serious fight against

stagflation involves nothing less than an effort to manage the capitalist business cycle in its latest form. This can be seriously attempted only by staking out a positive program aimed at price stability and guaranteed jobs (part-time as well as full-time) for all who are able, willing, and wanting to work for pay. The former objective requires not only certain fiscal and monetary policies but also government price controls and antispeculation measures; the latter, last-resort government job opportunities at good wages. If these two approaches are combined with major reductions in war spending, the conversion of military facilities to peacetime activities, and the development of soft energy resources, America could move from a situation of manipulated scarcity to one of planned abundance. Even with an expansion of labor-intensive work, it would be possible to shorten the official work week and provide more leisure time for those who want it.

2. *How can decentralized planning best be organized?* Many of those who grew to maturity during the period of the New Deal, Fair Deal, or Great Society think of planning in overcentralized terms. Fortunately, one of the encouraging aspects of American life in the 1980s is that many old-timers and new-timers are beginning to think of planning from the very bottom up—from neighborhoods, workplaces, towns, and regions. Only for a few doctrinaire sects does this mean the complete lack of national effort at integrating local plans. Besides, there are some operations —such as the reconstruction of a railroad network—that must be conceived in national or even transnational terms to provide a framework for local planning. The one thing I am sure of is that decentralized planning cannot be left to dedicated civil servants and professional advisers, no matter how locally rooted they may be. Active participation by citizens' movements outside the formal channels of government is also essential. How to go about this is one of the great challenges of the 1980s.
3. *What about profits?* This is one of the hush-hush subjects in American debates on economic policy. Yet the Corporate Overseers oppose planning for guaranteed jobs and price stability mainly because they know that if effective, such planning would not only curb windfall gains from shortages but also tend to reduce the rate of profit on invested capital. I wish they would say so more openly; they are correct on both scores. But such planning would not destroy capitalism. In certain ways it might strengthen—as well as humanize—it. The controls involved in price stability would curtail paper profits. Guaranteed jobs, while tending to raise wage rates, would also provide the larger purchasing power needed for sustained profitability. In return for losing some of their freedom over the use of profits, the larger corpora-

tions might gain—as in Sweden—the opportunity to increase their aggregate profits.

4. *What about small business?* Both recessions and inflation are deadly enemies of small enterprises. Yet the controls involved in planning for price stability and guaranteed jobs could injure small business unless planners at all levels recognize this danger. They must also recognize that giant corporations invariably try to use small companies—subsidiaries, suppliers, or distributors—as pawns on the economic chessboard. Plans at all levels should aim at providing more opportunities for small ventures; this involves generous capital assistance, technical assistance and training. Any guaranteed-job program should include—as did the early versions of the Humphrey-Hawkins full employment legislation—planning for self-employment. Could not serious and continuing support of this type for small business promote a vital counterbalance against the dominant tendency toward corporate concentration?

DEMOCRATIZING THE SOCIAL BASE

Democracy is not brute numbers; it is a genuine union of true individuals . . . . I am an individual not as far as I am apart from, but as far as I am a part of other men. . . . Thus the essence of democracy is creating. The technique of democracy is group organization.

MARY PARKER FOLLETT [9]

The neighborhood movement potentially forms a vital strand of an emerging force for democratic change.

HARRY BOYTE [10]

I swear to the Lord
  I still can't see
Why Democracy means
  Everybody but me.

LANGSTON HUGHES,
The Black Man Speaks

If one focuses on the formal machinery of democratic government, it is hard to find democratic currents that provide much hope for the future. The picture is much less bleak, however, when one looks at the many social groupings that are bringing people together both to do things for themselves and use and protect the machinery of democracy.

The American labor movement, for example, although still representing a minority of the gainfully employed and would-be employed, is experiencing unique alterations. Within the old-line craft unions of the building and trucking industries—long-ridden by money-grubbing bureaucracies, corruption, and company-supported racketeering—a new generation of union leaders is rising. Industrial unionists have taken the leadership in forms of collective bargaining that try to protect the full range of wages, hours, and working conditions. New successes in unionization drives are occuring in the low-wage, anti-union bastions of the South, Midwest, and small-town America. The most successful trade union expansion is taking place among white collar workers—with government employees (including police and fire people) and teachers (including college professors) taking the lead. Important beginnings are under way among technicians, office workers, retail employees, custodial staffs, household workers, and migratory farm labor. All this holds forth the promise of a more democratic, more discrimination-free, more humanistically oriented, more intellectually alert, and more influential labor movement.

With partial support from labor unions, there has also been an important development unprecedented in the history of America or any other country: a huge proliferation of public-interest citizen groups. Some of these have huge attention spans. Among these are the long-lived Americans for Democratic Action, the Council on Economic Priorities, Common Cause, the Public Interest Economics Foundation, and the Exploratory Project on Economic Alternatives. "Ralph Nader's initial concern with automobile safety," Hazel Henderson reports, "has grown into a million-dollar conglomerate enterprise funded by small, individual contributions, which covers a range of systemic concerns from the drive to control corporate behavior by federal chartering, to battling for tax and regulatory reform and funding citizen and student-activist groups across the country." [11] Much of Nader's work has involved class-action law suits on behalf of people never before able to initiate court proceedings to defend their common interests.

Within each established religion, there are those—some militantly active, some timidly restrained—who go far beyond the rituals of prayer, preaching, and charity in opposing war, bias, poverty or pollution. Many scientists have brought support for such activities into their professional as well as their personal lives. This is evidenced by the work of such groups as the Federation of American Scientists, the Center for Science in the Public Interest, the Scientists' Institute for Public Information, and the Union of Concerned Scientists. Each of these covers a remarkably broad range of public interests. Public-interests groups have also been organized among college students at all levels including the professional school of social work, urban planning, architecture, law, and medicine. Even some professional groups heretofore most conspicuous for self-serving myopia and political passivity have been touched by these currents. Hence the formation of such groups as the Committee for Social

Responsibility in Engineering, the National Association of Accountants in the Public Interest and—lo and behold!—the National Affiliation of Concerned Business Students. And it was an employee from a Madison Avenue advertising firm who coined the slogan (for use against corporate advertising of the "free enterprise" system): "If You Think the System Is Working, Ask Someone Who Isn't."

Perhaps even more important than the above activities has been—to quote from a 1979 report by Frank Riessman—"a tremendous proliferation of local community groups, block associations (10,000 in New York City alone), tenants groups, housing self-management groups, neighborhood revitalization groups, and other community-based groups. . . . ACORN (Association of Community Groups for Reform Now) was operating in five states two years ago and is now in 13 states. . . . Massachusetts Fair Share in 1976 had eight affiliated groups around Boston with 600 members and now has 25 groups across the state with over 13,000 members."[12] More broadly, the Alliance for Volunteerism estimates 6 million voluntary associations; a study by ACTION indicates 37 million volunteers. In middle-class neighborhoods many of these groups are active in fighting blockbusting, red-lining, rent increases, condominium conversions, and supermarket ripoffs. In lower-class neighborhoods they fight on similar issues, but with more attention to planned shrinkage, welfare cuts, inadequate health and education; they set up rape crisis centers and battered women's shelters. Broadly, as Riessman points out in the same report, they "are anti-bureaucracy, anti-big, anti-waste, anti-elite, pro-participation, pro-accountability, and pro-productivity on the part of government."

If it were not for the impressive growth in citizen activism of all types—neighborhood organizations, public-interest groups and labor unions—I would be much more hesitant in talking about decentralized planning. History is full of too many cases in which sweet talk about bottom-up planning has been a facade for top-down domination. Besides, the smartest people among the Corporate Overseers are not only planners par excellence; they are well versed in the arts of decentralizing some things in order to build larger and more manageable empires. The best protection against these oligarchic arts is a thorough honeycombing of society through a wide variety of interrelated organizations that can at least resist top-down domination and at best countervail and substantially reduce the concentrated power of transnational corporations and the Chief Executive Network.

For the present, however, the processes of bottom-up honeycombing are far too weak. If they are to be strengthened, some tough questions must be faced. I shall simply list two of the most baffling questions:

- How can people's organizations be extended and strengthened?
- How can they avoid becoming bureaucratized or co-opted?

In addition, I shall briefly discuss these questions:

1. *What can be done to eliminate discriminatory barriers to participation?* Legal remedies against racism, sexism, ageism, and other forms of discrimination are important; and they must be used wherever necessary, not only against the dominant institutions of society but also against any people's organizations guilty of these sins. But legal remedies can be brought into being, enforced, or improved only through organization and agitation by those who have been victimized by discrimination. This means sustained and dedicated action by every group.
2. *What can be done to bring together the scattered fragments of citizen activism?* Single-purpose organizations are often self-defeating; they may reproduce at the lower levels of society the same fragmentation and particularism that are the side effects of large-scale bureaucratization. The remedy is the aggregation of diverse and mutually supporting interests through networks, coalitions, and joint or parallel operations. Often, this means taking part in partisan or "nonpartisan" politics. Is it possible to have a political party not dependent on financing by big corporations and the rich?
3. *What about improvements in the formal machinery of democracy?* The oligarchs of society are always involved in reorganizing democratic machinery to make it more responsive to their needs. That is why, in the absence of bottom-up honeycombing, I am suspicious of electoral, legislative, and judicial reforms. From the viewpoint of true democracy, however, the agenda for reform or reconstruction is staggering; it involves a reconsideration of almost every element of governmental machinery at all levels: the electoral system, the judiciary, legislatures, organizational structures and management methods.
4. *What about the protection of civil liberties?* Bottom-up honeycombing and use of democratic machinery, however, depend on the protection of civil liberties—both the older liberties of speech, assembly, and organization and the newer liberties of personal privacy, the right to know, and sexual rights. This, too, requires organization. I dread thinking of what the state of civil liberties in America would be today without the valiant efforts over many years by the American Civil Liberties Union, the National Emergency Committee on Civil Liberties, and the National Lawyers Guild. These organizations have defended thousands of people whose civil liberties were abridged; in so doing, they have made life more worthwhile for millions of others who have never known to whom they owed certain freedoms. Much more is needed in the days ahead—not only to defend the best elements in the status quo but to mount a positive offensive for the strengthening and extension of civil liberties, civil rights, and other human rights, both economic and political.

INFORMATION FOR HUMAN LIBERATION

Perseus wore a magic cap that the monsters he hunted might not see him. We draw the magic cap down over our eyes and ears as make-believe that there are no monsters.

KARL MARX[13]

Tell the truth and run.

YUGOSLAV PROVERB

During the 1960s the people of the civil rights and antiwar movements initiated a process of revelation more far-reaching than that of the so-called "muckrakers" of earlier years. By demanding that American society live up to its highest promises, they revealed the yawning gap between ideals and realities. As their early militancy subsided, many others joined their ranks. Consumer advocates, tax analysts, and environmentalists are now bringing to light the latest tricks in the exploitation of consumers, taxpayers, and the environment. Labor leaders are revealing how large corporations have depressed the level of real wages and the power of labor movements by price hikes, capital flight, and the building up of a large pool of surplus labor. Many others are identifying the tacit racism, sexism, and ageism built into the society's dominant values and institutions. Civil liberties groups have been doing more than ever before to bring to light the dirty linen of the Establishment's repressive actions in both past and present. They are sounding the warning bell repeatedly against recurrent assaults on the Bill of Rights. Critics of America's military and imperial operations have been repeatedly exposing this corruption and wastefulness of the Pentagon, the dirty tricks of the CIA and its allies, and the subversive activities here and abroad of many First World transnational corporations.

These efforts have invariably been helped by those whom Ralph Nader calls "whistle blowers." These are the private and public employees, who, in Nader's words, protest publicly against any evil—"from pollution to poverty to income erosion to privacy invasion"—perpetrated by their employers.[14] Their efforts have helped ease the work of investigative journalists, against-the-stream legislative investigators at all levels of government, and against-the-stream academics. Indeed, all the recent "books of revelation," including legislative hearings and reports, would easily fill a thirty-foot bookshelf. If more people around the world could read them, they would learn that America is much more the stuff that dreams are made of than CIA agents, Coca-Cola, neutron bombs, and TV addiction. If more Americans could read them, or better yet, if their messages were handled fairly by the mass media, the Establishment's ideologies and myths would be much less capable of hiding the monsters of the world.

But questions remain.

1. *Is more muckraking needed?* According to Murray B. Levin, revolutionary exposés have an unintended consequence: "Muckrakers receive wide publicity while attacking specific evils and specific companies (occasionally an entire industry) but they do not attack the patterns of property ownership. . . . Such attacks siphon emotions away from broader critique, hinder the development of critical theory, and create the belief that when the specific evil is remedied, all will be well." [15] Levin might have added that they may also serve to deepen feelings of apathy and helplessness. Nonetheless, I think America needs much more, and better publicized, revelationary activity. Levin's critique suggests the need for exposés that *do* attack basic patterns of control, direct emotions *toward* broader critiques, and nurture an awarness of the *limitations* of any specific remedy. I would go further. While the Establishment is the central source of muck, it enjoys no total monopoly. Corruption, deception, and error are found elsewhere also—even among the activists in people's organizations. They too should be exposed without fear or favor.
2. *What about better information on the state of the nation?* Abstractly, I am still attracted by the idea of some system of social accounting that would provide an ordered array of information—qualitative as well as quantitative—on the changing state of American life. Yet Establishment moves in this direction—as I have pointed out in "Managing Information and Minds" (chapter 12)—have tended willy-nilly to provide as many vindicators as indicators. Moreover, even the most sacrosanct of government statistics often turn out to be totally misleading, particularly when based on definitional categories frozen many years ago and never adjusted to meet the changing conditions of life. Therefore, I agree completely with S. M. Miller's view that "it would be wise to encourage counter-indicators and counter-analysis." [16]
3. *Could the new communication technologies be used to advance true democracy?* With cable television, the number of TV channels could be increased immensely and two-way communication could be provided between senders and receivers. Also, by turning a dial or pushing buttons one could plug into a great variety of previously-taped educational or cultural programs. Some people wax enthusiastic over these possibilities. I view them skeptically. Unless the control of these systems is radically changed, they would probably turn out to be new forms of mind management.

In the meantime, the most important advance would be for the winning of better access to the media by artistic groups, labor unions, schools, neighborhood groups, and health centers.

RELEASING HUMANISTIC VALUES

The God who saves us will not descend from the machine; he will arise once more in the human heart.

LEWIS MUMFORD [17]

Many people have entered the Eighties with new commitments to moral and esthetic values. Late in the 1970s, a Harris poll revealed a significant value shift. People were asked basic questions concerning the stress they would place on alternative approaches to values, rewards, interpersonal relations, and living standards. Majority and minority opinions were reported as follows:

The Majority	The Minority
Learning to appreciate human values more than material values: 63%	Finding ways to create more jobs for producing more goods: 29%
Finding more inner and personal rewards from work: 64%	Increasing the productivity of the work force: 26%
Spending more time getting to know people better on a person-to-person basis: 77%	Improving and speeding up our ability to communicate with each other through better technology: 15%
Teaching people how to live with basic essentials: 79%	Reaching a higher standard of living: 17%

As in most opinion polls, a certain amount of distortion was created by the phrasing of the questions. Thus, appreciation of human values was falsely contrasted with job creation, a distinction hardly to be appreciated by those suffering from the inhumanity of unemployment and job insecurity. Other opinion polls have shown that 75 to 90 percent of respondents favor last-resort government jobs as a response to unemployment. Better-balanced questions, therefore, would have probably increased the majority in the left-hand column. Other surveys tend to suggest marked progress in appreciating—although not yet overcoming—

the deep-rooted nature of racism, sexism, and ageism in American society. I think there has also been some progress in efforts to escape the *machismo* that undermines the well-being of many American families and the role of the United States in the family of nations.

1. *How can more democratic values be nurtured?* The usual response is to proclaim the decisive roles of childhood learning from early infancy, and of subsequent education in school. But this begs the question; it is in homes and schools that nondemocratic values are customarily instilled. How can the values of parents and teachers be improved? I see no serious answer in the assumption that more humanistic values will automatically "arise once more in the human heart" in response to concentrated power, as a result of brilliant preaching or as a natural evolution once survival needs are met. Like happiness, the values of true democracy emerge—I suspect—not by direct design, but rather as a byproduct of things people do. Perhaps they arise as people learn from each other.
2. *What are the potentialities for nonviolent action in America?* In opposing nuclear energy, some environmentalists have revived the nonviolent methods of social action developed by Mahatma Gandhi in India and adapted to American circumstances by Martin Luther King and other civil rights activists. Without suggesting nonviolence as an all-purpose alternative to every oppressive act on the "ladder of terror" (discussed in chapter 14), I still think its potentialities are enormous. Americans need a substitute for William James's quasi-militaristic motto that we need "a moral equivalent of war." That substitute can be found in nonmilitary forms of moral action. From this viewpoint, more might be learned from the examples of Gandhi and King than from the therapies of Keynes and Freud, let alone the cults of escapism and submission.
3. *How can deep anxieties be alleviated at their roots?* Like my comments on the previous two questions, my answer to this one cannot take the form of a prescription. If anxiety relief is sought through madness, the cults of submission, and the misuse of sex and drugs, little help is provided by efforts to stop the symptoms. Rather, people can help each other in trying to deal with the causes of alienation, helplessness, and the loss of meaning in life. Ralph Nader's whistle blowers, when confronted with wrongdoing within their organizations, look for allies within and outside the organization and then act in accordance with principles of morality higher than mere bureaucratic loyalty. They may "suffer the consequences" personally; in return, they can retain—or regain—their self-respect. Perhaps whistle-blowing can be thought of in broader terms. For example, are there not ways in

which the long-term unemployed—consigned to the degradation of public assistance, the street hustle, and ghetto-life indignities—can also blow the whistle?

TRUTH AND RATIONALITY

There are no whole truths; all truths are half-truths. It is trying to treat them as whole truths that plays the devil.

ALFRED NORTH WHITEHEAD [18]

The true problems of living—in politics, economics, education, marriage, etc.—are always problems of overcoming opposites.

E. F. SCHUMACHER [19]

An encouraging aspect of college teaching is the skepticism with which students react to any "whole truths" that professors may try to pump into their heads. To get the grades that may help them get financial aid or jobs, students may memorize ideological tidbits and half-baked facts while keeping their skepticism under tight control and abstaining from expression (or clarification) of their own views. But this adaptation to the rigors of "higher" education does not mean genuine acceptance of the "value-free" posturing of those social scientists who throw trivial data into computers or pretend that oracular truths may be deduced from mathematical models. More broadly, I see resistance to technocratic orientations that would limit rationality to means alone, leaving ends and side effects out of consideration. Some law students and lawyers have been bringing the Bar before the bar of moral judgment or public opinion. Some medical students and physicians have been laying the medical profession out on the operating table. Some physical scientists have been examining the internal politics of science's formal pressure groups, informal control networks, and ties to the military-industrial complex. Some management students and managers are beginning to think in terms of basic morality. And beyond the halls of academe, larger numbers of people are searching for more ethical ways of living. Whether they find it in organized religion, in personal worship, in meditation, or even in cults, one thing is clear: They are not exactly willing to separate means from ends, rationality from morality, or the True from the Good and the Beautiful.

None of this quite conforms to the adaptive rationality of the Hydra-headed Establishment, or to the unfolding logic of friendly fascism. Yet all of this is insufficient. The logic of true democracy involves *learning through doing*. "The essence of democracy is creating," writes Mary Parker Follett. When I showed these words to a high official in a mammoth bureaucracy, his eyes glazed over. "What does that mean?" he demanded. His reaction illustrated another part-truth, again from Follett: "Concepts can never be presented to me merely; they must be knitted into the structure of my being, and this can be done only through my own activity." [20] My activity and the structure of my being tell me a few part-truths that cannot be simply presented to others but that many others, I know, have learned from their own experience: that the real world is enormously complex; that unsought consequences may prove more important than central intentions; that democratic life involves the integration of opposites; that problems are attacked more than solved; [21] that wholes cannot be understood by trying to add up their parts; that good analysis (which divides things into pieces) requires imaginative synthesis (to bring pieces together); that many truths (in George Bernard Shaw's words) "enter the world as blasphemies"; that the deepest interests of most people are hard to fathom; that eternal values are eternally changing; that narrow rationality can lead to MAD and other forms of madness; that the rationality of democracy is one that brings new values into being; and that the logic of democracy requires the formulation of questions that have no quick, easy, or simple answers.

Two questions have lived with me for over four decades:

1. *What about democratic management in human affairs?* I worked for many years in developing some concepts of democratic management and planning.[22] In retrospect, I have learned that much of this has been absorbed into the rhetoric of nondemocratic elitism, the practice of co-optation, and the arts of protecting or expanding concentrated power. But still the question burns in my mind. Could not the best elements of so-called "scientific management"—perhaps blended with the "scientific workmanship" hinted at by Harry Braverman [23]—be used in the unending struggle for true democracy? And to quote an almost blasphemous truth by the author of *Small Is Beautiful* (a truth most of his followers have ignored): "Large-scale organization is here to stay." From his long experience on Britain's National Coal Board, Schumacher then goes on to suggest some principles that might help combine "the orderliness of *order* and the disorderliness of creative *freedom*." He concludes by asserting that any such principles must be developed by going to the practical people, learning from them, synthesizing their experience into theories, and then returning to the practical people who must put these principles into practice.[24] Any people who do this illustrate Follett's words on the essence of democracy.
2. *Is a truly humanistic capitalism possible in America?* Any answer to this question depends on how one defines "humanistic." For some, humanism is the compassion of the Ultra-Rich as they take money from the middle classes and throw crumbs to the poor; it

is the largesse of dictators who declare recurrent amnesties for some of those who have survived torture; it is the smile on the face of any friendly despotism. For me, a humanistic capitalism has always been one in which a choice of productive and fulfilling job opportunities is always available for those able and willing to work for pay, inflation is prevented, and a guaranteed minimum income is provided for anyone. Barrington Moore goes further in envisioning capitalism-with-a-difference. He suggests far-reaching social changes: major reductions in military expenditures, an end to the tragic human waste of urban and rural poverty, stronger protections against arbitrary authority, "a wholesale redirection of scientific efforts toward human ends . . . an end to compulsive and socially wasteful forms of consumption and a very large increase in the services and amenities provided by the public sector." [25] Ideals of this type appeal strongly to all those seeking basic reforms in America—including the stronger liberals in the Democratic party. American reformers—including the stronger liberals in the Democratic party—have long worked·to develop such ideals and translate them into action. Many have done this with the feeling that, in effect, they were trying to save capitalism. In return, they have continuously been branded "eggheads," "pinkos," or "crypto-socialists." For moving cautiously on even lesser reforms, President Franklin Roosevelt himself was branded "traitor to his class" and died as the most hated as well as the best loved of all presidents. The branders of today—in company with the more sectarian Marxists—consistently maintain that stability, guaranteed jobs, and guaranteed minimum income are inconsistent with capitalism.

Barrington Moore himself lugubriously concludes that his style of reformed capitalism is "extraordinarily unlikely." Its clientele would be too small and weak, and the resistance to it enormous. The bulk of the reforms would be bitterly opposed by those with vested interests in military production, in other forms of wasteful production and consumption, and in high differentials in prestige, income, and wealth. Popular support could easily be mobilized on behalf of these interests, particularly if serious foreign threats are found to exist or are created. The Establishment's leaders are more apt to consider concessions if they themselves have considerable leeway—and the existence of this leeway depends on "world hegemony and continued exploitation." [26] If the capitalist world continues to shrink, such leeway may also diminish.

Back in 1945 an old friend and colleague told a story to explain his belief that genuine full employment without inflation or militarism might be possible in America. A grandfather was explaining to his grandson how a frog tried to escape an alligator. The frog jumped from a log into the river, swam through the river and hopped on into the land—

as the alligator came closer and closer. The alligator finally cornered the frog under a tree and opened his mouth to swallow the frog. "But the frog looked up," the grandfather said, "and just as the 'gator's jaws were clamping down, the frog flew up into the tree." "But, Grandpa," said the little boy, "frogs can't fly." "Indeed, they can't, my grandson, indeed they can't," was the answer, "but this frog flew—*he had to*." [27]

Sweden is one country where capitalism *had to* change. Supported by an enormously powerful labor movement, the Swedish socialists could long ago have nationalized the largest sectors of Swedish capital. Instead, they used their power to obtain "concessions"—mainly, public participation in the use of profits and very high levels of welfare-state services—that the large capitalists have benefitted from enormously, but which they would never have conceded if they had not feared nationalization. So with less nationalization than any other West European (or Scandinavian) country, Sweden has a unique combination of relative price stability and high levels of both employment and profitability. Perhaps the reason is that, in Sweden, countervailing power based on local and national organizations does more countering than veiling. Or is it perhaps that a credible threat of socialism is necessary to make captialism work more effectively for both the capitalists and the majority of the people?

It is also important to note that in Sweden Big Business and Big Government work very closely together. The result, according to Roland Huntford, is that the Swedes have become "the new totalitarians." [28] What Huntford misses is the fact that Sweden—like Norway and Denmark—is one of the most open societies in the world; there are longstanding guarantees of the public's right to know. Above all, the Scandinavian countries enjoy what Eric Einhorn of the University of Massachusetts calls "a participant political culture." [29] According to Dankwort Rustow of City University of New York, the essence of democracy in these countries is "the habit of dissension and conciliation over everchanging issues and amidst ever-changing alignments." [30] This habit is rooted in a democratized social base, with widespread democratic participation in even the smallest of local decisions. This leads me to a question, the very asking of which makes me uncomfortable. If the base of American society were much more democratized—along such lines as I have briefly touched upon earlier in this chapter—would it be possible for the growing partnership between Big Business and Big Government to be counterbalanced and humanized? On such a fulcrum, would it be possible to nudge the United States toward becoming more of a good neighbor in a new world order? Would it be possible to move toward a democratized Establishment, a more balanced economy, the use of information for human liberation, the emergence of more humanistic values, and the development of a more rational rationality?

All I can say is that everything depends on what people do—which brings me to the next and final chapter of this book.

21

What Can You Do?

As life is action and passion, it is required of a man that he should share the passion and action of his time, at peril of being judged not to have lived.

OLIVER WENDELL HOLMES, JR. [1]

TODAY, POSING THE QUESTION "What is to be done?" is often a facile cover-up for doing nothing or passing the buck to others. Nor are matters clarified making the verb active and adding a vague or totally unidentified *"one, we,* or *you."*

"What can one (or we or you) do?" is usually a glib way of avoiding the multiplicity of ones, of actors, in the real world. It is emptier than a performance of *Hamlet* without the Prince of Denmark; it is like a play without any actors at all.

Or else it is a way of discussing what *they* should do. "What should public policy—or the public policy maker—do about stagflation? Or the draft? Or the MX missile? Or nuclear power?" asks the traditional teacher of so-called public policy. The de-animated *public policy* and the unnamed *policy maker* become fetishistic masks behind which usually stand the Corporate Overseers, the Ultra-Rich, the political leaders, or whichever technocratic experts may be "in" at the moment.

But when the question is seriously asked and seriously answered, specifics are needed as to just *who* is to do what, when, and how. In this spirit, let me raise the question "What can *you* do?"

YES, YOU . . .

In the early days of the Vietnam War, while my students were beginning to protest against American intervention, I was full of ideas about what *they* should or should not do. Many more thousands of Vietnamese and Americans were killed before I began to ask what *I* should do.

I have tried to learn something from that experience. Now, when someone asks what can *we* or *one* do, I answer that it all depends on which we or one is discussed. When someone asks "What can you do?" I accept the question as referring to me specifically. I answer by telling what I have been doing as teacher, writer, and sometime political activist. Reviewing the choices I see ahead of me, I ask what they think I *should* do. This helps bring the discussion down from the make-believe world of action without actors to the real word of identifiable doers. The question then becomes "What might *you* in your own capacity do now or later—here, there, or somewhere else?"

In this real world of specific doers, of course, it is usually *they* who do the more important things. The myths of citizen and consumer sovereignty hide the crude realities of semi-oligarchic or oligarchic power. Conventional technocratic wisdom escapes this impasse by hailing the vanguard role of the knowledge elites. Conventional radical wisdom, in turn, idealizes the vanguard role of the working class—with major disputes as to which part of the working class (old, new, or "under") may be the critical sector. Then there are those who, in the light of the 1960s and the early 1970s, still look for leadership to the blacks, young people, or women—any group that has suffered most conspicuously at the hands of the establishment. Alan Gartner and Frank Riessman, somewhat skeptical of these groups, suggest that as consumers are increasingly exploited a "consumer vanguard" may emerge. Interestingly, they see any vanguard as a group that serves to unite all the other progressive forces. This view is widely shared by those who look to broad liberal-radical coalitions as a major force in the defense and expansion of human freedom.

This line of thought goes very far to modifying, if not destroying, old premises, whether embodied in establishment ideology or in classic Marxist dogma, concerning the vanguard role of any narrowly defined group or class. In the sphere of socialist thought James Weinstein has commented on the absence of any one sector whose immediate needs are seen as a key to uniting all others. "At different times particular sectors of the working class will play a leading role in the movement—as students and blacks did in different ways during the 1960s and industrial workers did in the 1930s—no one sector is a strategic short-cut to convincing the majority of Americans about the need for socialism and a socialist party to take power." [2] Similarly, John and Barbara Ehrenreich, after discussing the fragmentation of work under modern capitalism, suggest that "there is no longer any reason, other than a romantic one, to insist on the unique centrality of the workshop as the locale for the development of class consciousness in the United States." [3] In the context of their discussion it should be understood that "class consciousness" refers to an awareness of common interests on the part of all people who are (or want to be) engaged in paid employment. This is an enormously heterogeneous set of persons and groups that make up at least 75 percent of the adult population. In the light of this heterogeneity, it becomes rather difficult to make a priori judgments as to the source of the most significant initiatives. May not anyone—whether follower or leader, no matter how humble or previously inactive, no matter where he or she is located in the social structure—exercise useful initiatives?

ANYONE ANYWHERE, REALLY?

> Anyone, anywhere can make a beginning; this is an arena where one person can count, as Rosa Parks counted in the civil rights movement . . .
>
> STAUGHTON LYND [4]

On December 1, 1955, after a hard day's work, Rosa Parks, a forty-three-year-old black seamstress of Montgomery, Alabama, was returning home in a crowded bus. She was sitting in the front part of the black section, directly behind the white section, which was fully occupied. When more whites entered the bus, the driver told all the blacks to move further back. This was an established custom, and the other blacks complied. Rosa Parks refused. The driver called a policeman, who arrested her at once. A few days later the Montgomery Improvement Association, led by Martin Luther King, Jr., organized a black boycott of all city buses. Within a few years' time, civil rights boycotts and demonstrations—usually with white participants—were being staged in hundreds of cities throughout the South.[5]

Did Rosa Parks really make this beginning? The mythology of all the civil rights movements answers "yes." But the real answer is "no." Many black persons throughout the South had earlier been arrested for having been "uppity" in a bus. In the same city of Montgomery a few years earlier Vernon Jones, a black preacher, had refused to vacate his seat under similar circumstances—and had gotten away with it.[6] Also, the boycott led by Martin Luther King had had its origins in the responses of other lesser-known—and now unremembered—blacks who felt that something must be done *this* time. In turn, King's vigorous leadership of tne boycott goes back to the wave of hope that swept over the South after May 31, 1954, when the Supreme Court, responding to many years of pressure by the National Association for the Advancement of Colored People, ordered school desegregation "with all deliberate speed." It was also rooted in decades of black admiration of the boycotts and civil disobedience campaigns led by Mohandas K. Gandhi against British domination of India. And it was far back in 1893 when Gandhi, sitting in a South African railroad car, was asked to move to make way for whites. Like Rosa Parks many decades later, he refused and was forcibly ejected. By the next morning, under the shock of this event, "Gandhi had evolved from a private citizen to a political actor."[7] Thus, Rosa Parks' refusal was a culmination of thousands of beginnings, some of which were recorded, most of which were forgotten, over many years; here was an unpredictable outcome of thousands of sparks that flickered briefly and at the time seemed to have no consequence.

Can *any* individual reaction to exploitation or manipulation have consequences?

Of course it can.

The first consequence is on one's self. Any protest or resistance is better than the narcissistic "retreat to personal satisfaction" described by Christopher Lasch,[8] or the self-absorption therapies which, according to Edwin Schur, treat the "individual (together with a few partners in direct interaction) as some kind of closed system."[9] I say this even though some personal plunges into activism may be little more than the working out in public of arrogant fantasies of personal omnipotence. In full-employment campaigns I have seen more than one activist who, in the words of Peter Marin, "excludes from consideration all felt sense of solidarity, community or the power of collective labor or responsibility."[10]

Another consequence is learning—or the unlearning that is often necessary before new things can be learned. One can learn a lot from errors and failures as well as successes. This is attested to by my experiences in two grueling campaigns for genuine full employment. Social learning can also take place. During the movement against the Vietnam War many people learned new modes of personal satisfaction through modest actions in cooperation with others. In neighborhood programs today many people are learning that they can be truly effective only if *enough* single individuals make important "beginnings" by refusing to take part in the retreat into narcissism.

Can ants really harm mighty elephants? At first thought, it seems unlikely. Elephants are customarily surrounded my myriads of insects of all types, none of which can penetrate the thick elephantine hide. Also, elephants snuff out the life of countless ants whenever, without even knowing it, they step on ant hills. Yet elephant trainers are eager to explain the wisdom behind the African proverb: a single ant will drive an elephant mad . . . *if* it crawls into the elephant's trunk. This is unlikely if there is only one ant in the neighborhood.

Any part of a modern establishment has many more vulnerable apertures than an elephant. These can be penetrated and exposed by all sorts of people—from disaffected executives, wives, and husbands to disillusioned scientists, professionals, and technicians; from blue-collar workers to shop stewards and higher union officials; from Girl Fridays and Man Fridays to the floor and window cleaners; from those who until now have had little reason for hope to those who, despite repeated failures, are everlasting wellsprings of long-range optimism. Wherever you may be, there are opportunities for action.

"I have four columns marching on Madrid," boasted General Francisco Franco back in 1937, "and one inside the city." With the help of this fifth column, he finally overthrew the republican government in Madrid. In today's First World establishments the difference between inside and outside is not so clear. Many outsiders work inside the walls. Some of the insiders, as I pointed out in "The Adaptive Hydra" (chapter 16), see themselves as outsiders boring from within. If this be a personal rationalization for those seeking a "handful of silver," it also suggests that under conditions of more acute crisis, many co-optees will change colors again. Indeed, it is hard to see how any capitalist establishment could be fundamentally reformed or replaced without help from insiders. No matter how many columns may move from outside, four or five "fifth columns" could make all the difference.

HIGH ASPIRATIONS, REALISTIC EXPECTATIONS

No one person can do very much. This is why broad networks, coalitions, and movements are important. It is also why the question "What can *you* do?" must be realistically faced in terms of exactly where and what you are, what your capabilities might be, and who and what you might want to become.

The range of possible action is enormous. It is only barely hinted at in the agenda questions posed in the previous chapter, "The Long-Term Logic of Democracy." Indeed, the opportunities for small victories—particularly in the United States—are enormous. Here, a blatantly neofascist legislative effort or judicial decision can be held up or diverted. There, improvements in public services can be won. Here, an environmental monstrosity can be stopped in its tracks. There, some conspicuous victims of injustice can be saved, freed, or retroactively rehabilitated. Here, an entire neighborhood can be mobilized to improve run-down buildings, establish or improve a health clinic, or upgrade a local school. Here, an entire classroom can be raised to the level where formal learning becomes a wondrous excitement. There, a careful research study can rip aside the shrouds of mystification and false consciousness. Here, people can learn how to work together on behalf of interests broader than, but including, their own. Here, there, and almost everywhere some people can find some portion (in Walter Lippmann's words) of "the kind of purpose and effort that gives to life its flavor and meaning."

But you should also be realistic. On the path to any victory, the organizers—including *you*—may themselves be co-opted into the Establishment. At the moment of victory, the motive power animating your associates—and *you*—may be dissipated. As psychologists have long pointed out, a gratified need is no longer a motivator. And any success itself may strengthen the Establishment by demonstrating its presumed perfectibility.

Realism has another dimension. People will tell you that if you use new ideas, nobody will understand you. If you do, you will be isolated. People will tell you not to aim too high. If you do, you are doomed to disappointment. This problem of expectations will confront you in any sphere of action—whether the organization of workers or neighborhoods, the elimination of discrimination, or campaigns against war, the arms race, unemployment, and inflation. It even arises in the field of civil liberties. Do you really expect that the FBI can soon be returned to its original task of fighting crime? Do you really expect that in this age of competing intelligence forces, covert operations, and computerized dossiers, your personal privacy can long be protected against the menace of monitoring? If you do, this is as unrealistic as to expect quick conversion of TV and radio networks into instruments of democratic, rather than oligarchic, communication. Anyone who expects such Monday morning miracles is doomed to quick frustration and apathetic withdrawal. Only with a realistic expectation schedule can one keep on going the rest of the week—or month, year, or decade . . .

Let me put the question still more frontally. Should the defenders of America's Bill of Rights stand foursquare for all civil liberties for everyone, even though this would place an intolerable burden on the existing system of courts, legal defense, and mass media? Should the advocates of capitalism-with-a-difference commit themselves wholeheartedly to reforms that are unlikely? Should Establishment response to crisis be countered by alternative responses that may be doomed to failure? Should valuable time be spent popularizing an alternative vision that is truly visionary? In short, is it reasonable to ask the opponents of friendly fascism to make the kind of demands that create unrealistic aspirations?

My answer to these questions is "Yes, *if* . . ."

The *if* relates to the vital distinction—usually ignored—between expectations and aspirations.

It would be a deception of one's self and others to foster expectations of the impossible. But whether you are engaged in passive defense, counterattack, or positive initiatives, it is essential to combine realistic expectations with high—sometimes rising—aspirations. You will, in fact, get more of what people really need if your actions start with an orientation toward those needs rather than being "realistically" trimmed in advance to what conventional wisdom says they can readily get. To be an effective actor instead of merely a reactor, you must help raise aspirations far beyond the level of current expectations.

The shrewdest heads in the Establishment understand this distinction very well. That is why they level furious attacks against high aspirations in general, and personal attacks against anyone who tries to articulate them specifically. If articulated aspirations are broad enough to include the needs of the great majority of the people, it may be more difficult to carry out the old divide-and-rule strategies. Instead of trying to get what they need and want, the reasoning goes, people should be brainwashed into wanting what they get. More apathy by the masses, they seem convinced, is the prerequisite for preserving democratic machinery.

Realistically, I see an increase in the height and scope of popular aspirations as vital to resolving the inescapable contradiction of any effort to expand human freedom. Only if the aspiration level is high enough can minor victories serve to increase rather than diminish motivations. Only thus can leaders be strengthened by minor victories rather than being led down the primrose path to co-optation. Indeed, if aspirations are high enough, there is less need to wait until things get worse before anything is done. If they are broad enough to include the needs of people everywhere, it may be easier to tolerate whatever reductions in First World living standards might result from contractions in foreign military operations and military spending at home. The more perfect accumulation of capital and power requires more acceptance and less resistance by those who are weakened in the process. If more people hope for more power over their own lives, they are less apt to be satisfied with reforms that enhance the power of faceless oligarchs. So long as expectations are realistic, the daily frustrations resulting from high aspirations may serve to fuel the patient anger and the impatient, long-range hopes that must animate all action against friendly fascism.

Many decades ago, in trying to bring straight talk into movements against classic fascism, Antonio Gramsci dealt with this distinction indirectly. "Pessimism of the intelligence," he advocated, but "optimism of the will." Today, extending Gramsci's remark, I suggest that optimism and pessimism have to be woven into *both* intelligence and will. Will must recognize the huge difficulties in the immediate future. Intelligence must be oriented toward the more hopeful possibilities at any time—particularly in the long run.

MY COUNTRY RIGHT AND WRONG

For me patriotism is the same as humanity. I am patriotic because I am human and humane. It is not exclusive. I will not hurt England or Germany to serve India . . . My patriotism is inclusive and admits of no enmity or ill-will.

MAHATMA GANDHI

Guard against the impostures of pretended patriotism.
GEORGE WASHINGTON,
Farewell Address

In Gertrude Stein's opera *The Mother Of Us All,* Susan B. Anthony, the women's rights pioneer, declares, "I am not puzzled; but it is very puzzling." In fact, she was deeply puzzled; that was Gertrude Stein's point. Similarly, one who applies intelligence and will in discovering and developing the logic of democracy must expect to face puzzlements. Anyone who tries to demystify or displace the Kafkaesque castles of power in the modern world creates another mystery if he or she pretends to know what exactly will happen next. Confronting the Golden International, the Ultra-Rich, and the Corporate Overseers, or even their smallest underlings is no tea party, picnic, or mere intellectual game. Any such effort involves uncertain opportunities and personal risks. No one who persists in attacking the Establishment and resists co-optation can expect to be rewarded by it on earth—although after death official tribute may be paid to his or her memory. The most immediate reward is to have not only one's competence but one's patriotism called into question.

This brings us to a deep puzzlement: what is patriotism really? I am not satisfied with Samuel Johnson's definition of 1775 "Patriotism is the last refuge of a scoundrel." And I can only partly accept Ambrose Bierce's re-statement in *The Devil's Dictionary:* "I beg to submit that it is the first." Rather, I favor George Washington's implied distinction between genuine and pretended patriotism. This is like the difference between true and "fool's gold" democracy. But it is a much more puzzling distinction. The rhetoric of false democracy has beclouded the atmosphere for only a few decades. The rhetoric of false patriotism is older than the nation itself. It was always used by the classic fascists. It is a favorite artifice of friendly fascism today.

I can easily understand why George Washington warned against pretended patriotism. The Declaration of Independence held forth the promise of more democracy than any country had ever yet attempted. But, in the words of Earl Robinson's "Ballad for Americans," "Nobody who was anybody believed it. Everybody who was anybody—they doubted it." The more conspicuous doubters, in the words of Tom Paine, were the "sunshine patriots" who shrank from the service of their country in time of crisis. Equally dangerous were the many speculators who made fortunes by charging extortionate prices for the arms, food, and clothing used by Washington's soldiers. During the entire struggle for independence, moreover, the social life of the new nation's cities was dominated by the rich "anybodies" still loyal to King George and the blessings of imperial monarchy. After the war, when Jefferson served as ambassador in Paris, he reported back on his difficulites with rich Americans: "Merchants are the least virtuous of citizens and possess the least of *amor patriae.*"[11] After serving two terms as president, Jefferson explained this phenomenon: "Merchants have no country. The mere spot they stand on does not constitute so strong an attachment as that from which they draw their gains."[12]

I think I understand the kinds and roots of false patriotism today. Some years ago Francis W. Coker of Yale University put his finger on the divisive and exclusive patriots who "insist that the country must always be set above the rest of the world" and "in the name of patriotism conduct a virulent propaganda against economic and political measures of which they disapprove," including the admission of "undesirable" foreigners but also the free expression of dissident views in schools, churches or the media.[13] In his *Militarism, USA,* a sober critique based on years of experience in the U.S. Marine Corps, Colonel James A. Donovan identifies the dangerous patriot: "the one who drifts into chauvinism and exhibits blind enthusiasm for military actions. He is a defender of militarism and its ideals of war and glory. Chauvinism is a proud and bellicose form of patriotism . . . which identifies numerous enemies who can only be dealt with through military power and which equates the national honor with military victory." With an insider's gift for telling detail, he relates this kind of dangerous patriotism to the vested interests of the "vast, expensive, and burgeoning military-industrial-scientific-political combine which dominates the country."[14] In *The Reason for Democracy,* published after his death in 1976, Kalman Silvert of New York University provided another pungent description of false patriots: "People who wrap themselves in the flag and proclaim the sanctity of the nation are usually racists, contemptuous of the poor and dedicated to keeping the community of 'ins' small and pure of blood, spirit and mind."[15] The people described by Coker, Donovan, and Silvert are the kind of scoundrels Samuel Johnson and Ambrose Bierce were referring to—and anyone acting in the spirit of true democracy should be prepared for opposition from them.

But there is more to it than that. Throughout the Establishment there are "anybodies" who define patriotism as loyalty to themselves, their organization, or the regime, not to the Constitution, the country, or any higher principles of morality. To them, the Nuremberg principle was never enunciated. Their ideal subordinates are little Adolf Eichmanns who, not bothering about right or wrong, carry out any policies or orders given to them. Then there are the technocratic patriots who, fully accepting the dominant values of the Establishment, compete with each other in working out the details of the policies or orders. Unlike Eichmann's, their evil is not banal. Like the patriotism of Albert Speer's technicians in the Nazi war machine, it is creative, adaptive, and innovative—and totally divorced from any sense of moral responsibility. And at the Establishment's pinnacle, connecting it with other castles of power in the

Golden International, are the movers and shakers of the giant transnational conglomerates and complexes. Like the merchants described by Jefferson, they have no country and the least of *amor patriae*. If Jefferson were alive today, I think he would amend his statement to point out that while standing on and drawing their gains from many spots, they have real attachments to none.

I think I also understand the questionable patriotism of flag-waving "nobodies" in the lower and middle classes. At the beginning of the 1970s some "hard hats" in the building trades thought they were being patriotic by beating up youthful demonstrators against the Vietnam War. For those of them whose families had come to America to escape conscription, war, and oppression in Old War countries, this was a crude way of demonstrating their thankfulness for being able to live in the greater freedom of the New World. For those who had never been able to go to college, who suffered the insecurities of the highly irregular and seasonal construction industry, and who felt the humiliations of manual labor in an increasingly white-collar culture, this was an opportunity to demonstrate their physical superiority over the college kids. At the beginning of the 1980s, some white- and blue-collar workers joined in waving the American flag while burning Iranian flags and beating up Iranian students. What they demonstrated was a very human—although somewhat pathetic—desire to rally around a cause in which they could believe. Here was an obvious wrongdoing to oppose, and a brief chance to join with others in expressing a common national purpose.

But I am puzzled as to why true patriots seem to hide their love for America. Perhaps, as Kalman Silvert wrote after criticizing flag-waving racists, people who "like to think about embracing all their fellow citizens are ashamed to use the symbols of nationhood." These have been sullied by the posturing of false patriots. Perhaps true patriots feel that love of country should be stated by actions alone—even though this means yielding up the words and the symbols to the impostors. Perhaps, as they struggle against huge odds to amend the flaws in American life, their attachment to America recedes into the background. The awareness of this attachment can only be further diminished when the people in America's central-city ghettos hear the words of "America the Beautiful" telling them: "Thine alabaster cities gleam/Undimmed by human tears."

Nonetheless, I am puzzled. In 1948, Alan Paton, the South African writer, published a great novel, *Cry, the Beloved Country*. I remember wondering then what could be so beloved about that country, a land of bondage and fear, in comparison with my own country. I still wonder why so many of my own countrymen—particularly my students—are hesitant to express their love. Perhaps they must live in other countries long enough, as I have done, to appreciate the glories of America and learn that there is no other place where they can be at home. Perhaps they are put off by examples of blind patriotism. "Our country right or wrong," the famous toast by naval officer Stephen Decatur, seems to hail the closing of eyes to the wrongs committed by some Americans in the name of America.

To love America is not to cover up the misdeeds done by people of this country. A good parent is one who sees the faults of children as well as their beauties. He or she tries to understand those faults and, where possible, help correct them. This does not mean withdrawing love and giving it back depending on how the child behaves. For him or her, it is "My child right and wrong, but my child." True love is never blind.

In Germany today the true patriots are those who, among other things, are trying to come to grips with the essence of past Nazi horrors. In the Soviet Union the true patriots are those who try to understand the nature and roots of Stalinism and the Stalinist legacy, rather than simply uttering some words about "the cult of personality" and running away from the subject. In America the true patriots are those who face the fact that Americans have always been both right and wrong and, instead of trying to squelch criticism, calmly take the position "My country right *and* wrong." They are those who defend the good, the true, and the beautiful in American life. They are willing to take risks in attacking what is wrong. And as I have been pointing out in earlier chapters, there is much wrong in the making today.

I came to maturity hating the wrongdoers of classic fascism. They were truly hateful. I cannot say that I hate the racists, chauvinists, sexists, polluters, interventionists, price fixers, labor-haters, academic frauds, false patriots, and corporate criminals and corrupters who are taking us down the paths toward friendly fascism. Hatred is *their* game. They hate people at home and abroad, and I suspect that many of them hate themselves. They are as much the victims as the beneficiaries of a system that needs some reconstructing. They need compassion. They also need their comeuppance. They must be fought in the factories and the fields, in the offices and the supermarkets, in the courts and the legislatures, at the ballot boxes, in the classrooms, on the picket lines, in the press and on the air waves. They must be fought with every nonviolent and nonwarlike means that the ingenuity of man, woman, or child can devise.

These are no simple tasks. With so much to be done and undone, there is room—and need—for anyone anywhere. There are endless needs for uncovering exploitation and abuses wherever they may occur, whether intended or unintentional; and for demystifying the mysteries that obscure the workings of concentrated capital and power. It is necessary to act even while knowing that any line of action may have unintended consequences and prove to be myopic, perhaps even blind. It is essential to learn from mistakes and false starts, and to begin again in an endless struggle to make things better rather than sit idly by, waiting until they become worse. It does not matter so much whether one prefers defending the best in the status quo, seeking a truly reformed capitalism or preparing the way for democratic socialism. It does not matter what crisis one responds to, what aspect of the democratic vision one cherishes most, or which portion of the democratic logic one acts on and develops. What matters is that one finds companions in journeys that may not be brief but should be joyous.

In the course of these journeys the dominant logic of today may be totally submerged by a new wave of a democratic future that seems improbable at present. This is the hopeful challenge behind all the puzzling entanglements of "What is to be done and undone?"

O brave new world that has such challenge in it!

Notes

Introduction: A Patriotic Warning

1. Kenneth Dolbeare, "Alternatives to the New Fascism," paper delivered at the American Political Science Association, September 1976.
2. Alan Wolfe, "Waiting for Rightie," *The Review of Radical Political Economics*, Fall 1973.
3. Anne Morrow Lindbergh, *The Wave of the Future: A Confession of Faith* (New York: Harcourt Brace 1940).
4. For the term "blind anti-fascism," I am indebted to Arnold Beichman, who in referring to Robert Heilbroner's attacks on "blind anti-communism," complains that progressives may not recognize the existence of "blind anti-fascism" or "blind anti-racism" in *Nine Lies About America* (New York: The Library Press, 1972). If Beichman's point is that myopia, blind spots and blindness are to be found at all points on the political spectrum, I thankfully agree.
5. The argument that the Employment Act of 1946—apart from any of its framers' intentions—has laid the legal basis for the modern corporate state is presented forcefully by Arthur S. Miller in *The Modern Corporate State: Private Governments and the American Constitution* (Westport: Greenwood Press, 1976).
6. Gunther Anders, "Theses for the Atomic Age," *The Massachusetts Review*, Spring 1962.
7. Alvin Toffler, *Future Shock* (New York: Random House, 1970).
8. William L. Shirer's statement was made in a press interview appearing in the *Los Angeles Times* in 1972.
9. Marvin Harris, *Cannibals and Kings* (New York: Random House, 1979).
10. For the distinction between the ignorance of the wise and the wisdom of the ignorant I am indebted to Mary Parker Follett: "There is the ignorance of the ignorant and the ignorance of the wise; there is the wisdom of the wise and the wisdom of the ignorant. Both kinds of ignorance have to be overcome, one as much as the other; both kinds of wisdom have to prevail, one as much as the other." *The New State: Group Organization the Solution of Popular Government* (New York: Longman's Green, 1918; reissued Gloucester, Mass.: 1965).
11. *Nine Lies About America.*

Chapter 1: The Rise and Fall of Classic Fascism

1. Roland Sarti, *Fascism and Industrial Leadership in Italy, 1919–1940: A Study in the Expansion of Private Power under Fascism.* (Berkeley: University of California Press, 1971).
2. Edward R. Tannenbaum, *The Fascist Experience, Italian Society and Culture, 1922–1945.* (New York: Basic Books, 1972).
3. R. L. Carsten, *The Rise of Fascism* (Berkeley: University of California Press, 1967).
4. David Schoenbaum, *Hitler's Social Revolution* (New York: Anchor Books, 1967).

5. William Manchester, *The Arms of Krupp, 1587–1968* (New York: Bantam, 1970).
6. William Shirer, *The Rise and Fall of the Third Reich* (New York: Simon and Schuster, 1960).
7. Masao Maruyama, "The Ideology and Dynamics of Japanese Fascism," in Ivan Morris, ed., Masao Maruyama, *Thought and Behavior in Japanese Politics,* 1963 (New York: Oxford University Press, 1969).
8. "The Ideology and Dynamics of Japanese Fascism."
9. *Fascism and Industrial Leadership in Italy, 1919–1940.*
10. *Fascism and Industrial Leadership in Italy, 1919–1940.*
11. Robert A. Brady, *Business as a System of Power* (New York: Columbia University Press, 1943).
12. Speech to Nuremberg Congress, September 3, 1933.
13. Hermann Rauschning, *The Voice of Destruction* (New York: Putnam's, 1940).
14. *The Rise and Fall of the Third Reich.*
15. *The Rise and Fall of the Third Reich.*
16. Robert Payne, *The Life and Death of Adolph Hitler* (New York: Praeger, 1973).
17. *The Life and Death of Adolph Hitler.*
18. *The Rise and Fall of the Third Reich.*
19. *The Rise and Fall of the Third Reich.*
20. Albert Speer, *Inside the Third Reich* (New York: Macmillan, 1970).
21. Hermann Rauschning, *The Revolution of Nihilism* (New York: Longmans Green, 1930).
22. *The Rise and Fall of the Third Reich.*
23. *The Wave of the Future.*
24. Lawrence Dennis, *Operational Thinking for Survival* (Colorado Springs: Ralph Miles Publisher, 1969).
25. Hugh R. Trevor-Roper, *The Last Days of Hitler* (London: Macmillan, 1956).
26. Carl J. Freidrich and Zbigniew Brzezinski, *Totalitarian Dictatorship and Autocracy* (New York: Praeger, 1961).

Chapter 2: The Takeoff Toward a New Corporate Society

1. "The Internationalization of Capital," *Journal of Economic Issues,* March 1972.
2. Zbigniew Brzezinski, *Between Two Ages* (New York: Viking, 1970).
3. Daniel Fusfeld, "The Rise of the Corporate State in America," *Journal of Economic Issues,* March 1972.
4. Charles L. Mee, Jr. *Meeting at Potsdam* (New York: M. Evans, 1975).
5. Amaury de Riencourt, *The American Empire* (New York: Delta, 1968).
6. Andrew Shonfield, *Modern Capitalism* (New York: Oxford University Press, 1965).
7. V. I. Lenin, "Introduction," Nicolai Bukharin, *Imperialism and World Economy,* 1915 (New York: Monthly Review Press, 1973).
8. *Imperialism and World Economy.*
9. V. I. Lenin, *Imperialism, the Highest Stage of Capitalism* 1916 (Moscow: Progress Publishers, 1970).
10. Susanne Bodenheimer, "Dependency and Imperialism," in K. T. Fann and Donald C. Hodges, eds. *Readings in Imperialism* (Boston: Peter Sargent, 1971).
11. General Golbery do Couto e Silva, quoted by Eduardo Galeano, "Brazil and Uruguay: Euphoria and Agony," *Monthly Review,* February, 1972.
12. Sylvia Porter "The New Monetary System," *New York Post,* September 13, 1971.
13. "Western Policies the Topic at Meeting of Elite," *New York Times,* April 25, 1977.
14. *Between Two Ages.*
15. Anthony Eden, "Getting the Free World Together," *New York Times,* May 5, 1972.
16. *Newsweek,* June 16, 1975.
17. Ralph Nader, Introduction to Morton Mintz and Jerry S. Cohen, *America, Inc.* (New York: Dial Press, 1971).

18. James O'Connor, *Fiscal Crisis of the State* (New York: St. Martin's Press, 1973)
19. Kenneth Boulding, *The Meaning of the Twentieth Century* (New York: Harper & Row, 1964)
20. Alvin Toffler, *The Third Wave.*
21. Lord Ritchie Calder, quoted by Alvin Toffler, *The Third Wave.*
22. National Science Foundation, Experimental Research Program on Appropriate Technology, Division of Intergovernmental Science and Applied Technology, approved by the National Science Board, January 17, 1980.
23. I have provided a more detailed review of productivity and efficiency indicators in my *Organizations and Their Managing* (New York: Free Press, 1968).

Chapter 3: The Mysterious Establishment

1. Herbert Gans, *Deciding What's News: A Study of CBS Evening News, NBC Nightly News, Newsweek and Time* (New York: Pantheon, 1978).
2. The most significant general books on the American power structure are these: G. William Domhoff, *Who Rules America?* (Englewood Cliffs: Prentice-Hall, 1967); *Who Really Rules? New Haven and Community Power Re-Examined* (Santa Monica: Goodyear Publishing, 1978); *The Powers That Be: Processes of Ruling Class Domination in America* (New York: Vintage, 1979); Gabriel Kolko, *Wealth and Power in America* (New York: Praeger, 1962); Ferdinand Lundberg, *The Rich and the Super-Rich* (New York: Lyle Stuart, 1968); C. Wright Mills, *The Power Elite* (New York: Oxford University Press, 1956); Morton Mintz and Jerry S. Cohen, *America, Inc.* (New York: Dial Press, 1971), and *Power, Inc.* (New York: Viking, 1976). There are also other books that deal with important aspects of the subject: Richard J. Barber, *The American Corporation: Its Power, Its Money, Its Politics* (New York: Dutton, 1970); Richard J. Barnet and Ronald Muller, *Global Reach* (New York: Simon and Schuster, 1975); John Blair, *Economic Concentration: Structure, Behavior and Public Policy* (New York: Harcourt Brace Jovanovich, 1972); Andrew Hacker, *The Corporation Take-Over* (New York: Harper and Row, 1964); Stanislas Menshikov, *Millionaires and Managers: Structure of U.S. Financial Oligarchy* (Moscow: Progress Publishers, 1969); and Andreas K. Papandreou, *Paternalistic Capitalism* (Minneapolis: University of Minnesota Press, 1972).
3. Robert Townsend: Review of Robert Heilbroner, et al. "In the Name of Profit," *The New York Times Book Review,* April 30, 1972.
4. Leonard Silk, *Capitalism, The Moving Target* (New York: Quadrangle, 1974).
5. Paul Samuelson, *Economics,* 9th Ed. (New York: McGraw-Hill, 1973).
6. *The Rich and the Super-Rich.*
7. Arthur M. Louis, "America's Centimillionaires," *Fortune,* May 1968.
8. *Report on Millionaires:* report by U.S. Trust Company of New York, June 27, 1979.
9. Herman P. Miller, "Inequality, Poverty and Taxes," *Dissent,* Winter 1975.
10. Murray Rothbard Letter to the Editor, *New York Times,* March 1, 1972.
11. *The Power Elite.*
12. Richard J. Barber, *The American Corporation* (New York: E.P. Dutton, 1970).
13. Gerald Colby Zilg, *Behind the Nylon Curtain* (Englewood Cliffs: Prentice-Hall, 1974).
14. Robert Heilbroner, *The Limits of American Capitalism* (New York: Harper Torchbooks, 1966).
15. *The American Corporation.*
16. Senator Lee Metcalf, Congressional Record, June 24, 1971, cited in Richard May, *The Wall Street Game* (New York: Praeger, 1974).
17. Andrew Hacker, *The End of the American Era* (New York: Atheneum, 1970).
18. Bertram Gross, "The Secret Success of Jimmy Carter: Profits Without Honor," *The Nation,* June 2, 1979.
19. Marriner Eccles, *Fortune,* January, 1961.
20. The chart is borrowed from G. William Domhoff, *The Powers That Be* (New York: Random House, 1979). My only addition is the title.
21. This discussion is based largely on Domhoff's *The Powers That Be.*
22. For background in Greenbriar Conference: Domhoff, *The Powers That Be;*

Wesley McCune, *Who's Behind Our Farm Policy?* (New York: Praeger, 1956); James Deakin, *The Lobbyists* (Washington, D.C.: Public Affairs Press, 1966); and Donald R. Hall, *Cooperative Lobbying—The Power of Pressure* (University of Arizona Press, 1969).
23. Andreas Papandreou, *Paternalistic Capitalism* (Minneapolis: University of Minnesota Press, 1972).
24. Daniel Bell, *The Coming of Post-Industrial Society* (New York: Basic Books, 1973).
25. John K. Galbraith, *The New Industrial State* (New York: Mentor, 1968).
26. Daniel P. Moynihan, "The Professionalization of Reform," *The Public Interest*, Fall 1975.
27. *The Rich and the Super-Rich.*
28. D. F. Fleming, *The Cold War and Its Origins* (New York: Doubleday, 1961).
29. James MacGregor Burns, *Roosevelt: The Soldier of Freedom, 1940–1945* (New York: Harcourt Brace Jovanovich, 1970).
30. Ronald Radosh, *Prophets on the Right* (New York: Simon and Schuster, 1975).
31. Walter Goodman, *The Committee* (New York: Farrar, Straus and Giroux, 1968).
32. Irving Howe and Lewis Coser, *The American Communist Party* (New York: Praeger, 1963 edit.).
33. Frank Friedel, *America in the Twentieth Century* (New York: Knopf, 1965).
34. Colonel James A. Donovan, *Militarism, U.S.A.* (New York: Charles Scribner's Sons, 1970).
35. Francis X. Sutton, Seymour Harris, Carl Kaysen and James Tobin, *The American Business Creed*, 1956 (New York: Schocken, 1962).
36. Carl Kaysen, "The Social Significance of the Modern Corporation," *American Economic Review*, May 1957.
37. C. L. Sulzberger, "Should the Old Labels be Changed?" *New York Times*, July 1964. Quoted in Ayn Rand, *Capitalism: The Unknown Ideal* (New York: Signet, 1967).
38. *Capitalism: The Unknown Ideal.*
39. Arthur Burns, *Looking Forward*, 31st Annual Report of the National Bureau of Economic Research, 1951.
40. Seymour Martin Lipset, *Political Man* (New York: Doubleday, 1960).
41. Daniel Bell, *The End of Ideology* (Glencoe, Ill.: Free Press, 1960).
42. *The Coming of Post-Industrial Society.*
43. John K. Galbraith, *The New Industrial State* (Boston: Houghton Mifflin, 1967).
44. John K. Galbraith, *Economics and the Public Purpose* (Boston: Houghton Mifflin, 1973).
45. Amitai Etzioni and Richard Remp, "Technological 'Shortcuts' to Social Change," *Science*, January 7, 1972.

Chapter 4: The Side Effects of Success

1. *New York Times*, May 7, 1973.
2. Charles Reich, *The Greening of America* (New York: Random House, 1970).
3. Stanislas Andreski, "On the Likelihood of the Possibility of a Collapse of the Political System of the United States of America."
4. James Reston, "Who Speaks for America?" *New York Times*, April 16, 1972.
5. "The Dirty Work," *Wall Street Journal*, July 16, 1971.
6. Report of a Special Task Force to the Secretary of Health, Education and Welfare, *Work in America* (Cambridge: MIT Press, 1973).
7. Robert Dubin, "Workers," *International Encyclopedia of the Social Sciences*, vol. 16 (New York: Macmillan, 1968).
8. John and Barbara Ehrenreich, "Work and Consciousness," *Monthly Review*, July-August 1976.
9. Vance Packard, *A Nation of Strangers* (New York: McKay, 1972).
10. Richard Goodwin, *The American Condition* (Garden City: Doubleday, 1974).
11. Edward Shorter, *The Making of the Modern Family* (New York: Basic Books, 1975).

12 Suzanne Gordon, *Lonely in America* (New York: Simon and Schuster, 1976).
13. Hannah Arendt, *The Origins of Totalitarianism* (New York: Meridian, 1958).
14. *The American Condition.*
15. Hans Morgenthau, "Reflections on the End of the Republic," *New York Review of Books,* September 24, 1970.
16. George Charles Roche III, *The Bewildered Society* (New York: Arlington House, 1972).
17. HEW, *Work in America.*
18. Studs Terkel, *Working* (New York: Pantheon, 1974).
19. Abraham Briloff, *Unaccountable Accounting* (New York: Harper & Row, 1972).
20. *Lonely in America.*
21. Donald W. Tiffany, James R. Cowan and Phyllis M. Tiffany, *The Unemployed* (Englewood Cliffs: Prentice Hall, 1970).
22. Harvey Brenner, *Mental Illness and Economy* (Cambridge: Harvard University Press, 1973).
23. Edgar Z. Friedenberg, *Coming of Age in America* (New York: Random House, 1965).
24. Margaret Mead, *Culture and Commitment* (Garden City: Doubleday, 1970).
25. Clayton Fritchey, "Crime and Politics," *New York Post,* May 4, 1976.
26. Abraham Lass, "1+1=Terror," *New York Times,* November 20, 1971.
27. Quoted by Robert N. Winter-Berger, *The Washington Pay-Off* (New York: Dell, 1972).
28. Herbert Robinson, "Discount Group Hears a Prediction of Wave of Pay-Offs," *New York Times,* May 23, 1972.
29. "Federal Agencies Press Inquiry of Housing Frauds in Big Cities," *New York Times,* May 8, 1972.
30. David Durk, "Viva La Policia," *New York Times,* December 29, 1971.
31. Edwin H. Sutherland, *White Collar Crime,* 1949 (New York: Holt, Rinehart and Winston, 1961).
32. *White Collar Crime.*
33. *The Rich and the Super-Rich.*
34. Jack Anderson, with Les Whitten, "Haldeman On His Mind," *New York Post,* September 13, 1975.
35. Ralph Nader, Introduction, *America, Inc.*
36. Michael Tanzer, *The Sick Society* (New York: Holt, Rinehart and Winston, 1971).
37. Ward Just, *Military Men* (New York: Knopf, 1970).
38. Arthur H. Miller, Alden S. Raine and Thad A. Brown, "Integration and Estrangement," *Society,* July/August, 1976.

Chapter 5: The Challenge of a Shrinking Capitalist World

1. Daniel Bell, "The End of American Exceptionalism," *The Public Interest,* Fall 1975.
2. Michael Harrington, *Socialism* (New York: Saturday Review Press, 1972).
3. United Nation Declaration on the Establishment of a New International Economic Order, 1974.
4. "One could say that a state of cold war has marked the relations of the Soviet Union with the other leading powers ever since the cessation of open conflict between the new Bolshevik regime and the 'imperialists' in the early 1920s." Henry L. Roberts, "The Cold War," in John A. Garraty and Peter Gay, eds. *The Columbia History of the World* (New York: Harper and Row, 1972).
5. "A Conversation with George Kennan," interview with George Urban, *Encounter,* September 1976.
6. "Review of Current Trends in Business and Finance," based on a report by the secretariat of the Economic Commission for Europe. *Wall Street Journal,* August 18, 1975.
7. Mary Kaldor, *The Disintegrating West* (New York: Hill and Wang, 1978).

Chapter 6: Old Crises in New Forms

1. "Notes on the U.S. Situation at the End of 1972," *Monthly Review,* January 1973.
2. Paul Samuelson, *Economics* (New York: McGraw-Hill, 1973, Ninth Edition).
3. William Safire, "What Recession?" *New York Times,* October 10, 1974.
4. This is my own interpretation, in "Welcome to Stagflation," *The Nation,* August 1979.
5. Walter Grinder, *Business Week,* August 4, 1974.
6. Frank F. Furstenberg, Jr. and Charles A. Thrall, "Counting the Jobless: The Impact of Job Rationing on the Measurement of Unemployment," in Stanley Moses, ed. *Planning for Full Employment,* The Annals, March 1975.
7. Quoted in Bertram M. Gross, "Anti-Inflation for Progressives," *The Nation,* June 23, 1979.
8. Gene Koretz, "Global Inflation: A Disease in Search of a Cure," *Business Week,* March 1974.
9. Stated for first time in "Welcome to Stagflation."
10. Stephen Hymer, "The Internationalization of Capital."
11. *Business Week,* September 24, 1979.
12. Harry Braverman, *Labor and Monopoly Capital* (New York: Monthly Review Press, 1974).
13. *The Fiscal Crisis of the State.*
14. David Bazelon, *The Paper Economy* (New York: Random House, 1963).
15. *The Economic Impact of Disarmament* (Washington, D.C.: U.S. Government Printing Office, January 1962).
16. Captain David M. Saunders, U.S. Naval Institute Proceedings, September 1965.
17. Robert Tucker, "Israel and the United States," *Commentary,* November 1975.
18. Hasan Ozbekhan, "The Role of Goals and Planning in the Solution of the World Food Problem," in Robert Jungk and Johan Galtung (eds.), *Mankind 2000* (Boston: Universitetsforlaget, 1969).
19. Robert Clarke, *The Science of War and Peace* (New York: McGraw-Hill, 1972).
20. J. B. Phelps et al., *Accidental War: Some Dangers in the 1960's* (Ohio: Mershon National Security Program, Ohio State University, 1960).

Chapter 7: The Unfolding Logic

1. Walter Laqueur, "Fascism—the Second Coming," *Commentary,* February 1976.
2. John D. Rockefeller, *The Second American Revolution* (New York: Harper and Row, 1973).
3. Ronald Steel, "Interview with Walter Lippmann," *Washington Post,* March 25, 1973.
4. Robert Michels, *Political Parties,* 1915, Eden and Cedar Paul, tr., (Glencoe, Ill.: Free Press, 1949).
5. C. L. Sulzberger, "Heart of U.S. Darkness," *New York Times,* March 31, 1974.
6. Michel Crozier, Samuel Huntington, and Joji Watanuki, *The Crisis of Democracy* (New York; New York University, 1975). Michel Crozier has informed me that he never agreed with Huntington on this point, and in his new book *On Ne Change Pas La Societe Par Decret* (Paris, Bernard Grosset, 1979), Crozier urges more democracy, not less.
7. Alan Wolfe, "Capitalism Shows Its Face: Giving Up of Democracy," *The Nation,* November 29, 1975.
8. Donald Zoll, "Shall We Let America Die?" *National Review,* December 16, 1969.
9. Maxwell Taylor, *Swords and Ploughshares* (New York: Norton, 1972).
10. Speech at the Virginia Convention, June 16, 1788.
11. Editorial, "Subverting America," *New York Times,* June 17, 1973.
12. "Sumitomo: How the 'Keiretsu' Pulls to Keep Japan Strong," *Business Week,* March 31, 1975.
13. Richard Falk, "A New Paradigm for International Legal Studies," *Yale Law Journal,* April 1975.

14. "The Specter of Weimer," *Commentary,* December 1971. A similar poin is made by Arnold Beichmann in *Nine Lies About America.*

Chapter 8: Trilateral Empire or Fortress America?

1. Victor Zorza, "Soviet Nightmares," *Washington Post,* March 5, 1976.
2. Margarita Maximova, *Economic Aspects of Capitalist Integration* (Moscow: Progress Publishers, 1973).
3. Sankar Ray, "U.S. and European Multinationals: Intensified Contradictions," *The Economic Times,* New Delhi, January 16, 1976.
4. Gabriel Kolko, "Vietnam and the Future of U.S. Foreign Policy," *Liberation,* May 1973.
5. "Angola: What is Moscow Up To?" *National Review,* March 19, 1976.
6. Irving Kristol, "Kissinger at Dead End," *Wall Street Journal,* March 10, 1976.
7. Peter Berger, "The Greening of American Foreign Policy," *Commentary,* March 1976.
8. C. L. Sulzberger, "Our Haphazard Empire," *New York Times,* March 17, 1977.
9. George Liska, *Imperial America* (Baltimore: Johns Hopkins, 1967).
10. Robert Osgood, "The Nixon Doctrine and Strategy," in Robert E. Osgood, et al., *Retreat from Empire?* (Baltimore: Johns Hopkins, 1973).
11. Robert Tucker, "The American Outlook: Change and Continuity," in Osgood, *Retreat from Empire?*
12. *Between Two Ages.*
13. George Liska, *Beyond Kissinger: Ways of Conservative Statecraft* (Baltimore: Johns Hopkins, 1976).
14. *Between Two Ages.*
15. Henry Kissinger, "Defense of 'Grey Areas'", *Foreign Affairs,* April 1955.
16. David Binder, "A Modified Soviet Bloc in U.S. Policy," *New York Times,* April 6, 1976.
17. Robert Pfaltzgraff, Jr., "The United States and a Strategy for the West," *Strategic Review,* Summer 1977.

Chapter 9: The Friendly Fascist Establishment

1. Amaury de Riencourt, *The Coming Caesars* (New York: Capricorn, 1964.
2. Eugene J. Kaplan, *Japan, the Government Business Relationship* (Washington, D.C.: U.S. Government Printing Office, 1972).
3. Richard F. Janssen, *Wall Street Journal,* April 24, 1972.
4. "The New Banking," *Business Week,* September 15, 1973.
5. *Future Shock.*
6. Arthur S. Miller, *The Modern Corporate State: Private Governments and the American Constitution* (Westport: Greenwood Press, 1976).
7. Paul Dickson, *Think Tanks* (New York: Atheneum, 1971).
8. This is a slight expansion of the analysis by Michael Klare in *War Without End* (New York: Vintage, 1972).
9. Richard Falk, "Exporting Counterrevolution," *The Nation,* Special Issue on Intervention, June 9, 1979.
10. Quoted by Colonel James A. Donovan in his *Militarism, U.S.A.*
11. Richard A. Gabriel and Paul L. Savage, *Crisis in Command: Mismanagement in the Army* (New York: Hill and Wang, 1978).
12. William W. Turner, *Power on the Right* (Berkeley: Ramparts, 1971).
13. Sasha Lewis, "The Far Right Plan for 1980," *Seven Days,* August 14, 1979.
14. Joseph Trento and Joseph Spear, "How Nazi Nut Power Has Invaded Capitol Hill," *True,* November 1969.
15. Falangist Party of America, *Prospectus,* Box 5, Crystal Bay, Minnesota, 1979.
16. This is discussed in Bertram Gross, "Anti-Inflation for Progressives," *The Nation.*
17. Americans for Democratic Action, *A Citizen's Guide to the Right Wing,* Washington, D.C., 1978.

18. Quoted by Steve Manning, "'New Right' Forces Expect to Win," *Guardian*, October 3, 1979.
19. Arno Mayer, *Dynamics of Counter-Revolution in Europe, 1870–1956* (New York: Harper Torchbooks, 1971).
20. "American Intellectuals and Foreign Policy," *Foreign Affairs*, July, 1967, reprinted in *On the Democratic Idea in America* (New York: Harper & Row, 1972).
21. "Capitalism 101," *Newsweek*, April 30, 1979.
22. Peter Steinfels, *The Neoconservatives: The Men Who Are Changing America's Politics* (New York: Simon and Schuster, 1979).
23. Robert Nisbet, *The Twilight of Authority* (New York: Oxford University Press, 1975).
24. Daniel Bell, *The Coming of Post-Industrial Society* (New York: Basic Books, 1973).
25. Philip Boffey, *The Brain Bank of America* (New York: McGraw-Hill, 1975).
26. Ida Hoos, "Models, Methods, and Myths—the Mystique of Modern Management," paper delivered at 1975 Winter Computer Simulation Conference, Sacramento, California, December 18, 1975.
27. Ida Hoos, *Systems Analysis in Public Policy: A Critique* (Berkeley: University of California, 1972).
28. B. F. Skinner, *Beyond Freedom and Dignity* (New York: Knopf, 1971).
29. Jose M. R. Delgado, M.D., *Physical Control of the Mind* (New York: Harper & Row, 1969).
30. Charles Merriam, *Political Power*, 1934 (Glencoe, Ill.: Free Press, 1950).
31. Daniel P. Moynihan, "The United States in Opposition," *Commentary*, March, 1975.
32. Walter Laqueur, "The Issue of Human Rights," *Commentary*, May, 1977.

Chapter 10: Friendly Fascist Economics

1. Irving Kristol, "The Worst Is Yet to Come," *Wall Street Journal*, November 26, 1979.
2. Daniel Fusfield, "Introduction," Arthur S. Miller, *The Modern Corporate State*.
3. Robert Theobald, "What New Directions for Society?" *Los Angeles Times*, May 24, 1970.
4. A. W. Phillips, "The Relation Between Unemployment and the Rate of Change of Money Wage Rates in the United Kingdom, 1861–1957," *Economics*, November 1958.
5. Steven Rattner, "Executives Fail Fed's New Policy," *New York Times*, October 15, 1979.
6. Herman Kahn, *The Next 200 Years* (New York: Morrow, 1976).
7. *The Next 200 Years*.
8. Barry Commoner, *The Poverty of Power* (New York: Knopf, 1976).
9. *The Next 200 Years*.
10. Jim Hightower, *Eat Your Heart Out* (New York: Crown, 1975).
11. Mihajlo Mesarovic and Eduard Pestel, *Mankind at the Turning Point* (New York: Dutton, 1974).
12. James Ridgeway, *The Last Play* (New York: Dutton, 1973).
13. Robert Engler, *The Politics of Oil* (Chicago: University of Chicago Press, 1961), and *The Brotherhood of Oil* (Chicago: University of Chicago Press, 1977); and John Blair, *The Control of Oil* (New York: Pantheon, 1976).
14. Quoted by Anthony Sampson in his vivid *The Seven Sisters: The Great Oil Companies and the World They Shaped* (New York: Viking, 1975).
15. Barry Commoner, *The Poverty of Power* (New York: Knopf, 1976).
16. Editorial, "Capping Third World Gushers," *The Nation*, July 28-August 4, 1979.
17. Barry Commoner, *The Closing Circle* (New York: Knopf, 1971).
18. Barry Weisberg, *Beyond Repair* (Boston: Beacon, 1971).
19. *Beyond Repair*.
20. *The Next 200 Years*.
21. Donella Meadows, et al. *The Limits of Growth* (New York: Universe, 1972).

22. *The Next 200 Years.*
23. Robert Heilbroner, "Ecological Armageddon," *New York Review of Books,* May 23, 1970.
24. Ozorio de Almeida, "Development and Environment," *The Founex Report,* Carnegie Endowment for International Peace, 1972.
25. David Burnham, "Presidential Panel Asks Curbs on Chemical Perils," *New York Times,* August 15, 1979.
26. Helen Caldicott, *Nuclear Madness* (Brookline, Mass.: Autumn Press, 1978).
27. Dr. John W. Gofman and Dr. Arthur Tamplin, quoted by Dr. Helen Caldicott in *Nuclear Madness.* Dr. Caldicott also cites the numerous publications of Dr. John W. Gofman.
28. *Nuclear Madness.*
29. Anthony Lewis, "Act Now, Pay Later," *New York Times,* December 6, 1979.
30. Vance Packard, *The Waste Makers* (New York: David McKay, 1960).
31. *Beyond Repair.*
32. *Eat Your Heart Out.*
33. "A. Dale Console," in Ralph Nader, et al., *Whistle Blowing* (New York: Grossman, 1972).
34. Dr. Richard Kunnes, *Your Money or Your Life* (New York: Dodd Mead, 1971).

Chapter 11: Subverting Democratic Machinery

1. Murray B. Levin, *Political Hysteria in America* (New York: Basic Books, 1971).
2. Thomas R. Nye and Harmon Ziegler, *The Irony of Democracy* (Belmont, California: Wadsworth, 1971).
3. Yvonne Karp, *Eleanor Marx,* Vol. Two (New York: Pantheon, 1977).
4. Lawrence Dennis, *The Coming of American Fascism* (New York: Harper, 1936).
5. Robert L. Peabody, "House Leadership, Party Caucauses and the Committee Structure," *Committee Organization in the House,* Vol. 2, Select Committee on Committees, 1974.
6. L. D. Solomon, "For New York a Time of Testing as the Nation Looks On," *New York Times,* February 21, 1976.
7. Roger Alcaly, "New York: Waiting for the Dough," *Seven Days,* October, 6, 1975.
8. "For New York a Time of Testing as the Nation Looks On."
9. Interview by Ronald Steel, "Walter Lippmann at 83," *Washington Post,* March 25, 1973.
10. Barrington Moore, *Social Origins of Dictatorship and Democracy* (Boston: Beacon, 1967).
11. Garry Wills, *Nixon Agonistes* (New York: Signet, 1972).
12. Interview with *New York Times,* November 10, 1972.
13. Murray Edelman, *The Symbolic Uses of Politics* (Urbana: University of Illinois, 1964).
14. *The Rich and the Super-Rich.*
15. Douglas Fraser, President of the United Automobile Workers Union, Public Statement, 1979.
16. Quoted by James Farmer in *The Hired Guns of De-Unionization* (Washington, D.C.: Coalition of American Public Employees, 1979).
17. Karl Polanyi, *The Great Transformation: The Political and Economic Origins of Our Time* (Boston: Beacon, 1957).
18. Debra Hauser, "The Union-Busting Hustle," *The New Republic,* August 25, 1979.
19. James Farmer, *The Hired Guns of De-Unionization* and Phyllis Payne, "The Plot To Subvert Labor Standards," *AFL-CIO American Federationist,* July 1979.
20. Personal comment, reported by Sidney Dean of New York City.

21. *The Rich and the Super-Rich.*
22. Edward Luttwak, *Coup D'Etat* (London: Penguin, 1968).

Chapter 12: Managing Information and Minds

1. Herbert Schiller, *The Mind Managers* (Boston: Beacon, 1973).
2. Arthur R. Miller, *The Assault on Privacy* (Ann Arbor: University of Michigan Press, 1971).
3. William A. Caldwell, *How to Save Urban America* (New York: New American Library, 1973).
4. Adolph Hitler, *Mein Kampf.*
5. George Gerbner, "Communications and Social Environment," *Scientific American,* September 1972.
6. *The Mind Managers.*
7. Aldous Huxley, *Brave New World* (New York: Harper & Row, 1958).
8. Fred W. Friendly, *Due to Circumstances Beyond Our Control* (New York: Random House, 1967).
9. Statement to the Author by Theodore Gross, editor of *Boston Phoenix,* and *Boston After Dark.*
10. Daniel Boorsteen, quoted in H. Falk, "The Sound and the Fury," *Wall Street Journal,* September 1971.
11. Statement to the author by Larry P. Gross at Annenberg School of Communications, University of Pennsylvania, January 1976.
12. *The Mind Managers.*
13. Harold Mendelson and Irving Crespi, *Polls, Television and the New Politics* (Scranton: Chandler, 1970).
14. Joe McGinniss, *The Selling of the President 1968* (New York: Pocket Books, 1968).
15. *Transaction,* July-August 1971.
16. Edmund Carpenter, *The Dick Cavett Show,* April 1971.
17. Fred W. Friendly, "Foreword" to Newton Minow et al., *Presidential Television* (New York: Basic Books, 1973).
18. Felicia Lampert, "Deprivacy," reprinted from *Look* in frontispiece to Arthur R. Miller, *The Assault on Privacy* (Ann Arbor: University of Michigan, 1971).
19. Joseph Meyer, "Crime Deterrent Transponder System," *Transmission on Aerospace of Privacy,* July 26, 1966.
20. Paul Baran, *Hearings before the House Special Subcommittee on Invasion of Privacy,* July 26, 1966.
21. Richard M. Nixon, Executive Order 11605, July 2, 1971.
22. James Mardian, Address to the Atomic Energy Commission Security Conference, October 27, 1971.
23. Kenyon B. De Greene, *Sociotechnical Systems* (Englewood Cliffs: Prentice Hall, 1973).
24. Abraham Briloff, *Unaccountable Accounting* (New York: Harper and Row, 1972).
25. Raymond A. Bauer and Daniel H. Fenn, Jr., *The Corporate Social Audit* (New York: Russell Sage Foundation, 1972).
26. William Nordhaus and James Tobin, "Is Growth Obsolete?" National Bureau of Economic Research, *Fiftieth Anniversary Colloquium,* 1972.
27. Paul Samuelson, *Economics,* 9th edition (New York: McGraw-Hill, 1973).
28. Bertram Gross, "The Social State of the Union," *Transaction,* November 1965; Bertram Gross, *The State of the Nation, Social Systems Accounting* (London: Tavistock, 1967). Also in Raymond A. Bauer, Ed., *Social Indicators* (Cambridge, MIT Press, 1966); and Bertram Gross, ed. A. broad review of social indicators and vindicators appears in Bertram Gross and Jeffrey D. Straussman, "The Social Indicators Movement," *Social Policy,* September/October 1974.
29. Richard Greeman, review of James Ridgeway, *The Closed Corporation: Universities in Crisis,* in Tom Christoffel et al. *Up Against the American Myth* (New York: Holt, Rinehart and Winston, 1970).

Chapter 13: Incentives for Systems Acceptance

1. B. F. Skinner, *Beyond Freedom and Dignity* (New York: Knopf, 1971).
2. Aldous Huxley, *Brave New World,* 1932 (New York: Perennial Classic Edition, 1969).
3. Reimut Reiche, *Sexuality and Class Struggle,* 1968, Susan Bennett, Tr. (London: New Left Review Edition, 1970).
4. *Brave New World.*
5. Norman Podhoretz, *Making It* (New York, Bantam Books, 1967).
6. Lewis Mumford, *The Pentagon of Power* (New York: Harcourt Brace, Jovanovich, Inc., 1970).
7. *Future Shock.*
8. Steffan B. Linder, *The Harried Leisure Class* (New York: Columbia University Press, 1970).
9. John K. Galbraith, *Economics and the Public Service* (Boston: Houghton Mifflin, 1973).
10. Frances Fox Piven and Richard A. Cloward, *Regulating the Poor* (New York: Pantheon, 1971).
11. Walter Sullivan, "Scientists Foresee a Longer Life Span, Mainly for the Affluent," *New York Times,* February 23, 1971.

Chapter 14: The Ladder of Terror

1. *Report of National Commission on the Causes and Prevention of Violence* (Washington, D.C.: U.S. Government Printing Office, 1969).
2. Albert Thayer Mahan, *Time,* August 4, 1958.
3. Herman Kahn, *On Escalation* (Baltimore: Penguin, 1968).
4. *Wall Street Journal,* March 17, 1972.
5. *Wall Street Journal,* May 2, 1976.
6. *Wall Street Journal,* May 2, 1976.
7. Richard Harris, "The New Justice," *The New Yorker,* March 25, 1972.
8. Ronald Reagan, cited by Kenneth Lamott, *Anti-California: Report from Our First Parafascist State* (Boston: Little Brown, 1971).
9. Alan L. Oten, *Wall Street Journal,* April 8, 1971.
10. Thomas Szasz, *The Manufacture of Madness* (New York: Harper and Row, 1970).
11. Eugene V. Walker, *Terror and Resistance* (New York: Oxford University Press, 1969).
12. Diane Henry, "CIA's Clandestine Work Assailed Here," *New York Times,* March 26, 1975.
13. Miles Copeland, "Is There a CIA in Your Future?" *National Review,* March 1975.
14. Walter Sullivan, testimony before Senate Select Committee on Intelligence Activities, *Intelligence Activities and the Rights of Americans* (Washington, D.C.: U.S. Government Printing Office, 1976), excerpted in *New York Times,* April 29, 1976.
15. *Intelligence Activities and the Rights of Americans.*
16. John W. Crewdson, "Ex-Operative Says He Worked for FBI to Disrupt Political Activities Up to '74," *New York Times,* February 24, 1975.
17. Homer Bigart, *New York Times,* "Ex-Operative Says He Worked for FBI to Disrupt Political Activities up to '74," March 23, 1972.
18. Nathan Glazer and Daniel P. Moynihan, *Beyond the Melting Pot,* 2nd edition (Cambridge: M.I.T. Press, 1970).
19. Andrew Hacker, *The End of the American Era* (New York: Athaneum, 1970).
20. Kanti C. Kotecha and James L. Walker, "Police Vigilantes," *Society,* March/April, 1976.
21. Alan Wolfe, "Extralegality and American Power," *Society,* March/April, 1976.
22. George Gerbner and Larry P. Gross, "Living with Television: The Violence Profile," *Journal of Communication,* April, 1976.

Chapter 15: Sex, Drugs, Madness, Cults

1. Wilhelm Reich, *The Mass Psychology of Fascism,* Vincent R. Carfagno, Tr. (New York: Farrar, Straus and Giroux, 1970).
2. Anselma Dell'Olio, "The Sexual Revolution Wasn't Our War," *MS.,* Spring, 1972.
3. Harrison Pope, Jr., *Voices from the Drug Culture* (Boston, Beacon Press, 1971).
4. Dr. Marshall Dumont, "Mainlining America: Why the Young Use Drugs," *Social Policy,* November/December, 1971.
5. Henry L. Leondar and Associates, *Mystification and Drug Abuse* (San Francisco: Jossey-Bass, 1971).
6. Charles Witter, *Trans-Action,* July/August, 1971.
7. *New York Times,* September 5, 1971.
8. Kenneth Clark, "Leadership and Psychotechnology," *New York Times,* November 9, 1971.
9. *Journal of the Cincinnati Lancet Clinic, 1889.*
10. Sigmund Freud, *Civilization and Its Discontents* (London: Hogarth Press, 1953).
11. Thomas Szasz, *Law, Liberty and Psychiatry* (New York: Collier, 1968).
12. Dr. Gerald Klerman, quoted by David Brand in "Beyond the Blues," *Wall Street Journal,* April 7, 1972.
13. Dr. David Rosenthal, *Report for National Institute for Mental Health,* April 1972.
14. G. Brock Chisholm, "The Psychiatry of Enduring Peace and Social Progress," *Psychiatry,* January 1946.
15. "Religious Cults," *U.S. News and World Report,* June 14, 1976.
16. Berkeley Rice, 'The Fall of Sun Moon," *New York Times Magazine,* May 30, 1976.
17. Leo Litwak, "Pay Attention, Turkeys," *New York Magazine,* May 2, 1976.
18. Carey McWilliams "The New Fundamentalists," *The Nation,* June 5, 1976.

Chapter 16: The Adaptive Hydra

1. Noah Chomsky, *American Power and the New Mandarins* (New York: Vintage, 1969).
2. *Inside the Third Reich.*
3. Phillip Selznick, *TVA and the Grass Roots* (Berkeley: University of California Press, 1949).
4. *Socialism.*
5. Mary McGrory, "Pleading and Bleeding," *New York Post,* May 6, 1972.
6. Joseph Clark, *Congress: The Sapless Branch* (New York: Harper and Row, 1964).
7. Samuel F. Yette, *The Choice* (New York: Putnam, 1971).
8. Alphonso Pinkney, Personal statement to the author.
9. *Terror and Resistance.*
10. Friedrich and Brzezinski, *Totalitarian Dictatorship and Autocracy.*
11. Paul Goodman, "1984," in Harold Jaffe and John Tytell, *The American Experience, A Radical Reader* (New York: Harper and Row, 1970).
12. Leopold Tyrmand, *The Rosa Luxembourg Contraceptives Cooperative* (New York: Macmillan, 1972).

Chapter 17: The Myths of Determinism

1. Karl Popper, *Unended Quest: An Intelligent Autobiography* (Glasgow: Fontana/Collins, 1976).
2. Corliss Lamont, "The Cassandra in America," *New York Times,* July 25, 1971.
3. Theodore Draper, Letters from Readers, *Commentary,* April 1972.
4. *Without Marx or Jesus.*
5. Friedrich Hayek, *The Road to Serfdom* (Chicago: University of Chicago Press, 1944).

6. Bertram Gross, "Friendly Fascism: Model for America," *Social Policy*, November/December, 1970.
7. Franklin D. Roosevelt, Address at Cambridge, Mass., June 19, 1941.
8. Winston Churchill, Speech on Dunkirk, House of Commons, June 4, 1940.

Chapter 18: It Hasn't Happened Yet

1. Sidney Hook, "The Fallacy of the Theory of Social Fascism," in Louis Filler, ed. *The Anxious Years* (New York: Putnam, 1963).
2. Felix Greene, *The Enemy: What Every American Should Know About Imperialism* (New York: Vintage, 1971).
3. Richard Grunberger, *A Social History of Nazi Germany, 1933–1945* (Holt, Rinehart and Winston, 1971).

Chapter 19: The Long-Term Logic of Democracy

1. William H. Hastie, quoted in George Seldes, ed., *The Great Quotations* (New York: Pocketbooks, 1967).
2. Bernard Smith, Introduction, *The Democratic Spirit* (New York: Knopf, 1941).
3. United Nations Educational, Scientific and Cultural Organization, *Democracy in a World of Tensions: A Symposium*, Richard McKeon, ed. (Chicago: University of Chicago Press, 1951).
4. Harold L. Wilensky, *The New Corporatism, Centralization and the Welfare State* (Beverly Hills: Sage, 1976) and G. David Garson, *The Future of American Public Administration*, A Working Paper, Center for Urban Affairs and Community Services, North Carolina State University, Raleigh, North Carolina.

Chapter 20: The Democratic Logic in Action

1. Vladimir Dedijer, "A Letter to Jean-Paul Sartre," *New York Times*, February 6, 1971.
2. Mary Parker Follett, *The New State* (New York: Longmans, Green, 1918; reprinted Gloucester, Mass.: Peter Smith, 1965).
3. Representative Jim Weaver (D.Ore.), "Weaver on the Draft," *The Reporter for Conscience's Sake*, Washington, D.C., April 1979.
4. James Fenimore Cooper, *The American Democrat: Advantages of a Democracy.*
5. Louis B. Brandeis, *Labor*, October 17, 1941.
6. Robert L. Heilbroner, "The Inescapable Marx," *New York Review of Books*, July 29, 1978.
7. E. F. Schumacher, *Small Is Beautiful: Economics As If People Mattered* (New York: Perennial, 1975).
8. *Economics and the Public Purpose.*
9. *The New State.*
10. Harry Boyte, "A Democratic Awakening," *Social Policy*, Special Issue on Organizing Neighborhoods, September/October, 1979.
11. Hazel Henderson, *Creating Alternative Futures* (New York: Berkeley, 1978).
12. Frank Riessman, "Will Local Populism Lead to a New Progressivism?" *In These Times*, June 13-19, 1979.
13. Karl Marx, Preface to *Capital*, Vol. 1.
14. Ralph Nader, "An Anatomy of Whistle Blowing," in Ralph Nader, et al., *Whistle Blowing* (New York: Grossman, 1972).
15. *Political Hysteria in America.*
16. S. M. Miller, "Police and Science," *Journal of Social Policy*, January 1974.
17. *The Pentagon of Power.*
18. Alfred North Whitehead, *Dialogues of Alfred North Whitehead*, as recorded by Lucien Price (New York: Atlantic Monthly Press, 1954).
19. *Small Is Beautiful.*
20. Mary Parker Follett, *Creative Experience* (New York: Longmans, Green, 1926).

21. Charles E. Lindblom and David K. Cohen, *Usable Knowledge: Social Science and Social Problem Solving* (New Haven: Yale University Press, 1979).
22. Bertram Gross, *The Managing of Organizations* (New York: Free Press, 1964) and "Planning in an Era of Social Revolution," *Public Administration Review*, May/June, 1971.
23. *Labor and Monopoly Capital.*
24. *Small Is Beautiful.*
25. Barrington Moore, Jr., *Reflections on the Causes of Human Misery and Upon Certain Proposals to Eliminate Them* (Boston: Beacon, 1970).
26. Barrington Moore, Jr., *Reflections on the Causes of Human Misery and Upon Certain Proposals to Eliminate Them.*
27. Story first told by Gerhard Colm, "Technical Requirements (for Full Employment)", in "Maintaining High Level Production and Employment: A Symposium," *American Political Science Review*, December 1945.
28. Roland Huntford, *The New Totalitarians* (New York: Stein and Day, 1972).
29. Eric S. Einhorn, "Denmark, Norway and Sweden," in Itzhak Galnoor, *Government Secrecy in Democracies* (New York: Harbor Colophon, 1977).
30. Dankwort A. Rustow, "Transitions to Democracy: Toward a Dynamic Theory," *Comparative Politics*, April 1970.

Chapter 21: What Can You Do?

1. Oliver Wendell Holmes, Jr., Memorial Day Address, 1884.
2. James Weinstein, *Ambiguous Legacy: The Left in American Politics* (New York: New Viewpoints, 1975).
3. John and Barbara Ehrenreich, "Work and Consciousness," *Monthly Review*.
4. Staughton Lynd, "Workers' Control in a Time of Diminished Workers' Rights," *Radical America*, September/October, 1976.
5. Lerone Bennett, Jr., *What Manner of Man: A Biography of Martin Luther King, Jr.* (New York: Pocket Books, 1965).
6. *What Manner of Man....*
7. E. Victor Wolfenstein, *The Revolutionary Personality: Lenin, Trotsky and Gandhi* (Princeton: Princeton University Press, 1967).
8. Christopher Lasch, "The Narcissist Society," *New York Review of Books*, September 30, 1976, p. 5.
9. Edwin Schur, *The Awareness Trap: Self-Absorption Instead of Social Change* (New York: Quadrangle, 1976).
10. Peter Marin, "The Human Harvest," *Mother Jones*, December 1976.
11. Thomas Jefferson, Letter to M. de Meunier, January 24, 1786.
12. Thomas Jefferson, Letter to Horatio G. Spafford, March 17, 1814.
13. Francis W. Coker, "Patriotism," *Encyclopaedia of the Social Sciences* (New York: Macmillan, 1933).
14. *Militarism, U.S.A.*
15. Kalman H. Silvert, *The Reason for Democracy* (New York: Viking, 1977).

About the Author

BERTRAM GROSS is a Distinguished Professor of Public Policy and Planning in the Urban Affairs Department of Hunter College, and a Professor of Political Science in the Graduate Program of City University of New York. He has served in government office, and has written extensively on political and social topics. Among his books is *The Legislative Struggle:* A Study of Social Combat, which won the Woodrow Wilson Prize of the American Political Science Association.

During the Roosevelt and Truman administrations, he served as an advisor in the areas of public housing, war-time price controls, small business, and post-war planning. He was the major architect of the orginal full-employment bills of 1944 and 1945, and of the Employment Act of 1946. With Rep. Augustus Hawkins and the Congressional Black Caucus, he developed the original versions of the Humphrey-Hawkins Full Employment and Balanced Growth Act of 1978. From 1946 to 1951, he served as Executive Secretary on the President's Council of Economic Advisors.

While working on legislation in Congress and the President's office, he wrote *The Legislative Struggle.* After this, he was a visiting professor at the Hebrew University. He has subsequently taught at the University of California, Berkeley, has been a fellow at the Center for Advanced Study in the Behavioral Sciences, a Leatherbee Lecturer at the Harvard School of Business Administration, and a Professor of Administration at Syracuse University's Maxwell School, where he completed work on his two-volume *The Managing of Organizations.* He was the founder of the Center for Urban Studies at Wayne State University, and has been the president of the Society for General Systems Research. In 1978, he received a Fulbright travel grant, which he used to travel and lecture extensively in India. As a consultant to the UN Division of Public Administration and Finance, he has written and traveled extensively in the Third World.

Bertram Gross has edited numerous books and publications in his field, and has contributed scores of articles. He helped to write *Toward A More Responsible Two-Party System* for the American Political Science Association. As a leader in the social indicator movement, he published *The State of The Union: Social Systems Accounting,* and edited a series of issues for The Annals, which were brought together in *Social Intelligence for America's Future.* As editor and contributor to a special issue of the *Public Administration Review,* his article on "Planning in an Era of Social Revolution" won the William E. Mosher Award of the American Society for Public Administration.

Bertram Gross has written for the *New York Times* and *Social Policy,* where his first piece on Friendly Fascism appeared. He is a regular contributor to *The Nation.*

Index

Acheson, Dean, 91
"Ad-hocracy," 189
Andreski, Stanislas, 102
Advertising, 72-73, 259
Affirmative action programs, 308
Africa, 121
  and Portugal, 121
"Ageism," 100, 367
Air pollution. *See* Pollution
Alienation, 107-108, 371
American Bar Association, 77
American Business Creed, 92
American Civil Liberties Union, 367
American Farm Bureau Federation, 77
American Institute of Certified Public Accountants, 275
American Medical Association, 77
Americum, 225
Anthony, Susan B., 383
Anti-communist movement, 88-89, 91-92
Anti-imperialism, 128-129
Antinuclear movement, 225
Anti-Semitism, 14, 24, 29, 86
Apathy, 329-330
Arendt, Hannah, 29
Arrests, 300-301
"Asia Firsters," 85, 89
Auschwitz, 22
Authority figures, decline of, 117

Bailey, Charles W., II, 252
Bazelon, David, 154
Behavior control, 202
Bell, Daniel, 51, 80, 94-95, 119, 201, 202
Berger, Peter, 175
Bickel, Alexander, 233
Biddle, Francis, 86
Bierce, Ambrose, 383
Bilderburg conferences, 76
Blacks, 145, 326-327, 342
Blair, John, 217
Boardroom planning, 66
Boffey, Philip, 201
Boumedienne, Houari, 132
Boy Scouts, 270
Brain drain, 37, 51
Braverman, Harry, 151, 373
Brazil, 38-39
Brenner, Harvey, 109
Browder, Earl, 272
Brzezinski, Zbigniew, 42-43, 177
Bukharin, Nikolai, 34-35
Bureaucrats, 77
Burnham, James, 72, 175
Burns, Arthur, 94
Burton, Joseph A., 307
Business Roundtable, 76

Capital
  and fascism, 29-30
  internationalization of, 174
Capital-accumulation imperative, 169
Capitalism
  humanistic, 373-374
  image of, 93
Carter, Jimmy, 69, 71, 118, 205, 218, 231, 248
Carto, Willis, 195-196
Castro, Fidel, 121, 126, 133
CBS, 261
Censorship, 261-263
Central Intelligence Agency, 70, 305-307
Chamberlain, Neville, 19
Chief Executive. *See* Presidency
China, 124, 180-181
Chomsky, Noam, 321
Chrysler Corporation, 151
Churchill, Winston, 19, 27, 32-33
CIA. *See* Central Intelligence Agency
CIO, 88
Cirino, Robert, 264
Citizen activism, 366, 367
Civil liberties, 367
Clark, Kenneth, 315
Classic fascism
  and friendly fascism, 169-170
Clifford, Clark, 69
Cloward, Richard A., 238, 288
Coal, 215
Cohen, Jerry S., 186
COINTELPRO, 306-307
Coker, Francis W., 384
Cold war, 133-134
Colonialism. *See* Neocolonialism
Commitment, involuntary, 304, 317
Commoner, Barry, 214-215, 217
Communism, 85, 90-91, 94-95, 335-336
  business with, 179-180
  capitalist support for dissident regimes, 179
  expansion of, 120-125
  and fascism, 30, 343
  and intercapitalist conflict, 174-175
  Soviet-China conflict, 180-181
  See also Anti-communist movement
Community groups, 366
Commuters, 105-106
"Complexes," 41-42
Congress, 231-233
Connally, John B., 186, 190
Conscription, 197, 323

Conservatives, 200, 205
Console, A. Dale, 227
Conspiracy theory, 58
Consumption, 285-288
  and aspirations, 99
Co-optation, 325-327
Copeland, Miles, 306
Corporations
  assets, 66
  employees, 67
  image of, 92
  management, 48-49
  sales, 67
Council of Economic Advisors, 275
Counterculture, 100-101, 333
Coup, preventive, 252-253
Crime
  and Blacks, 110, 111
  and business, 112
  corporate, 113-116
  and law enforcers, 112-113
  organized, 112
  in schools, 110
  and unemployment, 110-111
Croly, Herbert, 12
Crozier, Michel, 166
Cuba, 121, 126
Cults, 318-319
Czechoslovakia, 18, 19, 124

Data banks, 271
Davis-Bacon Act, 245
Decertification (unions), 244-245
Decision-making, 80-81
Decolonization, 33, 128
Delgado, José, 202
Dell'Olio, Anselma, 312
Democracy, 352-354
Democratic Socialist Organizing Committee, 359
Democrats, 240-242
Dennis, Lawrence, 26
Détente, 134, 135, 137, 155, 357
Dewey, Thomas E., 84
Dickstein, Samuel, 87
Dies, Martin, 87
Dies Committee, 88, 90
Dirksen, Everett, 86
Discrimination, 367
  See also Racism
Dolbeare, Kenneth, 2
Dollar surplus, 136 shortage, 136
Domestic repression (Axis countries), 21, 22-23
Domhoff, G. William, 56, 240
Donovan, James A., 384
Draft, 197, 235, 323
Draper, Theodore, 332-333
Drucker, Peter, 29
Drug therapy, 305
Drugs, 315-316
  age of user, 314
  and hyperactive children, 314-315
DSOC. *See* Democratic Socalist Organizing Committee
Dubin, Robert, 104
Dulles, John Foster, 129
Dumont, Marshall, 314
Durham, Henry, 300

Eastern Establishment, 84
Economic Bill of Rights, 143
Edelman, Murray, 239
Eden, Anthony, 43
Eisenhower, Dwight D., 84
Electronic editing, 272-273
Employment Act of 1946, 4, 144
Engels, Friedrich, 336
Engler, Robert, 217
Erhard Seminars Training, 319
Esser, Herman, 13
EST. *See* Erhard Seminars Training
Establishment, 56-59
  Eastern, 84
  lower levels, 78, 81-82
Ethnic conflict, *See* Racism
Etzioni, Amitai, 258
Eurocommunism, 127, 181
European Economic Community, 42
Eurosocialism, 127
Executive management, 72-78
Expediential fascism, 167
Exxon, 115, 218

Fair Deal, 45, 89
Falangist Party of America, 196
Falk, Richard, 172, 193
Family, nuclear, 106-107
Family wealth, 64
Farm population, 105
FBI. *See* Federal Bureau of Investigation
FDA. *See* Food and Drug Administration
Featherbedding, 151
Federal Bureau of Investigation, 112, 270, 306-307
Federal Reserve Board, 149
Federal Trade Commission, 115
Federalism, 236-237
Fiat Motor Company, 151
Floating currencies, 136
Food and Drug Administration, 227
Ford, Gerald R., 310
Fossil-fuel deposits, 214, 220
Foundations, 73

France, 125
Frauds, 112
"Free lunchers," corporate, 45-46
Friedman, Milton, 361
Friendly, Fred, 261, 267
Full Employment and Balanced Growth Act of 1978, 144

Galbraith, John Kenneth, 72, 80, 95, 362
Gandhi, Mohandas K., 378-379
Gartner, Alan, 377
General Motors, 225-226
Gerbner, George, 310
Germany, 13-14, 18, 28-30, 154
  anti-Semitism, 24
  domestic repression, 23
  fascists, 16-17, 25
  inflation, 146
  neo-Nazism, 172, 195
  storm troopers, 13, 14
  war crimes, 22
Glazer, Nathan, 308
GNP. *See* Gross National Product
Gold, 136
Goldwater, Barry, 84, 198
Goodman, Paul, 328
Goodwin, Richard, 106, 107
Gould, Jay, 307
Gramsci, Antonio, 382
Grand juries, 234-235
Grants, 75, 96, 243
Greece, 258, 338
Greene, Felix, 343
Gross, Larry P., 263, 310
Gross, Theodore, 261
Gross National Product, 147, 149, 154, 155, 276, 362
Group of Ten, 42
Grunberger, Richard, 343

Hacker, Andrew, 309
Harrington, Michael, 125, 325
Harris, Richard, 302
Havana conference, 133
Hayek, Friedrich, 336
Heilbroner, Robert, 221, 359
Herbert, Anthony B., 299
Hightower, Jim, 227
Hirobumi, Ito, 17-18
Hiss, Alger, 89
Hitler, Adolf, 13, 14, 18, 19, 21, 23, 24, 25, 27, 28, 29, 256, 259, 294, 343
Ho Chi Minh, 120
Holmes, Oliver Wendell, 92
Hoos, Ida, 202
Hoover, J. Edgar, 272, 298
Howard, Thomas M., 300
Humphrey-Hawkins full employment legislation, 76, 143, 364
Hungary, 124
Huntford, Roland, 375
Huntington, Samuel, 166, 207
Huxley, Aldous, 260, 282, 313

IAC. *See* Industrial Advisory Council
Ibarruri, Dolores, 337
IMF. *See* International Monetary Fund
Imperial expansion (Axis), 21
Income, average, 63
India, 39, 129, 224
Indochina, 120
Industrial Advisory Council, 76-77
Inflation, 146-150, 210-211, 212, 213, 364
Information technology, 50-51
Interest rates, 149-150, 213
International Monetary Fund, 42, 181
Internationalists, 83
Interventionism, 19-20, 27, 193-194
Isolationism, 83, 86, 175-176, 183
Italy
  and communism, 125
  decolonization, 33
  fascists, 11-12, 16-17, 25, 28-30
  socialists, 11-12

Janssen, Richard F., 186
Japan, 15, 18, 84, 120, 137, 154, 166, 171-172, 185-186
  decolonization, 33
  fascism, 15-17, 25, 28-30, 238, 252
  and Manchuria, 15, 19, 20
Jargon, 204, 206
Jefferson, Thomas, 383-384, 385
Jews, 14, 22, 24, 327
Jobs, guaranteed, 363-364
Johnson, Lyndon, 36, 45, 71, 118, 236, 276
Johnson, Samuel, 383
Jones, Vernon, 378
Juries, 234-235

Kahn, Herman, 214, 215, 220, 221, 295
Kaldor, Mary, 138
Kaplan, Eugene J., 185
Kass, Leon R., 292
Kaysen, Carl, 92-93
Kennedy, John F., 45, 177, 236
Keynes, Lord, 140-141
Khrushchev, Nikita, 134
King, Martin Luther, Jr., 378
Kissinger, Henry, 39, 68, 186, 207, 246
Kita, Ikki, 14-15
Klerman, Gerald, 317-318
Knebel, Fletcher, 252
"Knowledge elites," 51, 80, 95, 96, 201
Kolko, Gabriel, 175

Kotecha, Kanti C., 309
Kristol, Irving, 175, 199-200, 246
Krupp firm, 22
Ku Klux Klan, 195

Labor unions. *See* Unions
Lamont, Corliss, 332, 346
Lasch, Christopher, 379
LDC's. *See* Less developed countries
Lend-lease Act, 27
Lenin, 34-35
Less developed countries, 128, 133
Levin, Murray B., 369
Lewis, Sinclair, 3, 234, 235
Lindblom, Charles E., 324
Linder, Staffan B., 287
Lippmann, Walter, 238
Lipset, Seymour Martin, 94
Liska, George, 177, 187
Lobbyists, 76-77
Lobotomy, 304-305
Lockheed Aircraft, 115
Louis, Arthur M., 61
Loyalty boards, 89
Lublin, Joann S., 300
Luce, Henry, 19, 93
Lundberg, Ferdinand, 81, 240
Luther, Martin, 24
Luttwak, Edward, 252

MacArthur, Douglas, 36
McCarthy, Joseph, 87, 91, 272, 298
McCormack, John, 87
McGovern, George, 248
McKnight, John, 288
McLaren, Richard, 299
McWilliams, Carey, 319
MAD. *See* Mutual Assured Destruction
Maddox, John, 266
Madison, James, 350
Malthus, Thomas, 214
Management, 188-189
  corporate, 48-49
  executive, 72-78
Managerial revolution, 80
Mao Tse-tung, 134
March on Rome, 12
Marching, 25, 256
Marcuse, Herbert, 330
Marin, Peter, 379
Market research, 265
Marshall, George, 91
Maruyama, Masao, 15
Marx, Karl, 72, 141, 210, 229, 359
Mass transportation, 41-42
Maximova, Margarita, 174
Mayer, Arno J., 199
Meany, George, 153
Media, 178
  advertising, 72-73
  control of, 263-265
Medical technology, 50, 52
Merriam, Charles, 205
Methodology, 96-97
Mexico, 329, 357-358
Michels, Robert, 165
Militarism, 155-156, 191-195, 323
  Axis, 21
  overkill, 155-156, 193
  spending, 191-192
  transnational, 192
Miller, Arthur R., 258
Miller, Arthur S., 186, 189
Miller, Herman, 62
Miller, S. M., 369
Millionaires, 61-62
Mills, C. Wright, 83
Mintz, Morton, 186
"Mixed economy," 93-94
Monitoring, 268-270
Moon, Sun Myung, 319
Moore, Barrington, 374
Morgenthau, Hans, 108
Mossadegh, Prime Minister, 358
Moynihan, Daniel P., 80-81, 151, 176, 205, 233, 308, 325
Muckraking, 369
Mumford, Lewis, 282
Mundt, Karl, 89
Mussolini, Benito, 11, 12, 18, 19, 21-22, 28
Mutual Assured Destruction, 157, 194-195
Myth-making, 204-206

Nader, Ralph, 365
National Academy of Engineering, 201
National Bureau of Economic Research, 139
National Emergency Committee on Civil Liberties, 367
National Lawyers Guild, 367
National Socialist German Workers' Party, 13
Nationalization, 37-38
NATO. *See* North Atlantic Treaty Organization
Nazi-Soviet Pact, 18, 20, 21, 88
Nehru, 129
Neocolonialism, 35-37, 128
Neoconservatives, 200
Neofascism, 171, 195-196, 335-336, 338
Neo-Nazism, 172, 195
Neumann, Franz, 146
NEW (net economic welfare), 276
New Deal, 346

New International Economic Order, 132, 133
New Left, 100-101, 139, 355
New Right, 195-199, 205
New York City, 236-237, 258
New York Regional Plan Association, 258
NIEO. *See* New International Economic Order
Nisbet, Robert, 200
Nixon, Richard, 84, 88, 89, 118, 120, 134, 166, 231, 232, 236, 266
Nolte, Ernst, 29
Non-aligned movement, 129, 133
Noninterventionists, 20, 83, 85, 86
Nordhaus, William, 276
North Atlantic Treaty Organization, 42, 91, 155, 156, 192, 193, 338
Nuclear radiation, 222-225
Nuclear reactors, 223-225
Nuclear war, 134, 156, 157, 337, 338

Obsolescence, planned, 225-226
O'Connor, James, 152
OECD. *See* Organization for Economic Cooperation and Development
Oil, 215, 217-218
  embargo, 38
  prices, 38, 148, 218
OPEC. *See* Organization of Petroleum Exporting Countries
Opinion polls, 264-267
Organization for Economic Cooperation and Development, 42
Organization of Petroleum Exporting Countries, 41, 132, 140, 148, 217, 218
Orwell, George, 204, 212, 262, 268
Osgood, Robert, 177
Overseers, corporate, 64-66, 82, 230
Ozbekhan, Hasan, 156
Ozone, 221

Paine, Tom, 383
Parks, Rosa, 378-379
Paton, Alan, 385
Patriotism, 383-385
Peabody, Robert L., 232
Pfaltgraff, Robert L., Jr., 182
Pharmaceutical industry, 227-228
Pinkney, Alphonso, 327
Piven, Francis Fox, 238, 288
Plutonium, 224-225
Podhoretz, Norman, 284
Polanyi, Karl, 243
Police actions, 302, 304
Policy planning, 74-75
Pollution, 219-222
Pope, Harrison, Jr., 313
Popper, Karl, 58
Population control, 129, 132
Portugal
  and Africa, 121, 125, 129
  and communism, 124-125
Positive rewards, 294-295
Post-industrialism, 95
Poverty programs, 238-239
Presidency, 67-71, 189-191
  and business, 69
  and television, 267-268
Preventive purge, 298-299
Prior restraint (press), 234, 263
Productivity index, 53
Professionals, 80-81, 95, 104, 281-285
Profits, 363-364
Propaganda, 259
  Axis, 25
Psychosurgery, 305
Psychotherapy, 316, 317

Racism, 308, 367
  Axis, 14, 21, 23-24, 25
Radical Right. *See* New Right
Rand, Ayn, 93
Rattner, Steven, 211
Rauschning, Hermann, 25
Ray, Sankar, 174
Recessions, 140-143, 147, 149, 154, 210-211, 213, 364
Reich, Charles, 203, 282, 312, 333
Reich, Wilhelm, 311-312
Reiche, Reimut, 280-281
Religious cults, 318-320
Republicans, 240-242
Research, 75, 96
  grants, 96
  institutions, 74
Resource depletion, 214-219
Retirement communities, 106-107
Revel, Jean-Francois, 203, 333
Riessman, Frank, 366, 377
Riot control, 301
Roberts, Henry L., 133
Robinson, Herbert, 112
Roche, George Charles, 108
Rockefeller, David, 43
Rockefeller, John D. III, 163
Romney, George, 93
Roosevelt, Franklin D., 27, 70, 86, 143, 337, 346, 358, 374
Roosevelt, Theodore, 70
Roper Organization, 266
Rosenthal, David, 318
Ruggles, Richard, 271
Rustow, Dankwort, 375

Samuelson, Paul, 62, 139, 276

Sarti, Roland, 16
Sartori, Giovanni, 352
Schiller, Herbert, 259, 266
Schleicher, Kurt von, 13-14
Schools, 277-279
Schumacher, E. F., 362
Schur, Edwin, 379
Scientists. *See* Professionals
Secrist, Ronald, 300
Selznick, Phillip, 325
Sexual revolution, 311-313
Shapiro, Irving S., 211
Shirer, William L., 6, 14
Shortages. *See* Resource depletion
Shorter, Edward, 106
Silvert, Kalman, 384, 385
Skinner, B. F., 202, 294, 336
Smith Act., 86, 89
Smith, Adam, 62, 93, 215
Smith, R. Harris, 306
Socialism, 125-127, 133, 181, 335-336, 343
Solomon, L. D., 237
Sonnenfeldt, Helmut, 180
Soviet Union, 20-21, 91, 329
  and China, 124, 180-181
  grain, 216
  and India, 129
  involuntary commitment, 304
Spain, 124, 125
Specialization, 104-105
Speer, Albert, 25, 27, 233, 324, 384
Stagflation, 140, 147, 149, 182, 212, 362-363
Stalin, 20, 21, 27, 35, 85
"Starlighters," 104
Stein, Gertrude, 383
Steinfels, Peter, 200
Stimson, Henry, 19
"Straight talk," 207
Strikes, 152
Suburban migration, 105
Sullivan, Walter, 306, 307
Sulzberger, C. L., 93, 176
Surveillance, 268-270
  covert, 305-307
Sutherland, Edwin H., 113, 114, 115, 116
Sweden, 375
Sweezy, Paul, 139
Systems analysis, 202
Szasz, Thomas, 304, 316, 317

Taft, Robert A., 84, 87
Taxes, 213, 290-291, 360
  evasion, 60, 62, 73, 147
Taylor, Maxwell, 167
Technocracy, Inc., 80
Technological revolution, 50-52, 103
Technology assessment, 201-202
Television, 256-258, 265-267, 369
  presidency, 267-268
  violence, 310
Terkel, Studs, 108
Third World Countries, 36-37, 39, 128-129, 165
  and arms, 156
  and nuclear energy, 224
  and socialism, 126-127
  and trade, 132
  and unions, 243-244
Three Mile Island, 225
Throwaways, 286
Tito, 124, 133
Tobin, James, 276
Toffler, Alvin, 6, 50, 189, 286, 292
Toxic Substances Strategy Committee, 222
"Trade-off policy," 149, 210, 212
Transnationals, 40-41, 76, 120, 150, 164, 171, 205, 243
Transportation, mass, 41-42
Trilateral Commission, 43, 76, 166, 172, 207, 350
"Triplespeak," 204
Truman, Harry, 45, 71, 88, 89
Tucker, Robert W., 156, 175, 177
Tydings, Millard, 272
Tyrmand, Leopold, 329

Ultra-rich, 59-64, 82, 190, 211, 230
Un-American Activities Committee, 87, 88, 298
Unemployment, 109, 142-145, 149-150, 154, 210, 212, 284
  and crime, 110-111
  variable, 275
Unification Church, 319
Unions, 79-80, 88, 151, 243-245, 281, 364-365
  busting, 153
  decline of, 245
United Nations Conference on Trade and Development, 132
United States Information Agency, 93
USIA. *See* United States Information Agency

Value Added Tax, 213
Vandenberg, Arthur, 86
VAT. *See* Value Added Tax
Veblen, Thorstein, 80
Venezuela, 39, 133
  oil, 38, 39
Versailles treaty, 17, 20
Video editing, 273
Vietnam, 120, 136, 175, 299

Vigilantism, 309-310
Violence, domestic, 294, 295, 296-297
  television, 310
Viguerie, Richard, 198
Volunteers, 366
Voorhis, Jerry, 88
Voter apathy, 118

Wage-price policies, 148-149, 290, 291
Walker, James L., 309
Wallich, Henry, 63
War, limited, 154
  See also Nuclear war
Washington, George, 383
Watanuki, Joji, 166
Watergate conspiracy, 246-247
Weaver, Jim, 358
Weimar Republic, 13
Weinstein, James, 377
Welch, Robert, 91
Welfare state, 44-45
Weyrich, Paul, 198
"Whistle-blowing," 371-372
Whyte, William H., 282, 289
Wilkie, Wendell L., 84
Wilson, Charles, 92
Wire tapping, 269
Witch hunting, 87, 272
Wolfe, Alan, 166, 310
Women
  discrimination, 367
  liberation, 100
  unemployment, 145
Work
  fragmented, 103, 104
  health hazards, 103
Work slow downs, 151
World Bank, 42

Yette, Samuel F., 326
Yugoslavia, 124, 179

Zoll, Donald, 167
Zorza, Victor, 176

CHICAGO PUBLIC LIBRARY
W9-AOE-323

SCHUBERT

A Critical Biography

SCHUBERT: THE MEMORIAL BUST BY JOSEPH DIALER
Historische Museum, Vienna

SCHUBERT

A Critical Biography

BY

MAURICE J. E. BROWN

A DA CAPO PAPERBACK

Library of Congress Cataloging in Publication Data

Brown, Maurice John Edwin.
Schubert: a critical biography / by Maurice J. E. Brown.—Da Capo Press paperback ed.
(A Da Capo paperback)
Reprint. Originally published: London: Macmillan, 1958.
1. Schubert, Franz, 1797-1828. 2. Composers—Austria—Biography. I. Title.
ML410.S3B7 1988
780'.92'4—dc19
[B]
ISBN 0-306-80329-1 (pbk.) 88-15962

This Da Capo Press paperback edition of *Schubert: A Critical Biography* is an unabridged republication of the edition published in London and New York in 1978. It is reprinted by arrangementwith the author's executors and The Macmillan Press Ltd., London and Basingstoke

Published by Da Capo Press, Inc.
A Subsidiary of Plenum Publishing Corporation
233 Spring Street, New York, N.Y. 10013

Manufactured in the United States of America

To

OTTO ERICH DEUTSCH

CONTENTS

CHAPTER		PAGE
	Foreword	ix
I.	1797–1814	1
II.	1815–1817	32
III.	1818–1819	78
IV.	1820–1823	99
V.	1824–1825	146
VI.	The Artist	194
VII.	1826–1827	233
VIII.	1828	281
IX.	His Century and Ours	312
	Appendices	
	(i) The 'Gmunden-Gastein' Symphony	354
	(ii) Works not included in the 'Gesamtausgabe'	362
	(iii) The works in chronological order	368
	Indices	
	(i) General Index	399
	(ii) Index of Works:	
	1. Vocal Music	407
	2. Instrumental Music	411

ILLUSTRATIONS

1. SCHUBERT (the memorial bust by Dialer) *frontispiece*
2. STRING QUARTET no. 2, in C: slow movement *facing page* 20
3. TITLE-PAGE of MATIEGKA'S 'NOTURNO' 36
4. FERDINAND, COUNT TROYER 148
5. SCHUBERT (Passini's engraving, after Rieder) 196
6. SCHOOL REPORT OF FRANZ THEODOR SCHUBERT 260
7. RONDO in A, Op. 107 292
8. FERDINAND SCHUBERT 340

FOREWORD

An attempt is made in this biography of Schubert to present the composer in the light of a century of discovery and research, not only in so far as the discoveries concern him directly, but also in so far as they concern the aims and ideals of modern biography in general.

The views of nineteenth-century biographers on human nature and personality seem to us, today, to be altogether too naïve and superficial. Where the creative artist is concerned, their whole-hearted acceptance of the 'artist as hero', as a pure channel through which heaven's inspiration might flow, belongs, in our view, more to the realm of fairy-tale than to life itself. Schubert has suffered perhaps more than his fellow composers from this fairy-tale approach to the musical creator. We ask today for an interpretation of his character based on something deeper and more suggestive than that of the simple-hearted but idle Viennese Bohemian, who composed in a state of 'clairvoyance'.

The chance to present the interpretation was first given to the Schubert biographer by Otto Erich Deutsch in his great collection of the documents of the composer's life, a book which is discussed fully later on in this biography. Because those documents have now, at last, been so fully given to the world, it has not been felt necessary when quoting from them to do so *in toto*. I have, on the contrary, sought to digest the mass of records and filter the essential from the immaterial, to suppress, and even to destroy when desirable, the doubtful documentary addition which merely obstructs our view of the composer.

The reader who wishes to refer to original documents in their entirety will seek them in Deutsch's collection, and not in the pages of this particular biography, which seeks to go beyond the document or record to the interplay of motives behind it, and which attempts also an assessment of the composer's craft and achievement.

The term 'critical' of the subtitle gives the clue to the kind of biography I have attempted to write. I have, I realise, run the danger of failing to achieve either true biography or true aesthetic appraisement. Nevertheless, it is the kind of book on Schubert which I felt impelled to write, and I could not write it in any other way. We read again and again in the columns of reviewers that the fusion of 'Life' with 'Works' is an unsatisfactory solution. With Schubert, however, the two are so inextricably bound up that without the 'Works' the 'Life' is almost nothing. On the other hand, the 'Works' without the 'Life', of which we have had several examples in recent years, must deal with categories, e.g. PF. Music, Church Music, etc., and Schubert's artistic growth cannot then be fully examined. In this biography the reader must be prepared to encounter the major compositions twice in the course of a chapter: first as the biographical fact, then as the subject of musical analysis and appraisement.

I have not followed the accepted modern practice of giving a 'Bibliography' at the end of the book for the simple reason that every book and article on Schubert of importance will be found mentioned in the text and particulars are given there.

A number of items are published for the first time in this book, and others for the first time in any Schubert biography in English. I wish especially to thank Dr. O. E. Deutsch for personal encouragement, for several items of fresh information incorporated in the text, and particularly for permission to give an English translation of the recently recovered letter from Doppler to Schubert in Chapter III. Another letter, from Schubert to Anna Hönig, appears for the first time with the kind permission of Major S. L. Courtauld of Umtali, S. Rhodesia. Konsul Otto Taussig, Malmö, has kindly allowed me to reproduce the School Report from the hand of Schubert's father, and a page from the score of the String Quartet no. 2, in C major. I am also grateful to the 'Deutsche Staatsbibliothek', Berlin, to the 'Stadtbibliothek' and the 'Historisches Museum', Vienna, for permission to reproduce various manuscripts and pictures in their possession.

Extracts from contemporary documents, other than Schubert's own letters, are quoted from Deutch's 'Documentary Biography' by kind permission of its publishers, J. M. Dent & Sons, Ltd., London. The American Edition, entitled *A Schubert Reader*, is published by W. W. Norton & Co., Inc., New York, and to these publishers also I express thanks for their kind permission to quote from the book.

Whenever necessary for the purpose of exact identification of a particular composition, I have quoted the number of the work in the Deutsch 'Thematic Catalogue', another invaluable book of reference for the Schubert scholar which is fully discussed on a later page. Such a reference appears as, for example, D. 570. In time, no doubt, the 'Deutsch' numbers will displace all other means of reference to the works of Schubert, although, at present, certain well established opus-numbers may possibly be more convenient to the reader. I have left song-titles in the original German. There are no generally accepted equivalents amongst the several English versions of these titles, and to give yet more, and still different, English titles seemed more likely to confuse, than to clarify the position. Only in the case of the universally used *Erlking* have I felt that it would be pedantic to restore the original German.

Schubert has been for thirty years, and will be for forty years to come, spared the attention of centenary celebration, with its unavoidable exaggerations and distortions. The portrayal of the composer in the following pages is, as far as I have been able to make it, a true picture of how he appears to the musical world of the mid-twentieth century. It is a different picture from those of the nineteenth century, and it will differ in the same degree from those which will be drawn in the next hundred years. It is to be hoped, paradoxically, that the farther he recedes in time, the nearer each successive portrait may come to the truth.

M. J. E. B.

MARLBOROUGH
February 1957

SCHUBERT

A Critical Biography

I

1797-1814

I

Three aspects of Schubert's life give it a unique place in the annals of creative artists. It has, to begin with, no elements in it of the success story; no climax of recognition of his genius, or acknowledgement of it, breaks the continuous obscurity of his years. Hence the biographer of Schubert cannot achieve readability in his pages by holding out the promise of eventual, even if delayed, success. There is no gathering darkness to make the dawn so welcome, for there is no dawn. A contributory cause is that he made no public appearance as a performer or conductor. He had not, in any case, the ability to do so as a keyboard player, since the charm and expressiveness of his playing were not alone sufficient to impress the public. It is surprising when one reviews the lives of the great composers to realise that *all* of them, without exception, first impressed patron or public as performers or conductors. Schubert could not gain recognition in that way. There have been attempts recently to prove that recognition did come, in the end, by composition alone, and as evidence, reviews of his work from musical journals in Leipzig, Berlin and Dresden have been quoted. But notices of his songs and pianoforte pieces in the provincial press of Germany are only such as we find accorded to every young composer's work; it is misleading to quote them in isolation. Amongst the multitudinous reviews of new music in all the newspapers of Germany and Austria they would make no showing. It is sufficient to recall that the young English musician Edward Holmes, a friend of Keats and a biographer of Mozart, passed the spring of 1827 in Vienna, and there moved in musical circles determined to find out all that was worth finding out; and in his records he does not once mention Schubert's name. Yet, in

1827, that name was almost at the summit of what renown it was ever to have in its owner's lifetime. Three years later, in 1830, that is, after the death of Schubert, the French scholar Fétis published an article on the state of music in Germany in his 'Curiosités Historiques de la Musique'; there is not one mention of Schubert's name throughout.

In the second place, Schubert was never able to free himself entirely from *necessity* in composing; that is to say, throughout his life he composed because he strove for a foothold. He was never to know, except in the modest way which any of us can know, what it was to compose for an audience which would attend to his music with the anticipation and respect always given to the established artist. Instead, outside the immediate circle of his friends, he was given a polite, even patronising, interest: not unfriendly, but containing a hint of 'Is this not the carpenter's son . . . ?' about it. And because the musical world of Vienna was never sure of him, he could never be entirely sure of himself. That is why he could not wholly succeed in discarding the influence of the older masters on his work. An artist who is still struggling for recognition is bound to retain a tentative streak in his work. This is certainly not to imply that there is anything tentative in the great C major Symphony, or in the 'Death and the Maiden' String Quartet. But as a tendency in his work its presence cannot be denied. It does not seem to have occurred to his critics that the reason for the late development in his instrumental works, late, that is, in comparison with his songs, is that he would not let himself *be* himself in these works. He was still trying to be Haydn or Mozart or Beethoven—or even Hummel and Kozeluch. It is obvious, to give a concrete example, in the last of his early string quartets, the one in E major of 1816 (Op. 125: no. 2). Time and again the real Schubert appears, tender and imaginative, but is swept aside by the merest aping of the Beethoven externals. Even in the works of his last years, in the Mass in E flat, or in the Sonata in C minor, he is prone to revert to Beethoven's mannerisms. Accordingly there is no phase in Schubert's composing career in which he is, in the best sense of the term, the self-conscious artist, determined, in the first place certainly, to please others, but also to please himself. And at no time, as a result of this, is he self-conscious about his finished work: he never catalogues, nor records and documents it as all other composers have done.

The third, and most remarkable, aspect for the Schubert biographer, is the almost impenetrable obscurity which descended at his death, and which persisted, with so little mitigation, for forty or fifty years. The outcome of that obscurity was that Schubert's compositions, apart from his lyrical songs, never really became part of the nineteenth century's international heritage of music until that century was nearly passed, nor did he, as a composer, become part of that century's musical thought and philosophy. It is a commonplace to encounter the names of Bach, Mozart, Beethoven, Berlioz, Liszt, Wagner, and others, in the criticisms and philosophical essays of non-musical writers, that is, of writers not primarily concerned with music; the name of Schubert could not occur there. And because his work has not influenced, nor been illumined by, the intellectual writings of the nineteenth century, nor has it, by some queer form of exclusiveness, found its rightful place amongst musico-scholarly writings either. The musical scholar and critic, priding himself, rightly, on his acquaintance with non-musical criticism and philosophy, is never led to Schubert by any of it. The case of Berlioz illustrates the point. The extraneous problems and exploits of that composer's 'Romanticism'—extraneous, so to say, to the actual corpus of his music, fascinated the literary figures of his day. The result is that Berlioz's music is lifted to cognizance by two factors quite apart from what it achieves by its own intrinsic worth: the attention given to him by contemporary literary figures, and the interest aroused since then in critics, musical and otherwise, by the references to it in the writings of the poets, and novelists, and essayists, and diarists of Berlioz's time. Schubert's obscurity leaves no possibility of this happening to him. Dates in isolation rarely mean very much; let us illustrate a chosen one in the nineteenth century—1865. In that year the 'Unfinished' Symphony was brought to light and performed in Vienna; the symphony which, to most people, means 'Schubert'. In 1865, Mendelssohn and Schumann, both always ardently ready to disseminate knowledge of new Schubert works, had been dead for many years. Neither knew the symphony: neither knew even that it existed. By 1865, Berlioz's work was finished, Wagner had composed 'Tristan' and 'Die Meistersinger', and Sibelius was born. And not until that year, two thirds of the way through the century, was the 'Unfinished' Symphony played for the first time.

In reading Schubert's life, these three facts should be remembered; otherwise that life offers many puzzles, and presents all kinds of difficulties. And one of the chief of these is to see the real Schubert through the fog of sentimental distortions which has arisen from the efforts of Victorian biographers, who, because of his posthumous obscurity, were obliged to rely too much upon anecdote and reminiscence, because manuscript and document were not available. The matter will be dealt with more fully later, when Schubert's art is considered more closely, but one point at least, may be made here. We read again and again in the pages of Kreissle, Grove, Reissmann and other biographers, and in numerous short, critical essays in musical periodicals, of Schubert's rapidity and ease in writing: we read that he never sketched, was impatient of revision, and composed, as it were, by improvising on paper. It is a false picture. Certainly Schubert had a fluent pen, and he composed quickly, because, when he was engaged on a composition, he could devote undistracted days to the work and did not spare himself till it was done. But such feats of rapidity lost nothing in the telling, especially by the friend or acquaintance to whom the business of composition was such an arduous and prolonged process that Schubert's fertility and energy impressed deeply—Lachner, Doppler, Randhartinger and the rest. In a few cases the anecdotes deriving from these acquaintances are obviously, demonstrably, pure inventions: proved to be so when documents have made an incredibly delayed appearance. The truth, which is, of course, less sensational, shows that the accounts of Schubert's lack of preparation can be ignored; and the truth is the discovery—still continuing today—of innumerable sketches (the adjective is not lightly used) for the finished compositions. Songs, PF. Sonatas and dances, symphonies, chamber music, operas, Church music, there are sketches for all these works, and in the case of the songs as many as four versions before he was satisfied. The sketches for the 'Unfinished' Symphony are, most happily, preserved. Those for the C major Symphony, which were probably begun at Gastein in 1825, are lost. Ignorance of such matters is bound to produce erroneous conclusions in writing of the composer himself, his procedures, and his music.

II

Schubert was the fourth surviving son of a schoolmaster in Vienna. Both his parents had come to the city from northern provinces in Austria; that may have been a factor in drawing them together. His father, Franz Theodor Schubert (1763–1830), was born in Neudorf, a village in Silesia; at the time of his marriage, he was teaching in the Leopoldstadt suburb of Vienna. His mother, Elisabeth Vietz (1756–1812), was in domestic service (there is no definite evidence for the information occasionally given, that she was a cook) in the nearby Liechtental district. The memorial tablet for her birthplace in Zuckmantel, Silesia, was for many years affixed to the wrong house! They were married on 17 January 1785 in the parish church of Liechtental, a small but most attractive baroque church which we encounter many times in Schubert's boyhood and youth. Schubert was, it will be seen, of Silesian peasant origin, and the firmly rooted legend of his being Vienna's 'one native composer' must give place to a more temperate view. He, just as Beethoven, Haydn, Mozart and the rest had done, came to Vienna from outside provinces. His nature responded to the stimuli of Vienna's gaiety and melancholy in so far as those elements were present in him, but as for his being an embodiment of her virtues and characteristics, a native of the capital born to give her a voice and an utterance, this is only a half-truth. His nature had depths, epic and tragic, not characteristic of Vienna, whereas her passivity, her *laissez-faire*, were largely unknown to him. And has not Vienna always subconsciously realised this? Not Schubert, but Johann Strauss is her favourite composer, her darling. And it is the strains of the Strauss waltz, not of the Schubert song or symphony, which she uses as the expression of her rejoicing at national fête-days.

What kind of a Schubert should we have had if his parents had returned to Silesia when he was a child? A great composer, of course; but we can assess Vienna's contribution to his genius if we see it as an enriching, stimulating and provoking influence rather than as a fundamental element. It is the non-Viennese part of his nature that responded so readily to the appeal of German literature; his song-texts alone could call the 'native Viennese' theory into question.

Just over a year after his marriage, in June 1786, Franz Theodor was appointed to a school of his own in the Himmelpfortgrund, a small district in the Liechtental parish whose name is preserved today by a short flight of stone steps called the 'Himmelpfortgrundstiege'.

New facts have recently come to light about the school and its story under the care of Schubert's father. It had been founded many years before in a house called 'Zum roten Krebsen' ('The Red Crab') in the main street now known as Nussdorferstrasse. It was originally no. 42; this was changed to no. 72 a year before Schubert's birth, and is, today, no. 54. Schubert's father occupied the schoolhouse as early as 1786, not, as hitherto supposed, in 1796. The house was typical of the terribly overcrowded neighbourhood; it contained sixteen 'dwellings', on ground and first floor, each comprising one room with a kitchen. The Schubert family (for two children, Ignaz and Elisabet, were born by then) had two of these dwellings and in these two large and two small rooms a school of several classes was accommodated, and Schubert's mother bore twelve children and brought up the five who survived infancy. They were Ignaz (b. 1785), Ferdinand (b. 1794), Karl (b. 1795), Franz Peter (b. 31 January 1797) and Maria Theresa (b. 1801). Today the birthplace is a Schubert Museum, preserved by the City Authorities of Vienna. It is exquisitely 'groomed' and contains much of interest in the way of pictures including the original of Moritz von Schwind's drawing 'A Schubert Evening at Spaun's'. The courtyard, into which one steps with surprising suddenness from the busy Nussdorferstrasse, is, one imagines, very like what it was in Schubert's own day, and private dwellings lead off from it still. In the house itself it is still possible to identify in the structure, though it has been somewhat altered, the original one-room-plus-kitchen scheme of the many family apartments of those far off times. The 'alcove', Schubert's actual birth-room, according to his sister Maria Theresa, was clearly one of the 'kitchen' rooms.

When Schubert's father took over the school it had a bad reputation; but in a few years' time all this was changed. One cannot but admire the industry, tenacity and spirit of this man. Fees were very low and not paid regularly; as numbers increased he was obliged to have a two session day, and to make ends meet gave private coaching as well. When his school had lived down its bad name, and more and more boys came to him, frequently from distant suburbs, the extra assistants he had to employ swallowed up the increased income. It is not difficult to see why he persuaded his sons, as they grew old enough, to become assistants in his school. When Schubert was born there were nearly 200 boys in his father's charge. In 1801, by means of a mortgage, Schubert senior bought and moved into a bigger (though still small enough) house in a nearby side-street called the Säulengasse. This house still stands in Vienna—it is a garage, called by some quirk of deference, 'Schubert-Garage'. It is like the birthplace in the sense that a small courtyard is surrounded by a two-storey building; but it is crumbling and decayed. Nevertheless, if one is allowed to mount the stone stairway and stand in the room over the gateway, one is surrounded by the small rooms where the schoolboys—Schubert among them—were taught; there is no groomed look about the tall houses beyond the courtyard, and there is only a square of sky if one looks upward. But if not quite as Schubert saw it, it is very like; and to the imaginative visitor a sense of the real period and the real background to Schubert's life may be caught more readily than in the Birthplace-Museum. And it is here, not there, that the genius began to bud, and where we stand, looking down into the unkempt yard, the strains of *Gretchen am Spinnrade* were first hummed over. Opposite, on the other side of the Nussdorfer street, is the stone stairway down which Schubert, with his family, stepped to reach the Liechtental Church.

It is only fair to mention that the picture of a stern, industrious, all-work-and-no-play schoolmaster, so frequently drawn of Schubert's father, is only one facet of the truth. In the years of struggle, with hardly sufficient money for the needs of his own large family, he continually gave shelter and generous assistance to his own and to his wife's brothers and sisters, whose individual stories were not only those of penury and hardship, but frequently of tragedy. Music, too, obviously meant far more to Schubert's father than a subject in his school time-table. In a small book on Schubert, Ralph Bates, possibly a little guilty of the prevailing trend for the 'de-bunking' type of biography, concentrated on Franz Theodor's sexual capacities, drawing attention to his large family, his overhasty re-marriage, and the continuing succession of children in that second union.[1] If we are to draw conclusions about the sexual precosity of men from the philoprogenitiveness of the nineteenth century, few would 'scape whipping. It may be permissible to draw such conclusions, of course. But Franz Theodor's possibly oversexed nature is interesting only in so far as it illuminates Schubert. If there is a connection between it and a precosity of creative energy on the part of his gifted son, then the line of research must be followed far on, if it is to be of any help: this Ralph Bates does not do.

After the move into the Säulengasse schoolhouse, matters gradually improved until, in 1814, when his youngest son Franz was enrolled as his least considerable assistant, taking the 'Taferl' class ('Taferl' = a little slate on which the children learnt their ABC), he had six assistant teachers. There were then over 300 boys in the school.

The Liechtental parish where the Schuberts lived and worshipped is situated in north-west Vienna. The real heart of the city lay inside old, fortified walls surrounded by a sloping stretch of grass called the Glacis. During the last century the walls were

[1] 'Franz Schubert', Ralph Bates, London, 1934, p. 15, and elsewhere.

pulled down, and today they are covered by the noble boulevards of the Ringstrasse. A fifth of the population, some 50,000 people, lived in the Inner City, where, needless to say, the true life of the capital was concentrated. The streets were narrow and ran between high buildings. Here were the shops, the cafés, the theatres, the publishing houses, the University buildings, the palaces and grounds of the aristocracy, the convents and green copper domed churches, chief amongst them the towering spire of St. Stefan's Cathedral. And, surprisingly enough, open parks and gardens which gave grace and delicacy to the picturesque huddle of rooftops and towers in the City, so that foreign visitors said, in Schubert's day, that the view of Vienna from St. Stefan's tower was more beautiful than that of Paris from Montmartre, or Rome from Pincio.

The early years of the century in Vienna were clouded by the devastation and hunger caused by the Napoleonic campaigns and successive occupations. Like most occupations, Napoleon's brought nothing to Vienna of permanent value, but a great deal of temporary misery. When the phase passed a different Vienna emerged. What the overhanging threat of Napoleon had meant we can see in Beethoven's case. In the abiding good humour of Schubert's music we see what his Vienna craved—peace, and entertainment; pathos, the tears quickly dried, was not unwelcome, but nothing harrowing, no more tragedy.

We can, of course, seek too much in the background of Vienna to elucidate and illuminate the music of the Schubert who loved her so abidingly. It is not necessary to fill in that background with too many enriching details, otherwise his figure is detracted from rather than added to. There was that in him which responded to the spirit of Vienna; and that spirit, as we have suggested, was in revolt against tragedy and excitement. The 'Biedermeier' period, as it is conveniently called, cultivated the secure, the domesticated, arts and there was a great deal of sentimental verse-writing, of diaries and albums and journals, of charades and impromptu plays at home, of friendly associations in cafés, of music-making and dancing. The reaction in the arts against the epic, classical forms, its strength in the 'Storm and Stress' movement temporarily spent, gathered its forces in this strange little backwater of silver-lace borders and vignettes, before it sailed on down the broad waters of the 'Romantic' movement. The pathos, so fashionable a foil to the everywhere desired security and contentment, was exemplified in the figure of the youth who wandered the earth in a frustrated and unhappy quest for some ideal, or in that of the hopeless lover, or, occasionally, in a figure who combined the two —the man of Schubert's and Müller's 'Winterreise', for instance.

Apart from music Vienna offered to the cultivated taste little that was indigenous in the arts. It is incomprehensible that anyone should consider it a period of universal artistic achievement. Its architecture was undergoing a hygienic cleansing from the final orgies of the rococo period, and that does not make for greatness. Its painting was humble and decadent—of the 'illustration' *genre* and Schubert's friend Moritz von Schwind became its greatest exponent. Its theatres, undoubtedly fettered by the rigid censorship of the Chancellor, Prince Metternich, were given up to German dramatists, Goethe, Schiller, or Lessing, and foreigners like Shakespeare and Racine; or they were frivolously engaged in presenting farces by Bauernfeld and Castelli, fairy-tale plays by Raimund, and sentimental comedies by Kotzebue and Heinrich von Collin. The native dramatist, Grillparzer, is an isolated figure. Opera was frenziedly popular if it were Italian, and the lighter French operettas, like Hérold's 'La Clochette' and 'Marie' were well liked. The poetry of the day, in Austria, was almost negligible until many years after the death of Schubert. It was a time in which the happy-go-lucky, the *gemütlich*, the slippered, arts of Vienna might have disgusted a more tasteful and sensitive composer than Schubert and forced him into scornful silence. Instead, with his simplicity, his warm-hearted and friendly nature, his ready cheerfulness and ready tears, he *responded*; and he poured out his music in response to these various stimuli with a fecundity which never fails to amaze, and which is his unique possession. Happy such an artist: who can combine that spontaneous response with the assured technical facility to give it utterance.

The intensive cultivation of music in the houses of the middle-class Viennese families has been mentioned. Secular music was no longer the product and solace of the aristocratic patron; the prince and priest of the eighteenth century, whose establishments contained bands of musical servants hired to perform chamber and orchestral music, with a composer-servant at their head to provide that music—they were passing. Instead, the wealthy middle-classes were paying the piper, and they called the tune. The publishing houses were pouring out the songs and dance-music and pianoforte pieces which they loved and asked for. The piano was the centre of this music making, and in the large and comfortable houses of the merchants and lawyers and civil servants were held these musical evenings, often weekly, to which numbers of guests were invited, and at which part-songs and cantatas, songs, chamber-music, pianoforte duets and so forth were performed. Two aspects of this domestic music making must be stressed because of their influence on Schubert, although in fact nothing has been mentioned in the foregoing pages which has not its influence on the personality of the composer and his music: they are, the part-songs of the male-voice choirs, and the everlasting dancing. They danced the waltz, the Ländler, the galop, the cotillon, the écossaise. Of the Congress of Vienna in those days De Ligne wrote: 'Le Congrès danse, mais il ne marche pas!' It would be difficult to say which of the two forms of music, part-song or dance, was the more popular. To both the Viennese were as addicts, and Schubert no less than they. If we look at the composer against this background and try to see how it pervaded his thought and creative processes and what the music was which he poured out in response to its stimulus, the first thing that strikes one is this: he redeemed its triviality. He lent the inarticulate moods and desires of Vienna a voice—and through him they speak enduring things. When we read of the elderly Schwind returning at last to Vienna, seeking the lamplit alleyways, and the haunts of his youth, we feel that he sought, not a real city, but to recapture almost vanished impressions: the music of his friend's playing and old Vogl singing; the gatherings of the Schubertians in the drawing-rooms of Spaun and Bruchmann and Hönig to hear that music and those songs.

Although Vienna's tastes were mainly for the more entertaining side of music, Gluck, Haydn and Mozart of the immediate past, and Beethoven of the immediate present, were by no means neglected figures in her musical life. Schubert composed perforce, and published, a large amount of music in popular forms—waltzes and marches and variations—but he was also able to publish the more serious side of his work: three Pianoforte Sonatas, Opp. 42, 53 and 78, a String Quartet, Op. 29 and a Pianoforte Trio, Op. 100. The songs published in his lifetime were not only those in a lighter vein, *Die Forelle*, *Heidenröslein*, *Der Alpenjäger*, but also the ones by which his later fame grew, the profound, the dramatic, or the poignantly expressed ones such as *Gretchen am Spinnrade*, *Gruppe aus dem Tartarus*, *An Schwager Kronos*, the Harper's songs from Goethe's 'Wilhelm Meister'. Italian opera did indeed sweep Vienna off her feet, and the Rossini fever of 1816-1817 knew no reasonable bounds, but in addition the city gave a welcome to the German operas of men like Gyrowetz, Mosel, Hummel and Josef Weigl; it had known 'Fidelio', it was on the eve of witnessing the epoch-making 'Der Freischütz', and it was, in a not too distant future, to know 'Lohengrin'. If, it has been said, there is in Schubert a conflict between Rossini and Beethoven, it is because that conflict was part of the Viennese character. It was made more acute in Schubert because, in spite of his Viennese environment, it must not be forgotten that he was the child of peasants in whom was a strong Puritanical bent. We see the trait markedly in Schubert's brother Ferdinand, and in his sister, Maria Theresa. In Schubert it is the more earnest side of his nature, the side which responded to Beethoven and Goethe and produced those repeated declarations in his letters, and to his friends, that he was 'thenceforth dedicated to opera and symphony' and so forth. But the easy going and relaxed side of that nature would re-assert itself and duet-fantasias and songs and dances came readily once again from his pen.

III

In October 1808, the lad Schubert won a place in the choir of the Imperial Court Chapel. Candidates were examined in singing and other subjects. His education had been the responsibility of his father, his brother Ignaz, and the organist of the Liechtental Church, Michael Holzer, who had given him lessons in organ-playing, singing and composition, and who is reported to have said of Schubert that whatever he came to teach him, he knew already: a veritable legend-making remark. The fact that vacancies in this Imperial Choir were publicy advertised in a capital city such as Vienna and that the eleven-year-old Schubert obtained one in a competitive examination proves that these men had given him a grounding which was sufficiently thorough. His voice, and his musical abilities, were part of his natural endowment; but those alone, it is clear from the records of the event, would not have been enough. The advantage to the boy of this place in the choir was that it admitted him to the *kaiserlich-königliches Stadtkonvikt* (Imperial and Royal City Seminary: called so to distinguish it from a similar school in the Josefstadt suburb of Vienna, for the sons of the nobility), the principal boarding school of Vienna, where the choristers were given a general education, with systematic training in musical subjects. It is doubtful whether Schubert, not being of wealthy or noble parentage, could have had a finer education anywhere in Vienna than he obtained at this school. The lecturers were clerics, strict Piarists; the material comforts of the boarders were not studied; classrooms were very cold in winter, food was scanty, teaching hours were long. But the opportunities for a boy of Schubert's gifts were phenomenal. The elderly principal, Dr. Franz Innocenz Lang, was an ardent music lover and encouraged the practice of music amongst all the students (it was not an obligatory subject for the non-choristers). Under the leadership of a twenty-year-old law student, Josef von Spaun, an orchestra was formed among the seminarists. So excellent were their performances of overtures and symphonies that members of the public gathered thickly in the square outside the building on fine evenings to listen to them;

and many Viennese came to think of the school as a 'Conservatoire' devoted solely to the cultivation of musical studies. From the reminiscenses of his friends and the records of the *Stadtkonvikt* in the Vienna City archives, we can assemble these facts: the orchestra in Schubert's day consisted of 6 first and 6 second violins, 2 violas, 2 'cellos and 2 basses. There were 2 of each of the woodwind, flute, oboe, clarinet, and bassoon; and horns, trumpets, and drums in unspecified numbers. Amongst his fellow pupils at the *Konvikt*, who later on became his friends, or whose names we shall meet again, are Josef von Spaun, who played second violin and whose friendship with Schubert is one of the brightest and most attractive things which the composer's biographer finds in his material, Anton Holzapfel, 'cello, and amongst the first violins, Anton Hauer and Leopold Ebner, the second of whom made many copies of Schubert songs, which later on proved invaluable when the originals were lost. The musician, Benedikt Randhartinger, of whom we shall speak later, did not join the *Stadtkonvikt* until after Schubert had left. Three other fellow pupils who became his friends, musical, but not members of the orchestra, are Josef Kenner, Johann Senn, the poet, and Albert Stadler, a man of fine character, who lived at Linz, in Upper Austria, and who became a collector of Schubert manuscripts and copies, and a reliable source of information on the composer.

From a humble place in the second violins Schubert quickly showed his mettle and in a short while he was leading the orchestra; in the absence of the music master, Wenzel Ruczicka, he became its conductor. Schubert's musical studies were in the hands of this industrious, thorough and skilful man. Ruczicka (1758–1823), a Hungarian by birth, had come to Vienna in 1772 and was appointed Court Organist in 1793. He was also a violist at the Burg Theatre, and a modest composer. At some time after 1811, when Schubert finished his studies with Ruczicka, he began work with Anton Salieri, the famous Italian composer and teacher. It is more than possible that Salieri's interest was aroused by the composing activities of Schubert. It was probably not an everyday occurrence to find one of the choirboys so outstandingly gifted in music and able to show the scores of overtures for orchestra (performed by the students under his conductorship), string quartets and substantial songs. Some of these boyhood works have survived, and the song *Hagars Klage* of March 1811 is actually named by a few of his friends as the work which aroused the Italian's interest. On several of Schubert's manuscripts, that of the String Quartet in B flat (D. 36), which he began in 1812, and on the manuscript of the String Quartet in D (D. 74) of 1813, we find Salieri's handwriting. The title page of the second of these quartets, in D major, did not see the light until 1928, when it was found in Vienna among the family papers of a descendant of Spaun's. Against Schubert's writing of his master's name Salieri added: 'premier Maitre de Chapelle de la Cour Imp. et Royale de Vienne.' There is sufficient evidence that he looked over the young composer's work. We can discount both extremes in the memoirs of Schubert's friends and acquaintances when they record the association between Schubert and Salieri: the latter was not Schubert's master in any close, systematic or continuous sense of the word, but neither was his instruction so casual or so carelessly received as would seem from some accounts, that of Anton Schindler, for example: he wrote '... we know for certain that Salieri never gave regular lessons in composition. If Schubert had undergone the required studies with Salieri it would have been quite unnecessary for him to have taken lessons in counterpoint with Sechter. Salieri only gave him advice on the treatment of voices'. Schindler is an untrustworthy witness. The example quoted above of the two string quartets shows that he was mis-informed over the extent of Salieri's instruction. There is a large number of 3-part canons and settings of Metastasio by Schubert, dated on various occasions in 1813, all clearly pupil's work. The lessons extended beyond *Konvikt* days and continued till 1816.

Schubert took part in daily music making—songs, pianoforte duets, chamber music—in the practice rooms of the *Konvikt* with his fellows. In his own home during the long vacation of the school year, which came in the autumn, he played viola in a family string quartet. His father played the 'cello, his brothers, Ignaz and Ferdinand, the violins. In the theatres of Vienna, particularly in the Kärntnertor theatre (now the wonderful Staatsoper of modern Vienna) and in the Theater an der Wien, he could hear the finest opera in Europe; his first visit was probably with his friend Spaun to hear Josef Weigl's 'Die Schweizerfamilie' on 8 July 1811. If we step back a little and review the musical influences and pressures on this sensitive, gifted boy during the five years 1808–1813, in which he was a pupil at the *Konvikt*, it must be admitted that few other composers in their early teens have had such a rich and varied nurture. Between them, Vienna and the *Konvikt* poured out for him a profusion of music—from the richest masterpieces of Mozart and Beethoven downwards; this music, and his work in the school, not only awakened and stimulated his genius, but gave that genius the technical equipment by which it could express itself. What are we to say to the ill-informed criticism which attacks that technical equipment with head-shaking remarks such as that 'he was deficient in counterpoint' (Grove), 'the most completely lacking of all the great composers in the purely cerebral power which is the necessary concomitant of the highest artistic achievement' (Cecil Gray), 'a more exasperatingly brainless composition was never put on paper' (Bernard Shaw on the great C major Symphony), 'his pianoforte sonatas cannot, either by their comprehension or intellectual grasp, be placed by the side of Beethoven's' (Kreissle). These critics, and others like them, confuse academic techniques, such as the use of invertible counterpoint, fugal expositions, augmentation, and so forth, with true intellectual processes in music (unanalysable, and therefore unnameable), and hold good workmanship to consist in the avoidance of consecutive fifths and hidden octaves. They consider that counterpoint is only displayed if it is manipulative and self-conscious. All of them have left one essential factor out of the count; if genius, the imponderable, is present, then the other factors count for nothing. The question must be held in reserve for fuller consideration later. Meanwhile a word could be added here on the use of the fugato, the canon, the solemn 'chorale-tune' and other academically admired devices of the 'Romantic' composers. They were introduced when inspiration ran dry; they have been most cogently dubbed, by Paul Henry Lang, 'musical buoys'.[1] Even Beethoven, on occasion, keeps the progress of a musical finale going with a fugato 'buoy', not because *he* would have sunk without it, but because he momentarily stepped aside into contemporary practice. Schubert, never at a loss for ideas, felt no need to use these *dei ex machina*, fugato and the rest, to help his plots along. But the glory of the counterpoint which is there—unteachable, unacademic, intangible—should silence criticism:

If genius, however, is lacking, of what use is cerebral power, and faultless workmanship, and the rest? Writing of some lesser contemporaries of Beethoven and Schubert, Lang, in the article mentioned, wrote: 'The assuredness of (their) refined and orderly

[1] *Musical Quarterly*, New York, April 1953, p. 237.

craftsmanship led to playfulness and, in the end, to academicism.' If Schubert's fecund outpourings break through the prim barriers of classical form, it is an indication of the greatness of his genius: only the man of small talent is always in full control of his creations.

Assertions that Schubert neglected his other subjects in the *Konvikt* in order to devote himself mainly to composition are belied by the facts: his school reports are still preserved, and in them we can read Dr. Lang's comments on his studies. Making allowances for the limited vocabularly of schoolmasters when they pronounce on their pupils' progress, it is easy to see that the boy Schubert maintained a satisfactory standard in his general studies. But more than that, the music surviving from those years, carefully preserved by his father, is small in bulk. Schubert had not achieved that rapidity of composition so remarkable later on, nor was he able to devote himself for undisturbed hours to his music. His careful dating of some early chamber music proves this. On the one-movement Trio in B flat, oddly entitled 'Sonata' (D. 28), we read: '27 July–28 August 1812'; a string quartet in the same key (D. 36) occupied him from 19 November 1812 to 21 February 1813.

The music which he composed during his last three years at the *Konvikt* is a miscellaneous assortment, an experimental phase; even a fragmentary opera, 'Der Spiegelritter' ('The Looking-glass Knight') survives. There are three long PF. Duet Fantasias and an 'Overture' for string quintet, in all of which Mozart's chromaticism has almost obsessed the boy; each one of these works uses the basic phrases:

or sections of them, in a rather mechanically worked fashion. The prelude of his first extant song, *Hagars Klage*, is based on the first of these ready-made themes. Several pieces for PF. solo are still unpublished; amongst them is another Fantasia, in C minor, where the presence of Mozart is so obvious that one might call the work 'Schubert's Fantasia on Mozart's Fantasia in C minor, K. 475'. Here, as an instance, is the *Andantino* section of Schubert's fantasia:

A few items of Church music are negligible. It will be necessary to make this rather slighting comment on the composer's settings of liturgical texts at several points in his career. The tale of his works is littered with numerous, short anthems, motets, offertories and the like, which are largely *ad hoc* compositions. His words in a letter to his father '. . . I have never forced myself to devotion, and, unless I become overwhelmed by it involuntarily, have never composed such hymns or prayers (as the *Ave Maria*), and then it is usually the right and true devotion' are somewhat piously unreal, for they are discounted by dozens of perfunctory examples of devotional music which he turned out, and which clearly only touched the surface of his mind.

The titles of the few songs which survive—*Hagars Klage*, *Des Mädchens Klage*, *Klagelied*, etc., show that the morbid appeal of tearful poetry affected Schubert as it does most adolescents. The one attractive song is a setting of Pope's *The Dying Christian to his Soul* (*Vital spark of heav'nly flame*), translated by Herder as *Verklärung* (*Transfiguration*). For the first time we see Schubert beginning to achieve variety without losing the sense of the song as a unit.

The most interesting group of works is the set of five string quartets (1) in C major (D. 32) of September 1812, (2) in B flat major (D. 36) composed between 19 November 1812 and 21 February 1813, (3) in C major (D. 46) of March 1813, with an extremely able finale, (4) in B flat major (D. 68) of June and August 1813, from which the slow movement and scherzo are missing, but which has a first movement of superb quality, and (5) in D major (D. 74) composed between 22 August and September 1813. The score of this fifth quartet bears in the composer's hand 'Trois Quatours . . . composés par Francois Schubert . . .'; the other two quartets of this proposed group were probably the one in E flat of the following November, and that in B flat of a year later (Op. 168). These quartets are excellent examples of early Schubert which, with all their faults of exuberance, occasional weak organisation, and imitations of Haydn and Mozart, are alive from first to last. The history of the first one is similar to the history of many of Schubert's early works in four movements. During the years of obscurity it lay on publishers' shelves. By the end of the nineteenth century it had disintegrated; the slow movement and the first part of the finale were mislaid. The 'Gesamtausgabe' included it in the 1890 volume of String Quartets as a *two* movement work. The present writer identified the slow movement and the missing part of the finale among the autograph collection of Konsul Otto Taussig, Malmö, Sweden, in September 1950.[1]

The *Andante* of the early String Quartet in B flat (D. 36) is a pure Schubertian idyll: one of the most attractive little movements in the work of his 'prentice years and a model of ternary structure. The central section in C flat major (the tonic key is B

[1] The Quartet was published by Breitkopf & Härtel, Wiesbaden; Parts, March 1955; Score, September 1956. It was first performed by the Element Quartet in a broadcast concert on 23 December 1955.

FIRST PAGE OF THE SLOW MOVEMENT FROM STRING QUARTET NO. 2,
IN C MAJOR. SEPTEMBER 1812

Published 1955 *Herr Otto Taussig*

flat) is a remarkable anticipation of his future fondness for the so-called 'Neapolitan' relationship (see p. 222). He made several attempts at a theme for this movement before he was satisfied. His manuscript shows these rejected efforts:

The second one (*b*) is not a new idea. He had already used it as the basis of an *Andante* in C major for the first String Quartet, mentioned above, and rejected it altogether; he then arranged the movement as a short, pianoforte solo (D. 29). Why he should reconsider it here is a mystery. To some of the music in the fifth string quartet, in D major, we shall return later.

IV

In October 1813 Schubert was offered a further period of study at the *Stadtkonvikt* by means of a grant from an endowment fund (the 'Meerfeld' endowment) if he would improve his mathematics. But he refused the offer and left the school. This was probably in part due to his father's persuasion, in part the outcome of his own self-realisation. He now lived at home in the schoolhouse of the Säulengasse and by December was attending daily the St. Anna 'Normal-Hauptschule', a kind of Training College for primary teachers. We encounter two legends at this point of his life, both of which can be discounted. The first is that he ran away from the *Konvikt*. This story derives from a Viennese writer named L. A. Frankl, who was visited in 1868 by Schubert's friend Franz von Schober. After the visit Frankl wrote a memorandum of their conversation in which Schober is supposed to have told him of Schubert's action. Apart from its inherent doubtfulness, and the fact that Schober's story relates to a supposed event of over fifty years before, the report was strongly denied by Albert Stadler, who was, after all, at school with Schubert; Schober did not meet Schubert till two years after the supposed incident. The other legend, which is found in most biographies of the composer, is that he decided to become a schoolmaster to evade conscription. The period of conscription was seven years, and although there were many loopholes, no exception was made for schoolmasters. This alone disposes of the allegation. But the truth is that Schubert was too short. The minimum height for such military service was 1.58 metres (=5 Austrian feet); Schubert's height was 1.567 metres (=4.9 Austrian feet).[1]

During the month or so between his leaving school and starting work at the St. Anna Training College, he finished his first symphony, in D major. (Strictly speaking it is no. 2, since there is a partly completed score of the first movement of an earlier one in the same key. This was composed *c.* 1812.) It is said to be dedicated to Dr. Innocenz Lang, and intended for performance on his name-day, i.e. the day of his patron saint, St. Francis. Neither statement is correct. The name-day of Dr. Lang was 4 October (the same as Schubert's); the symphony was not completed until 28 October 1813. It is his second symphony, in B flat, which Schubert dedicated to his old principal. The first symphony is the culmination of the schoolboy compositions, an astonishing creation for a lad of sixteen. Absolutely in the idiom of its day, it is therefore reminiscent of Haydn and Mozart and early Beethoven, but only in the sense that each of these composers reminds us at times of the other two. Schubert's symphony is completely individual in content. In the slow movement particularly, tender, intimate, full of musical fancy, we hear his voice alone. It was

[1] The Austrian foot is slightly longer than the English foot, but this does not affect the issue. In English measure Schubert was 5 ft. 1½ in.

probably performed by the students' orchestra in the *Stadtkonvikt*; otherwise the first public performance took place in 1881, sixty-seven years after its composition, when August Manns gave it (complete) at the Crystal Palace Concerts.

Immediately his symphony was completed, Schubert began work on his first opera, 'Des Teufels Lustschloss' ('The Devil's Castle'), which occupied him intermittently for the next year. The words are by August von Kotzebue, the dramatist already mentioned. Kotzebue was enormously popular all over Europe. He was widely travelled, sophisticated and egotistical, a tasteless purveyor of fashionable dramas. In 1819 he was assassinated in Berlin on suspicion of being a Russian spy, an event whose more distant ripples were later to affect Schubert. Although his play is fifth-rate and calls for enormous mechanical resources on the stage, it was a 'stock' libretto; many settings of it had been made before Schubert took it up, so that we can hardly blame him for not seeing its unsuitability when many older and more experienced composers had accepted it. He finished his first act on 11 January 1814, the second on 16 March, and the work was completed by 14 May. He then took it to Salieri for advice. What his master said led him to revise the first and third acts. The second version of Act I was finished on 3 September, that of Act III on 22 October 1814 almost exactly a year after the beginning of his work. All these manuscripts are extant. It is an ambitious opera, with plenty of admirable music in it. It can best be discussed, however, with the later operatic work in Chapter III.

The work on this opera was, it has been said, intermittent. It was interrupted on many occasions, and during those interruptions Schubert produced works more congenial to the music lover. His String Quartet in E flat (D. 87) was the first of them, composed in November 1813. It was not published until after Schubert's death and the manuscript, a fragment, did not come to light until during the first World War. One of the oddest misdatings of a work by Schubert is the attribution of '1824' to this early quartet. Reasons for the mistake will be discussed later, but it persisted right through the nineteenth century. The work is a delightful one, with one of the best finales which Schubert penned this side 1819, but how could Schubertians, from Kreissle to Grove, and on into the 1900's, be deceived into grouping the boy's work with the man's—into grouping this E flat Quartet with the great one in A minor, Op. 29? Schubert did not himself publish the E flat Quartet and the placing of the Scherzo as a second movement is the publisher's arrangement (Czerny, Op. 125: no. 1); the composer was unfailingly orthodox over the order of the four-movement scheme. By the time the String Quartets were published in the 'Gesamtausgabe' (1890) doubts had arisen about the date '1824', and the quartet was given the tentative dating '*c.* 1817', which was certainly more plausible. The autograph manuscript, when it eventually re-appeared, was found to be dated 'November 1813'. A word might be added here on Schubert's meticulous dating of his manuscripts. In early works they are sometimes very detailed, the date appearing at the end as well as at the beginning (even when, in one case, it was the same day). Occasionally the time a work took him is triumphantly added: 'Done in 4½ hours' is written at the end of the first movement of the String Quartet in B flat, Op. 168. These accurate dates make the task of arranging his works chronologically a straightforward and congenial one. Grove has surmised that it was his father's methodical training which brought about the habit, but in actual fact the very early works are not so carefully dated as those which originated under the teaching of Salieri. It was probably the dating of these exercises written under supervision which induced the habit. In later years only the month and year were given; but the excellent practice persisted right up to the last work he wrote.

During his eight months training for teaching (December 1813 to August 1814) he wrote a number of songs much more attractive than the rather grim and long-drawn ballads of former years; Schubert's song volumes begin with a veritable iron age. The 1814 songs, however, include *Adelaide, Andenken* and *Geisternähe* (April), and *Der Abend* (July). The last song, a setting of words by Matthisson, is worth more than passing mention;

it is a rewarding example of secondary Schubert. The advent of *Gretchen am Spinnrade* three months later, so dramatic and epoch-making, eclipses the earlier songs of 1814. This is not quite fair to the graceful, serious little song of a doomed lover with its skilfully introduced *recitative* and the nocturnal atmosphere invoked so simply. At least these few songs do something to prepare us for *Gretchen*, as they certainly prepared Schubert.

A work which occupied him during February 1814 has become notorious. It is his so-called 'Guitar Quartet'. Actually it is Schubert's arrangement, with additional 'cello part, of a Trio for flute, viola and guitar by Wenzel Thomas Matiegka. Matiegka (1773–1830), resurrected from oblivion by this mis-attribution, was born at Chotzen in Bohemia. He studied music with the Abbé Gelinsk at Prague, went to Vienna in the early years of the century and worked there till his death. His Trio, entitled 'Noturno' (*sic*), was published as his Op. 21 by Artaria, Vienna, in 1807; it was, strange to note, dedicated by Matiegka to Count Johannes Esterházy, Schubert's future employer. Schubert's manuscript arrangement was discovered in 1918, and published eight years later in Munich under the editorship of Georg Kinsky, as an original work of the composer's. In the 'Zeitschrift für Musikwissenschaft', October 1928, O. E. Deutsch suggested that the work was spurious, and would prove to be an arrangement of someone else's Trio. His words were dramatically fulfilled. Three years later a well-known Danish guitar virtuoso, Thorwald Rischel, discovered an original edition of Matiegka's Op. 21 and realised that it was identical with Schubert's work. Rischel's is the only extant copy. Kinsky admitted the error, and Deutsch's acumen, in the 'Zeitschrift' of August 1932. It is surprising that anyone could accept the work as by Schubert, but many people did. The second Trio-section in the Menuetto is Schubert's own composition, and in the last movement—a set of variations—he has altered the order in the original, and turned Matiegka's Var. V into the major key, placing it first.

The genuine quartets of the year are for strings only: no. 7, in

D major, which is a slight work, and no. 8, in B flat major. This was published in 1863 as Op. 168. It was commenced as a String Trio, but Schubert changed his mind after a few lines were written. His interest in the string trio as a medium suggests that a trio of performers was readily available during these years, for we find two more examples later on, of excellent quality (both, incidentally, in B flat major again, a very favourite key). The String Quartet, Op. 168, shows his gradual emancipation from the 'mosaic' form typical of young men's work. The slow movement (*Andante sostenuto*) concludes with a remarkable 'Neapolitan' cadence—very prophetic of future uses, and the finale is an even more remarkable pointer to the future, suggesting in embryo the Scherzo of the great C major Symphony.

The summer months of 1814 were devoted to the composition of a Mass, his first completed setting, in F major. It was performed on 16 October at the Liechtental Church, and this was a great occasion for the young composer. His family and friends were there in force, and there is a well-known anecdote in which Salieri greeted Schubert after the performance with the words: 'You are my pupil, Franz, and will do me much honour.' Unfortunately a small doubt arises when we find that, by a strange coincidence, there is an entry in the diary of Wenzel Tomašcek for this very day. Tomašcek, a famous pianist-composer of that day, whose work will be mentioned later in this book since he was a forerunner of Schubert in the short, lyrical PF. piece, wrote in his diary that a Mass by Salieri was performed in the Court Chapel on that 16 October 1814. Salieri would almost certainly have been present in the Chapel for the occasion. The music of Schubert's first Mass occupied him from 17 May to 22 July. It is melodious, modest in conception and extremely competently written; it shows the influence of Haydn—there are distinct echoes of 'The Seasons' in it—and also the influence of those unnumbered and unnamed men who wrote the music for the services in the Imperial Court Chapel where Schubert had recently sung as a choirboy. That is to say, it is of its period, light, formal and devoid of any profundity and soul searching, as we should expect in a seventeen year old boy's work. It has the same easy-going, intimate style that is found in his music for the offices of the Church, which led to their brief dismissal a few pages back.

The soprano solos in the Mass in F were sung by a young woman of Schubert's acquaintance named Therese Grob. Her ancestors were Swiss, and the family lived near the Schubert home, managing a small silk factory. They were cultured, fairly well-to-do people. The mother was a widow and both her children, Therese and Heinrich, were musical. Schubert was a constant visitor to their home. His eldest brother, Ignaz, was married to an aunt of Therese's, and he was said to be in love with the plain faced, but tender hearted Therese herself. For Heinrich, who was a 'cellist, Schubert composed a few instrumental works; for Therese, a number of sacred solos including a fine *Salve Regina* (1815), and possibly many Lieder, were written. Her voice was high, a pure lyric soprano. The love affair between her and Schubert came to an end, it is said, because of his uncertain financial position and the unlikelihood of his ever being a reliable breadwinner. Therese made sure of her daily bread; she passes from the Schubert story on 21 November 1820 when she married Johann Bergmann, a master baker. The descendants of Heinrich, a family named Meangya, of Mödling, Vienna, possess a small collection of Schubert songs in a volume called 'Therese Grob's Album'; amongst them are three still unpublished songs which the family refuse to release. They are:

i. *Am ersten Maimorgen* (*The first of May*), words by Claudius, composed in 1816;
ii. *Mailied* (*May Song*), words by Hölty, composed in 1816;
iii. *Klage* (*Lament*) anonymous, composed 1817.

All three are charming examples of lesser Schubert songs, and the prohibition of the Meangya family is incomprehensible.

A second performance of the Mass may have followed ten days

later at the Augustinian 'Hofkirche' (Court Church), in the Inner City; it would be, therefore, a more important occasion, but accounts of this event differ. Therese Grob said in after years that she could not remember there being a second performance, and the anecdotes grow more and more confused and unsatisfactory. But more important in the history of Schubert's creative achievement than the composition and performance of this Mass, is the appearance on 19 October of his first masterpiece in song, that is, the appearance in music of the first great German song in the sense understood today: *Gretchen am Spinnrade* from Goethe's 'Faust'. It was Schubert's first encounter with the work of the poet and the impact was tremendous. Never before in music had a poem so deeply and sincerely felt been matched with music as deep and sincere. *Gretchen* may claim to be the first song in which the music presents and explains the words in a fashion that the poet-dramatist could not, even though that poet be Goethe. The way in which the monotonous figure in the pianoforte accompaniment, which is a musical symbol of the spinning-wheel, stops at the climax of the song, when the girl's transport robs her of the power of physical movement, is unforgettable; but so, too, is the broken, sobbing resumption of that figure on the piano, for Schubert gives us here not only the spasmodic starting of the spinning-wheel, but the painful return of everyday sensation after the tranced numbness of the girl's body:

> *Oh, dreadful is the check—intense the agony—*
> *When the ear begins to hear, and the eye begins to see;*
> *When the pulse begins to throb, the brain to think again;*
> *The soul to feel the flesh, and the flesh to feel the chain.*

Yet the musical form of the song, bound to a beautiful unity by the soft, whirring accompaniment, if looked at coldly, can bear microscopic examination. It has a three-fold structure, each section terminated by Gretchen's cry 'Meine Ruh' ist hin, mein Herz ist schwer' ('My peace is gone, my heart is heavy'). This structure was imposed on Goethe by Schubert; he repeats the refrain at the end to achieve it. But there is one quality in the song which Goethe imposed on Schubert, and which has been overlooked in the commentaries: it is the sense of rapid heartbeats, almost of excitement, in the lines which Gretchen speaks. One could imagine an actress uttering them breathlessly. In the middle section of the song Schubert writes the powerful emotional and musical climax, but each of the other two sections has a similar rise and relaxation. But the wonder of the song, and it comes from his greatest gift, is its melodic development. He is unrivalled in this ability to evolve a continuously significant, yet closely inter-related, melodic line from an initial melodic fragment. In *Gretchen* the first phrase is this:

Other melodies in the song, from first to last, in all their variety and passion, evolve from (*a*) or (*b*). It has been said that Salieri could not teach Schubert how to decide whether a play would make a suitably theatrical libretto; how to reject and alter and add until a promising libretto was certain of success on the boards. But this power of melodic evolution and development is something which neither Salieri nor anyone else could teach; it was part of Schubert's powerful endowment and no one could have given it to him by tuition. The tiny 'Menuetto' movement from the String Quartet in D major, mentioned a few pages back, shows how Schubert, in these minor and unconsidered instrumental works, had prepared his pen for these transports of his genius. Here is quoted the opening of the melody from the first violin part, and part of its later development:

Before the close of the year Schubert set five other poems from Goethe including a further extract from 'Faust'—the *Scene in the Cathedral.* The best of the five, and a song which became quite popular a few years later, is the *Schäfers Klagelied* (*Shepherd's Lament*). Again the musical form is flawless, and Goethe's rather stilted words (he was imitating, parodying almost, the words of a well-known folk-song) are given music beyond their worth.

Schubert was established as an assistant teacher in his father's school. The 'shades of the prison-house' may have been closing upon him, but he had, in good measure, one famous characteristic of the Viennese, the capacity to create a 'dream world' into which the individual may slip to escape the unpleasant—or uncongenial, at least—realities of life around him. With many Viennese the world is the world of music. It was so with Schubert. That he escaped from the realities of his uncongenial duties into a world of composition is only too evident from the overwhelming list of works which originated in the first two years which he spent behind the schoolmaster's desk. Perhaps he knew that escape from the *Stadtkonvikt* would release him for his desired task. Perhaps it was an unrealised urge which drove him. But the results, from whatever cause, have no parallel elsewhere in music.

II

1815-1817

I

His friendship with the staunch Josef von Spaun brought Schubert rich rewards. Not in the material sense, unless we accept that rather charming but improbable story that Spaun supplied him with desperately needed music-paper; as Brahms has pointed out, Schubert's extravagance with music-paper as shown in his *Konvikt* scores, does not suggest any shortage of it. But in propaganda, in introductions to new friends, in artistic encouragement, Spaun was tireless. He was a student of law, and at this period was studying with Heinrich Watteroth, a professor at the University of Vienna. Amongst Spaun's friends and acquaintances, fellow students of his in law, were Johann Mayrhofer, Franz von Schober and Josef Witteczek. All these men were sooner or later introduced to his friend, the young composer. In December 1814 Spaun had given Schubert a poem *Am See*, which had been set to music there and then. A day or so later Spaun took the poet, Mayrhofer, to the Säulengasse house and introduced him to Schubert using the song as an excellent reason for doing so. (It is a pity that this first song from so fruitful a partnership is not more endearing: after a promising start it becomes entirely uninteresting.) Mayrhofer was a sensitive, introspective man, incurably realistic, and hence a pessimist. 'Morbid' is a word frequently used to describe his philosophy as we see it in his poetry. It was an outlook due in part to chronic ill-health. He and Schubert became more and more friendly during the two years following their meeting.

A more dramatic encounter was with Franz von Schober. This young man was the same age as Schubert but his origin and upbringing were as different as could be imagined. His father was born in Saxony of Swedish parents, his mother was a Viennese woman, Katharina Derffel. Shortly after their marriage, Schober senior returned to Sweden with his young wife. Schober was born in Torup Castle, near Malmö, where his father was the estate manager. The ties between Axel Stiernblad, the owner of the Castle, and the Schobers must have been fairly close; they named their eldest son Axel in his honour, and when he died, Katharina von Schober, then a widow, inherited his money. She returned to Austria and enjoyed a period of wealthy retirement. Axel von Schober chose a career in the army, while Franz, his younger brother, attended the convent school of Kremsmünster, and then went to Vienna in the autumn of 1815 to study law. Here he met Spaun and heard of Schubert. Spaun denied in after years the statement in Kreissle's biography of Schubert that Schober had learnt to know Schubert's songs at Linz in 1813, and he is obviously right. There were only a few songs in existence then, and certainly not the kind that would spread Schubert's fame.

Schober did not wait for an introduction. He sought Schubert out in the Säulengasse schoolhouse, coming upon him actually in the schoolroom, teaching small children and surrounded by piles of manuscripts. So we read in Schober's reminiscences. But even if we ignore any details of their meeting the substance remains. To Schober's remonstrances, enthusiasms and encouragements, Schubert could not remain indifferent. Half-prepared already to abandon teaching and throw the reins to his genius, Schubert was won over, and from that meeting with Schober his days as a schoolteacher were numbered. For this we owe Schober a debt of gratitude. There are others. This must be said because Schober's influence on Schubert in after years did not always tend towards the fulfilment of his genius. Schober himself was a dilettante: with no necessity to consider ways and means he tried one thing after another, law, acting, writing, publishing and so on. Schubert was fonder of him than of any other of his friends. Another of the things for which we must also be grateful to Schober was his introduction of Schubert to the elderly singer Vogl.

In the spring of 1816, Schubert tried to obtain a post as music master at a training college—the 'Normal-Hauptschule'—at Laibach, now Ljubljana in Jugoslavia, an establishment similar to the college in the Annagasse, that is, one for the training of teachers for primary schools. His application was undoubtedly inspired by Schober's visit; it may have been equally due to his desire to improve his material prospects in order to be in a position to marry Therese Grob. The post was advertised in February. He received a testimonial from Salieri and in April applied for the situation. Four months later, in September 1816, he heard of his ill-success (the leisurely tempo of these transactions will be encountered again: it was not by any means exceptional).

The songs which Schubert had composed in 1814 and 1815, particularly the Goethe songs *Gretchen am Spinnrade* and *Erlking*, were by now becoming familiar and very popular with his friends. In April Spaun wrote a letter to Goethe at Weimar and with it sent a volume of songs (the texts all by Goethe) written out in fair copy by Schubert. The letter, so obsequious in tone that only a man whose head had been turned by praise would fail to be nauseated by it, is dated 17 April 1816. This approach to Goethe arose from an attempt by his friends in that year, to bring out a series of books containing the songs arranged according to the poets of the texts. The first two were to be of texts by Goethe, and comprised these songs:

BOOK I

Gretchen am Spinnrade
Schäfers Klagelied
Rastlose Liebe
Geistes-Gruss
An Mignon
Nähe des Geliebten
Meeresstille
Der Fischer
Wanderers Nachtlied ('Du der von dem Himmel bist')
Erster Verlust
Die Spinnerin
Heidenröslein
Wonne der Wehmut
Erlkönig
Der König in Thule
Jägers Abendlied

Schubert's manuscript of these fair copies, dated March 1816, is in the Prussian State Library, Berlin. It may not be quite complete; there is a possibility that one or even more songs are missing from the book. Book II contained these songs:

BOOK II

Nachtgesang	*Der Sänger*
Der Gott und die Bajadere	*Der Rattenfänger*
Sehnsucht ('*Was zieht mir das Herz so?*')	*An den Mond* (I)
Mignon	*Bundeslied*
Trost in Tränen	*Wer kauft Liebesgötter?*
	Tischlied

The manuscript of Book II, also fair copies by Schubert and dated May 1816, is partly in the Paris 'Conservatoire' Library and partly in the Vienna City Library.

Commenting on Spaun's action, Richard Capell has these unforgettable words:

> The songs were sent as offerings to the altar at Weimar, where the ageing Goethe was (while still falling in love) living half-deified. They were not acknowledged; and none of the throng of inspiring genies that wheeled invisible about the incomparable sage and bard whispered to him that through this Viennese bohemian's music and not otherwise would his poetry reach masses of the earth's population for whom without it Goethe would be nothing but a name. ('Schubert's Songs', 1928, p. 9.)

Goethe did return the books of songs to Spaun.

In May, Spaun, with his friend and fellow student Josef Witteczek, moved into lodgings in the house of Professor Watteroth in the Erdberggasse. Witteczek was courting Wilhelmine, Watteroth's daughter. Spaun introduced him to Schubert, and in later years he became an ardent Schubertian and amassed a superb collection of Schubertiana: first editions, manuscript copies of songs and instrumental works, newspaper cuttings, programmes, portraits. For a short while—possibly for a holiday only—Schubert lived there with them. According to Kreissle the manuscript of some dances of that period bore the words 'Composed while confined to my room at Erdberg, May 1816'; this was apparently a record of the rather worn practical joke of locking a composer in a room and keeping him there until he has written something. There is another example of Schubert having been subjected to this jest: it is in connection with the Overture in F for PF. Duet, and the story then was told by Josef Hüttenbrenner. Neither manuscript, however, survives with Schubert's words to confirm the anecdote.

We do possess a few pages from a diary which he was keeping that year. They are dated 'June' and 'September'. The diary was rescued from oblivion by the famous collector Alois Fuchs, who recorded that he found it being sold piecemeal by a second-hand bookseller. Later the leaves became a possession of Gustav Petter, also a collector, chiefly of Schubert manuscripts, and today they belong partly to the Vienna *Gesellschaft der Musikfreunde*, partly to the Vienna City Library. The pages are not very interesting. The composer had returned to teaching and was living again in the Säulengasse house. On the page dated 13 June 1816 we read:

> I played variations by Beethoven, sang Goethe's *Rastlose Liebe* and Schiller's *Amalia*. Unanimous applause for the first, less for the second. Although I myself consider my *Rastlose Liebe* more successful than *Amalia* it can't be denied that Goethe's genius for lyric poetry contributed much to the applause.

This extract, familiar from being often quoted, gains a little from a discovery made only a few years ago in a library of the Austrian town of Linz. This was of the original manuscript of *Rastlose Liebe* with its definite date '19 May 1815'. The song had always been ascribed vaguely to the year 1815. We now know that it was actually composed on the same day as *Amalia*, whose date of composition has always been accurately known. So Schubert, on that June day of 1816, may have sung the two songs from an album which contained the batch of songs he wrote in mid-May 1815.

The accounts of the composition of two cantatas this summer seem to occupy more room in the Schubertian biographies than they merit. The first was Schubert's musical contribution to the celebrations attending the fiftieth anniversary of Salieri's advent in Vienna. His pupils organised a concert of original music for

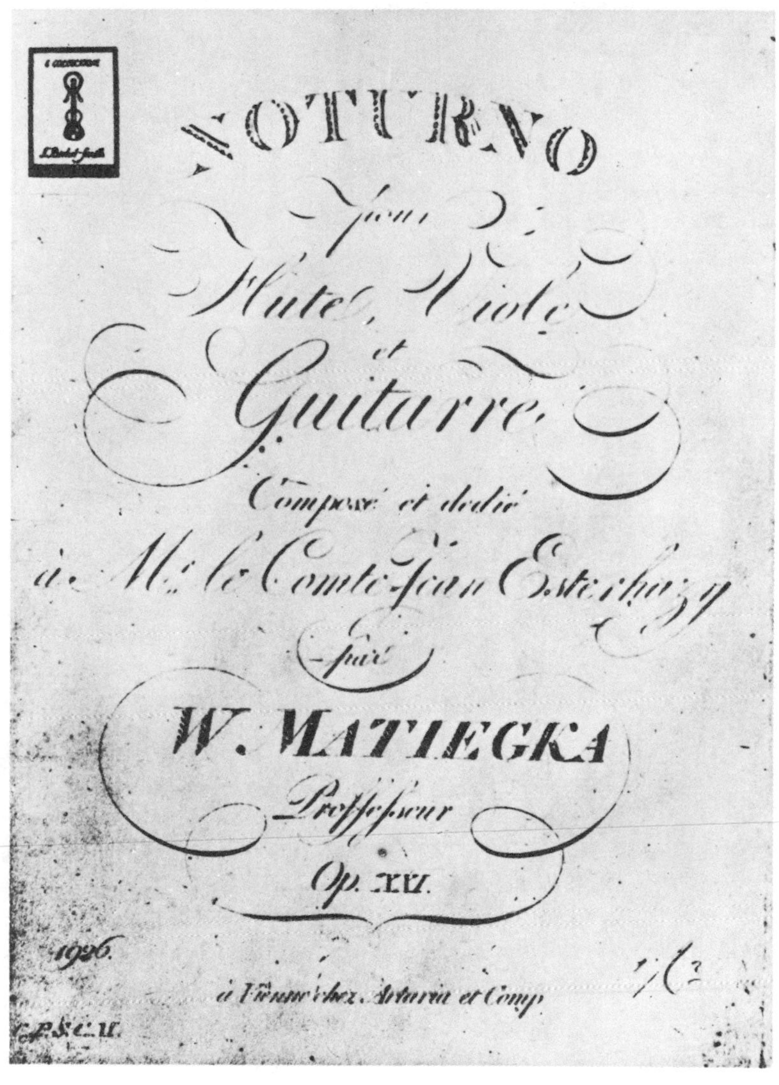

TITLE-PAGE OF THE 'NOTURNO', OP. 21, BY MATIEGKA
THE BASIS OF SCHUBERT'S SO-CALLED 'GUITAR' QUARTET
Mr. Thorwald Rischel

the day (evidently Schubert was considered, publicly and privately, his pupil). There are two versions, both extant, of the music which Schubert devised, but the cantata had only occasional value: little of it now strikes one as worthy of its author. The other cantata was likewise for the celebration of a teacher—for the name-day of Professor Watteroth.[1] His law students organised the affair and one of them, Phillip Dräxler, wrote the poem. It was called 'Prometheus' and contained delicate comparisons between the semi-divine craftsman and the professor himself. (It should be remembered here and later that in Schubert's day Prometheus was looked upon as a confident creator and craftsman, rather than as Shelley's bound and tortured Titan, hurling imprecations at Zeus.) Schubert obtained £4 from the students for his music and entered the fact—rather shyly—in his diary. The music consisted of solos, choruses and recitatives, and must have been of finer quality than the Salieri example, since it created a deep impression. We have no means of judging since the score was lost at the time of Schubert's death. Two law students who sang in the chorus made Schubert's acquaintance on the occasion. One was the poet Franz von Schlechta, an old student of the *Konvikt*, but who had attended after Schubert's time there. The other was Leopold von Sonnleithner, the son of a noted Viennese barrister, Ignaz; both father and son were ardent music lovers and in Ignaz Sonnleithner's house in the 'Gundelhof' weekly concerts of music were held to which large numbers of guests were invited. The name Sonnleithner is a familiar one in musical biography since the elder brother of Ignaz, Josef von Sonnleithner, was at one time a music publisher, and as Court Secretary had had a hand in the libretto of Beethoven's 'Fidelio'. Repeated efforts were made in the middle of the nineteenth century to find the lost 'Prometheus', until finally Leopold von Sonnleithner wrote a full account of the work, as he remembered it, told the story of its unhappy disappearance, appealed to the musical public for information, and even offered a reward for its recovery. There was no result. His account was published in

[1] This was apparently a Protestant name-day. Details are given in O. E. Deutsch's 'Documentary Biography', p. 67.

Fellners Blätter für Theater, Musik u. bildende Kunst, 5 March 1867. He wrote there that the cantata should have been performed on 12 July 1816 in the garden of the Erdberggasse house, but owing to bad weather the performance was actually given on 24 July. The score and parts were then sent to Johann Baptist Gänsbacher, the conductor of a Music Union at Innsbruck; many years later the work was retrieved from the Göttweih Monastery (*c.* 1825). It remained in Sonnleithner's possession until 1828, when Schubert himself took it back. The composer's death occurred a few months afterwards, and the work vanished without trace. It is clear that Schubert lent it to a professional acquaintance, and it is an ironical thought that it may have masqueraded in print under another name, ignored because that name was obscure, and then lost a second time!

Schubert may have been flattered by the appearance that year of two poems in his honour. The first was by Schlechta, written after the performance of 'Prometheus'; the other, more adulatory, was by his new friend Mayrhofer, entitled *Geheimnis: an Franz Schubert*. It begins

Say who taught thee songs
So caressing, so sweet?

Schubert, with no compunction, set the verses to music—a charming song this time.

Schober had been to Sweden during the summer to attend to family concerns connected with his mother's inheritance. He returned in the late autumn, and settled down in residence with his mother, in a house in the Landskrongasse. In December 1816 Schubert joined him, and this time it was not for a short holiday but for many months. It was the first step to freedom after two years of servitude.

II

But those two years had produced, in spite of the duties of training and teaching, such a bulk of work that the mind is almost stupefied in contemplating it. Hard work will not explain it; a thirst, a rapacity for composition, is suggested.[1] Some idea of how Schubert worked can be obtained if we devise a kind of calendar for one of the most productive months, that is, July 1815. There are several of these 'productive months' in the composer's career—December 1820 is another one, and June 1824. But none of them can compare with the July of 1815 as these details show:

July 1815

2nd. 'Lieb Minna' (Stadler).
5th. 'Salve Regina' in F, Op. 47, for soprano, orchestra and organ continuo.
Wandrers Nachtlied (I) (Goethe).
Der Fischer (Goethe).
Erster Verlust (Goethe).
7th. *Idens Nachtgesang* (Kosegarten).
Von Ida (Kosegarten).
Die Erscheinung (Kosegarten).
Die Täuschung (Kosegarten).
8th. *Das Sehnen* (Kosegarten).
9th. 'Fernando' (Stadler), one act operetta completed (it had been started on 22 June).
11th. 'Hymne an den Unendlichen' (Schiller) for accompanied S.A.T.B. Op. 112: no. 3.
First movement of Symphony no. 3, in D, resumed (it had been started on 24 May.)
12th. First movement of symphony finished.
15th. *Geist der Liebe* (Kosegarten).
Der Abend (Kosegarten).
Tischlied (Goethe).
Second movement of Symphony no. 3 commenced
19th. The whole symphony completed.
22nd. *Sehnsucht der Liebe* (Körner), revision of a song first composed in April 1813.
24th. *Abends unter der Linde* (Kosegarten)—first setting.
25th. *Abends unter der Linde* (Kosegarten)—second setting.
Die Mondnacht (Kosegarten).
Das Abendrot, vocal trio with PF. acc. (Kosegarten).

[1] The years 1815–1816 occupy 165 pages in O. E. Deutsch's 'Thematic Catalogue', that is, just over one-third of the book. 382 works are there listed.

26th. 'Claudine von Villa Bella' (Goethe). Three act operetta commenced.
27th. *Huldigung* (Kosegarten)
Alles um Liebe (Kosegarten).

Eighteen songs, it will be seen, were composed in this month alone. Although it is higher than the average monthly output, yet that year, 1815, saw the creation of a hundred and fifty songs; the next year there were over a hundred more, and the poets range from Goethe to Schubert's own versifying friends, and obscure scribblers like Schmidt, of Lübeck, who wrote the words of *Der Wanderer*.

The gibe that Schubert could set a bill of fare to music arose because it seems, at first glance, that he set uncritically any text that came his way. The over-abundant music appeared to be poured out over any verse, of whatever quality, provided that it treated of themes which appealed to him, of Nature in its burgeoning Springtime, the human heart and its cries. If sometimes the verses which we encounter in his songs seem pallid and pointless it is because German poetry in those days simply had not the wherewithal to supply the ardent young genius of Schubert. He had to make do with the second-rate for there was not enough of the first-rate to satisfy his needs. And those needs were clear cut in his own mind; there is every evidence that from the poetic almanachs and anthologies and collected 'Gedichte' available in Vienna, he made a careful and discriminating selection. He was well aware of what he wanted in a poem, second-rate or not, and nearly all his masterpieces, large and small, were born of poems which gave him what he wanted: a definite sentiment, a definite scene, and, if possible, a telling last verse—or even last *line*. It is not in his minor verse that these qualities are missing, but frequently in his choice of texts from the major poets—in the high-flown and rhetorical work of Schiller for instance. Amongst the 1815 Schiller songs is an attractive lyric *Lied: Es ist so angenehm, so süss*, and it is an ironical fact that Schiller's authorship is disputed. The words are probably by Karoline von Wolzogen, an early friend and patron of the poet.

In considering Schubert's choice of poetry, with its appreciable amount of indifferent verse, we are faced with two questions. The first is whether great poetry serves the ends of music at all well. Has it not such self-sufficiency, such verbal music of its own, that added music is apt to slow down the swift thought and nullify the melody of the words? Shelley's 'Music, when soft voices die' has attracted many composers, big and small, since it was penned. Its verse is so melodious, its thought of the essence of lyrical poetry. Is that not precisely why all its composers have failed in their settings? Take as an example from Schubert, Goethe's text *An den Mond.* This is a fine and famous poem, most deep in feeling and musically expressed. Schubert's first setting, of 19 August 1815, is a plain, strophic song, quite unenterprising. His second setting, written shortly afterwards, is 'onrunning', and ambitiously sets out to match Goethe. The music is certainly an evocation of the serene moonlight—soft, melancholy, and richly harmonised. Every care is lavished in the workmanship, especially in the 'river' stanza. But the song fails to reach the heart of the poem. Goethe's blended moods of content and unrest, and the expression of them, are beyond any music. Schubert catches the broad indication, but cannot possibly present the poet's detailed music.

The second question is this: is it not being wise after the event to condemn Schubert for a lack of discrimination in setting verses by his contemporary poets? Who of today could be certain, however sure his taste and judgement, of discriminating amongst modern poetry in a way that critics a hundred years hence would applaud? The young composer of today who sets to music the verses of Dylan Thomas and Robert Graves and Ezra Pound cannot be sure what the critics of A.D. 2058 will say of his taste in these matters. And if he, from time to time, should set to music those poems by relatively obscure people which he finds in the literary periodicals of today, he can be even less sure. But *we* should probably commend his taste. The music critics of Schubert's own day commended his choice of poetic texts, if they touched on the subject at all. As to Schubert's readiness to compose for any text which came his way—there is definite evidence to the contrary. He refused, almost obstinately, to set to music some half-a-dozen poems which were urged upon him by interested people, and not lightly urged. Two were poets: Johann Friedrich Rochlitz (1769–1842), the author of 'Der erste Ton', and Johann von Zedlitz (1790–1862), the author of the famous Napoleonic ballad 'Die nächtliche Heerschau'. Schubert refused both poems. The third of these persons was the singer Anna Milder-Hauptmann, who asked him, in her letters of 1825, to set Leitner's poem 'Der Nachtschmetterling' and if that did not please him, Goethe's 'Verschiedene Empfindungen an einem Platz'. But he ignored both her suggestions. Finally, an acquaintance, Albert Schellmann, an accomplished pianist, asked him to set his love poem 'Das Sternchen' to music so that it could serve as a valentine. But Schubert declined the request.[1]

German lyric poetry during the eighteenth century is represented in Schubert by widely diverse figures: Herder (1744–1803), Klopstock (1724–1803) and Johann Peter Uz (1720–1796). A consideration of Herder's supreme position can be left until Schubert's songs of later years. The young composer's settings of Klopstock and Uz are dutiful rather than inspired. *An Sie* and the engrossing *Die frühen Gräber* by Klopstock are two small songs of great charm: they contain workmanship so delicate that it goes unnoticed. *Die Sommernacht* is an unknown song because of its continuing exclusion from anthologies of the composer's songs. It needs an intelligent singer, for the episodic music requires skilful presentation; but the song is a lesser masterpiece. *Das Rosenband* (1815) and *Edone* (1816) are also rarely sung, but both, especially the second, are satisfying examples of his lyric forms—tuneful, with touches of poetry in the accompaniments. J. P. Uz wrote polished verses in the fashionable Anacreontic vogue of the day; unfortunately the best of Schubert's settings of six of his poems is the mutilated *An Chloen* (1816). Settings of Johann Georg Jacobi (1740–1814), like Uz an Anacreontic stylist, but more lyrical, are over-shadowed by the supreme and celebrated

[1] Since the above was written a lost letter from Schubert to the poet J. G. Seidl has come to light: 4 August 1828. Schubert declines a poem offered to him by Seidl since he could not discover in it anything at all which was suitable for music. ('Music & Letters', ed. by Eric Blom, October 1956.)

Litany for All Souls' Day (1816), but this is not perhaps fair to the delightfully fresh song *Die Perle*, a modest example of Schubert's thematic development, by which the whole song, accompaniment and melody, arises from the first two bars of the voice part.

A group of minor German poets, who were of the generation previous to Schubert, provided him in those years with some hundred poems, and they were clothed with a varied music which at no point touches sublimity, but is at all points charming, melodious and full of gentle poetry. L. C. Hölty (1748–1776) died even younger than Schubert; his small scale, fluent verses have none of the fire and strangeness of the 'Romantic' movement, yet foretell unmistakably that pathos and melancholy which were so fashionable in Schubert's Vienna after the upheavals of the Napoleonic wars. *Die Mainacht* is a strophic song in D minor, in which Schubert writes a characteristic, sad-sweet tune to match the poet's fluting nightingale; *Seligkeit* is a merry Ländler dance, which does not quite, perhaps, hit off Hölty's kind of bliss, but which gives one of its own—more intense and earthy. Two masterpieces are *An den Mond: Geuss, Lieber Mond* written on the same day as the previous song, 17 May 1815, and *Klage an den Mond* of almost exactly a year later. (Hölty's obsession with the moon as a poetic symbol is a psychological indication of much interest.) Each of these moon-poems is a good example of Schubert's 'modified-strophic' song, in which the endless changes he makes defy classification: one can only give instances. *An den Mond* has four verses; the first and last are set to a brooding tune in F minor (12/8), the second and third to a contrasting one in F major (4/4). *Klage an den Mond* is more refined; the 6/8 tune in F major for the first verse—the happy past—is differently, more poignantly, harmonised for the second verse—the regretful present; the third verse, which foretells the poet's early death, is newly composed but its melody has affinities with the former one. The music redeems the almost morbid sentiments.

Ludwig Kosegarten (1758–1818), a country priest in Rügen, North Germany, wrote of homely themes but with a somewhat pretentious style. Schubert was enthusiastically absorbed with his work during the summer and autumn months of 1815. On one day, October 19, he set seven of this poet's works to music, and in the 'calendar' for July, given above, we can see his engrossment. Two of the seven October songs are to the poet's lady, Rosa; *An Rosa*, I and II, are both short, and altogether overlooked. But they are melodious and warmly harmonised, and they lie in hand and voice so comfortably that a singer and a pianist would find them an excellent change in a Schubert programme. A third song from the incredible day is *Luisens Antwort*, which deserves a mention, since, apart from its own small merit, it has an outside interest. The poem was written by Kosegarten as an 'answer' to one by Klamer Schmidt called *Lied der Trennung*. Schmidt's pathetic poem is the heart-broken farewell of a lover to his Luise, certain that she will forget him. Kosegarten makes the girl answer with eternal vows of devotion. The interest lies in the fact that Mozart set the first to music in Vienna, on 23 May 1787, and Schubert set the pendant to music twenty-eight years later: Schubert answering Mozart. *Das Sehnen* is a more characteristic and passionate song, and in *Die Mondnacht* we have the best of the series, with touches of Schubertian harmonic piquancies and poetic fancy. The last song, the only Kosegarten setting in 1816, *An die untergehende Sonne* is rather cloying and too long drawn to challenge comparison with *Die Mondnacht*.

Friedrich von Matthisson (1761–1831), a native of Saxony, theologian turned poet, who earned his living as a Professor of Economics, had been praised by Schiller: perhaps a dubious recommendation where Schubert is concerned. He wrote Nature poetry, not leading to gentle melancholy and introspection like Hölty, but purely descriptive and eventually monotonous. He is the author of twenty of Schubert's texts. Oddly enough, the settings of 1814 are more interesting, on the whole, than the later ones of 1815 and 1816. The group is less attractive than those of Hölty and Kosegarten. The best of the Matthisson songs are the pure, nobly conceived *Entzückung* (1816) and the *Todtenkranz für ein Kind* with its very original harmonies (1815). He is the author of a number of Schubert's part-songs.

The last of this group of poets is Johann von Salis-Seewis (1762–1834), a Swiss poet; Schubert's settings of his poems are very slight, but there is solemnity in the music he wrote for the famous poem *Lied: in's stille Land*, and *Der Herbstabend* is beautifully written for the voice. Both songs are of March 1816. There was a last setting of Salis, five years later, *Der Jüngling an der Quelle*, which is wholly Schubertian and irresistable.

Goethe's advent in German literature can be compared with his advent in Schubert's cognisance. Just as Goethe's stature dwarfs the poets before him, so do Schubert's Goethe songs dwarf his previous efforts. Not that Schubert works always on the scale of *Gretchen am Spinnrade* and the *Erlking*. The song *Rastlose Liebe* of May 1815 is one of the great Goethe songs, as are the 'Harper' songs (from the novel *Wilhelm Meister*) and *An Schwager Kronos* of 1816; but there are smaller love songs and lyric moods which show equally his excited genius. *Am Flusse* of February 1815, in his stormy-melancholy key, D minor, is of the true Schubertian gold, but its patch-work construction makes it inferior to the second, serene setting of 1822 (see page 203). The D minor song is almost a miniature *Gretchen*, with a similar climax of emotional transport (at 'meiner Treue Hohn'). A more successful song on the same theme of regret for past love, less passionate, but flawlessly constructed, is the lovely *Erster Verlust* of July 1815. The lightly melodious *Heidenröslein* and *Die Spinnerin* of August, the two settings of *Meeresstille* of 20 and 21 June, are such perfect translations of the poems into musical images, and so in keeping with the poet's own pronouncements on the function of music in song, that one can only conclude that Goethe never looked at the volume which Spaun sent to him, nor sought anyone else's judgement in the matter.

At the other end of the scale there is a handful of Goethe songs which are entirely lacking in appeal. Such songs as *Der Rattenfänger*, *Der Gott und die Bajadere* and *Bundeslied* are frankly tedious.

In the September or early October of 1815 comes the most familiar incident in the Schubertian biography, the composition of the *Erlking*. Most familiar: because the *Erlking*, for a hundred years after its composition, was considered to be his supreme effort in song; and the grisly subject, a perfect example of 'Romantic' scare-mongering, perfectly written by Goethe, gave it a popularity over and above its music; and so his friends vied with each other in recording the incidentals of its composition. Unhappily, it is impossible, unless one shrinks from challenging them and allows oneself to be lulled into uncritical acceptance, to believe that they remembered and chronicled accurately. Genius, we know, is incalculable; but Schubert's fingers were not. How long would it take even him to write out the song—'to whelm it on to paper', 'to get it on to paper as quickly as he could write'? Remembering that copying a song may take longer than composing it—when the composer is Schubert—even so the act of writing out the *Erlking* would surely take three hours or so? He composed the song *Amphiaros* in March 1815, and on the manuscript he wrote 'in 5 hours'; *Erlking* is about three-quarters the length of *Amphiaros*. Let the reader experiment with a few bars. This makes Spaun's story (the chief source) at once improbable. He wrote that he and Mayrhofer called on Schubert one afternoon to find him pacing up and down a room excitedly ('glühend') reading the ballad; he then sat down and in the shortest time, as quickly as he could write, the magnificent song was on paper. Then the three hurried to the *Stadtkonvikt* (a matter of nearly an hour's walk), for Schubert, Spaun tells us, had no piano, and there the song was first sung, and Ruczicka explained and praised the famous dissonance between the semitones in voice and pianoforte at the boy's cry 'Mein Vater!' Spaun wished, and quite understandably, to convey a sense of urgency in his story of the incident, as if to correlate the rush of the rider through the midnight forest with Schubert's whelming the song on to paper. It was not a sheet of memoranda, it should be noticed, which would make the anecdote credible, for Ruczicka also played the song from the manuscript. But cold facts are against the story; we cannot imagine Spaun and Mayrhofer waiting for three hours while the song was written out, or if we can the interest evaporates. And could even Schubert achieve the perfect balance and artful workmanship in quite so impromptu a fashion? We know his almost unvarying practice (well established by 1815) of preliminary sketches: why should he abandon it for this important song? The truth is probably that we have in the records a telescoping of two or even more incidents: Schubert was pacing the room in the final stages of writing out the composition when the friends called, or else he 'whelmed' down some sketches for the song, and Ruczicka's playing came later on in the year.

The song was instantly popular in the Schubert circle; and after its publication (see page 104) continued to grow in popularity and esteem. Today perhaps we feel that Goethe's and Schubert's genius were both devoted in the ballad to elevating a fundamentally trivial idea. The assiduous attention given by later song writers to reality and psychological truth in the choice of song-texts increases our feeling that the *Erlking* is merely an artificial folk-ballad and its only emotion that of mock-horror (see how this modern tendency, however, gives greater lustre to *Gretchen am Spinnrade*). Schubert's harmonic boldness, his fresh and dramatic modulation, the vital melody in the *Erlking*—these are not one whit tarnished by our changed attitude to the text.

The exceeding difficulty of the accompaniment, graphic though it may be in conveying the horror of the ride, has contributed something to the fame of the song. Gustav Barth, a conductor of the Viennese Male-voice Choir Association ('Männergesang-verein'), told Friedländer in the 1880's that Schubert, when accompanying his father (Josef Barth), always played the right hand octaves as quavers, not triplets; Schubert said to Barth that others could play the triplets if they wished—they were too difficult for *him*. The story is vouched for by the existence of an autograph MS. in which the octaves are so written. It was probably Schubert's own copy which he used in accompanying singers of the ballad. As a contrast to this simplification of the composer's, it is on record that Liszt, whenever he accompanied the great French singer Adolphe Nourrit in the song, played the left hand runs in *octaves*.

In the two years 1815 and 1816 Schubert set most of the familiar 'Wilhelm Meister' songs. Mignon's pathetic and well loved song *Nur wer die Sehnsucht kennt* was composed three times, the first setting, of 1815, in F major is the best. *Kennst du das Land?* was also written in 1815; it remains an unloved setting of a much loved lyric. The third of Mignon's songs *So lasst mir scheinen*, from September 1816, is fragmentary. The three songs of the Harper were all written in that September. *An die Türen* was Schubert's first and only setting of the text, and was published as Op. 12: no. 3. But *Wer sich der Einsamkeit ergibt*, already attempted in 1815, is set again, this time magnificently. It is the well-known song, Op. 12: no. 1. Schubert's favourite of the three poems, whose words he must surely have applied to his own circumstances, is *Wer nie sein Brod mit Thränen ass*. He set this poem to music three times; all three settings, obviously evolving from each other, were written in the September of 1816, but he probably revised the third one in 1822 when it was published as Op. 12: no. 2. The first two settings are eclipsed by the third and this is a pity, for the second is a masterpiece equally as great as the third, although more rugged, perhaps, and unrestrained. Its tonality is unbelievable for its period. Compare this passage, for example, with anything by Beethoven from 1816 (his Sonata in A, Op. 101, would serve the purpose):

The criticism is sometimes made that Schubert did not fully understand Goethe. It would never have been made if it were not for the later, more elaborate, one could almost say, more obsequious, treatments of Goethe's texts. Schubert seeks always to evoke with his music a mood as close to the poet's as he can accomplish, as he did in *Gretchen am Spinnrade*, and in the song just considered. The evocation can occasionally convey the more vivid impression: in *Rastlose Liebe* the tempestuous beat of the music tells us more clearly what is in the poet's mind than his words dare do.

There remains the small group of songs which, in 1815 and 1816, Schubert composed on texts written by the friends of his own circle, chief among them Mayrhofer and Schober. The latter merely 'tried his hand' at poetry and had no serious vocational purpose like Mayrhofer. The first song in the tuneful series of Schober settings is the evergreen *Am Bach im Frühling* (1816). The great Mayrhofer songs were not written till 1817; the two outstanding ones of 1816 are the *Lied: an die Dioskuren* and the *Fragment aus dem Aeschylus*. The subjects of these two poems show Mayrhofer exploiting the short 'classical' revival which followed the *Storm and Stress* movement in Germany. Schubert used his dark, nocturnal key of A flat for both the songs; his noble and sombre style creates the mood of the two poems.

The song *Der Wanderer*, whose fame during the nineteenth century was exceeded only by the *Erlking*, was written in October 1816. On his early manuscripts Schubert gave the poet's name, wrongly, as Zacharias Werner, which is as it appeared in the anthology where he found the poem. It was an anthology of poems for public recitation, published in Vienna, 1815. In 1821, when the song was first published by Cappi & Diabelli, the poet's name was correctly given as Schmidt of Lübeck. There are two versions of the song, the earlier differing very slightly from the later one; it is called, however, *Der Unglückliche*. The poet altered the title later on to *Der Fremdling*. Schubert also altered the title, and called the second version of his song *Der Wanderer*. When he transposed the song into B minor for his employer, Count Esterházy, in 1818, he humorously added on the title-page:

Der Wanderer: or
Der Fremdling: or
Der Unglückliche.

He was never to know that it was introduced into France in 1835, by a baritone from the Opéra, as *The Wandering Jew*. The popularity of *Der Wanderer* in the nineteenth century was excessive; today it is abandoned. It is the same with *Ave Maria*, *Serenade* (words by Rellstab) and *Hark! hark! the Lark!*, whose worth remains as high as ever but whose appeal has, for today's listener, temporarily faded.

III

Four symphonies were composed during these two years of schoolmastering. They are:

no. 2, in B flat: 10 December 1814–24 March 1815,
no. 3, in D: 24 May–19 July 1815,
no. 4, in C minor: Spring 1816–completed 27 April 1816,
no. 5, in B flat: September–3 October 1816.

In all probability they were performed after composition by an amateur orchestral group which had grown out of the Schubert family string quartet. This orchestral society met first in the house of a merchant named Franz Frischling, who lived in the Dorotheergasse; the house was in the Inner City quite near the Augustinian Church. In the autumn of 1815, requiring more space, the orchestra moved to the residence of one Otto Hatwig, in the Schottenhof. Hatwig was a violinist at the Burg theatre and for two years or so he conducted the society. Schubert undoubtedly played the viola in this orchestra,[1] and two of the woodwind players, Josef Doppler (clarinet) and Ferdinand Bogner (flute) became his friends and we meet their names again in his story.

These early symphonies of Schubert, like the string quartets of the *Konvikt* years, are unmistakably the work of an original artist, using the familiar idiom of his day; they are not immature, and are not imitative of Haydn or Mozart or Beethoven (save possibly the first movement of the fourth, in C minor), and they are only separated from the later symphonies in B minor and C major, because they are the work of a young genius, who like all other young artists, grew, and enriched his resources, and deepened his thought. The vital melodic charm of these four works, their varied harmony and their orchestral fancy, give them an appeal which is often lacking in the mature symphonies of other composers. Schubert's stature grows when the true worth of these symphonic movements is admitted. When Dvořák was in America he wrote an article in 'The Century Magazine' deploring the neglect of these early symphonies of Schubert, and proudly stating the number of times he had conducted them at various concerts.[2]

The symphonies in B flat major (a key in which he can hardly go wrong) no. 2 and no. 5, are the best of the four. The variations of the earlier one, innocently happy, and transparently scored, and the ardent melodies of the *Andante con moto* in no. 5, provide the best music. The excellent development of his thematic material, especially in the finale of no. 2, and the first movement of no. 5, heralds the powerful work of the 1820's. His magnificent gifts in this sphere have been mentioned in connection with the

[1] Full details of the history of the orchestra were given by Leopold Sonnleithner in his memoirs; these were published in 1861–1863 in the 'Rezension und Mitteilungen über Theatre und Musik', Vienna. The issue for 15 June 1862 contains the orchestra's story.

[2] 'The Century Magazine', Vol. 48, no. 3, July 1894.

voice part of his songs; in instrumental work his full achievement is not so well known. Nineteenth-century judgements on it seem almost perverse; he prefers to repeat his themes, we are told, rather than attempting to develop them. Perhaps this book, by quotation and reference, may do something to modify that opinion.

The D major Symphony, no. 3, is a slighter, but charming work, and its finale is a madcap affair—one of the first of his orchestral movements to captivate an audience. The fourth symphony was given the title 'Tragic' by Schubert himself, but that was some time after its composition. It is the only symphony, apart from the 'Unfinished', whose first movement proper is in a minor key. The title, of course, goes appropriately enough with 'C minor' as an abstraction, but most inappropriately with Schubert's light-footed dance in the opening *Allegro Vivace*. This movement imitates certain procedures in the corresponding movement of Mozart's G minor Symphony, but not in a very assured fashion. But there is a superb slow movement. The expressive and shapely melody of this *Andante*, the *ostinato* accompaniment figure, which suddenly takes on a glorious life of its own, the contrasting section in F minor, and later, in B flat minor, all contribute to Schubert's greatest symphonic movement before 1822 brought the 'Unfinished' Symphony to birth. The contrasting section mentioned starts with a *staccato* theme in the first violins:

which is treated in imitation between the violins and 'cellos. An 'echo' phrase, very much in the manner of his songs, then appears, and suddenly his full lyrical and poetic powers take control. The phrase *b* of Ex. 8 above, 'echoed' between strings and woodwind, evolves into this cadence:

An air of contentment seems to settle over the orchestra, and the woodwind are given a long-drawn melody based on the cadential phrase quoted. The accompaniment derives from the phrase *a* in Ex. 8. It is a thoroughly Schubertian, thoroughly delightful, movement. The coda breaks away from pattering semiquaver figures into a slower, triplet rhythm in exactly the same way as the *Andante con moto* of the great C major Symphony. The last two movements fall below this standard.

Amongst the numerous dances—waltz, Ländler, écossaise—which he wrote for the piano during 1815 and 1816 there is the famous dance in A flat called by Schubert a 'Waltz' in one manuscript, a 'Deutscher', i.e. a 'Deutscher Tanz' ('German dance') in a second, and a 'Ländler' in a third, which became extremely popular in his own day. It was first published as no. 2 of the thirty-six dances in his Op. 9 in 1821, entitled by Diabelli, its publisher, the 'Trauerwalzer' ('Mourning Waltz'); this foolish name much amused the composer. It was re-printed several times, supplied with words, and even ascribed to Beethoven. Schubert had given his friend Anselm Hüttenbrenner a copy on 14 March 1818 and the dance in this version, combined with a waltz by Hummel, was published in 1826 by Schott's Sons, Mainz, as 'Sehnsucht' Waltz—by Beethoven! The error was quickly pointed out both by Anton Schindler, Beethoven's friend, and by an anonymous writer in the Leipzig 'Allgemeine Musikzeitung'. The waltz, still popular today, and known to the vast public of non-Schubertians by its use in the bastard 'Lilac Time' ('And she shall wear on her bosom, the fair lilac blossom'), is said to resemble an 'Arietta' in Henneburg's opera 'Der Jurist und der Bauer'.[1]

[1] This alleged resemblance was discussed in the Vienna 'Musik Zeitschrift' for February 1957. The quotation there of the 'Arietta' completely absolves Schubert of any plagiarisation.

It is a graceful example of his style in waltz-writing; but only in later years, with waltzes such as the delightful one in C sharp minor (Op. 50: no. 13), does he fully reveal how his melody could elevate and refine this homely form.

IV

1817 opens with Schubert installed in Schober's home in the Inner City. The house was called 'Zum Winter' and stood in the Tuchlauben. He hoped, doubtless, to earn his living by the sale of his compositions, by taking music pupils, by a success in the theatre. Schober, it is clear, provided him with lodging for which payments could be made whenever Schubert was in funds. It is not true that he gave Schubert room and board free; the debt to Schober of 190 florins (£19) which appears in Schubert's posthumous records, settled from the sale of his compositions within a year, was due for food and lodging. But at least the composer was free of the schoolroom routine, and his days were unhampered. He was doing what he wanted to do. If to his father and brothers his action seemed precipitate and fraught with uncertainty, and taken against all their advice and warning, it is because they were up against genius, and not talent. Talent compromises; but genius will get its own way. It tears the constraining bands; there may be agony in the doing, and the resulting wounds may profusely bleed, but nevertheless it tears them. We can only guess at Schubert's mental conflict in this rupture; his father's was more understandable. To Franz Theodor music in Vienna was not merely a precarious livelihood; it also meant that his youngest son would mix with a society of men whose moral laxity and standards of living were anathema to the strict Catholic that he was. It is fortunate that he was unable to foresee how his anxiety would be tragically realised.

In the early part of 1817, probably in March, Vogl and Schubert met. Schober's brother-in-law, Giuseppe Siboni, was an actor at the Kärntnertor Theater and through him Schober had made the acquaintance of the Court Opera singer Johann Michael Vogl. Vogl was nearing the end of a long, arduous and successful career on the boards. He was a cultured, dignified man, but in his earnestness there was, according to contemporary witness, a taint of charlatanism. Schober prevailed upon him to come to his home and meet Schubert and hear some of the young composer's songs. There are various records of the meeting. Schubert, who had as a boy venerated the singer, was discomfited by his rather stately presence. Vogl was on his guard. So many young composers had shown him their work; it did not do to encourage them too warmly when he could do so little to further their ambitions. But something happened as the two men talked and then tried over the songs. How could it not? Vogl was a composer himself, and of songs, and of quite interesting ones. He sang *Augenlied*, *Schäfers Klagelied*, and the just-composed *Ganymed*; he was impressed. He left Schubert with words of advice about not squandering ideas; he said the composer was 'zu wenig Comödiant, zu wenig Charlatan'—'too little of an actor, too little of a charlatan'! But soon after this first meeting, there were others, and now Vogl was seeking Schubert and exploring that treasury of songs. One career was over; the career by which he was to immortalise his name was about to begin.

Spaun wrote of Schubert in those days in his pamphlet 'Einige Bemerkungen' ('Some Observations'). His remarks were a kind of protest against the preliminary biographical sketch of the composer written by Heinrich von Kreissle and published in 1861. Spaun objected to the description of Schubert in Kreissle's work: he is there spoken of as having 'negroid' features, being a spendthrift and a contractor of debts, and an indulgent eater and drinker. The last accusation lingers on into modern biographies. Spaun's protests are convincing. He says Schubert was neither ugly, nor were his features 'negroid'. On the contrary, when he smiled or was talking ardently about subjects which interested him, his face glowed, his eyes lit up and he became almost handsome. Nor was he fat and paunchy: no sign of it, no talk of it, says Spaun. (In this connection we might wonder whether Schubert's later nickname of 'Schwammerl', which means a small mushroom, might not have referred to his diminutive stature as much as to his corpulence, as is usually assumed.) Spaun also asserts vigorously that he was moderate both in eating and drinking; they supped together daily for years, and only once during that time—a hot summer's day in the nearby village of Grinzing—did Spaun ever know Schubert to be the worse for drink. His nature was loyal and affectionate; and if his worst enemy had composed something beautiful he would have been delighted with it. These reminiscences of Spaun are full of interest and important as a source; they were written in 1864, but the manuscript was not recovered until May 1935, which accounts for their having no effect on nineteenth century biographies of the composer.

Schubert, according to Spaun, possessed no piano while he lived in the family house in the Säulengasse. Did access to an excellent instrument in the Schober's home lead to the series of pianoforte sonatas in the year 1817? We have no certain means of knowing but it seems very probable. There is also the fact that although the stream of *Lieder* still flows, it is obvious that even Schubert has exhausted for the time being his urge to song-writing. Another medium proved at once a powerful attraction. Up to this time Schubert had written very little sustained work for the piano. There are two fragmentary sonatas from 1815. The first, in E major, has no finale. There exists a sketch for the first movement, which was published in the supplementary volume of the 'Gesamtausgabe', in 1897; it is interesting to see from the sketch that Schubert actually toned down some of his first, startling modulatory ideas when he came to compose the final draft of the movement.

The second sonata, in C major, followed in September. It is an inferior work and it, too, lacks a finale, although the autograph manuscript suggests that there may have been a fourth movement, subsequently lost. When, in 1927, Walter Rehberg completed and published the sonata, he used an undated *Allegretto* in C major by Schubert (D. 346) as material for his finale. This *Allegretto* is a fragment, but it surely belongs to a later date than 1815. As a matter of fact, a fragment of the missing finale is almost certainly to be found on a rough draft of the 1815 setting of 'Nur wer die Sehnsucht kennt'. It is part of a 'Rondo' in C major, 2/4, for the pianoforte, dated 'October 1815'; the date is fairly convincing. A set of vigorous and characteristic variations known as the 'Ten Variations in F major' was another work of 1815 (February).

In August 1816 Schubert composed his third sonata, in E major. He was evidently not satisfied with the first scherzo, and so wrote a second for the work. Its five movements were published posthumously, and known for a very long time, as 'Fünf Klavierstücke' ('Five Piano-pieces'). Then, in 1930, a part of the autograph manuscript came to light, and was found to be entitled 'Sonata: August 1816'. The conjectural date previously given to the work was 1817. Ferdinand includes the sonata in the list of his brother's compositions (the key misprinted as F major), so that the manuscript was in his hands in 1839. By 1843 he had sold it to the Leipzig publisher, C. A. Klemm, who dropped the unfashionable title 'Sonata', and included *both* scherzos. Alois Fuchs also listed the work in his unpublished thematic catalogue of Schubert's compositions (prepared about 1842), but described it there as a fragment, consisting of first movement and part of an 'Allegro' (this would be the first scherzo). This is how the manuscript survives in America today, with a part of the finale in the Vienna City Library. If, in view of these fragments, and Fuchs' entry, we try to conjecture what, exactly, Ferdinand sent to Klemm at Leipzig, a mystery grows, for which there is no solution.

Why is the sonata ignored by pianists? The Schubert critic, Ludwig Scheibler, has protested that the composer's early pianoforte music (1815–1819) is largely neglected by pianists and piano-teachers. This Sonata in E major has a perfectly written first movement, intimate in tone, and richly inventive; the slow movement is a 'Nocturne', pathetic rather than passionate, and the finale is a most original movement called by Schubert 'patetico'. He never used the term but this once: he was probably using it, if we judge by the style of the music itself, as an equivalent of the German 'pathetisch', which means 'with pomp', 'oratorically', and not 'pathetic'. As for the scherzos: either is a worthy movement, and a player need not include both in a performance. Perhaps the first is the better of the two—an early masterpiece of Schubert's for the keyboard.

One other fragmentary piece was written during 1816, or possibly early 1817, although the manuscript is not dated. It is the start of a PF. Sonata in E minor. It has never been published and is quoted here complete for the first time:

The manuscript of this promising movement is in the Vienna City Library.

In 1817 Schubert obviously set out to explore the possibilities of the sonata as a form and the pianoforte as a medium. His newly won freedom, the brief respite from daily and uncongenial toil, produced a spate of compositions for the piano which are full of imaginative resource and variety, records of adventures into unexplored realms of music. There are, altogether, six PF. Sonatas of 1817. One is incomplete, having no minuet or scherzo, and another is fragmentary. Their composition extends from March till November. A great deal of research and scholastic sifting of evidence went on during the two Wars in connection with these six works, for in them reside nearly all the chronological problems and difficulties of the ordering of Schubert's sonatas. It is necessary to see the Schubert sonatas chronologically. 'Whoever follows Schubert by way of the sonatas in the order in which they were composed will assuredly see his life under a new aspect. For such a series of compositions is carved, as it were, from the master's very life—indeed a master's works *are* his true biography. They are the everlasting, into which the transitory is commuted.'[1]

His first sonata of the year, composed in March, is in A minor; it was not published until thirty-six years later, as Op. 164. Because the nineteenth century knew only Ferdinand's year-date —1817—it was placed at the end of the series of six sonatas and erroneous conclusions were drawn about its style and construction. The manuscript, in the Paris 'Conservatoire' Library, leaves no doubt as to the date of composition. The work is a typical example of early Schubert and forms an apt prologue to the subsequent five other sonatas, for its technical aspects, and its rather timid attempts at development and ornamentation, were all richly amplified in the following months. The first movement, for example, contains a device for building development sections, which in various forms may be found throughout his work: the repeated sequence of a basic idea that achieves harmonic, not melodic, shape by its repetitions:

[1] Professor Erwin Ratz, 'Schweizerische Musikzeitung', January 1949.

This is repeated in G major, then in F major, and leads to another sequential pattern. The detail is quoted to show that Schubert's exploration of harmonic colour in those days, led him to ignore the jolt to the ear of his chord juxtapositions. Thus, after the E major chord at the close of the phrase given above comes the dominant ninth in G major, i.e. a chord of D/F♯/A/E. This is the kind of brusque behaviour which we never find in Mozart, or Mendelssohn. But it leads to miracles of emotional and intellectual discovery. The theme of the slow movement, *Allegretto quasi Andantino* bears an interesting, but accidental, resemblance to the opening of the finale of one of Schubert's last three sonatas —in A major (Op. posth.)

The next two sonatas, dating from May, and June, are curiosities: the first because of its intrinsic music, the second for its extraordinary history. The Sonata in A flat, of May, is very slight in substance, but it has a finale in *E flat major*—an unprecedented departure from the classical tonal scheme. The work is in three movements and the minuet is probably lost; but that these three movements are an entity and not a haphazard assembly is proved by the existence of a very old copy made by, or for, Josef Witteczek in which they are also grouped under the heading 'Sonata'. Schubert's autograph copy is dated May 1817, but was not available when the work was first published, that is, in the 'Gesamtausgabe' volume of 1888. The copy is preserved in Vienna, in the Library of the *Gesellschaft der Musikfreunde.*

The fate of the next sonata, a work in a favourite key, E minor, is almost incredible. Schubert drafted a four movement work as follows:

i. *Moderato,* in E minor,
ii. *Allegretto,* in E major,
iii. *Scherzo and Trio*, in A flat and D flat major,
iv. *Rondo*, in E major.

His manuscript is dated June 1817. In this same month he started to revise the whole work, but after finishing the first movement he gave up the task. There were accordingly *two* autograph copies of the first movement. The work was not published by him and the batch of manuscripts came into the possession of his brother Ferdinand. The last movement was evidently detached from the rest, and Ferdinand did not suspect that it belonged to the other three movements. He sold it to Diabelli, who published it as Op. 145 in 1847; Diabelli prefaced the 'Rondo' with an 'Adagio', another Schubert sonata-movement. This was originally in D flat; it was cruelly, but not unskilfully, shortened and transposed into E major for the purpose of a prelude to the 'Rondo'. The story of the 'Adagio' movement can be told later (see page 68). In 1847 the conjunction of 'Adagio' and 'Rondo' was a highly fashionable pairing as can be seen from the contemporary publishers' catalogues and advertisements: Schubert's movements were butchered for the purpose of a ready sale. Meanwhile Ferdinand had sold the other three movements to the Leipzig publisher, F. Whistling, on 12 July 1842. A short while afterwards he sold the single copy of the revised first movement to Ludwig Landsberg, a well known collector of autographs. Whistling (he bought at the same time the score of the Fifth Symphony, in B flat) decided not to publish the truncated sonata and the manuscript disappeared for a time; in fact, no one knew that it existed. When, in 1888, the 'Gesamtausgabe' volume of the sonatas was printed, Landsberg's single movement was engraved, and so this Sonata in E minor appeared as a one movement work! But in 1907, in a manner by now not unfamiliar to the reader, Schubert's manuscript was unearthed from the Whistling archives; it was purchased by Professor Emil Preiger of Bonn. In May of that year Breitkopf & Härtel published the second movement, the E major *Allegretto*. Twenty-one years elapsed. In the Berlin periodical, 'Die Musik' of October 1928, as a Schubert Centenary Supplement, the third and remaining movement was published. If, to sum up, we now repeat Schubert's original scheme, with the dates of publication given beside his movements, we find this:

i. *Moderato:* published 1888,
ii. *Allegretto:* published May 1907,

iii. *Scherzo and Trio:* published October 1928,
iv. *Rondo:* published 1847.

This is surely a unique example in the history of music publication. The four movements were published as a whole, and for the first time, in 1948 by the British & Continental Music Agencies, London, edited by Kathleen Dale. It has been assumed throughout the recounting of this strange story of publication, that the 'Rondo' is, in actual fact, the finale of this Sonata in E minor. It will be recalled that the manuscript was detached. The evidence for the assumption is, first, that a copy of the movement in the Witteczek collection is headed—'Sonata: Rondo', and, second, that a short sketch for the Rondo exists on the back of a song, *Lebenslied*, dated December 1816. We know from these two facts that the movement is the finale of a Sonata, and that it was written after December 1816. The only one of Schubert's six works which could claim such a finale is the one in E minor.

The month of June also saw the composition of the fourth sonata of the year. It was his most ambitious effort. The key is D flat major, and the work opens with a soaring theme based—it is a feature of these 1817 sonata themes—on the notes of the common chord. He sketched the movement, revised it, composed a slow movement, almost finished the finale and then abandoned the work. Shortly after he transposed the sonata into E flat major, making a few changes of detail, and in this new key he finished the finale. A third movement, Minuet and Trio, in E flat, completed the scheme. The slow movement, *Andante molto*, first sketched in D minor, then transposed into C sharp minor for the first conception of the work, was left unchanged in detail; it was finally written in G minor for the second version of the sonata. The differences between the two versions of the first movement were examined by Hans Költzsch in his exhaustive study of Schubert's sonatas, 'Franz Schubert in seinen Klaviersonaten', published in 1928.[1] The E flat Sonata was published by Pennauer of

[1] There is a further examination by Harold Truscott, who was apparently unaware of Költzsch's work, in the 'Music Review', Cambridge, May 1953.

Vienna two years after Schubert's death, as Op. 122. It has been stated sometimes that the publisher transposed the work into E flat to help its sales, but this is not so. Schubert himself had completed the transposition at least by November 1817; we find the trio of the third movement also used in a 'Scherzo in D flat', clearly intended for the earlier version of this sonata but then discarded; the scherzo was dated November 1817. This dating has survived by mere chance, but since it has survived, it indicates when the transposition was finished. The sonata is the best known, and on the whole the best, of the six 1817 sonatas. It is a masterly little work, full of Schubertian melodies and of the sincerest feeling. If we consider the year of its composition, it is extraordinary to find it so free of the influence of Beethoven; or if not of influence, of imitation. We can admire the young genius, who lived in the brilliance of his great contemporary, and could yet emit his own light, and while so greatly loving and admiring the music of Beethoven (he called himself Beethoven's 'admirer and worshipper'), still be himself. If a critic occasionally gives the impression that he cannot accept Schubert's ability to fill a form called 'Sonata', so hallowed by Beethoven, with so completely different a music, he has not read Capell's cogent words—'How great our loss would be if Schubert, out of piety towards Beethoven, had felt himself restricted to composing Impromptus and Moments Musicaux!' Nineteenth-century Schubertians expressed regret that the composer transposed this sonata from D flat to E flat; but it is a 'Romantic' viewpoint. The music gains, if anything, a brightness and vivacity by being removed from the richer, darker key which was so beloved by the pianist-composers of the last century.

The fifth sonata, of July, is fragmentary; it consists only of an unfinished first movement, *Allegro moderato*, in F sharp minor. The key was not a favourite one of Schubert's. Apart from this sonata movement there is only one other instrumental movement in F sharp minor, the *Andantino* of the 1828 Sonata in A major. This may be the reason why Schubert's interest in the work failed before he completed it. It is a pity, because not only is the first movement so unlike the other five sonatas of the year, it is also uniquely different from the whole field of sonata-writing in the early nineteenth century. How stiffly imitative of Mozart and Haydn, and of each other, seem the sonatas of Hummel, Kuhlau, Dussek, Clementi and the rest, when we compare their talented efforts with the original work of this young genius; his is full of faults, it stumbles, it digresses, it is of little use for finger-practice. But it is alive, spontaneous, convincing:

For the last fifty years or so, the opinion has been held by Schubert scholars that two other short piano pieces by the composer belong to this sonata. They are the Scherzo and Trio, *Allegro vivace*, in D major and B minor, and an *Allegro* in F sharp minor (unfinished); both were published in the Supplement to the 'Gesamtausgabe', 1897. The suggestion was first made by the excellent Ludwig Scheibler,[1] and Walter Rehberg actually used the two pieces when he published a completed version of the sonata in 1928. Recently I examined for the first time Schubert's manuscript of these two pieces in the Vienna City Library, and at first it seemed as though the theory were untenable. The scherzo and finale are both written on the same folded sheet of music paper, and embedded between them is this cancelled fragment of a song:

[1] 'Die Rheinlande', Düsseldorf, 1905, p. 271.

Eventually I identified these bars as the continuation of the unfinished song *Lorma* (D. 327), composed on 28 November 1815. It seemed impossible to reconcile the co-existence of this 1815 song-fragment composed when Schubert was living at home, with two sonata movements written when he was lodging in Schober's house in 1817. But in an extraordinary fashion, this apparent contradiction is a strong support for the theory. The first movement itself, dated 'July 1817', was also written on manuscript paper containing music from 1815! This was part of the Mass in B flat of November 1815, the same *month* as *Lorma*. Schubert evidently economised at that period by using up half-empty sheets of music paper from the previous years. Such a practice keeps the Schubertian cataloguer intrigued—and wisely non-committal about dates and styles if there is any doubt.

The last work of the year in this form was composed, or at least sketched, in August. It is the Sonata in B major, published by Diabelli in 1843 as Op. 147. The manuscript sketch is in the possession of the *Gesellschaft der Musikfreunde*, Vienna, and is dated August 1817. It is possible that the sonata was not completed till the following year, since a copy made by Albert Stadler for a young woman named Josefine von Koller, an excellent pianist living, like Stadler, in Steyr, is dated 'August 1818'. Second only to the E flat Sonata in accomplishment and in the attractiveness of its melody, it exceeds even that in the poetry and fancy of its music. It is an epilogue, as fitting in its way as the A minor Sonata of March was for prologue, to the 1817 series of sonatas.

Of all Schubert's early compositions, these sonatas form the most distinguished group and show most clearly what he was to achieve in his maturity. They are, of course, the products of a young, still growing artist; but it is only in imagination and perception that we are conscious of his youth; in style, in structure, and in originality of material, he is already mature.

Before the sonatas of his maturity were written, those wonderful 'nine' commencing with the A minor Sonata, Op. 143, there are a few unfinished sonatas, tentative essays which failed to interest him very deeply; and there is one substantial fragment in F minor, composed at Zseliz in September 1818, which may be glanced at here. It is a wild, stormy affair, with tender episodes—Schubert's 'Sonata appassionata'. The first movement is of great promise, but breaks off at the point of recapitulation; it begins with this theme, pregnant with Beethovenian possibilities, but which, characteristically, produces instead a thoroughly original development section:

There is a magnificent scherzo, in E major, and the finale resumes the headlong rush of the first movement. A point of remarkable interest in connection with this sonata is the fate of its slow movement, an *Adagio* in D flat. This was possibly written later on when Schubert returned to Vienna (in November) and was used by Diabelli as the basis for the *Adagio* prelude for Op. 145; this work has already been discussed. The original form of the movement, before Diabelli's hack got to work on it, can be seen in the appropriate section of the 'Revisionsbericht' of the 'Gesamtausgabe', where it is printed in full. Schubert's original manuscript is lost, but a copy existed in the invaluable Witteczek collection and from this the printed version was made. We can deduce the fact that this *Adagio* in D flat *is* the slow movement of the F minor Sonata for this reason. An old manuscript catalogue of compositions by Schubert for the piano, and for piano and violin, compiled by Ferdinand for the publisher Diabelli, was still extant in 1930, and in the possession of Kreissle's descendants. In this catalogue the F minor Sonata is listed, and the *incipits* of four movements are quoted. That of the second movement is given thus (R. H. only):

but even with that error of copying the work is recognisable. It has never been included with the F minor Sonata; the editors of the 'Gesamtausgabe' did not know of Diabelli's catalogue, and although they did reprint the *Adagio*, they had no suspicion that it was actually part of the 1818 Sonata in F minor. But a future edition of Schubert's sonatas, in complete sequence, should restore the *Adagio* to its rightful place. It can be seen, too, how the key of D flat naturally links the key of the first movement, F minor, with the rather dramatic choice, for the scherzo, of the key of E major.

There is one final specimen in his early manner, the Sonata in A major, Op. 120. This short, sparkling and graceful work, the most popular perhaps of all his sonatas, cannot be dated exactly. For many years it was assigned to 1825, through a misinterpretation of early catalogues. As with similar misdatings of other works of his, no suspicions seemed to have been aroused until in 1906, Ludwig Scheibler challenged the date as absurd, and brought forward evidence that suggested an earlier one—1819.[1] He quoted a letter from Albert Stadler to Ferdinand Luib, written on 17 January 1858, in which we learn that Schubert wrote a sonata for Josefine von Koller while he was staying at Steyr. Vogl, visiting Steyr in later years, collected the manuscript sonata and took it back to Schubert in Vienna. Schubert stayed at Steyr in 1819, 1823 and 1825. Scheibler suggested that the sonata in question was probably that in A major, Op. 120, and further that 1819 was the most likely year. This date is now generally accepted, and is more reasonable than 1825. But the whole question is not a simple one. Stadler went on to say in his letter that he did not know what became of the sonata; this is a rather surprising statement since it was published in 1829, and by 1858, when Stadler wrote his letter, had become fairly well known. This raises the point—was he possibly writing about the B major Sonata, Op. 147, and not the Sonata, Op. 120? His memory may have been at fault, and the fact that he copied out the sonata in B major for Josefine von Koller may have become, after the lapse of forty years, the idea that Schubert actually composed it for her. This work in B major was also published by the time that Stadler wrote to Luib, but in the year of its publication, 1845, he moved from Linz to Salzburg, and was probably too occupied with his own affairs to take note of the publication. But whatever its date, the A major Sonata remains a gem amongst the Schubert sonatas, a fulfilment of the 1817 works, and one holding out the promise of future achievement which the last nine, in their turn, amply fulfilled.

V

A more obscure field explored by the composer in 1817, obscure, that is, in comparison with the sonatas, is that of the overture. It is an odd category; the form is a fluid one and most of

[1] 'Zeitschrift der Internationalen Musik Gesellschaft', Leipzig, pp. 485–487.

Schubert's work in it is not memorable. Throughout his life he wrote twelve unattached overtures: ten are for orchestra, and two for PF. Duet. The first to show any individuality, in B flat major, had been written in September 1816 for the small orchestral society already mentioned. Characteristics of the Schubert Overture can be found in it: the *Adagio* introduction, the use of 'Sonata-form' procedures for the *Allegro* section, and the shortened development section which becomes a kind of rondo-episode. The work in B flat imitates Beethoven but is not unattractive. There is a manuscript sketch for part of this overture (bars 87–118) which, having no title, remained unidentified. O. E. Deutsch erroneously lists it in his 'Thematic Catalogue' as part of a string quartet (D. 601).[1] From this sketch we are enabled to date the '*Andante* in A' for PF. Solo (D. 604), which is written on the back of the same paper, and thus belongs apparently to the autumn of 1816. It might, possibly, be another attempt at a slow movement for the Sonata in E major of that period.

In 1817 there were three overtures for orchestra, substantial works, and as good in their way as any of the symphonic finales which he wrote at the time. The first two are both in D major, the third in C major, and all three show quite strongly the influence of Rossini, whose popularity in Vienna had, by 1817, reached almost frenzied heights, although later on, in the 1822–1823 seasons, when Rossini himself came to the capital, the frantic enthusiasm passed all reasonable limits. We read in various documents and memoirs that Schubert liked 'Il Barbiere' and 'Tancredi', and that the last act of 'Otello' delighted him. The second and third of his 1817 overtures, in D and C, have in fact been nicknamed 'in the Italian style', but not by Schubert himself; that is, he has not so entitled them on his MSS., which is the impression one receives from printed editions, programmes and catalogues. The nickname was bestowed by Ferdinand. The 'Italian style' is, of course, unmistakable, and was remarked upon at once when the overtures were performed. One of the two, the

[1] There was a correction in Deutsch's article: 'Some additions and corrections to the Schubert Catalogue', Music & Letters, London, January 1953, p. 26.

key is not given in the programme, was performed in public at the Hall of the 'Roman Emperor ('Römische Kaiser'), Vienna, on 1 March 1818. It was a success, and was reported, very favourably, in newspapers of Vienna, and Dresden. In the Vienna 'Allgemeine Musikalische Zeitung' of 6 June 1818 the notice has the words '... it is fashioned in the Italian style'. All three of the 1817 overtures, no. 1 in D (May), nos. 2 and 3 (November) have an *Adagio* or *Maestoso* introduction, and after the main *Allegro* section, in sonata-form, they conclude with a *più mosso* coda. It would need extensive quotation to demonstrate how thoroughly the three are thematically and technically interlinked, but one obvious melodic connection can be quoted:

The *Adagio* introduction, and the *Vivace* coda of no. 2, in D major, were taken over and modified for use in a later overture, in C major, the one which Schubert wrote in 1820 for his incidental music to the play 'Die Zauberharfe'. This overture, although it was never played in Schubert's life-time under such a title, is now universally known as the 'Rosamunde' overture. This is because it was published in 1827 as part of Op. 26, which had been reserved for the items of music from 'Rosamunde'; it was then actually called 'Overture to "Rosamunde" '. Schubert also used the essence of the *Vivace* coda from the 'Italian' overture in D major, distilled by his mature genius, in the finale of the D minor String Quartet (1824) and in the first movement of the great C major Symphony (1828):

Soon after the composition of the two 'Italian' Overtures, he arranged them for PF. Duet, and these two arrangements at last found their way into print in 1872. The three 1817 overtures are strange works: productions of a genius, greater than the one he parodied; and yet, because of their immaturity, they cannot really vie with Rossini's mature and sparkling efforts.

Besides the sonatas and overtures of 1817 there are several fine pieces of chamber music for strings, and for pianoforte and violin. Altogether the three years from 1815 to 1817 were not rich in the production of chamber works, but those of 1817 form, in logical fashion, a culmination of the period. For strings alone Schubert composed the String Quartet in G minor (25 March–1 April 1815), the String Quartet in E major (probably, but not certainly, 1816), and two String Trios, both in B flat major, of which the first is unfinished (September 1816 and September 1817). The confusion in catalogues caused by the similarities between the last two works, in key, medium and dates, can be imagined.

The quartets are closely unified in style and musical content. The main theme of each first movement is a couplet: a bold, arresting figure, based on the notes of the common chord ('con brio' in G minor, 'con fuoco' in E major) is followed by a gentle, contrasting theme. The development of these elements shows a characteristic wayward quality, but it is excellently brought off, and in the E major Quartet, the instrumental colour, particularly the brilliant, wiry use of high chords on the upper strings, is admirable. The slow movements open with quiet, lyrical sections in 2/4 time, but a more dramatic interlude follows the subdued start. In the course of both slow movements there is a notable use of a technique which is to have very fruitful results in his later work for strings. The second violin and viola maintain a rhythmical accompaniment, while the 'cello and first violin sing a 'conversational' duet:

The first movements of the two String Trios are similarly alike: delicately written, lyrical from first to last, and within their slight compass, expressive of a wide range of emotion. The first String Trio (1816), contemporary with the Overture in the same key, B flat, gives an instance of Schubert's more exalted manner in a more exalted form. Both the String Trio and the Overture commence with very similar 'Allegro' subject themes, but the Trio is much more elevated in style. A few bars of the slow movement were written but the work was never finished. The second String Trio (1817) is complete. The slow movement, apart from a passage strongly imitative of Mozart, is highly original. It contains the first appearance of that passionate, stormily-lyrical interlude, which grew out of the dramatic, contrasting episodes in his early slow movements, and which Schubert loved to introduce into his mature slow movements for chamber music combinations, i.e. the *Andante con moto* of the PF. Trio in E flat (Op. 100), or the *Adagio* of the String Quintet. The finale of the String Trio starts cheerfully enough, but deepens as it goes on, and at the close there are two features of such interest that they call for mention. There is a climax built on rushing scale-passages in triplets, passed upwards from 'cello to viola, and viola to first violin, which we find repeatedly used in future string quartets; and there is a spontaneous episode clearly prompted when his mind was suddenly charmed by a chance cadential idea.

It is this uncalculated seizing of stray ideas, and their immediate, spontaneous expansion into poetical and emotionally wrought episodes, that proclaim the creative genius and give Schubert his charm, his enduring appeal. In this finale, the violin figure quoted above, with that slight 'differentness' in the rhythm at *a*, produces an extraordinarily fascinating sequence of ideas, and they lead to a second tense, but pianissimo, climax. This trio is the most important of the chamber works before the *Trout* Quintet.

Finally, there are four violin sonatas, and all, by the whim of publishers, were debased in their mis-namings:

1. Sonata in D major (March 1816),
2. Sonata in A minor (March 1816),
3. Sonata in G minor (April 1816),
4. Sonata in A major (August 1817).

The first three were published by Diabelli in 1836 as Op. 137, and called 'Sonatinas'; the last was published by the same firm in 1856, and called 'Duo'. In Schubert's autographs they are all entitled by him 'Sonatas', and this title should be restored. Only the first of the four is in three movements (there is no Minuet); all the rest are full scale works. It is, strangely, in the slow movements of the three 1816 sonatas that Schubert is least himself. The tentative quality of his work, which has been described, is here very apparent, and Mozart, again, is a dominating influence. The third sonata, in Schubert's most 'masculine' key—G minor—is a sturdy work, and the most popular of the three.

But the fourth sonata, in A major, Op. 162, is a different matter. It came at the end of a year which had been full of experiments with sonata-form, and together with the contemporary String Trio, it reflects the added technical assurance of its composer. The *Andantino* is a sad-sweet movement, brimming with alternate Schubertian ardour and pathos. The finale contains a theme which is a quotation from his *Cotillon* in E flat; it would justify a date of 1817 for the dance-piece.

It was said earlier in the chapter that although Schubert was more attracted to instrumental composition in 1817, nevertheless the stream of *Lieder* flowed unchecked. There were fifty or so songs that year, the largest group being eight songs on poems of Mayrhofer. These are nearly all on classical subjects, since Mayrhofer also dabbled in the fashionable practice of re-creating the ancient Greek and Roman myths, but naturally with none of Goethe's inspired psychological penetration. The 'Fahrt zum Hades' of January is a favourite piece of the Schubertian, unknown almost in the traffic of the concert-room. In March there followed six superb songs.[1] *Philoktet*, *Antigon und Oedip* and *Orest auf dem Tauris* exemplify his growing powers of comment in the pianoforte accompaniment and the fusion of dramatic recitative with pure melodic line in the voice part. These are more powerful still in *Der entsühnte Orest* and *Memnon* (although Memnon is a statue in Egypt, the name of the demi-god, and his legend, are Greek). The finest of the six songs is the neglected *Freiwilliges Versinken*, an address to Helios, the sun-god, in which Schubert's declamation—half song, half recitative—is magnificent. The accompaniment is a picturesque evocation of fading sunset and the rising moon.

But the best of the 1817 Mayrhofer songs is not based on a

[1] Two of these songs have hitherto been ascribed to September 1820 (*Der entsühnte Orest* and *Freiwilliges Versinken*). That date is of Schubert's *copies* of the songs, made later on.

Greek legend at all; it is much nearer home, much nearer Schubert's heart—*Auf der Donau—On the Danube*—of April. The poet's reverie on the passing of time as symbolised by the passing waters of the Danube, touched Schubert's sensitive mind deeply; a familiar sentiment, a familiar scene and the composer's response is in his best vein, a wholly admirable blending of PF. figuration and vocal melody into an indivisible whole.

To texts by Goethe there were numerous trifling songs, but also two excellent beginnings which were, unhappily, not carried through: *Gretchens Bitte* and *Mahomets Gesang*. Then there was the masterpiece of the year *Ganymed*, the song which won Vogl's allegiance, and we can understand that well enough. Goethe fashions the myth of Zeus seizing Ganymede to the Olympian heights into an image of the beauty of a summer morning catching the poet's heart to heaven. Schubert's song, in which a profusion of melodic ideas crowds the pages, suffers if it be given a finicking interpretation; singer and pianist must paint the picture in broad, generous strokes.

Another great song of the year is Schiller's *Gruppe aus dem Tartarus*. Schubert had tried his hand at the song the previous year; a fragment of his attempt is extant and reveals music of first-rate quality. But the 1817 song is yet finer. It is an almost terrifying picture—restless, chromatic, harsh—of the spirits of the damned. 'Eternity', with the image of the broken scythe of Time, is sung in C major, and the song dies away on to the muttered notes which we heard at the start, conveying the suggestion that the music circles on for ever and ever.

But the famous songs of the year are not these huge masterpieces; they are settings of minor poets like Schubart and Claudius. There is the remarkable song *An den Tod*, a setting of Schubart, but his name is perpetuated in the immortal, ever-fresh *Die Forelle* (*The Trout*). No fewer than five copies of this song, in Schubert's hand, are known (and more, we can be certain, are lost), showing its immediate popularity. Only in the last of the five copies by Schubert, in October 1821, is the 5-bar prelude of the PF. part to be found.

It is the same with two of Schober's poems which Schubert

set during March 1817. The first, *Trost im Liede*, is a serious and musicianly piece of writing, but it is *An die Musik* which immortalises the partnership of the two friends in song. The melody of this beloved address to music is as truly Schubertian as anything he wrote—intimate, ardent, and with that indefinable touch of pathos which goes to the heart. And yet, as Charles Stanford showed in a well-known piece of analysis, the constructional details of the masterpiece reward the searcher for them.[1] There are numerous autograph copies of this song also, and one of them, in the Paris 'Conservatoire' Library, written by the composer for an unknown friend, is enclosed in a small envelope inscribed—rather charmingly—'Manuscrit, très precieux'.

The third song in a trinity of popular favourites is *Der Tod und das Mädchen* (*Death and the Maiden*) to words by Claudius, composed by Schubert in February. This also deeply impressed its first hearers, and the fact that Schubert later on used the themes of *Der Tod und das Mädchen* and *Die Forelle* for variations indicates the continuing, widespread popularity of the two songs in the circle of his friends. The manuscript of *Der Tod und das Mädchen* was later on scissored into portions by his half-brother Andreas, and the relics distributed amongst friends as mementos. It was this person who cut away the opening of the early setting of J. P. Uz—*An Chloen* (p. 42)—leaving it as a fragment.

In August 1817 news that Schober's elder brother, Axel, was returning from France reached the family; Schubert's room was required and he was obliged to abandon his temporary refuge. The touching poem *Farewell* which he wrote, and set to music in Schober's 'Album', is dated '24 August 1817', but the 'distant land' to which friend Schober is said to be travelling was merely the French border; there he was to meet his brother. Schubert returned to his home in the Säulengasse, and resumed his classroom duties. One of the most depressing and frustrating periods of his life now began. The burden must have seemed doubly onerous after the months of freedom amongst those who were his own kind, in which his genius could command untrammelled days for its productions.

[1] 'Musical Composition', London, 1911.

III

1818-1819

I

Writing to his friends about the months which he passed in the Säulengasse house, once again bound to a routine, and excluded from easy contacts with the musicians and art-loving friends of the Spaun and Schober circles, Schubert spoke of himself as a 'frustrated musician'. At first the impetus of his creative work carried him on; the 'Italian' overtures were composed, the Sonata in E flat finally arranged to his satisfaction, a handful of songs to Schiller poems, including the *Gruppe aus dem Tartarus*, were written. There were two Mayrhofer songs, *Atys* and the charming *Am Erlafsee.* The second was printed as a supplement to a Viennese periodical devoted to poetry, music and painting, on 6 February 1818; it was Schubert's first appearance in print. But the creative fire began to die low. His sixth symphony was started in October 1817, but was not completed until the following February. It shows a great advance, in technical matters, on the previous five. The use of the orchestra is masterly, the movements are expertly organised to the point of glibness, all is crisp and competent. But there is no heart in the work; it is all externals. The expert craftsmanship is used on unattractive, trivial material, as a glance at the themes of each movement will show. A Sonata in C major, dated April 1818, remains unfinished. But for its date in Schubert's own hand one might consider it as belonging to his earliest days. The *Adagio* in E major, composed in the same month, April, is possibly the slow movement of the sonata. It was published separately in 1869 by a firm in Winterthur, and so became detached from the other two movements. The quality of the symphony and the sonata indicates the growing discontent and unhappiness of the composer in these early months of 1818. A seventh symphony, in D, was commenced in May. Schubert's sketches for the work are in PF. score and although none of his work on them was brought to a finished state, the pages of this 'sketch-book' are of tremendous interest and value. They show in an indescribable manner his methods of work, the imagination obsessed by a scrap of melody, or a rhythm, or a harmonic figure, evolving page after page from the impetic and generative theme. They also reveal the methods of genius, which does not wait for 'inspiration', nor waste its energies with the imposing, attention-catching, opening flourish, but *starts to work*: starts with anything that comes, confident that greatness will attend in its own time. Schubert's sketches in these early years show how from such ordinary and humble beginnings, his imagination worked on until 'inspiration' followed his efforts. The symphony sketches are very bulky, and contain twenty-five pages of closely written score. There are eight sketched movements, all related in key to the first, and from these the requisite four were to be chosen. The sketches were, of course, composed as the whim took him, but they are sorted out below and grouped into a standard four-movement scheme for the convenience of the reader:

I. First Movement:
   Adagio, D minor, 2/2, followed by *Allegro moderato*, D major, 2/2.

II. Slow Movements:
   1. D major, 2/4.
   2. *Andante*, B minor, 3/8.
   3. A major, 2/4.

III. Scherzo: D major, 3/4 and TRIO, G major, 3/4.

IV. Finale-Movements:
   1. Variant (*a*) D major, 4/4.
      Variant (*b*) *Maestoso*, D major, 4/4.
      Variant (*c*) D major, 4/4.
   2. Variant (*a*) D major, 2/4, first draft.
      Variant (*a*) D major, 2/4, later revision.
      Variant (*b*) D major, 2/4.
   3. D major, 2/4.

Only the *Andante* in B minor, an admirable, deeply serious movement which sounds the note of the 'Unfinished' Symphony, and the Scherzo, are anything like complete. The state of mind which would reject this mass of work can easily be deduced.

His friendship with Anselm Hüttenbrenner, a fellow-pupil with Salieri, deepened that year. For his friend he wrote a set of variations based on a theme from Hüttenbrenner's own String Quartet, No. 1, in E major, Op. 3. The variations are gracefully written but largely negligible. He also facetiously inscribed a copy of his so-called 'Trauerwalzer' for his 'wine-and-punch-brother, Anselm Hüttenbrenner, world-famous composer' on 14 March 1818. It seems ironical to us that Hüttenbrenner's vapid compositions should so readily find publishers in Vienna, whereas Schubert was then, and for years to come, quite unable to secure publication for any of his work.

Anselm's younger brother, Josef, also made Schubert's acquaintance during the spring. The composer sent him a copy of *Die Forelle* (*The Trout*) written at midnight on 21 February 1818. It is the famous autograph over which the sleepy Schubert shook the ink-bottle instead of the drying-sand. The manuscript was reproduced in facsimile in 1870 and then, incredibly, lost: a typically Hüttenbrennerish catastrophe as we shall see later on.

At the same period he composed and almost completed a *Rondo* in D major for PF. Duet, the first original work in this medium since his juvenile efforts of 1810-1813. His manuscript bears the simple indication '*Rondo* for 4 hands, 1818' (there is no month). Diabelli published an arrangement of the work in 1835 as Op. 138, calling it 'Notre amitié est invariable'. Until 1897, when the autograph was discovered, Op. 138 was taken to be an entirely original work of Schubert's. Diabelli had given the manuscript, together with a number of other Schubert and Beethoven MSS., to his son-in-law, Josef Greipel, who became *Kapellmeister* of the Peterskirche, Vienna, in 1847. Greipel remained in this position for fifty years, and as an old man with failing powers had no realisation of the value of his autograph possessions. These were all purchased at his death by the Nationalbibliothek, Vienna, but even then they remained obscure, and unexamined. Accordingly biographers and cataloguers, right down to the Deutsch Catalogue of 1951, have given the Rondo of 1818 as a complete Schubert work. O. E. Deutsch does label the MS. as a 'sketch', but even that is an inexact description. It is an incomplete fair copy, probably intended to be a playing copy for Schubert and a partner; although possibly not quite good enough for a publisher's engraver, it is certainly no first, rough draft. Schubert's *Rondo* is in the form A B A : *codetta*: A C A: *coda*. The 'C' section is not quite finished, but a few empty leaves in the manuscript show that Schubert intended to finish it. Diabelli's hack simply cut away the 'A C' portion and published the rest. The excised part was published as a supplement to an article on the Rondo by Leopold Nowak.[1] The fictitious title has been explained as an indication that the Rondo was Schubert's offering to his new friend, the pianist Josef von Gahy. He had recently been introduced to Gahy, who was a friend and colleague of Spaun, and he delighted to play PF. Duets with this new friend. At the close of the Rondo the players' hands cross, and this is supposed to be Schubert's gesture of friendship. Unfortunately, an examination of the manuscript shows that the hand-crossing is due to the rearrangement by Diabelli; there is no justification for it in the original, and it could not have been a gesture of Schubert's at all. But one of his scribbled notes about the work has a certain interest in this connection. He sent Spaun a rough copy of his song *Lob der Tränen* and on the bottom margin he has pencilled the words: 'Spaun! don't forget Gahy and the Rondeau'.[2] He was referring to this duet and perhaps Spaun was going to hear its first performance by the composer and his friend Gahy. The work is quite attractive; Ludwig Scheibler wrote of it as a 'Polonaise alla Rondo' which is a more congenial title than Diabelli's. It heralds a series of PF. Duets that year. They were the result of a new position which the composer took up in the following July.

This was the appointment, as music master, to the establish-

[1] 'Oesterreichische Musikzeitschrift', Vienna, November 1953.

[2] The song manuscript is in the Vienna *Stadtbibliothek*.

ment of Count Johann Karl Esterházy. The Count, his wife Rosine, and their children, Albert, Karoline and Marie, passed the winter months in their town residence in Penzing, just to the north of the Schönbrunn estate. In the summer months the family moved to their Schloss at Zseliz, on the river Gran, in Hungary. To that quiet retreat, in July 1818, the composer went to take up his duties. These were many and varied and not precisely defined: he gave Marie (born 1802) and Karoline (born 1805) lessons in pianoforte playing and some kind of instruction in musical theory, he wrote vocal exercises for the daughters and their mother, the Countess, who sang contralto, and he accompanied the Count's bass voice in various songs, including his (Schubert's) own. He composed PF. Duets for Marie and Karoline to play, and also, on occasion, partsongs for impromptu musical evenings. Although there are no records of such it cannot be doubted that he also improvised dance music for the modest balls and 'routs' that were held on summer evenings in the Zseliz Schloss.

Schubert, in a bounding reaction from his winter of discontent, wrote to his friends in Vienna that he lived and composed like a god; that he was without a care; that he lived at last, and it was high time, otherwise he would have become nothing but a frustrated (*verdorbener*) musician. To his father, who had at last received recognition from the City Authorities, having been promoted to a larger school in the nearby Rossau district, he wrote cordially and affectionately. Letters to and from his family and friends give a vivid quality to the year 1818, which is unusual in the composer's story. Since he lived always in Vienna, surrounded by his friends and relatives and business acquaintances, long letters were unnecessary, and this means a certain scrappiness in the personal documents of Schubert. The four years, 1818, 1819, 1824 and 1825, during which he lived for many months away from the capital, have a wealth of documentation which is welcome.

From his friend Josef Doppler he received the following letter giving various items of news—welcome and unwelcome—from Vienna. It is here published for the first time in English, since it was recovered only recently after many years of obscurity.[1] Doppler's punctuation is retained.

Vienna, 8 *October* 1818.

Friend of my heart,

I ought really to quarrel with you and to revile you, since you forget, for such a time, one of your best and devoted friends, but you need not fear although you are so neglectful that I can be like that too. Oh no! I am always working for you, and in order to give you a proof of it I announce to you at once, under the same cover, that since the Overture to Claudine Villa Bella cannot be produced at Herr Jaell's concert on account of its too great difficulties—that is to say, it must be because of the oboe and bassoon passages in it, which those fellows in Baden could not execute—it will now, however, be produced by an Imperial Court Chapel Orchestra surely with acclaim, accordingly I gave it to Herr Schneidel, conductor of the said orchestra, who will give it one of these days as the first overture at a concert which he will give for his benefit in the N. Austrian 'Landständischen' Hall, and is already posted up on the placards, and is being read by the eyes of all the world; a letter from me will report to you further particulars of it.

Herr v. Blahetka, whom you will presumably have heard of, or will know about through the playing of his small daughter, begs you earnestly to compose for his daughter a 'Rondo brillant', or whatever it is, which the aforesaid young lady could practise this winter and produce at a concert, that is to say, for the pianoforte with orchestral accompaniment. You may introduce difficulties, pranks, runs or anything that the devil inspires, as you like, only leave out the octave stretches, or such like, anything which is impossible for the shape of her hands.

Hr. v. Blahetka, who is now very famous as a poet, and produces many beautiful poems in the 'Theaterzeitung', is working on a grand oratorio of which two parts are already finished. The material is biblical history, and as I hear from many who have

[1] O. E. Deutsch, 'Wiener Zeitung', Vienna, 5 April 1953.

already read parts of it, very affecting and edifying and very well written for music since he himself is a good musician, I will transmit to you the whole of the poem since the end of the oratorio will soon be reached, so that you might set it to music, now what a first-rate thing that would be for you, if something by you should come to the light of day, I trust so, don't delay with the concerto for his daughter and apply yourself as soon as possible to the work, but transmit to me at once the completely finished score by post wagon. I will defray the expenses.

And now since the important commissions are all seen to, let us go on to secondary matters. Are you well? contented, happy? Are you busy composing worthwhile things? I must know all about what you have done, for given the opportunity these things might be produced. Answer all my questions and very soon; I hope that you will have a deep enough regard for my friendship not to put this letter aside without answering it.

As this was your name-day, I send my greetings, and wish you heartily all the good things which only friends can wish. I remain your loyal friend

Josef Doppler.

P.S. Our Orchestral Society has recently re-formed and is now on the point of becoming the best of its kind. . . . We are shortly going to do all your Masses since we have sufficient singers. More of this soon.

Nothing came of any of Doppler's invitations or promises in this letter. The overture was not performed then or at any subsequent time, nor did Schubert accept—on such airy invitation—the two Blahetka proposals. Doppler's words 'Are you well? . . . Are you busy composing things' chime in oddly with Schubert's remark that he was 'living and composing like a god'. But after a while the quiet, humdrum life in Zseliz, cut off from the stimulating music and society of Vienna, began to pall. 'My longing for Vienna grows daily' he wrote to his family. In November the return came, and Schubert took lodgings in the Wipplingerstrasse, sharing rooms with his friend Mayrhofer. He continued to give lessons to the Esterházy daughters throughout the winter. He lived cheaply and was able to make the payments from these lessons (and probably others) and the moderate fees from his summer duties suffice for his needs. But he was seriously contemplating music for the theatre as a means of livelihood, and he set to work immediately after settling down in his new lodgings on a one-act operetta 'Die Zwillingsbrüder' ('The Twin Brothers'). The play was based on a French original and written by Georg von Hoffmann. With the aid of Vogl's influence it was considered by the Kärntnertor Theater and later performed, but as we shall see it had no lasting success.

The 1814 song *Schäfers Klagelied* received some public performances in the spring of 1819 during the same series of concerts mentioned in connection with the 'Italian' Overtures. It was sung by Fritz Jäger, a tenor from the Theater an der Wien, the most imposing, but not the most important, theatre in Vienna; and it had a warm welcome. Schubert's name was becoming more widely known amongst private circles in Vienna. References to him, and to his songs are very frequent at that time in the friends' letters. Feeling, perhaps, that his presence in the capital during that period of rising interest was vitally necessary he resigned his position with the Esterházys and they left for Zseliz in the summer of 1819 without him. But his operetta was not, after all, given that season and he took a short holiday during July and August with Vogl, who always returned to his native town of Steyr in the summer months. Schubert delighted in the beauty of the countryside and wrote of it in enthusiastic letters to his brother Ferdinand and to Mayrhofer. He made the acquaintance of several musicians in Steyr, the clever young pianist Josefine von Koller, who may have inspired the Sonata in A major, Op. 120, and Sylvester Paumgartner, who was certainly responsible for Schubert's composing the PF. Quintet containing variations on the song *Die Forelle*, which song Paumgartner greatly esteemed. A short visit to Linz in August enabled Schubert to become more closely acquainted with Spaun's family, but a projected visit to Salzburg with Vogl did not take place. In September he and Vogl were back in Vienna, the singer to resume work with the Court Opera, the composer to his lodgings in the Wipplingerstrasse and to his dreams of conquering that Opera.

II

If we associate the years 1815 and 1816 with the composition of songs, and 1817 with sonatas, then 1818 and 1819 could be called the Pianoforte Duet years. A number of works for this medium were written, the first fruits of a rich production of PF. Duets composed during the next six years or so. It was a sociable medium one might say—and a substitute one. Schubert could play his duets with Gahy, or another friend, Franz Lachner, a Bavarian musician who came to Vienna in the autumn of 1822, or Johann Baptist Jenger, for the mutual pleasure of himself and his partner, or for the enjoyment of a circle of friends; a substitute medium, because it so conveniently adapts itself to orchestral arrangements. Nearly all of Schubert's overtures and symphonies were arranged by himself or his friends for PF. Duet, and he, like all other musicians, came to know intimately the symphonies of his predecessors, great and small, in a similar fashion. Some critics and other writers have even tried to enlarge the process and they hold that Schubert's original PF. Duets are orchestral works in disguise; a view with no evidence to support it and which can only be taken seriously because of the hold it has gained amongst music-lovers in general.

A few of the PF. Duets are known to have originated at Zseliz, and it is obvious why they did so. They formed teaching material for Marie and Karoline Esterházy. The first is a set of eight variations on a French Air in E minor. The 'Air' was a song *Le bon Chevalier* (*Der treue Reiter*), supposedly by Queen Hortense of Holland. It is a setting of words beginning

Reposez-vous, bon Chevalier!
Laissez-là votre armure. . . .

and in substance very like Sir Walter Scott's poem 'Soldier rest! thy warfare's o'er', which Schubert set at a later date. The variations are the finest of the early sets, with some notable modulations and vigorous writing in the final two or three. They were published in April 1822 as his Op. 10, dedicated to Beethoven by his 'admirer and worshipper, Franz Schubert'. Another less famous, and less worthy, set of variations for PF. Duet, which are almost certainly of that period, although possibly a little earlier than 1818, are those in B flat, published posthumously as part of his Op. 82. It is again in the last variation and the finale of the set that the individual Schubert is to be found. The *Rondo* in D major has been mentioned; its musical style and piquant rhythms are very like those in the 'Four Polonaises' for PF. Duet, published as the composer's Op. 75. Only of very recent years has it been possible to date these Polonaises, and to realise that they were written at Zseliz; a manuscript sketch for nos. 2 and 4, and the Trio of no. 3, turned up in the posthumous papers of the violinist Otto Dresdel, a friend of the composer Robert Franz. The sketch bore the date 'July 1818'. The Polonaises are charming dances, full of varied melodies and poetic fancies; their marked rhythms *alla polacca* give them strength and drive, and the graceful, fluid piano writing recalls Chopin. Why are they so neglected? In the sketch mentioned there is a fragmentary tune marked by Schubert 'Des' (=D flat). It runs as follows:

It evolved into the 'Trio' section of the third Polonaise, where it appears in this form:

But it also generated a second melody, more familiar to the reader, probably, than the Polonaise tune:

This is from the 'Trio' of the sixth piece in the 'Moments Musicaux', Op. 94, the *Allegretto* in A flat. It means that the date of composition of the *Allegretto* is round about 1818 and it is, therefore, the earliest of the 'Moments Musicaux'.

The first Duet Sonata, in B flat, Op. 30, was composed that year; the date '1824' is erroneous, and given because this early Sonata was associated with the second Duet Sonata, the more famous 'Grand Duo', in C major. Schindler gave the more acceptable date for the Sonata in B flat in his 'Catalogue of Schubert's Works' of 1857. The B flat Sonata for PF. Duet was published in 1823 by the Viennese firm of Sauer and Leidesdorf, and dedicated to County Pálffy, owner and director of the Theater an der Wien. The work is in three movements, there is no scherzo, and its shortness should recommend it to players. Again one asks: why is this sonata neglected? It starts with a Mozartean theme, it is true, but Schubert soon forgets his assumed accent and speaks in his own voice. The first movement has a *codetta* and a development section of great interest and imagination. The work teems with Schubertian melody, and the touches of unusual harmony, the original modulations, the imitations of thematic figures between the players, especially in the finale, should place the work occasionally in concert programmes. Instead of perhaps one more orchestration of the 'Grand Duo' Sonata, the bringing to light of this earlier one by two pianists would be a more rewarding effort.

The first of Schubert's many sets of 'Marches Militaires' for PF. Duet, was composed at that time and published in 1824 as Op. 27; the music of the three marches, in D, C and D, is a little obvious, but entertaining, and in the 'Trio' sections there is a quieter and more lyrical note. Like the overtures, the marches are all written to a pattern. But a fixed form is never a confining matter for Schubert, and his episodic departures from it usually produce music of great individuality. In later work in 'March' style there is music as thoroughly Schubertian as anything in the chamber music of the period.

The last two PF. Duets of the group are the Overtures in G minor and F major. The former work, composed in October 1819, was unknown to the nineteenth century. It came to light in 1896 in the posthumous papers of a friend of Ferdinand Schubert from whom he must have received the piece. The manuscript is a neatly written copy, and it has been suggested that the Overture was originally written for the orchestra. The PF. Duet may therefore be an arrangement. It was published in the supplementary volume of the 'Gesamtausgabe' (volume XXI). It is in the standard tripartite form: *Adagio* introduction, a main section in modified sonata-form, *Allegretto*, and an *Allegro vivace* coda. The Allegretto is a masterly piece of work having much in common with the Duet Sonata in B flat. It also shows a feature of Schubert's style in those years: a favourite harmonic clash between the diatonic seventh of a minor scale (F natural in the key of G minor) and the sharpened leading note (F sharp). Both Sonata and Overture derive tonal contrasts from the clash of F natural and F sharp—giving linkages between the keys D major/D minor/B flat major, and similar sets of keys. The second overture, in F major (with an *Adagio* introduction in F minor), was composed in November 1819 and published in 1825 as Op. 34. It is an extraordinary example of the inability of the individual to judge the merit of his own work that Schubert should have chosen to publish this markedly inferior composition rather than the previous Overture in G minor.[1] There is a legend, which originated with the untrustworthy Josef Hüttenbrenner, that Schubert composed the Overture in F in his (Hüttenbrenner's) lodgings in the Bürgerspital in three hours! This information, he said, was actually written by Schubert on his manuscript. Needless to say Josef was not able to produce the manuscript as evidence of his anecdote: it was lost. He even added that Schubert wrote the words '. . . and dinner missed in consequence'. The reader may judge for himself whether this overture, occupying a dozen pages of print, could have been so composed.

The two overtures, written for the piano in the autumn of 1819, had had a predecessor in February of that year, but it was an

[1] It is possible, however, that in 1825 he may no longer have had the manuscipt of the G minor Overture to hand. Friends, it is evident, borrowed the work, and it may have been temporarily mislaid.

Overture composed for orchestra. It is the last of Schubert's independent orchestral overtures: a work which, by reason of its being composed for orchestra, stands midway between his early compositions in that medium and the later work which begins, modestly enough, with the incompleted Symphony in E minor and major. The overture is in E minor. It received one or two performances in Schubert's lifetime, and then disappeared until it was published in the 'Gesamtausgabe', 1886. Alfred Einstein looks on the work as the true forerunner of the composer's maturity. It is a splendid composition, full of Schubert's powers of thematic development, original and telling harmonic effects, and significant melody. There are examples of those violent orchestral contrasts—full orchestral *fortissimos* sandwiching lightly accompanied solo passages, which Schubert inherited from Mozart and which are such a notable feature of his later work. The touches of poetical fancy are most moving:

But—and the unwilling modification must be added—too much of its magnificence evaporates when it leaves the paper for actual performance. Or perhaps it is when it leaves the piano for the orchestra. Schubert in these apprentice years failed to realise that kaleidoscopic harmonies so effective on the keyboard lose their colour in an orchestral version. The varied timbres of the orchestra, the notes of strings and wind, nothing if not sustained, seem to militate against quickly changing *fortissimo* harmonies. The 'Romantic' composers abandoned them at an early stage and substituted the far more effective device of contrasting orchestral sonorities. But the experiments of Schubert and Beethoven in harmonic contrasts enabled later composers to avoid what was ineffective, and to succeed with the contrasts of orchestral timbre. For all its weaknesses, the E minor Overture remains a peak in Schubert's early work and deserves more attention than it gets. In England, at least, it has never yet been given a carefully nurtured performance by a first-class orchestra under a pre-eminent conductor. Only under such conditions is a true judgement possible.

In the letter which Schubert wrote on 3 August 1818 from Zseliz, telling his friends that he was living and composing 'like a god', he mentioned that a song *Einsamkeit*, to words by Mayrhofer, was finished. He added that he believed it to be the best song he had written. This is another example of his inability to estimate fully the merits of his own work, for this song, an extremely long one, is an unequal piece of writing with 'two grains of corn hid in two bushels of chaff'. There are only half-a-dozen Mayrhofer settings in 1818 and 1819 and none of them has won and retained a hold on the interest of music lovers. *An die Freunde* has pages of excellent Schubert, and *Nachtstück* opens characteristically, but neither of them has the power or lyrical charm of the great 1817 group. Two 'nocturne' songs, *An den Mond in einer Herbstnacht*, composed during the unhappy spring of 1818, and *Abendbilder*, of February 1819, are both a shade too long to have attracted singers. But the Schubertian holds them dear. The first page of the address to the autumnal moon is from the heart of Schubert; the soft but stately march of the accompaniment is suggested by Alois Schreiber's line: 'Leis' sind deine Tritte durch des Aethers Wüste' ('Soft are your footfalls through the ethereal desert'). The other song, a reverie at dusk by Johann Peter Silbert, has further examples of Schubert's decorative accompaniments, musical imagery evoked by the bird-song, the evening bell, the moonlight on the church roof. From a group of songs to Schiller's poems, one—*Die Götter Griechenlands*—has won a fame which its own beauty could not bring it. This is because its opening bars contain a phrase in A minor which resembles the opening of the 'Menuetto' in the A minor String Quartet, Op. 29. As a result the popular quartet sheds some of its renown on the song; the point will be taken up again in connection with the chamber work. The song is melodious, and its pathetic tone reflects the poet's sigh for the golden age of the Grecian glory 'Fair World, where are you?'

There were only two settings of Goethe, both very different, but both entirely characteristic. *Die Liebende schreibt* is a sonnet in which the distant lover is begged for a love-token. It is a tender, moving song with a touch of colour in the tonality (B flat to G flat), a touch of the picturesque in the accompaniment for the tears that come and dry without falling. But it is eclipsed by its companion song, the wonderful *Prometheus*. The form of *Prometheus* is the *scena*, that is, a series of connected movements in varying tempos and keys, suggested by the various moods of the stanzas. Schubert's vocal line is a fusion of his dramatic melody and recitative, a true forerunner of Wagner's middle-period styles. The harmonic range and the freedom of modulation, however, are far in advance of anything in Wagner earlier than *Tristan und Isolde*. The Prometheus of Schubert and Goethe is rather the defiant creator of mankind than the tortured figure of Aeschylus: the point was made earlier. The only setting to challenge Schubert's is Hugo Wolf's (1889) and it is Wolf who has suggested the comparison for he considered that Schubert had misunderstood Goethe and wrote his song to show the correct interpretation.[1]

[1] The topic has been presented and explored by Gerard Mackworth-Young, 'Proceedings of the Royal Musical Association,' 1 March 1952.

One sphere in which Schubert was a prolific creator throughout his life is that of the part-song for male voices. It was an extremely popular medium in the early nineteenth century, but as a movement its strength dissipated itself, as the century passed, in the multitudinous associations of the 'glee club', and in the 'Liedertafel' of Germany and Austria, until the sheer bulk of mediocrity in production and performance alike smothered it. The beginnings of the movement appeared in the second half of the eighteenth century in Germany, Austria and Switzerland. It was a mutually fertilising growth in the three countries, although the prime impulse was not the same in each one. The 'Liederschule' of Berlin were offsprings of a union between the motets in the Church service and the choruses for male voices in opera: under the guidance of composers such as Johann Friedrich Reichardt and Johann Abraham Schultz they were responsible for the popularity of the male voice choir in Germany. The term 'Liedertafel' for these associations of male singers was used for the first time *c.* 1805 (see Zelter's letter of 26 December 1808 to Goethe). In Switzerland and South Germany the choirs and their music were inspired by the choral songs of the Reformation. The composer Hans Georg Nägeli, coming rather late on the scene, supported the singing of the male voice choirs so ardently that he brought about a revival of enthusiasm at a time when it was rapidly waning. We shall meet his name again later in Schubert's life, for he was a publisher as well as a composer. In Austria the earliest part-songs seem to have been arrangements of solo songs; an early manuscript in the Vienna City Library has arrangements by one Franz Schraub of some of Mozart's *Lieder*: *Das Veilchen*, *Abendempfindungen*, etc. The part-singing was taken up eagerly in Vienna. At the time when Schubert left the *Stadtkonvikt* the publishers were pouring out an enormous number of male voice part-songs. The lists can be seen in Whistling's 'Handbuch der musikalischen Literatur' (1787–1817). Josef and Michael Haydn, Mozart and Beethoven, particularly with the well known 'Canons' of various types, had fed the river of compositions, and Schubert exceeded them all. He composed close on a hundred part-songs for male voices. There are many 'Canons' in 1813, chiefly contrapuntal exercises for Salieri; in 1815 and 1816 his part-songs are strophic in form, but from 1817 onwards he uses the 'onrunning' form as well as the strophic, and in both styles he writes masterpieces quite worthy of being put alongside the best of his songs of the period. Most of them are unaccompanied, but there are several with pianoforte accompaniment, and a few with solo voices as well. His style in these part-songs is largely homophonic and he keeps the music going by bold changes of key and extraordinary harmonic strokes. Early work shows how keenly he responded to the grisly 'Romantic' theme: *Totengräberlied* of 1813 (Hölty) and *Der Geistertanz* of 1816 (Matthisson). This *Dance of Death* poem fascinated the boy Schubert; it is made tolerable only by the closing lines in which the capering dead explain the reason for their joy: that their hearts, being dead, no longer ache. Schubert tried his hand at three solo settings, one of them completed, as well as composing the vocal quartet. The part-songs of 1817 include a first setting of Goethe's great poem *Gesang der Geister über den Wassern*, another poem with a great attraction for Schubert. His quartet *Das Dörfchen* (words by Bürger) is very typical of the easy-going, sociable Schubert part-song and consequently very popular in his day; it was later revised and published as his Op. 11: no. 1 in 1822. He also published, in Op. 17, four quartets to texts by different poets; they are all secondary part-songs, but much worthier than the humble *Das Dörfchen*. The best two are the settings of Schiller's *Liebe* and an unknown poet's *Die Nacht*; both poems mention the murmur of streams at night and Schubert's sensitive music, his attempts with voices alone to depict the purling, shadowed waters, produce a charming pair of songs. The part-songs of Op. 17 are all quite short and would make an excellently varied concert item. Finally, in April 1819, Schubert composed the fourth setting of his beloved Goethe poem *Nur wer die Sehnsucht kennt* for men's voices. It is the greatest of his part-songs, a masterly setting of the words, warm in tone, varied in 'orchestration', and full of extravagant touches of colour, of harmonic adventure, of climax and repose. The main key is E major; the first section ends in a fortissimo F major and his clash of semitonal keys inspires the modulation throughout. It is Schubert's portrait in music of the hapless girl who is 'alone and cut off from all joys'.

III

One of the last works he composed in this period is the popular and famous *Trout* Quintet; the music is for piano and a quartet of strings (violin, viola, 'cello and double-bass). Albert Stadler, his schoolfellow and friend of those days, wrote many years after Schubert's death a letter to Ferdinand Luib in which he said that the work was commissioned by Sylvester Paumgartner, an enthusiastic 'cellist and one of the leading lights in the musical life of Steyr. Paumgartner, a wealthy bachelor, lived in a large house with a music room on the first floor where private musical parties were held, and a large music *salon* on the second floor, in which midday concerts and other musical activities took place under the stimulus of this benevolent patron. He also owned a well stocked music library. Apparently he required of Schubert a composition in the style of Hummel's PF. Quintet in E flat, Op. 87. He also admired the song *Die Forelle* and suggested the variations which form a favourite movement in the quintet. Schubert sketched some of his composition at Steyr, but the music was not completed until after his return to Vienna. Hummel's Quintet, which served Schubert as a prototype, is a short, straightforward work in four movements; the Menuetto is placed second, and the third movement, *Largo*, is only a page long and serves more as an introduction to the finale. It is excessively imitative of early Beethoven, or perhaps it would be truer to say that Hummel used the same idiom as Beethoven in an oppressively lifeless manner. It is sufficient merely to glance through the works of contemporaries such as Dussek and Hummel, to see Schubert's vitality and, although clearly influenced by Beethoven, his independent style. Very occasionally one sees a trait in Hummel's instrumentation which certainly appealed to Schubert: the piano is given a chance to sing, or it will enter effectively after silence to clinch a cadence.

But that is all there is in the meagre stretches of the work. Schubert's *Trout* Quintet, on the contrary, overflows with an abundance of musical-poetic fancies. Its melodies, their presentation and development, the instrumentation of the work, its irrepressible good spirits and sociability—not only have these qualities made it a greatly beloved work, but they stamp it as a universal masterpiece, the first of Schubert's chamber-works to claim the tributes not of Schubertians alone, but of all musicians. The great qualities of the early string quartets and trios, of the 'Duo' Sonata for PF. and violin, of the 1817 PF. Sonatas, may perhaps have their strongest appeal only to the Schubert lover; that is to say, their appeal is limited. But this is not the case with the PF. Quintet, whose appeal is for all. Even so, this first acknowledged masterpiece is not quite the whole Schubert, nor the fully mature composer. There is no point in over-praising it, nor in praising it for qualities which it has in small measure—the serious, dramatic power of the composer for instance. Its key is indeed a key to the work, for A major is Schubert's key of contentment; it always introduces a mood of expansive, friendly good-humour. A German critic has suggested that the countryside of Steyr, which Schubert himself called 'über allen Begriff schön'—'inconceivably beautiful'—is a 'secret collaborator' in the quintet.[1] Certainly Schubert's happiness that year may be responsible for the overflowing ideas of the work, but the thought of Paumgartner and four other players sociably enjoying his music is quite as acceptable a 'collaborator'.

> 'Those happy strains of wandering and roaming—the finale of the *Trout* Quintet is a good instance—do not suggest remote and solitary landscapes; there is always a feeling of town sociability behind them.' (Eric Blom.)

Technically the finest points of the quintet are the notable development of his main ideas in the first movement, the original rhythmic patterns of his slow movement, and the colourful modulations and counterpoints in the variations. The first of these points, the development of the main melodies in the opening *Allegro vivace*, could be examined more closely because Schubert's skill is so spontaneously charming that it goes—as it should of course—unnoticed. The violin states the first theme:

and a long passage based entirely upon it and the preliminary flourish of the pianoforte then follows. The quoted melody grows as a plant grows, throwing out subsidiary ideas and changing and adding to its own form, until finally the piano announces this version of it, played against a rhythmic accompaniment which derives from his early experiments with the medium of the string quartet:

[1] 'Schubert' (Willi Kahl), Cobbett's 'Cyclopedia of Chamber Music', Oxford, 1929.

The development section of this movement then builds up its powerful climaxes on the thematic ideas of Ex. 24, used thus against a throbbing background of the upper strings:

We are not told whether Paumgartner approved his gift when the parts were sent to him at the end of 1819—only that he made a very moderate showing at the 'cello part. The composition completely disappeared and no more was heard of it until ten years later. It was then sold by Schubert's brother Ferdinand to the publisher Josef Czerny, Vienna, and appeared in May 1829 as Op. 114. The auditors of the resurrected work, and they were not members of the Schubert circle, had the grace to realise its qualities. In an advertising notice of 21 May 1829 Czerny announced:

> This Quintet, having already been performed in several circles at the publisher's instigation, and declared to be a masterpiece by the musical connoisseurs present, we deem it our duty to draw the musical public's attention to this latest work by the unforgettable composer. . . .

But by that time Schubert was beyond all such adulation and the recognition of this early and beloved masterpiece came too late.

IV

1820-1823

I

The four years from 1820 to the close of 1823 were the critical ones in Schubert's artistic career and, for it does not follow, in his life also. At the commencement he was a young composer, unknown to Vienna at large, but appreciated by a circle of staunch and admiring friends. Amongst those friends were far-seeing and not uninfluential musicians such as Vogl and the Sonnleithners, father and son. Although he had experienced a number of setbacks, his life had brought him the satisfaction of achievement, recognition in a limited sense, and, at the start of 1820, several opportunities for the further advancement of his genius and its public acknowledgement. As the four years passed his name became more and more widely known in Vienna; two of his operettas were performed in its leading theatres; his songs were sung in public and created a profound impression; amateur and professional quartets repeatedly sang his male-voice part-songs and they were enthusiastically applauded; and finally the publication of his works started with the firm of Cappi & Diabelli: first of all songs on a subscription basis, then dances, then part-songs. His fame was spreading to Linz, Graz, the more distant parts of Austria, the provincial capitals of Germany; and patrons in distinguished walks of life were having their interest awakened in the young composer. Schubert's prospects were very favourable, and his head was slightly turned. His father and brothers became almost strangers, and friends of his boyhood, in so far as they were not part of the artistic circle in which he moved, were treated coolly. And then the event occurred from which, unless one deliberately underwrites it, the dramatic quality is difficult to remove. He became seriously ill at the end of 1822, and, as the tide of his affairs rose and success promised on all sides, he was obliged to withdraw from Viennese society, and in his wretched physical state watch opportunity after opportunity fail to materialise. 'They greatly praise Schubert' wrote Karl Beethoven in his uncle's conversation-book during August 1823, 'but it is said that he hides himself.' The close of the period saw one burst of effort, one meteoric blaze, as 'Rosamunde' was put on the boards. The play failed dismally, and the light is extinguished. At the beginning of 1824 Schubert was himself again; the days of aping the sophisticated man about town, and the brusque artist, were passed; affectionate relations with his father and brothers were resumed, his friendships regained their old warmth, the Viennese public quietly prepared to forget the young, disturbing theatre composer. One thing remained, and grew, until it reached an almost surfeiting climax: the publication in Vienna of his songs and, occasionally, instrumental works. But after 1823 the pattern of his life resumes the shapes and colours of the years and experiences before 1820, and we meet old names and old friends again in his story.

A rather startling event in the spring of 1820 was Schubert's arrest by the police under suspicion of subversive activities. The murder of Kotzbue the previous year, as a suspected Russian spy, had been carried out by a Berlin student, and from then onwards all Student Associations, first in Germany, and then in Austria, had been looked upon with suspicion by the police. Schubert's friend, Johann Senn, the Tyrolese poet, was arrested after resisting a police investigation into his papers, and Schubert, being present in Senn's lodgings during the affair, was arrested too. But it is clear that he was soon released. At the time of this unfortunate event he was engaged on the composition of a cantata for solo voices, mixed chorus and orchestra—an ambitious work. This was 'Lazarus, or the Festival of Resurrection', a static religious drama of a kind popular in eighteenth-century Germany, by August Hermann Niemeyer, a professor of theology at Halle University (died 1828). The drama is spoken by the characters Lazarus, Mary and Martha, the daughter of Jairus, Nathaniel, a priest, and Simon, a Sadducee. It was in three acts, of which Schubert probably composed the whole of the first two. Not all of the music has survived, but there remains a substantial fragment comprising Act I (complete) and most of Act II. The music was recovered during the middle of the nineteenth century from various owners by Alexander Thayer, the American Consul in Trieste, and author of a well known biography of Beethoven. The drama, 'Lazarus', is a meditation on Death, presented through the various emotions of the characters as they watch Lazarus die: despair and doubt (Martha), hope (Mary and Jairus' daughter), sceptism and fear (Simon), faith (Nathaniel). The poem is not without merit, but its gloominess cannot be redeemed even by the wonder of Schubert's music. And wonderful it is, the most intriguing of all his earlier choral works. The fusion of melody and recitative so remarkable in the song *Prometheus* is a feature of the vocal line of 'Lazarus' and it is supported by a most poetical and decorative style of writing in the orchestral accompaniment which suggests again and again the Wagnerian procedures in 'Die Walküre' and the first part of 'Siegfried'. The harmonic range is very wide. There are pages in 'Lazarus' which are akin to Schubert's operatic writing: the use of *recitativo* supported, not by chords, or decorated chords, as in all contemporary opera, but by a fluid use of short figures, almost *Leitmotive* in their cumulative effect. It is possible that we owe the non-completion of this interesting work to the advent of police and politics into Schubert's otherwise uneventful life; and that his arrest broke the continuity of his work on the cantata.

The operetta 'Die Zwillingsbrüder' was performed, eventually, on 14 June 1820. It was given in the Kärntnertor Theater, with Vogl doubling the parts of the twin brothers Fritz and Franz. The operetta was extensively reported, and on the whole well received. It was given a number of times throughout the summer, and then was never revived again. But as a result of its moderate success, Schubert was commissioned to compose the incidental music to another play, based on a similar French model, to be written by the same author: it was 'Die Zauberharfe' ('The Magic Harp'). The play—little more than a pantomime, as the word is understood today, with the same kind of scenic effects—was to be given in the rival theatre, the Theater an der Wien. The first performance took place on 19 August 1820, and although, again, Schubert's music pleased, the stupid libretto doomed the work to failure. Frankly, it bored the theatre-goers, and what chance had Schubert to alleviate that boredom with his occasional numbers? In October a last performance was given and the work heard no more. The Overture in C major, using, as has been said, material from the 'Italian' Overture in D major, is now known as the Overture to 'Rosamunde', and is as popular as any orchestral work of Schubert. It has, actually, nothing whatever to do with the play 'Rosamunde' of December 1823.

Between these two first performances of his operettas, in July 1820, Schubert spent a few days at Atzenbrugg, which lies some twenty miles north-west of Vienna. An uncle of Schober's managed estates in the neighbourhood, and to his house every summer between 1817 and 1824 Schober brought a band of young men and women, kindred spirits, for a country holiday; there were excursions into the neighbourhood, games in the adjoining fields and meadows, and charades and dancing in those rooms of the small castle at the disposal of the visitors. 1820 is the first year in which Schubert was a guest.

Two more of his songs were printed in December as supplements: the first was the 1819 song *Widerschein*, which appeared in an almanach called 'Taschenbuch zum geselligen Vergnügen' ('Pocketbook for Sociable Pleasures') from the firm of Göschen in Leipzig; the second was *The Trout*, given as a supplement to the Vienna 'Zeitschrift für Kunst', of 9 December 1820. Both songs were later on re-published by Diabelli: *The Trout* as Op. 32 in 1828, *Widerschein* as part of the 'Nachgelassene' songs in 1832. This second publication of *Widerschein* gave the song in B flat instead of the original D major, but this was the only alteration in the music (there is a slight change in the opening line of the words); the second publication is wrongly given as a second *version* in the Deutsch 'Thematic Catalogue'; the date 'May 1828' of this autograph is that of Schubert's copying of the song, possibly for the publisher.

The year closes with some outstanding work. The month of

December would be graced by the presence of the String Quartet Movement in C minor (the 'Quartett-Satz') alone, but there were, in addition, the superb motet 'Psalm XXIII' for S.S.A.A., written for a new friend, Anna Fröhlich, the extended solo cantata *Waldesnacht* (or *Im Walde*) for tenor and pianoforte, and two attempts, for male voices, of the Goethe poem *Gesang der Geister über den Wassern*. Both choral sketches are of excellent quality. The first of them, in C minor, with accompaniment for violas and 'cellos, was brought to a conclusion the following February. If only the same fortunate completion could have been the lot of the String Quartet! This quartet movement, in C minor, is the only movement in Schubert's instrumental work, prior to the 'Unfinished' Symphony, which prepares us for the greatness which bursts forth in that symphony. It was intended to be the first movement of a fully executed string quartet, and in its music Schubert at last combines his lyrical effusion, of which the *Trout* Quintet is so notable an example, with the darker, dramatic, and passionate qualities of his greater *Lieder*. The 'cello, for the first time in Schubert, is as free, as adventurous, as 'virtuoso' in technique, as the other three string parts; it seems to show that the work was not intended for performance by the Schubert family quartet, and the composer was no longer bound by the limited abilities of his father's cello-playing. The slow movement, an *Andante* in A flat, is full of promising ideas, but they never take wing, as it were, and after forty-four bars Schubert threw up his task.

The setting of Psalm XXIII, *The Lord is my Shepherd*, is fairly well known in England. It has that indefinable quality of greatness although the scope is small; and although, too, Schubert is using the secular idiom of his song-writing in composing this sacred work, the expression is so sincere, so delicate, that it creates an atmosphere of spiritual exaltation at the climax and an unearthly tranquillity at the close. The text is a translation into German by Moses Mendelssohn.

When the work was first performed in England, with English text, the 'Musical Transcript' of 2 September 1854 dismissed it with these words:

> ... the elevation of feeling, and the deep sanctity of the devotional spirit is absent. It is more operatic than sacerdotal, and its length is too protracted for the due expression of the sentiment. The restlessness of the accompaniment also damages the proposed effect.

Anna Fröhlich taught singing at the 'Conservatoire' of the *Gesellschaft der Musikfreunde*, an association of music lovers in Austria, which we shall meet with increasing frequency in Schubert's story. The Vienna branch of the association was housed in those days in the Tuchlauben, one of the larger streets in the heart of the Inner City. Psalm XXIII was composed for Anna's female singing-class there. She was one of four gifted sisters, the others being Barbara, Katharina (beloved by the poet Grillparzer, and through whom he met Schubert) and Josefine. At an evening concert in the home of Ignaz Sonnleithner, held on 1 December 1820, Anna Fröhlich accompanied the singer August von Gymnich in the *Erlking*; during January 1821 both singer and pianist again performed the song in a semi-public concert given by the *Gesellschaft*. The song was creating a deep impression. Ignaz von Mosel and Count Moritz Dietrichstein, two officials of the Imperial Court and both influential men, as well as the brothers Sonnleithner, were becoming interested in the young composer. A few weeks later, on 7 March 1821, at a public concert given by a 'Society of Ladies of the Nobility' for charitable purposes, Vogl sang the *Erlking* to Anselm Hüttenbrenner's accompaniment, with overwhelming success.

II

Schubert's own efforts to get the *Erlking* published had been unsuccessful. The Viennese firms were adamant about the difficulties of the accompaniment. The outcome of Spaun's efforts in the spring of 1817 to interest Breitkopf & Härtel of Leipzig in the song, was first told by Max Friedlaender in the Berlin journal 'Vierteljahresschrift für Musikwissenschaft' of July 1893. According to this, the Leipzig firm, doubtful of the authenticity of the composition, sent it for confirmation to the only Franz Schubert they knew, a composer in the service of the Dresden Court. This is the relevant part of his reply:

> . . . about ten days ago I received from you an esteemed letter in which you sent me a manuscript of Goethe's 'Erlking' supposed to be mine; with the greatest astonishment I inform you that this cantata was never composed by me; I shall retain the same in my keeping in order to find out who has sent you the rubbish in so rude a manner, and also to discover the fellow who thus misuses my name. . . .

But Leopold Sonnleithner, Josef Hüttenbrenner and a few others had determined that the song should be published, and had not only collected the money for its engraving, but, on offering it at one of the Sonnleithner musical evenings, a hundred copies were subscribed for. This meant money enough to have *Gretchen* also engraved. The success of Vogl's performance of the *Erlking* on the eve of the song's publication must have been very gratifying to the promoters of the venture. The firm of Cappi & Diabelli (the forerunners of Diabelli's firm) acted as agents, and Schubert's Op. 1 appeared on 31 March 1821. It was dedicated to Count Dietrichstein. About six hundred copies of the song were sold immediately. *Gretchen am Spinnrade*, Op. 2, dedicated to Moritz von Fries, appeared a month later, on 30 April 1821. This song had also had several successful performances at private and semi-public gatherings that spring. Nearly as many copies of *Gretchen* (between five and six hundred) were quickly sold. In a similar way Schubert published a number of songs in 1821 and 1822 comprising altogether seven opus-numbers. Amongst these twenty songs a few may cause mild surprise: in view of the masterpieces available it is hard to understand why such very minor works as *Morgenlied*, *Der König in Thule*, *Der Schäfer und der Reiter* and others, were chosen. But most of the greater Geothe settings were there, and *Der Tod und das Mädchen* was also included. We, naturally, are wise after the event.

The success of the first seven opus-numbers led Cappi & Diabelli to accept, on their own responsibility, publication of Opp. 8, 9, 10 and 11. Of these the first contains songs; the rest are '36 Waltzes' (Op. 9), 'Variations on a French Air' (Op. 10) and three part-songs (Op. 11). In December 1822 Schubert published three more sets of songs on his own initiative. These were Opp. 12, 13 and 14 containing the Harper's songs from 'Wilhelm Meister', and 'Suleika's First Song'. Cappi & Diabelli's venture with Opp. 8 to 11 was a modest enough beginning from Schubert's point of view, but it was, at least, a beginning. From then onwards publication proceeded regularly, but spasmodically, until by the time of his death, he had published works up to Op. 100. During April 1821, just before the appearance of *Gretchen*, he started to compose a duet for soprano and tenor to words by an unknown poet, *Linde Lüfte wehen.* It is sad that a duet of such charming promise should remain uncompleted. Since it has not been published in England, and never in an easily accessible form, it is quoted here:

Another invitation reached him in the spring of 1821 to compose music for the theatre. Two additional numbers were required for the Vienna *première* of Hérold's comic operetta 'La Clochette' ('Das Zauberglöckchen'), first produced in Paris in 1817. The two items were: a tenor aria for Azolin (*Der Tag entflieht, der Abend glüht*) and a so-called *Comic Duet* for tenor (Bedur) and bass (Zedir) (*Nein, das ist zu viel*). These were composed at once and performed on 20 June 1821. They were rather inappropriately exalted in style and prolonged in structure for the light and tuneful operetta which they supplemented, and made no mark at all.

The visit to Atzenbrugg soon afterwards assumes greater importance in the Schubert records than the preceding one of 1820, or the following one in 1822. A few German dances were composed there (Op. 9: nos. 1–3, and Op. 18: nos. 29–31) called the 'Atzenbrügger Deutsche', and incidents of the holiday are enshrined in drawings and paintings by Leopold Kupelwieser, a friend of Spaun's originally, but soon becoming an intimate of Schober and Schubert. There are two excellent watercolours, one depicting an excursion by coach through pastoral surroundings to nearby Aumühle, the other, an indoor scene, showing the party acting a charade. Schubert appears in both. There is also a pencil sketch of Schubert by Kupelwieser, not a favourite portrait but evidently an extremely good likeness. It was not discovered until Kupelwieser died in 1862 when it turned up amongst his posthumous papers, together with other sketches of members of the Atzenbrugg party, including Schober. They were published by Karl Kupelwieser (Leopold's son) in 1912. The two important watercolours, familiar now through frequent reproduction, were commissioned from Kupelwieser by Schober and remained in his possession until his death (1882). They were then purchased by that eminent Schubert collector and admirable Schubertian, Nikolaus Dumba, and on his death (23 March 1900) went to the City of Vienna. The equally well known, but inferior, landscape with figures, showing Schubert seated on the ground puffing a pipe, and entitled 'Playing ball at Atzenbrugg' is a composite affair: Schober, Schwind and the artist Ludwig Mohn, all had a hand in its production and this took place years after the event.

The private concerts at the Sonnleithners' residence, the 'Gundelhof', held every Friday evening in the early days of their organisation, were duplicated in middle-class residences all over the city. During the early 1820's a remarkable development of them occurred; by popular choice the whole of the music of the evening—songs, dances, pianoforte pieces and so on—was by Schubert. The concerts devised in this way were called 'Schubertiads'. The songs, naturally, were the chief part of the concert and Vogl's voice a powerful attraction; many of the songs of the 1820's were first performed at these 'Schubertiads'. They were held at the residence of the Bruchmann family, at Spaun's, and at two other friends' homes, Karl Hönig and Johann Umlauff (all these people were practising or studying or connected with law) and at many more houses too numerous to specify. Schubert was acquainted with the Bruchmann family because of his friendship with Franz Bruchmann, a young man of character who in after years abandoned law for Holy Orders and became an austere and forbidding cleric. His sister, Justina, was in those days secretly courted by Schober. Their father was a wealthy merchant, and besides their town house the family owned an attractive residence in the countrified suburbs of Vienna called 'The Caprice'.

The Hönig family lived near St. Stefan's Cathedral. Schubert was a friend of Karl Hönig, whose sister Anna (Nanette) was ardently courted by a young painter, Moritz von Schwind. Schubert had met Schwind through their mutual friend Josef Kenner, an old *Konvikt* pupil, and they quickly became intimate. The young painter, seven years younger than Schubert, idolised the composer, and their friendship was to prove a happy and fruitful one. Johann Umlauff, a law student, was another friend of the composer's, first meeting him in 1818. He it is who is responsible for the story of Schubert's composing in the morning, in bed. A guitarist of some accomplishment, he used to sing Schubert's songs to him, accompanying himself on the guitar. The legends which arose from such imperfectly remembered events are (1) that Schubert slept in his spectacles so as to waste no time looking for them in the morning, (2) that Schubert played the guitar and himself arranged the accompaniments of his songs for that instrument. The first of these legends is surely the silliest of all anedcotes invented about a great artist. How could it ever have been taken seriously? And yet it gave rise to one of the foulest gibes ever delivered against Schubert (page 345). Umlauff is also said to have disputed with Schubert the correct emphasis of the questioning line of *Der Wanderer*—'O Land, wo bist du? ('O Land, where art thou?'). He asserted that 'du' should be stressed and come on the first beat of the bar. Schubert, rightly, of course, held to his own stressing of 'bist'.

In the August of 1821, soon after his return to Vienna from Atzenbrugg, Schubert composed the Symphony in E minor and major; it is incomplete, and unperformable except in arrangements. The manuscript is a strange specimen of his methods of impromptu work, not frequently resorted to, and, as can be seen in this symphony, not successful. The *Adagio* introduction, in E minor, is fully scored; there follows the first movement proper, an *Allegro* in E major, which is scored fully up to the entry of the second subject in G major. This is at the end of a page. From there onwards, Schubert 'threads' the symphony right to the end. The score is left blank for subsequent filling in; the melody is indicated throughout, in Violin I, or Flute I, as a rule; the climaxes are sometimes more fully scored, sometimes indicated merely by a very high note (*sforzando*) in the first violin part. Too much remains for the 'arranger' to fill in, and the two best known completions, those of John Francis Barnett (performed at the Crystal Palace, 5 May 1883) and Felix Weingartner (performed at Vienna on 9 December 1934) are both failures. The music is in his early symphonic style, and there are few, if any, hints of the 'Unfinished' Symphony (which is only a year and two months ahead, as it were) but plenty of links with the Sixth Symphony, in C major, of 1818. The themes are still light-hearted to the point of triviality, and the 'Trio' of the third movement is very inferior. It is odd how the last three symphonic scherzos of Schubert, which have some degree of completion, are all in C major with a 'Trio' in A major (1818, 1821 and 1828) and that the transitional link between the 'Trio' and the recapitulated scherzo is, in all three cases, achieved by a sustained or repeated E natural. The slow movement, *Andante*, in A major, is an attractive movement, but short and slight. There is nothing in it to compare with the sketched *Andante* in B minor of the 1818 Symphony in D. Schubert was the least self-critical of composers, but he must nevertheless have felt that the score of his symphony was not worth completing: nor, frankly, is it. The development section of the first movement contains, as is often the way with other early, unfinished work, the best music in the symphony.

The manuscript was given to Mendelssohn by Ferdinand Schubert in March 1845. The first preformance of his brother's great C major Symphony at Leipzig in March 1839 had been due to Mendelssohn's enthusiasm for the work; Mendelssohn had also tried to secure performances in London and Paris. Ferdinand presented the score of the Symphony in E as a gesture of grateful acknowledgement. On 22 March 1845 Mendelssohn wrote a letter to Ferdinand, which has never been reproduced since it was first published in the Vienna 'Allgemeine Musikzeitung' of January 1848. Here is an English translation of it:

Dear Professor,

Yesterday I received through Doctor *Haertel* the symphony sketch by your brother, of which you have made me the possessor. What pleasure you give me through so fine, so precious a gift, how deeply grateful I am to you for this remembrance of the deceased master, how honoured I feel that you present so significant a specimen of his posthumous remains directly to me—all this you can surely put into words for yourself better than I, but I feel it necessary, although in few words, to express my gratitude to you for your gift. Believe me that I know how to esteem the magnificent gift at its true value, that you could have given it to no one who would have greater joy in it, who would be more sincerely grateful to you for it. In truth, it seems to me as if, through the very incompleteness of the work, the scattered, half-finished indications, that I became at once personally acquainted with your brother more closely and more intimately than I should have done through a completed piece. It seems as if I saw him there working in his room, and this joy I owe to your unexpectedly great kindness and generosity. Let me hope for an opportunity to meet you in the flesh, be it in Vienna or in this place here, and to make your personal acquaintance and then repeat to you by word of mouth, once again, all my thanks.

With respects

Yours faithfully,

Felix Mendelssohn-Bartholdy.

Frankfurt-am-Main,
22 *March* 1845.

On Mendelssohn's death, the manuscript passed into the ownership of his brother Paul. When, after many years, Paul Mendelssohn learned of Sir George Grove's interest in his brother's music, and of Grove's intention to write the lives of Schubert and Mendelssohn in his forthcoming 'Dictionary', he sent the manuscript as a gift to Grove. Grove received it in August 1868 and tells of his surprise at the reception of so bulky a manuscript in an appendix to Arthur Coleridge's English translation of Kreissle's 'Schubert' (London, 1869). The description of the music manuscript as it is given in that appendix, and in the 'Dictionary' itself, was written for Grove by William Rockstro. Grove's pronouncement on the symphony: '. . . it is probable that it did not occupy him more than a few hours' is incredibly silly, but his judgement of the *quality* of the work is, as always when he assesses Schubert, absolutely sound. He says: '. . . it is a work of the old school.' When Brahms learned that Paul Mendelssohn was sending the Schubert MS. to England he became alarmed, and begged Joachim to see that no 'Unzucht' (=lewdness, mischief) would result—referring to expected arrangements, constituting violation, by those inferior English musicians! (Letter of December 1868). Brahms himself had toyed with the idea of finishing the work, but realising the difficulties he abandoned the project; he may have heard in the meantime of Sullivan's intention of doing so. In the end a musician inferior to any of these men completed it. Barnett's account of his difficulties in filling up Schubert's blank score is set out in his paper to the Musical Association of 9 June 1891. There also he tells of the extraordinary occurrence whereby the MS. of the Symphony was nearly lost for ever. Apparently Rockstro brought the MS. back to Grove on a personal visit. He was met at the station and the two friends walked back to Grove's house together, discovering on arrival there that the score had been left in the train. Next morning it was discovered and returned to Grove. On his death the relic was acquired by the Royal College of Music, and is now housed in the British Museum.

III

In September 1821 Schubert left Vienna in the company of Schober to spend a few weeks at St. Pölten. The Bishop of St. Pölten was a relative of Schober's mother and he owned the neighbouring castle of Ochsenburg. The two friends, as far as is known, did not actually lodge in the Bishop's residence in St.

Pölten, although Schober's mother and sister were frequently guests there. But they certainly stayed for a while in the castle of Ochsenburg. Their purpose in seeking the retreat was to work together at an opera. This was 'Alfonso und Estrella', a grand opera in the full sense of the term as far as externals are concerned. It is the only one which Schubert wrote, since both 'Des Teufels Lustschloss' and 'Fierrabras' have spoken dialogue. Schubert has dated his first act '20 September 1821'. It was finished on 16 October and the second act started on 18 October. But after the month at St. Pölten the two friends returned to Vienna, and the music of Act II was finished there on 2 November. That day Schubert wrote a letter to Spaun and informed him with relish that his dedications on the early song publications had 'done their work'. That is to say, the gratified patrons had sent him sums of money as well as grateful acknowledgements. In an added page or two to this letter Schober told Spaun of their month in the 'half-town, half-country' district of St. Pölten and how the opera had come to be written, both friends, apparently, working in a communal study, Schober passing pieces of the libretto as he finished them across to Schubert for composing! Schober's letter also told of three 'Schubertiads' held during the month, one of them attended—so he wrote—by a princess, two countesses and three baronesses. The third act of 'Alfonso und Estrella' was finished on 27 February 1822; the overture was composed later than this, in February 1823. This was probably a first draft, and the manuscript is now lost.

Early in 1821 Schubert had moved from his lodgings with Mayrhofer to a nearby house in the same street. After the return from St. Pölten he lodged once again with the Schober family in the 'Göttweigerhof', situated in the street known today as the Spiegelgasse. The move may have been to continue the work on the opera, but he continued to live there some months after its completion.

Eduard Bauernfeld, a student of philosophy, a future playwright and satirist, and a noted translator of Shakespeare, met Schubert during January 1822. Schwind, the young painter, introduced them at a Schubertiad in the house of Vincentius

Weintridt. Both Bauernfeld and Schwind were great admirers of Weintridt, a noted freethinker of his day, and Schubert, too, evidently, found Weintridt's philosophy to his taste. The meeting between Schubert and Bauernfeld, ardently desired by the latter, was the start of a close and rewarding friendship.

The summer of 1822 is poor in compositions, an understandable reaction from the intensive work on the opera. The popular 'Military Marches', Op. 51, for pianoforte duet, were probably composed at that time; the first of the three, in D major, is one of the most attractive, melodically, of his works in the form, with a delicately modulated 'Trio' section. But if compositions were lacking, performances of his songs and the part-songs of Op. 11, were very numerous during the year in Vienna, and in other, provincial, towns. The three part-songs, *Das Dörfchen*, *Die Nachtigall* and *Geist der Liebe* seem to us today insipid to a degree, but their appeal for Schubert's generation was extraordinarily strong. They were repeatedly performed during his lifetime.

A document of Schubert's survives from the July of 1822 to which Ferdinand gave the title *My Dream*. It is a fanciful account in a rather elevated style of writing of a quarrel between the writer and his father. Reconciliation follows the mother's death, but the quarrel is renewed. Then a gentle maiden dies and after her burial there is a further, and one gathers, a final reconciliation. It struck the nineteenth century as a queer production—but nothing more than that. Then, following upon a suggestion by Schubert's half-brother Anton, the Schubertian Alois Fellner, and after him, Walter Dahms in his biography of Schubert (1912), treated the allegory as a chapter of autobiography. The document suddenly leapt into importance. For a quarter of a century all Schubert biographies and biographical essays developed the theme that Schubert and his father had quarrelled because of the young composer's absorption in music to the neglect of other studies at the *Konvikt*. Reconciliation came with the death of Schubert's mother. The further quarrel was when Schubert finally abandoned his tasks as a teacher and left for Hungary in 1818. There was a wild disregard of dates and facts to make these theories fit the tale *My Dream*. Schubert's mother died in

1812 during his years at the *Stadtkonvikt* before he had shown any sign of neglecting his general studies. After Schubert left the Rossau schoolhouse in 1818 his letters to his family show no sign whatever of estrangement—on the contrary. Nowadays the reaction against the autobiographical interpretation of the document is complete. Inspired by O. E. Deutsch's scorn of any such interpretation, modern biographers of the composer refuse to allow *My Dream* any basis in fact.

In all probability both extremes are equally at fault. Without fully subscribing to an autobiographical interpretation one might feel that there is something in the document of truth. Spaun, for example, in some notes on his relationship with Schubert, 'Ueber Franz Schubert', said:

> He told me that he often wanted to compose his thoughts in music, but his father mustn't know about it, for he didn't want his son to dedicate himself to music.

In manuscript recollections of Mayrhofer's we read:

> I often had to console Schubert's worthy father about his son's future, and I dared to prophesy that Franz would surely win through, nay that a later world would give him his due, slowly though it came to him at first.

Both Spaun and Mayrhofer wrote those remarks long before any autobiographical theories were spun about *My Dream*.

What are the origins of the allegory? It has been suggested that Novalis's flowery style, and contemporary German 'Romantic' tales are responsible. This is probably the case, and I have suggested elsewhere that, in particular, the work of Wilhelm Heinrich Wackenroder, which Schubert may have read at the *Stadtkonvikt*, is being closely imitated. Without wishing to add yet one more theory to those which already exist about *My Dream*, it has occurred to me that this production of Schubert's pen may have been the outcome of some exploit of the friends during the Atzenbrugg holidays. Its date 3 July 1822 lends some support to the idea, and so does the fact that a copy of the 'Dream' exists in

Schober's handwriting. They indulged in all kinds of 'pen-and-paper' games at Atzenbrugg castle; making poems on given words was one of them, making melodies from dots on a piece of paper was another. Possibly Schubert's *My Dream* was the best of the efforts during some similar, forgotten *jeu d'esprit* of the party, and Schober considered it worth preserving.

Schubert's pen was idle during the summer of 1822, but the astonishing burst of composition in the autumn gives the year outstanding importance. In September he took up the half-finished Mass in A flat which he had commenced in November 1819. It has always been assumed that he also abandoned the work in that November, but recently a pencil sketch of the song *Die gefangenen Sänger* dated January 1821 has come to light and on it there are also sketches of the 'Credo' for the Mass; the probability is that Schubert worked spasmodically on the Mass during the three years. At least he completed it in the September of 1822. Soon afterwards it was performed in the old Lerchenfeld Church, situated in east Vienna. In October he sketched, in PF. score, three movements of a Symphony in B minor. These sketches lay in obscurity amongst the mass of MSS. which passed into the possession of Ferdinand when Schubert died. They went on Ferdinand's death to one of his sons, Karl, together with a few other unfinished compositions of no saleable value, including the fragmentary duet 'Linde Lüfte wehen'. These manuscripts were discovered in Karl Schubert's possession by Max Friedlaender, in October 1883, and two years later the symphony sketches were purchased by Nikolaus Dumba. The sketches passed, on Dumba's death, into the Library of the *Gesellschaft der Musikfreunde*. The reason for recounting in detail this passing from hand to hand of the manuscript sketches will be justified later. Schubert began to score the work on 30 October. He completed two movements, but only the first page of the 'Scherzo' (not actually so called by Schubert) is written. Sometime in November 1822 the work was set aside and he never returned to it. This unfinished symphony, which was, after the lapse of half a century, to become the 'Unfinished' Symphony, so that to the whole musical world a peculiar evocative quality attached itself to the word 'unfinished', joined the other two unfinished works, in D and E, of previous years.

The subsequent history of Schubert's orchestral score of the 'Unfinished' Symphony is, as with many other works of his, almost unbelievable. In the following April (1823) the Styrian Music Society, whose headquarters were at Graz, elected Schubert as an honorary member, sending him a 'Diploma of Honour'. This honour was due to the activities of Johann Baptist Jenger, the secretary of the Society, a friend and admirer of the composer. The election and diploma were handed to Anselm Hüttenbrenner (an active musician in those days at Graz and, naturally, a member of the Society) for transference via Josef Hüttenbrenner, then in Vienna, to Schubert. The diploma was handed over to the composer in September 1823 on his return from a short holiday in Steyr and he at once acknowledged it and promised to send 'one of his symphonies in full score'. Josef stated in a letter written many years afterwards to his younger brother Andreas that Schubert handed him the score of the 'Unfinished' Symphony at the Schottentor (one of the gates leading through the walls of the Inner City: it is the one through which Schubert would naturally pass to and from his father's house and the Inner City) whence it eventually reached Anselm at Graz. This was probably in the October. From then onwards, for many years, the work disappeared from view. Schubert obviously thought no more about it; when he required one of his early symphonies he fell back on the 1818 work, in C major. Anselm Hüttenbrenner never bothered to get it performed at Graz, but perhaps this is understandable in view of its incomplete state. One might question, at this stage, Anselm Hüttenbrenner's action in appropriating a symphony score which had been sent as a gift to him, not as an individual, but as an official of a Society. After Schubert's death the Hüttenbrenners did not bother overmuch to let people know of the existence of this major work, although they themselves were only too well aware of its stature. In 1853 Anselm made a PF. Duet arrangement of the first two movements which he played with his brother. The manuscript of the Symphony was mentioned in the catalogue of Schubert manuscripts in his possession, which he made for Liszt in 1854. A few years later the work was referred to by Josef when he wrote to Johann Herbeck, the conductor of the Vienna 'Männergesangverein' and a director of the *Gesellschaft*. This letter of Josef's is dated 8 March 1860 and contains the words:

> (Anselm) possesses a treasure in Schubert's B minor Symphony, which we rank with his great C major Symphony, his instrumental swansong, and with all the symphonies of Beethoven—only it is unfinished. Schubert gave it to me for Anselm to thank him for having sent the diploma of the Graz Music Society through me....

Before the score was finally obtained from Anselm, and obtained in a way which almost suggests a wresting of it from his possession, there were two more references to the symphony The first was in Wurzbach's great biographical dictionary of the Austrian Empire in the section devoted to Anselm Hüttenbrenner; the second was the famous paragraph in Kreissle's biography (1865):

> There is an orchestral symphony in B minor, which Schubert presented, in a half-finished state, to the Musikverein at Graz, in return for the compliment paid to him of being elected an honorary member of that Society. Josef Hüttenbrenner is my authority for saying that the first and second movements are entirely finished, and the third partly. The fragment, in the possession of Herr Anselm Hüttenbrenner of Graz, is said, the first movement particularly, to to be of great beauty. If this be so, Schubert's intimate friend would do well to emancipate the still unknown work of the master he so highly honours, and introduce the symphony to Schubert's admirers.

As a result, when Herbeck visited Graz that same year (1865) Anselm was probably half prepared to yield up the work. Herbeck ingratiated himself by promising to perform a composition of Anselm's at Vienna during the coming winter season of concerts, and on mentioning, innocently, Schubert's name, the score of the 'Unfinished' was produced. Herbeck's account of the incident makes interesting reading. Preserving an air of disinterested calm he turned over the pages of the manuscript and gradually realised the beauty of the symphony. With a casual remark to the effect that it would be quite suitable for inclusion in the concert programmes he asked if he might have the score copied. 'Oh! take the manuscript back with you—take it!' said Anselm. Herbeck bore it off in triumph, and the opening two movements of the symphony were heard for the first time in Vienna on 17 December 1865.

Why was the Symphony in B minor never finished? It is one of the great enigmas in music, and there are three suggested answers to the question, each of which must be considered. The first is easily disposed of since it arose in the years immediately following the production of the work and was based on ignorance of the facts, namely, that Schubert intended the work to be a two-movement symphony, on the lines of, say, Beethoven's Sonata in F sharp major, Op. 78. The existence of an almost fully sketched 'Scherzo'-movement disposes of the argument.

The second theory, held widely in the early years of this century, suggests that self-criticism withheld the addition of a Scherzo and Finale: that the composer could not bring himself to add an unworthy pair of concluding movements to the two supreme ones he had already written. This is a sentimental view. It invests Schubert with emotions congenial to the observer, not with those which he could actually have felt. Schubert probably had no complete idea of the greatness and originality of the two symphonic movements he had just written; his cavalier treatment of them does not support the notion. Moreover, such a feeling did not prevent him, in the years following the 'Unfinished' Symphony, from occasionally adding an inferior Finale to first-rate preceding movements, in the PF. Trio in E flat, Op. 100, or in the G major PF. Sonata, Op. 78, to give two examples which spring to mind.

The third answer to the question is a more formidable, because a more acceptable one. It is that Schubert *did* finish the symphony and that Anselm Hüttenbrenner lost the MS. folios at the back of the unbound score: folios containing the end of the Scherzo and the Finale. This theory was expounded by Dr. T. C. L. Pritchard in the Music Review, Cambridge, February 1942. There are three factual pieces of evidence which, at first sight, lend support to the theory. The fully scored opening bars of the Scherzo end abruptly at the bottom of a page, and from the oboe part a 'tie' extends outwards and this suggests that another page of the score, at least, must have followed; the four blank pages at the end of the 'Unfinished' score suggest that a whole sheaf of papers has fallen out; and finally there is the well-known Hüttenbrenner fatality where MSS. are concerned. Dr. Pritchard points out the unlikelihood of Schubert handing over an unfinished work to the Graz Music Society, and goes on to say that Anselm kept quiet about the work for over forty years because he had lost the last part of it. Now one fact is missing from the above argument which makes a whole heap of difference when it is remembered. It is the existence of the preliminary sketches. These were never in the possession of the Hüttenbrenners and their history was recounted to show that they were never out of the hands of careful owners, from the time that Schubert died to the time they entered the Library of the *Gesellschaft*. There is no hint of a sketched finale in them; there is, on the contrary, an incompletely sketched third movement. The very fact that these sketches were preserved by Schubert suggests that he was intending to resume work on them. The three pieces of factual evidence may be answered as follows. The extending of a 'tie' or 'slur' was a mannerism of Schubert's handwriting. Any student of his manuscripts soon becomes aware of this fact. The signs are often so mechanical as to have no meaning: it was almost a mark of continuity in his composition. The fair copy of his 'Scherzo' was being made, after all, from a pre-existing sketch and Schubert was aware of the necessity for the tied note in the oboe part. Next, the sheaf of papers might have been removed by Hüttenbrenner simply because they were blank! This is more likely. But even if we allow that some of the Scherzo-movement has been lost it is doubtful whether a fully scored finale of Schubertian dimensions could possibly have disappeared from the score without trace. Thirdly, in the matter of losing and ill-treating manuscripts, Josef, not Anselm, was the offender. A piece of evidence which suggest that the Hüttenbrenners told the truth when they said that the work was unfinished is the visit of Schubert to Graz in 1827. Why was the symphony never mentioned between the friends, or the possibility of a performance discussed? We might suggest that it was because it was a fragment which Schubert had forgotten about, or could not take very seriously.

In considering the music of the symphony it is essential to examine the PF. sketches for the work which, unlike the sketches for all his other finished orchestral movements, have survived. Without explaining the mystery of genius they do exemplify the *multum in parvo* which is so noticeable in the first, tentative ideas which visit genius. This is especially remarkable with Schubert who, as was mentioned in connection with his PF. sketches of the 1818 symphony, hastily wrote down and uncritically accepted his ideas for fear that the others teeming in his brain should obliterate them. The ideas for the B minor Symphony are frequently raw and unpolished, but they are unmistakably the visitations of genius, and, in the final form of the two movements, reach perfection. There is a new quality in the sketches for the 'Unfinished' Symphony—it is difficult to define. It has something of assurance, something of authority. This is particularly evident with the *codetta* music in the first movement (bars 73–83). Two examples might be quoted from these sketches to show Schubert at work. In the first movement his original but very abrupt transition to G major for the second subject, achieved by the long sustained note on the horns and bassoons, has often been commented on: a *coup de théâtre* it has been called. Here is Schubert's original idea for this transition (from the recapitulation):

It is surely undeniable that this gradual and careful preparation is tedious compared with the arresting form it eventually took. The second quotation shows the development of an idea which

Schubert rejected from the final draft. It comes from the slow movement and is a treatment of the descending *pizzicato* scale of the opening two bars:

This foreshadowing of Brahmsian practices was not congenial, evidently, and it does, as one can readily see, strike a false note in the unselfconscious outpouring of tenderness and sadness in the incomparable movement.

Mention of Brahms brings to mind that one gross misprint re-copied again and again in the multiple scores of this symphony has been attributed to his editing. It occurs in bar 109 of the first movement, where the horns continue to play a B natural against a chord of the dominant seventh on strings and woodwind. The discord was too much for the ears of the 1860's and the first editor—if not Brahms, someone else—altered the note to C sharp. This is how it was printed by Spina in 1866 and how it appears in all subsequent editions. The text and its editions have been described thoroughly of recent years both in England and on the continent.[1]

The intimate tone and the strongly subjective emotions of his symphony were new in symphonic music, and the symmetry and formal beauty which enshrines this personal feeling cannot be too highly praised. Alfred Einstein has written:

> Not even Beethoven himself achieved anything more striking or more terse than the volcanic climax of the first movement of the 'Unfinished' Symphony. . . .

The excessive popularity of the symphony rests like a smear upon it; what are we to say, for instance, of a programme in which it is

[1] Ernst Hess: 'Zur Urtextfrage von Schuberts *Unvollendeten*', 'Schweizerische Musikzeitung', 1 March 1947. Adam Carse: 'Editing Schubert's Unfinished Symphony', 'Musical Times', March 1954.

sandwiched between Sullivan's 'Di Ballo' Overture and 'Tales from the Vienna Woods' of Johann Strauss? One feels that the manifold wonders of the symphony, whose music speaks so directly to the heart, have not received their full historical and scholastic acclaim. At first it seemed as if no acclaim at all was to be given to the work. One imagines that it must have leapt into instant popularity—but this is not quite so. A year elapsed before it was published. The Vienna music critic Hanslick asked whether the two movements were intended as a kind of background music for scenic effects in the theatre. Seven years later we find August Reissmann, in general a sound Schubertian, asking if these two movements should not be considered as part of the ballet music for a stage play—like that in B minor in the 'Rosamunde' music? How our estimation has changed! To quote Einstein once again: 'The "Unfinished" Symphony . . . that incomparable song of sorrow which we wrong every time we call it "Unfinished".' Strangely enough, in view of Reissmann's words, a composition by Schubert which has sometimes been used as a finale in performances of the symphony, and which is occasionally considered by critics and writers on music as a possibly unidentified finale to the work, is the 'Entr'acte in B minor' from the incidental music which Schubert wrote for the play 'Rosamunde'. There is much to commend the theory. The 'Entr'acte' is a true masterpiece, and would be a worthy companion to the other two movements. It was performed (on Grove's suggestion) at the Crystal Palace Concert of 19 March 1881 to serve as a finale to the symphony. It has been suggested that since Schubert was in such a hurry to complete the 'Rosamunde' music, he removed the finale of his symphony for use as an entr'acte. But the theory cannot be maintained against the facts. The manuscript paper of both scores has been minutely examined as a result of the theory, and the watermarks of both sheafs of paper are different. Although in itself this is not sufficient to disprove the suggestion, taken in conjunction with other contradicting statements it does so. For the symphony score was certainly in Graz at the time the 'Rosamunde' music was composed. Moreover, the heading of the music of the B minor Entr'acte, in Schubert's own hand, is 'No. 1:

Entre-Act nach dem 1. Aufz.' and it was certainly not an extracted finale movement that he headed so.

One actual fact which accounts for the setting aside of the symphony is his composition in November 1822 of the Pianoforte Fantasia in C major, Op. 15. It is a massively planned work in four sections corresponding to the four movements of a sonata, and universally known as the 'Wanderer Fantasia' although the name was not given to it by Schubert, nor ever used by him. The work is in C major—Schubert's 'epic' key—and we have evidence of the composer's love of what one might call 'Neapolitan' relationships in the choice of his keys. The 'Neapolitan' chord is built on the note a semitone above the key-note; in C major, for instance, C sharp (or D flat) is the basis of the chord, so that this note stands to C major in a 'Neapolitan' relationship. The *Adagio* of the Fantasia is in C sharp minor. The composer dedicated the work to Emmanuel, Edler von Liebenberg de Zsettin, a pupil of Hummel's and a wealthy landowner; it was published shortly after its composition by Cappi & Diabelli, in February 1823.

New, ornate, powerful pianoforte techniques were introduced by Schubert into this composition. The final movement, a rugged fugue, is almost *un*pianistic. Writing of the first movement Schumann said on 13 August 1828—that is, while Schubert was still alive:

> Schubert would like, in this work, to condense the whole orchestra into two hands, and the enthusiastic beginning is a seraphic hymn to the Godhead; you see the angels pray; the *Adagio* is a gentle meditation on life and takes the veil from off it; then fugues thunder forth a song of endless humanity and music.

The excessive ornamentation of the variations in the slow movement becomes almost guilty of display, but Schubert redeems it by anticipating in the baroque detail the theme of the next movement, the *Presto* Scherzo. The variations are written on an extract—much modified for the composer's purpose—from the song of 1816, the famous 'Der Wanderer', hence the name of the

Fantasia. Some critics have sought to interpret Schubert's Fantasia as a morbid exposition of the *words* of the extract, which are the despairing cry of the wandering exile, that life is empty and he is everywhere an outcast. But such an interpretation is itself morbid: it ignores the vigour and exuberance of Schubert's springtime music. The dramatic, yet broad, progress of the work belies its nickname, 'Wanderer'; from the start it knows where it is going and does not stray nor hesitate on its dynamic path. Sir Donald Tovey has said of this work that in its alternation of stormy development with quiet lyricism, and in its leisurely approach to climaxes, it looks back to the concertos of Bach (which Schubert, of course, did not know) and in its dexterous handling of the remotest possible key-relationships it looks forward to Wagner. The powerful climaxes of the work are helped and given sonority by Liszt's celebrated arrangement for Pianoforte and Orchestra; this alone would justify the later composer's version of what, to use his own words, he called: 'Schubert's splendid "Wanderer-Dithyramb".'

IV

1822 is the crisis of Schubert's life. It is during that year that we feel the real man is being buried beneath an assumed pose of the experienced, blasé man-about-town, and the off-hand, self-important artist. It was suggested at the beginning of the chapter that his head was slightly turned by the limited successes of that year and the previous one: the appearance of his work in the Viennese theatres, the publication of his songs and piano pieces, the adulation of the Schubertiads. Testimony to the state of affairs is not lacking, as the letters quoted below will show.

His friend of *Konvikt* days, Anton Holzapfel, wrote on 22 February 1822 to Albert Stadler:

> ... Schubert, as they say, made *bruit*, and he will likewise, as they say, make his *sort*. I rarely see him, nor do we hit it off very well, his world being a very different one, as it should be. His somewhat gruff manner stands him in very good stead and will make a strong man and a ripe artist of him; he will be worthy of art. ... Schubert

is working at an opera, the words of which are by Schober, a work at which they are said to have both laboured together in mutual understanding.

The 'gruff manner' is significant—how ill it goes with our picture of the gentle, goodnatured Schubert. But more telling is Spaun's heartfelt cry to Schober in a letter of 5 March 1822:

> ... Winter has gone by since then, and much that is of interest must have happened among you all, of which you should not deprive your far-off and dear friend. I am so very anxious to know all that the poetical-musical-painting triumvirate has produced. It cuts me to the soul that Schubert has ceased to sound for me....

A third letter is from Spaun's brother, Anton, to his wife. Anton was staying at Steyr during the summer of 1822 and had met Vogl there. He wrote home to Linz, on 20 July 1822:

> ... To me Vogl is extremely pleasing. He told me his whole relationship to Schubert with the utmost frankness, and unfortunately I am quite unable to excuse the latter. Vogl is very much embittered against Schober, for whose sake Schubert behaved most ungratefully towards Vogl and who makes the fullest use of Schubert in order to extricate himself from financial embarrassments and to defray the expenditure which has already exhausted the greater part of his mother's fortune. I wish very much that somebody were here who would defend Schubert at least in the matter of the most glaring reproaches. Vogl also says Schober's opera is bad and a total failure and that altogether Schubert is quite on the wrong road.

This is outspoken enough, and prepares us somewhat for the tragedy of the autumn. Schober's influence, not only on Schubert, but on all the members of his circle, was no secret. It is pretty clearly stated by many of these men in the letters they later on wrote to each other, and to biographers of Schubert, such as Ferdinand Luib and Liszt. Josef Kenner, in a letter to Luib of 1858, wrote of an episode in Schubert's life 'which only too probably caused his early death, and certainly accelerated it'. The episode is the contracting of venereal disease during the late autumn of 1822. O. E. Deutsch points out in the Schubert 'Documents' (page 287) that the disease was probably syphilis, although a clear distinction between various venereal diseases was not understood in Schubert's day. Certainly the course of the illness suggests that Schubert was suffering from it. The conventions of the nineteenth-century forbade any reference to the disease in the biographies of the composer; the complete absence of contemporary references, although the trouble was known to all his friends, suggests that documents, letters and so on, have been destroyed. Schubert's illness is mentioned, if at all, as a passing indisposition. Its effects on the composer, immediate and eventual, were deep and disturbing. The shock restored him to himself—the artificialities and assumptions of 1822 vanish like smoke. The six years till his death show bursts of abounding spirits, health and creative energy, but they alternate with periods of black depression, illness and stagnation.

The onset of this disease led to his leaving Schober's house. He returned in December to the schoolhouse in the Rossau district, and lived there for the next year. He sought his family, his brother Ferdinand; and he wrote a long, warm letter to Spaun telling him of his compositions, the PF. Fantasia, the Mass in A flat, the new Goethe songs. Two letters, both undated, but which from internal evidence belong to 1823, show the beginning of a withdrawal, almost of an indifference; the first is to Leopold Sonnleithner declining an offer to compose for the *Gesellschaft* concerts, the second to the music director of the St. Anna College declining to submit an orchestral overture for performance there.

His friendship with Josef Hüttenbrenner was closer than ever, in fact, Hüttenbrenner seemed to act as a kind of unofficial, and naturally unpaid, secretary and agent to Schubert. He kept the composer's accounts, wrote to publishers, and even made attempts to secure performances of Schubert's operas, including the juvenile 'Des Teufels Lustschloss'. Schubert himself was still sanguine about the chances of 'Alfonso und Estrella'. Weber at Dresden had expressed an interest in the work, and Schubert hoped that Ignaz von Mosel might propose the opera to him. In a letter to Mosel on 28 February 1823, Schubert wrote that he had completed the overture to 'Alfonso und Estrella' and asked if his opera might be personally recommended to Weber. At the Kärntnertor theatre, during 1822, the management had been taken over by Domenico Barbaja. He was not interested overmuch in German opera, and certainly not in the hazardous business of putting on the latest works of obscure composers. Schubert's hopes in his new opera were doomed.

His health grew worse, and the need for money became so urgent that in the early part of the year he sold outright to Diabelli his copyright in the early opus-numbers (Opp. 1–7). He received £32 for the transaction, and then asked Diabelli for £24 in exchange for his rights in Opp. 12–14. The publisher haggled over the sum and beat Schubert down, and this treatment, together with Schubert's suspicions of Diabelli's accounts of sales and so forth, led to a breach between them. The manuscripts which Schubert had already sold to the publisher came out as Opp. 16 and 17 (male voice quartets) and Op. 19 (songs including *An Schwager Kronos*) but there was no other connection between the composer and the publisher for several years.

In February Schubert was confined to the house and during the month of enforced rest he composed the first of his mature sonatas for PF. solo, the second in A minor, published posthumously as Op. 143. It opens with a stark, uncompromising movement in his grandest vein, and was subjected to the kind of revision which does not often occur in his work. The manuscript of the sonata, only recently emerging from obscurity, shows him going back to make alterations in the exposition of the first movement in the light of later changes in the recapitulation. The theme of the slow movement—one of his most original essays in this type of movement, and yet one praised in the nineteenth century for its 'Beethovenish' qualities!—was originally this:

The change in the note at * to A makes the melody unbelievably stronger.

Two sets of dances, sweet and lilting, were composed during this spring of wretchedness and ill-health (the capacity of the creative artist to detach himself from material circumstances is a constant surprise to the less gifted observer, and in Schubert's case the detachment is phenomenal). The dances were in the 'Deutsche' or 'Ländler' style, which is little else than a short, substantial waltz. One set appeared as Op. 33 in 1825, the second was not published until many years after his death, as Op. 171 in 1864. The sixth dance in Op. 171 might almost be a sketch for a later work, the Scherzo in the 'Death and the Maiden' String Quartet, and the third dance is a prophetic piece of writing whose fluid, chromatic harmony might easily be from the pen of Chopin:

A one-act *Singspiel*, 'Die Verschworenen', was composed during March and April while he was contending with pain and depression. And yet the music of the operetta is gay and high-spirited, and so suggestive of the legendary Vienna of the musical comedy stage, that it might be thought an outpouring of Schubert in the happiest of his days. The libretto is by Ignaz Castelli, one of a group of authors who wrote comedies for the Viennese theatres in which the basic idea was to explore the comic possibilities arising when ordinary citizens were placed against a fantastic background, such as the landscape of the moon, or fairyland, or, as in this *Singspiel*, of a sham medievalism which only existed in tales and stage plays. Castelli based his play on the 'Lysistrata' of Aristophanes. A number of disgruntled wives try to force their soldiering husbands to stay at home instead of everlastingly campaigning in the Wars of the Crusades, by denying them all matrimonial rights until they promise to give up war. Castelli published his play in February 1823 as the eighth number of a series of plays called 'Dramatische Sträusschen'. It contained a preface with these words addressed to composers:

> You are always asking for good opera librettos. Here is one! Now set it to music, gentlemen, and strike a blow for German Opera.

Schubert finished his setting at the end of April. A touchy political censorship disliked the title ('The Conspirators') and insisted that it be changed: it became 'Der häusliche Krieg' ('Domestic Warfare'). But the work was never accepted for performance at the Opera, and nearly thirty years passed before it was eventually staged. This took place at Frankfurt-am-Main in August 1861. There had been a concert version in Vienna during the March of that year and the aged Castelli was present sitting beside Hanslick. He confessed himself amazed at the sparkle and charm of the music. The operetta was performed in France[1] under the title 'La Crusade des Dames', translated into French by the famous Victor Wilder, in February 1868, and Wilder's version was later used in Vienna in preference to Castelli's original German text! The music may best be discussed later.

Schubert's illness reached a critical stage in May, and he was obliged to spend a short time in the Vienna 'General Hospital'. There is no real evidence at all that he commenced work on the 'Schöne Müllerin' song-cycle in this month; this was a later surmise. There is, on the contrary, such a bulk of existing compositions actually dated 'May 1823' that it is practically impossible for the 'Müllerin' songs also to belong to the month. The stronger probability is that he started the series of songs during August at Steyr. There are several other songs of May; they include no primary example of his work, although parts of the flower-ballade by Schober, *Vergissmeinnicht*, are delicious. He was on the look-out for a full length opera libretto; there are very long sketches for an opera called 'Rüdiger' or 'Rüdigers Heimkehr', the words by an unknown author, but whose story clearly deals with Rüdiger von Bechelaren. It is an episode from the

[1] It is surprising to find that as early as March 1863, 'Die Verschworenen' was given in Hoboken, New Jersey, U.S.A. This was much earlier than any performance in England.

Nibelungen sagas. But, as a critic has pointed out in another connection, the hour of the 'Ring' had not yet struck. Another very bulky sheaf of sketches by Schubert is preserved in the Vienna *Stadtbibliothek* for an untitled opera, in which the heroine is named 'Sofie'. The work may be attributed to this period since among the melodies Schubert wrote for the 'Sofie' opera is this one which he afterwards retrieved for the next opera, 'Fierrabras':

'Fierrabras' was a three-act opera written by Josef Kupelwieser, Leopold's brother. It is a lifeless story, as all these heavily 'Romantic' stories of the Spanish aristocracy are liable to be, since they deal with people, situations and events which never were, nor ever could be. Schubert's work was written in a short space of time—but the dates on his manuscripts have with very good reason been questioned. They are:

Act I: 25 May–30 May.
Act II: finished on 5 June.

Not even Schubert could have covered the enormous first act in five or six days. Walter Dahms has suggested that the dates for the conclusions of each act should read, respectively, 30 June and 5 August. This is rather too tidy a solution, but clearly something is wrong. Act III was finished on 26 September, and the Overture commenced on 2 October.

A word might be added here about the spelling of the title. Kupelwieser and Schubert and the writers of the nineteenth century contentedly used the double 'r'. Occasionally, as in Grove's catalogues, the spelling is 'Fierabras'. In the Schubert 'Documents', O. E. Deutsch instituted the single 'r'—'Fierabras' —since in the original Spanish he found that the word was so spelt. It means in that language 'Braggart' or 'Boaster'. Now this correction would have more force if the hero of the opera were such a character; but Fierrabras is simply a proper name, and should be spelt as Kupelwieser and Schubert spelt it. There is, moreover, evidence that in the sixteenth century (*c.* 1530) the name was 'Ferrbras'. On the whole, to use the original spelling seems the most satisfactory solution, and it will be so used here. The B.B.C. recently *translated* the title and announced the overture of Schubert's opera 'The Braggart'; this is fatuous. One might as well translate 'Faust' as 'The Pugilist'.

Recuperating from his weakness and wretched physical state, Schubert travelled to Linz and Steyr during July and August. He arrived in Linz on 25 July and was introduced by Spaun to the Hartmann family. Friedrich von Hartmann, an eminent civil servant, had two sons, Franz and Fritz; they went to Vienna in 1825, and their copious diaries contain many references to the day-by-day activities of the Schubert circle.

At Steyr, on 29 August, Schubert arranged a setting of Psalm VIII, 'O Lord, our God, how excellent is Thy name in all the earth', by the Abbé Maximilian Stadler, for string orchestra and organ. The original is for voice and pianoforte (or organ). It may have been commissioned by Sylvester Paumgartner, and it was performed in the Parish Church of Steyr by Vogl, whose copy of the voice part, in his own hand, has also survived with Schubert's copy of the same part.[1] The complete score of Schubert's arrangement, an autograph manuscript, was not discovered until May 1952.

Schubert altered a number of passages in both voice part and accompaniment; it is not a simple orchestration of the piece. He was clearly attracted to it, and strange to say there are decided Schubertian traits in the work—this phrase, for example, from bars 4–6:

[1] Max Friedlaender commented adversely on Vogl's alterations of the vocal part (an *idée fixe* of Friedlaender's); but they are Schubert's own this time.

which Schubert altered slightly to make even more intensely his own.

During August he continued work on Act III of 'Fierrabras', and probably this month in that summery countryside he began to compose the first songs of the cycle 'Die schöne Müllerin', which embowers, in an evergreen music, an idyll of young and tragic love in a valley, remote from the dust and traffic of the town. The evidence for August as the month of their commencement is not decisive, but it does exist: it is Spaun's remark in after years that Schubert started the 'Mill' songs at *Zseliz*. This place cannot be the right one, since Schubert was not there until a year later. But Spaun clearly had in mind that Schubert was not in Vienna, but in the country somewhere, and Steyr fits in with the fact, and the year 1823. Back in Vienna (in the middle of September) he continued to work on the songs, and the fifteenth one, *Eifersucht und Stolz*, survives in manuscript and is dated October 1823. On 30 November he wrote to Schober:

> I have composed nothing else since the opera (Fierrabras) except a few 'Mill' songs. The 'Mill' song-cycle will be published in four parts with vignettes by Schwind.

Trockne Blumen, the seventeenth song in the series, was used as the theme of a set of variations (flute and pianoforte), which Schubert composed in January 1824. The variations were written for his friend Ferdinand Bogner, evidently at his request. This suggests that Bogner had heard the song recently, so that its composition might have been in December 1823. Finally we have Schwind writing on 6 March 1824 to Schober: 'Of Müller's poems he has set two very beautifully'—which probably marks the end of Schubert's work on the cycle. The five books (not four as originally intended) were published by the August of 1824. The story told by Randhartinger in his old age that Schubert had encountered the poems through him is a pure fabrication (see page 330).

Wilhelm Müller's sequence of songs was published in Dessau two years before Schubert discovered them. 'Die schöne Müllerin' was the first part of the collection 'Poems found in the posthumous papers of a travelling horn-player' and was subtitled 'to be read in the winter'. It is said to have originated in a kind of play acted by members of Müller's circle, called 'Rose, the lovely maid of the mill'. Schubert omitted the poet's prologue and epilogue, as well as three poems from the main sequence; each of these comes from one of the three emotional phases of the cycle—hope, love, jealousy.

The music society at Linz, a more modest affair than the one at Graz, also elected Schubert as an honorary member during August. As far as Schubert knew this was the first of the honours, for it will be recalled that Josef Hüttenbrenner was unable to give the composer the certificate of election to Graz until he returned to Vienna the following month. He was still ailing, and there are frequent references to his state in letters to and from his friends. Schober (at Breslau) received news of his friend's serious illness from Schwind, from Anton von Doblhoff and from Spaun. Schubert himself wrote to Schober (the letter quoted on page 133) and of his own condition he said:

> For the rest, I hope to regain my health, and this recovered benefit will make me forget many sorrows. . . .

He also informed Schober that Weber's new opera 'Euryanthe' turned out badly, and in his opinion deserved its poor reception.

Schubert probably ruined his chances with Weber by his outspoken criticism of 'Euryanthe'. Spaun tells in his reminiscences that at first Weber was extraordinarily friendly, and promised because of Mosel's recommendation to bring 'Alfonso und Estrella' to performance in Berlin. When he enquired of Schubert how his opera had pleased him Schubert replied: 'Right well—but 'Freischütz' had pleased him better'. There was, in his view, too little melody in the new opera. Weber received this coldly, and there was no more talk of a production of 'Alfonso'. Spaun adds that he had all this from Schubert himself. But it is an exaggeration to say that Weber and Schubert quarrelled over the judgement. Later on, when Weber heard of the failure of Schubert's 'Rosamunde' he wrote frankly to Castelli, in Vienna, and said the fact gave him no pleasure, but only increased his embarrassment.

'Rosamunde' closes 1823 with a strange blend of success and failure, of renown and obscurity, of brilliance and darkness. The play was by Wilhelmine von Chézy, the authoress of 'Euryanthe', and it was given on 20 December. We hear nothing about it until the announcement on the day previous to its performance, but it is fairly obvious that Schubert wrote the music in a very short space of time—one account says five days.[1] Evidence is scanty, but not entirely lacking, that the music was composed without much time to spare. He used the overture he had already drafted for 'Alfonso und Estrella', writing the final score in December. Schwind, writing to Schober two days after the performance, said:

> Schubert had taken over the Overture he wrote for 'Estrella', as he thinks it too 'homespun' for 'Estella', for which he wants to write a new one.

There is the possibility, already discussed, that the entr'acte to be played after Act I was part of the 'Unfinished' Symphony; in any case one piece of ballet music was either used as the basis of this entr'acte, or was itself based on the entr'acte. In the second entr'acte, the very popular one in B flat, the interlude in B flat minor is an orchestrated version of an early song of his called *Die Leidende* (1816). A third entr'acte was based on one of the choruses in the play. The full list of Schubert's incidental music is as follows:

1. Entr'acte in B minor, after Act I.
2. Ballet music in B minor, similar to the previous entr'acte, Act II.
3. Entr'acte in D major, based on the 'Chorus of Spirits', after Act II.
4. 'Romance' for contralto, 'Der Vollmond strahlt', Act III.
5. Chorus of Spirits (Male voices), Act III.
6. Entr'acte in B flat, after Act III.

[1] Wilhelm von Chézy, son of the authoress: 'Erinnerungen', 1863.

7. Shepherd's melody in B flat for clarinets, horns and bassoons, Act IV.
8. Chorus of Shepherds (Mixed voices), Act IV.
9. Chorus of Huntsmen (Mixed voices), Act IV.
10. Ballet Music in G major, Act IV.

The actual play is lost, but a very full summary of the plot survives from contemporary records. There are some strange flowers in the rotting undergrowth of the 'Romantic' jungle-world, but nothing stranger than this play, with its secret passages, princesses brought up by fisher-folk, shipwrecks, poisoned letters, shephered princes and the rest. After two performances the play vanished from the boards. Schubert's music was fairly well received, the 'Overture'—one of his most successful overtures—was encored, and so was the Hunting Chorus. Some of the items were published soon after the performance as Op. 26, on 24 March 1824; Schubert arranged the orchestral accompaniments for the piano. The rest of the items followed at intervals and by 1867 the whole series had been published except the delightful little piece called 'Shepherd's Melody' (No. 7). The well-known anecdote of Grove and Sullivan digging in a dusty cupboard to find Schubert's 'Rosamunde' music, placed there after the second performance and undisturbed for forty-four years, needs to be modified a little. The two men were looking for, and they found, the orchestral parts for the items published as Op. 26, for which, it has been said, Schubert had arranged a piano part. The items were nos. 4, 5, 8 and 9 in the list above.

One of the most interesting aspects of the Grove and Sullivan story, and one which seems to have been overlooked, is that Edward Schneider's office, where the tied up sets of parts were discovered, was in the Tuchlauben. Now when Schubert died, the bulk of his manuscripts was in Schober's house, which was also in this same well-known street. So between 1828, when the composer died, and 1867, when the two Englishmen found the manuscripts, the music had wandered from place to place in Vienna, but had eventually found its way back to within a few yards of its original storing-place.

The two overtures, both called 'Rosamunde' Overtures, can now be seen to have no claim to the name. The earlier one, in C major, was written for the melodrama 'Die Zauberharfe', and has become associated with the play because it was published as 'Op. 26', reserved for the 'Rosamunde' items; the later one, in D minor and major, was written for 'Alfonso und Estrella', and has become associated with the play partly because it was played at the actual first performance of 'Rosamunde' in the Theater an der Wien, and partly because the editor of the Opera Volumes in the 'Gesamtausgabe', Johann Nepomuk Fuchs, printed it at the start of the incidental music for the play. Schubert never wrote an overture for the play, and he himself referred to the Overture to 'Alfonso' as 'his "Rosamunde" Overture' (see his letter to Ignaz von Seyfried, 23 November 1826).

It is not certain whether Schubert attended the first performance, but it seems from Schwind's letter dated 24 December 1823 as though he had been ill again. Written to Schober in Breslau the letter tells us:

> . . . Schubert is better, and it will not be long before he goes about in his own hair again, which had to be shorn owing to the rash. He wears a very cosy wig.

V

'Rosamunde' was the last serious attempt on Schubert's part to achieve a success in the Viennese theatres. That he never gave up hope is evident from the fact that he was engaged in sketching the music for Bauernfeld's libretto 'Der Graf von Gleichen' ('The Count of Gleichen') in the last years of his life. But these are only sketches, and there is nothing for the stage in any work of Schubert's last four years. It will be possible now to consider his achievement in this field, an achievement for which he laboured with much failure and very little success for ten years.

These operas of his, numerous and varied as they are, have been ignored by the world of music. Are they the heap of failures which most biographers and critics say they are? Who is to answer the question? How many musicians have acquainted themselves intimately with 'Alfonso und Estrella', say, from the full score, in order to find out if Schubert's one grand opera deserves its complete and utter neglect?[1] As one who has made the effort I would say that the score contains as much fine and outstanding music as any other full length opera ever written, if we judge the score purely as music. Schober's libretto, moreover, silly as it is, is not quite the absurd farrago that all the other Schubert operas, except 'Die Verschworenen', prove to be on examination, although even there, amongst the variety of plot and situation and dénouement, there are degrees of stupidity. But 'Alfonso und Estrella' would need skilful production, adequate setting and—if necessary—musicianly cutting, if it were to make its full effect: precisely, in fact, what most of the operas in the repertory need.

Schubert's librettos are all the productions of people to whom the fashionable 'Romantic' story was an obsession. Gothic, or pseudo-Gothic, lore is ransacked for the plot; the landscape of the medieval artist, natural to Dürer say, but falsified and sentimentalised by the third rate poets of the day, forms the background. Spain is the country of three of the operas, 'Alfonso', 'Fierrabras' and the early work 'Don Fernando', with castles and gardens and serenades and all the other Spanish equipment of history and legend. But no poetry or imagination uplifts the trend in these librettos. 'Romantic' characterisation and situations often tend towards puppetry: at least the danger is there. It needs the genius of Scott or Victor Hugo or Schiller to give the puppets life. Then poor Schubert!—dependent upon Kotzebue and Mayrhofer and, even worse, Stadler and Kupelwieser. Their people and situations have as much life as the *tableaux* in a wax-works.

There is, in Schubert's stage music, a tendency towards the exalted and profound manner which often leads him, so to say, to fall between two stools. On the trifling and unreal plots he bestowed the light, tuneful music that the Viennese theatres pur-

[1] At this point the reader should be warned against a vocal score of this opera, published in 1882 by Schlesinger, of Berlin. It is an abominable travesty of Schubert's work perpretrated by J. N. Fuchs, the man already mentioned as being the editor of the Opera Volumes in the Schubert 'Gesamtausgabe'.

veyed. He used standard forms—march, waltz, polonaise, the 6/8 metres of the *siciliano*, the rhythms of folk-song. But he cannot keep out of it all the depths, the sublimities, which are part of his genius. Whenever, momentarily, his librettos take on a semblance of life, the scene, say, where Mauregato realises his daughter's terror at the thought of being plighted to Adolfo ('Alfonso und Estrella', Act I), his music at once glows with invention and poetry. If only, one cries again and again when reading his operatic scores, if only he had met with a libretto containing some serious, real, credible persons and situations. What would *he* have made of 'Romeo and Juliet', 'Tristan and Isolde', 'Traviata', 'La Bohême', and so on? It is an idle speculation, but a tempting one. Had he met with librettos of this sort, we should have seen the same thing happening in the tale of his operas as happened when he encountered 'Gretchen' after the thirty or so early songs.

The 1815 operettas are these: 'Der vierjährige Posten' (one act), written in twelve days in May to words by his acquaintance Theodor Körner; 'Fernando' (one act), written in June and July, the play by his school fellow, Albert Stadler; 'Die Freunde von Salamanka' (two acts), written in November and December, the words by Mayrhofer. There is a fragmentary relic of a three-act operetta on the play by Goethe 'Claudine von Villa Bella'. The work was completed in the summer of 1815, but only the first act and fragments of the second survive. This is because the manuscript of the completed work passed into the hands of Josef Hüttenbrenner and, in after years, servants in his household used the pages of Act III and part of Act II to light fires. The irresistible question thrusts at us: do servants in a musician's household use music paper to light fires on their own initiative? One hesitates to answer.

The operettas all contain characteristic and picturesque pages, mostly at Schubert's secondary levels of interest, but all showing an incredible assurance and resource. In the aria *Einsam schleich' ich durch die Zimmer* sung by Olivia in 'Die Freunde von Salamanka' we have a song of much interest and perhaps of more than secondary value. There is a lovely modification of the theme in the 'da capo' section fully worthy of the composer's powers of thematic development.

The music of 'Claudine' contains songs having the sweet, pure expression of the smaller 1815 songs. This is most attractive in the number *Liebe schwärmt auf allen Wegen*, which has often been mistaken for one of his songs ever since Max Friedlaender included an arrangement of it in his Schubert song-volumes (Peters, 1886).

Schubert's 'apprentice years' in opera, as they might be called, include two more pieces, both left unfinished for lack of any incentive to complete them. The work 'Die Bürgschaft', composed in May 1816, is based (but remotely) on Schiller's ballad of that name. The second piece is 'Adrast' (1819), the words by Mayrhofer. Both 'Adrast' and Mayrhofer's other libretto, 'Die Freunde von Salamanka', were evidently not considered worthy of preservation by the poet; they are both lost, and in consequence Schubert's operettas, with the spoken interludes lacking, can never be performed without some adaptation. 'Adrast' has many worthy pages of music, rising at times to the levels of the Mayrhofer songs of that period.

The two stage works of his 'middle period', both of which were performed in Vienna, are neither of great interest. Schubert himself was said not to have cared for either. 'Die Zwillingsbrüder' was composed in late 1818 and early 1819. It contains much light, melodious music of an attractive nature; there is some piquant and witty orchestration as in Lieschen's Aria, no. 3: 'Der Vater mag wohl immer Kind mich nennen'; and depths of feeling here and there, notably in the treatment of 'alte Freunde' ('old friends') in Friedrich's Aria, no. 6: 'Liebe, teure Muttererde', show the real Schubert. But 'Die Zauberharfe', a Melodrama (the name was used in Schubert's day for pieces of musical declamation, words recited against a musical background) in three acts, contains almost nothing of note. It is a depressing experience to turn the pages of this score, and realise the immensities of hard work which Schubert put into the production of this music—with no result whatever.

All these early operettas, and the opera 'Des Teufels Lustschloss', have charmingly written and fully scored overtures. The one introducing 'Die Zwillingsbrüder' is particularly attractive. Would they not make a welcome change from the rather overplayed 'Rosamunde' Overture in C major?

The two major works, 'Alfonso und Estrella' and 'Fierrabras', were never performed in his lifetime, and have never been performed since. Liszt's famous production of 'Alfonso' on 24 June 1854 at Weimar was a sadly mauled and manipulated affair. And 'Fierrabras', produced at Karlsruhe on 9 February 1897, was given, we read, with text revised by one, and music revised by another, and all kinds of tomfooleries, it is evident, put in to make such a truncated result tolerable to an audience. There are beauties and splendours without number in both works, and the first act of 'Fierrabras' is second to nothing in the whole field of German Romantic opera. 'Alfonso' halts; there is no doubt that Schober was determined to provide an opera text which would draw out Schubert's powers in lyrical expression. The result is not what he intended. The characters stand about and sing songs. One longs for the end of their individual and concerted efforts. Abduction, rape, murder: Schober holds his villain back from the accomplishment of each of these actions in order that he may sing about them, his victim further postponing the event by her songs and recitatives. But what songs they are! *Doch im Getümmel der Schlacht* from Act I, *Von Fels und Wald umrungen* and the Verdian *Wo ist sie?* from Act II, are the peaks of the work. The beginning of Act II contains a song which Schober had already written; he then introduced it at this point in his play. Schubert's melody is astonishing, for the student coming upon it will recognise a 'Winterreise' song there! Schubert used the melody, years later, for *Täuschung*—the words of both poems are similar, and the resemblance is, of course, pure coincidence. It was first pointed out by Max Kalbech in his review of the Vienna production in 1882 ('Wiener Opernabende', 1884, page 82).

There is more action in 'Fierrabras', but Schubert obviously tired of his task. (This is also apparent in 'Alfonso'.) Act I of 'Fierrabras' teems with poetry and imaginative detail of rhythm, melody, harmony and orchestration. But apart from Florinda's

Aria (with male chorus) *Des Jammers herbe Qualen* in Act III, the second and third acts of the opera are on a lower and homelier —but still interesting—level.

The one quality which gives these operas such a powerful interest to the student (alas, not yet to the theatre-goer) is Schubert's gifted writing in the accompanied recitatives. This is not like, for instance, Handel's decorated *recitativo*, but displays a desire to enrich and yet unify the emotional background of the sung dialogue. It is a pointer, unknown and unacknowledged, to what Wagner was to accomplish. 'Fierrabras' uses spoken interludes; but even in that opera there is, on occasion, verse dialogue, with this exalted, declamatory music. What Schubert was struggling towards, of course, and what he nearly succeeded in reaching, was the 'Leitmotiv'. With his power of thematic exploitation and his musical response to the stimulus of words—what he would have made of it is beyond conjecture.

There remains 'Die Verschworenen', Castelli's witty, and racy, exposition of a very human situation. Schubert illustrates, with music as witty and pointed, the moves and countermoves in this game of love-lorn wives and war-infatuated husbands. He uses the march, the scherzo, the 'Romance', the polonaise, with skill, variety and gusto. And, when necessary, the music has a tenderness which brings tears. In recent years the work has been revived in London and Cambridge and charmed all hearers.

VI

During these years of Schubert's pre-occupation with the theatre there are, understandably, few Church works of any importance, but among them there is a famous, and thoroughly characteristic, setting of the words of the Mass. It is his fifth work, in A flat. Schubert's six settings of the sacred Latin text are usually divided into two groups, the first comprising the four early compositions, 1814–1816, the second the last two, mature works, in A flat and E flat. But to bring together, in this way, the Mass in A flat and the great Mass in E flat of Schubert's last year means that the earlier one is quite overshadowed. In many Schubertians the Mass in E flat arouses feelings of admiration; the Mass in A flat inspires affection. It is more lyrical, perhaps more sweet, than the final setting. It is certainly more fanciful; of all the six Masses, the fifth is most richly adorned with musical imagery, motif and piquant harmonic touch. Karl Kobald goes too far in writing of the music of the A flat Mass as a 'wreath of spring flowers, woven by the hands of fair maids, round the picture of the crucified Christ' for this gives an interpretation of the music which sentimentalises and belittles it. Yet it could be said that sections of this Mass—the 'Gratias agimus' and the 'Osanna in excelsis'—resemble a musical garland. The 'Et incarnatus est' of the 'Credo' presents one of Schubert's harmonic miracles, based largely—can one explain miracles?—on the use of the Neapolitan sixth. The music of the 'Crucifixis' is the finest in the Mass, and, at the end, the turn into A flat major after the prolonged cadence in A flat minor is a most poignant use of this favourite device. Every device of choral tone colour is used: solo voices, unaccompanied choir, occasional sub-division of the choir into eight parts, antiphony. The unprecedented key-scheme of the Mass deserves a word. From the A flat of the opening we pass to a 'Gloria' in E major; from this key Schubert passes to A major and A minor. The 'Credo' is in C major, and this provides an excuse for a 'Sanctus' in F major. The whole work again gives an instance of Schubert's fondness for what we have called a 'Neapolitan' key-relationship: A flat with A major, E major with F major.

It has been suggested that Schubert worked intermittently on this Mass between the date of its commencement (November 1819) and its conclusion in September 1822. The remark on the manuscript score, 'im 7b. 822 beendet' ('finished in September 1822') is not in Schubert's hand, but can be verified from his letter to Spaun of 7 December 1822. There are numerous sketches for the Mass in existence, and it is clear that Schubert revised it after its completion. The alterations can be seen on his autograph score in the Library of the *Gesellschaft der Musikfreunde*. That these alterations were made later than 1822 is clear from Ferdinand Schubert's copy, which was written soon after the completion of the Mass. It is said that Brahms once rehearsed the work from this copy of Ferdinand's, and was dissatisfied with certain passages; when he came to examine Schubert's revised MS. he found that the composer had altered the very passages which he found unsatisfactory.[1] The Mass in A flat heralds the series of compositions for the Church Offices, of which Leopold Nowak has written:

> One can say without fear of contradiction that in Schubert, Viennese sentiment and musical genius have been most beautifully revealed, not only in secular, but also in sacred compositions.

In conclusion there are the songs of these 'middle years'. They are dominated by the 'Schöne Müllerin' series, but considered as separate songs, none from this favourite song-cycle equals the settings of Goethe in 1821 or those of Rückert in 1822 and 1823. Individual songs such as *Grenzen der Menschheit* and the two songs of Suleika by Goethe, and *Dass sie hier gewesen* by Rückert, fully reveal Schubert's genius and in them it achieved its supreme manifestations. Nor, even in their own sphere, do the 'Mill' songs exceed the pathos and sweetness of the song, *Frühlingsglaube* (1820), or depict more graphically the sparkling water of the greatly loved *Auf dem Wasser zu singen* (1823). Schubert continued to draw on the poems of his friend Mayrhofer; the favourite song of the period is *Nachtviolen* (April 1822), but there is as well a pair of majestic songs called *Heliopolis*, I and II, which deserve mention. The mysterious 'No. 12' on Schubert's manuscripts of the two 'Heliopolis' songs can be explained thus: the two texts were drawn from the *twelfth* poem in the manuscript collection of Mayrhofer's poems. This collection is now in the Vienna *Stadtbibliothek*.

Two songs of 1823 have a richly endowed accompaniment and much ingenuity in the development of theme and motif. The one, *Der Zwerg*, has had perhaps a little more attention than it deserves; the other, *Lied*, a poem by Stolberg beginning 'Des Lebens Tag ist schwer', certainly too little attention. *Der Zwerg* owes part of its fame to the account given by Randhartinger of

[1] See the article on Schubert by Grove, 'Dictionary', first edition, page 336, col. ii, footnote.

its origins; he said it was scribbled down hurriedly before the composer accompanied him on a walk. But its portrayals of emotion—grief and horror, together with the almost Wagnerian treatment of short, musical phrases in the piano part, make a wonderful study. The other song, Stolberg's *Lied*, is stately in its measured progress; the harmonies, reaching to the future in their range, and handled with an assured technical facility, support a broad, noble melody inspired by the line 'Death's kiss is light and cool'. It is a song to which one returns with eager interest, discovering afresh, each time, its greatness and beauty.

'Death's kiss is light and cool'. There is a tendency in German commentary on Schubert to dwell rather heavily on the composer's fascinated interest in 'Death' poetry. It is easy to draw doubtful conclusions from it. But now and again a fatalistic element seems obvious in his choice of such poetry, as in the poem of Stolberg—

Life's day is hard and sultry,
Death's kiss is light and cool.

Schubert had indeed suffered a death-blow; although the desperate stages of his disease had passed his health would never be the same again. It is a new and strange thing to read that at the New Year celebrations of the friends on 31 December 1823, Schubert arrived accompanied by J. Bernhardt—his doctor.

V

1824-1825

I

After the dismal failure of 'Rosamunde' in the theatre, some revulsion against opera composition must have seized Schubert. He wrote no more, in fact, for the stage, beyond the half-hearted sketches for the opera 'Der Graf von Gleichen'. This reaction against the theatre may have been made keener by his acquaintance with two new friends whom he met at the home of the Sonnleithners, both first-rate instrumentalists. They were Ferdinand, Count Troyer, a clarinettist in the musical establishment of the Archduke Rudolph, and Ignaz Schuppanzigh. The latter, famous as a friend of Beethoven, had just returned from a tour in eastern Europe. He was the leader of an unrivalled string quartet, and the excellent playing of the four men turned Schubert's thoughts from the theatre into a new field of work. We find him in January 1824 beginning a series of chamber works, and absorbing himself wholeheartedly in them as if to thrust behind him the unhappy experiences of his failures with opera. The series opens with a set of variations for flute and pianoforte which Schubert composed for Ferdinand Bogner. His friendship with the flautist dated from the days when they had played together in the amateur orchestra which met at Hatwig's house, and it was maintained by Bogner's marriage to Barbara Fröhlich in 1825. The variations were based on the melody of *Trockne Blumen* from the 'Schöne Müllerin' song-cycle. The song, incidentally, had not then been published; it was the first one of Book V and so did not appear until the following August. The variations are of little interest; if there is anything to be said in extenuation of Schubert's use of such a song, it is that the aura of pathos and tenderness which *Trockne Blumen* has gathered over the years was not, in 1824, so obvious in its new-minted condition. He does not even give the song's title on the manuscript, and when the composition was eventually published, in 1850, it was entitled 'Introduction et Variations sur un théme original'. But in the three pieces of chamber music which he composed after the variations, there is such a quality of universal greatness and appeal that we can ignore the inferiority of the *Trockne Blumen* composition. These three works are the String Quartets in A minor and D minor (the latter known as the 'Death and the Maiden' Quartet) and the Octet in F major.

Both quartets were mis-dated during the nineteenth century. The A minor Quartet was considered to have been written in the summer of 1824 while Schubert was staying at Zseliz, and various 'Hungarian' influences were thought to be present as a result of this. The D minor Quartet was attributed to January 1826, a mistake which arose since the work was performed for the first time in that month, and Schubert may have revised it—but not very radically. The earlier quartet was more correctly dated from records of the first performance of it by Schuppanzigh and his colleagues on 14 March 1824. But Schubert probably composed it earlier than the March of that year (the date given by Deutsch in his 'Thematic Catalogue'), perhaps as early as the end of January. Schwind may be quoted in evidence: 'He writes quartets and German dances and variations without number' (letter to Schober of 13 February 1824). The date of the second quartet was not corrected until 1901, and in the usual rather dramatic fashion when a lost manuscript is found. The newly discovered autograph was fragmentary, containing only the first movement and part of the second, but the first page bore the date 'March 1824'. Sketches for it were doubtless being written earlier in the year, and may account for Schwind's 'variations without number'.

The Octet was commissioned by Count Troyer. It was finished on 1 March and performed at the Count's residence soon afterwards. He himself, of course, played the clarinet, and Ignaz Schuppanzigh was first violin. Another instrumentalist in the first performance of the Octet, who later became a notable enthusiast for Schubert's chamber work, was Josef Linke, a 'cellist.

The first months of 1824 contain various repercussions of the 'Rosamunde' performance. Weber, in spite of the coolness between him and Schubert, felt no elation at the news of the failure of 'Rosamunde', and the notice of the event, posted to Dresden by the editor of the Vienna 'Theaterzeitung' only embarrassed him. This adverse notice was sent to Weber for transmission to the editor of the Dresden 'Abendzeitung', Karl Winkler. Winkler wrote verse under the pen-name 'Theodor Hell' and was the author of one of Schubert's songs *Das Heimweh*, a pleasant, serious little song of July 1816; but it is hardly likely that he knew of Schubert's interest in his poem, and we cannot believe in any partisanship on Winkler's side. Nevertheless he refused to print the notice. Then the authoress of the play felt impelled to write an account of the possible reasons why it had failed to please, instancing lack of rehearsal, general frantic haste to stage the production, and new, inexperienced personnel at the theatre. One thing in Helmina von Chézy's favour must be said: she always, from the first, recognised the beauty, lyricism and power of Schubert's music for her play. In this 'Explanation' of hers, published by the Vienna 'Zeitschrift' on 13 January 1824, she referred to '. . . Schubert's glorious music . . . a majestic stream, winding through the poem's complexities like a sweetly transfiguring mirror, grandiose, purely melodious, soulful, unspeakably touching and profound . . .' and more in the same vein of flowery description, but obviously sincere beneath its flourishes. Publication of the favourite 'Romance' from the play, with Schubert's own arrangement of the accompaniment for pianoforte, took place on 24 March ('Axa's Romance', Op. 26). His publishers of those days, Sauer & Leidesdorf, promised the Overture, entr'actes and choruses shortly afterwards. In August Helmina von Chézy sent Schubert a revised copy of her play, and asked him what sum of money he would demand for the rights of the music. He asked for £10 and apparently received it, for after his death Helmina offered 'Rosamunde' and the incidental music to various theatres in South Germany, but without success.

An activity of the Schubert circle, initiated at the end of 1822, was the formation of 'reading parties' at which plays and novels

FERDINAND, COUNT TROYER

Oil by Johann Ender, 1826 *Baroness Alice Loudon*

of the day were read; it is not quite clear how the books were read, it seems as if Schober, as a rule, read the work aloud. In the early months of 1824 the parties were being held twice a week at the house of the painter Ludwig von Mohn. They became swollen in numbers by uncongenial associates and it was felt, too, that in the absence of Schober and Bruchmann, the two leading spirits, much of their attractiveness had gone. Occasional Schubertiads were held in conjunction with the readings, but Schubert's still uncertain health prevented the musical evenings from being all that they might be. The result was that the gatherings came to an end in April. The news was sent to Schober by Anton von Doblhoff, and to Kupelwieser, then in Rome studying painting, by his fiancée Johanna Lutz. She wrote:

> The reading parties have now come to an end and very quickly. It was easy enough to see it coming, for there were too many of them to last. (15 April 1824.)

The meetings were resumed when Schober returned to Vienna the following year. Their importance lies in the fact that through them Schubert encountered many authors whose verses either directly inspired his songs, or who stimulated his interest in various literary movements of the day, in Germany as well as in Austria. We certainly owe his Heine songs to the 'readings'.

The publication of Schubert's work was well under way in 1824. The earlier scheme of bringing out songs on a subscription basis seems a long way behind, and regular publication, payment and advertisement give a professional solidity to his standing in 1824 and 1825. Reviews and criticisms of his work were also appearing in music journals and Schubert, understandably enough, eagerly read these reports. He wrote to his father on 25 July:

> ... the favourable reception of 'Suleika' gave me just pleasure, although I wish I could have had a sight of the criticisms myself, in order to see if something could not be learnt from them; for however favourable a verdict may be, it may at the same time be equally laughable if the critic lacks the required understanding, which is not altogether rarely the case.

Franz Schubert senior, in his turn, made a point of informing his son during the following August:

> . . . the announcement of your 'Gondelfahrer' and 'Schöne Müllerin appeared in the 'Wiener Zeitung' on the 12th instant. . . .

As evidence of his new status, the appearance of the String Quartet in A minor might here be documented. We have been able from Schwind's letter to see the inception of the work in Schubert's mind and pen. He composed it because of his acquaintance with Schuppanzigh the violinist, and the subsequent promise of a performance. Schwind wrote again to Schober on 6 March 1824:

> A new Quartet is to be performed at Schuppanzigh's who is quite enthusiastic and is said to have rehearsed particularly well.

The performance took place on the afternoon of 14 March in the Hall of the *Gesellschaft der Musikfreunde* in the Tuchlauben. Schwind wrote a third time to Schober and said:

> Schubert's quartet has been performed, rather slowly in his opinion, but very purely and tenderly. It is on the whole very smooth, but written in such a way that the tune remains in one's mind, as with the songs, all feeling and thoroughly expressive. It got much applause, especially the *Menuetto* which is extraordinarily tender and natural. . . .

The term 'natural' here in Schwind's letter, recurs frequently throughout the nineteenth-century in connection with Schubert's music. 'A natural composer' they called Schubert. The implication is 'without art', and it had its associated terms: dilettante, amateur, unschooled and so forth. It is hard to bear, in view of the truth, and one can understand Spaun's anger at its use in connection with his friend. One can forgive Schwind his spontaneous use of the word in the above letter, but consider that very 'Menuetto', with its profundity of feeling, its highly wrought craftsmanship, its perfect technical finish and balance, and see how absurd is the application 'natural' to it—and to Schubert's work in general. The artist in Schwind should have warned him that 'smoothness' is only attained by the highest achievement in technical manipulation—so high, in fact, that it can conceal the very means by which it is achieved.

The reports of the performance in the newspapers were not appreciative. The Vienna 'Allgemeine Musikalische Zeitung' of 27 April said:

> New Quartet by Schubert. This composition must be heard several times before it can be adequately judged.

And the journal of Leipzig, with a similar title, two days later printed the well-known pronouncement 'not to be despised as a first born'. The phrase 'first born' is, to present-day readers, ironic: Schubert had actually written a dozen string quartets before the one in A minor; but it was, of course, the first one to come before the public. It was published by Sauer & Leidesdorf on 7 September 1824 under the title:

Trois Quattours
pour deux Violons, deux Altos et Violoncelle
par François Schubert.
Œuv. 29: no. 1.

The 'deux Altos' is a misprint; there is, of course, only one viola; the 'Trois Quattours' implies that Schubert was going to publish three quartets in this Op. 29 (this is a similar undertaking to the production of the early quartet in D major, see page 20). The second quartet, the D minor, was already written and its later publisher, Josef Czerny of Vienna, would have been justified in calling it 'Op. 29: no. 2'. The third quartet was composed two years later; this is the work in G major of June 1826. It was not published until 1851 and then called Op. 161.

Schubert received £4 from the publishers for his Op. 29. A similar sum was paid to him for other publications that year from the same firm: Op. 28, a part-song for T.T.B.B. called *Der Gondelfahrer*, a setting of Mayrhofer's poem, which appeared on 12 August, and Op. 27, three 'Marches Heroïques' for PF. Duet, published on 18 December. The five books of the 'Schöne Müllerin' songs were all published by August, in spite of the unhappy Schubert's complaint that they were so slow in appearing.

'It's a slow business with the "Maid of the Mill" songs, too: a book comes dragging out once every three months' (letter to Ferdinand from Zseliz, August 1824). These books were not altogether an arbitrary subdivision of the twenty songs into equal amounts, but make some attempt to present the five small 'Acts' of the play: I—the arrival at the mill (1–4), II—the falling in love (5–9), III—the brief idyll of happiness (10–12), IV—the jealousy and despair (13–17), V—the resignation and death of the young miller (17–20). It is doubtful whether Schober had any grounds for writing to Schubert on 2 December 1824: '. . . and your "Maid of the Mill" songs too failed to make a sensation, did they?' His words can only refer to the immediate reception of the cycle, for no songs of Schubert have been so consistently beloved and popular as these small but thoroughly typical specimens of his lyric genius. The five books were published as Op. 25 and Schubert dedicated the work to the young Baron Schönstein, a friend of Count Esterházy and a singer with a pleasant baritone voice, sympathetic and expressive in tone, so that he was an excellent interpreter of the Schubert song.

Besides these important publications numerous small commissions came to Schubert for songs and dances and short piano pieces, which brought him in a little money or helped to make his name better known. Sauer & Leidesdorf issued an 'Album Musical' in 1824; there were two editions, and Schubert was represented in both. The first, published on New Year's Day, contained an attractive PF. Solo in F minor, called 'Air Russe'; this has become celebrated through its re-publication later on as No. 3 of the 'Moments Musicaux', Op. 94. The variation which he had composed in March 1821 on the famous Waltz by Diabelli was published, as one among fifty others by various composers, on 6 June, and the short, but tremendously effective song to Death *An den Tod*, composed in 1817, formed a supplement to the Vienna 'Allgemeine Musikalische Zeitung' on the 26th of that month. The second edition of the 'Album Musical' followed in December. It contained another piece for the piano, in A flat, called 'Plaintes d'un Troubadour', afterwards included, as No. 6, in the 'Moments Musicaux' series. This piece, it has been suggested, may have been composed in 1818. A song was also included in the 'Album', the *Erinnerung* by Kosegarten which Schubert had written in July 1815.

Performances of the composer's part-songs were as frequent and popular as ever during 1824. They were usually part of a concert given by some celebrity, designed to serve as light relief, presumably, to the virtuoso seriousness of the soloist. Thus the young pianist, Leopoldine Blahetka, mentioned in the letter from Doppler to Schubert in 1818, and afterwards beloved by Chopin when he visited Vienna in 1830, included a vocal quartet of his in her recital of 21 March, and so, later on, did the violinists Hellmesberger and Schuppanzigh. The favourite quartet of that period was 'Die Nachtigall', words by Johann Karl Unger, which Schubert had composed in April 1821, and published as Op. 11: no. 2.

Amongst the Schubert documents of 1824, was a journal of his, which he kept in the March of that year. We know of it only through Bauernfeld, for the original is lost. Since Bauernfeld did not become acquainted with Schubert, to any degree of intimacy, until 1825, the actual wording of the extracts from Schubert's journal which he reproduced posthumously, in 1829, must remain suspect. They are all somewhat 'off centre' if we place them against our knowledge of the composer's character, and his own expression in letters. The most famous of them is a misquoted version of the original. Bauernfeld actually quoted Schubert as having written:

> What I produce is due to my understanding of music and to my sorrows; that which sorrow alone has produced seems to give least pleasure to the world.

Kreissle misquoted this as 'to give *most* pleasure', and it has been consistently misquoted ever since.

But a much more important document, authentic and extant, is a letter which he wrote on 31 March 1824 to his friend Leopold Kupelwieser in Rome. This letter is one of Schubert's most famous outpourings. It is usually quoted piecemeal, for so many topics in the work and thought of the composer have relevant support in the statements of his letter, that one can hardly avoid quoting from it when those topics are discussed. And so it has been thought necessary to quote it here in its entirety, so that any subsequent discussion of it may be easily followed. It is here newly translated.

Dear Kupelwieser,

I've been wanting to write to you for some time, but was so busy I hardly knew which way to turn. But now the opportunity has come through Smirsch and at last I can pour out my feelings again to someone. You are indeed so staunch and true. You will surely forgive me many things which others would take amiss. To put it briefly, I feel myself the most unfortunate, the most miserable being in the world. Think of a man whose health will never be right again, and who from despair over the fact makes it worse instead of better, think of a man, I say, whose splendid hopes have come to naught, to whom the happiness of love and friendship offer nothing but acutest pain, whose enthusiasm (at least, the inspiring kind) for the Beautiful threatens to disappear, and ask yourself whether he isn't a miserable, unfortunate fellow?

My peace is gone, my heart is heavy,
I find it never, nevermore. . . .

so might I sing every day, since each night when I go to sleep I hope never again to wake, and each morning merely reminds me of the misery of yesterday. So I should pass my days joyless and friendless, if it weren't for Schwind, who frequently visits me and sheds a light from those dear, departed days.

Our Society (Reading Society), as you probably know by now, being swollen with uncouth crowds for beer-swilling and sausage-eating, has committed suicide, for its dissolution takes place in 2 days, although since your departure I rarely went to it. Leidesdorf, whom I have come to know quite well, is indeed a really profound and good fellow, yet so deeply melancholy, that I am almost afraid I have profited from him in that respect more than I care to do; also, his and my affairs are going badly, so we never have any money. Your brother's opera (he did not do very well to leave the theatre) was pronounced unusable, and accordingly no claim has been made on my music. Castelli's opera, 'Die Verschworenen', has been composed in Berlin by a local composer, and received with acclamation.[1] In this way I appear to have composed, once again, two operas for nothing. I have done very little song-writing, but tried my hand at several instrumental things, for I have composed two quartets for violins, viola and 'cello, and an Octet, and want to write another string quartet, on the whole I want to prepare myself like this for grand Symphony.

The latest news in Vienna is that Beethoven is giving a Concert, at which he intends to produce his new Symphony, 3 pieces from the new Mass, and a new Overture. God willing, I also am thinking of giving a similar concert next year. Now I close, so as not to use too much paper, and kiss you a 1000 times. If you would write to me about your own enthusiasms and your life as well, nothing would more greatly please

Your

faithful friend

Frz. Schubert

My address, then, would be c/o Sauer & Leidesdorf, because I am going at the beginning of May to Hungary with Esterházy.

Farewell! Really well!!

Schubert's dejected spirits and ill-health are obvious from his words, and these are only wrung from his reserved nature because he trusts his correspondent—'You are indeed so staunch and true . . . things which others would take amiss' and so forth. We have in the spring of this year another example of the extraordinary detachment of the artist, for otherwise it is impossible to imagine the contentment and high spirits of the Octet born from this despairing mind. There was a sequel to Schubert's remark that he had composed two quartets, and that he wanted to write a third, and so prepare for a 'grand Symphony' in that manner. The two quartets, in A minor and D minor, were, as we

[1] This is not strictly true. The operetta, by Georg Abraham Schneider, conductor of the Opera House at Berlin, was given twice and then no more.

have said, considered by Schubertian biographers of the nineteenth century to have been composed *after* this letter was written. Thus they explained his words by dating the two quartets of Op. 125, E flat major (1813) and E major (1816), as early 1824. Even if we bear in mind the danger of dating works on stylistic grounds, nevertheless it is incomprehensible how such a date as '1824' could have gained any credence at all for the E major work, let alone for the earlier quartet in E flat, charming as many of its moments are. But the immature development of theme, and the generally flavourless slow movements, unmistakably proclaim their juvenile origins. It was not until O. E. Deutsch, in his valuable article 'The Chronology of Schubert's String Quartets' (Music & Letters, January 1943), assembled all the known facts in concise form, that critics and biographers became generally aware of the new discoveries, the new datings.

Significant, too, is Schubert's reference to a third quartet, which he intended to compose. This was not accomplished until two years later, when the superb Quartet in G major was written. The remarkable thing is that, although two years were to pass before he actually composed his third quartet, it was, in truth, *his next chamber work of any importance*. Only pianoforte sonatas, variations, and songs intervene between the D minor Quartet and the G major Quartet; the Sonata for Arpeggione and Pianoforte in A minor (November 1824) was not considered seriously by Schubert, and thrown off hastily for Vincenz Schuster, the inventor of the new instrument. Moreover, the 'grand Symphony', which was to be the culmination of these preparations, is clearly that in C major, of early 1828. These facts militate, in my opinion at least, against the theory that Schubert composed in 1825 a 'grand Symphony' at Gmunden and Gastein. He may have had one in mind then, and even written sketches for it, but the third quartet was to be written first. There are other factors, of course, to be considered in connection with the 'Gmunden-Gastein' Symphony, but they can be left until the appropriate time.

On 25 May 1824 Schubert left Vienna for Zseliz in Hungary, having, somewhat unwillingly, undertaken to join the Esterházy family once again in their summer retreat. According to Schwind he was resolved to write a symphony; this resolution of Schubert was common knowledge among his friends. Schwind several times mentioned it in his letters to Schober, even, at one point, confusing resolution-to-do with the actual deed. Hence the rumours and legend-promoting statements on the supposedly lost symphony, which if it existed at all could hardly have got beyond a sketched condition. A more tangible piece of luggage which Schubert took with him to Zseliz was an operetta libretto based on the epic poem of Ernst Schulze called 'The Enchanted Rose'; it was the same subject that Bauernfeld used later in the libretto he devised for Schubert on the exploits of the Count of Gleichen. But Schubert, though composing prolifically at Zseliz that summer, never worked on the operetta.

We can gather from a letter which his father wrote to him that he was received in friendly fashion by the members of the Esterházy family. They were not uninfluenced by Schubert's Viennese renown: their music master was a more considerable figure than the obscure musician of six years previous. He lived this time, not in the servants' quarters, but in a room in the castle itself. His salary was £10 per month: for those days, a generous one. On the whole he seemed fairly content. His health at last began to mend, his spirits rose. The two countesses were by this time quite accomplished performers on the piano and we owe to their abilities and enthusiasms the many compositions for PF. Duet which Schubert provided that summer. Marie, the elder sister, was about to become engaged; Karoline, now nearly twenty years old, was a child-like, delicate character, who undoubtedly inspired in Schubert a protective and affectionate regard, which may have been the beginning of love for her. But he could never have seriously entertained any idea of a love affair with her. His social position, his health, his prospects were all against it.

To his family, as usual, Schubert wrote affectionately and informatively. His father's replies raise a smile today, but a smile of respect and esteem as well as amusement. They are so full of typically paternal advice: he gently reminds Schubert of his duties to God, to himself, to his employers, to his patrons. He reminds his son of the honours bestowed by the Music Societies of Linz and Graz:

> If, contrary to all expectation, you should not yet have done so, let me urge you most earnestly, to thank them in a worthy manner. These noble societies show you exceptional love and respect, which may be very important for you. (14 August 1824.)

Schubert had, of course, acknowledged these distinctions by letter, but his father's 'in a worthy manner' suggests the offering of a major composition. It is odd to find that a few months after Schubert had composed two string quartets—the first completed ones for eight years—Ferdinand wrote to him to say that he had begun to perform again his brother's youthful quartets. In this letter of 3 July 1824 Ferdinand gave a list of songs which he had handed over to Ludwig von Mohn; he mentioned 'Fierrabras', the score of which he had lent to Kupelwieser, its librettist; and, in addition, he reported that he had sent off to Schubert a volume of Bach's '48 Preludes and Fugues'. These facts are mentioned because of the replies they drew from Schubert. The replies throw light on his feelings, usually so obscure, about his own compositions, and they are suggestive in connection with his development. The strong influence of Bach in the compositions of those months in Zseliz would be unaccountable had it not been for Ferdinand's chance remark. Schubert, doubtless using the preludes and fugues as teaching material for Marie and Karoline, absorbed and unconsciously expressed the techniques and textures of these keyboard masterpieces of Bach, giving them, at the same time, an unmistakably Schubertian character. The 'Eight Variations on an original Air', Op. 35, are full of this absorption in Bach. To Ferdinand's information on the early quartets, he modestly replied:

> . . . it would be better if you played other quartets than mine, for there is nothing in them, except that perhaps they please you, who are pleased with anything of mine.

On the mention of the songs by his brother, Schubert had this interesting comment to make:

> I comfort myself that only a few of them seem good to me, e.g. those included with 'Geheimnis'—'Wanderers Nachtlied' (II), and 'Der entsühnte Orest'. . . .

Schubert also wished to know, at once, why Kupelwieser wanted the opera score:

> Did Kupelwieser not mention what he intended to do with the opera? Or where he is sending it??

But Ferdinand was unable to give the composer any answer when he next wrote.

The letters show a deepening affection between the two brothers. From boyhood they were attached to each other—the much quoted letter written by Schubert at the age of 15 to Ferdinand, begging him for a few kreuzer to buy bread and apples and so eke out the scanty food rations at the *Stadtkonvikt*, is a good indication of the brothers' mutual affection. But Schubert's severe illness and his recent sojourn in the family home had drawn the ties closer. To whom else could Schubert unburden his grief and utter dejection of soul if not to a loved brother? Ferdinand wrote in his first letter that a musical clock in the coffeehouse called the 'Hungarian Crown' played waltzes by Schubert and, he told his brother, he was so surprised and moved that '. . . I involuntarily shed—'. Schubert replied 'Was it only the pain of my absence which made you shed tears, and could you not trust yourself to write the word? . . . Or did all the tears come to your mind which you have seen me weep?' We can understand why Ferdinand, for thirty years after his younger brother's death, remained a faithful guardian and advocate of his manuscripts, moved to continual pity by the thought of that gifted brother, so tragically dying before his name was made.

To Schwind and Schober there was a letter apiece, and it is in Schwind's letter that we get the only piece of evidence from Schubert himself that could possibly be interpreted as indicating a love for Karoline Esterházy. He wrote to Schwind that he longed damnably for Vienna in spite of the 'anziehenden bewussten Sternes' ('certain attractive star'). The star may be Karoline, but the remark hardly suggests the ardour of a lover. To Schober he opened his heart more than to Schwind, more even than to Ferdinand. As in the letter to Leopold Kupelwieser earlier in the year, he proclaims his longing for the days of his youth, particularly of that time which he and Schober had spent together composing 'Alfonso und Estrella'. To his friends and to his brother he mentioned the compositions of the summer; the Sonata in C major, for PF. Duet, known by the name which Diabelli bestowed on it, 'Grand Duo', when he published it as Op. 140 in 1838; the 'Eight Variations on an Original Theme', also for PF. Duet, which was published soon after he returned to Vienna, as Op. 35. The two duets were successfully played to the Esterházy family and their Hungarian friends, but Schubert wrote to Schwind:

> As I do not wholly trust the Hungarians' taste, I leave it to you and the Viennese to decide.

A third PF. Duet was written in September; it is the long, and very unequal 'Divertissement à l'hongroise'. Only a few years ago a preliminary sketch for part of the 'Divertissement' saw the light; it is for piano solo and consists of the *Allegretto* finale. Schubert called it 'Ungerische (*sic*) Melodie'. The manuscript bears in the composer's hand 'Zseliz, September 1824', which enables us to place and date the composition with certainty. The duet was published in April 1826 by Artaria of Vienna, as Op. 54. It was widely known in the nineteenth century with results which are not too happy; in many cases, e.g. Wagner's, it was practically the only instrumental piece of Schubert's to be known, and gave a wrong impression of his stature. Schumann wrote in his diary on 9 October 1836 that Mendelssohn 'stamped his feet' impatiently over the work.

Some Marches for PF. Duet were published the following year as Op. 40. Two of them, in G minor and B minor, are charmingly lyrical: the 'Trio' section of the first one is built on a melody so absolutely characteristic of its author in rhythm, harmony and contour, that it brings a smile to the face as if one were greeting an old friend. The fifth march, *funèbre* in style, in E flat minor, reminded a later friend of Schubert, Fritz von Hartmann, of his mother. He mentioned this in his diary and so conferred on this particular march a somewhat undeserved distinction.

Release from his not too congenial duties came in October. He travelled back to Vienna in the company of Baron Schönstein, a long letter from whom, describing the journey, has been preserved. They arrived on 17 October. It is an odd coincidence that the only two letters of Schönstein which have any relevance to the Schubert records are both of this year, 1824, and that the first gives us the exact date of Schubert's leaving Vienna for Zseliz and the second the exact date of his return to the capital—both trifling pieces of information and both quite incidental to the main points of the correspondence, but, at least, factually dependable.

Schubert was delighted to be back in his old haunts, and he and Schwind resumed their former intimacy, becoming almost inseparable. Schober wrote from Breslau and hinted at his speedy return to Vienna, but this did not take place until the following August. Best of all, Spaun visited Vienna for a few weeks' holiday and he and Schubert were re-united. At the end of the year, on 22 December, a new publisher's name appears, that of Thaddäus Weigl. In a 'Musikalische Angebinde' ('Musical Dedication'), a collection of new waltzes, Weigl included as No. 29, a waltz of Schubert. It was a charming piece, in E flat major, composed for PF. Duet in the previous July at Zseliz. Schubert arranged it in November for PF. Solo especially for Weigl's collection, and so business relations between the composer and the publisher were initiated. In a year's time Schubert was selling full scale work to Weigl.

II

In February 1825 Schubert moved his lodgings to a house next door but one to that of his young friend Schwind. The long, low apartment house is to the left of the Karlskirche and in those days pleasantly situated outside the Inner City and known as the 'Frühwirthaus'. 'As far as I can' Schwind wrote to Schober, 'I share his whole life with him'—and in that same February they gathered into their association the third member, the new friend, Eduard Bauernfeld. Schubert and Spaun had strolled out to the 'Moonshine' house on the previous Christmas Eve to visit Schwind, and had there found the young writer in Schwind's company: it was Schubert's first meeting with Bauernfeld, but a meeting long desired by the younger man, who greatly admired the music, especially the part-songs, of Schubert. The association was an uneasy and forced relationship *à trois*, and held together chiefly by the admiration which each of the younger men felt for Schubert's music. Bauernfeld was a facetious and light-minded friend. Both he and Schwind achieved solid renown in the middle years of the nineteenth century: Schwind as a 'Romantic' draughtsman and illustrator of German myth and folk-tale, Bauernfeld as a satirically humorous playwright and fablist, but in these years, when we meet them in the company of Schubert, neither is a very impressive figure. There is evidence, too, that Schubert felt for them both a tolerant, but by no means unseeing affection. Yet we owe much to both of them as 'recorders' of the composer; Schwind in his unrivalled illustrations of Schubert and Schubert's background, Bauernfeld in his biographical essays and memoirs. Schwind's illustrations are called 'unrivalled' and so, in bulk, they are. But actually, at that time, in May 1825, Schubert's protrait was painted by the water colourist, Wilhelm August Rieder, and it has become the favourite contemporary portrait, the one most frequently quoted. It is, however, surpassed in popularity by the engraving based upon it which Josef Kriehuber made in 1846. This gives a more masculine, a 'squarer', cast to the portrait of Rieder, and also flatters the composer a little.

Men and women throng the pages of Schubert's life during the early months of 1825. Schubertiads were held at least weekly and Vogl sang on these evenings the latest composed songs; they attracted many new admirers to the genius of the composer. Part-songs were performed in public and private; they, and the playing of the piano duets and dance music of the golden summer at Zseliz also won fresh friends. After Bauernfeld came the two Hartmann brothers, Fritz and Franz, with whom Schubert and Schwind drank 'brotherhood' soon after their arrival in Vienna.

Karl von Enderes, a lawyer and, later on, a notable Schubertian, also met the composer in the spring of that year.

Four women, three of them renowned actresses and singers, the fourth an obscure figure, play their part in the composer's life in those days. Johanna Lutz had no fame in the artistic world, we know her through Schubert's friend Leopold Kupelwieser to whom she was engaged. But her shrewd, kindly-affectioned comments on Schubert and his circle of friends are indispensable to our picture of the composer and his background. It was she who informed Kupelwieser of the unhappy conclusion of the 'Reading parties'. When Schubert returned to Vienna from Zseliz in November 1824 she reported to her fiancé that he and Schwind were much in each other's company and added that it was a good thing —'for if they are not of much use to each other, they do each other no harm'. She wrote in March 1825 of the activities of the Schubertians, complaining with amused, yet impatient, candour of the childish quarrels and feuds of the various cliques; 'Schubert' she wrote, 'is now very busy and well behaved, which pleases me very much.' As far as composition was concerned, Schubert was busy with song-writing; some of the songs from the 'Lady of the Lake' were probably composed during March and April, among them, for certain, the *Lay of the Imprisoned Huntsman.* He used a translation of Scott's text by Adam Storck. There were also the two nocturnal songs *Nacht und Träume* and *Die junge Nonne*, in which his melodic and dramatic power were not surpassed until the very last phase, in August 1828. The latter song contains more fascinating examples of his power of theme development: both voice and piano reveal the growth of the 'germ' motif and together give an unforgettable picture of the nun in her quiet cell—a point of physical and spiritual calm at the heart of the storm. The song was sung on 3 March 1825, *at sight*, it is said, by Sophie Müller, an actress of the Burgtheater, in her home at Hietzing, a village just to the west of Vienna. She was an accomplished singer, spoke English and loved English poetry; her youthful charm, her voice and her delightful acting were greatly to the taste of the Viennese and they idolised her. In her diary she records several visits by Vogl and Schubert, or Schubert alone, to the Hietzing residence during the early months of 1825. There both old and new songs were sung by her, or Vogl.

Another woman, attracted by the magic of Schubert's songs, was the remarkable actress, Katherina von Lászny. Schwind gave an awesome picture of this dying courtesan, still queening it over her little court, with the wreck of her beauty and charm still able to captivate the young painter, so that he wrote to Schober: 'What a woman! If she were not nearly twice my age and, unhappily, always ill, I should have to leave Vienna, for it would be more than I could stand.' After this meeting with Schwind she was taken ill and spat blood. But in spite of her enfeebled condition, and with indomitable spirit she continued to give parties and hold 'Schubertiads'. Schubert dedicated some songs and the Hungarian 'Divertissement' to her, a delicate compliment for her husband was a Hungarian. Before her marriage, Katherina also had appeared on the stage at the Burgtheater, but she was not so popular an actress as Sophie Müller: her numerous love-affairs scandalised the citizens of Vienna and Schwind concluded the account of his meeting her with the words: 'So now I know what a person looks like who is in ill repute all over the city, and what she does.'

In the previous December (1824) Schubert had received a letter from a great soprano whose performances in operatic roles at the Kärntnertor Theater had won his admiration as a boy. Anna Milder had settled in Berlin where she sang at the Court Opera, but she still kept in touch with Viennese circles, maintained a friendship with Vogl—it was with him that she had made her name in the Vienna Opera, and won Schubert's regard —and occasionally visited the city. She wrote to the composer inviting him to set to music a poem called 'Der Nachtschmetterling'. This he did not do, but he sent to her the second of the two songs of Suleika (*Ach, um deine feuchten Schwingen*), and with it a full score of the opera 'Alfonso und Estrella'. She replied on 8 March dashing any hopes which he entertained that the opera might be produced in Berlin. Frau Milder's reasons for its non-acceptance strike the present day reader of them as inadequate to say the least: she stated that its libretto was not in accord with the taste of the Berliners and *that* at a time when the variety of operas being staged makes it difficult to discover quite what was the desired type. But she very much approved of 'Suleika's Song' and sang it at her next concert, in the Jagor'sche Saal, Berlin. This took place on 9 June 1825, and was a brilliant success. Even the Berlin critics, for whom 'Lied' meant a strophic song in the tradition of Zelter and Reichardt, were captivated by the *Erlking* and the *Suleika* song; it would indeed be difficult to understand any coldness, in those days, towards those two exuberant settings of Goethe. But Schubert was not given unqualified praise; it was impossible for Berlin to accept wholeheartedly the 'durchkomponiert', i.e. onrunning, song, as a typical 'Lied'. For many years the Schubert song failed to capture this stronghold, and it was greeted there with sneers and neglect. It is ironical to think that nowadays the Schubert 'durchkomponiert' song has come to be synonymous with 'German song'. Anna Milder, triumphant with her successful concert, sent the cuttings to Schubert, who was then, in June, on holiday with Vogl in Upper Austria.

After the year of work, the year of holiday. In May he had departed from Vienna with Vogl, and the two friends arrived at Steyr on 20 May. The difference in his status at Steyr during 1825 compared with that during his first visit six years before is as marked as it was at Zseliz. In 1819 Schubert was an inconspicuous young musician, a protégé of Vogl. In 1825 he was a notable composer, the author of published songs which were loved and sung in the musical centres of Upper Austria as much as in those of Vienna. Everywhere Vogl and Schubert went their welcome was overwhelming. Theresa Clodi, sister of the young Max Clodi, a law student of Vienna who knew Schubert through Spaun, wrote to her brother from Ebenzweier Castle:

> Twice I have heard Vogl sing and Schubert play: it is and remains a divine pleasure to hear those two. (22 June 1825.)

The following 'journal' of Schubert's movements, and the documents of himself, his friends and admirers, may help to bring the summer holiday into perspective.

Steyr (20 May–4 June): Schubert stayed with Vogl in the house where the singer had been born, a flat-fronted building with a rather imposing, arched entrance at the side. It is today 32 Haratzmüllerstrasse in the Ennsdorf suburb. On 24 May the two friends visited Linz and journeyed on to the nearby monasteries of St. Florian and Kremsmünster. Schubert received an enthusiastic and warm-hearted welcome, for he was visiting people who already knew and loved his music and were prepared to honour its author. His reticent nature and still disconsolate spirits opened out under this warmth.

> In Upper Austria I find my compositions everywhere, especially in the monasteries of St. Florian and Kremsmünster, where, with the help of a worthy piano player I produced my four-handed Variations and Marches with gratifying success. (Letter to his parents, 25 July 1825.)

The 'worthy piano player' was the Dean of the Monastery, Father Heinrich Hassak. Schubert also performed alone the *Andante poco moto* variation-movement from his newly completed Sonata in A minor, published at the end of the year by Pennauer, as Op. 42. Vogl sang the new songs from Scott's 'Lady of the Lake', including the *Ave Maria*, a song which, it has been said, 'suffers today from its rather overpowering popularity of yesterday.' Schubert accompanied him, and the songs too had much success according to the composer's report in the letter quoted above. He and Vogl returned to Steyr on 27 May, remaining there until 4 June.

Gmunden (4 June–15 July): it is a small town on the shores of Lake Traun—'the environs of which are truly heavenly and deeply moved and benefited me' wrote the composer. He and Vogl lived with a merchant named Ferdinand Traweger, who greatly esteemed Schubert as man and musician, but whose advent into Schubert's life is a mystery. Traweger was fond of singing in male voice quartets, and while staying as his guest, Schubert composed for him two part-songs: the *Nachtmusik*, a setting of a serenade by Karl Seckendorf, and the Latin drinking-song *Edit*

Nonna, edit Clerus whose words were written in the sixteenth century. This racy text kept back the publication of the quartet; the censorship was not lifted until 1848. Schubert's setting is a full-throated enjoyment of the words, and the Latin tongue probably veils, for modern audiences, any offence in the words. We have Schubert's own word that he lived very pleasantly and freely at the Gmunden home. He became attached to Traweger's small, five-year old son, Eduard, and is supposed to have been the only one capable of allaying the boy's fears when, in the fashion of the day, leeches were applied as a remedy for fever. Eduard Traweger, who lived until 1909, was then the last surviving person to have known Schubert. From Gmunden the two friends visited Florian Clodi and his daughter Therese, whose home was Ebenzweier Castle, some three miles from Gmunden, on the lake shore. Therese, a gentle, devoted daughter —her father was blind—was a connection of Spaun's, and to the Schubertians she was known as the 'Lady of the Lake'. She managed the estate. It is a romantic picture, to imagine father and daughter listening to Schubert and Vogl performing the Walter Scott songs in a room of the castle, backed by the lake and its lovely shoreline.

The strangest and most perplexing report of these six weeks at Gmunden is the suggestion that Schubert composed there a symphony—the now entitled 'Gmunden-Gastein' Symphony. (That very title has a faint hint of the confusion which surrounds the subject.) The question will be considered later, so that it can suffice to say here that it is doubtful whether Schubert did anything more than sketch the work, although it may have been a substantial enough sketch for him to have considered it as good as finished, so far as the primal, creative impulse was concerned. Scoring and final details were for him, in 1825, routine matters, at his finger tips. But to say even that is to go beyond any documentary evidence which is reliable.

An old tradition in Gmunden says that while Schubert was there he watched a gang of pile-drivers at work and listened to their singing. These Austrian craftsmen had a repertory of songs whose very rhythmic nature helped the men to deliver a united 'hammer' blow on the pile at a strategic point in the music, actually on the *second* beat of the bar. The subject is of interest and was dealt with fully by Karl M. Klier in 1952.[1] Schubert, tradition has it, was intrigued by the song he heard and used it in his *Adagio* in E flat for PF. Trio, called a 'Notturno' and published as Op. 148. Here is the melody, said to be a pile-drivers' song, from the 'Notturno', supplied with arrows on the second beat, where the men would deliver the 'Niederschlag':

The most significant outcome of the story, if it has any truth, and its very strangeness suggests that it has, is that it gives us a chance to date the PF. Trio in B flat, Op. 99. The 'Notturno' in E flat has always been considered a rejected movement from the B flat PF. Trio, and since Schubert is not likely to have delayed using the song he heard, it is possible that the PF. Trio was begun as early as 1825. There is no other means whatever of dating it: the manuscript is lost and there are no contemporary references to it. Two dates have been deduced for its composition, 1826 and 1827. The piledrivers' song and its tradition make the earlier one, 1826, more probable.

Schubert and Vogl left Gmunden on 12 or 13 July and spent a night or two with acquaintances at Puchberg, a village near Wels.

LINZ (15 July–25 July): Schubert went on alone to Linz, his intention being to stay with Anton Ottenwalt and his wife Marie, the sister of Spaun. They were delighted to welcome him, and Ottenwalt wrote to Spaun (then at Lemberg) that Schubert looked so well and strong, so bright of appearance and genial in mood, that it was a pleasure to see him. On his arrival at Linz, however, and after a brief greeting, Schubert hurried off to Steyregg Castle, to pay his respects to the Countess Weissenwolf.

[1] 'Oesterreichische Pilotenschlägerlieder' in the 'Jahrbuch des österreichischen Volksliedwerkes I', Vienna, 1952. See also 'Music & Letters', April 1953, page 181.

The castle was five miles or so from Linz and Schubert spent several nights there. Sophie, Countess Weissenwolf, was a contralto and an eager Schubertian. Now she heard the 'Lady of the Lake' songs and was entranced with them. When they were published the following April they were dedicated to her—Schubert gratifying her pretty plain hint that such a dedication would be anything but disagreeable to her. He returned to the Ottenwalts on 19 July. When Vogl joined him there, three days later, he took the singer straightway on a visit to Steyregg Castle, staying there that time for two days. They were once more guests of the Ottenwalts on their return to Linz, and in a second letter to Spaun, Ottenwalt gives a very vivid account of the two friends, and describes the five solo songs to the Scott poems. The seven settings of lyrics from the 'Lady of the Lake' contain, of course, two part-songs: *Coronach* (female voices), which is an elegy foreshadowing the intensity of the 'Winterreise' songs, and *Bootgesang*, a trifling quartet for men's voices. Vogl sang all five of the solo songs, Ellen's as well. Ottenwalt wrote:

> We heard Vogl three times, and Schubert himself condescended to sing something after breakfast among ourselves, and also played his marches, two- and four-handed variations, and an overture on the pianoforte, compositions of such significance that one cannot trust oneself to discuss them.

The overture is probably that in F minor, Op. 34, for PF. Duet. An unexpected visitor to Ottenwalt's home, and one whom Schubert, without any doubt, welcomed warmly, was Albert Stadler, a friend from the *Stadtkonvikt* days.

STEYR (25 July–11 August): Schubert once again lived in Vogl's house in the Haratzmüllerstrasse and from there wrote the long and detailed letter to his father and stepmother which has already been quoted. Rainy weather kept him indoors, and one wonders whether he used the time to continue with the symphony sketches, or, more probably, to sketch the music for a new sonata, the one in D major, Op. 53. While at Steyr he received a letter from Schwind, which, apart from personal details, informed him of the arrival of Schober, back in Vienna from his travels in Breslau; of the imminent arrival of Kupelwieser, from Italy; and news of Bauernfeld, alternatively working for law examinations and at his poetry. The Schubert circle was in the process of re-forming.

A few days later Vogl and Schubert set off for Gastein, travelling there via Salzburg. For poor Vogl the visit to the Gastein spa was in the nature of a cure, and he took the waters for his painful gout; for Schubert, on the other hand, the trip was unalloyed holiday. They arrived on 14 August.

Gastein (14 August–4 September): a number of compositions originated at Gastein, all of them thoroughly typical of the composer in his over-abundant, rather lush vein, and, accordingly, not in the front rank of his works. The Sonata in D major was finished and written out; its autograph is dated 'Gastein. August 1825'. There are many pages of grand music in this sonata, but some which verge on the trivial. It is unusual to find Schubert using anything but conventional Italian for the expression marks of his movements, but we find the first movement bearing, in his autograph, the direction *un poco più lento e con capriccita* (bar 48). His requirement, as well as the wording of it, are both unusual. The four songs of the period are similarly luxuriant, but unequal pieces of work. Two of them are settings of poems by Johann Ladislau Pyrker, Patriarch of Venice, who was staying at Gastein that August. He and Schubert were already on a quite friendly footing, their acquaintance dated from 1821 when the composer had dedicated to Pyrker the songs of Op. 4. The Patriarch had interests at Gastein, among them a military hospital which he had founded and directed. The two songs are *Die Allmacht* and *Heimweh*, both, like the D major Sonata, full of exalted, Schubertian writing, but neither wholly successful; each in particular oversteps the limitations of the piano as an accompanying instrument. This is perhaps a cold verdict to pass on such warm, passionate art. Then let the fine words of Richard Capell (*loc. cit.*, page 213) on the song *Die Allmacht* serve as contrary opinion:

Schubert, exhilarated by his tour in the hills of Upper Austria, his thoughts . . . all set quivering by so many revelations of nature both benign and magnificent, found in this song the outlet for overflowing feelings. The Patriarch's verses could not have been happened on at a better moment. The subject, God apprehended in nature, went straight to Schubert's heart. There, with the hills round about him, he poured forth his blessing upon the health-giving air, and thanks to the Creator of life. The magnificent song is anything but a formal piece . . . it is intensely personal and rapturous. Schubert's temple was the hillside; and he brought all the sounds of the open-air, the torrent, the forest's murmur, the thunder-roll, into his hymn of praise. . . .

The other two songs are *Fülle der Liebe*, a setting of Friedrich von Schlegel's poem, showing remarkable affinities with the slow movement of the D major Sonata, and *Auf der Bruck*, Schubert's second setting of Ernst Schulze, a poet to whom he returned in the next two years and who inspired him with a series of deeply serious songs.

Vogl and Schubert left Gastein on 4 September, travelling via Werfen and the lakeside to Gmunden, where they again lodged with Traweger. Once settled there, Schubert began, on 12 September, a letter to Ferdinand, describing his journeyings and the impressions they had awakened in him. The famous account of his and Vogl's performance of the songs occurs in this letter:

The way in which Vogl sings and I accompany him, as though we were one at such a moment, is something quite new and unheard-of for these people. . . .

The composer and his singer paid another visit to Ebenzweier Castle, and a few days afterwards Vogl decided to return to Steyr. From there Schubert continued his brother's letter, but the detailed description proved too tedious for him. He threw up the task, and Ferdinand received the incomplete letter by hand when his brother arrived back in Vienna. Vogl had decided to go to Italy and the holiday for Schubert was drawing to an end. It seems fairly clear that since the movements of the two men were apparently determined by Vogl, Schubert was largely his guest on the holiday. Apart from the lodgings with Traweger and Ottenwalt, when both Schubert and Vogl were guests, the transport, and the hotels at Salzburg, Puchberg, Gastein and so on, were evidently paid for from Vogl's purse. On 17 September they returned to Steyr ('unfortunately' wrote Schubert in his brother's letter!).

STEYR (17 September–1 October): the quiet days here, at Vogl's house, produced four more songs. Two of them are modest pieces, but in some ways more successful than the ambitious work of the previous month, particularly the fresh *Wiedersehn*. This song remained unpublished until 1843, when it appeared obscurely in a symposium entitled *Lebensbilder aus Oesterreich* (*Pictures of Austrian Life*). The other two songs form a pair, textually related, for both poems were taken from a play entitled 'Lacrimas' by Wilhelm von Schütz, which Schubert must have found in Vogl's collection of dramatic literature. The first is *Florio*, a small, likable song in E major. But the other, *Delphine*, the outpouring of an impassioned woman, is a masterpiece, fully the equal of either of the Pyrker songs, and neglected, possibly, because of the over-riding demands on voice and intelligence.

On 1 October Vogl and Schubert arrived at Linz as the guests once more of the Ottenwalts. They found Stadler there on a second visit, and since Vogl was unable, or unwilling, to go to Steyregg Castle, Schubert went without him, taking Stadler as companion, to pay a third visit to Count and Countess Weissenwolf. Stadler shared a bedroom with Schubert, and years afterwards recalled the composer's amusement over an incident which occurred before they fell asleep. Schubert sang a tune from the 'Magic Flute', but Stadler could not remember the second part to it, and so was unable to join in the 'duet'. He also related how, in the morning, Schubert flatly refused to rise early and go for a walk with him into the inviting countryside.

The last 'recital' which Schubert and Vogl gave, in which some of the new songs of August and September were sung, as well as the much admired 'Lady of the Lake' series, took place at Anton Spaun's home on 3 October. Anton was a younger brother of Josef's. After this Vogl betook himself to Italy, and now he more or less drops out of the composer's story, save for a few isolated appearances. Schubert met Josef von Gahy at Spaun's little Schubertiad and returned with him to Vienna, where they arrived on 6 October.

'Schubert is back' wrote Bauernfeld in his diary. 'Inn and coffee house gathering with friends often until two or three in the morning.' Schober, Schwind, Kupelwieser, Bauernfeld, Schubert—they were together again, and there re-commenced the round of convivial parties, concerts, Schubertiads, with the autumnal Viennese background; the summer and the holiday were over, yet the social life to which Schubert gladly abandoned himself meant an end, for a while, of work. The next compositions bear the date December 1825.

The publications of that year were again numerous and varied and four publishers accepted his work. Diabelli eventually brought out a delayed Op. 19, containing the three Goethe songs *An Schwager Kronos*, *Ganymed* and *An Mignon*, which he had purchased before the rupture with Schubert. This may have acted as a kind of peace offering for negotiations were resumed soon afterwards and Schubert sold him a whole batch of work: his early Mass in C major, two offertories, a large number of waltzes and écossaises, and the fine 'Salve Regina' in F major, composed in 1815. These works Diabelli published as Opp. 45–50. Cappi, formerly a partner of Diabelli, now in business on his own, bought two batches of manuscripts from Schubert. The earlier one contained German Dances Op. 33, and the PF. Duet Overture in F, Op. 34; the latter a group of songs published as Opp. 36, 37 and 38. Of this group the most famous is Op. 36: *Der zürnenden Diana* and *Nachtstück*, which Schubert had dedicated to Frau von Lászny. But the masterpieces, instrumental and vocal, were published by more modest houses. From Sauer & Leidesdorf there came the superb set of variations for PF. Duet in A flat, Op. 35 and the six 'Grandes Marches', Op. 40, dedicated by Schubert to his doctor J. Bernhardt. Pennauer, a recently founded publishing house, brought out the Sonata in A minor, Op. 42, with which Schubert was charming his friends during the summer months in Upper Austria, and three songs: the second *Suleika* song as Op. 31 (a delayed publication) and the well nigh incomparable pair of nocturnes, *Nacht und Träume* and *Die iunge Nonne*, as Op. 43. Pennauer's recent establishment led his manager, Franz Hüther, to write rather appealingly to Schubert on 27 July 1825:

> Kindly fix the most exact price you can ask of a beginner....

The close of this sentence was translated in the nineteenth century 'as a beginner' and taken to refer to Schubert, whereat the hapless publisher was execrated for meanness. But Hüther was, of course, referring to his firm as the 'beginner', unable to pay extravagant fees.

There were a few trifling dances from Schubert's pen published in various 'Dance Albums' of the day, and hence completely lost until they were exhumed in the early years of this century. Diabelli re-issued the *Trout* (still without its opus number, 32); and *Der Einsame,* that most attractive of the fireside songs, appeared as a supplement to the *Wiener Zeitschrift* of 12 March 1825.

This was a large body of work to be published in one place by a composer in one year. The compositions are not shallow efforts designed to catch the interest of the moronic amongst the musical Viennese, such as the variations of Czerny, the dances and 'Morceaux' of Blumenthal and Weiss; they contain serious and significant works. Why, with the appearance of this music, ambitious and yet so likeable, did Schubert still fail to catch the ear of Vienna, and hence of musical Europe? One can only remind oneself, once again, of Schubert's inability to appear before the public in some executive capacity. There is no question of his obscurity. A glance through the pages of contemporary musical periodicals and publishers' announcements will show the wide international reputation of composers such as Herz and Pixis, who are not only abysmally inferior in our judgement to Schubert, but must have appeared at least moderately so to any informed music lover in their own day. But those two, or any similar composers one might select, were pianists, and the musical public knew them well in that capacity. It is possible that Schubert's very songs, which first opened the door to reputation for him, eventually proved, in his day, a drag on that reputation rather than a help to it. A song writer, however attractive his songs, is a lowly specimen in the world of music (just as an opera composer, however modest, is an important one). And although we can read in the Berlin 'Zeitung' of 11 June 1825:

> Rich enjoyment was afforded by the evening musical entertainment given by the Court Opera singer, Mme Milder, at Jagor's Hall on the 9th inst., which was numerously and brilliantly attended. . . .

and, again in the Dresden 'Abendzeitung' of 19 August 1825:

> The young, talented tone-poet Schubert, whose song compositions betoken the musical painter, continues to do excellent work in that unfortunately much neglected species. All his compositions testify to profound feeling combined with considerable musical theory. His songs find many purchasers. . . .

there is no escaping the conclusion that musicians could still agree with all this, and yet not consider Schubert seriously. The attitude persisted for decades and was held with particular obstinacy in England right up to the 1870's: merely a song-writer. In Vienna itself even song-writers, presumably, had a following of enthusiasts, outside their own circle of friends and patrons, for we find that Schubert received the mild honour of having his 'likeness' on sale in the Inner City. On 9 December 1825, Cappi announced the publication of his portrait, an engraving made by Johann Nepomuk Passini from the water colour by Rieder: it is the most famous of the contemporary Schubert portraits. 'An extremely good likeness' said the publisher's advertisement, 'of the composer of genius . . . who has so often enchanted his hearers with his vocal compositions. . . .' A *song* composer's portrait after all!

III

The music of 1824 and 1825 contains nothing for orchestra, that is if we exclude the problematical 'Gmunden-Gastein' Symphony from the sum of works. This is something very different from the years prior to 1824. Schubert's preoccupation with songs and chamber music, while undoubtedly satisfying his need for creative work and nourishing his genius, must equally have seemed to him the only way, after his abandonment of opera, to earn money. He composed what the publishers would accept, PF. Duets and Solos, songs and String Quartets, pouring into these works the highest he knew and was capable of.

The songs of the period fall into three major groups, the settings of texts by Sir Walter Scott, by Mayrhofer (the last of Schubert's songs on his old friend's poems), and by a new poet, Ernst Schulze. The Scott songs, especially those of the 'Lady of the Lake', were the most frequently performed and freely documented of all Schubert's songs in his lifetime, with the sole exception of the *Erlking*. None of them, except possibly *Coronach*, is first-rate Schubert, and all are eclipsed today. Something stilted and artificial in the Scott lyrics, which is mitigated by his picturesque word and phrase, stands exposed in the German translation without mitigation. And Schubert, dealing with the not-quite-genuine, never achieved the supreme touch.

This is made very clear when we glance at the Mayrhofer poems, which burn with sincerity however melancholy and despairing they may be. Mayrhofer, there is no doubt, was morbidly attracted to Death: the words of the song, *Der Sieg*, tell of his breaking the bondage of the flesh for the world of the spirit. The solemn chords of the opening and the passionate heart of the song (with a hint of 'Doppelgänger' technique) are in Schubert's 'grand style'; the song is a perfect vehicle for the bass singer. In the last of the four songs, *Auflösung*, the poet bids sun and springtime dissolve, for eternity's oblivion calls him. Schubert's music is an ecstatic flood—the great curves of the melody buoyed up by sweeping arpeggios on the piano. Ernst Schulze, a tragically doomed poet, is the author of five songs of 1825. *Um Mitternacht* is one of the endlessly varied nocturnes of that bright summer. It is a stylish, beautifully developed song, worked skilfully within modest limits. Schubert's finest settings of Schulze were yet to be: they came in the following year (1826).

We find Schubert several times in 1825 selecting a pair of poems from the work of various authors. After composing them it seems as if his interest in the poet was exhausted; he drew no further from his work. Pyrker's *Die Allmacht* and *Das Heimweh* are one example; the 'Two Scenes' from Schütz's *Lacrimas* are another. There are Jakob Craigher's *Die junge Nonne* and *Totengräbers Heimweh* as yet another pair of songs. *Die junge Nonne* ranks high among Schubert's great soprano songs and if its somewhat sentimental words prevent it from ranking quite so high as *Gretchen am Spinnrade*, it is easier to sing, and it is easier for the singer to stir an audience with its sentiments. Schubert's power of 'linear' development—the evolution of fresh and significant melodies from his initial 'germ-motif' is remarkably displayed in this song, and the treatment of his motif in the accompaniment is almost without peer amongst his 'onrunning' songs:

The obscure poet Karl Lappe is immortalised by Schubert's composition of two poems from his pen, *Der Einsame* and *Im Abendrot.* Grove has said the inevitably right word about the first, when he instances the recurrence of the group of four semiquavers in the accompaniment as imparting 'an indescribable air of domesticity to the fireside picture'. But it must not be thought that there is anything 'domestic' in the workmanship of the song, for that is filled with touches of genius: the crickets, the fall of the embers, the relaxed limbs of the rustic, are depicted graphically in the music, and detail after detail betrays Schubert's love for his song of 'true contentment'. As for *Im Abendrot*: one could argue reasonably, that the sheer beauty of its penmanship reveals a similar love on the part of the composer for his created work. The song is a miracle, for no amount of analysis or description seems to add one iota to an explanation of how these simple chords and diatonic phrases can achieve sublimity such as exists in this song of God in the hour of sunset: a Schubertian sublimity, a quality which no other composer but he possessed. It is a revelation of the aspiring spirit of man, which reaches its heaven through poetry alone.

In the letter to Leopold Kupelwieser quoted in full earlier, we read of Schubert's intention with regard to the two string quartets and the Octet of 1824: they were to be preparations for his 'grand symphony'. No one thinks of these three works as 'preparations' in any sense of the word; their greatness is self-evident and their function self-sufficient. The first quartet, in A minor, is a beloved work; in some ways we group it with the 'Unfinished' Symphony as giving us the heart of the composer. But with the quartet, as with the symphony, it is doing him an injustice to let the emotional directness, the poetry, the sheer beauty of the musical sound—which is ear-bewitching—prevent admiration and appreciation of his technical power: power used with masterly ease in development and formal construction. The adroit interplay of major and minor modes in the first movement, foretold so emphatically, and yet so persuasively, in the melody of the opening bars, the colourful use of the 'Neapolitan' sixth, the contrapuntal tissues, all these factors must also be appreciated. His power of theme-manipulation, now richly pouring into his instrumental forms from his song-writing techniques, gives a lyricism so elaborate and highly-developed that only the closest examination reveals the genetic relationship between the component parts. One of the more obvious examples is given here:

The slow movement is based on the Entr'acte in B flat from the 'Rosamunde' music; not merely the theme, but the whole of the first section is common to both pieces. The Entr'acte had, of course, been written only a month or so prior to the quartet movement; Schubert probably thought that he was rescuing the music from oblivion. In the third movement he dispensed with customary 'Scherzo' form, and reverted to the old-fashioned 'Menuetto', but he wrote a minuet unlike any other he had ever composed. The opening motif on the 'cello, taken up directly by the other three strings, is once again a germinating idea and it pervades the whole minuet, the 'Trio'-section as well. Is this 'cello motif taken over from his song *Die Götter Griechenlands*, an 1819 setting of Schiller's text? The point has intrigued writers on Schubert ever since it was raised by Willi Kahl in 1929.[1] It is more than possible that Schubert's mood in those days, of aching regret for the vanished days of his youth, a mood preserved for ever in the Kupelwieser letter, recalled Schiller's words to his mind:

Schöne Welt, wo bist du?
Kehre wieder, holdes Blüthenalter der Natur.

Fair world, where art thou?
Come again, O golden age of Nature.

And if the words were recalled, the music as well came to mind and pen. The song, like the 'Menuetto', veers between A minor

[1] Cobbett's 'Cyclopedia of Chamber Music'.

and major. If it is not merely fanciful to look upon A major as Schubert's key of contentment, then by association of ideas A minor is his key of yearning for lost contentment, of *Sehnsucht*. But full consideration of the Schiller song quotation will be taken up in connection with the octet.

The second quartet of that spring is the famous 'Death and the Maiden' String Quartet, in D minor. Its appellation derives from a mere song title, but as with the 'Wanderer' Fantasia of 1822, the temptation was irresistible, and unresisted, to weave fanciful interpretations and philosophies round the quartet by associating the music of *the whole work* with the subject of the poem which Schubert had set as a song in 1817. He selected the melody of the 1817 song and wrote variations on it for the slow movement of the string quartet; naturally, since the song embodies in music the mood of Death's words in the poem, these variations ring the changes on a limited range of emotions: noble, passionate, austere, sombre, and, at the end, consolatory. But the nineteenth century's incurable tendency to read meanings and fantasies and stories into all music prompted the theory that Schubert was, in the other three movements, also expounding some aspect of Death; the theory reaches absurdity in trying to account for the *siciliano* and tarantella rhythms of the finale. This, mark the word, is called a 'Dance of Death'. If Schubert, like many an artist of his day and race, was interested in the artistic possibilities of the 'Death' motif, it was always the most solemn and profound manifestations which inspired him. To imagine him extending this interest to the flippant and ghastly medievalism of the 'Dance of Death' is only possible to writers who know little of the composer's personality and outlook, and, it must be added, who ignore the *context* of the 'Death' variations. For there is much of grace, vivacity and charm in the quartet movements; much more, in fact, of a healthy artist's absorption in 'Life' than of a morbid one's portrayal of 'Death'.

All the techniques developed in his early quartet writing, perfected in the 'Quartettsatz' of 1820, show rich manifestations in the D minor Quartet. The music is urged forward with a powerful impulse by the pitting of the 'cello in its dramatic, high register, against the sonorities of chords high in the upper strings. Or if

Schubert's mood is lyrical, and the first violin is pouring out its song, he avoids a static congealing of the music's progress by remarkably buoyant figures of accompaniment in the middle strings. The finale of the quartet is perhaps overlong. But the rhythmic and metrical experiments are original to a degree, and although in discussing them similar experiments by Brahms have been mentioned there is little doubt that Schubert's spontaneous and incalculable pen produces results which bear little relationship to Brahms' somewhat deliberate, calculated rhythmic variants. The best of Schubert's experiments in this finale is too long to quote (pages 51 and 52 in the miniature Eulenberg score), but the poignant harmonies which introduce it might be quoted as revealing Schubert's deepening emotion: not pathos, nor the easily solaced sadness of *Erster Verlust*, but a savagery of grief seems to be portrayed here which was to lead to the heartbreak of the 'Winterreise' songs and of *Der Doppelgänger*:

Most musicians are agreed that the D minor String Quartet is Schubert's most successful piece of chamber music, and therefore one of the supreme accomplishments of all chamber music. Although the G major Quartet of 1826 and the C major Quintet of 1828 each contains isolated movements of greater value than the corresponding one in the D minor Quartet, neither of them is, as a whole, so sustainedly great. The finale of the quartet and the first movement of the quintet are inferior. Every single movement of the 'Death and the Maiden' Quartet is a masterpiece. The work was performed in January 1826, and then set aside, never played again, not published until after Schubert's death. What must his inward thoughts have been in considering this music and its—as far as he knew—oblivion? Is there any pain or frustration to be compared to that of the creative artist's, whose work is not so much misunderstood, as politely set aside as of not much account, and then forgotten?

Similar neglect, following upon a single performance, awaited the third piece of chamber music, the octet for clarinet, horn, bassoon, double-bass and string quartet in F major. The work may have been performed privately at Count Troyer's lodgings soon after its composition, but it received a public performance on 16 April 1827 at a concert given by Ignaz Schuppanzigh in the Hall of the 'Musikverein'. A report of the concert spoke well of the music, but grumbled rather at its duration: this is, in fact, nearly an hour. The music was then shelved and remained in obscurity for a quarter of a century, when C. A. Spina published a truncated version as Op. 166.

Schubert's scheme of movements in the octet follows its prototype, that is, Beethoven's Septet in E flat, Op. 20, composed in 1799 when Beethoven was 29 years old. Troyer, without doubt, requested that Beethoven's septet (very popular in Vienna at that time) should be Schubert's model, just as in the case of the *Trout* Quintet, Paumgartner had proposed Hummel's Op. 87. Schubert added a second violin to Beethoven's score, but otherwise he followed the older composer's work closely. The Septet in E flat has a six-movement scheme, Beethoven including a Scherzo as well as a Minuet, a set of variations as well as the conventional slow movement. The Octet in F major is similar, save that the Minuet and Scherzo movements change places. Both first movements and both finales have a slow introduction; in Beethoven these are *Adagio* (18 bars) and *Andante con moto alla marcia* (16 bars), in Schubert they are *Adagio* (18 bars) and *Andante molto* (17 bars). The variation-movement of each composer is *Andante*, 2/4 and placed in the dominant key of the respective work. Besides obvious points of resemblance such as these there are others more subtle; for example, Beethoven foreshadows in his *Adagio* prelude the main theme of the first movement:

and Schubert does the same thing in his first movement:

The publication of the octet in March 1853 omitted Schubert's variations and his minuet so that the work conformed to the four-movement scheme of orthodox 'Sonata-form'. The complete work was not published until 1875. Today, performances of the octet are very frequent. The wonder is that it is performed at all, instead of being, actually, one of his most popular pieces of chamber music. It is a late, 'Romantic' example of the classical 'Cassazione' or 'Divertimento', and a forerunner of the 'Suite' as a series of instrumental pieces not necessarily in dance-forms. This midway and 'transitional' status alone could be sufficient to damn it. Then, in view of its length, and of the players it requires for its performance, one could understand that it might be a rarity in chamber music programmes. When we are inclined to grumble at the neglect of this or that piece of Schubert's, it would be well to cast a glance at the octet, and be grateful that it is not one of them. The music of the octet is as varied as can be wished in such a long work. Schubert's moods range from the light-hearted dance of some of the variations,[1] and the pastoral measure of the 'Minuet', to the passion and ardour of the *Adagio* slow movement and the Finale. In some ways the world of the octet gives us Schubert's world more truly than anything else he wrote; the 'Death and the Maiden' Quartet spiritualises his world, the C major Symphony exalts it to a sublimity and majesty which it only in part possessed. The octet gives us Schubert's everyday Vienna: his bohemianism, his sociability, his exuberance, his easy-going 'bonhomie'; glimpses of the streets and fair-grounds of the city about him; a hint of the theatre, a snatch of song from the coffeehouse and beer-garden; and all conveyed together with the sudden inspirational flash when the poetry and picturesqueness of life in Vienna burn for a moment in his music. The intensely dramatic introduction of the finale (F minor), built on *tremolo* bases like drum-rolls, has more to it than mere preluding. For one thing it re-appears in the course of the main movement with great effect and carrying all kinds of possibilities for 'programme' interpretations. For another, it makes use of the figure from the song *Die Götter Griechenlands*. At this point we may resume discussion of the use of this motif in the 'Menuetto' of the A minor String Quartet. The two motifs from the quartet and the octet are here quoted together:

If the words of the song did, as was previously suggested, articulate a mood of Schubert's in that spring of 1824, then these two motifs may have been derived from the song itself:

[1] The theme of the variations is taken from his early operetta 'Die Freunde von Salamanka'. This was first pointed out by William Glock in his short life of the composer, 'Lives of the Great Composers', ed. A. L. Bacharach, London, 1936.

But it is also more than possible that all three ideas in the song, the quartet and the octet, derive from a common source. A source from which Schubert, while yet preserving his own unique individuality, drew again and again, sometimes consciously, but sometimes subconsciously; for to him, as to all musicians in Vienna, the source was in the heart of their musical being—Beethoven. He is a conscious factor in Schubert's creative work in the octet: is he possibly an unconscious factor too? If so, the source of these motifs is not hard to find:

This is the theme of the 'Trio'-section from Beethoven's Seventh Symphony, in A major, a work whose influence on Schubert was profound and pervasive; we find evidence of it throughout his creative life, in small songs, in large instrumental pieces. The above theme from the 'Trio' of the third movement of Beethoven's symphony was an influence as strong as that of the dactyllic rhythm of the second movement, the *Allegretto*, whose quality has been called 'positively Schubertian'.

IV

The three works, the two string quartets and the octet, form a cohesive group not only on stylistic grounds, but because they have in common their use of melodies from the composer's past—from 'Rosamunde', *Die Freunde von Salamanka*, *Die Götter Griechenlands*, *Der Tod und das Mädchen.* It gives a peculiar aura, a unity, to the trio of compositions. No other group of works by the composer has quite that unity; there is nothing like it in the several Pianoforte Duets which he composed in the summer of 1824 at Zseliz. They form, for all that, a very distinguished group. A set of six marches, the second and third of them the best he ever wrote, were published in May and September of 1825 as Op. 40 (Books I and II). The 'Eight Variations on an Original Theme in A flat' is Schubert's masterpiece in variation-form. It has a majesty, a warmth and a poetry which infuse every bar. The Hungarian 'Divertissement', published as Op. 54 in 1826, was fairly well-known in the nineteenth century and on the whole did not serve Schubert's reputation as an instrumental composer very well. Wagner's and Mendelssohn's derogatory judgements have been mentioned. They are not undeserved. Many of Schubert's faults are present in the duet: triviality (Wagner's complaint about the work), rhythmic monotony (Mendelssohn's complaint, due perhaps to the pseudo-Hungarian atmosphere), protracted repetition; but we find few of his virtues.

The group of duets is dominated by the Sonata in C major, published as the 'Grand Duo', Op. 140, in 1838, and dedicated by the publisher, Diabelli, to Clara Schumann. The term 'Sonata' had ceased to be commercially profitable by 1838, and the appellation 'Grand Duo' has apparently come to stay. It is a great example of the composer's epic style (observe the key), almost the supreme one, and each of its movements is so broadly planned and so generously filled with music, that the proportions of the work suggest a symphony rather than a sonata. The result is not surprising: writers ever since it was first published have wondered if it were a symphony in disguise. Schumann was the first one to propose the idea. He was of the opinion that Schubert had arranged a symphony for PF. Duet until the manuscript came into his wife's possession, a gift from Diabelli, and he saw for himself Schubert's own title: 'Sonata für Pianoforte zu vier Händen' ('Pianoforte Sonata for four hands'). But he could not give up the notion. 'A man who composes so much as Schubert' he wrote, 'is not too particular about the title he dashes down on his work, and it could be that he wrote SONATA at the head of his composition, whilst in his own mind he thought of it as a SYMPHONY.'[1] He then went on to talk of the 'symphonic' effects which are found in the duet, and the resemblances to Beethoven's symphonies: in particular the *Andante* of the Second Symphony, and the finale of the Seventh. His arguments ignore the facts: that Schubert was engaged in teaching two young piano pupils and providing them with material; that the manuscript of the work is beautifully written and represents Schubert's last word; that when he sketched a symphony in PF. score he did not hesitate to write at the top the word 'Symphony'; that all Schubert's big compositions for the piano, from the 'Wanderer' Fantasia at the beginning to the 'Lebensstürme' Duet at the end, teem with 'symphonic' effects, string *tremolandos*, horn and trumpet calls, drum rolls and woodwind 'solos', all of which Schumann spoke of as if they were only to be found in the one work alone. Nearer our own day Sir Donald Tovey follows Schumann. In his 'Essays in Musical Analysis', Volume I, he writes on Joachim's orchestrated version of the duet, and says: 'The GRAND DUO is unique among Schubert's four-handed works in the disconcerting nature of its orchestral style. Not even the FUNERAL MARCH FOR THE CZAR, Op. 55, is so full of the kind of orchestral things the pianoforte obviously cannot do, or so deficient in the things, pianistic or orchestral, that it can do with enjoyment.' Tovey then proceeds to enlarge on another problem altogether, which had, during the nineteenth century, become entangled with the other: whether or not the 'Grand Duo' was the lost 'Gmunden-Gastein' Symphony. Even to entertain the idea that it might be so is to ignore, or to be ignorant of, irreconcilable dates, and other uncompromising facts. Joachim orchestrated the 'Duo' in 1855; there are two other similar versions, by Anthony Collins (1939) and Karl Salomon (1946).

The most conclusive argument against the 'symphony-in-disguise' theory of the 'Duo' lies in the failure of any of these

[1] 'Neue Zeitschrift für Musik', Leipzig, June 1838.

orchestral versions to convince. In its orchestral garb the work betrays, only too obviously, its pianistic origins. Liszt's orchestral version of the 'Wanderer' Fantasia, without question conceived for the piano by Schubert, is more convincing. In so far as Schubert's organisation of a sonata differs from his organisation of a symphony, it is possible to see that the 'Duo' belongs to the former type of work. And its first movement is a close relation of the two solo sonatas, in A minor and C major, which Schubert wrote in the following spring.

All three, for example, open with a pregnant, octave phrase coupled with a few soft chords marking the cadence. They each have a bold, fanfare-like episode of clanging chords, which assumes great importance as the movement proceeds. In the opening movement of all three sonatas there is another feature which gives an underlying unity, almost persuading us that Schubert was writing in them a three-fold expression of one, prevailing, creative mood. It is the way in which the second subject is derived from the first. The two subjects could be looked upon not as contrasting themes, but as two variants of the same theme. The three pairs of themes are briefly quoted here to illustrate the point:

There was a similar evolution of the second subject in the first movement of the octet.

The Sonata in A minor not only preserves a wonderful unity between the parts of the first movement, each part evolving admirably from its predecessor so that the movement has a quality of inevitableness from the dreamy passages at the opening to the tremendous challenge of the last bars, it also possesses a unity from movement to movement. This is possibly deliberate, for the themes of the whole sonata are built on the interval of a third: minor in the first, third and last movements, major in the second movement. The variations of the second movement, the finest set from a prophetic point of view which he wrote, do not quite sound the emotional depths of those in Op. 35, but have all kinds of other advantages, being more concise, easier to play, and simpler of texture. The Scherzo is the best of all the sonata-scherzos and it presents splendid points of development, especially the way in which the rhythm of the opening is clothed with the poignant harmonies of the minor ninth (bars 29 *et seq.*), or delicate melody (bars 42–50). It is fascinating to see the influence of the fifth variation in Beethoven's 'Diabelli' set on Schubert's Scherzo:

Beethoven's 'Diabelli' Variations were re-published in early 1824 as the first part of a collection of variations on the publisher's waltz-theme. The second part contained Schubert's single variation together with the single variations of forty-nine other composers. It is not too much to suppose that Schubert had been playing Beethoven's celebrated '33 Variations' from this big publication, and that the work inspired his own interest in variation-form during these years when he wrote his best work in the form. Not only in the Scherzo of Schubert's sonata, but in the preceding variations-movement, and in the PF. Duet Variations of Op. 35, we find evidence of the deep impression made by Beethoven's 'Diabelli' set.

The companion sonata, unfortunately left incomplete by Schubert, is in C major. The manuscript, dated 'April 1825', was given by Ferdinand Schubert to Schumann on the occasion of his famous visit to Vienna in the spring of 1839. Schumann published the slow movement in his journal, the 'Neue Zeitschrift für Musik', the following December. At some later date his friend Adolf Böttger, divided the music up, and it is now scattered piecemeal over Europe. A page from the first movement (bars 71–135) is in the Fitzwilliam Museum, Cambridge, the rest of the movement is in the Vienna City Library. This Library also possesses the last part of the 'Menuetto' and the 'Trio'. But the whereabouts of the rest of the work is unknown. The last two movements are unfinished but in spite of that the sonata was published by the firm of Whistling, Leipzig in 1861 as 'Last (*sic*) Sonata'. It was given the title 'Reliquie', but the name has never caught on, nor has the work ever established itself in the concert room. Some writers have, with reason, advocated the performance of the first two, complete movements as an 'Unfinished' Sonata. Others consider that the remains of the 'Menuetto' and finale are too substantial to be silenced in this fashion, and attempts to launch the Sonata have been made with *ad hoc* conclusions provided by various pianist-composers; there is one, for example, by Ernst Křenek in 1921. But to no avail.

The first movement is in the composer's grandest style, and if the other movements had been on the level of this one, we should have had a sonata as eminent among its companions as the D minor String Quartet is in its particular sphere. As it is, the slow movement is rather easy-going Schubert, the 'Menuetto' is a fiery movement, with some striking, improvisatory passages in the second half, but the 'Rondo', *Allegro* in 6/8 time, is a trivial piece of writing. Schubert makes one or two noble attempts to deepen the significance of his 'Rondo' theme, and in one episode achieves with his material a sense of tranquillity and repose which proclaims the genius. But he was disheartened by the intractability of his themes and, it has been suggested, laid the work aside for good when he left Vienna for Steyr.

The two sonatas and the 'Duo' provide an excuse for a review of Schubert's pianoforte style in the middle 1820's. The bare octaves and unisons, strong but uncompromising, which he used for the first time in the Sonata in A minor of 1823, Op. 143, are more frequent in these later works, more frequent, but just as tense and unyielding. His piano techniques are simple ones and not altogether free of awkwardness. This lack of grace leads to the accusation 'unpianistic' but the point is that Schubert's techniques are entirely subservient to his material. Whereas Mozart and Beethoven would sacrifice something to shape their material to the demands of the player, Schubert sacrifices nothing. It leads to quite ungainly structures in the C major 'Reliquie' Sonata, which the reader of the music, or the private player, can ignore when lost in the contemplation of that music's grandeur, but which cannot be ignored by the professional pianist or concert audience. Schubert's fondness for broken chords, either supporting right-hand melodies, or themselves supported by striding unisons in the bass, often give a welcome grace to his musical progress especially when they fuse into a lyrically and harmonically developing pianism, grateful to the player's hands:

These extracts are both taken from the last of the three solo sonatas of 1825, the one in D major composed at Gastein in August, and published by Artaria in the following April as Op. 53. It is the least satisfactory of the eight sonatas of his maturity. The techniques mentioned, bare unisons and octaves, broken chords, fanfares of heavy chords, all embody rather second-rate material in this sonata, and Schubert's lush melody, apt to luxuriate in the summer of 1825—we have glanced at a few songs which fail because of it—runs to extravagant lengths in the slow movement and Scherzo of the work. The final Rondo contains a fragile, delicious tune, famous because of its use in the regrettable 'Lilac Time', which introduces a graceful and likeable finale hardly big enough to serve as a conclusion to the three preceding movements. It is a fault with many of his finales, not entirely redeemed in the great Sonata in G major of the following year, 1826. But before we resume Schubert's life in that year it would be profitable to survey his achievement and his powers as a creative artist at the summit of his career.

VI

THE ARTIST

To appreciate Schubert's achievement as an artist, that is, to view his work as a whole and estimate his originality, his workmanship and his range, and do so with a fresh and uninfluenced mind, is today difficult to the point of impossibility. So powerfully original a genius as his produced an ardent and adoring following, impatient of criticism; but it also provoked misunderstanding, misguided interpretation, and even hostility. The years following his posthumous fame abounded in these mixed emotions and very able spokesmen voiced them. Today, the judgements of the middle and late nineteenth-century critics on Schubert are accepted by the majority of music lovers, for, preserved in books and periodicals, these judgements have determined the twentieth century's approach to his music. To reach a portrait of the essential artist behind this firmly entrenched mass of mixed commentary is therefore impossible, for no one can rid his mind completely of it. But some of it must go—it genuinely obstructs a vision of the true Schubert.

It is difficult to keep out of one's words a note of protest in the clearing away of obstructions: but while, it is hoped, the protest will not grow shrill, one has to risk the accusation that a defensive note is unnecessary for Schubert's greatness, that he needs no protest. This is hardly true. No Schubert lover wishes his composer acclaimed for doubtful virtues or from dubious standpoints. Nor, on the other hand, can he leave ill-considered detractions unchallenged. Only from those who view his work steadily, and view it whole, can informed judgements be expected or acceptable. Otherwise distortions of the man and his music will continue to be repeated without challenge.

There is, first, the question of Schubert's 'education' or 'culture'. The point interested Vincent d'Indy and he wrote:

> Schubert must be considered as the type of genius without culture. In forms where a plan is indispensable his works are very unequal, not to say utterly defective....

And to this judgement of a minor French composer may be added that of a similar English one, Hubert Parry:

> Schubert is conspicuous among great composers for the insufficiency of his musical education. His extraordinary gifts and his passion for composing were from the first allowed to luxuriate untrained. He had no great talent for self-criticism, and the least possible feeling for abstract design, and balance and order....

One tries to read these passages patiently and avoid brushing them aside with a word, but they are too widely heeded to be so peremptorily dismissed. But what do d'Indy and Parry mean by 'culture', 'education' and 'training'? They were actually, whether aware of it or not, taking over the critical outlook of the previous generation, which had dubbed Schubert a 'natural' musician, 'untaught, unschool'd', who sang 'as the birds sing', and so forth, because his phenomenal genius and fertility were incomprehensible. But to believe that Schubert had no musical training, and to base arguments on it, is simply false: it ignores the facts. His education, both general and musical, was as thorough, as prolonged and as profitable as that of any of the composers whom Parry had in mind. For five years he attended the chief boarding school in Vienna, one, if not under the direct patronage of the Austrian Imperial Court, at least very closely attached to it. His music teachers were accomplished musicians and one of them, Antonio Salieri, internationally renowned. His friends were poets, painters and composers. Schubert, it is true, knew only Vienna: but what rival, in the world of music, had his city amongst the cities of Europe?

In a letter to Spaun, written during July 1825, Anton Ottenwalt has these words:

> Schubert and I sat together until not far from midnight, and I have never seen him like this, nor heard him: serious, profound, and as

> though inspired. How he talked of art, of poetry, of his youth, of friends, and of other people who matter, of the relationship of ideals to life, etc. I was more and more amazed at such a mind, of which it has been said that its artistic achievement is so unconscious, hardly revealed to, and understood by himself—and so on. Yet how simple was all this! I cannot tell you of the extent and unity of his convictions—but there were glimpses of a world outlook that is not merely acquired, and the share which worthy friends may have in it by no means detracts from the individuality shown by all this.

Both Parry and d'Indy in their remarks on balance and form are voicing the views of their day, a day in which any departure from Beethoven's and Mendelssohn's methods with sonata-form was looked upon almost as heresy: a viewpoint which is to us no longer tenable. It is Schubert's chief glory that he could be contemporary with a dominating figure like Beethoven, without slavishly imitating him. To be fair to Schubert, and despite these detractors, it is easy to name many of his mature works in all of which a 'plan is indispensable' and which display that plan, and which are neither unequal, nor in any way defective: the 'Unfinished' Symphony, the String Quartet in A minor, the last Sonata, in B flat major.

But quite apart from these tentative answers to such judgements on Schubert's 'culture', there is a third, devastating one. Genius is so powerful a factor in these matters, that other factors are, by comparison, negligible. Even if it were true that Schubert is a type of 'genius-without-culture', then that state is all-conquering, and 'talent-with-culture', even if the culture be gathered from the finest flower of the world's scholarship, droops and fails. If musical genius, without plan, or the least feeling for abstract order, can produce the D minor String Quartet, or the String Quintet in C major, then d'Indy's criteria are false ones, and we, and our judgements, are wrong.

The reason why Schubert is criticised on the grounds that his movements lack an organically planned structure, lies possibly in his poetic approach to the composing of music. He wished to feel intensely, and to express to the utmost of his powers, the present moment in his music: not for its significance as a link with what

SCHUBERT
COPPERPLATE ENGRAVING BY J. H. PASSINI FROM RIEDER'S AQUARELL, ON SALE IN VIENNA, DECEMBER 1825
Historische Museum, Vienna

has gone and what is to come, but for its momentary effect as sound, as pleasure for the listener. This is not to say for one moment that he was indifferent to the structural necessities of sonata-form, in fact, the contrary has been urged where his purely transitional passages are concerned; but drive and cohesion —the achievement of which was second nature with Mozart and Beethoven—are not Schubert's first consideration. His invention flows strongly; his themes and episodes and figuration are unified by it, they are not a succession of poetic notions, nor does he simply graft a series of intensely felt miniatures cleverly on to each other.

There are other obstacles in our way, if we wish to see the artist in Schubert clearly. There is the pronouncement, which seems so odd today, that he was deficient in counterpoint, and that this deficiency (somehow bound up with that supposed lack of education) is shown by the absence of *fugato* and *canon* and other academic piquancies in his instrumental work. The counterpoint in the slow movement of the 'Unfinished' Symphony, in the octet, in the 'Variations on an original theme in A flat', Op. 35, and in the slow movement of the great C major Symphony, is not only amply sufficient to dispose of the charge, it positively asserts that his powers as a contrapuntist are equal to those of any of the great composers, when vitality, and musical worth, are the points at issue. That *fugato* and *canon* were not congenial devices of his in composition is, actually, a tribute to his fertility and abundant creative energy. Composers of the post-polyphonic age often resort to antiquarian devices of the kind, and to *stretti*, augmentation, double counterpoint and other favourite scholastic structures, when their creative powers temporarily fail. The cogent words of P. H. Lang have already been quoted in this connection (page 17). Even Beethoven only rarely fuses his creative energy and the *fugato* device: one thinks immediately of the close of the 'Marcia funèbre' in the 'Eroica' Symphony, but parallels to that supreme example are not so common. Schubert was never so much at a loss for what to say as to be obliged to resort to these academic diversions. But he could, when his genius demanded it, use comparable contrapuntal devices to urge his music forward. A superb passage in the finale of the C major Symphony shows canonic tensions set up between trombones and violins at the climax of the development section:

Certain criticisms of his constructional methods are commonly found in analytical treatments of his first movements. They are these: that he writes 'development' episodes in the exposition section; that when he reaches the development section itself he repeats his themes in various keys rather than develop them. Evidence from here and there in his compositions can be adduced to support both of these statements, but they cannot stand against a total view of his work. J. A. Westrup has urged: 'By what rule is development forbidden in an exposition section?' And how, in the light of the superb thematic treatment in work after work of his maturity can he be said to repeat, rather than to develop, his themes? Consider the first movement of the String Quartet in G major: the fusion, the contrasting, of themes, in remote regions of music which his questing mind reaches while he is obsessed with the congenial opening theme—this manipulation is a matter for wonder. He has no formulae, no patterns upon which to build the 'free fantasia'; for him, as for Haydn and Mozart, each development section is an adventurous setting forth, and new challenges bring entirely new responses. Usually, Schubert's main theme, and its attendant subsidiary themes, form the basis of the section, as in all three mature string quartets; but sometimes, as in the String Quintet in C, a minor episode in the exposition section does service, and in the PF. Trio in E flat, a mere idea in the *codetta* of the opening section expands and flowers in the middle of the movement and completely dominates it. His development section may be pure poetry evolving from his stated material as in the PF. Trio in B flat, or it may become a closely argued, logical piece of prose as in the A minor Sonata of 1825, and certainly in the 'Unfinished' Symphony.

And if some of his transitions are accused of being abrupt, e.g. the celebrated presentation of the second subject in the first movement of the 'Unfinished' Symphony (see page 121), others, and they in the majority, are miracles of gradualness and inevitability. Sir Donald Tovey quotes one of them, the return of the main theme in the 1828 Sonata in B flat, praising it almost extravagantly in an essay on Schubert's tonality.[1] The three sonatas of that last year, of which the one in B flat is the third, are full of examples of this masterly transition from section to section.

That Schubert was repetitive, that his rhythmic obsession sometimes produced monotonous results, that his finales are generally inferior to the high level of the preceding movements, that his lengths are not always 'heavenly'—these criticisms can be admitted when they are qualified. For example, when Schubert is accused of being repetitive is it admitted that repetition is an essential ingredient of music in the eighteenth and nineteenth centuries, and that all composers repeat passages in their work, especially if they are pleased with them? Is Schubert more repetitive than Wagner, or Chopin?

When his finales are criticised as unworthy of the rest of the work, does the critic take into account that the importance and elevation of the final movement became established only after the death of Schubert, and that *all* composers prior to, say, Schumann and Mendelssohn wrote light-hearted finales to sonata and quartet and symphony. Beethoven's Ninth Symphony is an exception to the universal trend; but even in that work who would place the

[1] 'Music & Letters', October 1928, page 362.

choral finale in any other but the lowest place if the four movements were set in order of merit? The tendency to strengthen the character of the final symphonic movement, which reaches far out in Brahms and Sibelius, and in composers of the twentieth century, is, from an artistic point of view, sound theory. But in practice it makes heavy demands on the attention of the listener. Audiences of today are more capable, and more willing, to give that attention than were those of the early nineteenth century. As a point of irony it may be urged that Schubert's only mature movement of this kind—the finale of the C major Symphony—probably contributed as much as anything else to the rise in importance of the symphonic finale.

Schubert's exuberances, and trivialities, are occasionally attributed to a lack of 'taste'. Good taste, with no other quality to support it, is a limp attribute. The minor composer, who never offends with exuberances, and never reveals unexpected departures, either upwards or downwards, from a uniform level of achievement, avoids thereby the accusation of 'bad taste'; is this to be preferred to the adventuring, the questing, the vitality of music which refuses *no* path of exploration? Commenting on the music of Hummel, Kreuzer, Spohr, excellent examples of the 'minor' composer just specified, P. H. Lang, in the article already quoted has these words:

> There are no excesses in this music, no confusion, no controversy, no roughness of any kind, and no haphazard gestures—nothing but confidence in a well ordered tonal world, in the excellence of the métier.

When Schubert commences the finale of a PF. Sonata like this:

should 'good taste' have nudged his elbow and suggested more sober paths? Then we should have lost the deliciously tuneful and

May-time dance which originated with those bars, and which embodies the spirit of the Viennese countryside in sunshine and spring. Again one feels that the only satisfactory answer lies in the music itself.

Schumann is responsible for the phrase 'heavenly length' used of Schubert's instrumental movements. The length of a piece of music is not measured by the minutes it takes to play, or by the number of bars in its movements, but by a more intangible quantity—its power to interest the listener; and the issue is complicated by the fact that not all composers are equally interesting to music lovers. If and when Schubert fails to interest, his movement seems long—but duration of time has little to do with it. The fifty minutes of the Octet are unalloyed delight; the forty of the PF. Trio in E flat seem longer than their duration measured by the clock.

And with the mention of that work we may have reached, perhaps, the root cause of the Schubertian mis-judgements and aversions of the nineteenth century: the PF. Trio in E flat. It was a very famous work. It had formed the 'pièce de resistance' of the only public concert which Schubert ever gave, and to which his death, following so tragically soon afterwards, lent an added fame. It was his first composition to be published outside Austria. It was a favourite of Schumann's and he devoted an article to it in his journal 'Neue Zeitschrift der Musik', which was a long and glowing tribute. Years before Schubert's sonatas, quartets or symphonies were known in Germany, this trio was well known and well established. It contains music worthy of Schubert at his greatest, and such music exacted tribute, of course, from musicians everywhere; but it also contains, in greater measure than any other work of its period, the composer's faults. It is long-drawn; it is repetitive; it is diffuse; and its trivialities, the opening of the finale, for instance, seem all the more trivial against the sombre and passionate depths of the slow movement. Its length is exceptional in Schubert's chamber music; the Octet, not very much longer, contains, after all, two extra movements. In addition, where he almost always charms, in the Trio-section of the third movement, writing enchanting melody or devising imitation patterns, this time he fails, composing for the E flat Trio the most heavy footed and enigmatic bars in all the work of his later years. When early critics began to form judgements on Schubert's power as an instrumental composer, the E flat Trio loomed large in their view, and, we now see, too large.

II

It is pleasant to turn from this negative, defensive attitude, to a positive assessment of what Schubert the artist, as craftsman and pioneer, actually achieved, and to begin with what is perhaps his most endearing mass of work—the songs. For although his work in other fields has an equal claim to greatness, it was as a song-writer that he first became known, and as a song-writer that most people immediately think of him. His choice of poems, and the questions raised by that choice, have been discussed earlier. One of his glories is that he lifted inferior verse and sentiment to the heights of his genius, and gave to mild thoughts mildly expressed a universality and power that the poet never dreamed of. 'Winterreise' is the supreme example. Müller's poems relate the grief-crazed wanderings of a jilted lover, now crying out in anguish, now numbed with the thoughts of past happiness, tossed about by stormy weather, frozen by snow and icy winds. But the light of Schubert's genius shines steadily behind Müller's puppet-play until great shadows loom on the firmament; the unhappy lover assumes the tragic aspect of man himself, the wanderings become man's bewildered progress through life, tossed by winds of emotion, frozen by grief. 'Fremd bin ich eingezogen, fremd zieh' ich wieder aus . . .' sings the lover at the start: 'A stranger I came hither, a stranger I depart. . . .' The opening words of the little verse-tragedy, in Schubert's hands, take on the import of man's advent into this world, and his departure from it: the mystery unexplained. The song *Der Lindenbaum*, in which the lover broods on past happy hours with his sweetheart, is elevated by the wonderful music until it is the very essence of man's longing for the innocence of the golden past, of Dante's *Nella miseria*—'There is no unhappiness so great as remembering happier hours'. But 'Winterreise' has many parallels. Any handful of Schubert's masterpieces, *Die junge Nonne*, *Sei mir gegrüsst*, *Aufenthalt*, *Im Frühling*, all these show the miracle at work; the limited, commonplace words, the universal appeal of the song.

It is by seeing the whole corpus of his songs, composed throughout his life, from first to last, that we find the growth of his power in this direction. At first he obsequiously provided the poem with musical illustration; as time went on his composing of songs more and more resembled a process comparable to translation. He created in music the poem's literary values, and at times his music reached the poet's thought and expressed it more trenchantly than the poet himself had done. This differing approach was most tellingly and aptly displayed by Theodor W. Werner in his article on Schubert as a 'self critic'.[1] He discussed Schubert's two settings of Goethe's *Am Flusse*, the first composed in February 1815, the second in December 1822. The poem represents Goethe's emotion 'recollected in tranquillity'. Schubert's earlier setting is passionate, tortured; he gives it the direction *Wehmütig* ('Sorrowful'). The second one is serene, strophic: its equable flow is marked *Moderato*. Schubert in his mature years, it is seen, entered more fully into Goethe's mind—in Werner's phrase, he progressed from the poem to the poet.

The 1822 setting was referred to as 'strophic'. Schubert's varied forms of song are broadly classed into three groups: first, the strophic song, in which each verse is sung to the same melody, with the same accompaniment; second, the *scena* type of song, in which there are several clearly distinct sections with different key-signatures, and *tempo* indications; third, the 'on-running', or *durchkomponiert* song, in which the varying moods and ideas of the poem invoke different musical treatments, but in which a basic unity is obtained by a uniform type of accompaniment. The first group, the 'strophic', comprises also the so-called 'modified strophic' song, where Schubert, to obtain variety, departs from his repeated musical strophes so that on their return they are renewed and fresh to the listener. The well known songs of the 'Schöne Müllerin' song-cycle will serve admirably as illustrations of the various groups:

[1] 'Schubert als Selbstkritik', 'Musica', Cassel, May 1948.

i. *The simple strophic song:*
Mit dem grünen Lautenbande
ii. *The strophic song with refrain:*
Trockne Blumen
iii. *The strophic song with recitative:*
Am Feierabend
iv. *The 'modified' strophic song:*
Pause
v. *The 'scena' song:*
Der Neugierige
vi. *The 'on-running' song:*
Eifersucht und Stolz

It was not, however, Schubert's way to proceed from the strophic song, as an elementary form, to the 'on-running' type as the final crown, so to say, of his work. He wrote strophic songs to the very end of his life—*Am Meer* or *Die Taubenpost*, which is an admirably modified strophic song, are contemporary with *Der Doppelgänger*. It has already been suggested, too, that the strophic *Am Flusse* is a grander achievement than the earlier 'on-running' setting. There has been recently an attempt to review the strophic song, and to question whether the intensive, illustrative type of 'Lied' which was imitated from Hugo Wolf's methods, but without his genius, does not tend to an aridity and songlessness. Brahms asserted that composing the declamatory song was child's play compared with the devising of a satisfactory strophic melody for all the stanzas of the poem. Schönberg has said that he came nearer to the heart of the poem from Schubert's strophic settings than he did from a reading of the poem alone: an extravagant view perhaps, but most singers and students of the Schubert songs will have found that a musical passage has a sharpness which clarifies the poet's text, especially where it deals with deep emotions and sentiments that touch Schubert's sensitive spirit.[1] On many occasions Schubert sets to music a poem in which a repeated emotional pattern is perfectly served by a strophic setting.

[1] 'Das Verhältnis zum Text', in the 'Blaue Reiter', 1912, edited by Marc and Kadinsky.

In the poem 'Frühlingstraum', Müller writes two stanzas, each with a three-fold scheme; the first stanza may be summarised thus:

I dreamed of May and its blossoms/
The cockcrow violently woke me in the icy dawn/
Who painted the frost-flowers on the window pane?

and the second stanza runs:

I dreamed of loving a maiden/
The cockcrow violently woke me from my sore musings/
When the flowers on the pane blossom, shall I hold my love again?

The form of this poem, verse for verse, perfectly fits Schubert's strophic melody.

Because Schubert frequently used a loose, flexible organisation in his 'on-running' songs it would not be true to consider them planless altogether, and that he set them, as it were, piecemeal as he ran through the poem. His method of work was not the same in every case when he composed a song, but there are in existence many of his sketches for songs which he never completed, and it is possible to say that in most cases that method was invariable: his poem first engendered a *melody*. It was not necessarily a melody such as we find in *Die Forelle* or *Who is Sylvia?* The broken, passionate themes in *Gruppe aus dem Tartarus* or *Der Doppelgänger* could equally be the starting point of the song. On the first writing down the melody and its offshoots were shared between the voice and the right hand part of the pianoforte accompaniment, for Schubert indicated in this way the short interludes that were to fall between the vocal phrases. Bass notes were inserted in the left hand part where a touch of Schubertian remoteness in the harmony must not be forgotten. This method of work can be fully studied in the sketch for the unfinished song of 1827 called *Fröhliches Scheiden*. His many sketches also make it clear that modulatory harmony was part of his musical thinking and not born of improvising and exploring at the keyboard. This is particularly clear from the rapid sketch of Karoline Pichler's *Der Unglückliche*, where melody and bass only are written down by Schubert; yet, between them, they suggest all the tonal and harmonic colour which we have in the completed song. Schubert's extant sketches for the first part of the 'Winterreise' (nos. 1 to 12) are important; from them it is clear that the full conception of the song is present in embryo in his first writing down. It is the masterly refinement and added detail which one cannot deduce from these problematic sketches. How will he continue this? one asks. 'But it is the very essence of genius that it can, and does, solve the problems for which the rest of the world can envisage no solution.'[1] This should be remembered when judgements are passed on fragmentary sketches, e.g. those for the third movement of the 'Unfinished' Symphony; we do not know what Schubert might have done with those enigmatic pages.

Yet, when his work is finished, the problems solved, there is a simplicity and inevitability about the music that may deceive the naïve listener or student into imagining that it was all superficial and 'natural'. The very simplicity of means in Schubert's great songs enables him to bring off effects and sudden strokes which the elaborate and sophisticated techniques of later composers, particularly of the French school, miss completely. The poignancy of a climax is driven home with a steely point in a phrase of perhaps two semitones: in Gretchen's song at the words 'And ah! his kiss!' or in the 'Winterreise', when the wanderer ejaculates 'Oh! were the whole world dark!'

Ex. 47

(i) 'Gretchen am Spinnrade'

(ii) 'Einsamkeit'

[1] Winton Dean, 'Tempo', London, 1951–1952.

Harmonically, too, atmosphere can be created by a slight unusualness in the diatonic chords, quite impossible in the rich chromaticism of later epochs. The chord of C minor, for example, instead of an expected 6/4 on the dominant, produces in *Im Abendrot* an effect of piety and nocturnal meditation out of all proportion to the means used (A):

In view of the esteem and love which his songs aroused in his friends and acquaintances, and their ardent interest in his composition of them, it is wonderful that his own integrity, and his faith in himself, should have kept his method of work inviolate. Perhaps Schober's more trivial taste prompted many of Schubert's lighter, lyrical songs, but we need not grieve over that. Spaun, however, commented on Vogl's influence over Schubert by denying that it existed! Schubert's oldest friend was emphatic that no one had any influence over Schubert's compositional methods, and he was surely right. Some firm instinct, true and unerring, told Schubert that he was capable, as no man before him, of fixing in music the cry, the emotion of the human heart. He refused to be tempted away from his path.

III

His methods of work, which we have glanced at in his songs, but which are just as evident in his instrumental compositions, were not understood, and certainly not correctly presented by early biographers; as a result not very serious consideration has been given to Schubert as a craftsman. In those early biographies, Kreissle's, Grove's, Reissmann's, emphasis was laid on the more sensational aspect—his speed of working: a string quartet in a week, a symphony in less than a month, seven songs in one day, and so forth: and these are facts, of course, except that they give the extent of his fair copies of the particular compositions, and we do not know anything of preliminary work on them. But the reader is only too prone to assume that such *speed* of production must be attended by *carelessness* of production. In this connection Parry[1] can be quoted again:

> As a rule this speed of production was almost a necessary condition of Schubert's work in all branches of art. He had no taste for the patient balancing, considering, and re-writing again and again, which was characteristic of Beethoven.

More will be said later on about Schubert's re-writing again and again; here it is enough to say that, when discussing genius, no hard and fast rules can apply. We know today very much more about Schubert's procedures, and his work, than did the biographers of the nineteenth century. The new attitude began with Eusebius Mandyczewski in the 1890's, when every available song manuscript of the composer's was scrutinised and correlated and edited for the ten song-volumes of the 'Gesamtausgabe'. Mandyczewski was staggered to find how many manuscripts often went to the making of one song: two, three, even four versions were made by Schubert in his search for the ideal setting. We know of yet more of these manuscript preparations than Mandyczewski did, and it is a fairly sound surmise that Schubert sketched all his major works, and most of his minor ones, too, and did so throughout his life. Sometimes, in a burst of inspired writing, the sketch needed no radical revision, and so we have those hastily written songs like *Waldesnacht* of December 1820. But it is also obvious that other song manuscripts, for instance, *Der Leiermann* at the close of the 'Winterreise', are beautifully copied from a sketch no longer extant. For a number of Schubert's compositions we possess the finished work and the preparatory sketch, or sketches; those for the PF. Trio in E flat and the 'Unfinished' Symphony provide inexhaustible interest to a student. The sketches already mentioned for the Symphony in D, of 1818, enable us to generalise

[1] 'Studies of Great Composers', London, 1894, page 234.

a little on Schubert's methods with instrumental composition. As with his songs, he starts with a melody: ideas of accompaniment are sketched here and there, sometimes quite fully. Occasionally he will go back and insert the introductory bars. If he decides that, for the sake of balance or amplitude, a few bars must be inserted into music already written down, connecting signs are clearly marked over the insertion and its ultimate place in the sketch. These are 'aides-memoires' for his own benefit.

'His sketches' writes Gerald Abraham, 'are generally shorthand memoranda on a large scale, not germinal ideas to be watered with blood and tears like Beethoven's'; and while this is in the main true it must be pointed out that Beethoven's sketches do not, like Schubert's, tell the whole story: themes and transitions caused Beethoven to shed his blood and tears, but it is obvious that when these difficulties were overcome, he found large tracts of his movements rising as spontaneously and easily to his pen as ever Schubert did. Parry does not mention this fact.

When Schubert's melodic phrases begin to germinate, and ideas grow rapidly in his mind, his writing degenerates to a scribble—but never to illegibility. His mental excitement is obvious in the shaky handwriting. The difficulty which rises, when this kind of composition reaches its perfect expression in his finished work, is that of our intellectual apprehension. When he is intellectually on fire, so much arises in his mind and goes down on to paper at once, that it is impossible to apprehend the creative process: one gratefully accepts the result, but is left with a feeling that the process has elements almost of the supernatural in it. This explains why his friends attributed 'clairvoyance' to his methods, which is an explanation untenable today. In the last resort genius evades analysis, and one is thankful that it is so.

With later instrumental work Schubert's facility is astonishing and the pros and cons of what he intended to set down must have been debated and settled in his mind with hardly any delay. Even then afterthoughts refined and improved his initial ideas. In the manuscript of the Sonata in A minor of 1823 the episode immediately following the announcement of the main theme was revised and altered after its re-appearance in the recapitulation had shown Schubert a better way with it. The alteration in the melody of the slow movement has already been quoted. The change he made in the subject of the *Allegro ma non troppo* of the C major Symphony of 1828 is well known, but, for all that it is so familiar it is an extraordinary modification; being made after the whole movement was written it entailed literally hundreds of revisions of the score.

His alterations sometimes suggest a kind of subconscious cerebration, and certainly the progress of ideas from year to year shows that in the non-conscious depths of his mind there was a continual working at basic musical ideas—ideas, possibly, which he felt were not fully exploited when he first used them. From the string quartets the following two examples will show this process at work, although they show it at its most obvious. In the first 'couplet', the 'cello, pitted against the upper strings, plays a short phrase like a challenge.

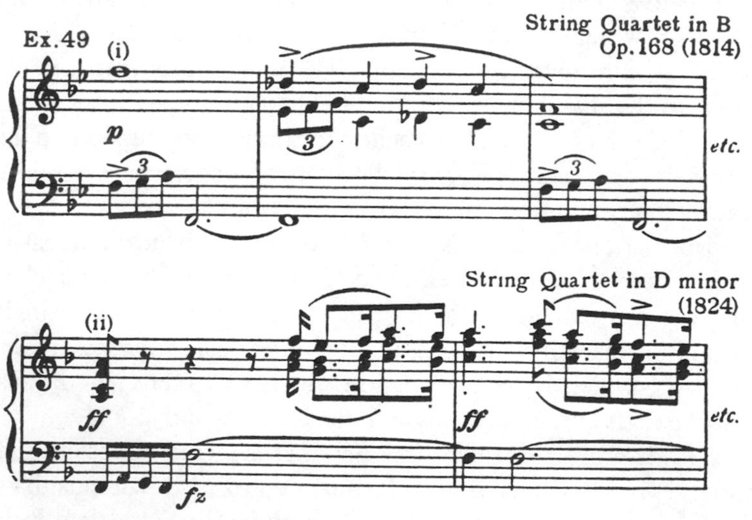

The second pair of extracts form a close parallel; the poignant theme in the first violin, played against *tremolo* strings, is shown in its earliest, and in its latest manifestation:

From his symphonic work the following three short extracts show a favourite type of imitation, which in his mind takes on a more and more dramatic form until in the finale of the last symphony it reaches the culmination of power and excitement:

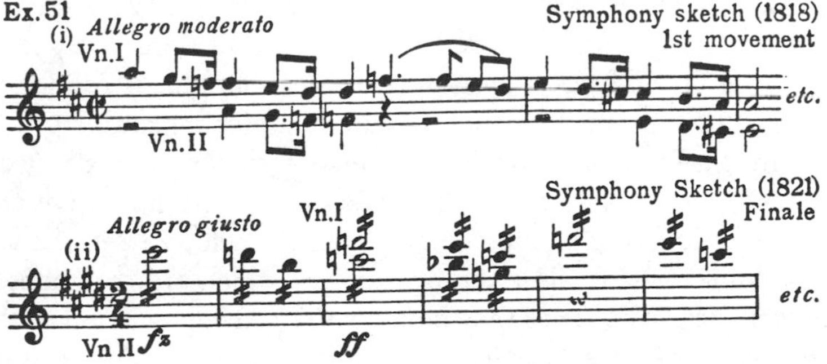

There are in his songs, also, many exemplifications of the unity of his work, the development, when his powers were mature, of embryo ideas which he could not fully use in his youth. The economy of *Der Doppelgänger* is only possible in the master whose youth flung out the extravagance of *Erlking*, and we are fortunate that Schubert encountered the Heine poem at the height of his genius, and the Goethe ballad in his inflammatory youth.

Mention of melodic ideas which re-appear in his work with deeper significance and a more defined emotion, brings the question of his melody, and its characteristics, into the discussion. Of inexhaustible variety and charm it is one of the primary factors of greatness in his music. Whether modern tendencies are really such as genuinely to set aside the basic importance of melody, or whether those tendencies are to set out in directions away from the 'vocal' melody as a basis for musical thought, it cannot be denied that only music which manifests an incomparable gift of melody survives, and that the one linking factor of all the great composers is their singular ability to charm with attractive and lovable melodies. The charm of Schubert's melody is, in the last resort, unanalysable, but certain features which are common to his melodies, in so far as they contribute to an appreciation of the artist at work, are worthy of mention. One striking feature generates a kind of tension, driving his melody onward it is this fondness for chromatic *appoggiaturas*. They have an almost anguished quality—the ear aches for the resolution, and is charmed and soothed when it comes:

The whole of this short waltz could be given as an example. There is a similar, quotable example in *Am Flusse* of 1822, where the A sharp sets up a melodic tension beautifully eased in the passing to A major on the words 'weave her hair'.

Further examples will be found in many of his dances, Op. 33: no. 10 and no. 15; Op. 18: no. 11; Op. 171: no. 3 and no. 5

(particularly in the last dance), and in numerous other songs of which *Letzte Hoffnung* provides excellent uses of the device.

The second subject of the Overture to 'Fierrabras' is perhaps the most rewarding example of this harmonic 'tension' which Schubert can set up in his melodies. The theme is quoted with the harmonic outline only:

The diminished seventh at 'A', a typical 'off-key' start to a theme in B flat major, gives the melody an initial impetus, but the unexpected move of the bass from F natural to F sharp in bar 4 forces the melody to take on shapes of G major and C major. The 'tension' created at 'B' is almost painful in its urgency. But how admirable the workmanship here! The cadence in C major, using the diminished seventh of the opening passes easily and naturally back to the tonality of B flat for a repetition of the tune. How still more admirable the whole 'build' of the overture when it is realised that (1) Schubert's intention all along had been to write a melody in C major, that being the orthodox dominant key of an overture in F major: the whole of the B flat tonality is itself an 'off-key' start to the theme, and (2) the first section came to a close in the required key, C major, but it was at once set aside by the powerful intrusion of a 'German sixth' E flat/G/B flat/C sharp; this chord leads quite naturally into the progression at 'A' in the above example.

A more difficult feature to define, but one which cannot be missed when we hear his melodies, is the strongly characteristic 'finger-print' in his melodic use of the minor mode. It is compounded of a fondness for decorating the dominant of the key with semitones above and below it. Thus, in C minor, the dominant G is approached from F sharp or A flat, and as a kind of corollary, the tonic C is similarly adorned with B natural or D flat. The close of the song *An den Mond* (Hölty) not only reveals both features, it will also serve to show how completely Schubert made these semitonal features a part of his melodic style: could anything be more purely Schubertian than the melody now quoted?

It is seen that the phrase proceeds from G minor (with A flat and F sharp adorning the tonic note) to its close in D minor (the dominant A now associated with G sharp and B flat). The tendency is, naturally, closely related to his partiality for the chord known as the 'Neapolitan' sixth. This chord is based on the semitone above the key note: in C minor it is the chord of D flat major (usually in its so-called 'first inversion', i.e. with F natural as its lowest note). And we find that these chromatic notes stand out like indices of the minor scale for Schubert, for his use of them in his melodies soon pervades his instrumental textures. In the variations of the Octet, a poignant passage in variation V could be quoted as an example. The key is C minor; the theme is played by 'cello and double bass in unison; the descant-like duet for first violin and clarinet in the quotation show the D flat and B natural grace-notes for the tonic note, C, and the dominant is decorated in like fashion by A flat and G flat (=F sharp):

The pathetic tone of the *Andantino* in the Sonata for PF. and violin, known as the 'Duo', is exquisitely conveyed by this 'pointing' of the semitones: in key A flat major, the mediant and the dominant are flecked with chromatic colour in this way (bars 61 to 66). The possibilities of modulation with these chromatic notes seem, in Schubert's hands, inexhaustible.

The so-called 'Hungarian' influence in his melody, and the various folk-song influences which writers from time to time try to persuade us went to the formation of his melodies, can all be largely discounted. Vienna in his day was a cosmopolitan city open to many influences at high and at low levels. The Italian sources and the Italian nourishing of her artistic exploits in architecture, painting and music, the French influences then supplanting those of Italy, the German and English influences on the dramatic and poetic literature of the time, all these higher influences were obvious and acknowledged. The dance rhythms and folk-songs of the Slav and Magyar peoples, nearer than just at Vienna's doorstep, in the house itself, made themselves felt at low levels. But Schubert probably fought consciously against these extraneous tendencies and pulls. To him Mozart and Haydn and Beethoven were the models for his music and, in later life,

Bach. He refused to succumb to Salieri's persuasion over the setting of Italian texts in preference to German, and Rossini's influence quickly passed; it merely stimulated, as suggested already, elements which were part of his innate musical being. When the composer actually used Hungarian themes and idioms he was fully conscious of the presence of them and labelled his work 'Divertissement à l'hongroise'. Themes sometimes quoted by writers as displaying an unconscious Hungarian influence, for instance, the subjects of the finales to the String Quartets in A minor (1824) and G major (1826) and to the E flat Trio (the theme in C minor, marked *L'istesso tempo*), show a facet of Schubert's own style. It appears in his songs, and in his marches for PF. duet written at various periods, and is apparent in work showing no trace of Magyar influences. He was not, apparently, averse to using folk or national songs on occasion but none of these uses is documented with any degree of reliability. The pile drivers' song of Gmunden mentioned in the previous chapter is traditionally spoken of as used in his 'Notturno', Op. 148, but we do not know the name of the song, or anything certain about it. Even less reliable is the suggestion that he used a Swedish song in the slow movement of the E flat Trio. This was first stated by Leopold Sonnleithner, but he did not call it a *folk-song*. The theme, so obviously Schubert's own that it is hard to take Sonnleithner's suggestion seriously, is supposed to have been taken by Schubert from the song 'The sun is sinking' by the Swedish composer Isaak Berg. It has never been traced. To the wrongly named 'Magyar' group, belongs a type of theme which Schubert wrote in later life, a kind of sublimation of those quoted just previously, containing great charm and originality. Little trace of vocal melody remains, the themes are purely instrumental, and depend for their full effect on the inseparably associated harmonic changes which accompany them. Two examples of this wonderful type of instrumental melody are found in the 'Notturno', Op. 148 and in the 'Fantasia' for PF. and violin, Op. 159. The finest example is the attractive theme which opens the 'Fantasia' for PF. Duet which Schubert dedicated to Karoline Esterházy:

Together with this late characteristic might be mentioned an early one. That is the unusual tendency in the years between 1818 to 1822 to repeat short phrases within the melody. The famous tune which forms the second subject in the first movement of the 'Unfinished' Symphony contains an excellent example of this feature, but it is found in many related works of the period:

Sequences, used freely but not obviously by Schubert, have as a rule a harmonic basis. In other words the repeated phrase does not always proceed up or down scalewise, but moves from one harmonic progression to another according to the scheme in Schubert's mind. The song *Who is Sylvia?* illustrates the point well, and here is another, less familiar one, from Estrella's aria *Von Fels und Wald umschlossen* in Act II of 'Alfonso und Estrella':

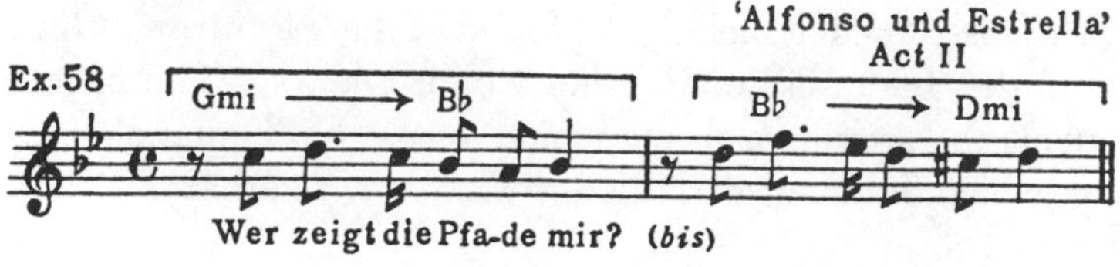

And it is in the extraordinary effects which he achieved by taking his sequences, on this harmonic basis, to extravagant lengths that we find so much to admire and to marvel at. Numerous instances could be quoted but the piquancy of the scheme can be seen in these bars from *Morgengruss* in 'Die schöne Müllerin':

Even more startling juxtapositions occur in the song *Die Liebe hat gelogen* (bars 8–11), where the scheme is C minor—A flat major: C sharp minor—A major. In the song *Delphine*, of 1825, there is an extended sequence of this nature leading to astounding harmonic shifts (from the words 'Wozu auch Blumen reihen und wässern' to '. . . wie verscheinen die Kleider!'). In his instrumental work these sequences are often purely harmonic, that is, they are deficient in, if not devoid of, melodic interest; there are examples in the 'Trio' section of the Scherzo in the 'Death and the Maiden' String Quartet, and in the first movement of the G major String Quartet (bars 210–225). They lead to the association of strangely assorted chords. Quite apart from harmonic sequences, however, there is a development in his later years of this jarring juxtaposition of unrelated chords and tonalities which produce a cold, or stark, emotional effect:

IV

Schubert's harmony is fundamentally that of his own day. He is perhaps overfond of the modulations possible to the diminished seventh chord, although he can use this accommodating 'pivot' in entirely fresh and striking ways (the passage, for instance, in the song *Stimme der Liebe* on a poem by Stolberg, at the words *Tränen der Sehnsucht*, and the *Crucifixus* of the E flat Mass). The chord which displaced the diminished seventh in the affections of the later 'Romantic' composers, namely the augmented fifth, is found occasionally in Schubert also. As a 'passing' chord, the augmented fifth has always been used, of course; it was its use as an unresolved discord, notably by Wagner, that gave it its peculiar significance and colour. But although, strictly speaking, Schubert's use of it is as a 'passing' chord, he dwells upon it at such length, and gives it such emphasis, that he was obviously attracted by its—to his ear—acid quality. There are exceptional uses of it in *Gruppe aus dem Tartarus* and in the *Nachthymne*. In Op. 171, the fifth dance, in B minor, has already been instanced as containing examples of the 'tensions' set up by chromatic discordances between melody and harmony; the same dance also contains a holding of the augmented fifth chord which is suggestive:

An even more emphasised lingering is found in the unfinished Sonata in F minor of 1818 (first movement):

And its repeated occurrences in the 'Sonnett III' of Petrarch (1818) give passing touches of weirdness to the music:

These harmonic resources are enriched by various chords of the sixth, the so-called 'French' and 'German' sixths, and the 'Neapolitan' sixth, mentioned previously, for all of which Schubert showed a marked fondness, especially for the third of these chords. In his young days Schubert's love of these colourful chords was an obsession; the secondary songs of 1815 and 1816, especially the longer ballads, use the progressions based on these sixths almost *ad nauseam*. In later life his use was more sparing, and more telling:

But of the chord of the 'Neapolitan' sixth—which is a *common* chord on the semitone above the key-note, he never tired. His uses of this chord, as a melodic 'spicing', as a cadence, as a harmonic progression, as a basis for modulation, are so numerous that one must put it at the head of all that is implied by Schubertian device and characteristic. One instance can be given here, his loveliest use of it, perhaps the most exquisite bars he ever wrote. They come from the first movement of the C major Symphony, in the recapitulation of the second subject. This is, with typical unorthodoxy, in C minor, and the return to the orthodox key of A minor is managed by this use of the 'Neapolitan' chord:

The music then moves at once into G minor, and the above bars are treated sequentially, so that G minor proceeds to A minor.

The most familiar of his practices, the shift from minor to major, and *vice versa*, and the drop to a key a third below his tonic key, have been so fully discussed, annotated and quoted by scholars, that a mere mention of them here is all that is necessary; they are so much a part of his musical thinking, and consequently so much a part of his musical heritage, that numerous references have, in any case, been made to them already. But another, less familiar feature, may be noted in connection with these shifts, and that is his frequent practice of starting outside his main key, and then swinging into it with a charming effect that may have a variety of emotional reactions. There may be surprise, as in the finale of the 'posthumous' Sonata in B flat, since the key seems to be established as C minor; there may be a darkening, tragic effect, as when the placid D flat harmonies which open the song *Memnon* unexpectedly drop into B flat minor; there may be a freshness, a vivacity, as in the Waltz, Op. 9: no. 29; or there may be a feeling of satisfaction, of homecoming, as in the 3rd Ländler of Op. 171, which has already been quoted on page 129. *Memnon* was quoted from the songs: there are many more similar uses there. In *Auf dem Wasser zu singen* the key of A flat minor at the start is held right through the song for the pure joy of a flood of bright tone-colour when the key of A flat major is reached, and the watery scene of the poem is bathed in sunset radiance. Depths of meaning and significance are achieved if he delays the main key because the poet's words suggest a refined use of the procedure. Both Tovey and Capell dwell affectionately, in this connection, on the wonderful way in which the main key of C major is held back in the song *Dass sie hier gewesen*, so that the preliminary remarks of the poet are given ambiguous harmonies, and the diatonic C major is not used until at length the words 'I know that she has been here' are sung. The chords at the start of the song—they have been called 'ambiguous' only in the sense that they are non-committal in the key of the song—form one example of Schubert's fondness for the occasional, inexplicable chord: others can be found in the coda of the first movement of the 'Death and the Maiden' String Quartet, and in the slow movement of the Sonata in A minor, Op. 143. They give his music a momentary darkness, a crudity, from which it emerges into his more usual sunny and equable moods with a renewed charm.

One feature of his harmony has no convenient label, except the vague one of 'chromatic'; yet once seized upon, and understood, it can exercise by its surprising originality and skill, a fascination which is like a spell. It is his supreme ability to sense the possibility of chromatic progressions, which are not obvious or implied, in the course of the diatonic notes in his melody. So skilful and delicate are these harmonic processes that it is not easy to discuss them in words. A simple example must be given, more obvious than most, to make the point plain. The melody which is quoted in the next example is simple and familiar: it is the close of the song *Hark! hark! the lark!*:

At 'A', Schubert's harmonies produce a modulation to D minor. Granted that many composers would avoid the tonic chord of C major at this point, it is doubtful whether anyone but Schubert would have avoided it in such an unusual way, but a way which, once discovered, seems inevitable. A song which will yield rich rewards in this field is the lightly regarded *Ungeduld* from the 'Schöne Müllerin' cycle, and an even more astonishing feat of unusual harmonic progression is brought off in the almost unknown *Totenkranz für ein Kind*. It would be a fascinating experiment to give this melody to a score of composers and see whether any one of them would hit upon Schubert's incredible cadences, drawn from the note progressions.

V

Schubert's piano techniques were briefly discussed in the previous chapter. They are not unassailable, and if it were possible to consider them apart from the material they embody, we might agree that he shows in them a 'half-mastery' of the keyboard, as it has been called. But in his orchestral and chamber-music techniques, he is a master among masters. The opportunities of his schooldays in the *Stadtkonvikt*, when intimate acquaintance with orchestras and chamber ensembles was an everyday experience for him, have been discussed. It is clear, right from the start, that such techniques were acquired easily and thoroughly from first-hand sources. Naturally, as his music gained individuality and depth with the passing years those techniques served a richer personality, but the first symphony and the first quartet are perfectly written for their respective mediums. These two mediums, the orchestral and the quartet, are chosen because by general agreement they represent the peak of a composer's technical achievement, and, in Schubert's case, his quartet techniques appear also in other chamber-music combinations. An individual feature of his orchestral writing is his partiality for violent contrasts, either of dynamics, or of instrumentation. This feature was one which he derived from Mozart. One of the most moving examples is the bar or two of quiet oboe melody which interrupt the progress of a *fortissimo* orchestral passage in the *Andante* of the 'Unfinished' Symphony, but equally effective contrasts between such solo and *tutti* passages add thrilling moments to the 'Alfonso und Estrella' Overture. His 'conversational' solos between the woodwind instruments are renowned, but they are a feature of his more mature works, first appearing markedly in the sketched Symphony in E, of 1821. The use, though, of three trombones, which did not appear in the Beethoven orchestra until the fifth Symphony, in C minor (1805), was Schubert's habit in the earliest orchestral works. It is in the advanced treatment of these instruments that his chief contribution to orchestral technique lies. They are not merely brought in to re-inforce climaxes, but are used with much expressiveness, often *pianissimo*, and the third trombone is frequently used as a bass for flutes and clarinets. Their solo entries in the first movement of the great C major Symphony are of the essence of epic poetry. He is fond of scoring his melodies for violins and bassoons in octaves, which gives a certain 'difference' to the *timbre* of his music, and the combination of horns and bassoons for dark, 'middle register' chords was a happy and original stroke; this tone colour opens the slow movement of the 'Unfinished' Symphony and, with the *pizzicato* bass strings, announces a different symphonic world from those of Mozart and Beethoven. Various individual points of orchestration are famous in his two mature symphonies. The 'call' phrases of the horn, in both the symphonic slow movements, in the episode leading to the recapitulation, are of the highest poetry and Schumann wrote a well-known and enthusiastic page on the second of them, likening the horn to a visitant from another world as it softly sounds among the even softer strings. There is an equally beautiful 'call' phrase given to the horn in the 'Kyrie' of the E flat Mass, at the same formal point.

Several references to his string quartet writing have been made in earlier chapters. As a contrast to the bold use of the 'cello in his later string quartets, we could instance his conventional and timid treatment of the viola. The emergence of the viola as the solo instrument of the string quartet is a feature of late nineteenth-century techniques: to Schubert (who himself played the viola), it was, in general, a filling-in instrument. One feature of his quartet writing, which persisted right to the very last, was his addiction to the use of *tremolo* bowing. This is usually not considered very good form in quartet technique, suggesting orchestral colour and procedure. But it depends on the quality of the music so scored: Schubert's parts are lively and complex; they are as frequently *pianissimo* as otherwise; the melodies so accompanied are elaborately phrased and divided between the instruments. It is a legitimate device if used, as he used it, powerfully, and no one would deny its attractive quality both to players and listeners. In the String Quintet of 1828, there is an interesting development of his quartet techniques. The device of the 'duet' for two stringed instruments is also a prominent characteristic of the Quintet. It is played by the two violins, or the two 'cellos, accompanied by the other three instruments. Alternatively, in the *Adagio*, the three 'middle' instruments play the theme and the 'outer' instruments first violin and second 'cello, embroider and decorate. His Quintet, in other words, resolves itself into a violin duet, or a 'cello duet, or a trio with violin and 'cello *obbligato*. In all three cases the viola is, if not negligible, subordinate. It is now of interest to contrast this technique with that of Mozart, who, in his String

Quintets uses an antiphony of two string trios; his two violins and first viola are contrasted with the two violas and 'cello. Mozart's first viola is now the bass of the first 'Trio', now the treble of the second 'Trio'.

Perhaps the most notable feature of Schubert's technical handling of the pianoforte in chamber ensembles is his treatment of it as a purely melodic instrument. This was mentioned in connection with the *Trout* Quintet, but further examples are to be found in profusion in the two PF. Trios, in B flat and E flat.

The criticism of his pianoforte style applies chiefly to his sonatas. A more lyrical pianism is used in the Impromptus, Moments Musicaux, and in the shorter, isolated pieces which he may have intended to publish as similar essays, such as the 'Drei Klavierstücke' of 1828. In these short pieces Schubert is famous as an innovator; he is looked upon as the forerunner of the 'Romantic' school, in which composers like Schumann and Chopin were able, through his example, to throw off the shackles of 'Sonata-form'. It is, of course, a greatly simplified view, and takes no account of the fact that minor composers such as John Field, Václav Tomašek and Johann Worzischek, had already established the short, piano piece in the early years of the century. Tomašek in particular is a forerunner of Schubert in this sphere, and his influence on the composer is much more certain than Schubert's, say, on Chopin. The very frequent use by Schubert of broken chords whose top notes coincide with the notes of his melody is a pure Tomašekian procedure, and even the lesser man's melodies contributed something to Schubert's. Here is the theme of Tomašek's 'Eclogue', Op. 51: no. 6, written in 1815:

We have only to think of the prelude to Schubert's song *Pause*, or the 'Trio' section of the Scherzo in the D minor String Quartet, to feel that the lesser composer's work had no inconsiderable effect on Schubert's development. But although, apart from his songs and lyrical pieces for the pianoforte, Schubert was not, from the point of view of 'Form', a pioneer, as far as harmonic and tonal range, and emotional content, are concerned, he is one of music's foremost innovators. The 'Romantic' movement in the arts sprang from the literary 'Storm and Stress' movement of the eighteenth century; it was held in check by the little reactionary movements which followed that tumult, and during which Schubert lived. But he is an initiator in emotional content, and in the 'atmosphere' which he evoked by his chromatic warmth and richness. When he wrote the theme of the 'Quartettsatz' in 1820, he produced a typical 'Romantic' theme whose echoes resound throughout the nineteenth century.

The shifting, melting chromaticism of his melody and harmony were to lead to the slow movement of Schumann's PF. Trio in D minor, Op. 63, and that, in turn, to the Prelude to 'Tristan und Isolde'.

It is not the formal changes in the 'Romantic' period which are so remarkable, but the re-orientation of musical thought, the different aims of composers in using their *materia musica*, and this is the sense in which Schubert is a pioneer. In matters of form, however much he may have distorted structures, he remains the last of the classical composers. He could not, living in the Vienna that had been the scene of Mozart's and Haydn's productions, which was even then witnessing the work of Beethoven, ignore his immediate past and escape from the pressure of his present. In matters of content, he may be perhaps the first of the 'Romantic' composers. But while his music cannot be looked upon simply as an Indian summer of the great Viennese classical period, nor can it be thought of simply as the precursor of the 'Romantic' school; both elements are present, the former the more strongly. There is in his work, as Alfred Einstein wrote, 'a lost paradise of purity, spontaneity and innocence.' And this suggests the 'Classical' master rather than the 'Romantic'. Whatever the 'Romantic' school was, it was not 'innocent'.

A word must be spared for one department of his music which, although not entirely neglected in performance, is strangely left out of account in consideration of his work as a whole, that is, the dance music. This vast mass of work, chiefly for the pianoforte, and extending from his very earliest years almost to the end of his life, is even yet not properly catalogued and identified. O. E. Deutsch, in his 'Thematic Catalogue', makes a brave effort, but leaving, as he does, the numerous dances in their haphazard assemblies as Opus-numbers, merely ignores the problem. Nor has the influence of these dances on his other work been adequately traced. For to Schubert, his short dance-pieces were the equivalent of the 'journals', the 'diaries', the 'note-books' of his fellow authors in the literary and artistic worlds. In them he jotted down ideas, he tried out pianoforte techniques, he sketched instrumental movements; and in them he embodied the moods and emotions of his passing days when larger work did not suit him. Much of his dance music was, we have it recorded by his friends, the fruit of hours of improvisation at the piano, while those friends danced. With a relaxed, but active mind, and busy fingers, and with the stimulus of an *ostinato* dance rhythm, the music welled up, and was embodied in the piano dances. It is fascinating to read through these 'journals', and to try to decipher them. One example of a sketched instrumental movement may be quoted. Here is the sixth dance of Op. 171, written in 1823; the continuation further on, in bar 7, is even more suggestive of the Scherzo in the D minor Quartet which it shortly became:

The quality of the music in these few bars indicates how far Schubert was prepared to take the simple music of the Ländler, in key, in style, and in thematic importance.

VI

The contrast between the pianistic style of writing shown in Schubert's sonatas and that in the Impromptus and dances is fundamental. To him the PF. sonata was, like the symphony and string quartet, an exalted form calling for more elevated and authoritative thought. The shorter pieces are more homely and intimate. It is true that one Impromptu, Op. 90: no. 1, opens in a manner suggesting a sonata, but the impression passes as the piece gets under way. No amount of taking thought would, of course, enable a minor composer to achieve the 'grand style', by which phrase Matthew Arnold designated the style of Shakespeare and Dante and Goethe. But Schubert shares with the other great composers of his race the supreme power of this 'grand style' of utterance by natural endowment. It is the non-Viennese quality in his physical and mental inheritance. He can, like Beethoven and Mozart, lay it aside temporarily, but it, and not the homelier, Viennese ways of speech, is his natural voice, and the more modest pieces and songs may at any moment swing up and out into music composed in this universal and timeless style of his. When Schubert wrote in his more unassuming vein, it was chiefly because he was being sociable, that is, he was accommodating his music to largely unmusical people, to those who danced, or worshipped, or wept and languished to his songs. For them he adopted the immediate idiom of his day, or even of his yesterday. He produced work without the true Schubertian fire, though unmistakably his. For with him art was never self-conscious. His technique was at his finger-tips, acquired and then forgotten. Dr. Walter Ford writing on these matters in connection with Schubert, states that 'self-consciousness fosters exaggerated sensibility and a limited outlook . . . idiosyncrasies of style [lapse] in the end into mannerisms and weaknesses'.[1]

Schubert's utter self-devotion to his genius made him abandon all regular methods of earning a living; it was not to spend his days in Bohemian idleness or conviviality, but to devote himself solely to the hard work of learning his craft as a composer. His decision makes the charge of 'dilettante', sometimes levelled at him, a preposterous accusation. This is how such an accusation was worded in the 'Edinburgh Review' of October 1883:

> His attitude towards the art was throughout his life that of a very gifted amateur, who wants art just as far as he can get enjoyment out of it, and turns away at the point where hard work begins. . . .

It is hard to refute this with patience. Josef Hüttenbrenner was probably telling the truth when he reported that the easy way of earning money by giving lessons was refused by Schubert who said that he would rather eat dry bread than do so, for lessons would interrupt the tireless application to his musical work, and deflect his energies. He never swerved from his high ideals; even though he was not entirely aware of the greatness and force of his own genius, he never, in order to earn a living, descended to the

[1] 'Music & Letters', London, October 1928.

easy production of inferior, catch-penny work, nor to the undertaking of regular hack-work, for that would have prevented the total dedication to his art. Anything less like the amateur, the dilettante, or the idling Bohemian of the arts can hardly be imagined. He was, and made himself so by hard work, the professional composer *par excellence*.

It might perhaps be a fitting conclusion to this chapter on Schubert's art, to consider in a brief paragraph what not to look for in Schubert. The very elements which many music lovers find most congenial are either absent altogether in his music, or only briefly encountered: wit, understatement, sophistication, picturesqueness, delicacy, bravura. These attractive qualities must be sought elsewhere, in the songs and piano pieces and orchestral suites of other men. Schubert's song-texts are neither erotic nor cynical. His expression is full-blooded, personal, extravagant, and the nearest he gets to humour, as Richard Capell has said, is good-humour; but it is not an urbane expression, nor an introverted one, and it is the power already spoken of, by which his music achieves sublimity, and radiates a 'light that never was on sea or land', that raises him above the level of the lesser composers, who are otherwise almost his equals in melodic charm and the affectionate spirit.

VII

1826-1827

I

A restless searching for a means of livelihood: that is the impression one gets from the records of these two years in Schubert's life; a means of livelihood which would leave him with leisure enough for his composing, and one which would not make such excessive demands on his powers as teaching had done. His words to Josef Hüttenbrenner, already quoted, were: 'I would rather eat dry bread than teach.' And we cannot wonder at this decision when we read Hüttenbrenner's further information that in his father's school, Schubert taught for nine hours a day. But neither would he now accept the kind of teaching post that had he done in 1824, as a music master to the Esterházy household. Instead he applied for positions as music director (Kapellmeister), sought a favourable play for an opera libretto, and wrote to publishing firms in Germany, offering them various compositions. In Vienna itself his work was being published at a rate which could not last: in 1826, twenty works were engraved and published, in 1827, twenty-two. Not that he was unable to keep up this rate of supply; he could easily have done so, but the public was surfeited, and the publishers grew cautious. Writing in those days from Vienna to a Leipzig music periodical, a journalist said of Schubert and his songs:

> He works almost too much at this species, and earlier excellent things are scarcely to be surpassed by the good ones which follow.

And yet the efforts to find a post, to establish himself in opera, or to make a name in Germany, misfired, and not altogether by an unlucky combination of circumstances; partly it was by reason of complex elements in his own character. The initial impulse was dissipated, and the slightest discouragement acted like a snub. Not for him the fighting persistence of Beethoven or Wagner, the dogged perseverance of Brahms. A factor which emerges from the reminiscences and memoirs of his friends and acquaintances, recorded years after his death, is that he was reluctant to invite them to his paternal home, and avoided, if possible, their calling on him there. His origins were of the humblest; there was in Vienna no social standing in the calling of a schoolmaster, and Franz Schubert senior was, in addition, desperately poor. The son, finding that his music opened doors into social circles far above him, did what many other artists have done before him, and since: without allowing it to change his affection for, or loyalty towards, the members of his family, he concealed those humble origins. But such concealment, and the sensitive pride which engenders it, are bound to take their toll of self-confidence. His shyness, remarked upon by strangers who met him, may well have been an involuntary defence against any advances which might penetrate his reserve in these matters. His modesty was, perhaps, the outcome of a conflict between two opposing emotions: unwilling shame over his lowly birth and upbringing and supremely confident belief in his own ability, and in the greatness of his own musical endowment. So the drive forward was made with initial confidence, and after a while the impetus was lost. Schubert, the musical giant, was time and again unable to put aside the insignificance attaching to the youngest son of a humble and penurious schoolmaster.

Actually, in the February of 1826, that humble schoolmaster received an overdue recognition of his tireless and unremitting work in Vienna's schools. As the conclusion of his forty-five years of teaching drew near, neighbours and fellow citizens in the Rossau district petitioned the Court that he be awarded the freedom of the City of Vienna. On 23 February 1826, Franz Theodor took the burgess's oath. But no word on the event from his son is extant.

Schubert's compositions of December 1825 and January 1826 were some half a dozen settings of poems by Ernst Schulze. They were written in his lodgings near the Karlskirche. Like the Säulengasse house, this dwelling place of Schubert's is still standing in Vienna, decayed but picturesque, and having an authentic suggestion of old Vienna in its ungroomed, unaltered antiquity. In addition to composing the Schulze songs there, he was that winter revising—it is not known how thoroughly—the D minor String Quartet. He had written of it, in 1824, as finished, and it is doubtful whether the revision was very extensive. The date 'January 1826' still attaches itself to the work because of this possible retouching. Schubert had only to lift his eyes from the pages of his manuscript to glimpse through his window the symbolical sculpture at the approaches to the Karlskirche. The 'Death' symbol of his quartet is precisely of the same kind as the huge skull which he could see amongst that sculpture. The trappings of Death were part of baroque decoration; to Schubert, in literature, they were the same. Neither in January 1826, nor at any other time, was he morbidly attracted to 'Death' poetry, nor 'Death' imagery.

The quartet was rehearsed on 29 and 30 January by a group of friends, the first violin being Josef Hauer, who later on related that at this rehearsal Schubert corrected the freshly written parts, and also cut out sections of the work. These were, of course, temporary cuts for the forthcoming performance; the score, the source of the work, was not in any way abridged. The work was first performed at the house of the lawyer Josef Barth, a friend of Spaun and of Schubert. He was an amateur musician and singer. For him, it will be recalled, Schubert played a simplified version of the accompaniment to the *Erlking*, and he also dedicated to Barth the part-songs of Op. 11. A second performance followed later on, in February, at the residence of Franz Lachner. The work remained in manuscript until Czerny of Vienna published it, posthumously, in July 1831.

The young comedienne and singer, Sophie Müller, entertained Schubert and Vogl several times during the course of the year at her villa in Hietzing; it is easily reached from the Karlskirche district and lies to the north of Schönbrunn.[1] Schubert took his songs to these social evenings and Sophie or Vogl sang them. Songs such as *Die junge Nonne* (which Sophie is said to have sung

[1] It is today the Hietzing suburb of the city.

at sight), *Die Rose*, Annot Lyle's and Ellen's songs from the Scott romances, were well suited to her voice and Anselm Hüttenbrenner wrote that she sang them 'most touchingly'. She died, tragically young, a year or so after Schubert's death.

In April Schubert applied for the post of assistant music director (*Vice-Hofkapellmeister*) to the Court Chapel. The vacancy was caused by the promotion of Josef Eybler to the principal Directorship, a position never filled by the Emperor since Salieri had left it in 1824. The fact of Schubert's application has always been known, but the actual document, in his hand, was not discovered until 1895. It was then found among papers in the possession of descendants of Maria Theresa, Schubert's younger sister, and published for the first time. It is couched in the usual obsequious terms which are used to ruling princes and their Court officials. The only points of interest in the list of facts provided by Schubert as evidences of his suitability for the post are (1) he claims that by his vocal and instrumental compositions his name has become known in the whole of Germany as well as in Vienna and (2) he states that he has to hand five Masses, all of which have already been performed in various Vienna churches. Usually he is so indifferent to the past works of his youth that to have these Masses correctly remembered and numbered is unique. That all had been performed is very likely; but there are no records in the case of the second and third (G major and B flat major). That his name was so widely known is an understandable exaggeration of the facts, but it does suggest that Schubert may have received, and read, the reports and reviews on his work which were being printed in various German periodicals. His application is dated 7 April 1826. Since the post had been vacant for two years without any serious dislocation of the music performances in the Court Chapel it is no surprise to find that the business of filling the post was taken at a pace even more leisurely than usual. On 19 December the final list of applicants was prepared for the Court Chamberlain, Prince Ferdinand Trauttmansdorff, the same man, incidentally, who had sanctioned Schubert's boyhood appointment to the choir of the Court Chapel. There were seven applicants besides Schubert and, with one obscure exception, all the names are familiar to readers of musical biography. But the eight men were passed over, and the candidate named for approval by the Court was Josef Weigl, the principal conductor of the Court theatres. A month later the appointment of Weigl was confirmed, and Schubert informed of his failure on 27 January 1827. Both Spaun and Bauernfeld mentioned the appointment in their memoirs, but in both records there is possibly more of their individual reaction to the affair, than an accurate memory of Schubert's own.

The coming of Franz and Fritz von Hartmann with their friend Ferdinand Walcher into the Schubert circle coincided with Spaun's re-appearance in Vienna. He returned on 20 April and was continually with Schubert. The composer had regained an old friend, but he lost a new one for Bauernfeld had left Vienna on 15 April for several months in Carinthia. Bauernfeld was not without a certain shrewd power of assessing a man's worth—his comments on Schober, Schwind and Schubert, written at various times in his journal, are apt and revealing; but he was volatile, satirical and facetious. He became famous in middle life as a writer of comedies, and even produced a mild, nineteenth-century equivalent of 'Animal Farm', in which the politics of his day were satirised in the form of a fable. As a youth, in Schubert's company, he was rather the self-appointed 'life-and-soul-of-the-party' and no friend, in the sense that Spaun was. Sometimes his suggestions and decisions showed a complete lack of wisdom, so that Schubert withdrew: there was the suggestion, for example, that he, Schwind and Schubert should live together and pool expenses. This they never did, and it was Schubert who discouraged the idea.

Bauernfeld's Carinthian tour was a prelude to his undertaking a position in a government department concerned with affairs in Lower Austria, so that it was partly business, partly pleasure. He had promised Schubert to write an opera libretto, and the composer's ardent interest in the progress of the work shows his eager grasping of this renewed opportunity to establish himself. But Bauernfeld's lack of wisdom is evident in the story he decided upon —'Der Graf von Gleichen'. The plot hinges on a bigamous marriage and would never have been passed by the censor of the day. Yet, half-knowing this, he persisted in his writing. Apart from its subject, it will be seen from the poet's journal what a dreary repetition of stock material he would present to the unlucky composer:

> ... I thought of the libretto for Schubert and set to work on 'Der Graf von Gleichen'. Dramatic and musical contrasts; orient and occident, janissaries and knighthood, romantic wooing and wedded love etc.—in short, a Turkish-Christian outline. The verses flow pretty easily for me.

After Schubert had sent in his application for the Court *Kapellmeister* position, it is possible that he may have tried to obtain a post as assistant conductor in the Kärntnertor theatre. The story was first related by Anton Schindler in 1857. According to this account Schubert composed a portion of an opera-libretto, and the music was then put into rehearsal. The ageing soprano, Nanette Schechner, broke down owing to the difficulty of his music and to the fact that her powers were failing. Schubert became obstinately angry, refused to alter anything, and left the theatre in a fury of disgust. Most of this is pure invention. In May 1826 Nanette Schechner was twenty years old and had just made her first appearance in Vienna. A letter of Schubert's was written that very month: it gives in an extraordinary fashion the *coup de grâce* to Schindler's inventions; he wrote to Bauernfeld in Villach that 'Mlle. Schechner has appeared here in "Die Schweizer Familie" and pleased enormously. As she looks very like Milder, she might be good enough for us'. Schober also wrote a month later to Bauernfeld and said: 'In matters theatrical I inform you only that Mlle. Schechner revolutionises the town by her wonderful singing in *German*. Since Milder it is said that no such voice has set the air vibrating, and she is still youthful, pretty and vivacious into the bargain. Schubert has heard her and chimes into the hymn of praise.' And it is this voice that we are asked to believe was unable, through age and incapacity, to perform some vocal music by Schubert. It is hardly necessary to add that Schindler was unaware of the existence of these two letters. We might also ask: if Schubert were applying for the post of an assistant *conductor*, why was he required to *compose* music? The obvious course would have been to ask him to conduct Mlle. Schechner in an aria of her own choice—say from *Die Schweizer Familie*.

And this suggests what is probably the truth of the matter, if there is anything in it at all. It was Schubert's conducting, not his composing, which failed to please the authorities, and it is quite possible that a singer could not accommodate her voice to arbitrary tempo or dynamics. The touch of obstinacy in Schindler's anecdote has an authentic ring, and if Schubert refused to slow down or to quieten his accompaniment, then the *prima donna* might very well break down.

II

Schubert tried no more for positions of the kind. An operatic success, publication of work, gifts from patrons, and perhaps a concert of his own music, these were now his aims. The last idea loomed larger in his mind as the time passed, and both Schwind and Bauernfeld urged the matter of a concert devoted solely to his compositions. As for publication, the stream rose steadily; in the first four months of 1826 five publishers were issuing his compositions. Pennauer brought out the Sonata in A minor, Op. 42; Matthias Artaria the Sonata in D major, Op. 53, and the seven Walter Scott settings as Op. 52; Cappi the 'Marche funèbre on the death of Alexander I' for PF. Duet, Op. 55; Thaddeus Weigl (brother of Josef, the yet to be successful candidate for the Court *Kapellmeister* position) the songs of Opp. 57 and 58; and Sauer & Leidesdorf the Overture to 'Alfonso und Estrella', arranged by Schubert for PF. Duet, Op. 69. This overture was overlooked and not re-published when the 'Gesamtausgabe' of Schubert's works was organised by Breitkopf & Härtel; it remains inaccessible. It was dedicated to Anna Hönig, sister of Karl Hönig, Schubert's lawyer friend. Schwind was her constant wooer, but her intensely religious views were leading to a slight friction between them. The reader of the Schubert 'Documents' will find a misleading description of the overture on page 510, where it is said to draw on themes from the opera. It suggests that here is a second overture, different from the earlier, well-known work. This is not the case. The duet is merely an arrangement of the familiar overture in D minor/major, in which none of the material is taken from the opera itself.

At the close of June, Schubert, whose pen had been idle for months, composed his last string quartet, in G major. It is a supreme work, flawed only in its over-facile finale; but the three preceding movements are of an unsurpassed greatness. Without the humanity of its predecessors, in A minor and D minor, and hence without their popular appeal, it has a grandeur and breadth of conception which their more modest dimensions could not compass. It was performed privately in Vienna, possibly by a quartet led by Josef Slavík, but the only recorded public performance was in Schubert's concert of March 1828, provided that the item in the programme called a 'New' String Quartet, meant the one in G major. As with the Octet, and the String Quintet in C, the score of the quartet lay undisturbed on Diabelli's shelves for over twenty years, until, following a performance in Vienna, it was published by Diabelli's successor, C. A. Spina, in 1851. The manuscript is still extant, and in the possession of the Vienna *Nationalbibliothek*. The quartet occupied Schubert ten days (20 to 30 June), days of absorbed and concentrated work. While he was so engaged, on 26 June, Vogl married. We learn the fact, not from Schubert or his friends, but from Sophie Müller, who wrote in her diary:

26 June 1826. Vogl, the singer, marries Rosa.

Vogl had returned from Italy, presumably restored in health, and after his marriage took his bride Kunigunde, the daughter of a painter Josef Rosa, to Steyr.

The Schubertiads of that year grew more frequent, and more numerously attended. They were held at the houses of Schubert's friends, Spaun, Witteczek and Enderes. Anton von Spaun, the younger brother, was passing through Vienna during June and wrote to his wife: 'A Schubertiad at Enderes, to which more than 20 people have been invited.' The new songs that were sung were to more poems of Schulze, and included the fascinating *Ueber Wildemann*, and the perfectly expressed music of *Im Frühling*, one of Schubert's masterpieces of song, in which the poet's mood of tender, but not harrowing, regret for the spring, and the love of youth, is ideally matched. Some four-handed marches for the pianoforte were also performed, but which ones they were is not known: O. E. Deutsch's surmise, that they were the two 'Characteristic Marches' of Op. 121 seems not to be likely. They were more probably the recently published 'Funeral' and 'Coronation' marches of Op. 55 and Op. 66. Schober mentioned these duet marches—but not naming them—in his letter to Bauernfeld of June 1826, written from a house in the village of Währing, where he and his mother were staying. It is to the north-west of Vienna, actually not very far from Schubert's birthplace. Schober had written in this letter the words already quoted about Mlle. Schechner. He then continued:

> If only Schubert would write an opera for her; perhaps yours would be suitable. If only he were not such a naïve barbarian. When I asked him recently why he had not come to see me during the whole of my illness, he answered innocently: 'But you are never to be found at home'. . . . Today Schubert is to come out here; I hope he will keep his word.

Schubert, with Schwind, visited the Schober house at Währing during the summer, and may even have slept there a night or two. But there was no prolonged stay as is evident from the fact that Schubert wrote letters from Vienna during June and July; he was, moreover, bored at Währing, according to Bauernfeld. But three or four songs were composed there in July, and two of them are as famous, in England, as anything he wrote: the settings of Shakespeare's *Hark! hark! the lark!* (from Act II of 'Cymbeline') and *Who is Silvia?* (from Act IV of 'The Two Gentlemen of Verona'). There is a third, more obscure, setting of a Shakespearian text from the same period, the drinking-song *Come! thou Monarch of the Vine* from Act II of 'Antony and Cleopatra'. It is of interest to watch the evolution of legend where the first, most popular, song is concerned. It became known amongst the friends that Schober's garden abutted on that of an inn 'Zum Biersack', where the noise of games and music frequently disturbed the Schobers and their guests. Hence the song was written, they presumed, with a background of noises from an inn garden. It was an easy step, as time passed, to place the writing of it actually *in* the inn garden, instead of beside it. Now Schubert's autograph of the three Shakespeare songs is in a small, rather 'home-made' booklet of plain paper, with music staves ruled in pencil. Enough! The story takes shape: Schubert's inspiration was so sudden that lines were hurriedly pencilled on a piece of paper to accommodate his muse, and what piece of paper more likely, in an inn garden (especially a Viennese inn, where every waiter is plentifully supplied with little plain-backed chits), than a bill of fare? The legend, in its final form, was told to Kreissle in all solemnity by Schubert's friend Josef Doppler, and faithfully reproduced in most subsequent biographies.

Schober, in those days, was managing a small lithography business in Vienna, and wrote to Bauernfeld that it was prospering pretty well. Bauernfeld was kept very well informed from Vienna during his Carinthian tour, and as a result we also are kept supplied with news in that plentifully-documented year. Schubert wrote again to him on 10 July warning him that a projected holiday with Spaun to Linz or Gmunden was impossible since he had no money. In view of his numerous publications in 1826 this does not suggest over-generous payment by the publishers. He informed Bauernfeld of Vogl's marriage, of Schwind's difficulties with the rigidly devout Anna Hönig, and of Schober's prospering business. There was also a renewed plea for the 'Graf von Gleichen' libretto, by which he hoped to make money, if not reputation. At the end of the month Bauernfeld returned to Vienna and handed over the book of the opera to Schubert. The composer never completed work on the music, but his sketches for it are very bulky, consisting of thirty-six large, and fifty-two small pages. In October 1826 the censor refused to license the play, but by then the composition of it had begun, and Schubert, rather pointlessly it seems, continued to work occasionally on it.

The publication of the Sonata in A minor as Op. 42 had brought some recognition of his powers as a composer for the pianoforte. In particular it had aroused the interest of Hans Nägeli, the Swiss composer, theorist and music publisher. On 18 June, in fact, Nägeli had written to his agent in Vienna, Karl Czerny, suggesting that Schubert might contribute to a series of pianoforte compositions to be published under the general title 'Musikalische Ehrenpforte' ('Musical Portal of Honour'). Czerny did so, and Schubert himself wrote on 4 July to Nägeli, expressing his willingness to comply with the commission, and offering a sonata for £12 in advance. Whether this modest demand was too much for the Zürich publisher, or for some other reason, the project hung fire. But doubtless we owe to it the composition soon afterwards of the Sonata in G major.

In August Schubert was ill and penniless. With a desperate effort to do something to improve his position he wrote to two Leipzig publishing firms on 12 August, to H. A. Probst and to Breitkopf & Härtel; the letters are very similar and Schubert expressed in both the wish to further his name in Germany. He offered the two firms songs, piano sonatas, string quartets and PF. Duets. He also singled out for mention the Octet, which shows that Troyer's commisssion did not carry proprietary rights in the compositions. The two string quartets yet unpublished were the 'Death and the Maiden' Quartet, and the recently composed Quartet in G major. The unpublished sonatas which he offered were the A major of 1819 and the A minor of 1823. He makes no reference to any PF. Trio, so the work in B flat major, Op. 99, may not have been completed. The replies from both firms arrived quite promptly. Probst evidently knew Schubert's work, and was a little afraid of it. But he did suggest that songs and pianoforte compositions would be considered. Schubert sent him three works via Artaria, the Vienna publisher. Breitkopf & Härtel said nothing of his work. But they clearly remembered the incident of April 1817, when a song called *Erlking*, by Franz Schubert, had been sent to them, and which they had mistakenly attributed to the Franz Schubert of Dresden. Their letter was written with a veiled tone of sarcasm. They offered a number of copies of the published work instead of a fee, and they claimed to be 'wholly unacquainted'—not with Schubert's compositions, they could hardly claim to be that—but 'with the mercantile success of your compositions'. The letter was, in the same contemptible manner, addressed to 'Franz Schubert: famous composer in Vienna'. Schubert had no more dealings with them.

A general lack of finances and an undercurrent of uncertainty about the future seem to have been the lot of each of the friends that summer and it was perhaps the reason for some trivial bickering and quarrelling amongst them, from which Schubert, if not quite immune, emerged without any serious breach. The air cleared temporarily during September when his friend, Leopold Kupelwieser and Johanna Lutz were married. We have read some of Johanna's friendly and affectionate comments on Schubert in earlier pages. He was clearly fond of both of them, and is said to have played the pianoforte for dancing at their wedding, and to have refused to let anyone else take his place there. An extraordinary development of this improvisation of nuptial dance music came to light only recently during the second World War. Richard Strauss in the course of a conversation with a lady discovered that she was a descendant of the Leopold Kupelwieser whom Schubert knew. She was Frau Mautner-Markhof, a granddaughter of Paul Kupelwieser, the second son of Johanna and Leopold. She then went on to tell Strauss of a strange family tradition. During Schubert's improvisation, one waltz tune so charmed the bride that she never forgot it. As the years passed her three sons grew up quite familiar with the tune, heard from their mother's singing and playing, and they, in turn, passed the tune on to their sons and daughters. Eventually, in 1943, Frau Markhof played it to Strauss. Here it is, a Schubert waltz melody preserved by ear for over a hundred years, which we owe in the first place to the admirable Johanna Lutz:

Strauss arranged it for PF. Solo: a rather luscious version of a Schubert waltz, with the melody, in G flat major, given to the 'tenor' voice, but attractively written for all that. His manuscript is now in the possession of the *Gesellschaft für Musikfreunde*.

Two very original part-songs for male voices, in Schubert's most graphic vein, are *Nachthelle* and *Grab und Mond*. The poems are by Johann Gabriel Seidl, a young Viennese poet personally acquainted with Schubert. Both poems are nocturnal. In the first the night is starry and serene, and Schubert's light, quick chords and the high, poised tenor melody depict the scene vividly: it is a difficult piece to perform but sheer delight to the listener. The second poem describes the moon shining into a grave, and the vague symbolism—the light never returning—seems to imply that death is the final end of man, and no word comes back to deny it. Schubert's unaccompanied part-song has an unearthly, hollow effect, with startling harmonic progressions and unresolved discords: a piece of impressionistic colouring inspired by the poet's scene—'silver-blue moonlight', and his question—'Quite mute?' The two pieces were composed in September 1826, probably for performance in Vienna; the only record of such a performance is of *Nachthelle*, sung in the following January.

At the end of the month Vogl and his bride returned to Vienna from Steyr, and the singer was heard once again in the Schubertiad evenings. His failing voice was eked out with much expressive 'word-singing' and gesture. Bauernfeld noted in his journal of 17 December 1826:

> Vogl sang Schubert songs with mastery, but not without dandyism.

This 'histrionic' attitude of Vogl was uncongenial to many of the circle; Schwind on occasion was contemptuously uncivil to him. It is certain, too, that Vogl introduced embellishments and ornaments in the melodies of the songs which could not have been very patiently borne either by Schubert or the more thoughtful of his audience.

The old schoolhouse in the Säulengasse was sold during October. Franz Schubert senior received £660 for the property and a small share—£20—came to Schubert. This break with one memory of his childhood was followed at once by a link with another one, for soon after the sale of the house he moved into lodgings in the Schober's new home, and this was a mere stone's throw from the *Stadtkonvikt.* Schober and his mother were now installed in a house in the Bäckerstrasse. Schubert began work on the Sonata in G major, probably intending it for Nägeli, or, failing him, for one of the various publishing houses in Germany should occasion arise. But whatever mercenary or 'celebrity' impulse ordered the composition of the sonata, once it was begun the impulse was primarily and purely artistic. The noble, exalted music of this great movement reveals the Schubert Sonata at its finest; the corresponding movement of the B flat Sonata of 1828 is exactly similar in style and treatment, and equally admired. The manuscript of the G major Sonata is a proud possession of the British Museum, and the sketches for the slow movement, remaining in Schubert's fair copy, give the autograph a more than normal interest. At bar 30 the slow movement was cancelled and restarted because the theme quoted in the next extract failed to satisfy its composer and was rejected out of hand:

Ex. 71

Further sketches for the slow movement are to be found at the back of the page containing the beginning of the 'Menuetto'.

One morning, just as Schubert was nearing the end of his work on the first movement of this sonata, Spaun called to see him. He made nothing of the interruption to his work, persuaded Spaun to sit down, and then he played the almost finished movement through to his friend. Spaun praised it highly and Schubert said: 'Since you like the sonata, you shall have it, for I like to do something to please you, when I can.' And eventually he placed the published work, dedicated to Spaun, in his old friend's hands. This incident was told by Spaun himself.

Several visits to Sophie Müller by Vogl and Schubert are recorded during October, and Jenger was also a visitor. No songs are actually named in the diary which Sophie kept, but doubtless the new Shakespeare songs were sung, and since Op. 59, containing the three wonderful Rückert songs, *Du bist die Ruh'*, *Lachen und Weinen* and *Dass sie hier gewesen*, had just been published, these songs would surely form part of the programme. In fact, not only does Sophie record buying some songs which were probably those of Op. 59, but one feels that she would find *Lachen und Weinen* irresistible, and that her singing of it would be wholly delightful. Another popular and cultured actress of the Burgtheater was Antonie Adamsberger, also, like Sophie, lost to the Viennese public through retirement. Although not in close touch with Schubert, she introduced Bauernfeld, from the Schubert circle, to Grillparzer, and during the October of 1826 she sang to the dramatist several songs by Schubert, including the Harper's song *Wer nie sein Brot mit Tränen ass* and *Ave Maria*. This was at the monastery of St. Florian. Grillparzer was returning to Vienna from a visit to Goethe at Weimar.

Many performances of Schubert's songs and part-songs had taken place at the evening concerts organised by the *Gesellschaft der Musikfreunde*, or the 'Musikverein', as it is also called. Schubert was in close touch with the association and esteemed by its officials: men such as Josef Sonnleithner and Rafael von Kiesewetter. At this period he promised to dedicate a symphony to the 'Musikverein'. In October the Committee voted Schubert 100 florins (£10) as a token of gratitude for his services to the musical activities of the Society and as an encouragement for further work. He acknowledged the gift on 20 October 1826. The series of Society minutes and the exchange of letters with Schubert have, in my view, been distorted by associating with them an undated letter of Schubert's referring to the score of a symphony which he was presenting to the Society. This association suggests that the 'Gmunden-Gastein' symphony was, by October 1826, in a finished and performable condition, a quite unjustifiable conclusion. The whole matter is considered in detail in the appendix (page 354).

III

At some time toward the end of November Schubert left the Schober family house and lived alone for a few months in lodgings near the 'Karolinentor'. This was a gate in the ancient, fortified wall leading to the Inner City, and is now demolished; it was opposite what is today the *Stadtpark* in Vienna, and not far from that section of the Ringstrasse known now as the 'Schubertring'. To get to his lodgings his friends walked on the wall, or Bastion, and they complained of 'the most frightful mud'.

He had resumed friendly relations again with the publisher Diabelli. Their renewed partnership was introduced auspiciously (or inauspiciously: it depends on the reader's point of view) by the 'Marches Militaires' of Op. 51, published in August; the first of the three marches, in D major, is Schubert's most popular, indeed, *only* popular, march. Pennauer also published some marches for PF. Duet: the ceremonial Op. 55 for the dead Tsar Alexander I, and the march, Op. 66, for the Coronation of his successor, Nicolas I. Amongst the various songs, the three Rückert settings of Op. 59, from the firm of Sauer & Leidesdorff, have been mentioned. The only other publication of interest is from Weigl, namely, the 'Divertissement in E minor, on French themes' published in June. This PF. Duet, called Op. 63: no. 1, was the first movement of a three-movement work. But its two companion movements, the 'Andantino varié' and a 'Marcia', were lost sight of for a year or so; when they were published, Weigl called them, not Op. 63: nos. 3 & 4, but by a new opus-number, 84: nos. 1 & 2. He thus effectively dissected the work for ever, for although this error has been repeatedly pointed out since the late nineteenth century, no attempt by publishers or performers has been made to assemble the scattered parts into a whole.

A young Bohemian violinist, Josef Slavík, mentioned earlier on in connection with a private performance of the String Quartet in G, had come to Vienna early in 1826 after a successful career in Prague. He hoped to make an international reputation. Schubert met him through the pianist Karl von Bocklet, and we owe to the advent of this violinist two works for violin and pianoforte, although neither is of any great moment. Slavík was a technician. He favourably impressed Paganini when the latter visited Vienna in 1828. A year later Chopin visited Vienna for the first time and he and Slavík became very friendly. Chopin wrote home that Slavík was a 'second Paganini', and added, awestruck, '36 staccato notes to a bow!' Schubert must have realised where Slavík's real achievement lay, for the two compositions he wrote for him tend to exploit the virtuoso style of violin-writing at the expense of musical values. The first was written in December 1826; it is the 'Rondeau Brillant' in B minor, planned on the usual lines for such a form: slow introduction leading to a 'Rondo allegro'. It could not, coming from Schubert at the end of 1826, be entirely without depth, but the various episodes are on the long side, and the inevitable repetitions involved in Rondo-form make it too protracted for its style and material. The same month saw the probable start of a large vocal composition which, to the Schubertian, is not a significant work, the 'German' Mass, as it is usually called. It was intended for celebrations of Low Mass in the vernacular and the words are by Johann Phillip Neumann, professor of physics at a Technical Institution in Vienna. The college is very near the Karlskirche where Schubert formerly lodged. Neumann was a cousin of Watteroth, through whom he became acquainted with Schubert. The Mass consists of eight separate religious songs to be sung by the choir and congregation during the intervals between the various stages of the Office: Introit, Gloria, Credo and so on. Schubert received £4 from Neumann for his composition.

Both text and music were published in 1827 without the authors' names, although naturally not without their permission. The reason why this slight and not unsentimental work has occupied so much space is that it became immediately, and has remained to this day in Vienna, very popular and greatly loved by the people. There are several arrangements to be had besides Schubert's own, and the first 'number', which begins *Wohin soll ich mich wenden?* is known and sung by many Viennese who have not the least idea that it is by Schubert, but who know it in numerous versions as a popular piece of Church music.

Performances of his works, songs and instrumental compositions, in private and semi-public concerts, were from now on very plentiful in Vienna. The December of 1826 saw three large gatherings of his friends, at Spaun's house near the Schottenkirche, at Hönig's, and at Witteczek's. The first, called by Franz von Hartmann in his diary 'a big, big Schubertiad' took place on 15 December 1826. It was a gathering of distinguished, middle-class people, who were named in welcome detail by the diarist. Besides the friends and acquaintances in Schubert's immediate circle, including the newly-wedded Kupelwieser and Vogl, with their wives, there were Grillparzer, Schlechta and many officials of the Imperial Court. Gahy and Schubert played the six marches of Op. 40, and Vogl sang song after song—over thirty of them. This evening Schubertiad inspired Schwind, years afterwards, to his very famous sepia drawing called 'Schubert evening at Spaun's'. The picture deserves more than the brief mention it can receive here, for it yields up much pleasure to those prepared to look beyond mere identification of the persons in the collective 'portrait'. The scene, Schubert at the piano, Vogl singing, and the men and women of the audience gathered about these central figures, is not a representational portrait of the particular party of 15 December 1826. It is an imaginative reconstruction of the many Schubertiads of the period. The original now hangs in Schubert's birthplace in the Nussdorferstrasse, saved for the city of Vienna by the efforts and pleas of O. E. Deutsch. There are one or two inferior and somewhat sentimental imitations by other painters of Schwind's noble conception.

Apart from the private parties there were the evening entertainments of the 'Musikverein' at which, during the winter session of 1826–1827 numerous songs, including *Der Zwerg, Der Einsame, An Schwager Kronos, Die junge Nonne*, and Psalm XXIII for female voices, were sung. At a concert in the Kärntnertor Theater on 2 December the Overture to 'Alfonso und Estrella' was revived. It received a notice in Berlin—somewhat equivocal —and one in the London music-journal 'Harmonicon', which was distinctly favourable: '... a revived overture by Schubert, full of striking effects, and worthy of being better known.' In the early days of 1827 Karl von Bocklet, the pianist to whom Schubert had dedicated the Sonata in D major, Op. 53, and Josef Slavík, performed the 'Rondeau Brillant' for Domenico Artaria, the music publisher. Schubert was present at the performance. This was a prelude to publication and Artaria brought out the piece during April 1827 as Op. 70.

A new friend of those days was Ferdinand Walcher, introduced to Schubert and his friends by the Hartmann brothers. Walcher, a young law student, came from Lower Austria; he was courting Sophie Kleyle, the daughter of a well-to-do Viennese family who lived, during the summer months, in a country residence at Penzing. Schubert visited the Kleyle family frequently and was a welcome and popular guest. Penzing lies to the north of Schönbrunn, and the pretty residence and gardens of the Kleyle's are still in existence today.

IV

During the latter months of 1826 and in the whole of 1827, the two brothers, Fritz and Franz von Hartmann, kept full diaries of their activities in Vienna. They were friends, in the first place, of Spaun, but the friendship soon embraced the whole of Spaun's circle; they encountered Schubert almost daily at the particular *Kaffeehaus* in favour with the circle of friends at the moment, and were at all the evening Schubertiads. Inevitably there are numerous references to Schubert in their diaries and these can all be found quoted fully in the pages of the Schubert 'Documents'. We do not meet the name Hartmann in the nineteenth-century biographies of the composer and it is due to O. E. Deutsch's researches that these diaries have been found, and the relevant entries published. In a few instances they correct error and supplement our information on the period. But most of the diary entries are the merest social chit-chat, and contribute very little that is vital. They do not tell us much that is new about Schubert's Vienna, being concerned almost entirely with the names of the people whom the two young men met, the *Kaffeehaus* to which they resorted in the evening, the practical jokes and jesting in which they indulged, and the time they went home. Naturally the Hartmanns were not gifted with second sight, nor were they aware how eagerly their pages would be scanned by future Schubertians. We cannot blame them for not watching Schubert more closely. He comes and goes in their pages like a ghost, he says nothing and does nothing except accompany his songs on occasion; we are not told what he looked like, how he played, what work he was engaged on, what he said about publishers, performers, concerts, plays, operas or books. Their comments on the Vienna *Kaffeehaus*, its atmosphere and its functions, are welcome. At that time the 'Grünanger' was the favourite haunt, a *Kaffeehaus* still standing today, in the district behind St. Stephen's Cathedral. The Viennese *Kaffeehaus* has no real counterpart in English life, yet an attempt must be made to understand its unique function, for it is an essential factor in the life of Schubert, as in the life of any Viennese of his day. Grove's attempt to equate it with the English 'club', to excuse Schubert's use of it, and to talk about the amount of drink consumed there, is no help at all. He based his conclusions on too scanty a supply of facts and a misinterpretation of those facts which were to hand. From the Hartmann diaries alone we can deduce that Schubert found these 'coffeehouses' simply a meeting place for congenial souls, and Grove's further statements about 'daybreak driving the friends back to their lodgings' and that 'few constitutions could stand such a racket' do not need the diaries to prove their absurdity. Distortions of this kind were to lead to preposterous misjudgements of Schubert. The coffeehouses of eighteenth-century London vanished during the next hundred years; in Vienna they survived and do so today.

When we read of these nightly gatherings, Schubertiads in private houses, discussions in the *Kaffeehaus*, the 'Musikverein' concerts, it is hard to find any relation between Schubert's outward life, which suggests a leisurely, almost lazy, progress from day to day, and the fire of creation which burned in him, the unremitting labour of composition which chained him to his desk during the day. It is this which gives his appearances in the journals and letters of his friends a ghost-like, unreal quality. He seems so quiet and controlled, almost insignificant, whereas we know all the time he is striving toward, and urging his powers to reach up to, the vision of the 'Winterreise'.

A truer picture of his moods can be found by reading a little below the surface of the comments made by his friends on his actions. Here, for example, are the allusions of the two Hartmann brothers to 4 March 1827:

> I went with Fritz to Schubert's, who had invited us, but never appeared at all. (Franz von Hartmann.)
>
> We went to Schober's, where we met Spaun, Schwind, Bauernfeld and Kriehuber with his wife and sister-in-law . . . because Schubert, who is Schober's lodger, had invited us to hear some new compositions of his. Everybody was assembled, but friend Schubert did not come. At last Schwind undertook to sing several of Schubert's earlier songs, which enchanted us. At half-past nine we all went to the 'Castle of Eisenstadt' where Schubert too arrived soon after us, and won all hearts by his amiable simplicity, although he had deceived our hopes by his artist's negligence. (Fritz von Hartmann.)

He was caught away from the actualities of daily life into the world of the 'Winterreise'—into *his* world, as it has been suggested, rather than Müller's. The flimsiness of social claims to keep him from his music is implied, if we read with understanding, in a further comment. This comes from a letter written to Ferdinand Walcher, then in Venice, by his fair friend Sophie Kleyle at Penzing:

> We do not lack visitors, for we have several each day; Angerer and Jenger come more often than usual, and Schubert too has given us the pleasure once already; he was most amiable and talkative, but escaped suddenly, before anyone had an inkling. . . . (1 June 1827.)

Besides the self-absorption in composition, or perhaps because of it, he had to bear both the lack of any promising situation or source of income, and wretched health. They were both, the financial outlook and his enfeebled condition, slowly growing less bearable. Schober in his old age passed on reminiscences of Schubert which were not too reliable, nor too kindly. He said of the early days of 1827 that Schubert was in love with Auguste Grünwedel, a young girl whom we find mentioned in the Hartmann diaries. Schober, one evening in the *Kaffeehaus* suggested to Schubert that he might marry her. Schubert rose angrily, made no reply, and hurried out of the place. Afterwards, in a calmer mood, he tried to answer the utterly tactless remark with a conventional parry, that he was convinced no woman would ever marry him.

Another incident of those days shows Schober in an equally vivid light. At a breakfast party on 6 January 1827 at Spaun's house, Gahy played two sonatas by Schubert and then some German dances. The dances were those of Op. 67, but we do not know which sonatas were played: it is almost certain that one of them was the work in G major, dedicated to Spaun. Schober joined the party halfway through and expressed his displeasure with the sonatas. Possibly a little jealousy embittered his remarks, for Spaun resented them, and the two men nearly quarrelled. Schober preferred Schubert's lighter, more lyrical vein. His attitude to the composer's more serious work, like the sonatas, contrasts strongly with that of Spaun. The reaction of each man tells us more about him than it does about the music which provoked the reaction. In the same way the type of music which Schubert wrote for each of his two friends, pleasing them with the kind they preferred, is revealing.

Another Schubertiad for a large gathering of people was held a few days after the 'breakfast' incident, again in Spaun's house. The Sonata for PF. Duet in C major, the 'Grand Duo', was played by Schubert and Gahy, followed by the 'Variations in A flat', Op. 35, a popular work amongst the Schubertians of that time. Vogl sang a series of songs including *Nacht und Träume* and *Im Abendroth* (which he sang twice).

A blow to Schubert's hopes came in the form of a polite rejection by Probst, the music publisher at Leipzig, of the proffered manuscripts (15 January). These were piano pieces, probably incorporated later on in the 'Moments Musicaux'. Probst claimed to be overburdened with work, since he was publishing the 'Complete Works' of Kalkbrenner! A different kind of letter came a few days afterwards from Ferdinand Walcher. He was the possessor of a pleasant, high baritone voice, and sang various Schubert songs, including *Auf dem Wasser zu singen*, with great charm. His letter enclosed two tickets for a performance of *Nachthelle* at the 'Musikverein', a part-song which, as Walcher wrote, is '. . . for a principal and damned high tenor'. The interest of his note—apart from the warm and affectionate terms expressed toward the dejected composer—lies in the opening paragraph. Walcher wrote a snatch of plainsong to the words 'Credo in unum Deum' and then continued: 'Du nicht, das weiss ich wohl, aber das wirst Du glauben . . .' and he then informed Schubert that Tietze would sing *Nachthelle* and so forth. Is there any point in hedging over this plain statement of Walcher's to Schubert? It means, in effect: ' "I believe in One God"—you do not, that I know well, but you will believe this. . . .' Schubert's unorthodox beliefs were known to his family and friends from quite early years, and his continuing association with like-minded professors and students in Vienna had, if anything, intensified them. It may be this unorthodoxy which vitiates his sacred music, and prevents it taking the last, clinching grip on the listener's admiration and attention. Walcher's 'Unum Deum' is the God of the Christian Church; Schubert was no sceptic where 'Gott in der Natur' was concerned. In that hymn to Nature's God, *Die Allmacht*, Schubert pours out a paean of praise from the depths of his soul. But there is no sacred music, or very little, of the same intensity in his Masses, or other settings of liturgical texts. It has been stressed that there was no conscious revolt in Schubert's attitude: one cannot imagine his being so positive as to adopt a belligerent unorthodoxy, and his position was partly subconscious, partly unapprehended. How, otherwise, can we account for his quite sincere words to his father:

> . . . they also wondered greatly at my piety, which I expressed in a hymn to the Holy Virgin and which, it appears, grips every soul and turns it to devotion. I think this is due to the fact that I have never forced devotion in myself and never compose hymns or prayers of that kind unless it overcomes me unawares; but then it is usually the right and true devotion. . . .

The hymn to which he refers here is, it is significant to note, the purely secular poem of Scott's *Ave Maria*, not the words of the angel's salutation to Mary. But for all Schubert's sincerity and simplicity, he is devoid of the implicit faith of Bach and Beethoven, and certainly of Bruckner, and hence incapable of the unarguable, unanswerable sublimity of assertion in their sacred music.

Walcher left for Venice in the spring of 1827 and as a farewell offering Schubert wrote in his album the delightfully fresh and original piece for piano known as the 'Allegretto in C minor' (D. 915) and inscribed it 'To my dear friend Walcher for remembrance, 27 April 1827'.

V

The manuscript of the first twelve songs of 'Winterreise' is dated 'February 1827', indicating the time at which Schubert started writing the fair copy of the first of them, *Gute Nacht*. He found these twelve poems (entitled 'Die Winterreise') in an almanach called 'Urania', published in Leipzig in 1823. The eagerness with which he started composing these songs, and the exhausted state in which their composition left him, show how congenial to his taste and to his gifts, were the straightforward and limpid verses of Müller. He was overjoyed to find another series of songs by the poet of the 'Schöne Müllerin' and he did not spare himself as poem after poem stimulated the creative power within him and—one might almost say—extorted musical scene after musical scene from his imagination, those incomparable scenes of despair and heartbreak, violence and numbness, in a landscape of snow and ice and bitter wind. In the late summer of 1827, after the first twelve songs were finished, Schubert encountered Müller's complete and final version of the cycle. This was included in a book entitled 'Poems from the posthumous papers of a travelling horn-player': 'Die Winterreise' was the second of the three parts in the book. It then contained twenty-four poems, but the new ones were not supplementary to the original twelve: they were inserted in various places. The book was dedicated by Müller to the 'Master of German Song, Karl Maria von Weber, as a pledge of his friendship and admiration'; he died in 1827 before Schubert's setting was published. When Schubert found Müller's final version he set to music the extra twelve poems, taking them as they came and placing them all together at the end of the twelve settings he had made in the spring of 1827. It has been said many times that Schubert *altered* the order of Müller's poems, but he did not do so deliberately as the above account makes clear.

Schubert's two manuscripts, with the whole series of twenty-four songs, has survived. The first one consists mostly of rough drafts, and is so full of alterations and additions that the publisher's engraver found it unreadable. Thereupon a fair copy was made and submitted to Schubert who not only corrected it, but radically altered it in a few places.[1] Since this copy, from which the first edition was printed, disappeared for many years, and since Schubert's 'foul papers' survived, several commentators, Max Friedlaender (1884), Mandyczewski (1894), Erwin Scheffer (1938) and others, have drawn attention to what they have deemed errors in the first edition. But Schubert himself made the changes. The copy made for the engraver is now in the *Stadtbibliothek* of Vienna. The manuscript containing the next twelve songs, from *Die Post* to *Der Leiermann*, Schubert's (not Müller's) Part II, is in fair copy; it is dated 'October 1827'. Only a fragmentary sketch exists for one of these songs, for no. 23, *Die Nebensonnen*.

Two of Schubert's friends mention these months in his life, and the composition of 'Winterreise'. Mayrhofer's paragraph is rather sentimental; his words that Schubert's winter had come upon him, hence the creation of 'Winterreise', take no account of the incredible detachment of the artist. How, otherwise, one

[1] The biggest change is in the second song, *Die Wetterfahne*, at bars 15–18.

might ask, if the winter were upon him, did Schubert come to write the ebullient, springtime music of 1828—the great C major Symphony, the String Quintet in C, the last three sonatas? Spaun's reminiscences of the 'Winterreise' period are more realistic. After relating the occasion when Schubert called the friends together, and sang the 'Winterreise' to them, he added:

> We who were near and dear to him knew how much the creatures of his mind took out of him, and in what anguish they were born. No one who ever saw him at his morning's work, glowing, and with his eyes aflame, yes, and positively with a changed speech, . . . will ever forget it . . . I hold it beyond question that the excitement in which he composed his finest songs, in particular the 'Winterreise', brought about his untimely death.

The music of the song-cycle heralds a new phase in his work, one which he did not live long enough to redeem from mere promise: a new power of intellectual depth in his treatment of thematic ideas, a new tranquillity, a richer imagery.

* * * *

In the way which we have noticed before, the 'fashionable' song of that period was *Der zürnenden Diana*; it was sung on several occasions in Vienna. Later on it was *Norman's Song* from the settings of the 'Lady of the Lake' lyrics. Another performance of Psalm XXIII was given by the singing pupils of the 'Conservatoire' on 18 March; it took place in the *Gesellschaft* concert-hall, a building situated in the Tuchlauben, which leads from the Graben. Schubert moved into lodgings in this same street soon afterwards, living again in the Schober household; their new residence was next door to the concert-hall. He had two rooms and a music-closet at his disposal—more comfortable quarters than he had ever enjoyed before.

On an occasion during February 1827 Beethoven, confined to his sickbed, had been given a batch of Schubert songs by Anton Schindler. Most of them were in printed editions, but a few were manuscript copies of published or unpublished songs made by Schindler. Beethoven examined them with great interest and according to Schindler (not, as we have seen, an entirely reliable witness) exclaimed at their number, length and variety.[1] Occasionally he uttered the ambiguous remark: 'If I had had this poem I would have set it'; was this pleasure in the poem, or dissatisfaction with Schubert's effort? Finally he pronounced: 'Truly in Schubert is the divine spark!'—which sounds very like a poetic invention on Schindler's part. The manuscript copies made by Schindler are not lost, and today, bound in one volume, are in the possession of Otto Taussig of Malmö. They comprise twenty-six songs, and contribute a few details of interest: most notably that the prelude of four bars in early editions of the song *Augenlied* was geniune Schubert, and not, as Mandyczewski considered, an addition of the publisher's. *Augenlied*, as copied by Schindler, is so ornate compared with the published song, that it is almost certainly an embellished version by Vogl. Similar ornate variants are to be found in other songs amongst the Schindler copies, also due to Vogl's efforts.

On 18 March Schubert is said to have gone in the company of Anselm and Josef Hüttenbrenner to visit the dying Beethoven. He had never met, nor spoken to Beethoven in all the years of his musical activities in Vienna. So much he told Spaun himself, and that disposes of many anecdotes, plausible and piquant though they may be, in which Schubert and Beethoven are supposed to have associated with each other.

Beethoven died on 26 March 1827. There is an extraordinarily vivid and detailed account of the dead composer in the pages of Franz von Hartmann's diary, quoted in the Schubert 'Documents', page 621. Schubert was one of thirty-six torch bearers at the funeral. Beethoven was buried in a small, square grave-yard known as the 'Friedort' ('Place of Peace') to the left of the Währingerstrasse as it leaves the city; in those days the cemetery lay beyond the city boundaries. After the funeral ceremony Schubert, Schober and Schwind, accompanied by the younger Hartmann, Fritz, visited the *Kaffeehaus*, 'Castle of Eisenstadt', and remained there discussing the dead composer until late into the night. The grisly story of the toast to Beethoven, followed by a

[1] Schindler wrote two accounts of the incident: (*a*) 'Allgemeine Theaterzeitung', Vienna, 3 May 1831, (*b*) 'Beethoven-Biographie', Münster, 1840.

second toast to the 'next one to die'—who was, in fact, Schubert himself—is an invention.

Soon after Beethoven's death, Schubert met at the house of Katharina von Lászny the pianist and composer Hummel, with his young pupil Ferdinand Hiller. Hummel was on the point of abandoning his career as a pianist. He delighted Schubert by going to the piano after Vogl had sung *Der blinde Knabe* and improvising on the theme of the song. The incident was related many years after the event by Hiller.[1]

April was full of performances of his work, new and old. One can well understand the frustration and depression which seized him when he encountered the apparently recalcitrant attitude of German publishers to his offers of compositions; he himself, in Vienna, was surrounded by every evidence of esteem and popularity. Or do we, in reading of these performances, isolated from the musical life of the city, gain a wrong impression? In that year, it will be remembered, the English musician Edward Holmes was in Vienna, recording fully the musical life of the capital, yet saying no word of Schubert. Even so, the following list seems favourable on any count: four part-songs (6 April), vocal quartet (12 April), the Octet, first public performance (16 April), 'Nachtgesang', for male voices and horns (22 April). There were also numerous performances of solo songs, and four Schubertiads, at one of which, on 21 April, Franz von Hartmann wrote that there was 'an enormous attendance'. Two days after that another of these popular gatherings was held at Witteczek's home. Schubert paid a grateful tribute to this loyal friend; it took the form of a dedication: the three settings of Seidl's nature-poems, the impracticable, but masterly *Im Freien*, *Das Zügenglöcklein* and *Der Wanderer an den Mond*, were 'offered in friendship to Josef Witteczek' and published as Op. 80 in May 1827 by Tobias Haslinger. This new name amongst Viennese publishers of his work appeared for the first time the previous month. In April, Haslinger had published the G major Sonata as Op. 78, but he did Schubert a disservice by calling the work 'Fantasia, *Andante*, Menuetto and

[1] 'In Wien vor 52 Jahren', and 'Kunsterleben', both accounts published in 1880.

Für die zweyte Classe

Von Seite der Pfarrschule in der Vorstadt Rossau wird hiermit bezeuget, daß *Joseph Haut* — Schüler der zweyten Classe sich in Sitten *sehr gut* verhalten, und die für den *zweyten* Curs vorgeschriebenen Gegenstände folgender Maßen erlernet hat:

Die Religionslehren . . . . *sehr gut*

Das bestimmte Stück aus dem II. Theile des Lesebuches . . . . . . *sehr gut*

Das Lesen mit Anwendung der Regeln des

Deutschgedruckten . . . .

Lateinischgedruckten . . . . } *sehr gut*

Deutschgeschriebenen . . . .

Lateinischgeschriebenen . . . .

Das Schönschreiben

Deutsch-current . . . .

Lateinisch . . . . } *gut*

Die Deutsche Sprachlehre . . . .

Das Recht- und Dictandoschreiben . . . . *sehr gut*

Das Rechnen in den 4 Rechnungsarten . . . . *gut*

Die Aussprache . . . . *sehr gut*

Dieser Schüler verdienet daher in die *erste* Classe *mit Vorzuge* gesetzt zu werden.

Wien am *15. May 1827.*

Franz Schubert

Schullehrer

SCHOOL REPORT MADE BY SCHUBERT'S FATHER FROM ROSSAU, MAY 1827

Herr Otto Taussig

Allegretto'. The title 'Sonata' was just beginning to lose favour, and for many years remained unfashionable, until, towards the end of the nineteenth century it re-emerged with an added *cachet* of distinction as the Viennese masters loomed larger above the wreck of the 'Romantic' movement. But Haslinger has fastened the label 'Fantasia' so firmly to this pure sonata-movement of Schubert's that it will remain there for all time. Diabelli published Op. 62, four settings of poems from Goethe's 'Wilhelm Meister', including the superb duet *Mignon und der Harfner*, which, since duet *Lieder* are so completely uncongenial today, is consigned to oblivion. Diabelli had also re-published the song *Auf dem Wasser zu singen* in March, as Op. 72: it had been a supplementary issue to the 'Wiener Zeitschrift' of December 1823.

During May and early June Schubert spent a few weeks at the village of Dornbach, which lay to the west of Vienna. He went with Schober and they lived in the inn 'Empress of Austria'. It was a charming spot, cupped by the wooded hills of the 'Wiener Wald'—the ideal place for the birth of the song *Das Lied im Grünen*, one of Schubert's most exhilarating songs of springtime. We know of no other compositions originating at Dornbach, but it is very likely that Schubert composed or sketched there some of the 'Impromptus' purchased during the late autumn by Haslinger and published as Op. 90. There would be money, in modest amounts, from Haslinger and Diabelli. The first published three sets of songs in May: *Die Allemacht* and *Das Heimweh* as Op. 79, *Im Freien* included in Op. 80, and the three songs to texts by Rochlitz, one of them the delicious little serenade *An die Laute*, as Op. 81. Diabelli re-published some supplements, *Der Wachtelschlag* as Op. 68, and *Die Rose* as Op. 73. This last publication is noteworthy as containing the very first list ever made of Schubert's published works, Opp. 1–74, thus including publications by firms other than Diabelli's. The last opus in the list, 74, is one of the Schubertian mysteries (Op. 82: no. 2 is another). Op. 74 is an arrangement made by the composer of a comic trio called 'Die Advokaten'; the music is by one Anton Fischer and Schubert's arrangement of it was made in 1812—when he was a boy of fifteen. It must therefore have been published without his knowledge, for he is hardly likely to have sold the trifling composition of another composer, when he had so much unpublished work of his own; but how Diabelli obtained the manuscript is almost incomprehensible. We must suppose that it was taken to the composer by one of the men on the fringe of his circle, Lachner, perhaps, or Schindler. There is no word from Schubert himself about the publication—no denial, no refutation.

Two short, but very typical songs, were given as supplements to the 'Wiener Zeitschrift' of 23 June 1827. *Wanderers Nachtlied* (the celebrated poem by Goethe beginning 'Ueber allen Gipfeln ist Ruh') and *Trost im Liede*. The first was re-published in Schubert's lifetime, but the second, a finer composition, was re-published by Probst, together with two other 'Zeitschrift' supplements, as a spurious Op. 101, in December 1828, just after Schubert's death.

On his return to Vienna in early June 1827, he was honoured by being elected a 'representative' of the *Gesellschaft der Musikfreunde*. It was a further acknowledgement of the regard in which his work was held by the Society; there were no duties required of him. But the distinction thus conferred may have spurred him on to the completion of the symphony sketched at Gmunden.

VI

The various threads which connect people living in social communities, and which, in Schubert's Vienna, weave an ever shifting web, now tightening, now breaking, now fastening again, suddenly form a pretty pattern during 1827, centring round the young and charming figure of Louise Gosmar. She was introduced to Fritz von Hartmann at a ball held in the residence of a wealthy merchant, a friend of her father's. Fritz and Louise discovered a mutual love for Schubert's music and talked of it while they danced. At that time Louise was a singing pupil in Anna Fröhlich's class at the 'Conservatoire', and soon found that Anna was a friend of Schubert's. Anna, knowing that Louise's parents wanted to give her a surprise for her birthday, went to Grillparzer and begged him to write a short birthday-ode in honour of the event. Grillparzer, in love with Katharina, Anna's younger sister, willingly complied with her request. Anna took the poem to Schubert, asking him if he would set it to music, and explaining why she wanted it.

The outcome is a well-known story in the Schubert records. He did compose the poem, a delightful serenade for a loved child, for contralto solo and chorus, just as Anna had asked him. But the chorus was for *men's* voices, and Anna wanted it, of course, for her female singing class. Schubert rectified his mistake at once, with a good-humoured acknowledgement of his foolish blunder. On 11 August the young ladies of the singing class were secretly conveyed to the Gosmar's residence at Döbling, a village to the north of Vienna, on the way to Grinzing. A piano was carried into the garden, and Schubert's and Grillparzer's 'Serenade' was sung by Josefine Fröhlich and her sister's pupils. It was a lovely summer's night and the effect created was unforgettable. Schubert was not present during the performance, but he heard the piece a few months later sung in Vienna and expressed his satisfaction with it. This 'Serenade', like the Mass in F major of 1814, and the 'Prometheus' Cantata of 1816, occupies a bigger place in the Schubert story than in the affections of the Schubertian. It has some utterly delightful and very characteristic moments, but it is too long drawn out for its material. As with many of Schubert's vocal pieces in the 1825-1827 period, a figure of accompaniment, original and striking at first, is kept going for page after page, and does not escape monotony. Thus, in the 'Serenade', the piano figuration, a vivid representation of the gentle knocking on the door of the sleeper's room, is played continuously until the ear wearies of it. The original form of the part-song, contralto solo and men's chorus, is preferable to the second, since the variety of *timbre* is welcome. Louise Gosmar, soon after the 'Serenade' birthday gift, fell in love with Leopold Sonnleithner, Schubert's friend and well-wisher. They were married in the following May.

Schwind was studying during 1827 at Munich; there is a possibility that he and Schubert were not quite so closely in touch since no letters were exchanged between them during the young painter's absence. But it was only a temporary loosening of the ties. Bauernfeld, too, working in his Government office is not so frequently encountered, but Schubert still worked spasmodically at his opera-text, 'Der Graf von Gleichen'.

A new haunt, called the 'Wolf preaching to the Geese', was favoured by the friends that summer; it was an inn rather than a *Kaffeehaus*, very near Schubert's and Schober's dwelling. But the endless discussions between the members of the circle continued just as ardently as they had at the 'Grünanger' and the 'Castle of Eisenstadt'. Schubert also visited Grinzing during the season to sample there the 'Heurige', the wine pressed that year. The centre of the village still looks today as it did in Schubert's day, and can easily be recognised from Schwind's well-known drawing, with Schubert drinking the 'new' wine in the company of Bauernfeld and Lachner. On 15 August 1827 he was met there by Hoffmann von Fallersleben, a chance meeting. Fallersleben, a poet and a collector of German folksong, best known, perhaps, for his authorship of 'Deutschland über alles', was on a visit to Vienna in the company of Heinrich Panofka. Years later he wrote a significant sentence in his autobiography 'Mein Leben' (1868) about this meeting with Schubert; he said: '. . . there was nothing in his face, or in his whole being, that resembled my Schubert.' It is, as already said, impossible to reconcile the externals of Schubert's being with the internal fire of creative energy which transformed him when he worked, as Spaun has pointed out. Vogl's wife, Kunigunde, writing to her daughter in 1850, also said that Schubert was 'a little, insignificant-looking man'.

VII

Through his friendship with Johann Baptist Jenger, Schubert was able to spend a short holiday that year at Graz, then a small township in south Austria, the capital of Styria. It was known to Schubert as 'Gratz', the name being altered in 1843. The town possessed a University, two fine Gothic churches and was within easy reach of lovely countryside. His hostess was Marie Pachler, an accomplished and cultured woman, whose piano playing had charmed Beethoven. Jenger had met her while staying at Graz. The visit had been long planned, in fact Schubert had been invited in 1826 but had had no money for the journey. Karl Pachler, his host, was a man of substance, kindly and just a little shy of his distinguished guest; he combined the activities of barrister and brewer, which sounds a fascinating conjunction of occupations. Schubert had promised, in a letter to Marie Pachler of 12 June 1827, that he would come to Graz with Jenger, and the two friends left Vienna on 2 September by coach.

The days he passed at Graz were the last period of holiday leisure and sunshine which Schubert was to know. He found nothing but friendliness, consideration and warm admiration there. His old friend Anselm Hüttenbrenner, who lived at Graz, was drawn into the circle, of course, and he, Jenger and Schubert made music for their own, and the Pachler's delight. The familiar coloured drawing by Teltscher of the heads of these three musicians was made at that time when the artist also visited Graz. Schubert heard the opera 'The Captivity in Egypt' by Meyerbeer at the Graz Theater, and was said to dislike it; a concert, at which *Norman's Song* was performed, was given in his honour (for he was, it will be remembered, an honorary member of the Styrian Music Society), and a comic play was staged for home performance by the Graz natives and their visitors.

There were several excursions, one to the castle of Wildbach, which was managed by an aunt of Pachler's. This visit greatly impressed not only the visitors but their hosts also. Among the people whom Schubert met at Wildbach was the father of Johann Nepomuk Fuchs, who afterwards made such a deplorable vocal score of 'Alfonso und Estrella', and who, instead of being execrated for such work, was appointed editor of the Opera Volumes in the 'Gesamtausgabe' of Breitkopf & Härtel. On 20 September Schubert and Jenger returned to Vienna, taking four days over the coach trip and seeing the towns of Fürstenfeld and Friedberg and climbing the summit of the Eselberg, before descending the valley road to Vienna via Schleinz.

Schubert wrote a warm letter of thanks to Frau Pachler, and said during the course of it:

> Above all, I shall never forget the kindly shelter, where, with its dear hostess and the sturdy 'Pachleros' as well as little Faust, I spent the happiest days I have had for a long time. . . .

Faust was the seven-year-old son of the house, a frail-looking, delicately formed boy. Schubert wrote a march ('Kindermarsch') for PF. Duet and sent it to him during October. He wrote on the manuscript a short letter to the boy's mother in which he warned her 'I fear I shall not earn his applause, since I do not feel I am exactly made for this kind of composition'. His self-distrust is not groundless; in attempting to write down to a young musician's level of understanding, he suppresses completely his own individuality. The 'Kindermarsch' is without any point of interest. Faust and his mother performed the march on 4 November, in honour of Karl Pachler; it was his name-day, and for this worthy occasion Schubert had promised the piece. He added in his letter to Marie Pachler that his 'usual headaches' were assailing him again, an ominous touch. A very different piece of music was also sent to Graz at that time; Schubert dispatched the full score of 'Alfonso und Estrella', since the possibility of a performance of the opera at the Graz Theater had been discussed. But this never materialised, although the score was hopefully kept by Karl Pachler for many years.

While he was at Graz Schubert composed two songs; the words of the first, *Heimliches Lieben*, were given to him by Marie Pachler, but those of the second song, *Eine altschottische Ballade*, suggest that it reached Schubert in a more round-about fashion. The Scottish ballad is 'Edward', from Bishop Percy's 'Reliques of Ancient English Poetry' and was translated into German by Herder. An examination of Schubert's text suggests that he used not a literary source at all but a song, namely, Loewe's setting of the ballad, his Op. 1: no. 1, published by Schlesinger of Berlin three years previously. Textual discrepancies in Loewe's text re-appear in Schubert's, but are not to be found in any one of Herder's own version of the poem, of which there are three.[1] Schubert had also composed at Graz some dances known as the 'Grätzer Walzer' and a single 'Grätzer Galopp'; the twelve waltzes were published in January 1828 by Haslinger, as Op. 91, and he included the 'Galopp' in a series of similar dances called

[1] See 'Monthly Musical Record', London, December 1955.

'Favorit Galoppe'. On his return to Vienna Schubert set the two poems *Das Weinen* and *Vor meiner Wiege*. They were by Karl von Leitner, a young poet who was a friend of the Pachler's and greatly admired by Marie. Schubert set the poems at her request. He included with them the two others he had composed at Graz, *Heimliches Lieben* and *Eine altschottische Ballade*, and intended to publish all four as Op. 106, dedicating the edition to Marie Pachler. The songs were lithographed by the Vienna 'Lithographisches Institut' but not, at first, given an opus-number. Moreover, at the last minute, the *Ballade* was removed and *To Silvia* substituted for it. Jenger wrote to Marie about the opus of songs, promising to bring her copies to Graz himself. But this he never did, and Marie received no copies from Schubert's own hands: instead she was obliged to buy her own.

Besides the manuscripts of the opera and the children's march there was at Graz another autograph of Schubert's: this was the sketch he wrote for the song *Die Nebensonnen*, which comes near the end of the 'Winterreise' song-cycle. The page was purchased from Faust Pachler many years later by Witteczek (October 1842). The second twelve songs of 'Winterreise' are fair copies in Schubert's hand, and are dated at the start 'October 1827'. If Schubert was working on *Die Nebensonnen* in September, it seems fairly clear that sketches for Part II of the song-cycle were being composed before the Graz holiday, that is, in August. But the final drafts and fair copies were being made during October although months passed before they were in the publisher's hands. No attempt was made by Schubert, or Haslinger, to re-assemble the twenty-four songs so that they corresponded with Müller's final order. The twelve songs from February were called 'Part I' and published in January 1828 as Op. 89: nos. 1–12. The next twelve, of October, were called 'Part II' and published after Schubert's death, in December 1828, as Op. 89: nos. 13–24. There is a faint possibility that the retaining of the original twelve songs as 'Part I' may have been deliberate on Schubert's part, and that he intended the cycle to be thought of, and performed, as in two parts; to give a literary analogy, we could cite Shakespeare's 'Henry IV'. It would ease the strain on both singer and audience to have either part of the cycle, and not both, in a public performance.

Further settings of Leitner, from the book of his poems which Schubert had received from Marie Pachler, were completed in November: *Der Wallensteiner Lanzknecht*, *Der Kreuzzug* and *Des Fischers Liebesglück*. The Leitner songs are an undistinguished group, while at the same time containing characteristic work. The poet's ideas are of a humdrum order—Capell calls them feeble-minded!—and they induced a certain spineless kind of writing from Schubert. The best of them is the erotic *Fischers Liebesglück* with its piano imagery, which suggests the swaying boat beneath the stars, but even that develops perfunctorily.

The month is graced by the composition of the second Trio for Pianoforte, violin and 'cello, in E flat. Schubert's sketches for the work, as well as his fair copy, are extant. It has been suggested that the work loomed too large in the nineteenth century, but this is not to belittle the achievement of its creation. It is a masterpiece and contributed much to the musical developments of 1828, particularly in the new organisation of the first movement, an organisation which Schubert had tried already in the G major String Quartet. The assertion made by Leopold Sonnleithner to Ferdinand Luib, in a letter written in 1857, that the theme of the slow movement was taken from a lost song by the Swedish composer Isaak Berg cannot be dismissed out of hand. Schubert did meet Berg in 1827 and heard some of his songs. But it would need the evidence of the song put before us to be convincing, for the C minor theme said to be derived in this way seems pre-eminently the composer's own. A manuscript copy of the Trio was in the possession of Karoline Esterházy at Schubert's death. He gave her the copy since the original had gone to the Leipzig publisher Probst, during 1828, for publication as Op. 100; this has since been lost. Karoline's manuscript suggests that Schubert had come into closer touch again with the Esterházy family, probably when Marie, the older sister, was married in Vienna on 1 December 1827. The surmise gains support from the fact that the Fantasia in F minor for PF. Duet, Op. 103, composed in January 1828 and published posthumously, was dedicated to Karoline.

The publications in 1827 included works for PF. Duet: Op. 75, the set of four Polonaises, from Diabelli, and two movements belonging to the 'Divertissement in E minor', mistakenly published by Weigl as Op. 84: nos. 1 and 2. A third PF. Duet was the rather showy set of variations on a theme by Hérold, which Haslinger published in September as Op. 82. This publisher also brought out during that same month Schubert's Op. 83, three Italian songs written for the great bass singer Luigi Lablache, and dedicated to him. They are undeservedly neglected, although this is perhaps understandable since they require the highest artistry as well as a noble voice. At the close of the year Haslinger published the first two of Schubert's famous series of Impromptus. They were called (eventually) Op. 90: nos. 1 and 2, the *Allegro molto moderato* in C minor, and the skimming *Allegro* in E flat. A year later the publisher advertised all four numbers of the opus, but the third and fourth pieces did not appear until 1857. By that time Tobias Haslinger was dead, and his son Karl published them. The third piece, the *Andante* in G flat major, was transposed into G major; the fourth is the *Allegretto*, which, like the song *Auf dem Wasser zu singen* is supposedly in A flat major, but commences in the minor key and postpones the resolution into the major key for as long as possible in order to delay the sheer, sensuous satisfaction of the change.

Schubert continued the series of 'Impromptus' until there were eight in all: the last four are dated December 1827 and actually entitled 'Impromptus' by the composer. This should dispose of the theory first announced by Schumann and supported by other writers, including Einstein, that the four pieces are a sonata, broken up to be more saleable. The four pieces, an *Allegro moderato* in F minor, the *Allegretto* in A flat major, the *Theme and variations* in B flat major, and the *Allegro scherzando* in F minor, seem to have an underlying key scheme such as would befit a sonata; but the key of the third is an awkward one to square with the others, and the first piece is certainly not a 'first-movement' from any formal point of view. The variations, a popular item, are based on a variant of Schubert's favourite theme from the 'Rosamunde' entr'acte in the same key. The four pieces were published complete by Diabelli, in two books, as Op. 142, in 1838. The influence of Schubert's 'Impromptus' on novel trends in pianoforte composition during the nineteenth century has been unduly stressed. Until 1838, it will be seen, only two of them had been published, and although they are not, in fact, movements from sonatas, there is little to distinguish them from Schubert's smaller sonata movements, that is to say, from his lighter slow movements, minuets and finales. The ironical fact, in my own view, is that they influenced Chopin, Schumann and Brahms, if at all, in their *sonata* writing, rather than in their shorter, lyrical pieces.

On 26 December the new PF. Trio was performed at a 'Musikverein' concert, and was given by Karl von Bocklet, Schuppanzigh and the 'cellist, Josef Linke. This performance doubtless inspired Schubert to make the final effort to give a concert of his own, and when, in fact, he did so, the PF. Trio in E flat was the chief item. The performance in December may also have inspired him to compose what was the last work of the year: a 'Fantasie' in C major, for PF. and violin, composed for Slavík and Bocklet. It is a full scale work, containing much vituoso writing for both instruments. But like the 'Rondo brillant' it fails to reconcile the claims of such technical display with those of his own genius. All four sections promise well at the start: the emotional undertones, the poised themes, the exalted atmosphere; but all too soon the rich embroidery begins and the music grows turgid. A set of elaborately decorated variations on his song *Sei mir gegrüsst* forms the third movement. At the first performance, in January 1828, Slavík was said to be unable to cope with the difficult part, and the piece failed to please. The 'Harmonicon' representative in Vienna was, for all that, again kind in his judgement: '... a new Fantasia for PF. and violin, from the pen of Franz Schubert possesses merit far above the common order.'

Reviews of this kind were frequent in the press of provincial Germany also, during 1826 and 1827. Before glancing at the four major works of the period, we might perhaps look at what Schubert's contemporary critics said about the music being published. The man who treated his work with the greatest seriousness wrote in the Leipzig 'Allgemeine Musikalische Zeitung'. He was

Gottfried Wilhelm Fink, a composer and writer on music, who had evidently taken a fancy to Schubert's Op. 21 (songs, including *Auf der Donau*) in 1824, and although not wholly approving, yet realised the young composer's gifts and appreciated the master touch in his music. Each successive work which reached his journal, Op. 42, Op. 39, Op. 59, was given the same serious regard, and the pages on Op. 42, the Sonata in A minor, are full of admiration. Finally, on the Sonata in G major, Op. 78, published and misnamed by Haslinger, he wrote a long and comprehensive study which was sensible and approving. Did Schubert see this review we might wonder? He would have appreciated the worth of the reviewer and enjoyed the well-considered praise. But a similarly named music journal in Frankfort dismissed the Sonata in a few lines; taking Haslinger's title as an indication that there were four separate pieces for the piano, it said of them: '. . . recommended for piano practice.' This Frankfort journal also reviewed regularly the Schubert song publications. It used a rather grudging tone, being unable to give up the basic idea in Germany of that day, that 'song' meant 'strophic song' and that there was something not quite *en règle* in Schubert's dramatic and richly wrought 'on-running' songs. Berlin was even more intransigent over the strophic song; but when the reviewer in the Berlin 'Allgemeine Musikzeitung' did encounter Schubert's use of that straightforward form, as in *Die Dioskuren*, he could not speak too highly of such settings. In Weimar and Munich, music periodicals reviewed the songs and spoke of them with moderate approval.

In Vienna itself there is seldom an independent voice to give us an insight into the reception there of Schubert's work, since most of the music critics were friends or partisans of his. But his songs were obviously popular with the general public, and his dance music was heard everywhere—even on the music-box mechanism of inn clocks.

VIII

There are, it has been suggested, four major works of this period—the String Quartet in G major, the Sonata in G major, the PF. Trio in B flat, all of 1826, and the second PF. Trio in E flat of 1827 (a year spent mostly in the composition of miniatures: songs, part-songs and piano-pieces).

The String Quartet in G requires four first-rate players in performance, and like the D minor Quartet, demands absolute unanimity of phrasing and interpretation between the first and second violins. It is music of the grandest, noblest order. The first movement ranks with the first movement of the C major Symphony of 1828 as one of Schubert's most successful essays in sonata-form. His method, in the quartet, the earliest definite and conscious use of it, is to write an opening theme of great breadth and nobility, which, we are persuaded, is more in the nature of an introduction since an obvious and energetic 'first theme' follows it at once. But as the movement proceeds and his purpose unfolds, we see the noble *motif* of the introductory bars assuming a greater importance. The 'energetic' theme is developed and worked in all kinds of imaginative ways, but above it, beyond it, as it were, is the majesty and power of the primary theme, lifting and ennobling the music. We find this 'double-theme' in other works of the last years, in the PF. Trio in E flat, in the String Quintet in C, in the last symphony, and in the second of the 1828 sonatas, the one in A major. It represents one aspect of the composer's artistic growth: early works display a double presentation of the one main them, the second more elaborate than the first, *cf.* the D minor String Quartet. This device grew into the finer, more satisfactory one we now consider. The String Quartet in G major opens with a held G-major chord which swells in a quick *crescendo* and breaks into rapid, G-minor figuration. This is repeated in the dominant key, D major. Its novelty is still a striking feature even today, when our ears are shocked by nothing. The apparent 'first theme', one of Schubert's loveliest inspirations, is now played by the first violin over softly thrummed chords in the lower strings, which move down through whole tones, G major to F major, F major to E flat major, and thence to G major:

Schubert's huge extension of dominant tonality (D major) for the 'second subject' section of his exposition is achieved by exploring the subsidiary keys of F sharp minor, B flat major and B minor. A lyrical theme is heard in all three keys, combined with a rising and falling *arpeggio* played with *tremolo* bowing. The development section exploits all four of these expositional ideas in writing which is coherent and well organised—but on fire. Nothing in the exposition but is transfigured and glorified in the wonderful sweep and ecstasy of these pages. Themes having no connection in the exposition are brought together to produce new situations, new emotions, just as two characters in a play might encounter and set going a tense, unexpected development of the plot:

The melodic tensions which Schubert can set up by unexpected harmonic changes and re-orientations in his themes are wonderfully realised in this movement, in, for example, bars 185–189, where a C flat instead of the normal C natural gives an aching unresolution to the melody. The tone-colour contrasts of the quartet, especially the rapid *tremolo* bowing set against the organ-like sounds of the sustained chords, show that Schubert was fully aware of his medium, and delighted with that one minor aspect of it. Broad, impassioned transitional episodes link the main sections of the movement; they have been described and quoted in the remarkable article on Schubert's tonality by Sir Donald Tovey mentioned earlier in this book. The *coda* to the movement might be read as a Schubertian 'Credo', for the music proclaims with no mental reservations at all his belief in the unity of the major and minor modes.

The slow movement in E minor is elegiac in tone, but contains the famous, almost notorious, episodes where classical tonality is completely thrown aside. Even if on paper Schubert's devices can be explained, in sound they are extraordinary. No attempt is made to placate the ear; while in the bass the strings move down from E minor to C sharp minor, and thence to B flat minor, the violin and viola reiterate a *staccato* phrase in an uncompromising G minor. There is a moving *coda* in E major, a foretaste of the Schubertian tranquillity of 1828, and in the key which was to embody that unearthly mood—his key of dreams and consolation.

The Scherzo, in B minor, is full of the rhythmic energy which animates the corresponding movement in the great C major Symphony, but the finale, similar in mood, and even in theme structure, is a little too superficial. The course of events had already been told, and told well, in the finale of the D minor Quartet. This time the tale does not grip. The best part of the movement is the C sharp minor passage, the theme shared between second violin and 'cello, in bars 322–354. This is in the mood of the Ernst Schulze songs of the period, and actually recalls one of them: *Ueber Wildemann.*

The sonata in the same key, written four months later, nowhere reaches the heights of the string quartet, but nowhere becomes as shallow as the finale of the chamber work. The expansive, hovering melody of the opening movement is built on a favourite sequential plan: a phrase in the tonic key followed by an almost identical phrase in the subdominant:

So natural and spontaneous are the results of this plan that it was probably a subconscious creative 'kink' of his. The unpredictable nature of Schubert's development-sections is borne out by this sonata. What would Beethoven have made out of the above theme? We can partly answer this question because a similar theme opens his G major PF. Concerto, Op. 58. He would, for the purposes of development, largely ignore it, using, if any part of it were used, only the mere opening half-bar figure. But Schubert used the whole stretch of the theme in imitative patterns, played *fortissimo* and gaining in power until they are thundered out in majestic and wide-spread chords.

Twice this huge crescendo is presented, but there are a number of significant changes of detail to be found in the second occurrence, for the climax and relaxation occur in keys so chosen that Schubert can return to the soft serenity of his recapitulation through a G minor to G major change.

Although the slow movement, an *Andante* in D major, is not a 'Theme and Variations', it has a remarkable resemblance to the variation-movement in the Sonata in A minor, Op. 42; there is the same song-like theme, and the same energetic, clangorous episodes in minor keys. The composer works at a scheme of rhythmic elaboration in this movement, and both themes are subjected to it; great variety is obtained within a short movement. The following quotation gives the outline of one theme's rhythmic development and evolution:

The 'Menuetto', a stately B minor movement, is marked *Allegro moderato*. To bring out the full effect of Schubert's *appoggiaturas* the *moderato* indication must be carefully observed. It seldom is in performance. The 'Trio' is a lyrical contrast in B major, derived from the close of the 'Menuetto' in a flash of genius, and appealingly beautiful in its miniature compass: one of the most lovable passages which Schubert ever penned. There is the same lowering of tension in the sonata-finale as there was in the string quartet; we have a homely, tuneful movement, completely individual in that it proclaims its composer throughout, but with few touches of poetry to lift it above its everyday level. One of these touches is found in the theme in C minor, which is decorated by short scale-like passages in a way prophetic of mid-nineteenth-century styles.

The two PF. Trios do not, in spite of the similarity of medium, suggest a unit in the way that the two string quartets of 1824, or the three sonatas of 1828, certainly do. If the story of the pile-drivers' theme is sufficient grounds for giving the earlier Trio the date '1826', then something like eighteen months separated the two compositions; in Schubert's life that was a reasonably long period. The style of the first movement of the B flat Trio would confirm the date (although alone it would be insufficient evidence). The main theme, a buoyantly lyrical and strongly characterised melody, is played at the outset, and followed by a complex modulatory episode based on a fragment from it, the triplet figure in bar 2. Then comes its second presentation, not more elaborate this time, but differently instrumented, a famous touch of Schubertian charm:

The use of the piano as the singer, with the strings providing a light background, is irresistible. The development has the same underlying plan as in the G major Sonata just considered. The melody is given *forte* in the minor key, builds up imitatively to a big climax and then yields to the second contrasting subject played in a soft, *dolce* episodic style, just as in the sonata. Towards the end of the development section of this movement, there is a remarkable 'false start' to the recapitulation; listeners with no sense of absolute pitch would be quite taken in, although the key is G flat, not the orthodox B flat. It serves the same purpose as a similar trick in the sonata—Schubert can glide from G flat into the fresh and sunny tonality of B flat for the 'real start'. And once there we realise that the G flat passage was a transposed version of the first presentation of the theme (bars 1–25).

In the E flat Trio, the opening is likewise a bold, typical theme, with the three instruments in unison, but the ground-plan of this movement belongs to his later styles of sonata-writing; the unison theme is introductory and is followed a few bars later by the 'main theme' of the movement. The two themes are quoted here in outline only:

The second subject is devoted to two vigorous themes in B minor and C minor, although the essential unity of the whole exposition is obtained—perhaps, according to strict classical procedure, wrongly—by references to themes (*a*) and (*b*) above. Then, in a remarkable way, the *codetta* is launched with a quiet little tune, harmonised with all his resource, which seems at first hearing to be an entirely new idea:

But examined, it can be seen to unite elements from the two themes of Ex. 78: the rhythm of (*a*), the melody of (*b*). The *codetta* theme is used as the basis of a long-drawn development section, a complete break with his procedures hitherto. The essential union of (*a*) and (*b*) into the *codetta* theme is clear when the introductory theme logically emerges from it, ready for the recapitulation. Lack of dramatic contrasts prevents the movement from taking a place in the front rank of Schubert's first movements, certainly it cannot compare with the first movement of the earlier Trio. But the next two movements, an *Andante con moto* in C minor, and a canonic Scherzo in E flat, are much finer than anything in the companion work. The threnodic march of the C minor movement heralds the *Andante con moto* of the last symphony. The finales of both Trios hardly deserve all the derogatory adjectives usually bestowed on them. They are, it is true, entertainingly written: dance-like metres, and heart-easing melodies produce lightweight movements. But, to begin with, the craftsmanship is admirable. Light movements, like Schubert's two finales, are not found so perfectly articulated and structurally sound, in the music of lesser men. Nor could Schubert, it has been repeatedly said in these pages, produce, in 1826 and 1827, music without moments of depth, and beauty, and passing wonder. The episodes in D flat and G flat, in the finale of Op. 99, where the pianoforte rises and falls, *pianissimo*, through three octaves, are delicious; and the introduction in the finale of Op. 100 of the C minor theme from the *Andante* movement, is a tremendously impressive passage, and one of the earliest instances in musical history of such a 'cyclic' device, a device to become so dear to the 'Romantic' period in the next thirty years.

The Trio in E flat was completed during November 1827, and, as already recorded, its first performance took place the next month. Schubert, in those days, was a sick and dispirited man. The disease contracted five years earlier was inwardly and inexorably undermining his health. To the headaches of which he had complained in the letter to Marie Pachler were added giddiness and nausea. Twice that autumn he cancelled arrangements because of ill-health. The second of these occasions was a party given by Anna Hönig. The letter he wrote to her has only recently been discovered. Its contents were known and are briefly stated in the Schubert 'Documents' (page 681). Here it is published for the first time in English:

[Outside] To Miss Nanette v. Hönig, *personal.*
[Inside]

I find it very difficult to have to tell you that I cannot give myself the pleasure of being at your party this evening. I am ill, and *in a way* which totally unfits me for such a gathering. With the renewed assurance that I am extremely sorry not to be able to oblige you

I remain,
Yours faithfully,
Frz. Schubert

Vienna, 15*th Oct.* 1827.

His material prospects had never been so gloomy; he seems to have lost heart where operatic composition was concerned, for can we imagine the music for 'Der Graf von Gleichen' hanging fire in the way it did if his heart had been in it—he who had set 'Fierrabras' in a few months? And the Viennese market was almost saturated with his work. We have seen that the anecdote is false, which tells of the toast he drank on the night of Beethoven's funeral. Schubert never toasted the 'next traveller' along the road of death. But a salutation as gloomy as this, and as prophetic, occurs in a poem of Bauernfeld's; he read it to the assembled friends on New Year's Day, 1828, in the house where Schober and Schubert were living. It contains this remarkable verse:

The spells of the poet, the pleasures of singing,
They too will be gone, be they true as they may;
No longer will songs in our party be ringing,
For the singer too will be called away.
The waters from source to the sea must throng,
The singer at last will be lost in his song.

Within the year the 'singer' was, in fact, called away, and only his songs remained to recall his image to the friends.

VIII

1828

I

Bauernfeld's prophecy bore an uncanny resemblance to the truth, but life itself outdid the poet in giving that truth an air of ordained doom. The pieces of the pattern seem to fall carefully into place as we look at the last year of Schubert's life: it has the elements of closure, and like all endings, it promises many beginnings. His friends, all of them, even the estranged Mayrhofer, were in Vienna, and in touch with him again. There was no holiday, and he remained in Vienna the whole year; he did not leave the beloved city even for a few weeks in the neighbouring countryside. The pace of composing was forced; masterpiece followed masterpiece in staggering succession. The stimulus of creating this superb music gave him life as few men know it. Then, as the year waned, his friends departed. He took up lodgings with his brother Ferdinand. It was like a homecoming, and there his last, fatal illness was to overtake him. The work of composing never ceased; the feverish power of his genius which exacted this music and drove him to such spiritual exaltation, in the end gave him death. When it came, death was like an exhausted sleep.

During January the Schubertians met at Bogner's café for their evening convivialities. Schubert was not always present, but it is clear enough that his music was the attractive force which held the men together. The friction between Spaun and Schober occasionally produced open disagreement. The two men were temperamentally poles apart, and even in their response to the music of their friend, it has been suggested, that temperamental difference was most marked. The earnest thoughfulness of Spaun was frequently at odds with Schober's mercurial spirits. But their mutual love for Schubert kept them together. 'Through him', Spaun wrote of Schubert, 'we were all brothers and friends.'

Throughout the early months of the year they met frequently —often once a week—in Schober's rooms for the 'reading-circles', now resumed after a lapse of four years. Various books of prose and poetry were read, usually by Schober, whose experience as an actor was doubtless an asset. The literature chosen was chiefly the work of minor 'Romantic' authors such as Tieck, but Kleist, Goethe and Aeschylus also figured in the readings. At one period the poems of Heine's 'Reisebilder' ('Travel Sketches') were read, and Schubert must have been present, for all six of his Heine songs are in the group so entitled. He may have sketched some of them during the spring of 1828. The two settings of Leitner, *Winterabend* and *Die Sterne*, each a different picture of the night sky, were composed in January, and Schubert also sketched during the month the 'Fantasia' in F minor, which is today gradually winning the esteem it deserves, as his greatest work for PF. Duet. Schubertiads continued to be as popular as in the previous autumn, although the composer was not always present. 'Schubert kept us waiting for him in vain' wrote one of his admirers, 'but . . . Titze sang many of his songs so touchingly and soulfully that we did not feel his absence too painfully.' The last Schubertiad to be held in Spaun's lodging's took place on 28 January, for the forty-three-year-old lawyer had at length become engaged to be married. His fiancée was Franziska Roner, whom Franz von Hartmann was delighted to describe in his diary as 'very nice, cultivated and pretty'. The Schubertiad was held in her honour. There seem to have been no songs, but the PF. Trio in B flat and the Variations in A flat, Op. 35, were played; the first by Schuppanzigh, Bocklet and Linke, the second by Schubert and Gahy. The evening ended with dancing until the small hours. Spaun and Franziska were married in the Peterskirche on 14 April.

During February Schubert was working on the C major Symphony. The month ascribed to it, 'March,' is written at the start of the full score; there must therefore have been preliminary work of an earlier date, and that this preliminary work was in an advanced stage is obvious from Schubert's letter of 21 February 1828 to the publishers Schott's Sons of Mainz. He mentioned in it a symphony, a completed work. This was in all probability the finished PF. sketch, begun at Gmunden in 1825, completed in Vienna by February 1828, and orchestrated in March. Later, presumably, in March, when the symphony was finished, he composed the setting of Grillparzer's poem *Mirjams Siegesgesang* (*Miriam's Song of Victory*). The music is for soprano and mixed chorus, but remains on modest levels of appraisement since the accompaniment was written for piano, not orchestra. It is a noble work, conceived on broad and balanced lines, with some vigorous and exciting passages when the text describes the Red Sea overwhelming Pharaoh and his host. The fugal treatment of the opening and closing choruses has been ascribed to the influence of Handel. The publisher Haslinger may have lent Schubert some of the oratorio scores of that composer: that he did so is purely conjectural. But we know that Schubert was reading and playing Bach's fugues from the '48', and the passages in *Miriam's Song* recall Bach rather than Handel. The cantata may have been intended by Schubert as the chief adornment of an ambitious project then engaging his mind. This was the organising of a concert consisting entirely of his own compositions. It would account for the piano accompaniment to the *Miriam* cantata—a practical issue. The concert evening was an ambition which had recurred to him at intervals for the past five years, but circumstances had not been favourable. Now, in this fatal year, obstacles melt away, and the dream becomes a reality.

We read in the Schubert records his petition of 6 March to the *Gesellschaft der Musikfreunde* for the use of their concert hall in the Tuchlauben premises. This was granted, and the concert, postponed from 21 to 26 March, was advertised in the Vienna 'Theaterzeitung'. Tickets at 2/6 each were sold by Diabelli and Haslinger, although the programme was headed 'Invitation to the Private Concert which Franz Schubert will have the honour of giving. . . .' The cantata, *Miriam's Song*, it is fairly obvious, was intended for the women's singing-class of Anna Fröhlich and the male-voice choir of the *Gesellschaft*, with Josefine Fröhlich singing the soprano solo part. Presumably it was not ready in time, for another setting of Grillparzer, the 'Serenade', which Schubert had composed for Louise Gosmar, was sung, and the men's chorus gave the long-drawn and rather uninspiring *Schlachtgesang* (*Battle Song*), to words by Klopstock. This composition, for double chorus, seems to be a grandiose expansion of a former setting dating as early as July 1816.

The instrumental items were both, from a modern point of view, dubious choices: the first movement of a string quartet (called 'new' in the programme, and presumably taken from the work in G major of 1826), and the whole of the PF. Trio in E flat. The string quartet movement ranks with his greatest work, but it is anything but 'popular' in its appeal, and the PF. Trio, with its leisurely progress, and of elegiac sadness in some of its moods, is hardly a winning item. Vogl, accompanied by Schubert, sang two groups of songs, and a new song with horn obbligato, called *Auf dem Strome*, was performed by Ludwig Titze and Josef Lewy.

A packed audience, all ardent admirers of the composer and determined to make the evening a success, applauded each item with shouts and stampings. Schubert, his fellow performers, and his close friends, were all elated by the triumphant progress of the evening.

The concert was reported briefly in Leipzig, Dresden and Berlin, but it is almost unbelievable that the Vienna papers ignored it altogether. The advent of the virtuoso violinist Paganini three days after Schubert's concert claimed their entire attention. Fate, having with one stroke cleared the way for that concert, was not concerned that the fruits of it be fortunate, and there is an ironic touch about the incidence of the concert of Paganini. One reads in a contemporary reference these astonishing words: '. . . minor stars [i.e. Schubert] paled before the radiance of this comet in the musical heavens [i.e. Paganini]'. The concert was not forgotten by the people who had attended and the editor of the Vienna journal 'Musikzeitung', Johann Schikh, wrote on behalf of a number of them, begging Schubert to repeat the occasion.

He made £32 from the concert. Unless a good deal of the sum went in settling debts, it is difficult to know why he was unable to leave Vienna as the summer approached for a much needed holiday. He pleaded lack of money when declining two invitations from the countryside. The first was from Ferdinand Traweger, the friend with whom he had stayed in Gmunden during 1825. It was a generous invitation making it clear that Schubert could stay in Traweger's house for as long as he wished, and in order not to embarrass the composer he asked a nominal sum for full board and lodging: it was 8d. a day! The second was from the Pachlers at Graz, again, a generous and accommodating offer. There were probably others, for Jenger wrote to Marie Pachler that Schubert had received several invitations from friends at Gmunden. But a short excursion into the Wiener Wald at the beginning of June, to Baden and the Heiligenkreuz Monastery, was the only break that year. Schubert was accompanied by Schikh and Lachner. At Baden, where they spent a night, Lachner organised a friendly competition, and he and Schubert each wrote a fugue for Organ Duet, which they played on the Abbey church organ the following day. Schubert's manuscript has been inscribed by some unknown friend 'Baden, 3 June 1828'. His fugue is in E minor and was published in 1844 as Op. 152; it is a mild, but not unattractive, piece.

Another 'occasional' composition, which, like the E minor fugue, is not without a certain wan charm, is the choral song *Glaube, Hoffnung und Liebe*, finished during August. Schubert wrote it for the consecration of a new bell at the 'Minorite' Church of the Holy Trinity in the Alsergrund suburb; the church was becoming famous, since Beethoven's funeral service had taken place there. It was situated in the Alser Strasse, not very far from Schubert's birthplace. The music of the processional chorus, accompanied by wind instruments, is in a slow 6/8 tempo which vividly suggests the rocking swing of a huge bell.

Glimpses of Schubert, his friends and the Viennese scene during August, like scenes through a peephole, are provided by the diaries of the Hartmann brothers and Bauernfeld. Schwind's brother was at home and the group of friends read 'Faust' at Schober's home on one evening, play-acted Kotzebue's one-act satire 'Die Unglücklichen' at Bauernfeld's on another, and, on most evenings, seated outside a favourite alehouse, 'Die Eiche', near St. Stefan's Cathedral, watched the moon rise over the city. At the beginning of September they all attended the première of Bauernfeld's comedy 'Die Brautwerber' ('The Suitors'), which had only a moderate success, but which Schubert found 'extraordinarily pleasing'. Soon after this Bauernfeld left Vienna, and Schwind departed for Munich the next month. Mayrhofer, after the brief appearance during the spring of the year, lost touch with Schubert, and the marriages of Vogl, Kupelwieser and Spaun meant an inevitable loosening of the ties between them and the composer. The Hartmann brothers also bade farewell to the capital and to the Schubert circle, leaving for Linz at the end of August.

II

These summer months spent in Vienna were devoted to composition. Schubert, instead of recuperating from his work in the spring, drove himself harder. His desire to initiate publication in Germany, which could only be achieved by piano or chamber works, led him to write several pieces of this sort in the early summer. The great 'Fantasia' in F minor was finished in April and played to Bauernfeld by Schubert and Lachner on 9 May. It has, in the highest degree, all those characteristic qualities of the composer which have endeared him to generations of music lovers, and the 'Scherzo' section is one of his finest stretches of writing for the piano. Two other duets, one of May and one of June, although published separately and usually considered as independent compositions may have been designed as movements from a third 'Sonata' for PF. Duet, designed but not completed by the composer. The first is the *Allegro ma non troppo* in A minor, published by Diabelli in 1840 and given the catchpenny title 'Lebensstürme' ('Life's Storms'). It is a strong, vigorous movement in sonata-form, and contains what is, in the opinion of many Schubertians, his loveliest melody. The melodic 'tensions', discussed in the previous chapter as being so remarkable a feature of the Schubert melody in the 1820's, lead, in this one, to some fascinating shifts from key to key. The second duet would have contributed, perhaps, the finale of the sonata. It is a 'Rondo' in A major, published by Artaria as Op. 107 a month or so after the composer's death. Schubert had written it for the publisher. Again, the melodic charm of the work is irresistible; Schumann, who thought this 'Rondo' one of Schubert's best compositions, has some remarkably interesting things to say of it (in a letter to Friedrich Wieck, 6 November 1829). In the last episode of the rondo (at the change to C major) Schubert uses the sequence-structure to achieve some most admirable harmonic and tonal effects, so new and, for their day, so revolutionary, that we can understand some of the concluding sentences in Schumann's letter mentioned above:

> I remember playing that very Rondo at an evening party at Herr Probst's, but at the finish both players and listeners stared at one another, rather at a loss to know what to think, or to know what Schubert meant by it all. . . .

In the letter which Jenger wrote on 4 July to Marie Pachler, warning her that Schubert and he would probably not, after all, be able to come to Graz that year, he added that the composer was in Vienna working at a 'new Mass'. None of the composer's manuscript sketches for this Mass, nor his fair copy, is dated, but it is evident from Jenger's letter that he had begun work on the Mass in E flat after his return from Baden in June. The music is for a quartet of solo voices, mixed chorus and orchestra. Schubert intended originally to 'figure' the 'cello and bass line for organ continuo, but changed his mind and struck out the words 'e organo' from his score. It is said that he meant the Mass for performance in the 'Minorite' Church; if so, the request to write a processional chorus for the consecration of the bell may be connected with his decision. The Mass was performed for the first time in the church nearly a year after Schubert's death, on 4 October 1829.

During August he completed a batch of songs on poems by Ludwig Rellstab. These were nine in number and Schubert may have intended them to form a kind of song-cycle: *Lebensmut*, *Herbst*, *Liebesbotschaft*, *Kriegers Ahnung*, *Frühlingssehnsucht*,

Ständchen, Aufenthalt, In der Ferne and *Abschied.* Schindler, in his reminiscences of Schubert, would have us believe that he found these poems of Rellstab among the posthumous papers of Beethoven, and that he handed them over to Schubert. Rellstab, years later, added a grace-note or two to the anecdote: he said that Beethoven had *asked* Schindler to give the poems to Schubert, and to suggest that he might set them to music. Dates, apparently so unimportant to these tale-spinners, will not square with the two stories.

The first two songs, *Lebensmut* and *Herbst*, are practically unknown. They were both composed earlier than the other seven. *Lebensmut* is considered a fragment, but is it actually so? A cursory glance at the song shows that Schubert's intention was to repeat the prelude of the song as a coda, although he has not written it out. This done we have a complete song, of a lively conception and much charm. Capell suggests that Schubert broke off because Rellstab's second stanza would not fit the music of the first, and this may be so: but there is no need to sing any more than the first stanza. The song is far too good to leave in obscurity. It was not published until 1872. The second song, *Herbst*, is an even finer work. The original draft was lost, and not until the song-volumes of the 'Gesamtausgabe' were practically completed, did a copy turn up. Schubert had written it during April 1828 in the album of the violinist Heinrich Panofka. It was published in the last volume of the songs in 1895. The stormy, E minor movement of the song recalls *Die Junge Nonne.* When the remaining seven songs were actually composed we do not know; the fair copy is dated 'August 1828'. They are as famous as their companions are obscure for they were published as the first part of the song series entitled by the publisher, Haslinger, 'Schwanengesang'. This so-called 'song-cycle' contains fourteen songs altogether, nos. 8–13 being six settings of Heine: *Der Atlas, Ihr Bild, Das Fischermädchen, Die Stadt, Am Meer* and *Der Doppelgänger*. The last song of the series was composed later, in October: it is *Die Taubenpost,* a setting of a poem by Seidl. This was added by Haslinger, without the composer's authorisation, surely to avoid the number thirteen; since it is actually Schubert's last song for voice and pianoforte, it rightly belongs there, at the close of his *Swansong*. The Heine songs were probably sketched and revised at intervals during 1828, from the time when Schubert had first heard them during the reading-circles. But final touches, and the fair copies, were made in August. It is also possible that Schubert intended to publish an opus consisting of the six Heine songs; Spaun wrote in his reminiscences that Schubert was then going to dedicate the collection 'to his friends'. With one possible exception each of these six songs is a masterpiece of the front rank. The assembling of the fourteen songs of the 'Schwanengesang' cycle is due to the association of Ferdinand and Haslinger, after the composer's death. They were not given an opus number and appeared in April 1829.

At the end of August Schubert took up lodgings with Ferdinand in his brother's new home. This lies to the south of the Inner City and was, in Schubert's day, a new suburb, the street in which Ferdinand's house was situated not even named. The move was recommended by Schubert's doctor, Ernst Rinna, who thought that the change of air was desirable. Schubert's health was dangerously impaired. He had complained for the last year of headache and nausea: his constant overworking, together with the haphazard conditions of living and eating, which were his daily existence, combined to bring him dangerously low. He probably adopted the doctor's suggestion with relief.

His brother's house still stands today. The street is now called the Kettenbrückengasse, and is situated in a district of populous thoroughfares, open market stalls and food shops, and dingy, tall apartment houses. The typically Viennese structure of Ferdinand's house shows a small courtyard surrounded by tall buildings. Schubert's room was on the right of the stairway.

As soon as he was settled in his new quarters he received the last of a long series of letters, written throughout that year from the publishers H. A. Probst of Leipzig and Schott's Sons of Mainz. Both men had written to him, by an almost incredible coincidence, on the same day, 9 February, offering to publish songs and pieces for piano solo or duet. The prolonged negotiations with Schott came to nothing. The composer refused to be brow-beaten into accepting niggardly fees for the proffered works. The vocal quintet *Mondenschein*, with an added PF. accompaniment, was sent to Schott's and retained by the firm, despite the fact that Schubert refused their offer of £3 for it. Three years after his death they published it—for nothing.

Probst accepted the PF. Trio in E flat, which had been so successfully received in the March concert. He gave Schubert £6 for it. The information imparted by Lachner to Grove that Schubert had received only 17/6d. for the Trio was an invention. The same source provides the false statement that Haslinger paid Schubert 10d. for each of the 'Winterreise' songs. Schubert wrote to Jenger during September saying that he had handed the second part of 'Winterreise' over to Haslinger for engraving. He had evidently completed these songs also during the autumn. The date ascribed to the second part of the song cycle is October 1827; but this is written above the fair copy of the first one, *Die Post*, and we do not know exactly when the others were composed. It is interesting to think that *Der Leiermann* may be contemporary with *Der Doppelgänger* and the other dramatic, Heine songs—or even later than they.

Besides the two large German publishing firms Schubert was approached by a more modest establishment, Karl Brüggemann, of Halberstadt, who also wanted pieces for piano solo or duet. These were to appear in a monthly album (a popular publishing device of the first half of the nineteenth century) called a 'Museum for PF. Music and Song'. Schubert expressed his willingness to contribute, but as in the similar affair with Nägeli, of 1826, nothing came of it, unless, as in the previous case, we owe to Brüggemann's invitation the sonatas of September 1828.

The few publications of 1828 in Vienna were an indication of his impossible situation there. He had reached a limit where Viennese firms were concerned. The first twelve songs of the 'Winterreise' were published as Op. 89: part I, by Haslinger, in January; three songs by Sir Walter Scott, *Lied der Anne Lyle*, *Gesang der Norna* and *Romanze des Richard Löwenherz* (the king's song from 'Ivanhoe'), appeared as Opp. 85 and 86 in March, from Diabelli; and the three well-known songs to poems by Goethe, *Der Musensohn*, *Auf dem See* and *Geistes-Gruss*, Op. 92, from Leidesdorf in July. Various songs had been privately lithographed and appeared during the summer. The only instrumental work of any importance is the 'Moments Musicaux' published in the spring by Leidesdorf as Op. 94. Moreover, when Schubert died there were very few publications impending: the group of songs known as Op. 108, containing the Schulz song *Ueber Wildemann*, was possibly designed by the composer, and, of course, there were the PF. Trio with Probst and the second part of 'Winterreise' with Haslinger which had yet to make their appearance. But his dealings with the Viennese firms were obviously declining, and after his death Ferdinand fought an unceasing but losing battle with publishers for nearly thirty years to get his brother's work accepted.

It is certain that his compositions, if not accepted by firms in Germany, were being sold there, and the reviews of some of his publications in the German papers were very definitely encouraging, and, on the whole, fair in judgement. The Leipzig 'Allgemeine Musikalische Zeitung' under its editor-reviewer G. W. Finck, was generous with space and praise in 1828, as it had been in 1827. In the three issues of 23 and 30 January, and 6 February, there were sensible and readable reviews of his songs in Opp. 79, 80, 81 and 83, and the 'Marie' Variations of Op. 82. The similarly entitled periodical of Berlin was, however, grudging in its praise of the Italian songs in Op. 83, and decidely satirical over the 'Winterreise' songs of Op. 89. This was for reasons already detailed; in Berlin 'German' song meant the strophic song and Schubert's bold schemes and modifications, and richly coloured accompaniments, disturbed and antagonised the Berliners. Munich and Dresden also reviewed various song publications, and if their praise is somewhat lukewarm, at least it is praise.

Besides letters from publishers, there were letters from distant friends and acquaintances who wrote of their admiration for his work and their appreciation of it. Johann Theodor Mosewius, music lecturer at Breslau University, wrote warmly of the two Müller song cycles. In an accompanying letter to Schober, their mutual friend, he added that he kept his pupils busy singing all the songs of 'Winterreise'. Princess Charlotte Kinsky, to whom

Schubert dedicated the four songs later known as Op. 106, wrote a cordial letter to him in July and enclosed a welcome gift of money. In Schumann's diary for 1828 there are numerous admiring references to Schubert, and this admiration was expressed in a letter to the composer which for unknown reasons he did not send. The long letter of 11 October from Anton Schindler, then in Pest, showed the same warm liking and respect for the composer's work and actually urged Schubert to go to Pest and repeat there the successful concert of the previous March.

But he was, by that time, wretchedly ill, his spirit beaten and almost broken. How is it possible to enter into the bleakness of his mood? Who can doubt but that he knew of his own powers? Could he who had composed the Symphony in C major, the Heine songs, the 'Winterreise', be unaware of the greatness of his genius? The utter indifference of the Viennese public towards those gifts must have induced at times a sick anger and frustration. And publishers like Schott's Sons, who halved his modest demands of payment for compositions, might be dealing with one of their own paid hacks. On 2 October he wrote desperately to Probst, who was still delaying the publication of Op. 100, the E flat Trio (and who went on doing so until Schubert was dead, so that he never saw a copy of his first publication outside Austria). This is his letter:

> I beg to inquire when the Trio will at last make its appearance? Is it that you do not yet know the opus number? It is Op. 100. I long for its appearance. I have composed, among other things, 3 sonatas for PF. solo, which I should like to dedicate to Hummel. I have also set several songs by Heine of Hamburg, which have pleased extraordinarily here, and finally written a quintet for 2 violins, 1 viola, and 2 violoncellos. I have played the sonatas in several places with much applause, but the quintet will be tried over only in the near future. If any of these compositions would perhaps suit you, let me know....

The reason why he composed a String Quintet, and particularly why he chose so unusual a combination of instruments, is a mystery. The three sonatas were marketable, and in spite of the slightly unfashionable aura beginning to gather round the term

START OF THE C MAJOR EPISODE FROM THE RONDO IN A MAJOR, OP. 107
SCHUBERT'S FIRST IDEA, ALTHOUGH CANCELLED, CAN STILL BE READ
Deutsche Staatsbibliothek

'sonata' he could have disposed of them reasonably quickly. But a big chamber work was another matter. It is, of course, little more than guesswork, but as he was then living with Ferdinand, one wonders if there may have been a revival of family quartet and quintet playing to suggest the composition of this work. His use of two cellos in the quintet had been the practice of Boccherini; but the combination had fallen into disuse in the early nineteenth century, when 'String Quintet', following the practice of Mozart and Beethoven, meant two violas and not two cellos. Schubert had played some of the sonata movements at an evening party held in the house of Dr. Ignaz Menz, on 27 September, but he is no doubt exaggerating a little in his report of their success 'in several places' for he wrote his letter only six days after the completion of the three sonatas. But the Heine songs had evidently been performed and had made their mark. Probst replied to this letter, but expressed interest only in the songs.

There is a note of tragic irony in Schubert's remark that the quintet would be tried over only in the near future. This work, of such supreme beauty and eloquence, lay unperformed for many a long day; not until 1850 was a cut version played in Vienna and not until three years after that was it published by the firm of C. A. Spina.

III

A short break in the routine of work occurred in early October, probably on the advice of his doctor. Ferdinand and Franz set off from Vienna on a walking tour of the district to the south of the city, to Unter-Waltersdorf, and then on to Eisenstadt, where Haydn's grave was their objective. They may have been accompanied on this excursion by friends, but it is not known for certain if this were so. In Schubert's weak and enfeebled condition the exercise could have had no beneficial effect.

After he returned to his lodgings he received Schindler's invitation to go to Pest, but such a venture was out of the question, and Schubert had no time even to acknowledge the letter for shortly after its arrival his last, fatal illness overtook him. His pen was not yet put aside, however, and in his last two songs, the miracle of detachment astonishes again. *Die Taubenpost* is a love-song, merry and tender and passionate by turns. *Der Hirt auf dem Felsen* he composed for Anna Milder-Hauptmann, yielding at last to her entreaties to provide her with a virtuoso vocal piece; the text is a composite affair drawn partly from Müller and partly from Wilhelmine von Chézy. The shepherd pipes to the spring, and so the song is provided with a clarinet obbligato. It is no empty showpiece, as the Victorians assumed rather too readily, declaring emphatically that *Die Taubenpost* was unquestionably Schubert's last song, as though *Der Hirt* was something to be hushed up. It has been sung a great deal during the last thirty years or so and has proved to be full of endearing Schubertian melody and sentiment; even the final coloratura raptures at the return of spring are filled with pure joy. The song was copied by Ferdinand after his brother's death and conveyed to Frau Hauptmann in September 1829 by Vogl. The very last productions are no fewer than four church compositions. He wrote a second, choral setting of the 'Benedictus', for his only published Mass, the one in C major, Op. 46; it was requested by Diabelli, the publisher of Op. 46, to serve as an alternative to the first setting if there were no soprano soloist available. There were two offertories, 'Tantum ergo' in E flat for vocal quartet, chorus and orchestra, and 'Intende voci' in B flat, for tenor solo, chorus and orchestra. The publication of these pieces gives yet another fantastic example to add to the chronicles of Schubert's published works. The two offertories were quite unknown during the nineteenth century. When the volume called 'Smaller Church Works' was published in the 'Gesamtausgabe' (Volume 14), in 1888, a short sketch for the first one was found and printed as a supplement in that volume. A little later someone discovered Ferdinand's copies of the vocal and instrumental parts for this 'Tantum ergo', and also for the other, then unknown, offertory, 'Intende voci'. Full scores were made up from these parts and the two works were published in 1890 by Peters of Leipzig. Later still, both of Schubert's own manuscripts were discovered, and these were published, as authentic versions, in the supplementary volume (No. 21) of the 'Gesamtausgabe', in 1897.

The fourth liturgical work was the final version, with accompaniment for woodwind and brass, of the 'Hymn to the Holy Ghost', commenced in the previous May. The text is by A. Schmidl. It was published by Diabelli in 1847 as Op. 154. All these church compositions were doubtless written with the object of strengthening his hand if ever the opportunity came of obtaining a position in the imperial or city churches of Vienna; no primary impulse, such as drove him that month to compose *Die Taubenpost*—slight though it is, dictated the composition of the four church works. The chords move in harmonic clichés, *religioso*, and the melodies are solemn and conventional. It was an indifferent epilogue to the year's work but it would hardly be possible to provide such a series of masterpieces with any epilogue at all which was not something of an anticlimax.

IV

In reviewing that series it is fitting to start with the first one of the year, the great[1] C major Symphony. The work is by general agreement the summit of his achievement in music. It might be mentioned, in passing, that the symphony seems in an almost uncanny way to have been approached by numerous tentative preparations. Right through the body of Schubert's work runs the prophetic promise of the symphony. This is not the place to consider the numerous foreshadowings but they give the symphony a strange sense of fulfilment. It is a fulfilment in other meanings of the word. The Schubertian device of the main theme which 'broods' over the movement is nowhere so marvellously exploited as in the first movement, where the *Andante* horn theme of the opening bars gradually assumes a greater and greater authority until it is played at the close of the movement with the

[1] 'Great' is, strictly speaking, simply a translation of the German word 'gross', used conventionally in Schubert's day for works scored for full orchestra, or otherwise using full scale musical forces. It can also be translated as 'Grand', e.g. 'Grand Opera', 'Grand Mass'. It was retained in the case of this symphony, after the general disuse of the term, to distinguish the work from Schubert's 'Little' Symphony in the same key of 1818. Nevertheless, the other connotation of the word—witness the small 'g'—is always present, for the world of music thereby pays tribute to the greatness of the symphony.

full panoply of the orchestra. Nor does any other movement of Schubert's exemplify so well his ability to bring together contrasting ideas so that they generate new emotions and new patterns, nor his equally skilful power of fusing those ideas into a unified whole. There are perhaps five separate ideas which are so blended or opposed in the first movement and the development section leads the listener through wonderfully varied experiences, from light, lyrical pleasure to highly dramatic excitation of feeling. The famous trombone entries in the *codetta* leading to the development section have always been looked upon as recalling the listener's attention to the opening theme of the work. Strings and woodwind build up a patterned background, using material from the second subject, when the three trombones enter with their stately phrases. William McNaught, however, considers that these were 'freshly minted' by the composer, and not derived from the opening horn theme.[1] It is possible, surely, for them to be both: a sudden inspiration, the wonder of which is that it threw up phrases so remarkably like the generative theme of the movement. We have evidence here that the theme was hovering in Schubert's mind as he conceived the evolutionary progress of the movement. A small point, overlooked in performance, is the importance of the oboe phrases at the start of the *Allegro ma non troppo*; they complete the violin themes and should not be allowed to disappear into the background.

Schubert's chromatic harmony and the harmonic 'tensions' set up in his melodies have frequently been mentioned, so that it is pleasant, as a contrast, to be able to draw attention to the purity

[1] 'The Symphony', ed. Ralph Hill, London, 1949, page 157.

and charm of the clear, diatonic harmony in this movement (bars 268–274, for example).

The slow movement is the whole world of Schubert: his poetry and passion, his tender response, his technical gifts of thematic development, his use of the orchestra which is without equal in the sphere of non-pictorial music, and, above all, that subjective, intensely personal approach to the listener which woos and wins his affection. An episode which deserves the highest admiration in its technical handling is the A major recapitulation of the second theme, the one first heard in F major. The novel treatment of the brass instruments, that is, as utterers of poetic ideas instead of mere reinforcers of noise, won the willing tributes of the nineteenth century, although its orchestras refused to play the work. The child who conducted the *Stadtkonvikt* orchestra was the father of a man who became an absolute master of the orchestra as a medium for his thought.

The Scherzo is written in full 'sonata-form', an unusual scheme for that time, but one which elevates this section of the symphony to an importance which is hardly warranted, since a relaxation of tension would have been a welcome thing here. But the relaxation comes with the A major Trio, for here we listen to one of Schubert's sustained melodies, sumptuously harmonised and orchestrated.

The finale has been called a 'poem of speed'. It is a volcanic outpouring of music: neither the *tarantella* rides of the quartet finales, nor the lavishly written rhythmic and melodic episodes of the PF. Sonatas, nor the varied dance measures of the Octet and PF. Trios, contributed more than a trifle to this new and colossal movement. It exploits rhythmic patterns:

The differing lengths of these phrases will be noticed; the danger of a monotonous, 'four-square' rhythm in the finale is avoided by skilful uses of the irregular rhythms in the above example, and by an overlapping of melodic phrases. Just as in the first movement Schubert fused his melodic fragments into a new and varied music, so in this movement he fuses his rhythmic elements. Melodies, continually varied and modified, embody the rhythms, and their combined counterpoints. In the development section the use of canon and imitation between the subject themes is admirable on paper and electrifying in performance. At the close ot this section there is the inspired, and celebrated swerve into E flat major for the recapitulation. It is quite unorthodox, but inevitable, springing as it does from the Schubertian trick of passing to a key a third below the tonic key, by two downward steps (G to F, F to E flat). And the fact seems to have been missed by his critics, that he was repeating the similar process by which he had reached his development section (G to E flat) and achieving in that way a remarkable tonal unity.

Unity of another kind is obtained between the four movements by the use in each one of a similar ascending and descending *motif*, which is used in all four of them as a foil to the main theme or themes:

Schubert, as is well known, revised the symphony by erasures and alterations, after it was scored and completed. There was a good deal of preliminary revision too, and in nearly every case he strengthened and refined his melodic and thematic writing. He offered the score, as he had promised, to the *Gesellschaft der Musikfreunde*, and it is more than likely that he then sent the letter usually ascribed to 1826. There is no record of the work being rehearsed, but this must have been undertaken, and it was found too difficult. Schubert withdrew it and replaced it by his earlier C major Symphony. After his death it remained with Ferdinand until Schumann's historic visit to him on 1 January 1839. Then, at last, and because of Schumann's advocacy, the symphony was performed (in a considerably 'cut' version) at Leipzig on 21 March 1839 under Mendelssohn's conducting. The performance was part of the last subscription concert of the season at the famous Gewandhaus. The work was published in 1840 by Breitkopf & Härtel in parts, and in an arrangement for PF. Duet. Nine years later the score was published. The rejection of the symphony by the orchestral players of the *Gesellschaft* in the spring of 1828 was repeated in melancholy fashion again and again as time passed. In 1836, and in 1839, Viennese orchestras refused to play it. When Habaneck in Paris, in 1842, and Mendelssohn in London, in 1844, tried to rehearse the symphony, the players would not go on with it. There is no point in simply dubbing these men 'orchestral tyrants' as Grove did; there was a great deal to be said for them—ask any orchestral string player today (especially a cellist!) who has played in the symphony. The overall impression which we have of the symphony's greatness and sublimity takes no account of the sweat and boredom of string players coping with the work and obliged to play the same accompanying figure for bar after bar—running sometimes to lengths of over a hundred bars. William McNaught, in the essay already quoted, remarks with cogency: 'So the wheels go round, while we enjoy the journey. The players of 1844 could not know, as today's players know, that this was the whirring and breathing of a new creation!'

The first performance in England was a private one. It took

place at Windsor Castle in 1844 and was given at Prince Albert's instigation by his private orchestra.[1] He had obtained the MS. score and printed parts from Mendelssohn. In France the symphony was first given on 23 November 1851. Berlioz wrote of the performance: '... this Symphony ... is, to my thinking, worthy of a place among the loftiest productions of our art.' Whether his compatriots agreed with him is doubtful, for the *second* performance of the symphony did not take place in France for another forty-odd years—on 17 January 1897.

Today criticism is stilled. But no other work of the period, of comparable greatness, has so divided opinion, and inspired almost malicious derogation as well as affectionate esteem.

Equally poetic uses of the orchestra, although possibly not so apt, touch the Mass in E flat with colour. This is his master work in the six settings of the Mass which he composed. The most exalted moments in the liturgical text had inspired the best music in all the earlier Schubert Masses, and did so again in the last of them: such passages as the 'Et incarnatus est' and the 'Crucifixus' in the 'Credo', the 'Sanctus', the 'Agnus Dei'; he responded to their appeal as ardently as ever, and with masterly results. In the 'Crucifixus'—a 12/8 setting in A flat minor—the trembling rhythms of the strings invoke a kind of shuddering horror at the picture of the crucified Christ, and the final cadence in A flat major after the prolonged preparation in the minor key is very moving. The 'Agnus Dei' is overpowering in its effect; orchestral and choral masses of sound are piled up into *fortissimo* climaxes which die away to a whispered 'miserere'. It is as if the burden of sin were too heavy and these 'miserere' interludes have the peace of exhaustion. The threefold 'Holy! Holy! Holy!' of the 'Sanctus' besieges the ear with the juxtaposition of key-changes: E flat major, B minor, G minor and E flat minor pass in the space of seven bars. The final 'Dona Nobis' achieves the same effect at the end of the Mass as the 'miserere' choruses of the 'Agnus Dei': it suggests the exhaustion which follows a paroxysm of grief. It will be observed that Schubert is attracted by the *humanity* of the

[1] There are, unfortunately, no documentary records of any kind, concerning this performance, in the Royal Archives at Windsor Castle.

words of the Mass, if that rather vague word may be permitted. The universal quality of the two great Masses of Bach and Beethoven, in which the sufferings and aspirations of man as symbolised in Christ are transcended into an act of worship is absent in Schubert's E flat Mass. Not the sin and suffering of mankind, but the Babe of Bethlehem, the dying and risen Christ, human adoration and the prayer for peace are the living images in his mind and in his music.

In considering the work of his last year it is difficult to avoid the belief that the composition of the songs of the 'Winterreise' had a profound effect on his musical sensibilities and techniques. The new, *intellectual* quality in the development sections of his movements, although there were signs of it before the composition of the song-cycle, becomes very noticeable, in the 'Lebensstürme' PF. Duet, and in the PF. Duet Fantasia in F minor, for example, as well as in the sonata-movements of the C major Symphony and the String Quintet. It derives from the styles and procedures in the 'Winterreise' songs such as *Die Wetterfahne*, *Auf dem Flusse* (this song particularly), *Irrlicht* and *Der Wegweiser*. Another feature which was born in the 'Winterreise' pervades the work of 1828: the tranquillity, the dream-like serenity of the *Lindenbaum*. It is found in the slow movement of in the Trio-section of the Quintet, in the slow movement of the Sonata in B flat, in the melodic interludes of the 'Lebensstürme'.

The use of the five stringed instruments in the Quintet has been discussed earlier. The blending of the tranquil emotion of the *Adagio* in this great piece of chamber music with the passionate outburst at the heart of the movement is achieved with a new assurance, and the 'wellnigh incredibly lovely sounds' evoked by the *pizzicato* decorative work of the first violin and cello combine to make this one of the loveliest *Adagios* in all music. 'I hold the very look on paper of this E major *Adagio* to be beautiful' wrote Richard Capell.

A word can be given here in connection with the end of the exposition of the first movement, where the double bar is reached.[1] This is what Schubert wrote:

[1] This was first discussed by Dr. Eric Blom, 'Observer', 4 May 1952.

In performances, the players often treat the dominant seventh in the fourth bar above as if it were a 'first ending' chord, that is to say, since they are not observing Schubert's repeat-signs, they omit the chord altogether and pass from the G major chord in the third bar to the diminished seventh in the fifth bar. This preserves the soft tones of the whole passage, it is true, but Schubert obviously intended the *fz* explosion of the omitted chord to be echoed by the *forte* chord of A major in the seventh bar of the quotation. To leave out the chord in performance is a violation of his intention and an arbitrary interference with his music.

The plaintive Trio-section, which foreshadows Bruckner, contains the deepest feeling in the whole work. It is of the same essence as the 'Miserere' and 'Dona Nobis' of the E flat Mass, and even nobler than they. It speaks vividly of the development of Schubert's art, that this Trio, filled in previous works with the slightest of material—air or Ländler—should be so profoundly elegiac.

The last instrumental works of the year, and, accordingly, the last he ever penned, were the three pianoforte sonatas, in C minor, A major and B flat major. They are in a signally fitting manner his last compositions, for Schubert was a pianist all his life. The very first extant work of his that we possess is a pianoforte piece, and before that there were variations and dances for the piano, now lost. His friends knew him as a pianist, as a solo player, as a duettist, as an accompanist—rarely as a singer, never as a conductor. The long series of PF. Sonatas is richly epilogued in these three of September. The first, in C minor, is the most Beethovenish of his works, but in externals only, for Beethoven was always an abiding influence under the surface of his thought. This first sonata is full of 'hard sayings' especially in the chromatic episodes of the first movement. But how the thematic power of these passages gains from the harmonic 'tensions' set up in them!

The second sonata opens nobly with one of Schubert's 'gestures', and its humble beginnings are worth looking at. Sketches for all three of these sonatas are extant; considering that they are long, full-scale works, and that the sketches are ample preparations, the staggering industry of the composer seems beyond the capacity of normal beings. Here is his first idea for the A major Sonata—a *multum in parvo* passage without question:

The slow movement is a soothing cradle-song, but this, also, has a central episode which is chromatic and abstruse. The finales of the two sonatas are both extended movements. They teem with all manner of captivating ideas: the harmonic strokes of the C minor *Allegro* and the huge span of the music in the development section of the A major Rondo (*Allegretto*), being wholly admirable. But each concludes a sonata which is already of big dimensions, and so makes heavy demands on a listener's response. The position is not, however, made easier by well intentioned pianists who play these two finales at a breakneck speed in the hope that hereby the duration will be shortened. For the minute or two saved, most details of Schubert's thought and imagination are sacrificed.

The finale of the third sonata, in B flat major, is shorter, and although more in the composer's 'Impromptu' vein, achieves an equally acceptable music. This last sonata is a general favourite. The inspired and masterly use of tonality in the first movement, achieving an unconventionality of progression by the simplest of devices, was greatly relished by Sir Donald Tovey and led to one of his finest essays.[1] There is much in common between the first movement of the Sonata in B flat, and that of the G major Sonata, Op. 78, of 1826. Both use a broad dignified theme in the opening bars, and this is partnered by a lilting dance-tune later in the movement; and in both movements unexpectedly powerful structures are built up on these themes. But it is because the serene slow movement (in C sharp minor) and the finale rank as partners equal in greatness to the first movement, that we can award the palm to this last sonata as the finest which Schubert composed.

The 'Schwanengesang' is not, of course, a song-cycle in the accepted sense of the word. In comparing its artistic achievement with that of the 'Winterreise' a different standpoint is necessary. The whole of the 'Winterreise', it has been said, is greater than the sum of its parts, and the whole is supreme; but no individual song in the cycle approaches the two great Heine songs of the 'Schwanengesang'—those tragic vignettes, *Die Stadt* and *Der Doppelgänger*. In these fourteen songs Schubert's invention was never more vivid, more sanguine. The tragedy of the death of young genius becomes more poignant in the case of Schubert, for no other creator who died, as he did, so early in life, produced just before his death work so novel and challenging as we have in the 'Schwanengesang'.

The Rellstab songs are especially picturesque, and although, with the exception of *Aufenthalt*, none quite taps the depths in

[1] 'Music & Letters', London, October 1928.

Schubert, they are all very attractive and well known. Each one gave the composer a definite scene: a summer brook, a sleeping camp, night and the nightingale, storm-swept mountains; and a definite sentiment: contented or aspiring love, apprehension, despair; and to such verses Schubert instantly responded with songs of abiding value. The Heine poems intensify the emotion and give the scene greater reality. The sting of tears in the eyes, the salt sea-wind on the lips, the oppressive agony of frustrated love in the midnight watches—Heine creates life, not flights of literary artifice. The result is a series of firm, first-rate songs from *Der Atlas* to *Der Doppelgänger*. There is an extraordinary sense of Nature as a factor in man's tragedy—the sea as a symbol of grief and unhappy love in *Am Meer*, the mist pierced by the sun's ray as a picture of sudden self-knowledge in *Die Stadt*, the darkness of midnight, embodying the heart's loneliness, in *Der Doppelgänger*.

The titles of these Heine songs were provided by Schubert himself. It should be noted that he called the first song, not *Atlas*, but *The Atlas*; in other words, the poem is not about the mythical Titan who bore the world on his shoulders, but about a man bowed down with the burden of unrequited love. *Das Fischermädchen*, although a charmingly tuneful song, is perhaps the only one of the six not created *en un jour de largesse*. There is a deeper note of irony in the words than Schubert saw, or chose to see. This ironic, mocking tone in Heine, so appealing to English tastes, is not so well appreciated by German speaking races. In Heine the combination of Jewish descent and French sympathies is too much for the German critic. But in the last three songs Schubert catches the ironic note to perfection—the music reveals the suffering and the satire. With the incomparable *Doppelgänger* he inaugurated a new, and dangerous, way of composing songs, the 'recitative' song, in which the vocal line has the dramatic qualities of speech and in which all the genial elements of a song—melody and pulsing rhythm—are suppressed in favour of the predominating atmosphere and drama of the lyric. He should have placed a signpost on that path: 'For the genius only.' Too many indifferent composers have set forth on the path and lost themselves in unmusical morasses.

The Schubertian treasury of song begins with *Gretchen am Spinnrade* and ends with *Doppelgänger* and there is the same integrity of emotional feeling in both, and in all the span of great songs between. *Die Taubenpost*, Schubert's last song, belongs neither in body nor in spirit to either the Rellstab group or to the Heine group of songs; for all that it can inspire an affectionate response in the Schubertian. It is in the style of the 'Mill' songs and its syncopated, throbbing accompaniment represents the lover's heartbeats, not anxious as in *An mein Herz*, but keenly anticipatory. Sometimes the emotion changes and the lover pours out his confident love in a charming melody; the broken phrases, passing between voice and piano, speak of the rapt mind when he confesses that the *Carrierpigeon* of the title is *Love's yearning*, and are most imaginatively composed. The song proves, if proof were needed, that Schubert, as time passed, would have written another song whose character would be determined solely by the poem in his hands, not by the discoveries and revelations of the Heine music. But there was no more time left for him.

V

Amongst the performances of his songs and part-songs in Vienna in 1828 there was again a favourite piece: it was the setting for a quartet of female voices of Psalm XXIII. It was fatally apt; the shadow of death lay across the composer's path during that autumn. In the new district where Schubert lodged with Ferdinand, the water supply and drainage were far from satisfactory and in October Schubert contracted typhoid fever from infected water. His debilitated condition undoubtedly allowed the disease to gain so rapid a hold. The first signs that he was seriously ill appeared on 31 October when, with his brother, he visited a tavern situated near the old family home in the Säulengasse. He was nauseated by the fish he tried to eat, and from then onwards till his death he seems to have eaten almost nothing. For a day or two he worked on, and one of the most incredible events of his life must now be recorded. He arranged with the well-known theorist, Simon Sechter, to take a course of instruction in fugue, and even attended the first lesson, on 4 November, in the company of a fellow composer, Josef Lanz. What lay behind this fantastic decision? Was it the insistence of friends like Lachner, that he was a 'natural' composer, just because the overflowing abundance of his work did not fit in with their little scale of 'form'? Was it the report that his Masses did not please the Emperor, because they were not 'in the Imperial style'? Did he think to unlearn his genius, and absorb the talent for writing neat, contrapuntal fugues? Whatever the reason, he soon became too ill to continue with the studies and on 11 November took to his bed. It cannot have been easy for Ferdinand and his wife to be burdened with this sick man. Their apartment consisted of a large living-room and two small rooms, one of which was occupied by Schubert. There was also a twelve-year-old child Therese. Profesfesional nurses were employed and Schubert's little step-sister, the thirteen-year-old Josefa, also helped to nurse him.

He wrote to Schober the well-known letter which is so moving to read, appealing for books, especially by Fenimore Cooper. It is odd for English readers to contemplate Schubert absorbed in those days of sickness with 'The Last of the Mohicans' and 'The Pilot'. Schober, perhaps remembering Schubert's behaviour to him in the days of *his* sickness, did not come near: he said it was because he feared infection. Bauernfeld, Lachner, Spaun, and possibly Josef Hüttenbrenner, visited the dying composer. With Bauernfeld Schubert discussed their projected opera, the 'Graf von Gleichen', but various incidents recorded by other writers in the nineteenth century as having occurred at this time are dubious. On 16 November two doctors, Josef von Vering and Johann Wisgrill conferred over the illness and diagnosed typhoid fever.[1] His regular doctor, Rinna, was himself ill at the time. Schubert's illness could not have been an uncomplicated business with the deep-seated trouble still present from the disease of 1822, and it is surely not a coincidence that one of the two doctors above, Vering, was a specialist in venereal diseases. One of the last tasks

[1] 'Bauchtyphus' in German, and translated erroneously by nearly all nineteenth-century biographers of Schubert in English as 'typhus fever'. The mistake would probably have persisted still had it not been for the investigations of Frank Walker into the question: see his 'Schubert's last illness', 'Monthly Musical Record', London, November 1947.

Schubert undertook was the correction of the proofs of Part II of the 'Winterreise', which was due to be published, and actually appeared a few weeks after the composer's death, on 30 December 1828.

The end was near. On 17 and 18 November Schubert became delirious and at times was restrained with difficulty in his bed. During his wandering he asked Ferdinand, 'Why do you let me lie in this black hole?' His room was dark and probably not particularly inviting during those mid-November days. At 3 o'clock in the afternoon of 19 November he died, turning to the wall with the words: 'Here, here is my end.'

The following day his father announced the death from the house in Rossau. On Saturday, 22 November, the body was taken to St. Josef's Church in the Margarete district and was there consecrated. Schober, at the request of the Schubert family, had written new and appropriate words to be sung to Schubert's melody for his poem 'Pax Vobiscum' and this was performed in the Margarete church. After the service the body was taken to the Währing suburb, and was buried in the cemetery there. Shortly before he died, Schubert, in his delirium, had whispered to Ferdinand words such as 'Beethoven does not lie here' and his family took them as meaning that he wished to be buried near Beethoven. Only two graves separated those of the two composers. The Währing District Cemetery is a small graveyard lying to the left of the Währingerstrasse as it leads out from the Schotten Ring of the Inner City. Today it is called a 'Schubert Park' and preserves still an air of peace and antiquity although the bodies of the composers have long since been removed to more honoured graves.

His family and his friends were half prepared for the tragedy of his end, but when it came the shock was great. Their emotions may be summed up in the words which Schwind wrote to Schober, when the news reached him in Munich on 24 November:

> I have wept for him as for a brother, but now I am glad for him that he has died in his greatness and has done with his sorrows. The more I realise now what he was like, the more I see what he has suffered.

And Jenger wrote to Marie Pachler at Graz:

> . . . that I am still unable to conquer my sorrow over the death of my good friend Schubert, and have been feeling unwell since his death, Baron Grimschitz will likewise tell you.

The small possessions left by Schubert were valued at £6 and among them was some 'old' music. What this music actually was is not known: the designation 'old' suggests used, printed music. It was certainly not his accumulation of manuscripts, which were still at Schober's house in the Tuchlauben. His juvenilia would be in his father's house in the Rossau district, and the newly composed songs, string quintet and sonatas, of little worth in the eyes of the official evaluators, were not even inventoried. Shortly after Schubert's death, Schober transferred all the composer's manuscripts to Ferdinand's apartment in the Kettenbrückengasse.

The expenses of Schubert's illness and funeral were heavy for the pinched resources of his father and brother. From Ferdinand's detailed records we derive the fact that Schubert possessed nearly £5 at the time of his death, and the total money paid out for doctors, nurses, medicines and so forth, came to £13. The funeral and other posthumous expenses paid by his father increased this amount to £60. In seven months these debts were cancelled by the sales of his last compositions. From Haslinger, in December, Ferdinand received £15 as a first instalment for the 'Schwanengesang' songs; from Czerny he received that same month £10. Further fees followed from these two publishers, and from Diabelli, amounting to £20. In June he was able to submit an account to his father showing that he had received altogether £64 in publisher's payments. Ferdinand's biggest stroke of business was with Diabelli in 1830; this transaction must be considered in detail in the next chapter, but the sum of money involved can be mentioned here in connection with the other fees: it was £240. There was then no need for Ferdinand or Franz Theodor Schubert to have had any qualms about the funeral outlay in which they were involved. Nor was this the last of the incoming money. Ferdinand was his brother's heir by courtesy only; Schubert left no will. But his careful custody of the huge mass of manuscripts, his ceaseless endeavours to publish the works, his efforts to interest editors and impresarios and conductors in the larger compositions, symphony, opera and Mass, cannot be ascribed entirely to cupidity. His love for Franz and his pity over the hapless fate of so gifted a brother, was undoubtedly the stronger urge.

There were memorial poems in Schubert's honour published in various Vienna journals, and soon the first obituary notices began to appear. A subscription fund to erect a memorial stone over his grave was opened under the direction of Schober, Jenger and Grillparzer, and a concert was organised by Anna Fröhlich to help the funds. It was held in the hall of the 'Musikverein'—where his own concert had been so successfully given a few months earlier—and amongst the items performed were *Mirjams Siegesgesang* and the PF. Trio in E flat. Sufficient money was raised to swell the subscription funds to the required amount, and the plan was put into operation. The memorial was designed by Schober and executed by the architect Christian Friedrich Förster. A bust of Schubert, perhaps based on a death-mask, was carved by Josef Alois Dialer, an acquaintance of the composer, and cast in iron; it was not bronzed over until a later date. Grillparzer wrote the much-criticised epitaph. He made one or two attempts at it, all of which show, first, that Schubert's reputation was almost entirely that of a song-writer; second, that he was a considered to have been cut off by death before he had accomplished anything of supreme value.

In July 1830 the memorial was completed, the bust—a very fine piece of work and a congenial likeness of the composer—installed, and pilgrims to the grave could read what Grillparzer had finally written of Schubert:

THE ART OF MUSIC HERE ENTOMBED A RICH POSSESSION
BUT EVEN FAR FAIRER HOPES

The Vienna journal 'Allgemeine Musikalischen Anzeiger' of 6 November, wrote of the memorial:

> The tombstone is simple—as simple as his songs; but it conceals a profound soul, as they do.

And now the darkness descended. At the end of 1830 the memorial had been erected, the vast bulk of his manuscripts was stored on Diabelli's shelves, his operas, symphonies, and Masses slumbered in the big iron chest which Ferdinand bought for safe storage. His friends were scattered, and leading Viennese musicians, to whom he never meant very much, almost forgot the humble composer who had moved amongst them. When Chopin visited Vienna in 1829 and again in 1830, Schubert might never have existed if we judge by what the young Pole found in the musical life of the capital, and Karl Czerny, in the 'Reminiscences' of his life in musical Vienna up to 1832 makes no single mention of Schubert's name.

The slow gathering of light during the nineteenth century until the noonday of his reputation in the twentieth, requires a chapter to itself.

IX

HIS CENTURY AND OURS

I

When Schubert died, his unpublished manuscripts, an enormous number of them, lay in various places scattered about Vienna, Graz and Linz. His juvenile pieces, dating back to 1810, were still in the Rossau district, at the schoolhouse in the Grünetorgasse. The works of the 1820's were in the music closet of his rooms in Schober's house, in the Tuchlauben. Ferdinand in the Kettenbrückengasse apartment had the songs, the sonatas, the string quintet and the offertories, composed during the autumn just before the composer died. In a short time these three large collections were brought together and in Ferdinand's possession. It might be of interest to glance now at the whereabouts of other small collections of Schubert manuscripts in that November of 1828, of whose existence Ferdinand was probably unaware.

At Graz, the Hüttenbrenner brothers, Anselm and Josef, possessed between them a sizeable collection containing the scores of the 'Unfinished' Symphony, the operettas 'Claudine von Villa Bella', and 'Der Spiegelritter', the opera 'Des Teufels Lustschloss', the '13 Variations on a theme by Anselm Hüttenbrenner', numerous vocal trios, and several songs, including the 'blotted' copy of *Die Forelle*, and *Der zürnenden Diana*. Also at Graz were the scores of 'Alfonso und Estrella' and the 'Kindermarsch', both with the Pachlers. A second copy of 'Alfonso und Estrella' was in Berlin, in the Library of the Court Opera.

At Linz both Spaun and Stadler owned Schubert manuscripts. Stadler possessed quite a number of part-songs, including the *Ruhe, schönstes Glück der Erde* and the magnificent five-part *Nur wer die Sehnsucht kennt*. He also had the manuscripts of the early PF. Duet Fantasia in C minor (D. 48) and four solo songs, *Der*

Kampf, Thekla, Der Strom and *Das Grab*. Spaun had merely the parody called *Die Epistel* and the *IV Canzonets* said (but erroneously) to have been written for his wife.

Karoline Esterházy, at Zseliz, owned a number of Schubert manuscripts, most of them dating from 1818 and 1824, when Schubert was her music master. The instrumental pieces were the PF. Trio in E flat, several dances composed in January and October 1824, two PF. Duet Overtures, in C major and D major (the 'Italian' Overtures). She owned a few songs, *Blondel zu Marien, Abenlied, Ungeduld, Die Blumensprache, Das Abendrot* (composed for her father), and *Das Geheimnis*. Other song manuscripts were in the possession of various friends: Josef von Gahy (*Der Blumenbrief, Das Mädchen* and *Bertha's Lied*), Witteczek (the wonderful *Waldesnacht*), Schober (*Jägers Liebeslied*), Streinsberg (*Grablied für die Mütter*), and one Freiherr von Stiebar had been given by Schubert the fifth autograph copy of *Die Forelle*—the only one containing the 5-bar introduction. Two cantatas, *Gebet* and the *Deutsche Messe*, were also in private ownership: the first was with Baron von Schönstein, the second with the author of the text, J. P. Neumann. Karl Pichler, Holzer's successor at the organ of the Liechtenthal Church, had come into possession of the manuscripts of the Mass in C and the *Tantum Ergo* (D. 460). The female choruses *Gott in der Natur* and 'Psalm XXIII' were owned by Anna Fröhlich, and numerous PF. Solos, e.g. the '*Allegretto* in C minor' written for Ferdinand Walcher, were to be found in the albums of various friends of the somposer. One 'album', belonging to Therese Grob, contained several songs, among them three which have remained unpublished to this day.

It is impossible to trace the separate destinies of all these little collections. Some of the manuscripts are now lost, some are still in private possession, some are in the national libraries of London, Paris, Berlin, Vienna and Washington, others are in the hands of dealers. But the fate of Ferdinand's manuscripts, although mysterious in a few cases, can be given with some certainty. He gave several of them to his son Karl; these were unfinished fragments or sketches, which one can hardly avoid noticing were unsaleable.

The sketches for the 'Unfinished' Symphony and for the Symphony in D of 1818 were among Karl's manuscripts. A year or so after Schubert's death, in early 1830, the publisher Anton Diabelli finally accepted Ferdinand's offer of the Schubert manuscripts: it was the second time he had approached Diabelli, the first being only a few days after his brother's death. The publisher, for the sum of £240, acquired so numerous an assemblage of pieces, that publication of them went on regularly, if spasmodically, right through the nineteenth century, and on into the twentieth. Today, nearly a hundred and thirty years afterwards, publication is still incomplete: eighty pieces remain to be published.[1] As far as bulk alone is concerned, in the mere number of musical compositions, Schubert outdid all his peers, even though his life was shorter than that of any of them. Ferdinand's catalogue as he revised it for his offer to Diabelli is given here:

A. All the solo songs in his possession.
B. Pianoforte music, comprising:
   1. *Adagio* and Rondo, for PF. and String Quartet [*recte* 'Trio'],
   2. Sonata for PF. and Arpeggione,
   3. Three Sonatinas for PF. and Violin,
   4. Sonata in A, for PF. and Violin,
   5. Set of Variations,
   6. Sonata in D (composed at Gastein),
   7. Four Sonatas,
   8. Fugue in E minor, PF. or Organ Duet.
C. Chamber music, comprising:
   1. Trio for violin, viola and 'cello.
   2. Nine String Quartets,
   3. String Quintet in C,
   4. *Adagio* and Rondo in F, for PF. Quartet [identical with B. 1],
   5. Concerto in D, Violin and Orchestra,
   6. Octet, for 2 violins, viola, cello, bass, horn, clarinet, bassoon.

His concluding paragraph gives the items which were excepted from the sale: 1. the Operas, 2. the Oratorios, 3. the Cantatas

[1] See Appendix II.

with full orchestra, 4. the Part-songs, 5. the Symphonies, 6. the Overtures, 7. the Masses. The whole catalogue is not a complete record of the items which changed hands, even if allowances are made for an understandable generalisation, and Ferdinand must have reconsidered the exceptions above, for he later included the part-songs, the overtures, and some of the cantatas with orchestral accompaniment. Quite apart from the unspecified songs, there were numerous PF. Solos and pieces of chamber music not given in the catalogue. An attempt is made here to supplement the rather broad lines of the statement with a few details. The songs sold to Diabelli numbered approximately 250. They were published as follows: 137 songs in 50 sets or volumes ('Lieferungen') under the general title 'Nachgelassene musikalische Dichtungen' ('Posthumous Musical Poems') between 1830 and 1850; another 17 songs published with opus numbers between 1850 and 1867; from the rest many were sold to the firm of J. P. Gotthard in Vienna, which published another 50 or so between 1868 and 1872. A few more were purchased piecemeal by various firms up to 1894, but the bulk went to Breitkopf & Härtel for publication in the song-volumes of the 'Gesamtausgabe' (1894 and 1895).

The 'PF. Music' section mentions a set of variations and four sonatas. The variations were those of 1815, known as 'Ten Variations in F' (D. 156); the sonatas were three of 1817, in A flat, B major and A minor, and one of 1823, in A minor (D. 784). It is ironical to see Diabelli receiving, at last, this Sonata in A minor, which Schubert had withdrawn in a fit of dudgeon in the spring of 1823. Other items of pianoforte music not mentioned by Ferdinand, although they were passed on to the publisher, are these: *Adagio* in D flat, Rondo in E major, Fantasia in C minor (D. 993) and several Minuets in various keys.

Amongst the items of chamber music there are nine string quartets. These are as follows: (1) in C minor, 1812; (2) in B flat, 1813; (3) C major, 1813; (4) in B flat, 1813; (5) in D major, 1813; (6) in D major, 1814; (7) in B flat, 1814; (8) in G minor, 1815; (9) in G major, 1826. Besides these nine there were two others, unnamed by Ferdinand. They were (*a*) a quartet in C major (D. 3) and (*b*) a quartet in C minor (D. 103). When Diabelli bought these eleven quartets they were all complete. Between 1830 and 1890 three of them—all written on loose leaves—had disintegrated: the fifth of the nine above, in B flat, and the two unnamed quartets. The missing movements of the quartet in C major have been recovered, but those of the other two quartets, in B flat and C minor, were irretrievably lost.[1] All that remained of these two quartets has now been published; of the B flat Quartet there were the first movement and the finale, and these were published in the 'Gesamtausgabe' in 1890; of the C minor Quartet, only the first movement (*Grave* introduction, followed by an *Allegro*) survived and was published in Vienna in 1939.[2]

Additional unnamed pieces include several part-songs for male voices, among them the powerful setting of Goethe's 'Gesang der Geister über den Wassern' with its sombre accompaniment for bass strings; a number of liturgical works such as the offertories of October 1828, and the 'Magnificat' in C, of 1816; and numerous orchestral overtures including the two 'Italian' Overtures in D and C of 1817, the third overture of that year, in D, the overtures to 'Alfonso und Estrella' and 'Fierrabras', and the very early overture to the play 'Der Teufel als Hydraulikus'. Strangely enough, there were also in this large collection of pieces some sketches for an early overture (in D major) and the first of all his symphony sketches, based on this very overture, and dating, in all probability, from *Stadtkonvikt* days; these sketches were almost certainly included by error, for they were quite unpublishable, and of no interest to such a firm as Diabelli's. Slowly, as the century wore on, piece by piece made its appearance. At some time in the 1840's Diabelli handed over several manuscripts of compositions which had been published to his son-in-law, Josef Greipel, organist at the Peterskirche, Vienna. Greipel died in 1897 and his manuscripts were purchased by the Vienna *Nationalbibliothek*. Apart from these most of the manuscripts are still in private possession, quite a large number still in the hands of the

[1] See page 20.

[2] The manuscript of the two published movements of the String Quartet in B flat has recently seen the light after many years of obscurity. It is in the possession of J. H. Farrer, Haslemere.

Cranz brothers, the last successors to Diabelli in the publishing business.

Ferdinand was left with the scores of all his brother's operas and other stage works, all his Masses, his symphonies and his oratorios, numerous small works not considered in the sale to Diabelli, and all the duplicate copies made by Schubert. He sold the 'Reliquie' Sonata in C major and the Symphony no. 5, in B flat, to the Leipzig publisher Whistling, in July 1842. Two years later, in 1844, he was visited by the well-known collector of autographs, Ludwig Landsberg, and sold to him a number of the smaller manuscripts. These included the first movement (a duplicate manuscript) of the 1817 Sonata in E minor. Landsberg bequeathed his Schubert MSS. to the Berlin State Library. In 1859 Ferdinand died. His collection of manuscripts, the still unpublished symphonies, operas, Masses, and so forth, he left, not to his son Karl, but to his nephew, Eduard Schneider, the son of his, and Franz's, younger sister Theresa. Schneider was a lawyer whose offices were in the Tuchlauben. The Schubert autographs were stored in the roomy cupboard of his sanctum and it was there, in 1867, that Grove and Sullivan were shown them. As a custodian Schneider was conscientious, and fully aware of the value of his inheritance. There had been some talk in the city about his unsuitability as the guardian of such a treasure, and this imputation he much resented. On 10 March 1861 he wrote to Johann Herbeck, the well-known conductor of the Vienna 'Philharmonic' Orchestra;

> ... there is no cause for any art-lover to regret that Schubert's manuscripts have come into my possession.

Nor was there. In course of time, they were all purchased by Nikolaus Dumba, and after publication in the volumes of the 'Gesamtausgabe', Dumba bequeathed them, either to the Library of the *Gesellschaft der Musikfreunde*, or to the *Stadtbibliothek* (City Library) in Vienna. The sketches, given away by Ferdinand to his son Karl, were also bought by Dumba and from him they too reached the *Gesellschaft* Library.

Two other important collections of Schubert manuscripts in

Vienna must be mentioned in conclusion. They were the copies he had sent to the publishers Haslinger and Artaria, both of whom kept the music after they had published it. Other publishers, as we have noticed, destroyed it. Artaria's possessions found their way chiefly to the Berlin State Library; amongst them is the Rondo in A major for PF. Duet, Op. 107. But Haslinger's manuscripts, including the priceless 'Winterreise', and the 'Impromptus', are still, in the main, in private possession. The autograph of the Sonata in G, Op. 78, however, is in the British Museum.

II

If we view the progress of Schubertian publication, performance and scholarship during the nineteenth century, we find that there are two epochal years. The first closes the forty or so years after his death, during which time, with no external aids at all, no propagating societies, no advocating critics or performers, his music had to make its own way into the hearts of the coming generation; in 1864 the first full-length biography, that of Kreissle von Hellborn, was published in Vienna, and within a twelvemonth the 'Unfinished' Symphony was discovered and performed. The second climactic year is 1897, the centenary of his birth, when with the last volume of the 'Gesamtausgabe' his total major output was at last available in print, and it became obvious, with the close of a century's sifting and assessment, during which the perishable had vanished from music, that Schubert's reputation as a great master was expanding yearly and striking ever deeper roots.

In the first of these periods, up to 1864, his songs, naturally, kept his name alive, although the more contemporary values and idioms of the songs of Schumann, Robert Franz, Loewe, and hosts of song-composers now forgotten, left Schubert no longer unchallenged in his own field. In the few years following his death publication of his work was comparatively plentiful. As Grove had written: 'Death always brings a man, especially a young man, into notoriety, and increases public curiosity about his works.' The collection of songs called by Haslinger 'Schwanengesang' was followed by the *Trout* Quintet, Op. 114, the PF.

Sonata in A major, Op. 120, and the two PF. Duets, Fantasia in F minor, Op. 103 and Rondo in A major, Op. 107. By the end of 1829 these instrumental pieces, together with twenty-two songs, brought his published works to Op. 120. Nine works followed in 1830, including the PF. Sonata in E flat, Op. 122, the two very rousing marches for PF. Duet, Op. 121, two ill-assorted String Quartets, in E flat (1813) and E major (1816), Op. 125, and the song with clarinet obbligato, familiar in England today as *The Shepherd on the Rock*, which Schubert had composed just before his death for Anna Milder-Hauptmann. The String Quartet in D minor, and Psalm XXIII for female voices appeared in 1831. A few volumes of the 'Posthumous Musical Poems' had also been published. Public curiosity was satisfied, and publication almost ceased. The three Sonatas for PF. and Violin, called 'Sonatimas', were published as Op. 137 in 1836, and two years later the 'Grand Duo' in C major, Op. 140, the cantata of 1828, *Mirjams Siegesgesang*, the early Mass in B flat, and the last three PF. Sonatas appeared. For the next six years or so there was nothing. Schubert had wished to dedicate the last three sonatas to Hummel, but by 1838, when they were published, that famous pianist-composer was dead. Diabelli decided, aptly enough, to dedicate them to Schumann. Soon after the honour thus paid to him, towards the end of 1838, Schumann visited Vienna for the first time. Quite casually, according to his memoirs, he remembered that Ferdinand Schubert was still living there, and on impulse he visited him. It was on New Year's Day, 1839. In spite of the enormous number of manuscripts which Ferdinand had sold to Diabelli, there was still the greater part in his possession, and when the lid of that iron chest was lifted Schumann must have been staggered at the quantity of music lying there. He looked at the symphonies and appreciated at a glance the value and importance of the great C major Symphony. Ferdinand was persuaded to copy it and send the score and parts to Mendelssohn in Leipzig. The outcome of all this is well documented in the Schubert annals. Mendelssohn gave the symphony on 21 March 1839. Even in its 'cut' version the work was considered to be rather long; but its success was unquestionable. A year later Breitkopf

& Härtel published the work, in parts.[1] This was Schubert's second important publication outside Austria.

Schumann was, at that time, the editor of the Leipzig music journal 'Neue Zeitschrift für Musik', and he published in the issue for February 1839 several Schubert documents which he had received from Ferdinand: *My Dream*, the poem which Schubert wrote in September 1820 called *Der Geist der Welt*, and the pitiful cry *Mein Gebet* of May 1823. In addition four letters from Schubert were printed for the first time: one of them being the very first he wrote; it was to Ferdinand from the *Stadtkonvikt*. Schumann also persuaded Ferdinand to write a series of biographical articles on his brother; these important sources of information on Schubert's life were published in the 'Neue Zeitschrift' between 23 April and 3 May 1839. They conclude with a catalogue of compositions, arranged chronologically, containing several items which later biographers would have done well to observe, for many misdatings could then have been avoided.

Ferdinand hoped by his catalogue to draw the attention of publishers and public to the store of works still available. The occasional appearance in those years of new publications by Schubert, containing works of the magnitude of the 'Grand Duo' and the three 1828 sonatas, as well as the many small, charming songs, kept the composer's name before the public, even if that public's interest was not very active, but there was no response whatever to the catalogue, in spite of Schumann's added appeal, and his offer to act as an intermediary between owner and publisher. In 1842, the attempts made by Leopold Sonnleithner and Alois Fuchs to find the lost cantata 'Prometheus', even by advertising in the Vienna 'Musikzeitung', provoked Schumann into writing this paragraph:

> . . . if only the unprinted things of Schubert, which he is known to have composed, could be brought to light! For instance, in the library at Berlin, there is a grand Opera ('Alfonso und Estrella') and in Vienna over fifty works of still greater value. These things cannot

[1] See 'The Discovery of Schubert's C major Symphony', by Otto Erich Deutsch. 'Musical Quarterly', New York, April 1953.

print themselves: those whose chief business it is ought to give themselves some trouble, that the world may at last come to a full and correct appreciation of the value of Schubert.

The songs published in the 'Posthumous Musical Poems' continued to appear regularly, but it was not until 1845 that two more instrumental works were published: the Sonata in B major, Op. 147 and the *pastiche Adagio* and Rondo, Op. 145. But soon after that period of silence the activities of two musical organisations in Vienna renewed general interest in his work and gave a fillip to the publication of it. To one of these organisations *Schubert* was a golden name: it was the 'Association of Male Voice Choirs' ('Männergesangverein'). His choral part-songs for male voices are not known today, but they were loved and admired then. In 1847 a congress of these choral societies was held in Vienna and a whole-hearted and enthusiastic resolution was passed by all the members to hold a Schubert Festival Concert on 19 November, the anniversary of his death. Gustav Barth, son of Schubert's friend Josef, was the conductor, and a varied programme of chamber works and part-songs was given. The second of the two organisations was a famous String Quartet team, whose leader was Josef Hellmesberger; he and his colleagues gave a session of chamber music concerts in Vienna annually, the first in 1849; the concerts continued for many subsequent years. Hellmesberger was a member of a famous Austrian musical family, and his quartet of string players achieved international renown as sensitive interpreters of the classic string quartet. From time to time he brought forward the Schubert chamber music, first the two published quartets in A minor and D minor, then also the unpublished works, the String Quintet in C, the String Quartet in G major, the Octet. Hellmesberger's efforts would not win our admiration today. He gave the Schubert compositions with heavy 'cuts', and with passages from other quartets interpolated. Nevertheless the compositions were undoubtedly successful and publication slowly followed the concert performances: the G major Quartet, Op. 161, in 1852; the Quintet, Op. 163, in 1853; the Octet, Op. 166, in 1854.

Again the stream of publication dried up, having awakened

little other than local interest. Eight years passed, with practically no publication of any importance. In 1862 the 'Reliquie' Sonata was published, a year afterwards the early String Quartet in B flat appeared as Op. 168. But the years of obscurity were past. In December 1864 Kreissle's important biography of the composer made its appearance. Its full, circumstantial detail, and the admirably complete catalogues of printed and unprinted work, classified into various sections, songs, PF. music, orchestral music, and so forth, placed the whole vague business on to a scientific and easily consultable basis. The book was not, however, entirely without preliminary studies, and we might now glance at the work of Kreissle's predecessors which led to his achievement.

III

Ferdinand's biographical essays have been mentioned. They were the first to appear after the phase of the 'obituary-biography' had passed. In the year following Schubert's death there had been four of these obituaries, by Bauernfeld, Leopold Sonnleithner, Mayrhofer and Spaun. Each year that passed produced an occasional report of performances of Schubert's compositions, or reviews of his published works, but between 1829 and Ferdinand's 'From Franz Schubert's Life' of 1839 there was nothing of substance. In 1840 Anton Schindler's biography of Beethoven was published; it contained a few anecdotes referring to Schubert, but none of them is at all reliable. A year later Wilhelm von Chézy and Franz Grillparzer both published work in which they related memories of their dead friend and his music. Two Viennese musicians, Alois Fuchs and Ludwig Neumann, were both busily collecting material for a life of Schubert and the former compiled, in connection with his projected biography, a 'Thematic Catalogue' of Schubert's works, seeking the collaboration of Ferdinand in that particular task. Neither project came to anything. The next biographical work of any size was written by Schindler and published in the 'Niederrheinische Musikzeitung' of March 1857. As biography it is valueless, containing no new facts but much dubious anecdote, for instance, the story of Schubert's application for the post of assistant conductor at the Kärntnertor

Theater. But Schindler did give in connection with his biography a long, chronologically ordered catalogue of Schubert's works. This was much fuller than Ferdinand's, since Schindler, in 1831, had had access to Diabelli's purchases of Schubert MSS., and his list is valuable and authentic. Here then was a dated catalogue which could have saved later biographers many a crass error. As late as 1907 Ludwig Scheibler drew attention to this forgotten catalogue made by Schindler (which was 'often ignored', he wrote) and pointed out that the dates given there for these three works:

1. String Quartet in E flat, Op. 125: no. 1, 1813
2. String Quartet in E major, Op. 125: no. 2, 1816
3. PF. Duet Sonata in B flat, Op. 30, 1818

were much more plausible than those attributed by the editors of the 'Gesamtausgabe' volumes, and other writers.

The biographical material gathered by Fuchs and Neumann was acquired by Ferdinand Luib, a Viennese scholar and musician, who set about the task of writing Schubert's life with exemplary thoroughness. He got into touch with all surviving friends and acquaintances of Schubert—some whose connection with the composer was very slight—and sent them short questionnaires and appeals for information. His plan never materialised, but from among the many answers he received, those of the Hüttenbrenners, Stadler, Bauernfeld, Anna Fröhlich and Ebner are still preserved, although unpublished, and contain plenty of supplementary though hardly vital information. The 'Luib' letters are preserved in the Vienna *Stadtbibliothek*. Finally, the biography was undertaken by a man great enough to sustain the interest and labour necessary for such an enterprise, Heinrich Kreissle von Hellborn. Appropriately enough, when we realise the preponderance of lawyers and law-students in the Schubert circle, Kreissle was a Viennese lawyer, who held high office in the Austrian Court's Department of Finance. A fine musician, and a director of the *Gesellschaft*, he was the ideal man for the task. His biography has not been dimmed by the passing years, at least, it should not be considered as entirely set aside by subsequent work. It is still an encyclopedic mine of information. Naturally, in the course of a hundred years, much more information about the composer and his music has seen the light and Kreissle's artistic judgements were based upon imperfect knowledge and an insufficient realisation of Schubert's true stature. These deficiencies he shared with all musicians of that day. But as a source book for the lives and personalities of the men and women who surrounded Schubert, as an account of the composer's music and manuscripts, as a picture of the mid-nineteenth century and its attitude to the man and his music, it is an invaluable book. It had been preceded by a 'Sketch'; Kreissle wrote a short biography in 1861 which was published serially in the Leipzig music journal 'Die Signale für die musikalische Welt'. This sketch provoked Spaun's wonderfully intimate study of his friend entitled: 'Some Observations on the Schubert biography of Kreissle von Hellborn'. This study was not published however, and so, unfortunately, had no bearing on Kreissle's final work.

IV

In France and England we find, perhaps understandably, nothing like the interest in Schubertian performances and publication as in Austria and Germany, mild enough there. His songs made their way and won a lasting esteem in both countries. In 1831 the great dramatic soprano, Wilhelmina Schröder-Devrient sang the *Erlking* in London and it was published that year by Wessel & Co. This London firm then began a serial publication called 'Series of German Songs' and by 1839 thirty-eight of Schubert's songs had appeared in it. It was in that year that the very famous passage was printed in the 'Musical World' expressing suspicion at the number of Schubert songs pouring from the press when, it said, 'one would think his ashes were resting at peace in Vienna.' One thinks, ironically, in reading this passage today, of the vast treasures still awaiting publication when those words were penned, and of the surprise of the writer if he could have been told that *three hundred songs* were yet to appear. Wessel included in his 'Series' songs such as *Der Wanderer*, *Ave Maria*, *Die Forelle*, *Die junge Nonne* and so on. They were spoken highly of in contemporary journals, but the performances of them would probably bring a wry twist to the mouth today. There was always the insufferable Victorian inability to leave anything alone, if it were not immediately of the present, as we have seen in the case of the Hellmesberger Quartet performances. When Margarete Stockhausen at a London concert on 13 February 1840 sang *Gretchen am Spinnrade*, this was her text:

Let me weep again,
My heart is sore,
Since Damon hath left me
For evermore. . . .

and in the programme the words are said to be '. . . by Mr. Oliphant, imitated from Goethe'. The 'Musical World' pronounced the song to be '. . . a very pretty German melody by Schubert'. But the instrumental works made no headway at all in England. The Overture to 'Fierrabras', given in June 1844, was dubbed by the 'Musical Examiner', 'an absolute nullity,' and Mendelssohn's complete failure that same year to persuade the orchestra even to rehearse the great C major Symphony for one of the Philharmonic Society's concerts in London has been discussed. John Ella performed the 'Death and the Maiden' Quartet and the two PF. Trios, Opp. 99 and 100, at the 'Musical Union' Concerts of 1848, and occasionally an Impromptu or one of the 'Moments Musicaux' was included in the programmes of London pianists. But it is depressing to come across a very denigatory account of his pianoforte works by J. Davison in the 'Musical World' of 9 February 1850. This is full of the usual clichés of the partially informed writer on Schubert, and is particularly hard to stomach in its context—an adulatory discussion of the supremacy and eternal values of Mendelssohn's 'Songs without Words'. Joachim wrote from London on 22 May 1852 to Liszt:

> Schubert is regarded here as an upstart in instrumental composition and people are inclined to doubt his fitness for work in this branch.

When August Manns undertook the conductorship of the concerts given in the Crystal Palace, in 1856, he decided to introduce the great C major Symphony to the English public. It was given in two parts on 5 April and 12 April 1856. The programme announced this dichotomy with these words:

> Though often performed and much admired in Germany Schubert's Symphony is never heard in this country; the cause is, doubtless, its great length. In order that this may not be felt, the first three movements only will be given today, and on Saturday next the *Andante* and *Scherzo* will be repeated with the closing movement of the composition.

August Manns persuaded the secretary of these concerts to come and listen to the music of the symphony at rehearsal, and that was how George Grove first heard the music of Schubert, and when it first took hold of his imagination and won his allegiance.

In France both chamber music and songs obtained a fairer hearing than in England. As early as September 1830 the *Trout* Quintet was performed in Paris. The two great string quartets, and the PF. Trios were heard there before they were in England. The songs also were much more popular in Paris than in London. This was due in part to the singing of the famous tenor Adolphe Nourrit, who had been first attracted to Schubert in 1833 by hearing Liszt perform his arrangement of the *Erlking*. Nourrit sang Schubert's songs in the Paris salons for the next five years until his death in 1839, and won countless admirers for them. Nourrit was a friend of Chopin. At his funeral service in Marseilles, Chopin, returning from the ill-fated sojourn in Majorca, played the Schubert song *Die Gestirne* on the cathedral organ. In that same year the Paris firm Simon Richault published an 'Album musicale de François Schubert' and another publisher, Maurice Schlesinger, started a series of song-volumes on 7 July 1839. By 17 December, when Volume 8 appeared, the total number of songs published was 185. Schubert's 'Lieder' were considered in those days by Parisian critics to have killed the 'Chanson' or 'Romance'. This assertion, very debatable then, is today no longer true. The 'Lied', originating in Schubert and culminating in Hugo Wolf, is nowadays a dead form, and the 'Chanson', the 'Romance' and the 'Ballad', so vigorous before Schubert, are as vigorous today.

It is ironical to have to record the fact that much of the continuing popularity of the Schubert songs in France during the 1840's was due to the song *Adieu!* This had been composed by August von Weyrauch and published in Paris in 1824; but somehow or other it had become associated with Schubert's name, and although it was of the very type of 'Chanson' already considered as 'killed' by Schubert, its popularity was widespread. The words are excessively sentimental and well calculated to appeal to the shallower type of music-lover. Weyrauch re-published *Adieu!* in Berlin in 1846 with an indignant preface calling attention to the misattribution of his song; he added that the style of the melody alone should have been enough to make it readily identifiable as *his* work and not Schubert's!

By 1850 the number of songs printed in Paris reached the astonishing total of 367; this was keeping pace with Germany and Austria and there must, by then, have been simultaneous publication in all three countries. But no greater success attended the attempts in those days to procure a performance of the C major Symphony in Paris; at rehearsals conducted by Habaneck in 1842, the orchestra simply refused to go on with the work. Not until 23 October 1851 was the symphony given in Paris. This was, at least, five years before the London performance, but even so, later than two already given in America: Boston, in 1849, and New York, in the spring of 1851.

In Vienna a plaque had been affixed to the walls of the Birthplace. The ceremony took place on 7 October 1858 and was organised by the 'Männergesangverein'. Ferdinand died a few months afterwards on 26 February 1859 and his death again brought to public notice the large amount of unpublished work passing into the keeping of his nephew Eduard Scheider. In the October of 1863 the bodies of Beethoven and Schubert were disinterred, their remains were measured and photographed and they were re-buried side by side (but still in the Währingerstrasse Cemetery). The biography of Kreissle, the discovery of the 'Unfinished' Symphony, its subsequent performance, and the publication of the important Mass in E flat: all these incidents were cumulative. The forty years of obscurity and neglect and hard won recognition for anything but his most popular songs were over. During the next forty years the light brightens and his reputation gathers strength and stature in overwhelming measure.

V

The appearance of Kreissle's great book produced a spate of reminiscences by all kinds of people who had known Schubert, and who felt, possibly, that their knowledge of him had not been sufficiently drawn upon for the compilation of the composer's biography. Often the connection between Schubert and these tellers of tales was extremely tenuous and in a few cases has been greatly exaggerated. Moreover, if the truth be told, many of their anecdotes were inventions, and can be demonstrated as false by comparison with associated documentary evidence. Since the many biographers of the composer, writing between 1864 and 1947 (the date when Deutsch published his Schubert 'Documents') have, in all innocence, woven these anecdotal reminiscences into the fabric of Schubert's life, it is proposed to deal here with the false informants and their inventions. There are six chief offenders: the brothers Hüttenbrenner, Anselm and Josef, Franz Lachner, Josef Doppler, Anton Schindler and Benedikt Randhartinger. The two Hüttenbrenners have figured in earlier chapters and have made there a poor showing as custodians of Schubert manuscripts. The fundamental trouble lay in Anselm's deep-seated jealousy of Schubert's growing reputation, and resentment at what he considered the musical world's perverse unawareness of his own gifts. The ambivalent relationship—a professed veneration and love for a composer who was his friend, and the unspoken envy of that composer's gifts and the spread of his reputation, produced a morbid, unbalanced state of mind. Josef, fond of his older brother, and loyal to his aspirations as a composer, shared Anselm's resentment and sometimes spoke bitterly against the love shown for Schubert's songs when his brother's, he held, were equally admirable. Towards the end of his life Josef became weak in mind, but continued to write about Schubert and Anselm, his brother, in letters which are almost incoherent. From Anselm Hüttenbrenner we have the fantastic story of Schubert's visit to the dying Beethoven in March 1827. The composer, from his deathbed, is supposed to have said: 'Anselm you have my mind (Geist), but Franz has my soul (Seele)'. Schubert's visit to Beethoven is recorded by two untrustworthy witnesses and there is no other evidence that he was ever in the company of Beethoven. On the contrary, Schubert's own statement has been mentioned in an earlier chapter—he told Spaun that he had never met, nor spoken to, Beethoven. Hüttenbrenner's story was designed to boost his own status. It was related in a biographical sketch of him written by Karl von Leitner, the poet, and published in the Graz 'Tagespost' of June 1868. Most of his reminiscences of Schubert, written for Liszt's and Luib's projected biographies, must be checked against existing documents before being accepted: they are all subtly coloured by the prevailing desire to deflate Schubert and inflate himself, although both processes are carried through with a deceptively mild pen.

Josef is responsible for the story, already quoted, that Schubert composed the Overture in F, Op. 34, in his rooms in three hours; and that on the manuscript (non-existent today) Schubert recorded the fact and added '. . . and dinner missed in consequence'. There are more fanciful decorations to this story. Josef also reported Schubert's great admiration for various compositions by his brother Anselm, the Requiem Mass in C minor, for example, which was chosen for performance in the Memorial Service after Schubert's death.

More seriously misleading than the Hüttenbrenner anecdotes however, because they have affected the attitude towards Schubert's compositional methods, are those of the other men. Josef Doppler, a friend of Schubert's youth, with whom he had little to do after 1818, was in touch with Kreissle and passed on several rather sensational stories based on half-remembered reports of carelessly told news. He gives another version of the anecdote mentioned above concerning the hastily written overture, cheapened by circumstantial additions. The composer is supposed to be returning from a performance of 'Tancredi'. He resents his friends' praise of Rossini's music, saying that it is the easiest thing in the world to write overtures like Rossini's. His friends take him at his word, and promise him a glass of good wine if he will write such an overture. Thereupon he sits down . . . and so on. This time, however, it was the 'Italian' Overture in D major which he produced. Doppler, of course, had no realisation of the craft of composition, and no idea of Schubert's seriousness of purpose in his vocation. He is responsible for the similar story of the composition of *Hark! Hark! the Lark!* in the beer-garden at Währing. This 'dashing-off' of songs and overtures is the non-musical person's idea of how a composer goes to work. Doppler's story of the break between Schubert and Salieri is as follows. Salieri cut out and corrected all the passages in the Mass in B flat which reminded him of Mozart and Haydn. Schubert came to Doppler with the defaced manuscript of the Mass, flung it down angrily, and said as he did so that he would have nothing more to do with Salieri as a teacher. The Mass was written in 1815; the manuscript is in the British Museum, available for anyone to see that there are no alterations or defacements of the nature indicated by the story. There was no 'break' with Salieri; the association merely ended as all pupil-teacher relationships eventually end. And that was certainly later than 1815. Schubert was, of course, not aware of how Doppler would one day tell these stupid tales, but some words he once wrote to Ferdinand have, to our ears, an ironic ring:

> I merely marvel at the blind and wrong-headed zeal of my rather clumsy friend Doppler, whose friendship does me more harm than good. (29 October 1818.)

Benedikt Randhartinger attended the *Stadtkonvikt* in the years following Schubert's leaving it. He claimed a much closer relationship with the composer than he actually enjoyed and decorated it with fanciful stories. The best known one deals with the inception of the song-cycle 'Die schöne Müllerin'. According to this, Schubert called on Randhartinger, then the secretary of Count Ludwig Széchényi, and being left alone for a moment, picked up a book of poems. He became interested, pocketed the book, and left before Randhartinger returned. The next morning he proffered several of the 'Müllerin' songs, already completed, as a peace-offering for what he had done. Here are the facts: the first songs of the 'Müllerin' cycle were composed in the summer (probably August) of 1823; Randhartinger's appointment as the Count's secretary was in 1824. The two dates cannot be reconciled to give the story any veracity. In the same way Randhartinger invented the account of Schubert's composing *Der Zwerg* in the few minutes while he kept his friend waiting for a walk. Another story of those 'dashed-off' compositions which will not bear the light of truth.

Either from Randhartinger, or from Franz Lachner, came the tale of the toast drunk at the 'Mehlgrube' inn on the night of Beethoven's funeral. It was first recorded in Kreissle's biography (Vol. II, page 269). Schubert's true movements on that memorable evening are recorded in the diaries of the Hartmann brothers. He was not at any time in the company of Randhartinger nor Lachner, nor did he visit the 'Mehlgrube' inn. Lachner, an associate of the composer in the years between 1823 and early 1828, wrote in 1881 some dubious stories about the composer, and passed on several more, by word of mouth, to Grove. His written reminiscences contain an absurd anecdote. It tells how Schubert was inspired by the sound of a coffee-mill to write the first theme of the D minor String Quartet. This, wrote Lachner, was early in 1826. Again, incompatible dates give him the lie. He based the date of his story, naturally, on the date given everywhere in 1881 for the commencement of the string quartet. Schubert's manuscript, discovered years afterwards, shows the beginning of the quartet to date from March 1824.

Lachner is responsible, too, for the 'locked drawer'—a story of Schubert's composing, thrusting the finished work in a drawer, locking it, and then forgetting all about it. It is an apt story of a man like its inventor, whose composition was a mere decoration of a busy musical life, but utterly unbelievable of a working composer like Schubert, who lived by selling his work. In the late 1870's (probably 1878) Grove's friend C. A. Barry visited Munich.

Grove begged him to get all the information on Schubert he could from 'old Lachner', who was then conductor of the Court Opera. The tales Barry received included the one just mentioned, another that Haslinger paid Schubert 10d. for each of the 'Winterreise' songs, and that he received from the publisher H. A. Probst, of Leipzig, the sum of 17s. 6d. for the PF. Trio in E flat, Op. 100. But Lachner's crowning effort is his statement to Barry about the compositions of the first twelve of the 'Winterreise' songs. 'Half-a-dozen', he remembered, 'were written in one morning.' This, after fifty years, shows a good memory. It is true that Schubert composed six or seven songs on one day in his 'teens. They were short, very lyrical songs, of no great moment. Examination of the autograph manuscript of the 'Winterreise' songs in question reveals a very different state of affairs and suggests days of work.

Several 'incidents' in early biographies of the composer originate with Anton Schindler. He was much addicted to the 'Romantic' period's ideal of a composer: a divinely-inspired, Byronic figure, who could strike noble attitudes of defiance, or prophetic utterance, or even, on occasion, of self-abnegation. His story, for example, of Weber giving the score of 'Euryanthe' to Beethoven, and praying him to make 'such alterations as he pleased' has been quite discredited. Yet his similar inventions about Schubert still linger on in modern biographies of the composer. The distorted story of Schubert and the Kärntnertor Theater conductorship is gradually disappearing; not so the visit to Beethoven in 1822 with the score of the 'Variations on a French Air', Op. 10, under his arm. We need not discuss whether or not Beethoven, as Schindler said, pointed out a fault in the harmony to the utter discomfiture of Schubert, for we know that the two composers never met. And Schindler's invention here is probably matched by a similar invention over the alleged remark of Beethoven: 'Truly in Schubert is the divine spark!' A favourite anecdote, first told by Schindler, tells of the efforts of Schubert's friends to persuade him to prepare and revise his compositions more thoroughly, more in the manner of Beethoven with sketches and modifications. Their efforts on the stubborn composer, applied evening after evening, were in vain. Schubert would sit down and resentfully say to them: 'Go it, I beg you!', implying that he was ready to suffer, but would ignore, their imprecations. This is the way in which Schindler tries to account for what he considered the lack of 'science' in Schubert's work, a view so dear to mid-nineteenth-century opinion. Who among Schubert's friends, one might ask, would have done this upbraiding? And there is another question that suggests itself: Was anyone, outside of Beethoven's closest circle, aware of his compositional methods in the early 1820's? It is extremely doubtful if any of Schubert's friends and associates knew of them. Schindler knew nothing of Schubert's own methods and preparation. He, like Lachner, was inclined to exaggerate the closeness of his friendship with Schubert, and some such thought was at the back of his mind when he invented the incidents connected with the composition of the songs in the 'Schwanengesang'. Details were given in the previous chapter, but the continuation of Schindler's story shows its falsity. Two days after he received the poems, Schubert took the completed settings of *Liebesbotschaft*, *Kriegers Ahnung* and *Aufenthalt* to Schindler, so we read. These songs were completed in August 1828, when Schindler was living at Pest.

There are other stories, too numerous to mention, which bear the same stamp of spuriousness. But one of these stories must, in concluding the dismal count, be refuted. It originated with Baron Schönstein. He said that Vogl took a recently composed song of Schubert's, transposed it into a more suitable key, and a fortnight afterwards put it in front of the composer. They tried it over together and at the close Schubert is supposed to have said: 'A good song. Whose is it?' Schönstein told the story to illustrate the popularly held idea that Schubert was 'clairvoyant', by which was meant that he composed in a state of hyper-physical, trance-like excitement: a kind of unknowing vehicle for the Muses who forgot his work when it was out of his system. It is a view commonly held amongst the more primitive music-lover, and even fostered by the more theatrical type of composer. It is perhaps hardly necessary to add that Schönstein, when pressed, could not remember *which* song it was. I have suggested elsewhere that if there is any truth in the incident at all, then Schubert was uttering a mild rebuke. He well knew what Vogl's 'transpositions' entailed: embellishments, and ornamentation of all kinds in the vocal part. 'Whose is it?' in that case would mean: 'Is the song mine—or yours?'

These tales are, in themselves, trivial and each alone not worth bothering about. But the cumulative effect of them is tremendous. What a picture they create: a composer who could throw off composition after composition without thought or revision, in a transport, and who would listen to nothing or nobody in his obstinate determination to pursue his own course. It is a false picture, and against it Schubert's true friends continued to protest in vain.

VI

Kreissle's catalogue of unpublished works brought about a result which Ferdinand Schubert, Schumann and other friends, urging the point in the 1840's, were unable to do. It awakened people's interest in the 'rich treasure' which Grillparzer, in his epitaph for Schubert, said was buried with the composer. He was almost telling the truth. The store was yielding, year by year, its 'rich treasure', and after the discovery of the 'Unfinished' Symphony and its subsequent publication, things at last began to move. One of the most amazing events in the record of Schubert's posthumous recognition is the outburst of publication and republication in Leipzig in the years 1868–1870. Leipzig had always been favourable to Schubert. From the days when Fink reviewed his songs in 1827 and 1828, on to the performance of the C major Symphony, and, later, to Schumann's warm-hearted advocacy of his songs and sonatas, there had always been a welcome there for his work. In 1868 every music publisher in Leipzig—and there were many such—began a series of song-volumes, besides republishing the three song-cycles. Piano arrangements of his symphonies and chamber music, and re-issues of that chamber music, were on sale, and liberally advertised in all the journals. New compositions, as well as old, were published, and these include 'Lazarus' (1866), the 'Quartettsaatz' in C minor (1870), the 'Arpeggione' Sonata, the String Quartets in D (D. 94) and G minor (D. 173) (1871), the Mass in A flat (1875).

In 1874 Gustav Nottebohm published his famous 'Thematic Catalogue' of Schubert's works. It was claimed to be 'of the printed works' ('Thematisches Verzeichniss der im Druck erschienenen Werke von Franz Schubert') but there were substantial supplements giving the unpublished works as well. The book was in three main sections, (*a*) Works with opus numbers, 1 to 173: (*b*) the 'Posthumous Musical Poems', fifty volumes; (*c*) Works published without opus numbers. The third part of a supplementary section gave a fairly full list of the yet unpublished music, based mainly on Kreissle's lists. There were also lists of Schubert's publishers, portraits, and books about him. It was an invaluable reference-book for the Schubert student and presented in an easily accessible form the material collected by three predecessors in that field—Diabelli's catalogue of 1851, Kreissle's, in the biography, of 1864, and the lists given by Reissmann in his biography of 1873. Nottebohm performed his task admirably, and today his book is only superseded because of the fuller, more accurate, and chronologically ordered catalogue of Otto Erich Deutsch.

The decade between 1880 and 1890 was the period of the 'Critically Revised Complete Edition' (the 'Gesamtausgabe'). Breitkopf & Härtel of Leipzig had produced these editions of the works of Beethoven, Mozart, Haydn, Schumann and Chopin and other less considerable figures. In 1884 the decision was taken to produce a similar 'Collected Edition' of the works of Schubert. It was a vast undertaking since much of the work would be published for the first time, and for sheer bulk it would exceed all the others. An editorial board was formed including such men as Brahms, Hellmesberger, Ignaz Brüll and so on, and, as a kind of 'General Secretary', Eusebius Mandyczewski. This was a most happy choice, for Mandyczewski was a musicologist, thorough, capable and industrious. Between 1884 and 1895 the volumes were slowly published, and Masses, Operas, Symphonies were at long last available in print. The supreme achievement of the edition, and it is due to Mandyczewski's efforts, is the ten volumes of songs. These, in spite of certain opinions to the contrary, were given chronologically, and whenever Mandyczewski found more than one version of a song he published it. The amazing number of Schubert's songs—already a source of wonder in the volumes published by other firms, which included as many as 367—was now found to be 603: two hundred or so published for the first time.

For the centenary of Schubert's birth, 1897, Breitkopf & Härtel published a 'Supplement' Volume which brought the total number of volumes to thirty-nine. The 'Supplement' contained all kinds of compositions, some fragmentary, some which had turned up after the appropriate volume had been published, for instance, the String Trio in B flat of 1817, some which were alternative versions of works already included in previous volumes, and some which were sketches for finished work. It is, for the Schubert student, a fascinating collection of pieces.[1]

Although arrangements of the early symphonies for PF. Duet had been published in the 1860's, no curiosity or desire to hear them in their original form was aroused. The fourth symphony, in C minor, because of its title 'Tragic', inevitably won more attention than the rest. The slow movement was published in score, and the whole work had been performed in Leipzig on 19 November 1849—a death anniversary—from manuscript parts. The sixth symphony, the 'Little' C major, had been performed as early as 1828 and it, too, was given in Leipzig soon after the performance of the 'Tragic' Symphony. In the case of the 'Little' C major Symphony it was felt, no doubt, that being the last of the early symphonies it was therefore the best: a surmise, unfortunately, which the merits of the work do not confirm. The general inferiority of these two best known symphonies produced the same effect upon public opinion as, earlier, the PF. Trio in E flat had done, and no attempt was made to perform the other four early symphonies. Brahms was 'Artistic Director' of the 'Musikverein' in 1873, when the famous 'World Exhibition' took place in

[1] The full story of the 'Complete Edition' of Schubert's works is given by O. E. Deutsch in 'Music & Letters', July 1951, page 226.

Vienna. He was invited to conduct a Schubert concert as part of the Festival activities, but he declined to do so. It would be strange, he said, excusing himself, to fill a concert with the works of one composer and besides, there were very few works by Schubert suitable for performance 'en grand style'. But Manns and Grove in England, their enthusiasm aroused during rehearsals of the 'Great' C major Symphony in 1856, eventually obtained the manuscript parts of all the early symphonies of Schubert. The honour of first performing them belongs to England, for Manns conducted the whole series during the seasons of the 'Crystal Palace Concerts'. The dates on which these symphonies were performed are these: no. 1, in D major, 30 January 1880; no. 2, in B flat, 20 October 1877; no. 3, in D major, 19 February 1881; no. 5, in B flat, 1 February 1873. The symphonies never became really established in the concert repertoire; in the closing decades of the nineteenth century, contemporary music, as represented by the work of Wagner, Strauss, Brahms, Tchaikowsky and others, was popular in a degree which we cannot imagine today. The comparative rarity of concerts, and the vast amount of music to be drawn upon, completely excluded the early Schubert symphonies. Only with the coming of broadcasting, and the multiplicity of concerts which resulted from it, did these early works win a hearing and, more than that, enable the Fifth Symphony, in B flat, to endear itself to the musical public as a thoroughly worthy forerunner of the two later symphonies, the 'Unfinished' and the 'Great' C major.

The operas were not so fortunate. They, with the exception of 'Die Verschworenen', have never been performed. So called 'first performances' of 'Alfonso und Estrella', 'Fierrabras', and others, are nothing of the kind. Liszt wrote enthusiastic letters about 'Alfonso und Estrella'—'cette charmante musique . . . le succès, et un succès populaire et productif, est indubitable . . .'; he wrote thus to Escudier on 21 January 1854. But he gave a severely cut version at Weimar five months after this, and it won, in that form, no success at all. The travesty of the opera published in vocal score by Haslinger in J. N. Fuchs arrangement has been discussed already. Today the full length operas are still unperformed, and judgements on their merits or otherwise, should remain in abeyance until they are given in their entirety, in a first class production.

VII

Schumann's famous visit to Vienna in 1839 can be paralleled by Grove's in October 1867. Ferdinand showed the amazed Schumann the store of accumulated manuscripts in his possession; the same store, only slightly diminished, was shown by Ferdinand's nephew, Dr. Schneider, to the equally astonished Grove. Just as Schumann returned to Leipzig, full of enthusiasm for what he had seen, arranged for a performance there of the C major Symphony, and wrote ardently in his journal of the composer and his music, so Grove returned to London, laden with the missing 'Rosamunde' part-songs, primed with information about the early symphonies, and determined to obtain performances of the 'Rosamunde' and other orchestral music. He too wrote of what he had found. When Arthur Duke Coleridge published in 1869 an English translation of Kreissle's 'Schubert', Grove wrote for the second volume a masterly appendix describing his Vienna visit and giving a *catalogue raisonné* of all the symphonies, including the E minor and major sketch, then in his possession. Eventually his researches and the accumulated experiences of his concert activities and his abiding love for Schubert produced the 'Life' of Schubert which he wrote for the 'Dictionary of Music and Musicians', published in 1882.[1] His article has been translated into German, by Hans Effenberger, but never published there. Between Kreissle (1864) and Grove (1882) there were two major biographies of the composer. The first is the work of the Berlin composer and scholar, August Reissmann. He published his book 'Franz Schubert: sein Leben und seine Werke' in 1873. It contained, as supplements, about six unpublished works quoted in full; others, such as the Quintet Overture (D. 8) for 2 violins, 2 violas and 'cello, composed by Schubert in June and July 1811, were merely referred to and briefly quoted. Amongst these works

[1] The 'Dictionary' had been published in instalments; the work, in four volumes, was published as a whole in 1883.

is the String Trio in B flat (1817), and in view of this reference it seems inexcusable for the editors of the 'Gesamtausgabe' to have forgotten it; they were forced to include it in the 'Supplement' volume. Reissmann, writing before Nottebohm's 'Thematic Catalogue', is also the first scholar to give a comprehensive chronologically ordered list of Schubert's works. He perpetrated several errors, it is true, which were taken over by Nottebohm and persisted into the twentieth century: these mistaken dates have already been discussed; they concern the two quartets of Op. 125, the two mature quartets of 1824, the Sonatas in D major, Op. 53 and A major, Op. 120, and the PF. Duet Sonata in B flat, Op. 30. Grove, later on, gave a most admirable catalogue of this kind. At the close of his dictionary article he printed eleven columns of full, detailed information, listing there 1,131 compositions. It was an intolerable deletion when future editors of 'Grove's Dictionary' cut out this catalogue in favour of an abbreviated summary of contents from the 'Gesamtausgabe', especially as Grove's list was without its equal anywhere in Europe. The fifth edition of 'Grove', under the editorship of Dr. Eric Blom, gives a full, dated list of works arranged in categories, with detailed information of publication, first performances, text sources and the like.

The second biography of importance published in the years between Kreissle's and Grove's is that written by Constantin von Wurzbach as an entry in his famous 'Biographical Lexicon of the Austrian Empire', 1876.[1] His article was based largely upon Kreissle, and contained in addition some facts from Anselm Hüttenbrenner; but a few valuable references to contemporary publications provide documentary facts of some importance.

Beside the biographers, major and minor ones, there arose a body of Schubertians who were fired, like the original band of men round the composer himself, purely by love of his music. These men inspired performance, publication and scholarship; they prompted memorials and suggested commemorative plaques on the various residences of Schubert in Vienna and other buildings (the Liechtenthaler church, for example) connected with his activities there. They also collected and preserved his manu-

[1] 'Biographisches Lexikon des Kaisertums Oesterreich', Vienna, 1876.

scripts. An early collector of this kind was Karl Pinterics, a friend of Schubert who amassed invaluable memoranda, first editions and copies of unpublished songs. On his death in 1831 his collection passed to Witteczek who added it to his own. Although there were few original manuscripts in the collection there was a large number of copied songs the originals of which had been lost. On Witteczek's death, in 1859, the collection was bequeathed to Spaun who also possessed an individual collection of Schubertiana. When Spaun died, six years after Witteczek, his entire collection, fed by so many subsidiary libraries, passed into public ownership for he left it to the Library of the *Gesellschaft der Musikfreunde*. It was, of course, an important source for the 'Collected Edition'.

Two other men who were collectors of manuscripts, and who owned many of Schubert's pieces, were Ludwig Landsberg discussed earlier in this chapter, and Gustav Petter. But the greatest of all these collectors, a man to whom the world of Schubert scholarship owes an incalculable debt, was Nicolaus Dumba, a wealthy Viennese merchant of Greek descent, and a cultured musician. He bought the entire mass of manuscripts in Dr. Schneider's possession, and others belonging to various descendants of Schubert, adding to these, many manuscripts of already published works which he obtained from the original publishers. Not only did he urge forward the project of the 'Collected Edition', he also aided its inception by a gift of money. On his death, 23 March 1900, the manuscripts in his possession were bequeathed to 'his beloved city of Vienna', most of them going to the *Stadtbibliothek*; but the 'Unfinished' Symphony, together with the sketches for the work, was left to the *Gesellschaft der Musikfreunde*. He had purchased the Kupelwieser water-colours and these, too, went to the *Stadtbibliothek*.

The Schubert manuscripts in the Berlin Library were admirably listed and described by Robert Lachmann ('Zeitschrift für Musikwissenschaft', November 1928) although several more Schubert manuscripts have been acquired since then. The Paris 'Conservatoire' possesses a large number of autograph manuscripts by Schubert which were the gift of Charles Malherbe. He

FERDINAND SCHUBERT

Lithograph by Kriehuber, 1852 *Historische Museum, Vienna*

was the archivist at the Paris 'Opéra' and an ardent manuscript collector. This collection was catalogued in exemplary fashion by Jacques Gabriel Prod'homme, who published his account in the 'Revue Musicologique', November 1928. The most sizeable collection of Schubert manuscripts still in private possession belongs to Konsul Otto Taussig, of Malmö, Sweden. Many of his manuscripts have come from the residue of Diabelli's purchases in 1830, which passed to successive owners of the original firm; this residue is now jointly owned by the brothers Alwin and Albert Cranz, the first in Vienna, the second in Brussels. Herr Taussig's collection thus contains unpublished work. This great collector also owns many autographs of subsidiary interest, such as documents written by Schubert's father, copies of the songs made by Enderes and Stadler (the only sources in many cases, since Schubert's originals are lost), and the copies made by Schindler which the dying Beethoven saw.

VIII

Grove's advocacy of Schubert met with general success in England, but it was not quite unqualified. Prejudice died hard, and many factors had contributed to it. For so long had the composer been looked upon as a songwriter, who had failed in his attempts to master instrumental forms, that the musical world of the day was half-reluctant to accept Schubert as a writer of masterpieces in all other spheres. But gradually his music conquered. In 1870 the first of the succession of 'Schubert Societies' was founded in London and gave many concerts of obscure or little-known works. In Manchester Charles Hallé performed a series of eight sonatas and these were then published by Augener's in London. Further volumes of piano-music followed. The 'Octet' was given at the 'Popular Concerts', and in 1881 the whole cycle of eight symphonies was given at the Crystal Palace. Two years later, on 5 May 1883, Barnett's completion of the symphony-sketch in E was performed.

In France the initial burst of song performance and publication did not lead to an interest in Schubert's other work such had arisen in England; there was to be no French counterpart of Grove. The 'Unfinished' Symphony was performed for the first time in 1873, but it was not until 1897 that the C major Symphony received a second performance. The Sonata in G major, Op. 78, was performed in 1875 (it was pronounced 'too orchestral, too long'), and various chamber works, Op. 100 and the D minor String Quartet, appeared occasionally in Paris concerts of the 1870's, but the biographical article on Schubert, written for 'Larousse' of 1875, deals with him solely as a song-writer and ignores his instrumental music altogether. It was possible for Ernest Legouvé, a well-known French singer, to write in his 'Souvenirs', published in Paris in 1885: 'Today, Schubert is almost forgotten.' Schubert occupies in France a position similar to that of Bruckner in England. Lip service is paid to his eminence, but performance of his work is infrequent, and then more dutiful than desired. Occasionally there is an ardent tribute from a French musician but not all Schubertians, and certainly not all musicians, will agree with the following comment of L. A. Bourgault-Ducoudray in his book 'Les musiciens célèbres', although it may perhaps be quoted as an antidote to Legouvé's lugubrious remark above. This is what Ducoudray wrote in 1908:

> La musique de Schubert n'est pas faite pour provoquer la fine analyse d'un intellectuel, ou pour exercer le scalpel d'un dilettante. *C'est un cadeau fait par Dieu, en un jour de largesse*, qu'on accepte sans discussion et sans reflection.

In Vienna the 'Männergesangverein', pursuing its ardent course of homage to the composer, collected funds for a monumental statue to be erected in the *Stadtpark*. The park lies just beyond the Ringstrasse (that section of it now named 'Schubertring') and the statue was carved by Karl Kundmann. It is a seated figure, and Schubert is looking up, pen poised, in the act of composing. It was unveiled on 15 May 1872 and at the ceremony Dumba delivered the address of homage. On 22 June 1888 Schubert's body was again exhumed, for the last time, and re-buried in the 'Grove of Honour', in the Central Cemetry. A bas-relief of the composer, with one of the Muses holding a laurel-wreath above his head, stands over his grave; the sculptor was again Karl Kundmann. Above the empty grave in the Währingerstrasse Cemetery, called today the 'Schubertpark', a copy of Dialer's bust was erected (1925); the original bust now stands in the Birthhouse, in the 'alcove-room' where, according to tradition, he was born.

During those slow years when the song-writer was being revealed as so much greater an artist, worthy of being named in the same breath as Mozart and Beethoven, critical opinion was likewise undergoing a peculiar transitional phase. Kreissle, for all his enthusiasm and knowledge, is naturally unable to dissociate himself entirely from the opinions and attitudes of his contemporaries and often pronounces judgements which seem strangely jarring to our ears. After admitting that the last Mass, in E flat, is not known outside Vienna, he gives, as his opinion, the view that the noblest of the other five Masses is that in G major, Schubert's second setting of the office. This short work has great charm, but his placing of it above the later one in B flat, and the mature fifth setting, in A flat, is hard to understand. He calls the *Trout* Quintet 'mindless' ('geistlos') and leaves it at that; the first and last movements of the 'Wanderer' Fantasia are 'uncouth' in construction; the finale of Op. 100 has a 'poor subject' and is worn threadbare by exceeding length. On the other hand he praises work such as the Fantasy for PF. and violin, Op. 159, and the 'Rondo' of Op. 145, in terms which would be considered nowadays as extravagant.

The reluctance in England to accept the great C major Symphony as a masterpiece of the first rank was not fully overcome until well into the twentieth century. The critic J. W. Davison, writing in the 'Musical World', seemed unable to appreciate any music which was not by Beethoven or Mozart or Mendelssohn (his especial favourite); his vitriolic attacks on Chopin were notorious. After a performance of Schubert's symphony by the Musical Society in London during the 1859 season, he wrote:

> The ideas throughout it are all of a minute character, and the instrumentation is of a piece with the ideas. There is no breadth, there is no grandeur, there is no dignity in either; clearness, and contrast, and beautiful finish are always apparent, but the orchestra,

> though loud, is never massive and sonorous, and the music, though always correct, is never serious or imposing.

Grove, quoting this passage, asks: 'Is it possible for criticism to be more hopelessly wrong?'

But Grove himself sometimes errs. It is not a congenial thing to have to say, but the nineteenth century's unanimous tributes to Grove's biographical article on Schubert cannot, in honesty, go unchallenged today. Grove's excellent researches led to the discovery of unpublished letters, unrecorded dates on manuscripts and much factual evidence which was new at that time, and all this is admirable. But not only was Grove, like Kreissle, unable to view Schubert apart from the prejudice and spirit of those times, his writing is also, in a rather disturbing way, coloured by the Victorian ideals and limitations of the 1880's. He is occasionally arch, occasionally facetious, and sometimes a little too much the 'English Gentleman'. A careful and close re-reading of his article will reveal at once that he was a generous and warm-hearted soul, but his drawing of Schubert's character, his accounts of Schubert's methods of composition, his description of the music itself, his portraits of the composer's friends, are all slightly false. From start to finish he just misses the mark of truth. He is uncertain when he comes to tackling the music of Schubert because he himself was not sure of technical facts. These criticisms can be illustrated by his own words: the following extracts are from his letter to Mrs. Edmond Wodehouse, written on 18 March 1882 while he was writing the discussion of Schubert's music which closes his biographical article.[1] He wished, he wrote to Mrs. Wodehouse,

> . . . to bring out the fact that in listening to Schubert one never thinks of the cleverness or the contrivance, as one often does even in Beethoven, but simply of the music itself—the emotions it raises in you and the strong personal feeling it excites towards the composer. Easy enough to put it in that way, but hitherto impossible to work it out in proper terms. It's quite curious how innocent he is of innovation or experiment or of trying aesthetic contrivances as Schumann, Mendelssohn, Spohr, even Beethoven himself do. His sym-

[1] 'Life of Sir George Grove', Charles Graves, London, 1903, page 282.

phonies and sonatas are just in the old form as far as arrangement of movements go, etc., and in the construction of each movement, if he wanders from the form, it is not from any intention of neglecting it and setting up something fresh, but just because he goes on pouring out what he has to say and so gets into all kinds of irregular keys and excrescences.

This is bad enough, but worse follows:

Remember the splendid effects, the beautiful instrumentation, &c., and then recollect that every piece was written without note or sketch as hard as his pen would go, and you form some idea of the skill and technical ability of the man with all his want of learning.

Is it to be wondered at, that if Grove adopted this line in discussing Schubert, and if, in addition, he quotes without question all the rather foolish anecdotes by Schubert's friends, that he was the cause of similar serious misunderstanding on the part of other music lovers? The dictionary article appeared in 1882 and in October 1883 it was reviewed in the 'Edinburgh Review'. The review is anonymous in the journal, but it was actually written by H. Heathcote Statham. It is a poisonous effort, and it deeply upset Grove, although he had only himself to blame. Statham draws from Grove's biography conclusions about Schubert based upon the anecdotal aspect already deplored: he finds Schubert to be a lower-class ruffian, uncouth, dirty in his habits (for, Statham asserts, if he wore his spectacles all night we know what that tells us about his habits of cleanliness), drunken, and one who merely played at his art. Grove wrote a letter of remonstrance to the editor of the 'Edinburgh Review', Henry Reeve. But Reeve replied to Grove that he agreed with Statham, and the review exactly expressed his own opinions. In his letter (26 October 1883) he continued:[1]

No one admires his [Schubert's] natural genius and vocal power more than I do, but as your biography proves, it was genius growing in a Vienna beer-shop, with a slender amount of education, a low social standard, and more facility than application. Wonderful but incomplete. . . .

[1] *loc. cit.*, page 293.

Grove's account of the composer and his composing greatly influenced musical opinion in England during the years from 1890 onwards, and we see the outcome, even so late as 1928, from the pen of a man who, although he cared deeply for Schubert and sang his songs in an almost incomparable fashion, reveals by his writing on the composer that his first hand knowledge and true apprehension are lamentably weak. Here is Plunket Greene, and the hand of Grove lies heavily upon him:[1]

> He burned no midnight oil. There is hardly a correction in his Mss.; he dashed them off in the white heat of his genius. It is no exaggeration to describe him as the most inspired of all composers, for what he did he did almost in spite of himself. His technical equipment was comparatively limited (he had arranged to take lessons in counterpoint just before he died). His harmonic range was *small*. He had certain tricks which almost amount to *clichés*. He rang the changes on alternating minor and major so often as almost to render them suspect to our modern ears....

The repeated assertion that Schubert never altered or corrected his manuscripts was made by people who seem to be unaware of the fact that fair copies rarely do show such alterations. These critics show no knowledge of the existence of the composer's very numerous sketches.

IX

1897 revealed to the musical world at the close of the nineteenth century the true greatness of Schubert, and pointed to the fuller appreciation of his genius which was to develop in the twentieth century. Publication of his work (with the exception of numerous minor pieces) was complete at last, performances of all his instrumental masterpieces, for piano, for orchestra and for chamber music combinations, were regular occurrences and many of these masterpieces were firmly established in the concert repertory. His songs had never suffered any eclipse, and although the tremendous possibilities which he had opened up by his exploration of the 'Lied' had been developed, in their individual fashions,

[1] 'Music & Letters', London, 1928, page 317.

by Schumann, Brahms and Hugo Wolf, none of these composers did more than follow out the implications in the Schubert 'Lied': none of them produced anything so original in song-form that it led to yet further developments. And the Schubert 'Lied' is as beloved today, and as frequently performed, as it was in the 'Schubertiad' evenings of old Vienna.

With the dawn of the twentieth century there arose in the field of Schubertian scholarship and criticism, a man whose character, percipience and industry produced the greatest contribution to that field of study which it had ever known. Otto Erich Deutsch, studying the art of Moritz von Schwind, was drawn to the work of Schwind's friend Schubert, the greater artist. That was how Deutsch's work on Schubert began. In 1905 his first book was published: it was a 'Schubert Brevier', a collection of the sayings, letters, documents, dates, of the composer's life. It was an omen. Deutsch has never been drawn to the aesthetic discussion of music. A child of his time, he has concentrated on the factual and documentary basis of a composer's life and music. In Schubert there was an enormous sphere for his activities. Anecdote was largely rejected. Instead, Deutsch collected all the appropriate documents he could lay his hands on. Published letters, poems, inscriptions in albums and manuscripts were first assembled. Then he got into touch with the descendants of Schubert's relatives, his friends, his biographers, his publishers, and collected from them diaries, reports, accounts, letters, photographs and pictures. All the accumulated manuscripts of the archives and offices of the City of Vienna were combed through, and the back numbers of journals and periodicals were ransacked for advertisements and reviews. The harvest was rich. Deutsch then did a surprisingly simple thing. He assembled all his documents in chronological order and let the results speak for themselves. His book was called 'Franz Schubert: die Dokumente seines Lebens', and published by Georg Müller, Leipzig, in 1914. It was intended to be the second in a series of four works; the first to be a German translation of Grove's biographical article, the third a pictorial book ('Sein Leben in Bildern'), the fourth a thematic catalogue. The pictorial volume was actually published first, in 1913; if readers do not know this volume, let me urge its value, importance and fascination. Copies are rare and expensive, but most of the bigger libraries contain a copy and it is worth going to some trouble to consult it; very few persons, places or things which one encounters in the Schubert story are without their representation in the book. Deutsch's work corrected all the established errors of chronology, and proved many of the old, favourite stories to be myths. His standard of accuracy, that ruthless objectivity where facts were concerned, placed him in the forefront of Schubert authorities. We are concerned here only with his work on Schubert; in other fields, research on Handel, Haydn and, particularly, Mozart, his renown is as great.

The fourth volume, the thematic catalogue, was published in England in 1951. It is a companion volume to the English translation of the 'Documents' which had appeared four years earlier.[1] The reason for this fortunate conjunction of two books so vital to the English Schubertian, was that Deutsch left Vienna because of the German *Anschluss* of Austria in 1938 and sought refuge in England; he settled eventually in Cambridge.

Between 1897 and 1928 biographies of the composer continued to appear, impelled by a new vigour from the fact that all his music was by then available in the 'Gesamtausgabe' volumes. Two were outstanding, not so much from a biographical point of view, as from the fact that both contained extensive reproductions of manuscripts and manuscript-sketches, which were new to the musical public, and from their excellent analytical treatment of the whole corpus of composition. They are 'Franz Schubert', by Richard Heuberger (Berlin, 1902), and 'Schubert', by Walter Dahms (Leipzig, 1912). If, biographically, they contribute nothing new, it is because Deutsch's work now sets a much higher standard in such matters.

Apart from his documentary books, Deutsch published between 1902 and 1928 many works by Schubert which had escaped the notice of the editors of the 'Gesamtausgabe' or which were

[1] 'Schubert: A Documentary Biography', translated by Eric Blom, London, 1947.

discovered in various odd and interesting ways in homes and museums all over Europe. A list of these works has never been given, and the one provided here is supplied with dates of publication:

1. Six Ländler in B flat (1816). Graz, 1902.
2. Four Ecossaises (1815). 'Die Musik', Berlin, 1912.
3. *Lied in der Abwesenheit*, song (1816); Two Ländler in E flat (?1820). 'Moderne Welt', Vienna, 1925.
4. Three Trios for men's voices, poems by Matthisson (1816):
   (*a*) *Andenken*,
   (*b*) *Erinnerungen*
   (*c*) *Widerhall.* Vienna, 1927.
5. Psalm XIII, song, translation by Moses Mendelssohn (1819). Vienna, 1927.
6. Eight Ländler in F sharp minor (1816). Vienna, 1928.
7. 'Ungarische Melodie' in B minor, PF. Solo (1824). Edition Strache, Vienna, 1928.
8. Polonaise in B flat, violin solo and orchestra (1817). Edition Strache, Vienna, 1928.

Other scholars had published various unknown Schubert works in New York, Munich, Leipzig and Berlin. Chief amongst them are a 'Salve Regina' in F major, for soprano solo and orchestra (1812) published in Vienna in 1928, a Trio in one movement in B flat, for PF., violin and 'cello (1812), published in 1923, and a charming song *Jägers Abendlied*, a setting of the Goethe poem written in 1815, which Mandyczewski published in 'Die Musik', January 1907.

On 22 May 1908 the City Authorities of Vienna purchased the 'Birth-house' from its owner, Rudolph Wittmann, and the decision was taken to turn the first floor of the house into a Schubert museum. It was opened on 18 June 1912 and is today a worthy place of pilgrimage. The most precious exhibits are Dialer's bust of Schubert from the original memorial stone, Schwind's sepia drawing 'A Schubert Evening at Spaun's', and various articles from the original furnishings of the parental home, or from Ferdinand's apartment: things such as bureaus, tables, a pianoforte, all of which Schubert knew and possibly used. His spectacles are there, together with an inkstand said to be his, and sundry other possessions.

In 1928 came the centenary celebrations of Schubert's death. Apart from concerts and festivals of all kinds, the world over, there was in Vienna an important exhibition of his work. It included many manuscripts and first editions such as could not, earlier, have been seen assembled in one place, pictures and manuscripts of his friends, his poets, publishers and biographers. There were numerous pictures of old Vienna, and of associated subjects. The beautifully prepared catalogue of this exhibition is a useful item in the Schubertian bibliography and as such appears in all recent lists of this kind.

Publication of scholarly studies of his music appeared in all musicological journals of the world, some of them, indeed, preparing a special issue devoted exclusively to essays on various aspects of his work. From the mass of studies so written one or two emerge as vitally important. Two essays by Sir Donald Tovey can safely be said to voice in an authoritative manner the new appreciation and the new veneration for Schubert which had grown from its beginnings in 1897. The first is the essay on the composer's tonality, already quoted on several occasions in previous chapters of this book, and the other is a full length study of the music entitled 'Franz Schubert'.[1] Finally, the book on Schubert's songs by Richard Capell must be mentioned. This, like Tovey's essay on Schubert's tonality, has been frequently quoted here. It is an affectionately written, but penetrating study of the songs, and of all aesthetic studies of the composer, in any language, it gets nearest to the heart of Schubert. Again and again Capell says things about the songs and their composer, phrased in his incomparable fashion, which, being once said, bear the stamp of imperishable truth and endear themselves to the Schubertian as an inseparable comment on the particular song or feature of the song. His introductory remarks to the 'Winterreise' have no equal in the Schubertian literature.

[1] 'Heritage of Music', Oxford University Press, 1927.

X

The enormous number of essays and books written for the 1928 centenary can be assessed from Willi Kahl's catalogue of all the writings on Schubert between 1828 and 1928. The first hundred years, to the end of 1927, produced, according to Kahl, nearly 2,000 items. One year later, in December 1928, this had risen to over 3,000 items. An inevitable period of reaction set in, but not a prolonged one. In the 1930's, in spite of the growing tension and unrest in Europe, biographies, notably Walter Vetter's 'Franz Schubert' of 1934, discoveries of letters and manuscripts, and literary studies of his music, continued to enrich the Schubertian heritage. A collection of newly-found dance music, 'Deutsche Tänze', was published in Vienna in 1930, edited by Alfred Orel and O. E. Deutsch; the charming dances composed in October 1824 at Zseliz, were published in 1931 from the manuscript which Schubert gave to Karoline Esterházy; a 'Tantum Ergo' in C major, for chorus and orchestra, edited by Karl Geiringer, followed in 1935; the first movement of a String Quartet in C minor (D. 103) from which the other movements had been lost, was edited by Orel and published in Vienna in 1939. After the outbreak of war, in 1940, Orel's book, 'Der junge Schubert', appeared. It contained a large number of Schubert's settings of Metastasio texts, written as exercises for Salieri, the manuscripts having formed part of Dumba's great collection. The book usefully concentrated on Schubert's juvenilia, and catalogued them in careful detail.

In England, a thorough survey of his work in all categories, excluding biography and concentrating on the music alone, was written by a group of scholars and published under the editorship of Gerald Abraham in 1947. This was 'Schubert: a symposium' and in it, for the first time, a serious attempt to examine the music of the operas was made by A. Hyatt King. A similar approach, 'Works' without 'Life', was made by Alfred Einstein in 1951. His book, 'Schubert', is an objective study by a first-class scholar who was not, primarily, a Schubertian specialist. The book on Schubert which forms part of the 'Master Musicians' series is by Arthur Hutchings, a most attractively written and thoughtful study.[1]

Discoveries of his manuscripts still continue. The 'deep suspicion' of the 'Musical World' in 1844, at the fact that new songs by a composer sixteen years dead continued to be published, might well be felt by any journal today, for not a year goes by but a new manuscript of Schubert's is discovered somewhere; lost for a hundred and thirty years or so, and then found again on a library shelf, in a collection of old music, in the posthumous papers of a dead musician. Most of the recent discoveries have been already described in the appropriate place in earlier chapters.

Breitkopf & Härtel are eventually to publish a second supplementary volume to the 'Gesamtausgabe'. It will contain all the still unpublished work and in 'Appendix II' of this book the ideal form of the volume, not necessarily the one it will take, is suggested.

Another publication promised for the near future is Deutsch's collection of the Schubert 'Memoirs', a convenient though not particularly accurate term used to describe the writings and reminiscences of the men and women who knew Schubert, or who were closely associated with people who knew him. It will be an invaluable source-book, although calling for careful handling, for it records all the anecdotes, genuine and otherwise, which arose in the mid-nineteenth century.

In 1955 a facsimile reproduction of the autograph manuscript of 'Winterreise' was published in Cassel, Germany, by the Bärenreiter Verlag. The publication was reviewed by 'C. v. D.' (Charlotte von Dach) in 'Der Bund', Berne, Switzerland on 26 May 1955. The closing paragraphs of that review sum up, in a most admirable fashion, the attitude of the mid-twentieth century to that Viennese composer who lived so short a life, and died in obscurity and poverty completely oblivious of the immortal name he was leaving behind him.

> Perishable leaves, fading traces of work and of what were once the realities of a man's life: he who examines them with the heart,

[1] J. M. Dent & Sons Ltd., London, edited by Eric Blom.

and not with the clumsier outward intelligence, to him they are magic mirrors, in which such a thing as the creative spirit is to be perceived.

They are precious, they are lovely, these leaves; and they have also a great moral significance: they show us the places in a man's soul where spirit wrestles with matter; the eternal struggle towards the light, the sacred toil to shape the pure form of the Divine out of the transitoriness of the human spirit.

For that reason we shall love and reverence these pages of grey paper on which Schubert penned his 'Winterreise'.

APPENDIX I

THE 'GMUNDEN-GASTEIN' SYMPHONY

It is not possible to come to a definite conclusion when considering the problem of this alleged composition by Schubert. One can assemble pieces of evidence from existing documents and make some attempt to assess the merit, or force, of each one, in itself and in its relationship to the others. And in the attempt one must keep in mind such imponderable factors as Schubert's own methods of composition (especially the composition of symphonies), his friends' often hazy knowledge of what he was actually working on at any given period, and their even hazier knowledge of his particular methods of work.

But these scraps of evidence, considered as impartially as possible, incline one to believe that to the question: Did Schubert compose a symphony at Gmunden and Gastein in 1825?—neither the definite 'Yes' nor the definite 'No' would be a satisfactory answer.

There are, altogether, ten documents to be brought forward as witnesses, and they group themselves fairly neatly into four sections.

I

1. Schubert to Leopold Kupelwieser, 31 March 1824

This has been quoted in full on page 154. The revelant extract is as follows:

> I have tried my hand at several instrumental works, for I wrote two quartets for violins, viola and 'cello, and an Octet, and I want to write another quartet, in fact, I intend to pave my way towards grand symphony in that manner....

2. Schwind to Leopold Kupelwieser, 31 May 1824

After telling Kupelwieser that Schubert had left Vienna for Zseliz, taking an opera libretto with him, Schwind adds:

> ... he has also resolved to write a symphony.

3. Anton Ottenwalt to Spaun, 19 July 1825

This was written while Schubert was on holiday in Upper Austria. The composer had just arrived from Gmunden to stay in Linz, and Ottenwalt, his host, wrote enthusiastically of the pleasure his songs had given them all. Then Ottenwalt informs Spaun:

> By the way, he had worked at a symphony in Gmunden, which is to be performed in Vienna this winter....

4. Schubert to his father and stepmother, 25 July 1825

The composer was at Steyr for a short while. He describes his days at Gmunden:

> I lived at Traweger's, very free and easy. Later, when Councillor von Schiller was there, who is monarch of the whole Salzkammergut, we (Vogl and I) dined daily at his house and had music there as we also often did at Traweger's house.

5. Schwind to Schubert, 14 August 1825

This was written from Vienna and Schubert received it at Gastein. Schwind refers to Schubert's symphony in these words:

> About your symphony we may be quite hopeful. Old Hönig is dean of the faculty of jurisprudence, and as such is to give a concert. That will afford a better opportunity of having it performed; indeed we count upon it.

These five passages give the preliminary references to the symphony, and we might pause here and consider what they imply. We find that Schubert intended to write a symphony, that he told his friends so, and that they discussed the matter amongst themselves. It is true that he wanted to write a third string quartet first, and that his resolve to compose the symphony at Zseliz in 1824 was not carried through, but the idea is in the air. A year later, at Gmunden, there is no question—he worked at this symphony and must himself have told Ottenwalt so.

But how seriously did he apply himself to the task in view of his own account of the way he passed his days at Gmunden in the letter to his parents? There is no word from the composer himself, in any of his letters written during the period (and they are not few), about the symphony. At least the work was not finished, for no concert in Vienna that winter contained the performance of a new Schubert symphony. It is fairly safe to conclude that at Gmunden he composed sketches for a symphony, and took them back to Vienna with him in the autumn. How substantial they were there is no means of knowing, but they were set aside for the time being.[1]

II

Reference must be made here to a batch of documents belonging to the autumn of 1826, when, it was known, Schubert had announced his intention of dedicating a symphony to the *Gesellschaft der Musikfreunde*. These documents concern the transactions between the *Gesellschaft* and Schubert, in connection with a gift of £10. It was a token of the Society's sense of obligation to the composer and a generous acknowledgement of his work. It was presented on 12 October 1826. Schubert wrote an official receipt and courteous thanks on 20 October 1826. It has been suggested, when this period of Schubert's life was discussed, that the whole simple business has been befogged by associating with those straightforward documents an *undated* letter from Schubert to the Society in which he 'dedicated' a symphony to it:

6. Schubert to the 'Gesellschaft der Musikfreunde', NO DATE

To the Committee of the Austrian *Gesellschaft der Musikfreunde.*

Convinced of the noble intention of the Austrian 'Musikverein' to support any artistic endeavour as far as possible, I venture, as a native artist, to dedicate to them this, my symphony, and to commend it most politely to their protection.

With all my respects,
Your devoted
Franz Schubert

[1] The alternative possibility should be taken into account, that Schubert might have abandoned any idea of completing the symphony and used his material for the Sonata in D major, composed at Gastein in 1825 and published as Op. 53 the following year.

It seems from Schubert's words here, that the score of the symphony was dispatched with the note. The *Gesellschaft* has no record of receiving any such symphony in 1826, nor has it any symphony score from that year, nor, in the letter offering the gift of money, sent to Schubert by the President, Raphael Kiesewetter, is any thanks offered for the work, which would be an omission not to be credited. On the other hand, the Society did receive the score of the great C major Symphony in 1828, and recorded the fact (Catalogue mark: xiii. 8024). At rehearsals the work was found too difficult, whereupon Schubert withdrew the larger symphony and offered to the Society the smaller, 1818 work in the same key. The undated letter just quoted, one feels, *must* belong to 1828, and have accompanied the score of the great C major Symphony. One small factual piece of evidence might be mentioned. Schubert's undated letter is still extant and in the archives of the Society. All documents of those early years were given a consecutive numbering—no date was added. The original number on this letter has been altered, which has a faint suggestion that its position has been moved in the early files, possibly to bring it into line with the transactions over the donation to Schubert and the rumours that he intended to dedicate a symphony to the Society. It is now to be found in the 'October 1826' section, from which it is quoted in the Schubert 'Documents' (page 559); the attribution there 'Early October 1826' has, however, nothing to support it.

III

But it seems permissible to draw the conclusion that the gift of £10 from the *Gesellschaft*, together with the fact that in June 1827 he had been elected as a 'representative' of the Society, inclined Schubert's thoughts to the composition of a symphony, so long in his mind and now, at last, taken in hand. The third string quartet, which he had wished to write before undertaking the 'grand symphony', had been composed in July 1826. The symphony sketches started at Gmunden meant that the work had, at least, begun to take shape on paper. During the autumn of 1827, after his return from Graz, he may have worked on his sketches to their conclusion. Early in 1828 the work was finished (probably in draft) for he himself mentioned it in a letter.

7. Schubert to B. Schott's Sons, Mainz, 21 February 1828

The composer offered a number of his instrumental and vocal works to the publisher. He concludes with these words:

> ... this is the list of my finished compositions, excepting three operas, a Mass, and a symphony. These last compositions I mention only in order to make you acquainted with my striving after the highest in art.

The next month, in March, the fair copy of the C major Symphony was begun. On its completion it was sent to the *Gesellschaft* with the result already related.

IV

After Schubert's death there were references to the C major Symphony in two of his obituary notices. These tend to confirm the possibility that the sketches made at Gmunden and Gastein were afterwards worked up into the symphony intended for the *Gesellschaft*, and that in their complete form we have the great C major Symphony.

8. Josef Spaun's 'On Franz Schubert' in the Linz journal 'Oesterreichisches Bürgerblatt fur Verstand, Herz und gute Laune' of 27 and 30 March and 3 April 1829

Spaun writes the following words in the course of his biographical article:

> ... in 1825, at Gastein, a grand symphony for which the composer himself had a vast preference....

but he makes no subsequent reference to the C major Symphony of 1828. This would be incomprehensible if he knew of the two symphonies as separate works, and he certainly knew of the existence of the 1828 symphony. To him the '1828' symphony originated at Gastein. He gives '6 Symphonies' as the composer's total, and since neither he, nor any of Schubert's friends in Vienna, knew of the existence of the 'Unfinished' Symphony, then at Graz, it is pointless to try and identify the six of which he was thinking. Later on, he writes of this 'Gastein' Symphony as a most beautiful work, a judgement which he could not have passed upon it since it was unknown on paper and in performance. He was obviously referring to the 1828 work.

9. Eduard Bauernfeld's 'On Franz Schubert' in the 'Wiener Zeitschrift für Kunst' of 9, 11 and 13 June 1829

Bauernfeld, basing his account on Spaun's already published obituary, named the 'Gastein' Symphony as composed in 1825. He gives a short account of Schubert's operas, and then continues:

> To the larger works of the last years belongs further a symphony written at Gastein in 1825 for which its author had a special liking, and the Mass of the year 1828 . . . his last work.

He then goes on to discuss a Symphony in C major, but this turns out to be the earlier work, for Bauernfeld gives its date of composition, 1817. Then he concludes:

> Perhaps the 'Gesellschaft' will by and by make us acquainted with one of Schubert's later symphonies, possibly with the 'Gastein' Symphony.

His brief mention of a 'Last Symphony' in 1828, of which he says nothing at all in his article, occurs in his catalogue, and is clearly designed to amplify Spaun's; it is not based on his knowledge of two separate symphonies.

One significant fact, which is generally overlooked in discussions of this question, is that Ferdinand nowhere makes any reference to a symphony in the last six years of his brother's life, other than the great C major Symphony, which he assigns, of course, to 1828. If there had been a symphony other than this, from the weeks at Gmunden and Gastein, and if the existence of such a symphony had been vaguely known to Schubert's friends, it would surely have been known also to Ferdinand. But he makes no mention of it.

10. Thematic Catalogue: manuscript notes made in 1842 by Aloys Fuchs.

That the symphony which Schubert intended to dedicate to the

Gesellschaft der Musikfreunde was, in fact, the work of 1828, is proved by a reference in this catalogue of Fuchs. He compiled it in collaboration with Ferdinand Schubert. Against his entry of the Symphony in C major, 1828, he writes:

> . . . for the Vienna 'Musikverein'.

This information must have been confirmed by Ferdinand and seems to represent the truth in the matter.

The acceptance of the last symphony as the only work in that form written in Schubert's mature years was general until Grove raised the matter in 1881. He was preparing to write his biographical article for the 'Dictionary' and during his preliminary work on the subject he had pondered over Bauernfeld's entry: '1825. Grand Symphony.' He came to the conclusion that a symphony had been written by the composer in that year and soon afterwards lost. He expressed his views in a letter to the 'Times' of 28 September 1881. The secretary of the *Gesellschaft* in those days, C. F. Pohl, misinterpreted a passage in Grove's letter as an accusation against the authorities of the Society for negligence and careless handling of a score entrusted to their care. Pohl wrote a protesting reply to Grove, denying the charge: his letter was published in the 'Neue Freie Presse' of 7 October 1881. He stated categorically that the symphony dedicated to the Society was not lost, being, in fact, the great Symphony in C of 1828. As for the 'Gastein' Symphony, he did not believe in its existence:

> . . . it would have been entered at once, in 1826, in the Archive-Catalogue, considering the punctilious care of Baron von Knorr, then the Society's Archivist. . . . neither Sonnleithner, the sisters Fröhlich, Baron Schönstein, Bauernfeld, Spaun, nor his own brother Ferdinand, ever heard of it. Especially as Dr. Leopold Sonnleithner was, in 1826, witness at all the meetings of the Society, it seems impossible to believe that that man who has earned such honour over Schubert should during forty-nine years (he died in 1873) have never remembered the existence of this symphony.

Pohl erred, we can see, in saying that Bauernfeld and Spaun knew 'nothing of the symphony', but as the facts quoted above make clear, their knowledge was extremely hazy compared with that of such a witness as Leopold Sonnleithner.

In a letter to the 'Times' of 17 October 1881, Grove made haste to correct Pohl's wrong impression, but the subject had, through this irrelevant exchange of letters, forcibly thrust itself on the attention of the musical world, and since that day there has been an inconclusive discussion of the pros and cons of the existence of an earlier symphony from 1825–1826.

The collecting of the documents above cannot, as was implied in the introductory paragraph, decisively settle the issue. Paradoxically the answer seems to be, after all, that Schubert did not write a symphony at Gastein and Gmunden, nor was it subsequently lost!

APPENDIX II

WORKS BY SCHUBERT NOT INCLUDED IN THE 'GESAMTAUSGABE'

Most of these compositions are still unpublished. The publication of the others has been either in the form of supplements to Austrian, German or Swiss periodicals, or from Continental publishing houses with only local reputations. Even the published works are therefore largely inaccessible. The works are classified here according to the general plan of the *Gesamtausgabe* ('Complete Edition)' of Breitkopf & Härtel, to which they could well form a second Supplementary Volume (Serie XXII). Short fragmentary compositions, unsuitable for publication, are given in a paragraph at the end of the list of works.[1]

A. ORCHESTRAL WORKS

(*a*) Overture in D major. Fragment. (?) 1812.

(*b*) Symphony in D major: first movement. *Adagio* leading to *Allegro con moto*. Fragment, based on the material of (*a*). 1812.

(*c*) Movement in D major. Fragment. 1813.

(*d*) Polonaise in B flat for solo violin and strings. September 1817.

(*e*) Symphony in D. Sketches in pianoforte-score for eight movements. May 1818.

(*f*) Symphony in E. Sketches for four movements in full-score. August 1821.

(*g*) Sketch for, and the partly completed full-score of, third movement of the 'Unfinished' Symphony. October 1822.

B. CHAMBER WORKS

(*a*) String Quartet in G major: first movement. Fragment. (?) 1810.

[1] The list is a revised version of my article 'Supplement no. 2 for the Schubert *Gesamtausgabe*', published in the 'Monthly Musical Record' of February 1954. The material of that article is used here with the kind permission of the editor.

(*b*) Overture in C minor, for String Quintet (2 violins, 2 violas, 'cello). 29 June/12 July 1811.

(*c*) *Allegro* for piano, violin and 'cello called by the composer 'Sonata'. 27 July/28 August 1812.

(*d*) Second and fourth movements of a string Quartet in C major. *Andante* (A minor) and *Allegro con spirito* (C minor/major). September 1812. (The first and third movements were published in the *Gesamtausgabe* as 'String Quartet no. 2': V, 2; part of the fourth movement is given in the *Revisionsbericht*.)

(*e*) Trio-section of a minuet for flute, guitar, viola and 'cello. February 1814. (The original contribution to the so-called 'Guitar' quartet.)

(*f*) String Quartet in C minor: first movement. *Grave* leading to *Allegro*. April 1814.

(*g*) String Quartet in C minor: slow movement in A flat. Fragment. (The second movement to the famous 'Quartettsatz'.)

C. PIANOFORTE DUET

(*a*) Three German dances (one in E minor, two in E major). Summer 1818. (The first dance has two Trios, and the one in G major is published in the *Gesamtausgabe*, XII, 10.)

D. PIANOFORTE SOLO

(*a*) Fantasia in C minor. (?) 1810.

(*b*) Two minuets: i. C major, ii. F major. (?) 1810.

(*c*) Two fugues for 4 voices: i. D minor, ii. B flat. 1813.

(*d*) Two minuets and four trios. November 1813. (Two minuets probably lost from the MS.)

(*e*) Trio-section in E major (for the Waltz, Op. 127: no. 3). 1815.

(*f*) Waltz in C sharp major. 1815.

(*g*) Trio-section in (?) F major (for the unfinished Sonata in C major). 1815.

(*h*) Eight Ländler in D major. January 1816.

(*i*) Eight Ländler in F sharp minor. 1816.

(*j*) Four écossaises (F major, B flat major, two in A flat major). 1816.

(*k*) Sonata in E minor: first movement. Fragment. (?) 1817.

(*l*) Sonata in E minor: second, third and fourth movements of the Sonata no. 6. June 1817. (First movement published in the *Gesamtausgabe*: X, 4.)

(*m*) Écossaise in E flat. 1817.
(*n*) Ländler in E flat. (?) 1820.
(*o*) Eight Ländler (various keys). (?) 1820.
(*p*) PF. arrangement of the Overture for 'Alfonso und Estrella'. November 1822.
(*q*) Écossaise in D major. January 1823.
(*r*) Ungarische Melodie in B minor. Zseliz, 2 September 1824. (PF. sketch of the *Allegretto* from Op. 54.)
(*s*) Three écossaises (B flat, two in D major). September 1824.
(*t*) Six German Dances (three in A flat, three in B flat). Zseliz, October 1824.
(*u*) Two German Dances (F major and G major). April 1825.
(*v*) Four Waltzes (A flat, B minor, two in G major). 1825–1826.

E. CHURCH MUSIC

(*a*) 'Salve Regina' in F major (Sop. solo, orch. and organ continuo). June 1812.
(*b*) *Kyrie* of a Requiem in E flat. Fragment. (July ?) 1816.
(*c*) 'Tantum ergo' in C major (Chorus, orch. and organ continuo). August 1816.
(*d*) German Requiem (author unknown) in G minor (four voices and organ accompaniment). Zseliz, August 1818.
(*e*) 'Tantum ergo' in B flat (Vocal quartet, chorus and orch.) August 1821.
(*f*) *Kyrie* of a Mass in A minor. Fragment. May 1822.

F. DRAMATIC MUSIC

(*a*) *Adrast* (text: Johann Mayrhofer). Six numbers unpublished in the *Gesamtausgabe*. (?) 1819.
(*b*) *Claudine von villa Bella* (text: Goethe). Arietta and duet. Both fragments. July 1815.
(*c*) *Sakuntala* (text: J. P. Neumann after Kalidasa). Sketches for Acts I and II. October 1820.
(*d*) Two arias (nos. 8 and 13) (from *Alfonso und Estrella*); (PF. accompaniment arranged by the composer). 1822.
(*e*) *Sofie* (?): sketches for Act I of an unnamed opera. (?) 1823.
(*f*) *Rüdiger* (author unknown). Aria with chorus: duet. May 1823.
(*g*) *Der Graf von Gleichen* (text: Bauernfeld). Sketches (short score) for Acts I and II. June 1827/1828.

G. CANTATAS AND PART-SONGS

(*a*) *Dithyrambe* (text: (Schiller). Tenor solo, mixed chorus, solo voices, PF. accompaniment. March 1813.

(*b*) *Ewig still steht die Vergangenheit* (text: Schiller). Canon for three voices. July 1813.

(*c*) *Die Schlacht* (text: Schiller). Male voices. First sketch. August 1815.

(*d*) *Trinklied* (author unknown). T.T.B.B. unacc. 1816. (The original PF. accompaniment is lost.)

(*e*) *Erinnerungen* (text: Matthisson). T.T.B. unacc. May 1816.

(*f*) *Widerhall* (text: Matthisson). T.T.B. unacc. May 1816.

(*g*) *Andenken* (text: Matthisson). T.T.B. unacc. May 1816.

(*h*) *Leise, leise, lasst uns singen* (author unknown). T.T.B.B. unacc. 1819.

(*i*) *Viel tausend Sterne prangen* (text: A. G. Eberhard). Mixed chorus, PF. accompaniment. 1819.

(*j*) *Linde Lüfte wehen* (author unknown). S.T., PF. accompaniment. Fragment. April 1812.

(*k*) *Mondenschein* (text: Schober). T.T.B.B.B., PF. accompaniment. January 1826. (The *Gesamtausgabe* gives the version without accompaniment.)

(*l*) *Das stille Lied* (text: J. G. Seegemund). T.T.B.B. unacc. Fragment. May 1827.

(*m*) Sketches for *Mirjams Siegesgesang* (text: Grillparzer). March 1828.

H. SOLO SONGS

(*a*) *Ich sass am einer Tempelhalle* (text: (?) Salis-Seewis). Fragment. 1811.

(*b*) *Jägers Abendlied* (text: Goethe). 20 June 1815.

(*c*) *Meeresstille* (text: Goethe). 20 June 1815.

(*d*) *Der Graf von Hapsburg* (text: Schiller). Fragment. 1815.

(*e*) *An den Mond* (author unknown). Fragment. 18 October 1815.

(*f*) *Lorma* (text: Ossian—trans. Harold). Fragment. 28 November 1815.

(*g*) *Gruppe aus dem Tartarus* (text: Schiller). Fragment. March 1816.

(*h*) *Lied in der Abwesenheit* (text: Stolberg). Fragment. April 1816.

(*i*) *Am ersten Maimorgen* (text: Claudius). 1816.

(*j*) *An Chloen* (text: Uz). Fragment. 1816.

(*k*) *Mailied* (text: Hölty). November 1816.

(*l*) *Song without title or words*. May 1817.
(*m*) *Der Leidende* (author unknown). 1817.
(*n*) *Psalm XIII* (trans. Moses Mendelssohn). June 1819. (The last six bars are missing.)
(*o*) *Abend* (author unknown). Fragment. 1819.
(*p*) *Greisengesang* (text: Rückert). First version, substantially differing from the well-known setting. (?) 1822.
(*q*) *O Quell, was strömst du?* (text: Schulze). Fragment. 1826.
(*r*) *Fröhliches Scheiden* (text: Leitner). Fragment. 1827.

I. MISCELLANEOUS WORKS

(*a*) Seven exercises in counterpoint. *c*, 1812.
(*b*) Multiple settings of four passages from Pietro Metastasio. Autumn 1812.
  i. 'Quell' innocente figlio' (the angel's aria from *Isacco*), for S., S.S., S.A.T., S.A.T., S.A.T.B., S.A.T.B., S.A.T.B.
  ii. 'Entra l'uomo' (Abraham's aria from *Isacco*), for S., S.A., S.A.T., S.A.T.B., S.A.T.B., S.A.T.B.,
  iii. 'Te solo adoro' (Achior's aria from *Betulia liberata*), for S.A.T.B.
  iv. 'Serbate, o Dei custodi' (chorus from *La Clemenza di Tito*), for S.A.T.B. (two versions: both in D major), S.A.T.B. (C major), Tenor with bass continuo (two versions: both in C major).
(*c*) i. Six Ländler in B flat. February 1816.
  ii. Four 'Komische Ländler' in D major. 1816. (The treble stave only of these ten dances is preserved.)
(*d*) Verses from St. John's Gospel (ch. vi, vv. 55–58), for Sop. solo and figured bass. 1818.
(*e*) i. Two Ländler (A major, E major). 1819.
  ii. Two Ländler (both D flat). May 1821. (The treble stave only of these four dances is preserved.)
(*f*) Canon for six voices. January 1826.

The following items are very fragmentary. The last one is given here for the sake of completeness since it certainly contains traces of original work by Schubert; it could hardly be published as his work.

1. 35 bars from the first movement of a String Quartet (? in F major). *c*. 1813.

2. Offertory in C major ('Clamavi ad te'). *c.* 1813. (The soprano part only is preserved. The fact that it was copied by Schubert from a completed work, now lost, is proved by his insertion of the number of 'rest' bars between the vocal phrases.)
3. Two fragmentary arias from an unnamed opera. 1814.
4. Sketch (6 bars) for the opening of a setting of Mignon's song *So lasst mich scheinen.* (A flat, 2/4). September 1816.
5. Fragment (11 bars) from a completed setting of Mignon's song *So lasst mich scheinen.* (G major, 4/4). September 1816.
6. Sketches for 3 Polonaises from Op. 75: nos. 2, 3 and 4. *c.* 1818.
7. Arrangement for voice and orchestra of Maximilian Stadler's setting of Psalm VIII for voice and PF. August 1823.

APPENDIX III

THE WORKS IN CHRONOLOGICAL ORDER

This list of Schubert's works, chronologically arranged, is based upon primary research, and in all cases where it departs from the 'Thematic Catalogue' of O. E. Deutsch, there are good reasons for the departures. They may be due to further information from Dr. Deutsch himself, to recent discoveries, or to my own examination of various Schubert manuscripts. The results of Dr. Fritz Racek's careful description of the Schubert manuscripts in the Vienna 'Stadtbibliothek'[1] are also incorporated here.

I have omitted from the list some fifty items which are given in the 'Thematic Catalogue'. They comprise those works which are irretrievably lost, arrangements by Schubert of his own or of other composer's works, small fragments, dubious compositions, and one or two duplicates which, by acquiring dates differing from their originals, are masquerading as independent works, e.g. the song *Widerschein*.

In order to preserve a realistic chronology an approximate date has been assessed to those works which cannot be dated with certainty. It has in every case been carefully indicated. By this means it has been possible to avoid placing a number of undated works at the end of the list and the final works there are, as they should be, the last the composer wrote. With a similar aim in view works whose only date is that of the *year* of composition have been placed in the middle of that year's work, not at the beginning or end. Since they must be placed somewhere it seemed less desirable, to give an actual example, to break the sequence of December 1815 and January 1816, than that of June and July 1816.

[1] 'Von der Schubert Handschriften der Stadtbibliothek,' Fritz Racek, in the 'Festschrift zum hundertjährigen Bestehen der Wiener Stadtbibliothek' ('Wiener Schriften', IV), Vienna, 1956.

1810

Fantasia in G, PF. Duet (8 April–1 May).

1811

Hagars Klage (Schücking) (30 March).
Des Mädchens Klage (Schiller) (? March).
Eine Leichenphantasie (Schiller) (? March).
Overture in C minor, Str. Quintet (29 June–12 July).
Fantasia in G minor, PF. Duet (20 September).
Der Vatermörder (Pfeffel) (26 December).

1812

Overture in D, Orchestra (26 June).
Salve Regina in F, Soprano, Orchestra, Organ (28 June).
Klaglied (Rochlitz).
Der Spiegelritter, Operetta in 3 acts (Kotzbue): 1 act written.
Overture in D, Orchestra (Introduction in D minor).
Der Geistertanz (Matthisson).
Quell' innocente figlio (Metastasio), various settings.
String Quartet ('mixed keys')
Movement in B flat for PF., vn. and 'cello (called *Sonata*) (27 July–28 August).
Viel tausend Sterne prangen (Eberhard) (? August).
Der Jüngling am Bache (Schiller) (24 September).
Kyrie for a Mass in D minor, Chorus, Orchestra, Organ (25 September).
Overture (?) in D, Orchestral fragment (? 1812).
Overture to 'Der Teufel als Hydraulicus' (Albrecht), Orchestra (? 1812).
String Quartet in C major (September).
Andante in C, PF. Solo (9 September).
Twelve 'Wiener Deutsche', PF. Solo.
Entra l'uomo (Metastasio) various settings (September–October).
Te solo adoro (Metastasio) (5 November).
Serbate, o Dei custodi (Metastasio) (10 December).
String Quartet in B flat (19 November–21 February 1813).

1813

Totengräberlied (Hölty) (19 January).
Kyrie for a Mass in B flat, unacc. Chorus (1 March).
String Quartet in C (March).

Dithyrambe (Schiller), mixed voices, Tenor, PF. (29 March).
Fantasia in C minor, PF. Duet (2 versions) (April–10 June).
Kyrie for a Mass in D minor, Chorus, Orchestra (15 April).
Die Schatten (Matthisson) (12 April).
Unendliche Freude (Schiller), T.T.B. (15 April).
Sehnsucht ('Ach! aus dieses Tales') (Schiller) (15–17 April).
Vorüber die stöhnende Klage (Schiller), T.T.B. (18 April).
Unendliche Freude (Schiller), Canon, T.T.B. (19 April).
Selig durch die Liebe (Schiller), T.T.B. (21 April).
Sanctus, canon with coda (21 April).
Hier strecket (Schiller), T.T.B., (29 April).
Dessen Fahne (Schiller), T.T.B. (May).
Verklärung (Pope, tr. Herder) (4 May).
Hier unarmen (Schiller), T.T.B. (8 May).
Ein jugendlicher Maienschwung (Schiller), T.T.B. (8 May).
Thronend auf erhabnem Sitz (Schiller), T.T.B. (9 May).
Wer die steile Sternenbahn (Schiller), T.T.B. (10 May).
Majestät'sche Sonnenrossse (Schiller), T.T.B. (10 May).
Schmerz verzerret (Schiller), T.T.B. (11 May).
Kyrie for a Mass in F, Chorus, Orchestra, Organ (12 May).
Frisch atmet (Schiller), T.B.B. (15 May).
Fantasia in C minor, PF. Solo (? 1813).
Overture in D, Orchestral fragment (? 1813).
Symphony in D, Orchestral fragment based on above (? 1813).
Liebe säuseln die Blätter (Hölty), vocal trio (? 1813).
Fugue, 4 voices, PF. Solo (? 1813).
Allegro moderato in C, Andante in A minor, PF. Duet (? 1813).
String Quartet in B flat (2 movements) (8–16 June, 18 August).
Variations in F major, PF. Solo (? 1813).
Totengräberlied (Hölty), T.T.B. (? 1813).
Ich sass an einer Tempelhalle (? Salis) (? 1813).
Twenty Minuets, PF. Solo.
Miserero pargoletto (Metastasio).
Dreifach ist der Schritt (Schiller), T.B.B.
Dreifach ist der Schritt (Schiller), canon à tre (8 July).
Ewig still (Schiller), canon à tre (8 July).
Die zwei Tugendwege (Schiller), T.T.B. (15 July).
Minuet and Finale in F, 2 ob., 2 cl., 2 hn., 2 bn. (18 August).
Thekla (Schiller) (22–23 August).
String Quartet in D (22 August–September).

Trinklied ('Freunde, sammelt') (?) (29 August).
Pensa, che questo istante (Metastasio) (13 September).
Der Taucher (Schiller) (17 September–5 April 1814).
Son fra l'onde (Metastasio) (18 September).
Eine kleine Trauermusik, 2 cl., 2 bn., db. bn., 2 hn., 2 trb. (19 September).
Kantate zur Namensfeier des Vaters (Schubert), T.T.B. and guitar (27 September).
Auf den Sieg der Deutschen (?), solo with 2 vn. and 'cello (Autumn).
Two Minuets, PF. Solo (? 1813).
Symphony no. 1, in D (finished 28 October).
Zur Namensfeier des Herrn Andreas Siller (?), solo with vn. and harp (28 October–4 November).
'Des Teufels Lustschloss', Opera in 3 acts (Kotzebue) (30 October–22 October 1814).
Minuet in D, strings (? November).
String Quartet in E flat, Op. 125: no. 1 (November).
Verschwunden sind die Schmerzen canon, T.T.B. (15 November).
Five Minuets (6 trios) for String Quartet (19 November).
Five 'German' dances (7 trios) with coda, for String Quartet (19 November).
Two Minuets (4 trios), PF. Solo (22 November).
Don Gayseros (Fouqué) (? 1813). } *Don Gayseros*
Nächtens klang die süsse Laute (? 1813) } *Don Gayseros*
An dem jungen Morgenhimmel (? 1813) } *Don Gayseros*
Allegro moderato in C, PF. Solo (? 1813).
Andantino in C, PF. Solo (? 1813).
Fugue, 4 voices, PF. Solo (? 1813).

1814

Trio of a Minuet for fl., va., guitar and 'cello (included in the so-called 'Guitar' Quartet). (26 February).
Trost. An Elisa (Matthisson) (? April).
Andenken (Matthisson) (April).
Geisternähe (Matthisson) (April).
Erinnerung (also called *Totenopfer*) (Matthisson) (April).
Grave and Allegro, String Quartet in C minor (23 April).
Die Befreier Europas (?) (16 May).
Mass no. 1, in F, S.A.T.B., Chorus, Orchestra, Organ (17 May–22 July).

Minuet in C sharp minor, PF. Solo (? June).
Salve Regina, B flat, Tenor, Orchestra, Organ (28 June–1 July).
Lied aus der Ferne (Matthisson) (? July).
String Quartet in D.
Adelaide (Matthisson).
Der Abend (Matthisson) (July).
Lied der Liebe (Matthisson) (July).
Wer ist gross? (?), Bass, T.T.B.B., Orchestra (24–25 July).
String Quartet in B flat, Op. 168 (5–13 September).
An Emma (Schiller) (17 September).
Erinnerungen (Matthisson) (mid September).
Die Betende (Matthisson) (mid September).
Das Fraulein im Türme (Matthisson) (29 September).
An Laura (Matthisson) (2–7 October).
Der Geistertanz (Matthisson) (14 October).
Das Mädchen aus der Fremde (Schiller) (16 October).
Gretchen am Spinnrade (Goethe) (19 October).
Nachtgesang (Goethe) (30 November).
Trost im Thränen (Goethe) (30 November).
Schäfers Klagelied (Goethe) (30 November).
Sehnsucht (Goethe) (3 December).
Am See (Mayrhofer) (7 December).
Ammenlied (Luibi) (December).
Symphony no. 2, in B flat (10 December–24 March 1815).
'Szene aus Goethe's "Faust" ' (12 December).
An die Natur (Stolberg) (? December).
Lied (*Mutter geht*) (Fouqué) (? December).

1815

Bardengesang (Ossian, tr. Harold) (20 January).
Trinklied ('Brüder, unser Erdenwallen') (Castelli) (February).
Auf einen Kirchhof (Schlechta) (2 February).
Minona (Bertrand) (8 February).
Als ich sie erröten sah (Ehrlich) (10 February).
Der Sänger (Goethe) (February).
Lodas Gespenst (Ossian) (February).
Sonata no. 1, in E major (11 February–21 February).
Das Bild (?) (11 February).
Ten Variations in F major (finished 15 February).
Écossaise in F, PF. Solo (21 February).

Am Flusse (Goethe), 1st setting (27 February).
An Mignon ('Ueber Tal') (Goethe) (27 February).
Nähe des Geliebten (Goethe) (27 February).
Sängers Morgenlied (Körner), 1st setting (27 February).
Sängers Morgenlied (Körner), 2nd setting (1 March).
Amphiaros (Körner) (1 March).
Mass no. 2, in G major, S.T.B., Chorus, Strings, Organ (2–7 March).
Begräbnislied (Klopstock), S.A.T.B., PF. (9 March).
Trinklied vor der Schlacht (Körner) (12 March).
Schwertlied (Körner), Solo with Chorus (12 March).
Gebet während der Schlacht (Körner) (12 March).
String Quartet in G minor (25 March–1 April).
Das war ich (Körner) (26 March).
Stabat Mater in G minor, Chorus, Orchestra, Organ (4–6 April).
Die Sterne (Fellinger) (6 April).
Vergebliche Liebe (Bernard) (6 April).
Adagio in G major, PF. Solo (8 April).
Liebesrausch (Körner) (8 April).
Sehnsucht der Liebe (Körner) (8 April).
'Tres sunt', Offertory in A minor, Chorus, Orchestra, Organ (10–11 April).
Die erste Liebe (Fellinger) (12 April).
Trinklied ('Ihr Freunde') (Zettler) (12 April).
'Benedictus es, Domine', Gradual in C, Chorus, Orchestra, Organ, Op. 150 (15 April).
Second 'Dona Nobis' for the Mass in F major, S.A.T.B., Chorus, Orchestra, Organ (25 April).
'Die vierjährige Posten', 1 act *Singspiel* (Körner) (8–19 May).
Des Mädchens Klage (Schiller), 2nd setting (15 May).
Der Jüngling am Bache (Schiller), 2nd setting (15 May).
An den Mond (Hölty) (17 May).
Die Mainacht (Hölty) (17 May).
Die Sterbende (Matthisson) (May).
Stimme der Liebe (Matthisson) (May).
Naturgenuss (Matthisson) (May).
An die Freude (Schiller) (May).
Rastlose Liebe (Goethe) (19 May).
Amalia (Schiller) (19 May).
An die Nachtigall (Hölty) (22 May).

An die Apfelbäume (Hölty) (22 May).
Seufzer (Hölty) (22 May).
Mailied ('Gruner wird') (Hölty) 2 voices or 2 hn. (24 May).
Symphony no. 3, in D major (24 May–19 July).
Mailied ('Der Schnee zerinnt') (Hölty), 2 voices or 2 hn. (26 May).
Der Morgenstern (Körner), 2 voices or 2 hn. (26 May).
Jägerlied (Körner), 2 voices or 2 hn. (26 May).
Lützows wilde Jagd (Körner), 2 voices or 2 hn. (26 May).
Liebeständelei (Körner) (26 May).
Der Liebende (Hölty) (29 May).
Die Nonne (Hölty) (29 May: revised 16 June).
Der Liedler (Kenner) (June–12 December).
Klärchens Lied (Goethe) (3 June).
Adelwold und Emma (Bertrand) (5–14 June).
Der Traum (Hölty) (17 June).
Die Liebe (Hölty) (17 June).
Jägers Abendlied (Goethe) (20 June).
Meeresstille (Goethe), 1st setting (20 June).
Meeresstille (Goethe, 2nd setting (21 June).
Colmas Klage (Ossian) (22 June).
Grablied (Kenner) (24 June).
Das Finden (Kosegarten) (25 June).
'Fernando', 1 act *Singspiel* (Stadler) (27 June–9 July).
Mailied ('Grüner wird') (Hölty), T.T.B.
Mailied ('Der Schnee zerrinnt') (Hölty), canon à tre.
Ballade ('Ein Fraulein schaut') (Kenner).
Waltz in C sharp major, PF. Solo.
2nd Trio for the Waltz in E major, PF. Solo, Op. 127: no. 3.
Klage um Ali Bey (Claudius), S.S.A. with PF.
Der Mondabend (Kumpf).
Geistes-Gruss (Goethe).
Waltzes for Op. 127, PF. Solo.
Minuet in A, PF. Solo.
Eight écossaises, PF. Solo.
Der Graf von Hapsburg (Schiller) (? 1815).
'Totus in corde', Offertory in C, Op. 46: Sop., Orchestra, Organ.
Lacrimoso son io (?), 2 settings as canon à tre.
Lieb Minna (Stadler) (2 July).
Salve Regina in F major (Second Offertory), Sop., Orchestra, Organ, Op. 47 (5 July: revised 28 January 1823).

Wanderers Nachtlied ('Der, du von dem Himmel bist') (Goethe). (5 July).
Der Fischer (Goethe) (5 July).
Erster Verlust (Goethe) (5 July).
Idens Nachtgesang (Kosegarten) (7 July).
Von Ida (Kosegarten) (7 July).
Die Erscheinung (also called *Erinnerung*) (Kosegarten) (7 July).
Die Täuschung (Kosegarten) (7 July).
Das Sehnen (Kosegarten) (7 July).
Hymne an den Unendlichen (Schiller), S.A.T.B. with PF. (11 July).
Der Abend (Kosegarten) (15 July).
Geist der Liebe (Kosegarten) (15 July).
Tischlied (Goethe) (15 July).
Abends unter der Linde (Kosegarten), 1st setting (24 July).
Abends unter der Linde (Kosegarten), 2nd setting (25 July).
Das Abendrot (Kosegarten), Vocal Trio with PF. (25 July).
Die Mondnacht (Kosegarten) (25 July).
'Claudine von Villa Bella' (Goethe), 3 act *Singspiel* (started 26 July
Huldigung (Kosegarten) (27 July).
Alles um Liebe (Kosegarten) (27 July).
Das Geheimnis (Schiller), 1st setting (7 August).
Hoffnung (Schiller) (7 August).
Das Mädchen aus der Fremde (Schiller) (12 August).
Trinklied in Winter (Hölty), T.T.B. (? August).
Frühlingslied (?), T.T.B. (? August).
Willkommen, lieber schöner Mai (Hölty), 2 settings as canon àtre (? August).
An den Frühling (Schiller) (August).
Die Bürgschaft (Schiller) (August).
Die Spinnerin (Goethe) (August).
Lob des Tokayers (Baumberg) (August).
Punschlied (Schiller) (18 August).
Der Gott und die Bajadere (Goethe) (18 August).
Der Rattenfänger (Goethe) (19 August).
Der Schatzgräber (Goethe) (19 August).
Heidenröslein (Goethe) (19 August).
Bundeslied (Goethe) (19 August).
An den Mond (Goethe), 1st setting (19 August).
Wonne der Wehmut (Goethe) (20 August).
Wer kauft Liebesgötter (Goethe) (21 August).

Die Fröhlichkeit (Prandstetter) (22 August).
Der Morgenkuss (Baumberg) (22 August).
Cora an die Sonne (Baumberg) (22 August).
Abendständchen: an Lina (Baumberg) (23 August).
Morgenlied (Stolberg) (24 August).
Trinklied ('Auf! Jeder sei nun froh') (?), T.T.B.B., with PF. (25 August).
Bergknappenlied (?), T.T.B.B., with PF. (25 August).
Das Leben (Wannovius), S.S.A., with PF. (25 August).
An die Sonne (Baumberg) (25 August).
An die Sonne (Tiedge) (25 August).
Der Wieberfreund (Abraham Cowley, tr. Ratschky) (25 August).
Lilla an die Morgenröte (?) (25 August).
Tischerlied (?) (25 August).
Totenkranz für ein Kind (Matthisson) (25 August).
Abendlied (Stolberg) (28 August).
Punschlied (Schiller), T.T.B., with PF. (29 August).
Cronnan (Ossian, tr. Harold) (5 September).
An den Frühling (Schiller), 2nd setting (6 September).
Lied ('Es ist so angenehm') (Schiller) (6 September).
Furcht der Geliebten (Klopstock) (12 September).
Selma und Selmar (Klopstock) (14 September).
Vaterlandslied (Klopstock) (14 September).
An Sie (Klopstock) (14 September).
Die Sommernacht (Klopstock) (14 September).
Die frühen Gräber (Klopstock) (14 September).
Dem Unendlichen (Klopstock) (15 September).
Lied nach dem Falle Nathos (Ossian, tr. Harold) (September).
Sonata in C major (September).
Das Rosenband (Klopstock) (September).
Das Mädchen von Inistore (Ossian, tr. Harold) (September).
Shilric und Vinvela (Ossian, tr. Harold) (20 September).
Namensfeier (Vierthaler): or *Gratulations-Kantate*, S.T.B., Chorus, Orchestra (27 September).
Hoffnung (Goethe) (? September).
An den Mond (Goethe), 2nd setting (? September).
Twelve écossaises, PF. Solo (3 October).
Liane (Mayrhofer) (October).
Lambertine (Stoll) (12 October).
Labetrank der Liebe (Stoll) (15 October).

An die Geliebte (Stoll) (15 October).
Wiegenlied (Körner) (15 October).
Mein Gruss an den Mai (Kumpf) (15 October).
Skolie (Deinhardstein) (15 October).
Die Sternenwelten (Fellinger) (15 October).
Die macht der Liebe (Kalchberg) (15 October).
Das gestörte Glück (Körner) (15 October).
Nur wer die Sehnsucht kennt (Goethe), 1st setting (18 October).
Hektors Abschied (Schiller) (19 October).
Die Sterne (Kosegarten) (19 October).
Nachtgesang (Kosegarten) (19 October).
An Rosa I (Kosegarten) (19 October).
An Rosa II (Kosegarten) (19 October).
Idens Schwanlied (Kosegarten) (19 October).
Schwanengesang (Kosegarten) (19 October).
Luisens Antwort (Kosegarten) (19 October).
Der Zufriedene (Reissig) (23 October).
Kennst du das Land? (Goethe) (23 October).
Hermann und Thusnelda (Klopstock) (27 October).
Erlking (Goethe) (October).
Ländler and écossaises from Op. 18 (October).
Klage der Ceres (Schiller) (9 November: finished June 1816).
Mass no. 3, in B flat, S.A.T.B., Chorus, Orchestra, Organ, Op. 141 (started 11 November).
Harfenspieler: Wer sich der Einsamkeit ergibt (Goethe) (13 November).
'Die Freunde von Salamanka' (Mayrhofer), *Singspiel* in two acts (18 November–31 December).
Lorma (Ossian, tr. Harold), 1st setting (28 November).
Die drei Sänger (?) (23 December).
Das Grab (Salis), 1st setting (28 December).

1816

Eight Ländler in F sharp minor, PF. Solo (January).
Eight Ländler in D major, PF. Solo (January).
Four 'Komische' Ländler in D major (? PF. Solo) (January).
Six Ländler in B flat, (? PF. Solo) (February).
Der Tod Oskars (? Ossian, tr. Harold) (February).
Lorma (Ossian, tr. Harold), 2nd setting (10 February).
Das Grab (Salis), 2nd setting (11 February).
Eight Ländler in B flat, PF. Solo (13 February).

Salve Regina (German text) in F major, S.A.T.B., Organ (21 February).
Three Minuets for PF. Solo (Trio to the third unfinished) (22 February).
Morgenlied (?) (24 February).
Abendlied (?) (24 February).
Stabat Mater (Klopstock) in F minor, S.T.B. soli, Chorus, Orchestra (28 February).
Salve Regina in B flat, Chorus, Organ (March).
Sonata ('Sonatina') in D major, PF. and vn., Op. 137: no. 1 (March).
Sonata ('Sonatina') in A minor, PF, and vn., Op. 137: no. 2 (March).
Frühlingslied (Hölty) (13 March).
Auf der Tod einer Nachtigall (Hölty) (13 March).
Die Knabenzeit (Hölty) (13 March).
Winterlied (Hölty) (13 March).
Ritter Toggenburg (Schiller) (13 March).
'Die Schlacht' (Schiller), Cantata, PF. (March).
Laura am Klavier (Schiller) (March).
Des Mädchens Klage (Schiller), 3rd setting (March).
Die Entzückung an Laura (Schiller), 1st setting (March).
Die vier Weltalter (Schiller) (March).
Pfügerlied (Salis) (March).
Die Einsiedelei (Salis), 1st setting (March).
Gesang an die Harmonie (Salis) (March).
Lebensmelodien (Schlegel) (March).
Der Flüchtling (Schiller) (18 March).
Lied: In's stille Land (Salis) (27 March–April).
Wehmut (Salis) (End of March–April).
Der Herbstabend (Salis) (End of March–April).
Abschied von der Harfe (Salis) (End of March–April).
Der König in Thule (Goethe) (? April).
Jägers Abendlied (Goethe), 2nd setting (? April).
An Schwager Kronos (Goethe) (? April).
Sonata ('Sonatina') in G minor, PF. and vn., Op. 137: no. 3 (April).
Die verfehlte Stunde (Schlegel) (April).
Sprache der Liebe (Schlegel) (April).
Daphne am Bach (Stolberg) (April).
Stimme der Liebe (Stolberg) (April).
Entzückung (Matthisson) (April).
Geist der Liebe (Matthisson) (April).
Klage (Matthisson) (April).
Lied der Abwesenheit (Stolberg) (April).

Symphony no. 4, in C minor ('The Tragic') (finished 27 April).
Stimme der Liebe (Stolberg) (29 April).
Julius an Theone (Matthisson) (30 April).
'Die Bürgschaft' (?), Opera in 3 acts (unfinished) (started 2 May).
Klage an den Mond (Hölty) (12 May).
Twelve 'German' dances ('Deutsche'), PF. Solo (? May).
Six écossaises, PF. Solo (May).
Naturgenuss (Matthisson), T.T.B.B. (May: PF. acc. in February 1822).
Andenken (Matthisson), T.T.B. (May).
Erinnerungen (Matthisson), T.T.B. (May).
Trinklied im Mai (Hölty), T.T.B. (May).
Widerhall (Matthisson), T.T.B. (May).
Minnelied (Hölty) (May).
Die Erwartung (Schiller) (May).
Die frühe Liebe (Hölty) (May).
Blumenlied (Hölty) (May).
Der Leidende (?), 1st setting (May).
Der Leidende (?), 2nd setting (May).
Klage ('Trauer umfliesst mein Leben') (?) (May).
Seligkeit (Hölty) (May).
Erntelied (Hölty) (May).
Rondo in A major, Vn. solo and str. orch. (June).
An die Sonne (Uz), S.A.T.B., with PF. (June).
Chor der Engel (from Goethe's 'Faust'), S.A.T.B. (June).
Cantata for the 50th Jubilee of Salieri (Schubert.
1st setting, T.T.B.B., Ten., PF. (? June).
2nd setting, T.T.B., Ten., PF. (June).
Das grosse Halleluja (Klopstock) (June).
Schlachtgesang (Klopstock) (June).
Die Gestirne (Klopstock) (June).
Edone (Klopstock) (June).
Die Liebesgötter (Uz) (June).
An den Schlaf (? Uz) (June).
Gott im Frühlinge (Uz) (June).
Der gute Hirt (Uz) (June).
Fragment aus dem Aeschylus ('Oreste', tr. Mayrhofer) (June).
'Prometheus' (Dräxler) [Lost]: Cantata, Soli, Chorus, ? PF. (17 June).
Mass no. 4, in C major, S.A.T.B., Chorus, Orchestra. Organ, Op. 48 (June–July).

Der Entfernten (Salis), T.T.B.B. (? 1816).
Minuet in E major (two Trios), PF. Solo (*c.* 1816).
Die Einsiedelei (Salis), T.T.B.B.
An den Frühling (Schiller), T.T.B.B.
An mein Klavier (Schubart).
Allegretto in C major, PF. Solo (? 1816).
Der Entfernten (Salis) (? 1816).
Fischerlied (Salis) (? 1816).
Licht und Liebe ('Nachtgesang', Collin) (? 1816).
String Quartet in E major, Op. 125: no. 2
Trinklied ('Funkelnd im Becher') (?), T.T.B.B., with PF.
Gold'ner Schein (Matthisson), canon à tre.
Die Nacht (Uz).
An Chloen (Uz).
Am Bach in Frühling (Schober).
Waltzes from Op. 127 and Op. 9.
Romanze (Stolberg).
Fischerlied (Salis), T.T.B.B.
Freude der Kinderjahre (Köpken) (July).
Ländler PF. Solo (publ. 'Gesamtausgabe', XII, 10).
Requiem Mass (*Kyrie*) in F major, S.A.T.B., wind band (? July).
Osterlied (Klopstock), S.A.T.B. with PF. (? 1816).
Grablied auf einen Soldaten (Schubart) (July).
Das Heimweh ('Th. Hell'—K. G. Winkler) (July).
An die untergehende Sonne (Kosegarten) (July–May 1817).
Aus Diego Manzares (Schlechta) (30 July).
An den Mond (Hölty) (7 August).
Sonata in E major (publ. as 'Fünf Klavierstücke') (August).
Adagio in C major, PF. Solo (? August).
'Tantum ergo' in C major, Chorus, Orchestra, Organ (August).
'Tantum ergo' in C major, S.A.T.B., Chorus, Orchestra (August).
An Chloen (Jacobi) (August).
Hochzeitlied (Jacobi) (August).
In der Mitternacht (Jacobi) (August).
Litanei auf das Fest Aller Seelen (Jacobi) (? August).
Trauer der Liebe (Jacobi) (August).
Die Perle (Jacobi) (August).
Pflicht und Liebe (Gotter) (August).
Overture in B flat, Orchestra (September).
Andante in A major, PF. Solo (? September).

String Trio in B flat, one movement (September).
Symphony no. 5, in B flat (September–3 October).
Cantata (for Josef Spendou), S.A.T.B. soli, Chorus, Orchestra, Op. 128 (September).
Liedesend (Mayrhofer) (September).
Abschied: nach einer Wallfahrtsarie (Mayrhofer) (September).
Rückweg (Mayrhofer) (September).
Alte Liebe rostet nie (Mayrhofer) (September).
Orpheus (Jacobi) (September).
Harfenspieler I: Wer sich der Einsamkeit ergibt (Goethe) (September).
Harfenspieler II: An die Türen (Goethe) (September).
Harfenspieler III: Wer nie sein Brot (Goethe),
1st setting (September).
2nd setting (September).
Nur wer die Sehnsucht kennt (Goethe),
2nd setting (? September).
3rd setting (September).
Der Sänger am Felsen (Karoline Pichler) (September).
Lied: Ferne von der grossen Stadt (Pichler) (September).
Magnificat in C major, Soli, Chorus, Orchestra, Organ (15 or 25 September).
Adagio and Rondo concertante in F major, PF., vn., va., 'cello (called 'Klavier-Konzert') (October).
'Auguste jam coelestium', in G major, Sop., Ten., Orchestra (October).
Der Wanderer (Schmidt von Lübeck) (October).
Der Hirt (Mayrhofer) (October).
Lied eines Schiffers an die Dioskuren (Mayrhofer) (? October).
Geheimnis: an Franz Schubert (Mayrhofer) (October).
Zum Punsche (Mayrhofer) (October).
Am ersten Maimorgen (Claudius) (? November).
Mailied ('Grüner wird') (Hölty) (November).
Der Liedende (?), 3rd setting (? November).
Konzerstück in D major, Vn. solo and Orchestra (? November).
Lied: Ich bin vergnügt (Claudius), 1st setting (? November).
Phidile (Claudius) (November).
Lied: Ich bin vergnugt (Claudius), 2nd setting (November).
Bei dem Grab meines Vaters (Claudius) (November).
An die Nachtigall (Claudius) (November).
Abendlied (Claudius) (November).

Am Grabe Anselmos (Claudius) (4 November).
Der Geistertanz (Matthisson), T.T.B.B. (November).
Abendlied der Fürstin (Mayrhofer) (November).
Wiegenlied: Schlafe, schlafe, holder, süsser Knabe (?) (November).
Herbstlied (Salis) (November).
Rondo in E major, PF. Solo, Op. 145 (the finale of the Sonata in E major, 1817) (? December).
Skolie (Matthisson) (December).
Lebenslied (Matthisson) (December).
Leiden der Trennung (Metastasio, tr. H. v. Collin) (December).
Vedi, quanto adoro (Metastasio: Didone's aria) (December).

1817

Frohsinn (?) (January).
Jagdlied (Werner) (January).
Die Liebe (Leon) (January).
Trost ('Nimmer lange weil ich hier') (?) (January).
Der Alpenjäger (Mayrhofer) (January).
Wie Ulfru fischt (Mayrhofer) (January).
Fahrt zum Hades (Mayrhofer) (January).
Schlaflied (Mayrhofer) (January).
Augenlied (Mayrhofer) (? January).
Sehnsucht (Mayrhofer) (? January).
La pastorella al prato (Goldoni) (January).
La pastorella al prato (Goldoni), T.T.B.B., with PF. (? January).
Fischerweise (Schlechta) (? January).
Die Blumensprache (Platner) (? January).
Eight écossaises, PF. Solo (February).
Écossaise in E flat, PF. Solo.
An eine Quelle (Claudius) (February).
Der Tod und das Mädchen (Claudius) (February).
Das Lied vom Reifen (Claudius) (February).
Taglich zu singen (Claudius) (February).
Die Nacht (?, tr. Harold) (February).
Lied: Bruder, schrecklich brennt (?) (February).
Sonata in A minor, Op. 164 (March).
Gesang der Geister über den Wassern (Goethe), T.T.B.B. (March).
Der Schiffffer (Mayrhofer) (? March).
Am Strome (Mayrhofer) (March).
Philoktet (Mayrhofer) (March).

Memnon (Mayrhofer) (March).
Antigone und Oedip (Mayrhofer) (March).
Auf dem See (Goethe) (March).
Mahomets Gesang (Goethe) (March).
Ganymed (Goethe) (March).
Der Jüngling an den Tod (Spaun) (March).
Trost im Liede (Schober) (March).
An die Musik (Schober) (March).
Orest auf Tauris (Mayrhofer) (March).
Der entsühnte Orest (Mayrhofer) (? March 1817).
Freiwilliges Versinken (Mayrhofer) (? March 1817).
Die Forelle (Schubart) (? April).
Pax vobiscum (Schober) (April).
Hänflings Liebeswerbung (Kindl) (April).
Auf der Donau (Mayrhofer) (April).
Uraniens Flucht (Mayrhofer) (April).
Song: no title, no words (? May).
Overture in D major, Orchestra (May).
Sonata in A flat (May).
Liebhaber in allen Gestalten (Goethe) (May).
Schweizerlied (Goethe) (May).
Der Goldschmiedsgesell (Goethe) (May).
Nach einem Gewitter (Mayrhofer) (May).
Fischerlied (Salis), 2nd setting (May).
Die Einsiedelei (Salis), 2nd setting (May).
Gretchens Bitte (Goethe) (May).
Sonata in E minor (June).
Sonata in D flat (June).
Sonata in E flat, Op. 122 (revised and transposed version of previous sonata) (June).
Der Strom (?) (? June).
Das Grab (Salis) (intended for male voices) (June).
Die abgeblühte Linde (Széchényi) (? 1817).
Der Flug der Zeit (Széchényi) (? 1817).
Der Schäfer und der Reiter (Fouqué).
An den Tod (Schubart).
Sonata in F sharp minor. (July).
Lied im Freien (Salis), T.T.B.B. (July).
Iphigenia (Mayrhofer) (July).
Sonata in A major, PF. and vn. (called 'Duo'), Op. 162 (August).

Sonata in B major, Op. 147 (August).
Thirteen Variations on a theme by Anselm Hüttenbrenner in A minor, PF. Solo (August).
Die Entzückung an Laura (Schiller), 2nd setting (August).
Abschied von einem Freunde (Schubert) (24 August).
Polonaise in B flat, vn. solo, str. orchestra (September).
String Trio in B flat, vn., va., 'cello (September).
Gruppe aus dem Tartarus (Schiller) (September).
Elysium (Schiller) (September).
Atys (Mayrhofer) (September).
Am Erlafsee (Mayrhofer) (September).
Wiegenlied: Der Knabe in der Wiege (Ottenwalt) (September–November).
Der Alpenjäger (Schiller) (October).
Symphony no. 6, in C major (October–February 1818).
Overture (in the Italian style) in D major, Orchestra (November).
Overture (in the Italian style) in C major, Orchestra (November).
Six 'German' Dances, PF. Solo (XII, 13).
Three 'German' Dances, PF. Solo (XII, 15).
Two 'German' Dances, PF. Solo (XII, 17).
Scherzo in B flat, PF. Solo (November).
Scherzo in D flat, PF. Solo (November).
Der Kampf (Schiller) (November).
Thekla (Schiller), 2nd setting (November).
Lied eines Kindes (?) (November).
Das Dörfchen (Bürger), T.T.B.B. (December: revised and lengthened *c.* 1819).

1818

Lebenslust, S.A.T.B., with PF. (January).
Trio in E major, PF. Solo (for an unidentified Minuet) (February).
Auf der Riesenkoppe (Körner) (March).
Sonata in C major (First movement and Finale) (April).
Adagio in E major, PF. Solo (probably the slow movement of the previous item) (April).
An den Mond in einer Herbstnacht (Schreiber) (April).
Symphony sketches (D major): eight movements sketched (May).
Grablied fur die Mutter (?) (June).
Four Polonaises, PF. Duet, Op. 75 (? July).
Three Marches: B minor, C, D, PF. Duet, Op. 27 (? July).

Introduction and variations on an original theme in B flat, PF. Duet, Op. 82: no. 2 (posth.) (? July).
Fantasia in C major, PF. Solo (? 1818).
March in E major, PF. Solo.
St. John's Gospel, vi. 55–8, Sop., with figured bass.
Sonata in B flat, PF. Duet, Op. 30 (? August).
'German' Dance with two trios and coda, PF. Duet (? August).
Einsamkeit (Mayrhofer) (August).
Deutsche Trauermesse ('German Requiem') (?), S.A.T.B., Organ (August).
Der Blumenbrief (Schreiber) (August).
Das Marienbild (Schreiber) (August).
Eight variations on a French air, in E minor, PF. Duet, Op. 10 (September).
Sonata in F minor (September).
Adagio in D flat (slow movement of preceding sonata).
Rondo in D major ('Notre amitié est invariable'), PF. Duet, Op. 138 (? September).
Blondel zu Marien (?) (September).
Allegretto in A flat (no. 6 of the 'Moments musicaux'), PF. Solo (? October).
Das Abendrot (Schreiber) (November).
Sonnet I (Petrarch, tr. Schlegel) (November).
Sonnett II (Petrarch, tr. Schlegel) (November).
Sonnett III (Petrarch, tr. Gries) (December).
Waltzes and écossaises from Op. 9 and Op. 18, PF. Solo.
Lob der Thränen (Schlegel) (? December).
Blanka (Schlegel) (December).
Vom Mitleiden Mariae (Schlegel) (December).

1819

Die Gebüsche (Schlegel) (January).
'Die Zwillingsbrüder' (Georg v. Hoffman), 1 act *Singspiel* (finished January).
'Adrast' (Mayrhofer), Opera, text lost: (unfinished) (? February).
Overture in E minor, Orchestra (? for 'Adrast') (February).
Der Wanderer (Schlegel) (February).
Abendbilder (Silbert) (February).
Himmelsfunken (Silbert) (February).
Das Mädchen (Schlegel) (February).

Berthas Lied in der Nacht (Grillparzer) (February).
An die Freunde (Mayrhofer) (March).
Sonata in C sharp minor (First movement: unfinished) (April).
Nur wer die Sehnsucht kennt (Goethe), T.T.B.B.B. (April).
Ruhe, schönstes Gluck der Erde (?), T.T.B.B. (April).
Marie (Novalis) (May).
'Hymnen: I, II, III, IV' (Novalis) (May).
Psalm XIII (tr. Moses Mendelssohn) (June).
Sonata in A major, Op. 120 (? July).
Two Ländler (? PF. Solo).
Der Schmetterling (Schlegel).
Die Berge (Schlegel).
Ruhe (?), T.T.B.B.
Sehnsucht ('Ach, aus dieses Tales Gründen') (Schiller).
Hoffnung (Schiller).
Der Jüngling am Bache (Schiller), 3rd setting.
'German' Dance in C sharp minor, PF. Solo.
Écossaise in D flat, PF. Solo.
Cantata (for J. M. Vogl's birthday), S.T.B., with PF., Op. 158 (publ. as 'Der Frühlingsmorgen') (August).
PF. Quintet in A major (*The Trout*), Op. 114 (started September).
Overture in G minor, PF. Duet (October).
Beim Winde (Mayrhofer) (October).
Die Sternennächte (Mayrhofer) (October).
Trost (Mayrhofer) (October).
Nachtstück (Mayrhofer) (October).
Die Liebende schreibt (Goethe) (October).
Prometheus (Goethe) (October).
Widerschein (Schlechta).
Overture in F minor and major, PF. Duet, Op. 34 (November).
Salve Regina in A major (Third Offertory), Op. 153, Sop., Orchestra (November).
Die Götter Griechenlands (Schiller) (November).
Mass no. 5, in A flat, S.A.T.B., Chorus, Orchestra, Organ (November–September 1822).

1820

Nachthymne (Novalis) (January).
Vier Canzonen (Vitorelli and Metastasio) (January).

'Lazarus: the Feast of Resurrection' (Niemeyer), Cantata in 3 acts (2 only finished), S.A.T.B., Chor., Orch. (February).

Die Vögel
Der Knabe
Der Fluss
Der Schiffer
} (Schlegel) (March).[1]

Die Sterne (Schlegel) (? March).

Namenstaglied (Stadler) (March).

Six Antiphons for Palm Sunday, Chorus (April).

Five écossaises in A flat, PF. Solo (May).

'Die Zauberharfe' (Hofmann), incidental music to a 3 act play (June, July ?).

Ueber allen Zauber Liebe (Mayrhofer).

Morgenlied (Werner).

Twelve Ländler (E flat and D flat), PF. Solo.

Liebeslauschen (Schlechta) (September).

Frühlingsglaube (Uhland).

'Sakuntala', Opera in 3 acts: sketches only (Neumann) (October).

Der Jüngling auf dem Hügel (H. Hüttenbrenner) (November).

String Quartet in C minor, 1 movement ('Quartettsatz') (December).

Gesang der Geister über den Wassern (Goethe), male voice octet, 2 va., 2 'cello. Sketch. (December).

Gesang der Geister über den Wassern (Goethe), T.T.B.B., with PF. Sketch. (December).

Psalm XXIII (tr. Moses Mendelssohn), S.S.A.A., with PF., Op. 132 (December).

Der zürnenden Diana (Mayrhofer) (December).

Im Walde ('Waldesnacht') (Schlegel) (December).

1821

Die gefangenen Sänger (A. W. v. Schlegel) (January).

Der Unglückliche (Pichler) (January).

Gesang der Geister über den Wassern (Goethe), 4 T., 4 B., 2 va., 2 'cello, D.B., Op. 167 (February).

Versunken (Goethe) (February).

'German' Dance in G flat, PF. Solo (8 March).

Grenzen der Menschheit (Goethe) (March).

Suleika I ('Was bedeutet?') (Goethe) (March).

Suleika II ('Ach um deine feuchten Schwingen') (Goethe) (? March).

[1] These four songs may have been composed in March 1823.

Geheimes (Goethe) (March).
Mahomets Gesang (Goethe) (March).
Variation in C minor on the Diabelli Waltz, PF. Solo (March).
Frühlingsgesang (Schober), T.T.B.B. (PF. acc. added in 1822).
Im Gegenwärtigen Vergangenes (Goethe), T.T.B.B., with PF.
Aria and Duet, T. and T.B., Orchestra: for Hérold's 'La Clochette' (Spring).
Die Nachtigall (Unger), T.T.B.B. (April).
Linde Lüfte wehen (?), Mezzo Sop. and Ten., PF. (April).
Heiss mich nicht reden (Goethe), 1st setting (April).
So lasst mich scheinen (Goethe), 1st setting (April).
Johanna Sebus (Goethe) (April).
Der Jüngling an der Quelle (Salis).
Atzenbrügger 'German' Dances, Op. 18 (July).
Symphony in E minor and major: sketch (August).
Tantum ergo in B flat, S.A.T.B., Orchestra (16 August).
Der Blumen Schmerz (Mayláth) (September).
'Alfonso und Estrella' (Schober), Opera in 3 acts (20 September–27 February 1822).

1822

Geist der Liebe (Matthisson), T.T.B.B. (January).
Am Geburtstag des Kaisers (Deinhardstein), S.A.T.B., Orchestra (January).
Epistel: Herrn Josef Spaun (M. v. Collin) (January).
Tantum ergo in D major, Chorus, Orchestra, Organ (20 March).
Die Liebe hat gelogen (Platen) (Spring).
Nachtviolen (Mayrhofer) (April).
Heliopolis I: Im kalten rauhen Norden (Mayrhofer) (April).
Heliopolis II: Fels auf Felsen (Mayrhofer) (April).
Kyrie for a Mass in A minor (May).
Three 'German' Dances (XII, 14) (? 1822).
Four quartets, T.T.B.B., Op. 17 (? 1822).
 i. *Jünglingswonne* (Matthisson),
 ii. *Liebe* (Schiller),
 iii. *Zum Rundentanz* (Salis).
 iv. *Die Nacht* (? Krummacher).
Der Wintertag (?). T.T.B.B., Op. 169 (PF. acc. lost (? 1812).
Three Military Marches, Op. 51, PF. Duet.
Der Wachtelschlag (Sauter).

Galop and eight écossaises, Op. 49, PF. Solo.
Tantum ergo in C major, Chorus, Orchestra, Organ, Op. 45.
Sixteen Ländler and two écossaises, Op. 67, PF. Solo.
An die Leier (Bruchmann).
Im Haine (Bruchmann).
Am See (Bruchmann).
Du liebst mich nicht (Platen) (July).
Gott in der Natur (Kleist), S.S.A.A., with PF. (August).
Todesmusik (Schober) (September),
Wer nie sein Brot (Goethe), 3rd setting (? October).
Symphony in B minor (The 'Unfinished') (October–November).
Fantasia in C major (The 'Wanderer'), PF. solo, Op. 15 (November).
Schatzgräbers Begehr (Schober) (November).
Schwestergruss (Bruchmann) (November).
Des Tages Weihe (?), S.A.T.B., with PF., Op. 146 (22 November).
Sei mir gegrüsst (Rückert).
Selige Welt (? Senn).
Schwanengesang (Senn).
Ihr Grab (Engelhardt).
Die Rose (Schlegel).
Der Musensohn (Goethe) (December).
An die Entfernte (Goethe) (December).
Am Flusse (Goethe), 2nd setting (December).
Willkommen und Abschied (Goethe) (December).

1823

Twelve écossaises, PF. Solo (January).
Écossaise in D major, PF. Solo (January).
'German' Dances, and two écossaises from Op. 33 (January).
Der Zwerg (M. v. Collin) (? January).
Drang in die Ferne (Leitner) (? January).
Wehmut (M. v. Collin) (? January).
Sonata in A minor, Op. 143 (February).
Waltzes from Op. 127, PF. Solo (February).
Two 'German' Dances (XII, 18), PF. Solo.
Dass sie hier gewesen
Du bist die Ruh
Lachen und Weinen
Greisengesang
} (Rückert) (? February)

Waltzes from Op. 50, PF. Solo (? February).
Der zürnende Barde (Bruchmann) (February).
Viola (Schober) (March).
Abendröte (Schlegel) (March).
Die Verschworenen (later: *Der häusliche Krieg*) (Castelli), 1 act *Singspiel* (March–April).
Lied: Des Lebens Tag ist schwer (Stolberg) (April)
Pilgerweise (Schober) (April).
Twelve 'German' Dances, Op. 171, PF. Solo (May).
'Rüdiger', Opera sketches (?) (May).
Opera sketches (unnamed: 'Sofie' (?)) (May).
Vergissmeinnicht (Schober) (May).
Das Geheimnis (Schiller), 2nd setting (May).
Der Pilgrim (Schiller) (May).
Two 'German' Dances in D flat, (XII, 17), PF. Solo (? 1823).
'German' Dance in D major, PF. Solo (XII, 20) (? 1823).
Three 'German' Dances, PF. Solo (XII, 16) (? 1823).
Wanderers Nachtlied: Ueber allen Gipfeln (Goethe).
'Fierrabras' (Kupelwieser), 3 act Opera (May–October).
Die schöne Müllerin (Müller), song-cycle, (August–early 1824).

i. *Das Wandern.*
ii. *Wohin?*
iii. *Halt!*
iv. *Danksagung an den Bach.*
v. *Am Feierabend.*
vi. *Der Neugierige.*
vii. *Ungeduld.*
viii. *Morgengruss.*
ix. *Des Müllers Blumen.*
x. *Thränenregen.*
xi. *Mein!*
xii. *Pause.*
xiii. *Mit dem grünen Lautenbande.*
xiv. *Der Jäger.*
xv. *Eifersucht und Stolz.*
xvi. *Die Liebe Farbe.*
xvii. *Die böse Farbe.*
xviii. *Trockne Blumen.*
xix. *Der Müller und der Bach.*
xx. *Des Baches Wiegenlied.*

Allegro moderato in F minor (no. 3 of the 'Moments musicaux'), PF. Solo.

Auf dem Wasser zu singen (Stolberg) (? autumn).

'Rosamunde', Play in 4 acts (Helmina v. Chézy), incidental music (November).

1824

Introduction and variations in E minor on 'Trockne Blumen', Fl. and PF., Op. 160 (January).

String Quartet in A minor, Op. 29 (? January).

Two 'German' Dances, PF. Solo (XII, 18) (? January).

Octet in F major, Strings and wind, Op. 166 (February–1 March).

Der Sieg (Mayrhofer) (March).

Abendstern (Mayrhofer) (March).

Auflösung (Mayrhofer) (March).

Gondelfahrer (Mayrhofer) (March).

Der Gondelfahrer (Mayrhofer), T.T.B.B., with PF. (March).

String Quartet in D minor ('Death and the Maiden') (March).

Salve Regina in C major, T.T.B.B., Op. 149 (April).

Waltzes from Op. 50, PF. Solo.

Waltzes from Op. 127, PF. Solo.

'German' Dances from Op. 33 (May: arr. for PF. Duet in July).

Dithyrambe (Schiller).

Sonata in C major, PF. Duet ('Grand Duo'), Op. 140 (June).

Eight variations on an original theme in A flat, PF. Duet, Op. 35 (July).

Four Ländler, PF. Duet (XII, 27) (July).

Gebet (Fouqué), S.A.T.B., with PF. (September).

Three écossaises, PF. Solo (September).

Ungarische Melodie in B minor, PF. Solo (2 September).

Divertissement à la hongroise in G minor, PF. Duet, Op. 54 (September).

Six Grand Marches, PF. Duet, Op. 40 (October).

Six 'German' Dances, PF. Solo (October).

Sonata for PF. and Arpeggione (in A minor) (November).

'German' Dances from the set published as *Gesamtausgabe*, XII, 10, orig. for PF. Duet (November).

Lied eines Kriegers (?), Bass and Chorus (31 December).

1825

Lied der Anne Lyle (Scott) (? January).

Gesang der Norna (Scott) (? January).

Des Sängers Habe (Schlechta) (February).

Wehmut (Hüttenbrenner), T.T.B.B. (February).

Nacht und Träume (M. v. Collin).

Die junge Nonne (Craigher).

Im Abendrot (Lappe) (February).

Der Einsame (Lappe) (February).

Im Walde (Schulze) (March).

Der blinde Knabe (Colley Cibber, tr. Craigher) (April).

Bootgesang, T.T.B.B., with PF.
Coronach, S.S.A., with PF.
Ellens Gesang I: Raste Krieger } (Scott) (Spring).
Ellens Gesang II: Jäger, ruhe
Ellens Gesang III: Ave Maria

Lied des gefangenen Jägers (Scott) (4 April).

Two 'German' Dances, PF. Solo (April).

Albumblatt: Waltz in G major, PF. Solo (16 April).

Totengräbers Heimwehe (Craigher) (April).

Sonata in A minor, Op. 42 (April) .

Sonata in C major ('Reliquie') (April).

Normans Gesang (Scott) (? June).

Trinklied aus dem XVI. Jahrhundert (Latin text), T.T.B.B. (July).

Nachtmusik (Seckendorf), T.T.B.B. (July).

Sonata in D major, Op. 53 (August).

Cotillon in E flat, PF. Solo.

Waltz in A flat, PF. Solo.

Das Heimweh (Pyrker) (August).

Die Allmacht (Pyrker) (August).

Auf der Bruck (Schulze) (August).

Fülle der Liebe (Schlegel) (August).

Wiedersehen (A. v. Schlegel) (September).

Abendlied für die Entfernte (A. v. Schlegel) (September).

Florio
Delphine } from the play 'Lacrimas' (Schütz) (September).

Six Polonaises, PF. Duet, Op. 61 (Autumn).

Divertissement in E minor, PF. Duet, Op. 63: no. 1 and Op. 84: nos. 1 and 2 (Autumn).

'Abschied von der Erde', musical monologue (Pratobevera) (Autumn).

Grande Marche funèbre (on the death of Alexander I) in C minor, Op. 55 (December).

An mein Herz
Der liebliche Stern
Um Mitternacht } (Schulze) (December).

1826

Tiefes Lied (Schulze) (January).
O Quell, was strömst du (Schulze) (January).
Mondenschein (Schober), T.T.B.B.B., with PF., Op. 102 (January).
Four songs from 'Wilhelm Meister' (Goethe), Op. 62 (January):
i. *Mignon und der Harfner* (*Nur wer die Sehnsucht*),
ii. *Heiss mich nicht reden*,
iii. *So lasst mich scheinen*,
iv. *Nur wer die Sehnsucht keent.*
Canon à sei (January).

Am Fenster
Sehnsucht: Die Scheibe friert
Im Freien } (Seidl) (March).

Im Frühling (Schulze) (March).
Lebensmut (Schulze) (March).
Ueber Wildemann (Schulze) (March).
Twelve 'Valses Nobles', PF. Solo, Op. 77 (? 1826).
Waltz in G major, PF. solo (? 1826).
Two waltzes (G major, B minor), PF. Solo (? 1826).
Grande Marche heroïque (for the coronation of Nicholas I), in A minor, PF. Duet, Op. 66 (Spring).
Two 'Marches caractéristiques' in C major, PF. Duet. Op. 121 (Spring)
String Quartet in G major, Op. 161 (20–30 June).

Come thou Monarch of the Vine
Hark! Hark! the Lark!
Who is Silvia? } (Shakespeare) (July).

Hippolits Lied (Gerstenbergk) (July).
Widerspruch (Seidl), T.T.B.B., with PF. (? 1826).
'Four refrain-songs' (Seidl), Op. 95 (? 1826).
i. *Die Unterscheidung*,
ii. *Bei dir allein*,
iii. *Die Männer sind méchant*,
iv. *Irdisches Glück.*

Wiegenlied (Seidl) (? 1826).
Der Wanderer an den Mond (Seidl).
Das Zügenglocklein (Seidl).
Totengräber-Weise (Schlechta).
Das Echo (Castelli).
Nachthelle (Seidl), Ten. solo., T.T.B.B., with PF., Op. 134 (September).
Grab und Mond (Seidl), T.T.B.B. (September).
Sonata in G major, Op. 78 (October).
Deutsche Messe (including 'The Lord's Prayer') (Neumann), Chorus, wind band, Organ (late Autumn).
PF. Trio in B flat, Op. 99 (end of 1826?).
Adagio in E flat, PF., vn., 'cello ('Notturno'), Op. 148 (end of 1826 ?).
Rondo in B minor, PF. and vn., Op. 70 (December).

1827

Romanze des Richard Löwenherz (*Ivanhoe*: Scott) (January).
Zur guten Nacht (Rochlitz), Bar. solo, Male voices with PF. (January).
Alinde (Rochlitz) (January).
An die Laute (Rochlitz) (January).
Der Vater mit dem Kind (Bauernfeld) (January).
Eight variations on a theme from Hérold's 'Marie', in C major, PF. Duet, Op. 82 (February).
Jägers Liebeslied (Schober) (February).
Schiffers Scheidelied (Schober) (February).
'Winterreise' (Müller), song-cycle (Book I, February: Book II, October).

Book I:

i. *Gute Nacht*,
ii. *Die Wetterfahne*,
iii. *Gefror'ne Thränen*,
iv. *Erstarrung*
v. *Der Lindenbaum*,
vi. *Wasserflut*,
vii. *Auf dem Flusse*
viii. *Rückblick*,
ix. *Irrlicht*
x. *Rast*,
xi. *Frühlingstraum*,
xii. *Einsamkeit*,

xiii. *Die Post*,
xiv. *Der greise Kopf*,
xv. *Die Krähe*,
xvi. *Letzte Hoffnung*,
xvii. *Im Dorfe*,
xviii. *Der stürmische Morgen*,
xix. *Täuschung*,
xx. *Der Wegweiser*,
xxi. *Das Wirtshaus*,
xxii. *Mut*,
xxiii. *Die Nebensonnen*,
xxiv. *Der Leiermann*.
} Book II

Schlachtlied (Klopstock), Double Male-voice Chorus, (28 February).
Nachtgesang im Walde (Seidl), T.T.B.B., 4 hn. (April).
Frühlingslied (Pollak), T.T.B.B. (April).
Frühlingslied (the above arr. for voice and PF.) (April).
Allegretto in C minor, PF. Solo (27 April).
Das Lied im Grünen (Reil) (June).
'Der Graf von Gleichen' (Bauernfeld), 3 act Opera (sketches started mid-1827).
Ständchen (Grillparzer)
i. Contralto solo, T.T.B.B., with PF. (July).
ii. Contralto solo, S.S.A.A., with PF. (July).
Gott im Ungewitter (Uz), S.A.T.B., with PF. (? 1827).
Gott der Weltschöpfer (Uz), S.A.T.B., with PF. (? 1827).
Wein und Liebe (Haug), T.T.B.B.
Four Impromptus, Op. 90, PF. Solo (Summer ?).
Allegretto in C minor, PF. Solo (XXI, 16).
Three Italian Songs (first two: Metastasio, third: ?), Op. 83.
Heimliches Lieben (Klenke) (September).
'Edward: eine altschottische Ballade' (Percy, tr. Herder) (September).
Twelve 'Grazer' Waltzes, Op. 91, PF. Solo (September).
'Grazer' Galop, PF. Solo (September).
Kindermarsch in G major, PF. Duet (11 October).
Das Weinen.
Vor meiner Wiege
Fröhliches Scheiden.
} (Leitner) (? October).
PF. Trio in E flat, Op. 100 (November).
Der Hochzeitsbraten (Schober), S.T.B., with PF. (November).

Der Wallensteiner Lanzknecht (Leitner) (November).
Der Kreuzzeug (Leitner) (November).
Des Fischers Liebesglück (Leitner) (November).
Moments musicaux, nos. 1, 2, 4 and 5, Op. 94 (? November).
Fantasia in C major, PF. and vn., Op. 159 (December).
Four Impromptus, Op. 142, PF. Solo (December).
Cantata ('for the recovery of Irene v. Kiesewetter') (?), S.A.T.T.B.B., with PF. Duet (26 December).

1828

Der Tanz (Schnitzer), S.A.T.B., with PF. (? January).
Der Winterabend (Leitner) (January).
Die Sterne (Leitner) (January).
Fantasia in F minor, Op. 103, PF. Duet (January: finished April).
Symphony in C major (the 'Great') (February: finished March).
Mirjams Siegesgesang (Grillparzer), Sop. solo, S.A.T.B., with PF. (March).
Auf der Strom (Rellstab), acc. for PF. and hn. (March).
Lebensmut (Rellstab) (? March).
Herbst (Rellstab) (April).
Drei Klavierstücke, PF. Solo (XI, 13) (May).
Hymn an den heiligen Geist (Schmidl), T.T.B.B., with Male-voice Chorus (May).
Allegro in A minor ('Lebensstürme'), Op. 144, PF. Duet (May).
Fugue in E minor, Op. 152, PF. or Organ Duet (3 June).
Mass no. 6, in E flat, S.A.T.B. soli, Chorus, Organ (June).
Rondo in A major, Op. 107, PF. Duet (June).
Psalm XCII (Hebrew text), Bar. solo, S.A.T.B. Chorus (July).
Glaube, Hoffnung, Liebe (Reil), S.A.T.B. Chorus, with wind band (August).
Glaube, Hoffnung, und Liebe (Kuffner) (August).
'Schwanengesang', song 'cycle':

i. *Liebesbotschaft*,
ii. *Kriegers Ahnung*,
iii. *Frühlingssehnsucht*,
iv. *Ständchen*,
v. *Aufenthalt*,
vi. *In der Ferne*,
vii. *Abschied*,

} (Rellstab) (August).

viii. *Der Atlas*,
ix. *Ihr Bild*,
x. *Das Fischermädchen*,
xi. *Die Stadt*,
xii. *Am Meer*,
xiii. *Der Doppelgänger*
} (Heine) (August).

xiv. *Die Taubenpost* (Seidl) (October).

String Quintet in C major (2 vn., va., 2 'cellos) (September).

Sonata in C minor,
Sonata in A major,
Sonata in B flat major.
} (September)

Second 'Benedictus' for Mass no. 4, in C major, S.A.T.B., Chorus, Orchestra, Organ (October).

Tantum ergo in E flat, S.A.T.B., Chorus, Orchestra (October).

Offertory in B flat ('Intende voci'), Ten. solo, Chorus, Orchestra (October).

Hymnus an den heiligen Geist (Schmidl), double Male-voice Chorus, Soli and Chorus, with wind band, Op. 154 (October).

Der Hirt auf dem Felsen (Müller and H. v. Chézy), with acc. for PF. and cl., Op. 129 (October).

(i) GENERAL INDEX

Abraham, Gerald, 209, 351, (362)
Adamsberger, Antoine, 247
Adieu (Weyrauch), 327
Advokaten, Die, 261
Aeschylus, 92, 282
Albert, Prince Consort, 300
'Album Musicale', 152
Aristophanes, 129
Arnold, Matthew, 230
Artaria (Vienna), 25, 160, 239, 243, 251, 287, 318
Atzenbrugg, 102, 107, 109, 116
Augener (London), 341

Bach, 3, 217, 256, 283, 301
  48 Preludes and Fugues, 158, 283
Barbaja, Domenico, 128
Barnett, John Francis, 110, 112, 341
Barry, Sir Charles A., 331
Barth, Gustav, 47, 321
Barth, Josef, 47, 235, 321
Bates, Ralph, 8
Bauernfeld, Eduard, 10, 113, 153, 162, 170, 173, 237–9, 241–2, 245, 247, 263, 280–1, 285–6, 307, 322, 323, 359–60
Beethoven, 2, 3, 5, 12, 16, 17, 22, 36, 37, 51, 53, 64, 87, 91, 93, 146, 155, 185, 187, 196, 197, 209, 216, 226, 229, 231, 234, 256, 258–60, 264, 275, 280, 288, 293, 301, 303, 308, 322, 327, 329, 331, 332, 335, 343, 344
  'Diabelli' Variations, 189–90
  Fidelio, 12
  PF. Concerto in G major, 275
  Septet, 182
  Sonata in F sharp major, 119
  Symphony no. 3, 197
  Symphony no. 5, 225
  Symphony no. 7, 185
  Symphony no. 9, 199
Beethoven, Karl, 100
Berg, Isaak, 217, 268
Berlioz, 3, 4, 300
Bernhardt, J., 145, 173
'Biedermeier' Period, 9
Blahetka, Josef von, 83
Blahetka, Leopoldine von, 83, 153
Blom, Eric, 42, 97, 301, 339, 348, 352
Blumenthal, Jacob, 174
Boccherini, Luigi, 293
Bocklet, Karl von, 249, 251, 270, 282
Bogner, Ferdinand, 51, 133, 146
Böttger, Adolf, 190
Bourgault-Ducoudray, Louis, 342
Brahms, 112, 122, 143, 181, 200, 204, 234, 270, 335, 336, 337, 347
Breitkopf & Härtel (Leipzig), 104, 239, 243, 265, 299, 315, 319, 335–6, 352, 362
British Museum, 112, 246
Bruchmann, Franz, 12, 108, 109, 149
Bruchmann, Justina, 108
Bruckner, Anton, 256, 302, 342
Brüggemann, Karl (Halberstadt), 290
Brüll, Ignaz, 335
Burg Theater, Vienna, 14, 51, 163, 164
Bürger, Gottfried, 94

Capell, Richard, 35, 170, 223, 232, 268, 301, 350
Cappi & Co. (Vienna), 173, 175, 239
Cappi & Diabelli (Vienna), 50, 99, 105–6, 124
Carse, Adam, 122
Castelli, Ignaz, 10, 129–30, 134
Chézy, Wilhelm von, 322
Chézy, Wilhelmina von, 135, 148, 294

Chopin, 129, 153, 199, 227, 249, 270, 311, 326, 335, 343
Claudius, Matthias, 76
Clementi, Muzio, 65
Clodi, Florian, 167
Clodi, Max, 165
Clodi, Therese, 165, 167
Cobbett, William: 'Cyclopedia of Chamber Music', 97
Coleridge, Arthur Duke, 112, 338
Collin, Heinrich von, 10
Collins, Anthony, 187
Cooper, Fenimore, 307
Cranz, Albert & Alwin, 317, 341
Crystal Palace Concerts, 23, 110, 123, 325, 337
Czerny, Joseph (Vienna), 98, 235, 309
Czerny, Karl, 174, 242, 311

Dach, Charlotte von, 352
Dahms, Walter, 114, 131, 352
Dale, Kathleen, 63
Dante, 230
Davison, James William, 325, 343
Dean, Winton, 206
Deutsch, Otto Erich, 25, 37, 39, 70, 81, 83, 115, 126, 156, 229, 240, 250, 252, 261, 320, 328, 336, 347–8, 351, 368; *see also under* 'Schubert: Thematic Catalogues'
Diabelli, Anton, 68, 294
Diabelli & Co. (Vienna), 53, 74, 80, 128, 173, 174, 186, 240, 248, 269, 270, 283, 286, 290, 309, 314–17, 319, 323, 341
Dialer, Josef Alois, 310, 343, 349
Dietrichstein, Moritz von, 104, 105
Doblhoff, Anton von, 134, 145
Doppler, Josef, 4, 51, 82, 153, 242, 328, 329–30
Dräxler, Phillip, 37
Dresdel, Otto, 87
Dumba, Nikolaus, 108, 317, 340, 342, 351
Dürer, Albrecht, 138
Dussek, Jan Ladislav, 65, 95
Dvořák, Anton, 51

Ebner, Leopold, 14
'Edinburgh Review', 345
Effenberger, Hans, 338, (347)
Einstein, Alfred, 90, 123, 229, 269, 351
Ella, John, 325
Enderes, Karl von, 163, 240
Esterházy family, 156–7, 233
Esterházy, Count Johannes, 25, 50, 82, 152, 155
Esterházy, Countess Rosine, 82
Esterhàzy, Albert, 82
Esterhàzy, Karoline, 82, 85, 159–60, 268, 313, 351
Esterházy, Marie, 82, 85, 268
Eybler, Josef, 236

Fallersleben, Hoffmann von, 264
Farrer, J. H., 316
'Faust', 285
Fellner, Alois, 114
Fétis, François Josef, 2
Fink, Gottfried, 271, 291, 334
Fischer, Anton, 261
Field, John, 227
Fitzwilliam Museum, Cambridge, 190
Ford, Walter, 231
Förster, Christian Friedrich, 310
Frankl, L. A., 21
Franz, Robert, 87, 318
Friedländer, Max, 47, 104, 116, 132, 140, 257
Fries, Moritz von, 105
Frischling, Franz, 50
Fröhlich, Anna, 103, 104, 262–3, 283, 310, 313, 323, 360
Fröhlich, Barbara, 104, 146
Fröhlich, Josefine, 104, 263, 283
Fröhlich, Kathi, 104, 262
Fruhwirthaus, Vienna, 161
Fuchs, Alois, 36, 57, 320, 322–3, 359
Fuchs, Johann Nepomuk, 137–8, 265, 337

Gahy, Joseph von, 81, 86, 173, 250, 254, 282, 313
Gänsbacher, Johann Baptist, 38

Gastein, 5, 156
Geiringer, Karl, 351
Geist der Welt, Der (Schubert), 320
Gesellschaft der Musikfreunde (Vienna), 36, 61, 67, 245, 247, 251, 255, 258, 262, 270, 283, 299, 310, 317, 323, 340, 356–60
Glock, William, 184
Gluck, 12
Goethe, 10, 12, 34, 35, 40, 41, 42, 45, 49, 76, 93, 139, 165, 230, 247, 262, 282, 290, 325
Gosmar, Louise, 262–3, 284
Gotthard (Vienna), 315
Graves, Charles, 344
Graves, Robert, 41
Gray, Cecil, 16
Greene, Plunket, 346
Greipel, Josef, 80, 316
Grillparzer, Franz, 10, 104, 247, 250, 262, 283, 310, 322, 334
Grob, Heinrich, 27
Grob, Therese, 27, 34, 313
Grove's Dictionary, 144, 338, 339, 345
Grove, Sir George, 4, 16, 111, 112, 123, 136, 207, 299, 317, 318, 326, 331, 337, 338, 341, 344–6, 360–1
Gründwedel, Auguste, 254
Gymnich, August von, 104
Gyrowetz, Adalbert, 12

Habaneck, François, 299, 327
Hallé, Charles, 341
Handel, 283
'Harmonicon' (London), 251, 270
Hartmann, Franz von, 132, 162, 237, 250, 253, 259, 260, 282, 285–6, 331
Hartmann, Fritz von, 132, 161, 162, 237, 251, 253, 259, 262
Haslinger, Karl (Vienna), 269
Haslinger, Tobias (Vienna), 260–1, 266, 267, 269, 271, 283, 288, 290, 291, 309, 318, 332, 337
Hassak, Heinrich, 166
Hatwig, Otto, 51
Hauer, Anton, 14
Hauer, Josef, 235
Haydn, 2, 5, 12, 20, 22, 26, 51, 65, 93, 198, 216, 229, 330, 335
The Seasons, 26
Haydn, Michael, 93
Heine, Heinrich, 149, 282, 288, 292, 305
Hell, Theodor, 148
Hellmesberger, Johann Georg, 153
Hellmesberger, Josef, 321, 335
Henneberg, 53
Herbeck, Johann, 118, 317
Herder, Johann Gottfried von, 19, 42, 266
Hérold, Ferdinand, 10, 269, 291
La Clochette, 107
Herz, Heinrich, 174
Hess, Ernst, 122
Heuberger, Richard, 248
Hill, Ralph, 296
Hiller, Ferdinand, 260
Hoffmann, Georg von, 85
Holmes, Edward, 1, 260
Hölty, Ludwig, 43, 44
Holzapfel, Anton, 14, 125
Holzer, Michael, 13, 313
Hönig, Anna, 109, 239, 242, 280
Hönig, Karl, 12, 108, 109
Hönig, Ludwig, 355
Hortense, Queen, 86
Hugo, Victor, 138
Hummel, Johann Nepomuk, 2, 12, 53, 65, 124, 182, 200, 260, 292, 319
PF. Quintet, Op. 87, 95
Hutchings, Arthur, 352
Hüther, Franz, 174
Hüttenbrenner, Andreas, 117
Hüttenbrenner, Anselm, 53, 80, 104, 117, 120, 236, 259, 265, 312, 328, 339
Hüttenbrenner, Josef, 26, 80, 89, 105, 117, 120, 127, 134, 233, 259, 307, 312, 323, 329

Indy, Vincent d', 195–6

Jacobi, Johann, 42
Jaeger, Fritz, 85
Jaell, Eduard, 83
Jagor'sche Saal, Berlin, 165
Jenger, Johann Baptist, 86, 117, 247, 264, 267, 285, 287, 290, 309, 310
Joachim, Josef, 112, 187, 325
'July 1815': calendar, 39

Kahl, Willi, 97, 179, 351
Kalbech, Max, 141
Kalkbrenner, Friedrich, 255
Karlskirche, Vienna, 161, 234, 249
Kärntnertor Theater, Vienna, 16, 54, 85, 101, 128, 164, 238, 251, 322
Kenner, Josef, 14, 109, 126
Kiesewetter, Rafael von, 247, 357
King, A. Hyatt, 351
Kinsky, Princess Charlotte, 291
Kleist, Heinrich von, 282
Klemm, C. A. (Leipzig), 57
Kleyle, Sofie, 251, 253
Klier, Karl, 168
Klopstock, Friedrich, 42
Knorr, Baron von, 360
Kobald, Karl, 143
Koller, Josefine von, 67, 69, 85
Költzsch, Hans, 63
Konvikt, see *Stadtkonvikt*
Körner, Theodor, 139
Kosegarten, Ludwig, 43, 44
Kotzebue, August von, 10, 23, 100, 138, 285
Kozeluch, Leopold Anton, 2
Kreissle von Hellborn, Heinrich, 4, 16, 33, 55, 68, 112, 118, 153, 207, 242, 318, 322–4, 327, 329, 338, 343–4
Křenek, Ernst, 190
Kreutzer, Conradin, 200
Kriehuber, Josef, 162
Kuhlau, Friedrich, 65
Kundmann, Karl, 342–3
Kupelwieser, Josef, 131
Kupelwieser, Karl, 108, 154, 158
Kupelwieser, Leopold, 108, 148, 153–5, 160, 163, 170, 173, 178, 244, 250, 340, 354
Kupelwieser, Paul, 244

Lablache, Luigi, 269
Lachner, Franz, 4, 86, 235, 262, 264, 285, 286, 290, 307, 328, 331–2
Lachmann, Robert, 340
'Lacrimas' (Schütz), 172, 177
Landsberg, Ludwig, 317, 340
Lang, Franz Innocenz, 13, 18, 22
Lang, Paul Henry, 17, 197, 200
Lanz, Josef, 307
Lappe, Karl, 177
Larousse: 1875, 342
Lászny, Katherina von, 164, 173, 260
Legouvé, Ernest, 342
Leidesdorff, Maximilian, 154, 291
Leitner, Karl von, 42, 267, 268, 282, 329
Lerchenfeld Kirche (Vienna), 116
Lessing, Gotthold, 10
Lewy, Josef, 284
Liebenberg de Zsettin, Emanuel von, 124
Leichtentaler Kirche, Vienna, 5, 6, 8, 13, 26, 313, 339
Liechtental district, Vienna, 5, 8
Lied der Trennung (Mozart), 44
Liedertafel, 93
Ligne, Prince Charles Joseph de, 11
Linke, Josef, 147, 270, 282
Linz Music Society, 134, 158
Liszt, 3, 47, 118, 126, 141, 325, 329
  Wanderer Fantasia arrangement, 125, 188
  Erlking arrangement, 326
Loewe, Karl, 266, 318
Luib, Ferdinand, 69, 95, 126, 268, 323, 329
Lutz, Johanna, 149, 163, 244

Mackworth-Young, Gerard, 92
Malherbe, Charles, 340
Mandyczewski, Eusebius, 208, 257, 259, 335, 349
Männergesangverein (Vienna), 47, 321, 327, 342

Manns, August, 23, 325, 337
Matiegka, Wenzel, 25
Matthisson, Friedrich von, 44
Mautner-Markof, Frau, 244
Mayrhofer, Johann, 32, 38, 46, 49, 75, 84, 91, 113, 115, 139, 140, 144, 176, 257, 281, 286, 322
McNaught, William, 296, 299
Meangya family, 27
Mein Gebet (Schubert), 320
Mendelssohn, Felix, 3, 110, 160, 196, 199, 299, 300, 319, 325, 343, 344
  Songs without words, 325
Mendelssohn, Moses, 103, 349
Mendelssohn, Paul, 111, 112
Menz, Ignaz, 293
Metastasio, Pietro, 15, 351
Metternich, Prince Clemens, 10
Meyerbeer, Giacomo, 265
Milder-Hauptmann, Anna, 42, 164–5, 175, 294, 319
Mohn, Ludwig, 108, 149, 158
'Monthly Musical Record', London, 266, 307, 362
Mosel, Ignaz von, 12, 104, 127
Mosewius, Johann Theodor, 291
Mozart, 2, 5, 12, 16, 20, 22, 44, 51, 52, 65, 73, 75, 93, 197, 198, 216, 226, 227, 229, 231, 293, 330, 335, 343
  Abendempfindung, 93
  Magic Flute, The, 172
  Veilchen, Das, 93
Müller, Sophie, 163–4, 235, 240, 247
Müller, Wilhelm, 10, 133, 202, 256–7, 267, 294
'Music & Letters', London, 42, 156, 168, 199, 231, 304, 336, 346
'Music Review', London, 119
'Musical Examiner', London, 325
'Musical Quarterly', New York, 17, 320
'Musical Union' Concerts, 325
'Musical World', London, 324–5, 343, 352
Musikverein, see *Gesellschaft der Musikfreunde*
My Dream (Schubert), 114–15, 320

Nachgelassene musikalische Dichtungen, see 'Posthumous Musical Poems'
Nachtschmetterling, Der, 164
Nägeli, Hans Georg, 93, 242, 246, 290
Napoleon, 9
Nationalbibliothek, Vienna, 80, 240, 316
Neumann, Johann Phillip, 249, 313
Neumann, Ludwig, 322–3
Niemeyer, August Hermann, 100
Nourrit, Adolphe, 47, 326
Nowak, Leopold, 81, 144

Orel, Alfred, 351
Ottenwalt, Anton, 168, 195, 355
Ottenwalt, Marie, 168

Pachler, Faust, 265–6, 267
Pachler, Karl, 264, 266
Pachler, Marie, 264–5, 267, 279, 285, 287, 309
Paganini, Nicolo, 249, 284
Pálffy, Count Ferdinand von, 88
Panofka, Heinrich, 264, 288
Parry, Hubert, 195, 208, 209
Passini, Johann Nepomuk, 175
Paumgartner, Sylvester, 85, 95, 98, 132, 182
Pennauer, Vienna, 166, 173, 239, 248
Peters, Leipzig, 294
Peterskirche, Vienna, 80, 282, 316
Petter, Gustav, 36, 340
Pichler, Karl, 313
Pichler, Karoline, 205
Piledrivers' Song (Gmunden), 167
Pinterics, Karl, 340
Pixis, Johann Peter, 174
Pohl, Carl Ferdinand, 360–1
Pope, Alexander, 19
'Posthumous Musical Poems', 315, 321, 335
Pound, Ezra, 41
Preiger, Emil, 62
Pritchard, T. C. L., 119

Probst, H. A., Leipzig, 243, 255, 262, 268, 289, 292–3, 332
Prod'homme, Jacques Gabriel, 341
Pyrker, Johann Ladislaus, 170, 177

Racek, Fritz, 368
Racine, Jean, 10
Raimund, Ferdinand, 10
Randhartinger, Benedikt, 4, 14, 133, 144, 328, 330–1
Ratz, Erwin, 60
Reading Parties, 148, 154, 163, 282
Reeve, Henry, 345
Rehberg, Walter, 56, 65
Reichardt, Johann, 93
Reissmann, August, 4, 123, 207, 338
Rellstab, Ludwig, 287–8
Richault, Simon (Paris), 326
Rieder, Wilhelm August, 162, 175
Rinna, Ernst, 289, 307
Rischl, Thorwald, 25
Rochlitz, Johann, 42
Rockstro, William, 112
'Roman Emperor' Hall, Vienna, 71
Roner, Franziska, 282
Rosa, Kunigunde, *see* Vogl, Kunigunde
Rossau, Vienna, 82, 115, 127, 234
Rossini, 12, 70, 72, 217
  Tancredi, 330
Royal College of Music, London, 112
Rückert, Friedrich, 144
Ruczicka, Wenzel, 14, 46

St. Pölten, 112
Salieri, Anton, 14, 15, 26, 34, 36, 80, 94, 195, 217, 236, 330, 351
Salis-Seewis, Johann von, 44
Salomon, Karl, 187
Sauer & Leidesdorff, Vienna, 88, 148, 151, 152, 173, 239, 248
Schaeffer, Erwin, 257
Schechner, Nanette, 238, 241
Scheibler, Ludwig, 57, 65, 69, 81, 323
Schellmann, Albert, 42
Schikh, Johann, 284–5
Schiller, 10, 36, 40, 44, 76, 138, 140, 179
Schiller, Councillor Franz von, 355
Schindler, Anton, 15, 53, 88, 238–9, 258, 262, 288, 292–3, 322–3, 328, 332–3
Schlechta, Franz von, 37, 38, 350
Schlegel, Friedrich von, 171
Schlesinger, Paris, 326
Schmidl, (?Adolf), 295
Schmidt, Georg Philipp (of Lübeck), 40, 50
Schmidt, Klamer, 44
Schneider, Eduard, 136, 317, 327, 338, 340
Schneider, Georg Abraham, 155
Schneidl, Herr, 83
Schober, Axel von, 33, 77
Schober, Franz von, 21, 32, 38, 49, 54, 56, 76, 102, 108, 109, 113, 115, 126, 133, 134–5, 147–9, 152, 157, 159, 161, 164, 170, 173, 207, 237, 241–2, 246, 248, 254, 259, 280, 281, 291, 307–8, 310, 312, 313
Schober, Katherina von, 33
Schönberg, Arnold, 204
Schönstein, Baron Karl von, 152, 161, 313, 333, 360
Schott's Sons, Mainz, 53, 283, 289, 290, 292, 358
Schottentor, Vienna, 117
Schraub, Franz, 93
Schröder-Devrient, Wilhelmina, 324
Schubart, Christian, 76
SCHUBERT:
  Applications for posts, 34, 236, 238
  Birthplace, 6, 327, 343, 349
  Catalogues (1) Deutsch, 39, 70, 81, 102, 147, 335, 348, 368
    (2) Diabelli, 261, 335
    (3) Fuchs, 57, 322
    (4) Grove, 339
    (5) Kreissle, 322, 334, 335
    (6) Nottebohm, 335, 339
    (7) Reissmann, 335, 339
    (8) Schindler, 323
    (9) Schubert, Ferdinand, 320

Conscription, 22
'Documentary Biography', 239, 251, 259, 280, 328, 348, 357
Dream, My, 114–15, 320
Diary, 36, 37, 152
Gesamtausgabe, 20, 89, 90, 239, 265, 294, 315, 316–17, 318, 335, 339, 340, 348, 362
Poems: *Abschied*, 77
Geist der Welt, Der, 320
Mein Gebet, 320
Schubertiads, 108, 113, 149, 162, 164, 173, 240, 245, 250, 254, 260, 282
Spectacles, 109, 345, 350
Schubert, Elisabeth (mother), 5, 114
Schubert, Elisabeth (sister), 6
Schubert, Ferdinand, 6, 12, 16, 68, 70, 98, 110, 116, 127, 143, 158–9, 190, 281, 289, 291, 294, 299, 306–9, 312–17, 319–20, 322, 327, 334, 338, 350, 359–60
Schubert, Franz (of Dresden), 104, 243
Schubert, Franz Theodor (father), 5–8, 13, 16, 82, 114, 150, 157, 171, 234, 245, 308, 355
Schubert, Ignaz, 6, 12, 16, 27
Schubert, Josefa, 307
Schubert, Karl (brother), 6
Schubert, Karl (Ferdinand's son), 116, 313, 317
Schubert, Maria Theresa, 6, 7, 13, 236, 317
Schubert, Therese, 307
Schultz, Johann Abraham, 93
Schulze, Ernst, 157, 171, 176, 234, 240
Schumann, Clara, 186
Schumann, Robert, 4, 124, 160, 186, 190, 199, 201, 226, 227, 229, 269, 270, 287, 292, 299, 318, 319–21, 334, 335, 338, 344, 347
Schuppanzigh, Ignaz, 146–7, 150, 153, 182, 270, 282
Schuster, Vincenz, 156
Schütz, Wilhelm von, 172
Schwind, Moritz von, 6, 10, 11, 109, 113, 133, 134, 135, 137, 147, 150, 154, 157, 159, 161–3, 164, 169, 173, 237, 239, 241, 245, 250, 259, 263, 286, 308, 347, 349, 354, 355
Scott, Sir Walter, 86, 138, 167, 176, 290
Sechter, Simon, 15, 306–7
Seckendorff, Karl, 166
Seidl, Johann, 42, 245, 288
Senn, Johann, 14, 100
Seyfried, Ignaz von, 137
Shakespeare, 10, 113, 230, 267
Shaw, George Bernard, 16
Shelley, 37, 41
Sibelius, Jean, 4, 200
Siboni, Giuseppe, 54
Silbert, Johann Peter, 92
Slavík, Josef, 240, 249, 251, 270
Sonnleithner, Ignaz von, 37, 99, 104, 108
Sonnleithner, Josef von, 37, 247
Sonnleithner, Leopold von, 37, 51, 99, 105, 127, 146, 217, 263, 268, 320, 322, 360
Spaun, Anton von, 126, 172, 240
Spaun, Josef von, 12–15, 32, 34, 45, 46, 55–6, 81, 85, 104, 108, 113, 115, 126, 127, 134, 143, 150, 161, 168, 195, 207, 235, 237, 240, 241, 247, 250–1, 254, 258, 259, 264, 281, 289, 307, 312, 322–4, 340, 355, 358, 360
Spina, C. A., Vienna, 182, 240, 293
Spohr, Louis, 200, 344
Stadler, Albert, 14, 22, 67, 69, 95, 125, 138, 169, 172, 312, 323
Stadler, Maximilian, 132
Stadtbibliothek, Vienna, 35, 59, 81, 144, 257, 317, 323, 340
Stadtkonvikt, Vienna, 13–18, 21, 22, 31, 46, 93, 114, 159, 169, 225, 246, 297, 320, 330, 368
Stanford, Charles, 77
Statham, H. Heathcote, 345

Stiebar, Freiherr von, 313
Stiernblad, Axel, 33
Stockhausen, Margarete, 325
Stolberg, Count Leopold, 144
Storck, Adam, 163
Strauss, Johann, 5, 123
Strauss, Richard, 244, 337
Streinsberg, Josef von, 313
Styrian Music Society, Graz, 117, 158, 265
Sullivan, Arthur, 112, 136, 317
Széchényi, Count Ludwig, 330

Taussig, Konsul Otto, 20, 259, 341
Tchaikowsky, 337
Teltscher, Josef, 265
Thayer, Alexander Wheelock, 101
Theater an der Wien, Vienna, 16, 85, 88, 102, 137
Thomas, Dylan, 41
Tieck, Ludwig, 282
Tietze (*or* Titze), Ludwig, 255, 282, 284
Tomašek, Václav, 227
Tovey, Donald, 187, 199, 223, 274, 304, 350
Traweger, Eduard, 167
Traweger, Ferdinand, 166, 167, 285, 355
Trauttsmandorff, Prince Ferdinand, 236
Troyer, Count Ferdinand, 146–7, 182, 243
Truscott, Harold, 63

Umlauff, Johann, 108–9
Unger, Johann Karl, 153
Uz, Johann Peter, 42, 77

Vering, Josef von, 307
Vetter, Walter, 351
Vienna City Library, *see Stadtbibliothek*
Vogl, Kunigunde, 240, 264
Vogl, Michael, 12, 33, 54–5, 69, 76, 85, 99, 101, 104, 105, 108, 126, 162, 164, 165, 207, 240, 242, 245, 247, 250, 259, 260, 284, 294, 333, 355

Wagner, 3, 4, 92, 160, 199, 234, 337
Lohengrin, 12
Siegfried, 101
Tristan und Isolde, 92, 229
Walküre, Die, 101
Währing, nr. Vienna, 241, 308
Walcher, Ferdinand, 237, 251, 253, 255–6, 313
Walker, Frank, 307
Watteroth, Heinrich, 32, 35, 37, 249
Watteroth, Wilhelmina, 35
Weber, 127, 148, 257, 332
Euryanthe, 134
Freischütz, Der, 12, 134
Weigl, Josef, 12, 16, 237
Weigl, Thaddeus, Vienna, 161, 239, 248, 269
Weingartner, Felix, 110
Weintridt, Vincentius, 114
Weiss, Franz, 174
Weissenwolf, Countess Sofie, 168–9, 172
Werner, Theodor, 203
Werner, Zacharias, 49
Wessel & Co., London, 324
Westrup, Jack A., 198
Weyrauch, August von, 327
Whistling, Leipzig, 62, 190, 317
Whistling's *Handbuch*, 93
Wieck, Friedrich, 287
Wilder, Victor, 130
Windsor Castle, 300
Winkler, Karl, 148
Wisgrill, Johann, 307
Witteczek, Josef, 32, 35, 61, 63, 68, 240, 250, 260, 267, 313, 340
Wittmann, Rudolph, 349
Wodehouse, Mrs. Edmond, 344
Wolf, Hugo, 92, 204, 326, 347
Wolzogen, Karoline von, 40
Worzischek, Johann, 227
Wurzbach, Konstant von, 118, 339

Zedlitz, Johann von, 42
Zelter, Karl Friedrich, 93
Zseliz, 67, 82, 84, 91, 156–61, 313, 354
Zuckmantel, 5

(ii) INDEX OF WORKS

1. VOCAL MUSIC

Abend, Der, 24
Abendbilder, 91
Abendlied, 313
Abendrot, Das, 313
Abschied, 288
Adelaide, 24
Adrast, (Opera), 140
Alfonso und Estrella (Opera), 113, 127, 134, 135, 137, 141, 160, 164, 218, 265–6, 312, 320, 337
Overture, 225, 239, 251, 316
Allmacht, Die, 170, 177, 255, 261
Alpenjäger, Der, 12
Altschottische Ballade, Eine, 266
Am Erlafsee, 78
Am ersten Maimorgen, 27
Am Flusse (I), 45, 203–4
Am Flusse (II), 203–4, 213
Am Meer, 204, 208, 305
Am See (Mayrhofer), 32
Amalia, 36
Amphiaros, 46
An Chloen, 42
An den Mond (Goethe) (I), 35, 41
An den Mond (Goethe) (II), 41
An den Mond (Hölty), 43, 215
An den Mond in einer Herbstnacht, 91
An den Tod, 76, 152
An die Dioskuren, 49, 271
An die Freunde, 91
An die Laute, 261
An die Musik, 77
An die untergehende Sonne, 44
An mein Herz, 306
An Mignon, 34, 173
An Rosa (I) and (II), 44
An Schwager Kronos, 12, 45, 128, 173, 251
An Sie, 42
Andenken, 24
Andenken (Part-song), 349
Annot Lyle's Song, 236, 290
Antigon und Oedip, 75
Atlas, Der, 288, 305
Atys, 78
Auf dem Flusse, 301
Auf dem See, 290
Auf dem Strome, 284
Auf dem Wasser zu singen, 144, 223, 255, 261, 269
Auf der Bruck, 171
Auf der Donau, 76, 271
Aufenthalt, 203, 288, 304, 333
Auflösung, 176
Augenlied, 55, 259
Ave Maria, 50, 166, 247, 256, 324

Benedictus (for the C major Mass), 294
Berthas Lied, 313
Blinde Knabe, Der, 260
Blondel zu Marien, 313
Blumenbrief, Der, 313
Blumensprache, Die, 313
Bootgesang (Part-song), 169
Bundeslied, 35, 45
Burgschaft, Die (Opera), 140

Cantata for Salieri's Jubilee, 37
Canzonets, IV, 313
Claudine von Villa Bella (Opera), 83, 139, 312
Come, thou Monarch of the vine, 241
Coronach (Part-song), 169, 176

Dass sie hier gewesen, 144, 223, 247
Delphine, 172, 219

Dioskuren, Die, see *An die Dioskuren*
Doppelgänger, Der, 176, 181, 204, 205, 212, 288, 290, 304–5
Dörfchen, Das (Part-song), 94, 114
Du bist die Ruh', 247

Edit Nonna (Part-song), 166
Edone, 42
Edward (Eine altschottische Ballade), 266–7
Eifersucht und Stolz, 133
Einsame, Der, 174, 177, 251
Einsamkeit, 91
Enchanted Rose, The, 157
Entsühnte Orest, Der, 75, 159
Entzückung, 44
Epistel, Die, 313
Erinnerung, 153
Erinnerung (Part-song), 349
Erlking, 34, 45–7, 49, 104, 165, 176, 212, 235, 243, 324
Erster Verlust, 34, 45, 181

Fahrt zum Hades, 75
Fernando (Opera), 138–9
Fierrabras (Opera), 113, 131, 133, 141–2, 158, 280, 337
  Overture, 214, 316, 325
Fischer, Der, 34
Fischermädchen, Das, 288, 305
Fischers Liebesglück, Des, 268
Florio, 172
Forelle, Die, 12, 76, 80, 102, 174, 205, 312, 313, 324
Fragment aus dem Aeschylus, 49
Freiwilliges Versinken, 75
Fremdling, Der (Der Wanderer), 50
Freunde von Salamanka, Die, 139, 140, 184, 186
Fröhliches Scheiden, 205
Frühen Gräben, Die, 42
Frühlingsglaube, 144
Frühlingssehnsucht, 287
Frühlingstraum, 205
Fülle der Liebe, 171

Ganymed, 55, 76, 173
Gebet (Part-song), 313
Gefangenen Sänger, Die, 116
Geheimnis: an Franz Schubert, 38
Geheimnis, Das, 159, 313
Geist der Liebe (Part-song), 114
Geisternähe, 24
Geistertanz, Der (Part-song), 94
Geistes-Gruss, 34, 290
Gesang der Geister über den Wassern (Part-song)
  (I), 94
  (II) Sketch: 103
    Complete version, 316
  (III) Sketch: 103
Gesang der Norma, 290
Gestirne, Die, 326
Glaube, Hoffnung und Liebe (Part-song), 285
Gondelfahrer, Der (Part-song), 150, 151
Gott in der Natur (Part-song), 313
Gott und die Bajadere, Der, 35, 45
Götter Griechenlands, Die, 92, 179, 184, 186
Grab, Das, 313
Grab und Mond (Part-song), 245
Grablied für die Mutter, 313
Graf von Gleichen, Der (Opera sketches), 137, 146, 237–8, 242, 264, 280, 307
Grenzen der Menschheit, 144
Gretchen am Spinnrade, 12, 25, 28, 34, 45, 47, 49, 105, 177, 206, 306, 325
Gretchens Bitte, 76
Gruppe aus dem Tartarus, 12, 76, 78, 205, 220
Gute Nacht, 256

Hagars Klage, 15, 18
Hark! Hark! the Lark!, 50, 224, 241, 330
Harper's Songs from *Wilhelm Meister*, 12, 45, 106
  (I) *An die Türen*, 48
  (II) *Wer sich der Einsamkeit ergibt*, 48
  (III) *Wer nie sein Brot*, 48, 247
Häusliche Krieg, Der, see *Verschworenen, Die*

Heidenröslein, 12, 34, 45
Heimliches Lieben, 266–7
Heimweh, Das (Hell), 148
Heimweh, Das (Pyrker), 170, 177, 261
Heliopolis, I, and II, 144
Herbst, 287, 288
Herbstabend, Der, 45
Hirt auf dem Felsen, Der, 294
Hymn to the Holy Ghost (1828), 295

Ihr Bild, 288
Im Abendrot, 177–8, 207, 254
Im Freien, 260, 261
Im Frühling, 202, 240
In der Ferne, 288
Intende Voci, 294
Irrlicht, 301

Jägers Abendlied (I), 349
(II), 34
Jägers Liebeslied, 313
Junge Nonne, Die, 163, 174, 177, 203, 235, 251, 288, 324
Jüngling an der Quelle, Der, 45

Kampf, Der, 313
Klage, 27
Klage an den Mond, 43
Klagelied, 19
König in Thule, Der, 34, 105
Kreuzzug, Der, 268
Kriegers Ahnung, 287, 333

Lachen und Weinen, 247
Lady of the Lake, The (songs), 163, 166, 169, 172, 176, 236, 239, 258
Lazarus (Cantata), 100, 334
Lay of the imprisoned huntsman, 167
Lebenslied, 63
Lebensmut (Rellstab), 287, 288
Liedende, Der, 135
Leiermann, Der, 208, 257, 290
Letzte Hoffnung, 214
Liebe (Part-song), 94
Liebe hat gelogen, Die, 219
Liebe schwärmt auf allen Wegen, 140
Liebende schreibt, Die, 92
Liebesbotschaft, 287, 333
Lied (Schiller), 40
Lied (Stolberg), 144
Lied der Anne Lyle, see *Annot Lyle's Song*
Lied eines Schiffers an die Dioskuren, see *An die Dioskuren*
Lied im Grünen, Das, 261
Lied in der Abwesenheit, 349
Lied: in's stille Land, 45
Linde Lüfte wehen, 106, 116
Lindenbaum, Der, 202, 301
Litany for All Souls' Day, 43
Lob der Tränen, 81
Lorma (II), 66
Luisens Antwort, 44

Mädchens Klage, Des, 19
Magnificat in C, 316
Mahomets Gesang, 76
Mailied, 6, 27
Mainacht, Die, 43
Masses:
F major, 26, 263
G major, 236, 343
B flat major, 66, 236, 319, 330
C major, 173, 313
A flat major, 116, 142–4, 335
E flat major, 2, 142, 220, 222, 226, 287, 300–1, 302, 327, 343
Deutsche Messe, 249, 313
Meeresstille, 34, 45
Memnon, 75, 223
Mignon's songs:
(*a*) *Kennst du das Land?*, 47
(*b*) *Nur wer die Sehnsucht kennt* (1815), 35, 47
(*c*) *Nur wer die Sehnsucht kennt* (Part-song), 94, 312
(*d*) *So lasst mich scheinen*, 48
Mignon und der Harfner, 261
Miriam's Song (Cantata), 283, 310, 319
Mondenschein (Part-song), 290
Mondnacht, Die, 44
Morgenlied, 105
Musensohn, Der, 290

Nacht, Die (Part-song), 94
Nacht und Träume, 163, 174, 254
Nachtgesang, 35, 360
Nachthelle (Part-song), 245, 255
Nachthymne, 220
Nachtigall, Die (Part-song), 114, 153
Nachtmusik, Die (Part-song), 166
Nachtstück, 91, 173
Nachtviolen, 144
Nähe des Geliebten, 34
Nebensonnen, Die, 257, 267
Norman's Song, 258, 265
Nur wer die Sehnsucht kennt, see under Mignon's songs

Orest auf Tauris, 75

Pause, 227
Pax vobiscum, 308
Perle, Die, 43
Philoktet, 75
Post, Die, 257, 290
Prometheus, 92, 101
Prometheus (Cantata), 37, 263, 320
Psalm XIII, 349
Psalm XXIII (Part-song), 103, 251, 258, 306, 313, 319

Rastlose Liebe, 34, 45, 49
Rattenfänger, Der, 35, 45
Rosamunde (Incidental music), 100, 102, 123, 134–7, 146, 147, 186, 338
Overture, 71, 102, 141
Romanze ('Der Vollmond strahlt'), 135, 148
Rose, Die, 236, 261
Rosenband, Das, 42
Rüdiger (or *Rüdigers Heimkehr*), (Opera sketches), 130
Ruhe, schönstes Glück (Part-song), 312

Salve Regina (1812), 349, (1815), 27, 173
Sänger, Der, 35
Scene in the Cathedral (*Faust*), 30
Schäfer und der Reiter, Der, 105
Schäfers Klagelied, 30, 34, 55, 85
Schlachtgesang (Part-song), 284
Schöne Müllerin, Die (Song-cycle), 130, 133, 144, 150, 151–2, 203, 219, 330
Schwanengesang (Song collection), 288–9, 292, 304–6, 309, 318, 333
Sehnen, Das, 44
Sehnsucht (Goethe), 35
Sei mer gegrüsst, 203, 270
Seligkeit, 43
Serenade (Part-song: Grillparzer), 263, 284
Serenade (Rellstab), 50, 288
Shepherd on the Rock, The, see *Hirt auf dem Felsen, Der*
Sieg, Der, 176
Sofie(?) (Opera sketches), 131
Sommernacht, Die, 42
Sonnett III (Petrarch), 221
Spiegelritter, Der, (Opera), 18, 312
Spinnerin, Die, 34, 45
Stadt, Die, 288, 304–5
Ständchen, see *Serenade* and *Hark! Hark! the Lark!*
Sterne, Die (Leitner), 282
Stimme der Liebe (Stolberg), 220
Strom, Der, 313
Suleika (I), 106, 144, 149, 164–5
(II), 144, 174

Tantum ergo (I) (1816), 313
(II) (1816), 351 (1828), 294
Tubenpost, Die, 288, 294, 295, 306
Teufels Lustschloss, Des, 23, 113, 127, 140, 312
Thekla, 313
Tischlied, 35
Tod und das Mädchen, Der, 77, 105, 186
Todtenkranz für ein Kind, 44, 224
Totengräberlied (Part-song), 94
Totengräbers Heimweh, 177
Trockne Blumen, 133, 146
Trost im Liede, 77, 262
Trost in Tränen, 35
Trout, The, see *Forelle, Die*

Über Wildemann, 240, 274, 291
Um Mitternacht, 176
Ungeduld, 224, 313
Unglückliche, Der (*Der Wanderer*), 50
Unglückliche, Der (Pichler), 205

Vergissmeinnicht, 130
Verklärung, 19
Verschworenen, Die (Opera), 129, 138, 142, 155, 337
Vierjährige Posten, Der (Opera), 139
Viola, 258
Vor meiner Wiege, 267

Wachtelschlag, Der, 261
Waldesnacht (*Im Walde*), 208, 313
Wallensteiner Lanzknecht, Der, 268
Wanderer, Der (Schmidt), 40, 49, 50, 109, 324
Wanderer an den Mond, Der, 260
Wanderers Nachtlied (I), 34
Wanderers Nachtlied (II), 159
Wegweiser, Der, 301
Weinen, Das, 267
Wer kauft Liebesgötter?, 35
Wetterfahne, Die, 257, 301
Widerhall (Part-song), 349
Widerschein, 102, 368
Wiedersehn, 172
Winterabend, 282
Winterreise, 10, 181, 202, 206, 253, 256–8, 267, 290, 291, 292, 301, 304, 308, 318, 332, 350, 352–3
Wohin soll ich mich wenden?, 250
Wonne der Wehmut, 34

Zauberharfe, Die (Opera), 71, 101, 137, 140
Zügenglöcklein, Das, 260
Zürnenden Diana, Der, 173, 258
Zwerg, Der, 144 251, 331
Zwillingsbrüder, Die (Opera), 85, 101, 140–1
Zwillingssterne, Die, see *An die Dioskuren*

2. INSTRUMENTAL MUSIC

Adagio in D flat, PF. Solo, 315
Adagio in E major, PF. Solo, 78
Adagio and Rondo in E major, Op. 145, 62, 321
Adagio and Rondo in F major, PF. Quartet, 314
Allegretto in C minor, 256, 313
Andante in A major, 70
Andantino varié, PF. Duet, 248
'Arpeggione' Sonata, 156, 313, 335
Atzenbrügger Deutsche, 107

Ballet Music (*Rosamunde*), 135–6

Concerto in D major, Vn. & Str. Orch., 314
Cotillon in E flat, 75

Deutsche (German Dances):
Op. 33, 173
Deutsche Tänze (published 1930), 351
'October 1824', 351
Divertissement à l'hongroise, Op. 54, 160, 164, 186, 217
Divertissement on French themes, Op. 63: no. 1, 248
Op. 84, 269
Drei Klavierstücke, 227
Duo, Grand, *see* 'Sonatas'
Duo in A major, Vn. & PF., *see* 'Sonatas'

Écossaises (1815), 349
Entr'actes (*Rosamunde*)
in B minor, 123, 135

Entr'actes (*Rosamunde*) (*cont.*)
in B flat major, 135, 179, 269

Fantasias for PF. Solo:
in C major (The *Wanderer*), Op. 15, 124, 180, 187, 343
in C minor, 19, 315
Fantasies for PF. Duet:
in G major, 18
in G minor, 18
in C minor, 18, 312
in F minor, Op. 103, 217, 268, 282, 286, 301, 319
Fantasia in C major, Vn. & PF., Op. 159, 217, 270, 343
Fünf Klavierstücke, 57
Fugue in E minor, Org. or PF. Duet, 285, 314

'Gastein' Symphony, *see under* 'Symphonies'
Grand Duo, *see under* 'Sonatas'
Grätzer Gallop and *Walzer*, 266
'Guitar' Quartet (spurious), 25

Impromptus, PF. Solo, 227, 318, 325
Op. 90, 230, 261, 269
Op. 142, 269–70

Kindermarsch, 266, 312

Ländler, PF. Solo:
Op. 67, 254
6 in B flat, 2 in E flat, 8 in F sharp minor, 349
Lebensstürme, PF. Duet, 187, 286, 301

Marches, PF. Duet:
Marches heroïques, 88, 151
Marches militaires, 114, 248
Grandes marches, 160, 164, 173, 186, 250
Marches caractéristiques, 240, 319
Funeral March for Alexander I, 187, 239, 241, 248
Coronation March for Nicolas I, 241, 248
Marcia on French themes, Op. 84, 248
Kindermarsch, 266, 312

Moments musicaux, PF. Solo, Op. 94, 88, 152, 227, 255, 291, 325

'Notre amitié est invariable', PF. Duet, 80
Notturno, PF. Trio, Op. 148, 168, 217
Noturno (Matiegka) (spurious), 25

Octet in F major, Op. 166, 147, 155, 178, 197, 201, 215, 243, 260, 314, 321, 341
Overtures for orchestra:
Der Teufel als Hydraulikus, 316
D major (sketch), 316
B flat major, 70
D major (1817), 70, 316
D major ('in the Italian style'), 70, 78, 85, 102, 316, 330
C major ('in the Italian style'), 70, 78, 85, 316
E minor, 89–91
For Opera Overtures: *see under the work in* 'Vocal Music'
Overtures for PF. Duet:
D major (arr. from the 'Italian' overture), 72, 313
C major (arr. from the 'Italian' overture), 72, 313
G minor, 88
F minor/major, 36, 89, 169, 173, 182–5, 329

Pianoforte Quintet ('The Trout'), 95, 98, 103, 182, 227, 318, 326, 343
Pianoforte Trios:
B flat ('Sonata'), 18, 349
B flat, Op. 99, 168, 199, 227, 243, 272, 277–8, 252, 325
E flat, Op. 100, 12, 74, 119, 199, 201, 208, 217, 227, 268, 270, 272, 278–9, 284, 290, 291, 292, 310, 313, 325, 332, 342, 343
Adagio in E flat, *see Notturno*

Polonaise in B flat, Vn. & orch., 349
Polonaises, PF. Duet, Op. 75, 87, 269

'Reliquie' Sonata, *see under* 'Sonatas'
Rondeau brillant, PF. & Vn., 249, 251
Rondo in E major, Op. 145, 315, 343
Rondos for PF. Duet:
in D major, Op. 138, 80, 87
in A major, Op. 107, 287, 318, 319

Scherzo in D flat major, PF. Solo, 64
Sehnsucht Waltz, 53, 80
Sonatas for PF. & Vn.:
D major, Op. 137: no. 1, 74, 314, 319
A minor, Op. 137: no. 2, 74, 314, 319
G minor, Op. 137: no. 3, 74, 314 319
A major ('Duo'), 74, 75, 96, 216, 314
Sonatinas for PF. & Vn., *see above* Sonatas for PF. & Vn.
Sonata for PF. & Arpeggione, 156
Sonatas for PF. Duet:
B flat major, Op. 30, 88, 89, 323, 339
C major (Grand Duo), 88, 160, 186–8, 254, 319, 320
Sonatas for PF. Solo:
1. E major (1815), 56
2. C major (1815), 56
3. E major (Fünf Klavierstücke), 57, 70
4. E minor (fragment), 58
5. A minor, Op. 164, 60, 67, 315
6. A flat major, 61, 315
7. E minor (1817), 61–3, 317
8. D flat major, 63
9. E flat major, Op. 122, 63, 78, 319
10. F sharp minor, 64
11. B major, Op. 147, 66, 69, 315, 321
12. C major (1818), 78
13. F minor, 67, 221
14. A major (1819?), 68, 85, 243, 319, 339
15. A minor, Op. 143, 67, 128, 209, 223, 243, 315
16. A minor, Op. 42, 12, 166, 173, 188–90, 199, 239, 242, 271, 276
17. C major ('Reliquie'), 188, 190–1, 317, 322
18. D major, Op. 53, 12, 169–70, 192, 239, 251, 314, 339, 356
19. G major, Op. 78, 12, 119, 243, 246, 254, 260, 271, 274–7, 304, 318, 342
20. C minor (1828), 2, 292, 303–4, 320
21. A major (1828), 64, 292, 302–4
22. B flat major (1828), 196, 199, 223, 246, 292, 301, 302–4, 319
String Quartets:
C major (1812), 20, 225, 315
B flat major (1812–13), 15, 315
C major (1813), 20, 315
B flat major (1813), 20, 211, 315
D major (1813), 15, 18, 20, 29, 151, 315
E flat major, Op. 125: no. 2, 20, 23, 156, 319, 323, 339
D major (1814), 26, 315, 335
B flat major, Op. 168, 20, 24, 26, 210, 322
C minor (1814), 315, 351
G minor (1815), 72, 315, 335
E major, Op. 125: no. 1, 2, 72, 156, 319, 323, 339
C minor (Quartett-Satz), 103, 180, 228, 334
A minor, Op. 29, 12, 92, 147, 150–1, 155, 178–80, 184, 196, 217, 321, 339
D minor ('Death and the Maiden'), 2, 71, 147, 151, 180–2, 184, 196, 210, 217, 219, 223, 227, 235, 243, 319, 321, 325, 326, 339, 342

String Quartets (*cont.*)
G major, Op. 161, 151, 156, 181, 193, 198, 211, 219, 240, 243, 249, 268, 271–4, 284, 315, 321, 357
String Quintets:
'Overture' in C minor, 18, 338
C major, Op. 163, 74, 181, 196, 199, 226, 258, 292, 301, 314, 321
String Trios:
B flat major (1816), 72–3
B flat major (1817), 72–3, 314, 336, 338
Symphonies:
D major (sketch), 316
1. D major, 22, 225, 337
2. B flat, 50, 51, 337
3. D major, 50, 52, 337
4. C minor ('Tragic'), 50, 52, 336
5. B flat, 50, 51, 62, 317, 337
6. C major (the 'Little'), 78, 110, 117, 295, 299, 336, 357
7. D major (sketches), 79, 110, 208, 211, 217, 314
8. E minor/major (sketches), 90, 109, 211, 225, 338, 341
9. B minor (the 'Unfinished'), 3, 5, 51, 52, 103, 110, 116–24, 178, 196, 197, 199, 206, 208, 217, 225, 312, 314, 318, 327, 334, 337, 340, 342, 358
10. C major (the 'Great'), 2, 5, 51, 53, 71, 184, 197, 198, 210, 212, 222, 225, 258, 274, 282, 292, 295–300, 301, 319, 320, 325–6, 327, 337, 338, 342, 343, 357–61
'Gmunden-Gastein' Symphony, 167, 175, 187, 248, 354–61

Trauerwalzer, 53, 80

'Unfinished' Symphony, *see above* 'Symphonies: B minor'
Ungarische Melodie, 349

Variations:
Ten Variations in F major, 57, 314, 315
on a Hüttenbrenner theme, 80, 312
on *Die Forelle*, 85, 95
on a French Air, Op. 10, 86, 105, 332
on an original theme in B flat, Op. 82, 87
On *Der Wanderer*, 124
on *Trockne Blumen*, 133, 146
on a waltz by Diabelli, 152, 190
on an original theme in A flat, Op. 35, 158, 160, 166, 173, 186, 190, 197, 254, 282
on a theme from Hérold's 'Marie', 269, 291
on *Sei mir gegrüsst*, 270

Waltzes, PF. Solo:
Op. 9, 105, 223
Op. 18, 213
Op. 33, 129, 213
Op. 171, 129, 213, 220, 230
'Johanna Lutz', 244
'*Grätzer Walzer*', 266
see also under *Trauerwalzer* and *Sehnsucht* Waltz

PRINTED IN GREAT BRITAIN BY ROBERT MACLEHOSE AND CO. LTD
THE UNIVERSITY PRESS, GLASGOW